PENGUIN REFERENCE
The Penguin Latin Dictionary

'Just as Latin is coming back into fashion, here is a fresh and unintimidating guide for anyone wanting to read or write in that beautiful language. It's a piece of cake – in fact it's a *fragmentum placentae!*'
Boris Johnson

'Impressive … An excellent linguistic tool for any serious student of Latin.'
Dr Rosanna Omitowoju, Faculty of Classics, Cambridge University

Robert Shorrock was born in Lancashire in 1972. He was educated at Clitheroe Royal Grammar School and Durham University, and went on to gain a PhD in Classics from Christ's College, Cambridge. He spent time as an undergraduate supervisor at Cambridge University and MA lecturer at King's College, London, before taking up his current position as a Classics teacher at Eton College, Windsor. He has published widely on epic poetry and the Classical tradition and is co-editor of the journal *Greece & Rome*. He lives near Slough with his partner, the archaeologist Vedia Izzet, and their three young children.

David Butterfield was educated at Lancaster Royal Grammar School, where he was first introduced to the Classical languages. He studied Classics as an undergraduate and graduate at Christ's College, Cambridge, where he was recently pre-elected to a research fellowship at the age of twenty-one. His primary area of Classical research is Latin textual criticism, with particular focus on Lucretius, and he has a number of publications in the field. His wider interests lie in the history of Classical scholarship, Latin and Greek verse composition and antiquarian book-collecting.

The Penguin

LATIN
DICTIONARY

Compiled by R. Shorrock and D. J. Butterfield

PENGUIN BOOKS

PENGUIN BOOKS

Published by the Penguin Group
Penguin Books Ltd, 80 Strand, London WC2R 0RL, England
Penguin Group (USA) Inc., 375 Hudson Street, New York, New York 10014,
USA Penguin Group (Canada), 90 Eglinton Avenue East, Suite 700, Toronto, Ontario,
Canada M4P 2Y3 (a division of Pearson Penguin Canada Inc.)
Penguin Ireland, 25 St Stephen's Green, Dublin 2, Ireland (a division of Penguin Books Ltd)
Penguin Group (Australia), 250 Camberwell Road, Camberwell, Victoria 3124, Australia
(a division of Pearson Australia Group Pty Ltd)
Penguin Books India Pvt Ltd, 11 Community Centre, Panchsheel Park, New Delhi – 110 017, India
Penguin Group (NZ), 67 Apollo Drive, Rosedale, North Shore 0632, New Zealand
(a division of Pearson New Zealand Ltd)
Penguin Books (South Africa) (Pty) Ltd, 24 Sturdee Avenue, Rosebank, Johannesburg 2196, South Africa

Penguin Books Ltd, Registered Offices: 80 Strand, London WC2R 0RL, England

www.penguin.com

First published 2007
2

Set in StoneSerif & StoneSans
Typeset by Data Standards Ltd., Frome, Somerset, UK
Printed in England by Clays Ltd, St Ives plc

ISBN: 978-0-141-01555-2

Contents

Acknowledgements   vii
List of Maps   viii
Introduction   ix
How to Use the Dictionary   xi
Parts of Speech   xiv
Grammar Essentials   xvi

Latin–English Dictionary   1
English–Latin Dictionary   317

Latin Words and Phrases in Common Use   397
List of Latin Proper Names   405
Chronology of Roman Emperors   412
Chronology of Latin Writers (from Plautus to Suetonius)   415
Maps   417

For P, D and I

For L

hic cito, qui linguam soleant adamare Latinam,
omnibus auxilium grande libellus eat!

Acknowledgements

Samuel Johnson in his 1755 *Dictionary of the English Language* famously defined the noun 'Lexicographer' as 'a writer of dictionaries; a harmless drudge, that busies himself in tracing the original, and detailing the signification of words'. It remains to be seen what harm this dictionary might cause to its readers; as to the suggestion of drudgery, Johnson clearly exaggerated – but it is certainly true that it is a much easier thing to start a dictionary than to finish one! We are grateful to Nigel Wilcockson who commissioned the dictionary back in 2003 and to the subsequent Penguin editors who have patiently overseen the project on its long journey towards completion, most particularly to Kristen Harrison for her encouragement and sound advice over the last year. Monica Schmoller – whose eye for detail at the copy-editing stage greatly improved the manuscript – and Ellie Smith – who has kept schedules on track despite our best efforts to slow things down – also deserve our warmest thanks, as do the two proofreaders Pat Bird and Mark Handsley.

When Johnson embarked on his dictionary, he was entering into *terra incognita*, with few works of reference to assist him in his attempt to trace the 'signification of words'. In writing this Latin dictionary we have been able to enjoy the support and guidance of a formidable lexicographical tradition. In particular, acknowledgement should be made to the 2,126 pages of the *Oxford Latin Dictionary* (ultimately edited by P. G. W. Glare), which has been a constant and invaluable source of reference throughout. The linguistic excellence of the *OLD* itself rests on impressive foundations and we have often consulted the rich 'word-hoards' of earlier dictionaries, most notably Jacob Bailey's 1828 edition of the *Totius Latinitatis Lexicon* by Facciolati and Forcellini, and E. A. Andrew's influential revision of *Freund's Latin Dictionary*.

RECS and DJB

List of Maps

1. Roman Italy   417
2. The Roman Empire (under Trajan)   418–19
3. Roman Britain   420
4. The City of Rome   421–2

Introduction

The history of Latin lexicography has been a long and distinguished one, with *Lewis and Short* and *The Oxford Latin Dictionary* being two familiar English jewels in its crown. In spite of the existence of these great (in both size and learning) tomes, the field has long sought a dictionary that is at once small in size but broad in compass. We believe that the present work attempts to fill this notable gap. Indeed, no dictionary of this size is more comprehensive in its selection of Latin words. This book should therefore serve as a valuable tool to the Latin learner, the advanced student of Classics and the interested general reader.

The dictionary is able to achieve the breadth that it does by its exhaustive inclusion of all words used by the core canon of Latin authors. Such comprehensive lexicographical coverage of the central spine of Roman literature provides a robust, accurate and wide-reaching repertory of Classical Latin. The linguistic and semantic diversity of the language is documented from the comic poets of the early second century BC through to the biographer Suetonius of the early second century AD. The dictionary records the complete vocabulary of the following authors:

Plautus	Virgil (and the *Catalepton*)	Persius
Terence	Horace	Lucan
Nepos	Livy	Martial
Cicero	Tibullus	Statius
Caesar	Propertius	Tacitus
Lucretius	Ovid	Juvenal
Sallust	Seneca the Younger	Pliny the Younger
Catullus	(*Tragedies, Letters*)	Suetonius (*Lives of the Caesars*)

The Penguin Latin Dictionary provides full coverage for any reader of Latin engaging with these key authors and their varied texts, whether prose or poetry. Analysis of so great a volume of Latin that covers so expansive a period allows the reader to gauge the semantic spectrum that individual terms can possess. Likewise, words which only occur once in surviving Latin literature nevertheless find a place in the dictionary, whether it be a Plautine term to describe one who desires to profit by wicked means (*turpilucricupidus*), Cicero's dismissive term for an excessive lust for women (*mulierositas*) or even Persius' word for the noise produced by popping one's cheeks (*scloppus*)!

For reasons of space and ease of usage, the respective authors of Latin words are not recorded. If such information is required, it can be readily found in the larger Latin lexica. Although the dictionary covers comprehensively the vocabulary of the afore-mentioned authors, an exception has been made with regard to proper names, as their full citation would have caused the dictionary to swell to mammoth proportions. Instead, a selection of the most important proper nouns is offered at the close of the book.

The dictionary also includes a streamlined English to Latin section. Since the number of students who engage in the art of prose composition is now lamentably small, the focus of this part of the dictionary is towards readers and learners who seek an accurate and clear list of Classical Latin translations for key English terms. By avoiding the unnecessary practice of recording synonymous and archaic English words as entries, the list is succinct and to the point.

To close this brief introduction, it is worth recording a small but positive fact. Whatever the lamentations of those who believe Classics to be dying or the complaints of those who regard the subject as outmoded, a stream of young students with keen minds and fresh perspectives continues to flow into Classical research from diverse corners of the world. Though not immense in number, their willingness and ability to engage with the Classical world and its myriad facets – not least the Latin language – is now more noticeable than ever. If this dictionary can help aid the researches of this new wave, then the labour expended upon it will, we believe, have been more than justified.

R. Shorrock
D. J. Butterfield

How to Use the Dictionary

Headwords

Headwords are printed in bold type in both the Latin to English and the English to Latin sections. All Latin words have long vowels marked with a macron (i.e. **ā, ē, ī, ō, ū, ȳ**); all vowels not so marked are short in quantity. In a few instances where there is potential ambiguity, short *i* and *u* are marked as **ĭ** and **ŭ**. If two or more homonyms exist (regardless of differences in vocalic quantity) they are distinguished by superscript numerals (e.g. **malus**[1], **-a, -um** *adj.*; **mālus**[2], **-ī** *m.*; **mālus**[3], **-ī** *f.*). If a form of a word is unattested it is printed between square brackets.

Verbs
Latin verbs are listed in the *first person singular present active indicative* followed by their conjugation number (e.g. **amō** 1.). If the verb is of the third conjugation, or if it is of the other conjugations but slightly irregular, then the following two forms are also listed: the *first person singular perfect active indicative* and the *supine* (if they exist). If a verb is fully irregular its *present active infinitive* is also recorded as the second item (e.g. **sum, esse, fuī** *v.irreg.*). The use of a hyphen in principal parts represents the stem of the verb: in **abrādō, -sī, -sum** 3. the hyphens signify the letters *abrā*.

A summary of the forms of each conjugation and of the five primary irregular verbs is offered in the Grammar Essentials section.

English verbs are listed in the *first person singular present active indicative* alone.

Nouns and adjectives
Latin nouns are listed in the *nominative singular*, after which is printed the genitive singular and the gender of the noun (e.g. **rex, rēgis** *m.*). Latin adjectives are listed in the *nominative singular* with the *masculine*, *feminine* and *neuter* forms recorded in that order. If all three forms are identical, the genitive singular is instead offered (e.g. **ingens, -ntis** *adj.*). The use of a hyphen in nominal and adjectival entries represents the root of the noun or adjective: in **abrogātiō, -ōnis** *f.* the hyphen signifies the letters *abrogāti*.

A summary of the forms of the five declensions of nouns is offered in the Grammar Essentials section. The declensions of adjectives can be derived from this section.

Other entries
All other headwords are followed by their respective parts of speech in italic type (e.g. **absurdē** *adv.*). The abbreviations and their meanings are given below.

Supplementary material

If a verb, adjective or preposition takes a certain case or introduces a certain construction, this information is provided in brackets after the conjugation number or part of speech (e.g. **dē** *prep.* (+*abl.*); **queō, quīre, quīvī (quiī)** 4. (+*inf.*)).

Entries

Meanings provided in the entries are separated by commas, if they are roughly synonymous; if they are different senses, they are separated by semi-colons (e.g. **abdōmen, -inis** *n.* belly, paunch; gluttony). If further indication of a meaning is required, this is provided in italics and in brackets (e.g. **fulcrum, -ī** *n.* headrest (*of a couch*)). Paraphrases or further explanations of a word are also provided in brackets but in roman (e.g. **lōmentum, -ī** *n.* skin lotion (made from bean-meal)). Under certain entries a Latin phrase involving the headword is introduced. Such phrases are printed in bold type.

Abbreviations

1.	verb of the 1st conjugation
2.	verb of the 2nd conjugation
3.	verb of the 3rd conjugation
4.	verb of the 4th conjugation
1. *dep.*	deponent verb of the 1st conjugation (etc.)
1. *impers.*	impersonal verb of the 1st conjugation (etc.)
abl.	ablative case
acc.	accusative case
adj.	adjective
adv.	adverb
compar.	comparative
conj.	conjunction
dat.	dative case
esp.	especially
exclam.	exclamatory/exclamation
f.	feminine (noun)
f.adj.	feminine only adjective
gen.	genitive case
imper.	imperative
impers.	impersonal
indecl.adj.	indeclinable adjective
indecl.n.	indeclinable neuter noun
indic.	indicative mood
inf.	infinitive
interj.	interjection
interrog.	interrogative

m.	masculine (noun)
m.adj.	masculine only adjective
n.	neuter (noun)
nom.	nominative case
part.	particle
pass.	passive
pf.	perfect
pl.	plural
prep.	preposition
pron.	pronoun
refl.	reflexive
rel.	relative
sbst.	substantive
sg.	singular
sim.	similar
sthg	something
subj.	subjunctive mood
superl.	superlative
usu.	usually
v.irreg.	irregular verb
voc.	vocative case

Parts of Speech

For the purpose of traditional grammatical analysis, Latin words are classified into eight separate parts of speech (noun, pronoun, adjective, verb, adverb, preposition, conjunction, interjection); to this list may also be added the particle.

A **noun** refers to a person, place, thing or an idea. Nouns in Latin are varied by number (singular or plural), gender (masculine, feminine or neuter) and case (nominative, vocative, accusative, genitive, dative or ablative). Some words also possess a locative case. The five declensions of nouns are listed in the Grammar Essentials section. An appendix of proper nouns, providing the name of specific people or places, can be found at the end of the dictionary.

A **pronoun** is a word used in place of a noun. Personal pronouns (e.g. **ego** or **tū**) stand in place of the names of people. Demonstrative pronouns (e.g. **ille** or **hīc**) describe the spatial or hypothetical location of entities. Relative pronouns (e.g. **quī**) refer back to a noun mentioned in the previous clause or sentence. Possessive pronouns (e.g. **meus** or **tuus**) relate a noun to its owner. Pronouns are modified by number, case and (where appropriate) gender.

An **adjective** describes a noun or a pronoun. An adjective assumes the number, case and gender of the noun or pronoun that it modifies. Adjectives can also be made comparative (e.g. **laetior** *happier*) or superlative (e.g. **laetissimus** *happiest*). For the declension of adjectives consult the first, second and third declensions of nouns in the Grammar Essentials section. An adjective can sometimes stand in place of a noun rather than modifying it and in such instances is termed a **substantive** (e.g. **laeta** *happy things*).

A **verb** indicates the occurrence or performance of an action or the existence of a given state. Verbs can be divided into three persons, in both singular and plural. Latin verbs are arranged into six tenses (present, future, imperfect, perfect, future perfect, pluperfect), four moods (indicative, subjunctive, imperative, infinitive) and two voices (active and passive). Latin possesses four conjugations of verbs, the forms of which are recorded in the Grammar Essentials section. Transitive verbs are those that take a direct object (e.g. **amō tē** *I love you*); intransitive verbs do not take a direct object but can nonetheless be followed by an indirect object (e.g. **pāreō** *I obey* or **pāreō illī** *I obey that man*). Certain verbs can be both transitive and intransitive. Latin also possesses a set of verbs termed **deponent**. These are grammatically passive in form but active in meaning. An **impersonal** verb is one which cannot have a human subject. Instead, its subject is an inanimate third person (e.g. **pluit** *it rains*). Participles and gerundives are varied by number, gender and case.

An **adverb** is a word that modifies the nature of a verb (e.g. **saltō rapidē** *I dance rapidly*). Adverbs are not modified by number, gender or case but nonetheless can be made comparative (e.g. **rapidius** *more rapidly*) and superlative (**rapidissimē** *most rapidly*).

A **preposition** is a word that relates a noun or pronoun grammatically to the rest of the sentence (e.g. **est aqua in flūmine** *there is water in the river*). Prepositions are indeclinable. They can introduce three cases (accusative, genitive or ablative) and this determines in what case the following noun or pronoun stands.

A **conjunction** is a word that joins words, phrases or clauses. Conjunctions are indeclinable. Certain conjunctions are coordinating, i.e. they put two things in a similar syntactic relation (e.g. **ego et tū** *I and you*), whereas others are subordinating, i.e. the conjunction introduces a word, phrase or clause that is dependent upon what precedes (e.g. **saltō quod sum laetus** *I dance because I am happy*).

An **interjection** is a word – typically an expression of emotion – that can be introduced at any stage in a sentence or can stand alone (e.g. **eheu!** *alas!*). Interjections are indeclinable.

A **particle** is a word that brings extra meaning to a sentence but does not stand in grammatical relation to any part of it (e.g. **vērō** *indeed* or **nempe** *truly, to be sure*). Particles are indeclinable.

Grammar Essentials

Declension of Nouns

First declension
(*mostly feminine*)

Singular

Nom.	puella
Voc.	puella
Acc.	puellam
Gen.	puellae
Dat.	puellae
Abl.	puellā

Plural

Nom.	puellae
Voc.	puellae
Acc.	puellās
Gen.	puellārum
Dat.	puellīs
Abl.	puellīs

Second declension
(*mostly masculine and neuter*)

Singular	*m.*	*m.*	*n.*
Nom.	servus	liber	bellum
Voc.	serve	liber	bellum
Acc.	servum	librum	bellum
Gen.	servī	librī	bellī
Dat.	servō	librō	bellō
Abl.	servō	librō	bellō

Plural			
Nom.	servī	librī	bella
Voc.	servī	librī	bella
Acc.	servōs	librōs	bella
Gen.	servōrum	librōrum	bellōrum
Dat.	servīs	librīs	bellīs
Abl.	servīs	librīs	bellīs

Third declension
(masculine, feminine and neuter)

Singular	f.	m.	f.	m.	n.
Nom.	urbs	leō	nāvis	pater	opus
Voc.	urbs	leō	nāvis	pater	opus
Acc.	urbem	leōnem	nāvem	patrem	opus
Gen.	urbis	leōnis	nāvis	patris	operis
Dat.	urbī	leōnī	nāvī	patrī	operī
Abl.	urbe	leōne	nāve (-ī)	patre	opere
Plural					
Nom.	urbēs	leōnēs	nāvēs	patrēs	opera
Voc.	urbēs	leōnēs	nāvēs	patrēs	opera
Acc.	urbēs	leōnes	nāvēs (-īs)	patrēs	opera
Gen.	urbium	leōnum	nāvium	patrum	operum
Dat.	urbibus	leōnibus	nāvibus	patribus	operibus
Abl.	urbibus	leōnibus	nāvibus	patribus	operibus

Fourth declension
(masculine, feminine and neuter)

Singular	f.	n.
Nom.	manus	genū
Voc.	manus	genū
Acc.	manum	genū
Gen.	manūs	genūs
Dat.	manuī	genuī
Abl.	manū	genū
Plural		
Nom.	manūs	genua
Voc.	manūs	genua
Acc.	manūs	genua
Gen.	manuum	genuum
Dat.	manibus	genibus
Abl.	manibus	genibus

Fifth declension
(mostly feminine)

Singular	f.	f.(/m.)
Nom.	rēs	diēs
Voc.	rēs	diēs
Acc.	rem	diem
Gen.	reī (rēī)	diēī
Dat.	reī	diēī
Abl.	rē	diē
Plural		
Nom.	rēs	diēs
Voc.	rēs	diēs
Acc.	rēs	diēs
Gen.	rērum	diērum
Dat.	rēbus	diēbus
Abl.	rēbus	diēbus

Conjugation of Verbs

First conjugation: *amō* I love

Active
Indicative

Singular	*Present*	*Future*	*Imperfect*
1st person	amō	amābō	amābam
2nd person	amās	amābis	amābās
3rd person	amat	amābit	amābat
Plural			
1st person	amāmus	amābimus	amābāmus
2nd person	amātis	amābitis	amābātis
3rd person	amant	amābunt	amābant

Singular	*Perfect*	*Future perfect*	*Pluperfect*
1st person	amāvī	amāverō	amāveram
2nd person	amāvistī	amāveris	amāverās
3rd person	amāvit	amāverit	amāverat
Plural			
1st person	amāvimus	amāverimus	amāverāmus
2nd person	amāvistis	amāveritis	amāverātis
3rd person	amāverunt (-ērunt, -ēre)	amāverint	amāverant

Subjunctive

Singular	*Present*	*Imperfect*	*Perfect*	*Pluperfect*
1st person	amem	amārem	amāverim	amāvissem
2nd person	amēs	amārēs	amāveris	amāvissēs
3rd person	amet	amāret	amāverit	amāvisset
Plural				
1st person	amēmus	amārēmus	amāverimus	amāvissēmus
2nd person	amētis	amārētis	amāveritis	amāvissētis
3rd person	ament	amārent	amāverint	amāvissent

Imperative

Singular	*Present*	*'Future'*
2nd person	amā	amātō
3rd person		amātō
Plural		
2nd person	amāte	amātōte
3rd person		amantō

Infinitive

Present	*Perfect*	*Future*
amāre	amāvisse	amātūrum (-am, -um *etc.*) esse

	Present participle	*Future participle*
	amans (-ntis)	amātūrus (-a, -um *etc.*)

Passive
Indicative

Singular	Present	Future	Imperfect
1st person	amor	amābor	amābar
2nd person	amāris (-re)	amāberis (-re)	amābāris
3rd person	amātur	amābitur	amābātur

Plural			
1st person	amāmur	amābimur	amābāmur
2nd person	amāminī	amābiminī	amābāminī
3rd person	amantur	amābuntur	amābantur

Singular	Perfect	Future perfect	Pluperfect
1st person	amātus (-a, -um) sum	amātus (-a, -um) erō	amātus (-a, -um) eram
2nd person	amātus (-a, -um) es	amātus (-a, -um) eris	amātus (-a, -um) erās
3rd person	amātus (-a, -um) est	amātus (-a, -um) erit	amātus (-a, -um) erat

Plural			
1st person	amātī (-ae, -a) sumus	amātī (-ae, -a) erimus	amātī (-ae, -a) erāmus
2nd person	amātī (-ae, -a) estis	amātī (-ae, -a) eritis	amātī (-ae, -a) erātis
3rd person	amātī (-ae, -a) sunt	amātī (-ae, -a) erunt	amātī (-ae, -a) erant

Subjunctive

Singular	Present	Imperfect	Perfect	Pluperfect
1st person	amer	amārer	amātus (-a, -um) sim	amātus (-a, -um) essem
2nd person	amēris	amārēris	amātus (-a, -um) sīs	amātus (-a, -um) essēs
3rd person	amētur	amārētur	amātus (-a, -um) sit	amātus (-a, -um) esset

Plural				
1st person	amēmur	amārēmur	amātī (-ae, -a) sīmus	amātī (-ae, -a) essēmus
2nd person	amēminī	amārēminī	amātī (-ae, -a) sītis	amātī (-ae, -a) essētis
3rd person	amentur	amārentur	amātī (-ae, -a) sint	amātī (-ae, -a) essent

Imperative

Singular	Present	'Future'
2nd person	amāre	amātor
3rd person		amātor

Plural		
2nd person	amāminī	
3rd person		amantor

Infinitive

Present	Perfect	Future
amārī	amātum (-am, -um *etc.*) esse	amātum īrī

Perfect participle	Gerundive
amātus, -a, -um	amandus, -a, -um

Second conjugation: *habeō* I have

Active
Indicative

Singular	*Present*	*Future*	*Imperfect*
1st person	habeō	habēbō	habēbam
2nd person	habēs	habēbis	habēbās
3rd person	habet	habēbit	habēbat

Plural			
1st person	habēmus	habēbimus	habēbāmus
2nd person	habētis	habēbitis	habēbātis
3rd person	habent	habēbunt	habēbant

Singular	*Perfect*	*Future perfect*	*Pluperfect*
1st person	habuī	habuerō	habueram
2nd person	habuistī	habueris	habuerās
3rd person	habuit	habuerit	habuerat

Plural			
1st person	habuimus	habuerimus	habuerāmus
2nd person	habuistis	habueritis	habuerātis
3rd person	habuerunt (-ērunt, -ēre)	habuerint	habuerant

Subjunctive

Singular	*Present*	*Imperfect*	*Perfect*	*Pluperfect*
1st person	habeam	habērem	habuerim	habuissem
2nd person	habeās	habērēs	habueris	habuissēs
3rd person	habeat	habēret	habuerit	habuisset

Plural				
1st person	habeāmus	habērēmus	habuerimus	habuissēmus
2nd person	habeātis	habērētis	habueritis	habuissētis
3rd person	habeant	habērent	habuerint	habuissent

Imperative

Singular	*Present*	*'Future'*
2nd person	habē	habētō
3rd person		habētō

Plural		
2nd person	habēte	habētōte
3rd person		habentō

Infinitive

Present	*Perfect*	*Future*
habēre	habuisse	habitūrum (-am, -um *etc.*) esse

	Present participle	*Future participle*
	habens (-ntis)	habitūrus, -a, -um

Passive
Indicative

Singular	Present	Future	Imperfect
1st person	habeor	habēbor	habēbar
2nd person	habēris (-re)	habēberis (-re)	habēbāris
3rd person	habētur	habēbitur	habēbātur

Plural			
1st person	habēmur	habēbimur	habēbāmur
2nd person	habēminī	habēbiminī	habēbāminī
3rd person	habentur	habēbuntur	habēbantur

Singular	Perfect	Future perfect	Pluperfect
1st person	habitus (-a, -um) sum	habitus (-a, -um) erō	habitus (-a, -um) eram
2nd person	habitus (-a, -um) es	habitus (-a, -um) eris	habitus (-a, -um) erās
3rd person	habitus (-a, -um) est	habitus (-a, -um) erit	habitus (-a, -um) erat

Plural			
1st person	habitī (-ae, -a) sumus	habitī (-ae, -a) erimus	habitī (-ae, -a) erāmus
2nd person	habitī (-ae, -a) estis	habitī (-ae, -a) eritis	habitī (-ae, -a) erātis
3rd person	habitī (-ae, -a) sunt	habitī (-ae, -a) erunt	habitī (-ae, -a) erant

Subjunctive

Singular	Present	Imperfect	Perfect	Pluperfect
1st person	habear	habērer	habitus (-a, -um) sim	habitus (-ae, -a) essem
2nd person	habeāris	habērēris	habitus (-a, -um) sīs	habitus (-ae, -a) essēs
3rd person	habeātur	habērētur	habitus (-a, -um) sit	habitus (-ae, -a) esset

Plural				
1st person	habeāmur	habērēmur	habitī (-ae, -a) sīmus	habitī (-ae, -a) essēmus
2nd person	habeāminī	habērēminī	habitī (-ae, -a) sītis	habitī (-ae, -a) essētis
3rd person	habeantur	habērentur	habitī (-ae, -a) sint	habitī (-ae, -a) essent

Imperative

Singular	Present	'Future'
2nd person	habēre	habētor
3rd person		habētor

Plural		
2nd person	habēminī	
3rd person		habentor

Infinitive

Present	Perfect	Future
habērī	habitum (-am, -um *etc.*) esse	habitum īrī

Perfect participle	Gerundive
habitus, -a, -um	habendus, -a, -um

Third conjugation: *regō* I rule

Active
Indicative

Singular	Present	Future	Imperfect
1st person	regō	regam	regēbam
2nd person	regis	regēs	regēbās
3rd person	regit	reget	regēbat

Plural			
1st person	regimus	regēmus	regēbāmus
2nd person	regitis	regētis	regēbātis
3rd person	regunt	regent	regēbant

Singular	Perfect	Future perfect	Pluperfect
1st person	rexī	rexerō	rexeram
2nd person	rexistī	rexeris	rexerās
3rd person	rexit	rexerit	rexerat

Plural			
1st person	reximus	rexerimus	rexerāmus
2nd person	rexistis	rexeritis	rexerātis
3rd person	rexerunt (-ērunt, -ēre)	rexerint	rexerant

Subjunctive

Singular	Present	Imperfect	Perfect	Pluperfect
1st person	regam	regerem	rexerim	rexissem
2nd person	regās	regerēs	rexeris	rexissēs
3rd person	regat	regeret	rexerit	rexisset

Plural				
1st person	regāmus	regerēmus	rexerimus	rexissēmus
2nd person	regātis	regerētis	rexeritis	rexissētis
3rd person	regant	regerent	rexerint	rexissent

Imperative

Singular	Present	'Future'
2nd person	rege	regitō
3rd person		regitō

Plural		
2nd person	regite	regitōte
3rd person		reguntō

Infinitive

Present	Perfect	Future
regere	rexisse	rectūrum (-am, -um *etc.*) esse

	Present participle	Future participle
	regens (-ntis)	rectūrus, -a, -um

Passive
Indicative

Singular	Present	Future	Imperfect
1st person	regor	regar	regēbar
2nd person	regeris (-re)	regēris (-re)	regēbāris
3rd person	regitur	regētur	regēbātur

Plural			
1st person	regimur	regēmur	regēbāmur
2nd person	regiminī	regēminī	regēbāminī
3rd person	reguntur	regentur	regēbantur

Singular	Perfect	Future perfect	Pluperfect
1st person	rectus (-a, -um) sum	rectus (-a, -um) erō	rectus (-a, -um) eram
2nd person	rectus (-a, -um) es	rectus (-a, -um) eris	rectus (-a, -um) erās
3rd person	rectus (-a, -um) est	rectus (-a, -um) erit	rectus (-a, -um) erat

Plural			
1st person	rectī (-ae, -a) sumus	rectī (-ae, -a) erimus	rectī (-ae, -a) erāmus
2nd person	rectī (-ae, -a) estis	rectī (-ae, -a) eritis	rectī (-ae, -a) erātis
3rd person	rectī (-ae, -a) sunt	rectī (-ae, -a) erunt	rectī (-ae, -a) erant

Subjunctive

Singular	Present	Imperfect	Perfect	Pluperfect
1st person	regar	regēbar	rectus (-a, -um) sim	rectus (-a, -um) essem
2nd person	regāris	regēbāris	rectus (-a, -um) sīs	rectus (-a, -um) essēs
3rd person	regātur	regēbātur	rectus (-a, -um) sit	rectus (-a, -um) esset

Plural				
1st person	regāmur	regēbāmur	rectī (-ae, -a) sīmus	rectī (-ae, -a) essēmus
2nd person	regāminī	regēbāminī	rectī (-ae, -a) sītis	rectī (-ae, -a) essētis
3rd person	regantur	regēbantur	rectī (-ae, -a) sint	rectī (-ae, -a) essent

Imperative

Singular	Present	'Future'
2nd person	regere	regitor
3rd person		regitor

Plural		
2nd person	regiminī	
3rd person		reguntor

Infinitive

Present	Perfect	Future
regī	rectum (-am, -um *etc.*) esse	rectum īrī

	Perfect participle	Gerundive
	rectus, -a, -um	regendus, -a, -um

Fourth conjugation: *audiō* I hear

Active
Indicative

Singular	Present	Future	Imperfect
1st person	audiō	audiam	audiēbam
2nd person	audīs	audiēs	audiēbās
3rd person	audit	audiet	audiēbat

Plural			
1st person	audīmus	audiēmus	audiēbāmus
2nd person	audītis	audiētis	audiēbātis
3rd person	audiunt	audient	audiēbant

Singular	Perfect	Future perfect	Pluperfect
1st person	audīvī (audiī *etc.*)	audīverō (audierō *etc.*)	audīveram (audieram *etc.*)
2nd person	audīvistī	audīveris	audīverās
3rd person	audīvit	audīverit	audīverat

Plural			
1st person	audīvimus	audīverimus	audīverāmus
2nd person	audīvistis	audīveritis	audīverātis
3rd person	audīverunt (-ērunt, -ēre)	audīverint	audīverant

Subjunctive

Singular	Present	Imperfect	Perfect	Pluperfect
1st person	audiam	audīrem	audīverim	audīvissem
2nd person	audiās	audīrēs	audīveris	audīvissēs
3rd person	audiat	audīret	audīverit	audīvisset

Plural				
1st person	audiāmus	audīrēmus	audīverimus	audīvissēmus
2nd person	audiātis	audīrētis	audīveritis	audīvissētis
3rd person	audiant	audīrent	audīverint	audīvissent

Imperative

Singular	Present	'Future'
2nd person	audī	audītō
3rd person		audītō

Plural		
2nd person	audīte	audītōte
3rd person		audiuntō

Infinitive

Present	Perfect	Future
audīre	audīvisse	audītūrum (-am, -um *etc.*) esse

	Present participle	Future participle
	audiens (-ntis)	audītūrus, -a, -um

Passive
Indicative

Singular	*Present*	*Future*	*Imperfect*
1st person	audior	audiar	audiēbar
2nd person	audīris (-re)	audiēris (-re)	audiēbāris
3rd person	audītur	audiētur	audiēbātur

Plural			
1st person	audīmur	audiēmur	audiēbāmur
2nd person	audīminī	audiēminī	audiēbāminī
3rd person	audiuntur	audientur	audiēbantur

Singular	*Perfect*	*Future perfect*	*Pluperfect*
1st person	audītus (-a, -um) sum	audītus (-a, -um) erō	audītus (-a, -um) eram
2nd person	audītus (-a, -um) es	audītus (-a, -um) eris	audītus (-a, -um) erās
3rd person	audītus (-a, -um) est	audītus (-a, -um) erit	audītus (-a, -um) erat

Plural			
1st person	audītī (-ae, -a) sumus	audītī (-ae, -a) erimus	audītī (-ae, -a) erāmus
2nd person	audītī (-ae, -a) estis	audītī (-ae, -a) eritis	audītī (-ae, -a) erātis
3rd person	audītī (-ae, -a) sunt	audītī (-ae, -a) erunt	audītī (-ae, -a) erant

Subjunctive

Singular	*Present*	*Imperfect*	*Perfect*	*Pluperfect*
1st person	audiar	audīrer	audītus (-a, -um) sim	audītus (-a, -um) essem
2nd person	audiāris	audīrēris	audītus (-a, -um) sīs	audītus (-a, -um) essēs
3rd person	audiātur	audīrētur	audītus (-a, -um) sit	audītus (-a, -um) esset

Plural				
1st person	audiāmur	audīrēmur	audītī (-ae, -a) sīmus	audītī (-ae, -a) essēmus
2nd person	audiāminī	audīrēminī	audītī (-ae, -a) sītis	audītī (-ae, -a) essētis
3rd person	audiantur	audīrentur	audītī (-ae, -a) sint	audītī (-ae, -a) essent

Imperative

Singular	*Present*	*'Future'*
2nd person	audīre	audītor
3rd person		audītor

Plural		
2nd person	audīminī	
3rd person		audiuntor

Infinitive

Present	*Perfect*	*Future*
audīrī	audītum (-am, -um *etc.*) esse	audītum īrī

	Perfect participle	*Gerundive*
	audītus -a, -um	audiendus, -a, -um

Irregular verbs
(*all active only*)

sum, esse, fuī to be

Indicative

Singular	*Present*	*Future*	*Imperfect*
1st person	sum	erō	eram
2nd person	es	eris	erās
3rd person	est	erit	erat

Plural			
1st person	sumus	erimus	erāmus
2nd person	estis	eritis	erātis
3rd person	sunt	erunt	erant

Singular	*Perfect*	*Future perfect*	*Pluperfect*
1st person	fuī	fuerō	fueram
2nd person	fuistī	fueris	fuerās
3rd person	fuit	fuerit	fuerat

Plural			
1st person	fuimus	fuerimus	fuerāmus
2nd person	fuistis	fueritis	fuerātis
3rd person	fuerunt (fuērunt, fuēre)	fuerint	fuerant

Subjunctive

Singular	*Present*	*Imperfect*	*Perfect*	*Pluperfect*
1st person	sim	essem	fuerim	fuissem
2nd person	sīs	essēs	fueris	fuissēs
3rd person	sit	esset	fuerit	fuisset

Plural				
1st person	sīmus	essēmus	fuerimus	fuissēmus
2nd person	sītis	essētis	fueritis	fuissētis
3rd person	sint	essent	fuerint	fuissent

Imperative

Singular	*Present*	*'Future'*
2nd person	es	estō
3rd person		estō

Plural		
2nd person	este	estōte
3rd person		suntō

Infinitive

Present	*Perfect*	*Future*	*Future participle*
esse	fuisse	futūrum (-am, -um *etc.*) esse	futūrus, -a, -um

mālō, mālle, māluī to prefer

Indicative

Singular	Present	Future	Imperfect
1st person	mālō	mālam	mālēbam
2nd person	māvīs	mālēs	mālēbās
3rd person	māvult	mālet	mālēbat

Plural			
1st person	mālumus	mālēmus	mālēbāmus
2nd person	māvultis	mālētis	mālēbātis
3rd person	mālunt	mālent	mālēbant

Singular	Perfect	Future perfect	Pluperfect
1st person	māluī *etc.*	māluerō *etc.*	mālueram *etc.*

Subjunctive

Singular	Present	Imperfect	Perfect	Pluperfect
1st person	mālim	māllem	māluerim	māluissem
2nd person	mālīs	māllēs	mālueris	māluissēs
3rd person	mālit	māllet	māluerit	māluisset

Plural				
1st person	mālīmus	māllēmus	māluerimus	māluissēmus
2nd person	mālītis	māllētis	mālueritis	māluissētis
3rd person	mālint	māllent	māluerint	māluissent

Present infinitive	Perfect infinitive
mālle	māluisse

Present participle
mālens (-ntis)

possum, posse, potuī to be able

Indicative

Singular	Present	Future	Imperfect
1st person	possum	poterō	poteram
2nd person	potes	poteris	poterās
3rd person	potest	poterit	poterat

Plural			
1st person	possumus	poterimus	poterāmus
2nd person	potestis	poteritis	poterātis
3rd person	possunt	poterunt	poterant

Singular	Perfect	Future perfect	Pluperfect
1st person	potuī *etc.*	potuerō *etc.*	potueram *etc.*

Subjunctive

Singular	Present	Imperfect	Perfect	Pluperfect
1st person	possim	possem	potuerim	potuissem
2nd person	possīs	possēs	potueris	potuissēs
3rd person	possit	posset	potuerit	potuisset

Plural				
1st person	possīmus	possēmus	potuerimus	potuissēmus
2nd person	possītis	possētis	potueritis	potuissētis
3rd person	possint	possent	potuerint	potuissent

	Present infinitive		*Perfect infinitive*	
	posse		potuisse	

Present participle
potens (-ntis)

---

volō, velle, voluī to want

Indicative

Singular	Present	Future	Imperfect
1st person	volō	volam	volēbam
2nd person	vīs	volēs	volēbās
3rd person	vult (volt)	volet	volēbat

Plural			
1st person	volumus	volēmus	volēbāmus
2nd person	vultis (voltis)	volētis	volēbātis
3rd person	volunt	volent	volēbant

Singular	Perfect	Future perfect	Pluperfect
1st person	voluī *etc.*	voluerō *etc.*	volueram *etc.*

Subjunctive

Singular	Present	Imperfect	Perfect	Pluperfect
1st person	velim	vellem	voluerim	voluissem
2nd person	velīs	vellēs	volueris	voluissēs
3rd person	velit	vellet	voluerit	voluisset

Plural				
1st person	velīmus	vellēmus	voluerimus	voluissēmus
2nd person	velītis	vellētis	volueritis	voluissētis
3rd person	velint	vellent	voluerint	voluissent

	Present infinitive		*Perfect infinitive*	
	velle		voluisse	

Present participle
volens (-ntis)

nōlō, nōlle, nōluī not to want

Indicative

Singular	Present	Future	Imperfect
1st person	nōlō	nōlam	nōlēbam
2nd person	nōn vīs	nōlēs	nōlēbās
3rd person	nōn vult (volt)	nōlet	nōlēbat

Plural			
1st person	nōlumus	nōlēmus	nōlēbāmus
2nd person	nōn vultis (voltis)	nōlētis	nōlēbātis
3rd person	nōlunt	nōlent	nōlēbant

Singular	Perfect	Future perfect	Pluperfect
1st person	nōluī *etc.*	nōluerō *etc.*	nōlueram *etc.*

Subjunctive

Singular	Present	Imperfect	Perfect	Pluperfect
1st person	nōlim *etc.*	nōllem *etc.*	nōluerim *etc.*	nōluissem *etc.*

Imperative

Singular	Present	'Future'
2nd person	nōlī	nōlītō
3rd person		nōlītō

Plural		
2nd person	nōlīte	nōlītōte
3rd person		nōluntō

Present infinitive	Perfect infinitive
nōlle	nōluisse

Present participle
nōlens (-ntis)

LATIN–ENGLISH DICTIONARY

ā see **ab**

ā(h) *interj.* cry of pain, joy *or* appeal

ab or **ā** *prep.* (+*abl.*) from; away from; by (the agency of); since

abactus, -ūs *m.* theft of cattle

abacus, -ī *m.* sideboard; counting-board

ābaetō see **ābītō**

abaliēnātus, -a, -um *adj.* estranged, alienated

abaliēnō 1. to transfer possession of; remove; alienate

abavus, -ī *m.* great-great-grandfather; distant ancestor

abdicātiō, -ōnis *f.* abdication, resignation

abdicō[1] 1. to abdicate, resign; disown

abdīcō[2], **abdixī, abdictum** 3. to reject omens

abditus, -a, -um *adj.* hidden, out of the way; abstruse, obscure; *n.pl.sbst.* secret places

abdō, abdidī, abditum 3. to hide; cover, bury; remove

abdōmen, -inis *n.* belly, paunch; gluttony

abdūcō, -uxī, -uctum 3. to lead away, remove; cause to deviate

abeō, abīre, abīvī (abiī), abitum 4. to go away, depart; change into; die; **abī in malam rem** to hell with you!

abequitō 1. to ride away

aberrātiō, -ōnis *f.* (+*ab* +*abl.*) relief (from); diversion (from)

aberrō 1. (+*ab* +*abl.*) to wander (from); digress; differ (from); make a mistake, do wrong

abhinc *adv.* from this time, ago; from this place, hence

abhorreō 2. (+*ab* +*abl.*) to shrink back (from); be disinclined (towards); be inconsistent (with)

abhorridus, -a, -um *adj.* unsightly, repellent

abiciō, abiēcī, abiectum 3. to throw down *or* away; give up; degrade

abiectē *adv.* without spirit, abjectly; humbly

abiectiō, -ōnis *f.* dejection, depression

abiectus, -a, -um *adj.* downcast, despondent; unimportant; low, base

abiegnus, -a, -um *adj.* made of fir-wood

abies, -etis *f.* silver fir; wood of the silver fir; javelin; ship

abigō, abēgī, abactum 3. to drive away; remove; deter (from); **partum abigere** to procure abortion

abitiō, -ōnis *f.* going away, departure

ābītō 3. to go away, depart

abitus, -ūs *m.* going away, departure; place of egress, way out

abiūdicō 1. to remove something with a judicial sentence

abiungō, -xī, -ctum 3. to unyoke; separate, detach

abiūrō 1. to deny on oath, abjure; disavow

ablēgātiō, -ōnis *f.* sending away on duty

ablēgō 1. to send off *or* away; remove

abligurriō 4. to lick away, eat up; squander

ablocō 1. to let out on lease

ablūdō 3. to differ from, be unlike

abluō, -uī, -ūtum 3. to wash off *or* away; bathe

abnatō 1. to swim off *or* away

abnegō 1. to refuse; deny (*someone sthg*)

abnepōs, -ōtis *m.* great-great-grandson; distant descendant

abneptis, -is *f.* great-great-granddaughter

abnoctō 1. to stay out all night

abnormis, -is, -e *adj.* deviating from the norm, belonging to no school *or* sect

abnuō, -uī, -ūtum 3. to refuse by a nod of the head; deny; decline

abnūtō 1. (+*dat.*) to shake the head repeatedly (at)

aboleō, -ēvī, -itum 2. to destroy; do away with, dispel

abolescō, -lēvī 3. to vanish, pass away

abolitiō, -ōnis *f.* abolition, annulment (*of a law*); amnesty

abolla, -ae *f.* thick woollen cloak

abōminandus, -a, -um *adj.* ill-omened; abominable; *n.pl.sbst.* detestable things

abōminor 1. *dep.* to deprecate an unfavourable omen; hate, detest

aborior, abortus 4. *dep.* to die away, fade out

aboriscor 3. *dep.* to fade away, perish

abortiō, -ōnis *f.* premature delivery, abortion

abortīvum, -ī *n.* means of procuring abortion, abortifacient

abortīvus, -a, -um *adj.* born prematurely, aborted

abortus, -ūs *m.* premature delivery, abortion; failure to fertilize

abrādō, -sī, -sum 3. to scrape away; shave off; extort (*money*)

abripiō, -ipuī, -eptum 3. to snatch away, remove; drag off

abrogātiō, -ōnis *f.* repeal of law

abrogō 1. to repeal, revoke; take away

abrumpō, abrūpī, abruptum 3. to break off, break; cut short

abruptiō, -ōnis *f.* breaking off; tearing away

abruptus, -a, -um *adj.* steep, sheer; cut short; rash; stubborn

abs see **ab**

abscēdō, -cessī, -cessum 3. to go away; withdraw; retire

abscessiō, -ōnis *f.* separation, loss

abscessus, -ūs *m.* going away, withdrawal; absence

abscīdō, -dī, -sum 3. to cut off; separate

abscindō, -idī, -īssum 3. to tear off *or* away; break off; separate

abscīsus, -a, -um *adj.* steep, precipitous

absconditē *adv.* obscurely, abstrusely

absconditus, -a, -um *adj.* hidden; abstruse; disguised

abscondō, -ī(dī), -itum 3. to hide, conceal; keep secret

absens, -ntis *adj.* absent

absentia, -ae *f.* absence

absiliō 4. to fly away *or* apart

absimilis, -is, -e *adj.* dissimilar, unlike

absinthium, -(i)ī *n.* wormwood

absistō, abstitī 3. (+*ab* +*abl.*) to go away, withdraw (from); cease (from)

absolūtē *adv.* completely; simply

absolūtiō, -ōnis *f.* acquittal; completion; perfection

absolūtōrius, -a, -um *adj.* of *or* relating to acquittal

absolūtus, -a, -um *adj.* complete, finished; pure, absolute

absolvō, -vī, -ūtum 3. to free; acquit; complete; relate

absonus, -a, -um *adj.* inharmonious; incongruous

absorbeō, -buī or **-psī, -ptum** 2. devour; engulf; engross

absque *prep.* (+*abl.*) without, except

abstēmius, -a, -um *adj.* sober; self-restrained

abstergeō, -sī, -sum 2. to wipe off *or* away; expel

absterreō 2. to frighten away; keep from

abstinens, -ntis *adj.* (+*abl.*/+*gen.*) abstaining from; self-restrained

abstinenter *adv.* abstinently; scrupulously

abstinentia, -ae *f.* abstinence, self-restraint; integrity; starvation

abstineō 2. to restrain, keep back; abstain; fast

abstō 1. to stand aloof; keep away

abstrahō, -xī, -ctum 3. to drag away; remove; separate

abstrūdō, -sī, -sum 3. to conceal

abstrūsus, -a, -um *adj.* hidden, concealed; reserved; abstruse

abstulō 1. to take away

absum, abesse, āfuī *v.irreg.* (+*ab* +*abl.*) to be absent, distant (from); be free (from)

absūmēdō, -inis *f.* consumption, squandering

absūmō, -umpsī, -umptum 3. to consume; use up; take away

absurdē *adv.* discordantly; absurdly, irrationally

absurdus, -a, -um *adj.* discordant; absurd, inappropriate; incapable

abundans, -ntis *adj.* overflowing; abundant; (+*gen./abl.*) abounding (in)

abundanter *adv.* abundantly; copiously

abundantia, -ae *f.* overflowing; abundance; wealth

abundē *adv.* in abundance; exceedingly

abundō 1. to overflow; (+*abl.*) abound (in)

abūsiō, -ōnis *f.* flawed use of a synonym

abusque *prep.* (+*abl.*) right from; ever since

abūsus, -ūs *m.* wasting

abūtor, abūsus 3. *dep.* (+*abl./acc.*) to use up, waste; misapply; exploit

ac see **atque**

acalanthis, -idis *f.* small song-bird

acanthus, -ī *m.* the plant bearsfoot; gum tree

acapnus, -a, -um *adj.* burning without smoke

accantō 1. (+*acc.*) to sing to; sing at

accēdō, accessī, accessum 3. (+*dat.* or +*ad/in* +*acc.*) to approach, come to; agree with; enter upon; be added

accelerō 1. to hasten, quicken; hurry

accendō, -dī, -sum 3. to kindle, set on fire; inflame, excite

accenseō, -um 2. to count in addition

accensus, -ī *m.* attendant; *pl.* supernumerary soldiers

acceptātus, -a, -um *adj.* acceptable

acceptiō, -ōnis *f.* receiving, accepting

acceptō 1. to receive

acceptor, -ōris *m.* believer

acceptrix, -īcis *f.* female who receives, receiver

acceptum, -ī *n.* receipt of money; credit

acceptus, -a, -um *adj.* welcome, pleasant; (*of money*) credited, received

accessiō, -ōnis *f.* approaching; attack; addition

accessus, -ūs *m.* approach; attack; way in; admittance

accidens, -ntis *n.* chance occurrence, accident

accidō[1], -ī 3. to fall down; occur, befall; **accidit ut** (+*subj.*) it is the case that

accīdō[2], -dī, -sum 3. to cut into, hack at; weaken, diminish

accingō, -nxī, -nctum 3. to surround, gird; equip, prepare

acciō 4. to summon, send for

accipiō, accēpī, acceptum 3. to receive, accept; welcome; learn

accipiter, -tris *m.* hawk; one who snatches

accipitrīna, -ae *f.* snatching theft

accītus[1], -a, -um *adj.* imported

accītus[2], -ūs *m.* summons

acclāmātiō, -ōnis *f.* shout

acclāmō 1. to shout at; protest; applaud

acclārō 1. to make clear, reveal

acclīnis, -is, -e *adj.* (+*dat.*) leaning on *or* against; inclined (to)

acclīnō 1. (+*dat.*) to lean on, rest on; incline

acclīvis, -is, -e or **-us, -a, -um** *adj.* uphill, inclined upwards

acclīvitās, -ātis *f.* ascent, steepness

accognoscō 3. to recognize

accola, -ae *m./f.* neighbour

accolō, accoluī, accultum 3. to live near

accommodātē *adv.* agreeably, suitably

accommodātiō, -ōnis *f.* adjustment, fitting; courteousness

accommodātus, -a, -um *adj.* (+*ad* +*acc.* or +*dat.*) appropriate, suited (to)

accommodō 1. to fit, adjust; adapt

accommodus, -a, -um *adj.* (+*dat.*) fit (for), adapted (to)

accrēdō, -didī 3. (+*dat.*) to believe

accrescō, accrēvī, accrētum 3. to grow, increase; rise; accrue

accrētiō, -ōnis *f.* increase

accubitiō, -ōnis *f.* reclining (*at meals*)

accubitus, -ūs *m.* lying, reclining

accubō 1. to lie, recline; rest

accubuō *adv.* lying down

accūdō 3. to coin further

accumbō, -buī , -bitum 3. to lie down; recline (*at table*); (+*dat.*) sleep (with)

accumulātor, -ōris *m.* one who heaps up, accumulator

accumulō 1. to heap up, accumulate; load; increase

accūrātē *adv.* carefully, precisely

accūrātiō, -ōnis *f.* carefulness, accuracy

accūrātus, -a, -um *adj.* carefully prepared, exact

accūrō 1. to prepare with care; treat carefully

accurrō, -(cu)rrī, -rsum 3. (+*ad* +*acc.* or +*dat.*) to run (to), hurry (to); occur; attack

accursus, -ūs *m.* running to; attack

accūsābilis, -is, -e *adj.* blameworthy, reprehensible

accūsātiō, -ōnis *f.* accusation, indictment

accūsātor, -ōris *m.* prosecutor, accuser; informer

accūsātōriē *adv.* in an accusing manner

accūsātōrius, -a, -um *adj.* of *or* relating to the prosecution; denunciatory

accūsātrix, -īcis *f.* female prosecutor

accūsitō 1. to accuse repeatedly

accūsō 1. (+*gen. of charge*) to charge; censure, reproach

acer, -ris *n.* maple; maple wood

ācer, ācris, ācre *adj.* sharp; shrill; keen; intense; fierce

acerbē *adv.* bitterly; harshly; prematurely

acerbitās, -ātis *f.* harshness; bitterness; suffering

acerbō 1. to aggravate; embitter

acerbus, -a, -um *adj.* sour, bitter; harsh; distressing; premature

acernus, -a, -um *adj.* of maple wood

acerra, -ae *f.* incense-box

acersecomēs, -ae *m.* long-haired youth

acervālis, -is, -e *adj.* proceeding by accumulation

acervātim *adv.* in heaps; summarily; haphazardly

acervātiō, -ōnis *f.* heaping up, accumulation

acervō 1. to heap up

acervus, -ī *m.* heap, pile; mass

acescō, acuī 3. to become sour

acētābulum, -ī *n.* small cup (*for juggling*)

acētum, -ī *n.* sour wine, vinegar; quick wit

achātēs, -ae *f.* agate

acidus, -a, -um *adj.* sour, vinegary; sharp-tongued; unpleasant

aciēs, -ēī (-ē) *f.* sharp edge; insight; sight; eye; battle-line; battle

acīnacēs, -is *m.* short Persian sword

acinus, -ī *m.* berry, grape; stone of a berry

acipenser, -eris *m.* or **-sis, -sis** *m.* sturgeon (*or sim. luxury fish*)

aclys, -ydis *f.* light javelin

acoenonoētus, -us, -um *adj.* without common feeling

aconītum (-on), -ī *n.* kind of poisonous plant; poison (of this plant)

acor, acōris *m.* bitter or tart item

acquiescō, -ēvī 3. to rest, repose; subside; die; (+*in* +*abl. or* +*abl.*) find comfort (in); be pleased with

acquīrō, -sīvī, -sītum 3. (+*ad* +*acc. or* +*dat.*) to obtain; acquire (for)

acrātophorum, -ī *n.* vessel for holding unmixed wine

acrēdula, -ae *f.* unknown bird

ācriculus, -a, -um *adj.* somewhat shrewd

ācrimōnia, -ae *f.* energy, vigour

ācriter *adv.* keenly, intensely; harshly; violently; clearly; attentively

acroāma, -atis *n.* piece of oral *or* musical entertainment; entertainer

acroāsis, -is *f.* public lecture

acta, -ae *f.* seashore

actiō, -ōnis *f.* action; performance; speech; proposal; legal suit; accusation

actitō 1. to do repeatedly *or* habitually; be an actor in

actiuncula, -ae *f.* short speech

actīvus, -a, -um *adj.* active, practical

actor, -ōris *m.* drover; performer; actor; advocate; manager

actuāria, -ae *f.* swift boat

actuāriola, -ae *f.* small swift boat

actuārius[1], -a, -um *adj.* swift, agile

actuārius[2], -ī *m.* shorthand writer

actum, -ī *n.* act; achievement; decree; *pl.* record of events (*esp. of the senate*)

actuōsē *adv.* energetically, in a lively manner

actuōsus, -a, -um *adj.* energetic, full of activity

actus, -ūs *m.* driving of cattle; right of way; movement; progress; activity; duty; behaviour

actūtum *adv.* immediately, instantly

acula see **aquola**

aculeātus, -a, -um *adj.* stinging; pointed

aculeus, -ī *m.* sting; dart; spur

acūmen, -inis *n.* sharp point; sting; shrewdness; pointedness

acuō, acuī, acūtum 3. to sharpen; intensify; incite

acus, acūs *f.* pin, needle; hair-pin; curling-iron; pipefish, needlefish

acūtē *adv.* clearly; acutely, shrewdly

acūtulus, -a, -um *adj.* somewhat shrewd, acute

acūtus, -a, -um *adj.* sharp, pointed; keen; sagacious; clear; shrill; violent

ad *prep.* (+*acc.*) to, towards; by, near, at; up to, before; according to; concerning; for

adactiō, -ōnis *f.* compulsion, obligation

adactus, -ūs *m.* thrust

adaequē *adj.* equally; (+*ut*/*atque*) in like manner (as)

adaequō 1. (+*dat.*) to make equal (to), level; equal; be in equality (with)

adaestuō 1. to rush up; boil up

adamantēus, -a, -um *adj.* of steel; adamantine

adamantinus, -a, -um *adj.* of steel; adamantine; **adamantina saxa** diamonds

adamās, -antis *m.* hardest substance, adamant; diamond

adambulō 1. (+*ad* +*acc.*) to walk (near)

adamō 1. to admire deeply; fall in love with; covet

adaperiō, -uī, -tum 4. to open fully; open up; reveal

adapertilis, -is, -e *adj.* that may be opened

adapertus, -a, -um *adj.* open; overt

adaptō 1. to adapt; (+*dat.*) adjust (to)

adaquō 1. to get water; supply with water

adauctus, -ūs *m.* increase, growth

adaugeō, -xī, -ctum 2. to increase, augment; magnify

adaugescō 3. to become greater, increase

adaugmen, -inis *n.* addition, increase

adbibō, -ī 3. to drink in addition; absorb

adbītō 3. to come near

adc- see **acc-**

addecet 2. *impers.* it is fitting, proper

addenseō 2. to make more dense

addīcō, addixī, addictum 3. (+*dat.*) to assign (to); sell (to); award (to); support; be propitious (towards); sentence

addictiō, -ōnis *f.* assignment, adjudication

addictus¹, -a, -um *adj.* (+*dat.*) addicted (to); bound (to); *m.sbst.* addict

addictus², -ī *m.* person enslaved for debt

addiscō, addidicī 3. to learn in addition

additāmentum, -ī *n.* additional element

addō, addidī, additum 3. to add; attach to; confer; increase; go on to say

addoceō 2. to teach something in addition

addormiscō 3. to fall asleep

addubitō 1. to doubt, be uncertain;

addūcō, adduxī, adductum 3. to bring to, draw; induce; tighten; contract

adductē *adv.* strictly, closely

adductus, -a, -um *adj.* grave; strict; compressed

adedō, adesse, adēdī, adēsum *v.irreg.* to eat into; eat up; erode; squander

ademptiō, -ōnis *f.* taking away, seizure

adeō¹, adīre, adiī, aditum 4. (+*dat.* or +*ad*/*in* +*acc.*) to come to, approach; visit; incur; engage in

adeō² *adv.* to such a degree; (+*ut*/*quin* +*subj.*) so (much) (that); moreover, besides; indeed; (+*dum*/*donec* +*subj.*) up to the time (when)

adeptiō, -ōnis *f.* obtaining, acquisition

adequitō 1. (+*ad* +*acc.*) to ride (to)

aderrō 1. (+*dat.*) to wander towards

adēsuriō 4. to feel very hungry

adf- see **aff-**

adg- see **agg-**

adhaereō, -sī, -sum 2. (+*dat.* or +*in* +*abl.*) to cling (to), adhere (to); keep close (to); adjoin

adhaerescō, -sī , -sum 3. (+*dat.* or +*in* +*abl.*) to stick (to); keep close (to); be fixed; run aground

adhaesiō, -ōnis *f.* link

adhaesus, -ūs *m.* adherence, adhesion

adhibeō 2. (+*dat.* or +*in*/*ad* +*acc.*) to put (to); direct (to); apply (to); provide (for); bring in

adhinniō 4. (+*dat.* or +*ad* +*acc.*) to whinny (at); (+*acc.*) whinny to

adhōc see **adhūc**

adhortātiō, -ōnis *f.* encouraging *or* persuasive speech

adhortātor, -ōris *m.* one who exhorts, encourager

adhortor 1. *dep.* to urge on, exhort

adhūc *adv.* so far, as yet; still; yet further

adiacens, -ntis *adj.* adjacent, neighbouring; *n.pl.sbst.* neighbouring regions

adiaceō 2. (+*dat.* or +*ad* +*acc.*) to lie near (to); be adjacent (to); live near (to)

adiectiō, -ōnis *f.* addition; increase; repetition

adiectus, -ūs *m.* contact

adiciō, adiēcī, adiectum 3. (+*dat.* or +*in*/ *ad* +*acc.*) to throw (at); apply (to); add (to)

adigō, adēgī, adactum 3. (+*dat.* or +*in*/*ad* +*acc.*) to drive (to); thrust (into); bring forward; compel; stimulate

adiiciō see **adiciō**

adimō, adēmī (adempsī), ademptum 3. (+*dat.* or +*ab* +*abl.*) to take away (from), remove (from); deprive of; kill

adipātum, -ī *n.* rich dish (*esp. for children*)

adipātus, -a, -um *adj.* bombastic

adipēs, -um *m.pl.* obesity, fat

adipiscor, adeptus 3. *dep.* to arrive at; overtake; (+*acc.*/*gen.*) acquire, attain

aditiālis, -is, -e *adj.* inaugural; **aditiālis cēna** banquet given by magistrate on entering office

aditiō, -ōnis *f.* act of approaching

aditus, -ūs *m.* approach; access; way in; attack; opportunity

adiūdicō 1. (+*dat.*) to award (to) as a judge; ascribe (to)

adiūmentum, -ī *n.* help, aid, assistance

adiūnctiō, -ōnis *f.* union; combination; qualification

adiūnctor, -ōris *m.* one who proposes in addition

adiūnctus, -a, -um *adj.* (+*dat.*) adjacent (to); related (to); cognate; pertinent; *n. sbst.* collateral circumstance; attribute

adiungō, -nxī, -nctum 3. (+*dat.* or +*ad* +*acc.*) to harness (to); attach (to); add (to); apply (to)

adiūrō 1. to confirm by oath; swear by

adiūtābilis, -is, -e *adj.* helpful

adiūtō 1. to help, assist

adiūtor, -ōris *m.* helper, assistant

adiūtōrium, -iī *n.* help, assistance

adiūtrix, -īcis *f.* female accomplice

adiuvans, -ntis *adj.* contributory

adiuvō, adiūvī, adiūtum 1. to help, assist; augment; aggravate

admātūrō 1. to hasten to maturity

admētior, admensus 4. *dep.* to measure out

admigrō 1. (+*ad* +*acc.*) to go to

adminiculō 1. to support with props

adminic(u)lum, -ī *n.* prop, stake; human support; tool

administer, -trī *m.* helper, assistant

administra, -ae *f.* female assistant

administrātiō, -ōnis *f.* handling; administration; oversight; official duty

administrātor, -ōris *m.* manager, director

administrō 1. to assist; perform; manage, administer

admīrābilis, -is, -e *adj.* admirable; astonishing; paradoxical

admīrābilitās, -ātis *f.* admiration; remarkable quality

admīrābiliter *adv.* admirably; paradoxically

admīrandus, -a, -um *adj.* admirable; astonishing

admīrātiō, -ōnis *f.* admiration; astonishment; remarkable quality

admīrātor, -ōris *m.* admirer

admīror 1. *dep.* to admire; wonder at

admisceō, -scuī, -xtum 2. (+*dat.* or +*in* +*abl.*) to mix (in or together); combine (with); involve

admissārius, -(i)ī *m.* lewd man; sodomite

admissiō, -ōnis *f.* audience

admissum, -ī *n.* offence, crime

admissūra, -ae *f.* breeding

admittō, admīsī, admissum 3. to let in; receive; allow; release

admixtiō, -ōnis *f.* admixture

admoderātē *adv.* suitably, conformably

admoderor 1. *dep.* (+*dat.*) to moderate

admodum *adv.* very much; rather; altogether

admoeniō 4. to besiege

admōlior 4. *dep.* to struggle to; lay on

admoneō 2. to remind; advise; warn; admonish

admonitiō, -ōnis *f.* reminder; advising; warning; rebuke

admonitor, -ōris *m.* one who reminds

admonitum, -ī *n.* advice

admonitus, -ūs *m.* reminder; advice; warning; admonition

admordeō, ad(me)mordī, admorsum 2. to bite at; extract money from

admorsus, -ūs *m.* biting at, gnawing

admōtiō, -ōnis *f.* application

admoveō, admōvī, admōtum 2. (+*dat.* or +*ad* +*acc.*) to move (to); apply (to); bring up; place near

admūgiō 4. (+*dat.*) to low (to)

admurmurātiō, -ōnis *f.* murmur (*of an audience*)

admurmurō 1. to murmur in response

admutilō 1. to clip close; fleece

adnarrō 1. (+*dat.*) to relate (to)

adnatō 1. (+*dat.*) to swim to or by

adnectō, -xuī, -xum 3. (+*dat.* or +*ad* +*acc.*) to attach (to); connect (to); tie up; implicate

adnexus[1], -a, -um *adj.* contiguous (to)

adnexus[2], -ūs *m.* fastening; connection

adnītor, adnixus or **adnīsus** 3. *dep.* (+*dat.*) to rest on, lean upon; (+*inf.* or +*ut*/*ne* +*subj.*) strive hard (to)

adnō 1. (+*dat.*) to swim to or near; sail to

adnotātiō, -ōnis *f.* note, comment

adnotātor, -ōris m. one who makes notes, annotator

adnotō 1. (+dat.) to note; mark; notice; designate

adnūbilō 1. (+dat.) to cast clouds against

adnumerō 1. to pay out; count among; enumerate

adnuntiō 1. to announce

adnuō, -uī, -ūtum 3. to nod assent; signal; grant

adnūtō 1. to order by nodding

adoleō, adultum 2. (+dat. or +ad +acc.) to make a burnt offering (to); (+abl.) burn (on)

adolescō¹, adolēvī, adultum 3. to grow; mature; gain strength

adolescō² 3. to blaze

adopertus, -a, -um adj. covered; hidden; clothed; shut

adopīnor 1. dep. to conjecture

adoptātīcius, -(i)ī m. adopted son

adopt(āt)iō, -ōnis f. adoption (of a child)

adoptīvus, -a, -um adj. adopted; adoptive; ingrafted

adoptō 1. to adopt; assume; select

ador, adōris n. grain

adōreus, -a, -um adj. made of emmer wheat

adōria (-ea), -ae f. glory, renown

adorior, adortus 4. dep. to attack; assail; set to work on; (+inf.) attempt to

adornō 1. (+dat.) to prepare, get ready (for); (+abl.) furnish (with), adorn (with); honour (with)

adōrō 1. (+dat.) to appeal to, beg; honour, worship; hail

adp- see **app-**

adq- see **acq-**

adr- see **arr-** (other than below)

adrādō, -sī, -sum 3. to shave closely; trim; fleece

ads- see **ass-** (other than below)

adsum, adesse, affuī v.irreg. (+dat. or +ad +acc.) to be present (at/for), be at hand; attend; appear in support (of)

adūlans, -ntis adj. adulatory

adūlātiō, -ōnis f. act of fawning; adulation; obeisance

adūlātor, -ōris m. flatterer

adūlātōrius, -a, -um adj. of adulation

adulescens¹, -ntis adj. young; the younger

adulescens², -ntis m./f. young male/ female, youth

adulescentia, -ae f. youth; youthfulness

adulescentula, -ae f. (dear) young woman

adulescentulus¹, -a, -um adj. rather young

adulescentulus², -ī m. rather young man; mere youth

adūlor 1. dep. or **adūlō** 1. to fawn on; flatter; show servility to

adulter¹, -erī m. adulterer

adulter², -era, -erum adj. adulterous

adultera, -ae f. adulteress

adulterīnus, -a, -um adj. counterfeit; false

adulterium, -(i)ī n. adultery

adulterō 1. (+acc.) to commit adultery (with); counterfeit; corrupt; change

adultus, -a, -um adj. adult; mature; fully grown; at full strength

adumbrātim adv. with shadowy outline

adumbrātiō, -ōnis f. sketch

adumbrātus, -a, -um adj. sketchy, unsubstantial; feigned, counterfeit

adumbrō 1. to sketch, outline; feign

aduncitās, -ātis f. curvature

aduncus, -a, -um adj. curved; hooked

adurgeō 2. (+dat.) to press hard (upon)

adūrō, adussī, adustum 3. to burn; singe; freeze

adusque prep. (+acc.) as far as; up to

adustus, -a, -um adj. burnt, scorched; dusky

advectīcius, -a, -um adj. imported

advectō 1. to import

advectus¹, -a, -um adj. imported; immigrant

advectus², -ūs m. importation

advehō, -xī, -ctum 3. (+dat. or +ad +acc.) to bring, convey (to); pass. to travel (to)

advēlō 1. to veil

advena, -ae m./f. foreigner; immigrant; stranger; adj. foreign, alien

adveniō, advēnī, adventum 4. (+ad/in +acc. or +dat.) to reach, arrive (at); arise

adventīcius, -a, -um adj. extraneous; foreign; accidental; **cēna adventīcia** banquet held to celebrate a guest's arrival

adventō 1. to approach, draw near; arrive; impend

adventor, -ōris m. visitor; customer

adventōrius, -a, -um adj. **cēna adven-**

tōria banquet held to celebrate a guest's arrival

adventus, -ūs or **-ī** *m.* approach; arrival; onset; attack

adverberō 1. to strike against

adversāria[1]**, -ae** *f.* female opponent

adversāria[2]**, -ōrum** *n.pl.* day-book (*for accounts*)

adversārius[1]**, -a, -um** *adj.* opposed; inimical; of the opposition party

adversārius[2]**, -(i)ī** *m.* adversary, opponent; rival

adversātrix, -īcis *f.* female adversary

adversitor, -ōris *m.* slave who escorted his master

adversō 1. to direct

adversor 1. *dep.* (+*dat.*) to oppose; be inconsistent (with); be contrary (to)

adversum, -ī *n.* opposite direction *or* position; contrary; difficulty; hindrance

adversus[1]**, -a, -um** *adj.* facing towards; opposed; contrary; sloping away; *m.sbst.* opponent

adversus[2] **(-um)** *prep.* (+*acc.*) facing; opposite; in the direction of; against

adversus[3] **(-um)** *adv.* facing; in opposition; (+*v. of motion*) to meet

advertō, -tī, -sum 3. (+*dat.* or +*ad/in*+*acc.*) to turn (towards); direct (towards); heed

advesperascit 3. *impers.* it becomes evening

advigilō 1. watch over; be vigilant

advīvō, advixī, advictum 3. to be alive

advocāta, -ae *f.* female supporter

advocātiō, -ōnis *f.* advocacy; body of legal advocates; postponement (*esp. of a trial*)

advocātus, -ī *m.* legal advocate; counsellor; assistant

advocō 1. to summon; call upon; invoke; plead a case; cite

advolātus, -ūs *m.* flying towards

advolō 1. (+*dat.* or +*ad/in*+*acc.*) to fly towards; rush towards; swoop (upon)

advolvō, -vī, -ūtum 3. (+*dat.*) to roll towards; (+*dat./acc.*) grovel before

adytum, -ī *n.* innermost part of a temple; holy shrine

aedicula, -ae *f.* little room; *pl.* little house

aedificātiō, -ōnis *f.* act of building; building

aedificātiuncula, -ae *f.* little building project

aedificātor, -ōris *m.* builder; creator

aedificium, -(i)ī *n.* building

aedificō 1. to build, construct; build upon

aedīlicius, -a, -um *adj.* of *or* relating to an aedile *or* an ex-aedile; *m.sbst.* ex-aedile

aedīlis, -is *m.* Roman magistrate responsible for overseeing certain public matters (*buildings, markets, aqueducts etc.*), aedile

aedīlitās, -ātis *f.* aedileship

aedis (-ēs), -is *f.* temple; *pl.* house, household

aedituens see **aeditu(m)us**

aeditu(m)us, -ī *m.* temple-keeper; sacristan

aēdōn, -onis *f.* nightingale

aeger, aegra, aegrum *adj.* sick; injured; weary; troubled; difficult; painful; corrupt; *m.sbst.* sick person

aegis, -idis *f.* shield (*esp. of Jupiter or Minerva*)

aegrē *adv.* with difficulty; grudgingly; **aegrē ferre** to be vexed about; **aegrē facere** (+*dat.*) to cause trouble (to)

aegreō 2. to be sick

aegrescō 3. to become sick; be distressed; worsen

aegrimōnia, -ae *f.* grief; anxiety

aegritūdō, -inis *f.* sickness; grief; anxiety

aegror, -ōris *m.* sickness

aegrōtātiō, -ōnis *f.* sickness; disease

aegrōtō 1. to be sick; diseased

aegrōtus, -a, -um *adj.* sick; diseased; love-sick

aegrum, -ī *n.* diseased part

aelinon *interj.* alas (for Linus)!

aelūrus, -ī *m.* cat

aemula, -ae *f.* female rival

aemulātiō, -ōnis *f.* ambition; rivalry; imitation

aemulātor, -ōris *m.* imitator

aemulātus, -ūs *m.* rivalry

aemulor 1. *dep.* to rival; imitate; be jealous of

aemulus[1]**, -a, -um** *adj.* (+*gen./dat.*) rivalling; envious (of); comparable (to)

aemulus[2]**, -ī** *m.* rival; imitator

aēn(e)ātor, -ōris *m.* trumpeter

aēneus, -a, -um *adj.* made of bronze; from bronze; bronze-coloured

aenigma, -atis *n.* allegory; riddle

aēnum, -ī *n.* bronze vessel; cauldron

aēnus see **aēneus**

aequābilis, -is, -e *adj.* equal; uniform; just
aequābilitās, -ātis *f.* uniformity; equality
aequābiliter *adv.* uniformly; smoothly; equally; justly
aequaevus, -a, -um *adj.* equal in age, coeval
aequālis[1], -is, -e *adj.* equal; coeval; uniform; universal; smooth
aequālis[2], -is *m.* contemporary; equal; equivalent
aequālitās, -ātis *f.* equality; uniformity; smoothness
aequāliter *adv.* in equal measure; equally; uniformly; steadily
aequanimitās, -ātis *f.* goodwill; equanimity
aequātiō, -ōnis *f.* equal distribution
aeque *adv.* equally; similarly; justly
aequilībritās, -ātis *f.* equilibrium
aequilībrium, -(i)ī *n.* equilibrium
aequinoctiālis, -is, -e *adj.* of *or* relating to the equinox
aequinoctium, -(i)ī *n.* equinox
aequiperābilis, -is, -e *adj.* comparable
aequiperō 1. to regard as equal, liken; (+*dat.*) become equal (with)
aequitās, -ātis *f.* justice, equity; balance; **aequitās animī** contentment, equanimity
aequiter *adv.* equally
aequō 1. to make level; equalize; (+*dat.*) liken (to); be equal (to); rival; **(solō) aequāre** to destroy entirely
aequor, -oris *n.* level surface; plain; sea; *pl.* waters
aequoreus, -a, -um *adj.* of *or* by the sea; marine
aequum, -ī *n.* level ground; equality; what is fair
aequus, -a, -um *adj.* level; balanced; equal; fair; tranquil; (+*dat./gen.*) favourable (to); reasonable
āēr, āeris *m.* air; atmosphere; sky; breeze; scent; mist
aerāria, -ae *f.* copper mine
aerārium, -(i)ī *n.* public treasury (*esp. that in the temple of Saturn at Rome*)
aerārius[1], -a, -um *adj.* of copper; of *or* relating to money; **tribūnus aerārius** the lowest class of Roman citizens
aerārius[2], -(i)ī *m.* coppersmith; Roman citizen of the lowest class

aerātus, -a, -um *adj.* made of bronze; fitted *or* armed with bronze
aereus, -a, -um *adj.* made of copper *or* bronze
aerifer, -era, -erum *adj.* bronze-bearing
aeripēs, -pedis *adj.* bronze-footed
aerisonus, -a, -um *adj.* sounding with bronze
āerius, -a, -um *adj.* of *or* from the air; lofty; heavenly; airborne
aerūgō, -inis *f.* rust; envy, avarice
aerumna, -ae *f.* task; trouble, distress
aerumnābilis, -is, -e *adj.* distressing
aerumnōsus, -a, -um *adj.* full of suffering; distressing
aes, aeris *n.* copper, bronze; money; copper *or* bronze tool; bronze tablet, statue; **aes aliēnum** debt
aesar *n.* Etruscan deity
aesculētum, -ī *n.* oak forest
aesculeus, -a, -um *adj.* of oak
aesculus, -ī *f.* oak tree, durmast
aestās, -ātis *f.* summer; summer heat *or* sky; year
aestifer, -era, -erum *adj.* heat-bringing; hot
aestimābilis, -is, -e *adj.* possessing value
aestimātiō, -ōnis *f.* valuation; estimation; assessment of legal penalty; esteem
aestimātor, -ōris *m.* appraiser; estimator
aestimātus, -a, -um *adj.* under a financial forfeit
aestimō 1. to estimate, value; assess; reckon; consider
aestīva, -ōrum *n.pl.* summer military camp; season for campaigns, campaigns; summer pastures
aestīvē *adv.* in a summery manner
aestīvō 1. to spend the summer
aestīvus, -a, -um *adj.* of summer; used in summer; summery
aestuārium, -(i)ī *n.* coastal area flooded at high tide, estuary
aestum- see **aestim-**
aestuō 1. to be hot, blaze; boil up; burn (*with love*); be agitated; vacillate
aestuōsē *adv.* blazingly
aestuōsus, -a, -um *adj.* very hot, sweltering; seething; tossing
aestus, -ūs *m.* heat; summer; fire; tide; swell, surge; tumult; fever; passion

aetās, -ātis *f.* age; age group; period of life; lifetime, era; time

aetātula, -ae *f.* early age, youth; young person

aeternitās, -ātis *f.* eternity; immortality

aeternō[1] 1. to immortalize

aeternō[2] *adv.* forever

aeternum *adv.* forever, perpetually

aeternus, -a, -um *adj.* infinite; everlasting, immortal; permanent; **in aeternum** forever, perpetually

aethēr, -eris *m.* heaven, ether; sky; daylight; the gods

aetherius, -a, -um *adj.* heavenly, ethereal; divine; aloft; earthly (*not subterranean*)

aethra, -ae *f.* splendour; bright sky

aetiologia, -ae *f.* explanation of causes, aetiology

aevitās see **aetās**

aevum, -ī *n.* time; long time; lifetime; age; eternity

affābilis, -is, -e *adj.* affable, friendly; sympathetic

affābilitās, -ātis *f.* affability

affabrē *adv.* skilfully

affatim *adv.* satisfactorily, sufficiently; *sbst.* (+*gen.*) sufficiency (of); *adj.* ample, sufficient

affātus, -ūs *m.* address, conversation

affectātiō, -ōnis *f.* (+*gen.*) striving after; affectation

affectātor, -ōris *m.* (+*gen.*) seeker (of)

affectiō, -ōnis *f.* condition; (**animī**) **affectiō** mood, predilection, disposition; relationship

affectō 1. to strive after; contend; (+*inf.*) attempt, endeavour (to); try to conquer; lay false claim to; **spem affectāre** to cherish a hope

affectus[1]**, -ūs** *m.* state, emotion; disposition; affection; eagerness

affectus[2]**, -a, -um** *adj.* affected; impaired, ill; (+*abl.*) endowed (with); (+*ad* +*acc.*) related (to); (+*adv.*) minded (in such a way)

afferō, afferre, attulī, allātum *v.irreg.* to bring to; contribute; bring about; apply; report; allege

afficiō, affēcī, affectum 3. to affect, influence; harm; (+*abl.*) stir, affect (with); endow (with)

affīgō, affīxī, affīxum 3. (+*dat. or* +*ad* +*acc.*) to fix on, attach (to); nail (to); pierce; impress on

affingō, -nxī, -ctum 3. (+*dat.*) to make and add (*a part*) (to); embellish; ascribe (to), associate (with)

affīnis[1]**, -is, -e** *adj.* (+*dat.*) adjacent (to); related by marriage *or* descent (to); connected (with); subject (to)

affīnis[2]**, -is** *m.* neighbour; relative by marriage

affīnitās, -ātis *f.* relationship by marriage; connection

affirmātē *adv.* with assurance, positively

affirmātiō, -ōnis *f.* affirmation; assertion; conviction

affirmō 1. to assert, aver; confirm, corroborate; (+*acc.*+*inf.*) affirm (that)

afflātus, -ūs *m.* exhalation; breeze, draught; inspiration

affleō 2. to weep at

afflictātiō, -ōnis *f.* torment, affliction

afflictō 1. to buffet, toss about; vex, harass; oppress

afflictor, -ōris *m.* one who overthrows *or* subverts

afflictus, -a, -um *adj.* shattered, ruined

afflīgō, -līxī, -lictum 3. to knock down; strike; damage; vex, distress; overthrow, subvert

afflō 1. (+*acc.*) to breathe to *or* upon; (+*dat.*) blow (upon), waft; poison; infuse; inspire

affluens, -ntis *adj.* (+*abl.*) abounding (in); plentiful (in); favourable

affluenter *adv.* abundantly; extravagantly

affluentia, -ae *f.* abundance; extravagance

affluō, -xī 3. (+*dat.*) to flow in *or* towards; drift along; (*of people*) come flocking; (+*abl.*) abound (in)

affor 1. *dep.* to address, speak to

afformīdō 1. to be afraid

affrangō 3. (+*dat.*) to crush (against)

affricō 1. (+*dat.*) to rub on; smear on

affulgeō, -sī 2. to shine; (+*dat.*) look favourably upon

affundō, affūdī, affūsum 3. (+*dat. or* +*ad* +*acc.*) to pour upon; shed; flow by; spread over; (+*dat.*) *pass.* prostrate oneself (before)

āfluō, -xī 3. to flow from; (+*abl.*) abound (in)

agāsō, -ōnis *m.* stable-boy; horse driver; low servant

agellus, -ī *m.* small piece of land

agēma, -atis *n.* division of soldiers in the Macedonian army

ager, agrī *m.* field, piece of land; estate; countryside; district

āgerō 3. to take away, remove

aggemō 3. (+*dat.*) to groan with

agger, -ris *m.* mound; pile; rubble; rampart; pier, dam; bank; ridge

aggerō¹ 1. to pile up; heap over; (+*dat.*) heap on

aggerō², -ssī, -stum 3. (+*dat. or +ad +acc.*) to bring *or* bear (to); heap up; heap on

aggestus, -ūs *m.* bringing; terrace

agglomerō 1. (+*dat.*) to join (to), mass together (with)

agglūtinō 1. (+*dat. or +ad +acc.*) to stick, attach (to)

aggravēscō 3. to worsen, become serious

aggravō 1. to burden, oppress; aggravate, make worse; exaggerate

aggredior, -ssus 3. *dep.* to advance; approach; attack; seize; (+*inf.*) begin (to)

aggregō 1. (+*dat. or +ad +acc.*) to join together (with), associate (with); reckon among; implicate (in)

aggressiō, -ōnis *f.* opening (*of a speech*)

agilis, -is, -e *adj.* nimble, agile; energetic; alert; stirring

agilitās, -ātis *f.* nimbleness, swiftness

agitābilis, -is, -e *adj.* light, mobile

agitātiō, -ōnis *f.* disturbance, shaking; movement; exercise, practice

agitātor, -ōris *m.* one who drives, drover

agitātus, -a, -um *adj.* lively

agitō 1. to move, drive; hunt; perform, practise; live; agitate, vex; discuss, argue; consider

agmen, -inis *n.* stream; band, train; marching column, line of troops; army

agna, -ae *f.* ewe lamb

agnascor, agnātus 3. *dep.* (+*dat.*) to be born in addition (to)

agnātiō, -ōnis *f.* consanguinity through a father

agnātus, -ī *m.* male blood relation by the father's side; subsequent child

agnellus, -ī *m.* lambkin

agnīna, -ae *f.* lamb (*the meat*)

agnīnus, -a, -um *adj.* of a lamb

agnoscō, agnōvī, agnitum 3. to recognize; realize; accept, admit to

agnus, -ī *m.* lamb

agō, ēgī, actum 3. to drive; rouse; do; transact; go; emit; attend to; aim at; live; pass; discuss; think; **lēge agere** to go to law; **grātiās (-tēs) agere** (+*dat.*) to thank; **age** come!

agōn, agōnos *m.* contest; public games

agorānomus, -ī *m.* market inspector

agrārius, -a, -um *adj.* of *or* relating to the division of public land; *m.pl.sbst.* political party that proposed dividing public land among the people

agrestis¹, -is, -e *adj.* of *or* relating to fields; rural, wild; unsophisticated, coarse

agrestis², -is *m.* countryman; boor

agricola, -ae *m.* farmer

agripeta, -ae *m.* one who seeks out land

āh see **ā(h)**

aha *interj.* aha! (*exclam. of surprise, denial or laughter*)

ahēn- see **aēn-**

ai *interj.* ah! (*exclam. of grief*)

āiens, -ntis *adj.* affirmative

āiō *v.irreg.* say; assert; agree, say yes; talk about

āla, ālae *f.* wing; upper arm, armpit; wing of an army; cavalry squadron; reef of a sail; band of warriors

alabaster, -trī *m.* or **alabastrum, -ī** *n.* perfume casket

alacer, -cris, -cre *adj.* lively, nimble; eager

alacritās, -ātis *f.* liveliness; enthusiasm

alapa, -ae *f.* slap, smack

alāris, -is, -e or **-ius, -ia, -ium** *adj.* of the auxiliary cavalry; *m.pl.sbst.* cavalry; auxiliaries

ālātus, -a, -um *adj.* winged

alauda, -ae *f.* Gallic legion of Julius Caesar

albātus, -a, -um *adj.* clothed in white

albens, -ntis *adj.* white, grey; pale; clear

albeō 2. to be white; be pale; lighten

albēscō 3. to become white *or* grey; become bright *or* light

albicapillus, -a, -um *adj.* white-haired

albicō 1. to be white

albidus, -a, -um *adj.* white

albitūdō, -inis *f.* whiteness

albulus, -a, -um *adj.* white, hoary

album, -ī *n.* white; whiting; white tablet; register, list of judges selected by the quaestors

albus, -a, -um *adj.* white, grey; pale, fair; clear, bright; favourable

alcē, -ēs (*nom.pl.* **alcēs**) *f.* elk

alcēdō, -inis *f.* kingfisher, halcyon

alcēdonia, -ōrum *n.pl.* halcyon days

alcyōn, -onis or **-onē, -ēs** *f.* kingfisher, halcyon

alcyonēum, -ī *n.* medicine made from the halcyon's nest

ālea, -ae *f.* gambling game; betting stake; risk

āleārius, -a, -um *adj.* of *or* relating to gambling

āleātor, -ōris *m.* gambler

āleātōrius, -a, -um *adj.* in *or* from gambling

āleō, -ōnis *m.* gambler

āles¹, ālitis *adj.* winged; swift

āles², ālitis *m./f.* large bird, fowl; augury; winged god *or* beast; constellation

alescō 3. to grow

alga, -ae *f.* seaweed; water-plant

algens, -ntis *adj.* cold, chilly

algeō, alsī 2. to be cold; withstand cold; be neglected

algidus, -a, -um *adj.* cold

algor, -ōris *m.* cold

algōsus, -a, -um *adj.* covered with seaweed

algus, -ūs *m.* cold

aliā *adv.* by another route

aliās *adv.* at another time; in other circumstances; besides

āliātum, -ī *n.* food made with garlic

alibī (-bi) *adv.* in another place; in other respects

alica, -ae *f.* emmer groats; emmer porridge; fish sauce

alicārius, -a, -um *adj.* of porridge making

alicubi *adv.* somewhere, anywhere; occasionally

alicula, -ae *f.* light cloak

alicunde *adv.* from somewhere; from some other place

alid see **alius**

aliēnātiō, -ōnis *f.* transference of ownership; estrangement; stupor

aliēnigena, -ae *m.* foreigner, alien; *adj.* foreign

aliēnigenus, -a, -um *adj.* foreign, alien

aliēnō 1. to transfer, alienate; estrange, make hostile; alter the identity of; deprive

aliēnus¹, -a, -um *adj.* of another; foreign; (*+dat./abl.*) unrelated (with); irrelevant (to); unfavourable (to); insane; *n.sbst.* land, property *or* affairs of others

aliēnus², -ī *m.* slave of another; foreigner; stranger

ālifer, -era, -erum *adj.* winged

āliger, -era, -erum *adj.* winged

alimentum, -ī *n.* food; fuel; *pl.* sustenance, alms

alimōnium, -(i)ī *n.* nurture, rearing

aliō *adv.* to another place, to elsewhere; another subject *or* purpose

aliōquī(n) *adv.* in other respects; otherwise; in any event, besides

aliorsum *adv.* in another direction; in a different sense

ālipēs, -edis *adj.* with winged feet; swift; *m.sbst.* horse; the god Mercury

ālipilus, -ī *m.* slave who plucked another's armpit hair

aliptēs, -ae *m.* master of wrestlers *or* gymnasts

aliquā *adv.* in some way or other

aliquam *adv.* rather (many)

aliquamdiū (-ndiū) *adv.* for some time

aliquandō *adv.* at times; once; at some time; at last

aliquantillum, -ī *n.* very little amount

aliquantisper *adv.* for some time

aliquantō *adv.* to some extent

aliquantulum¹, -ī *n.* little amount

aliquantulum² *adv.* to a small extent

aliquantum¹, -ī *n.* certain amount, some part

aliquantum² *adv.* to some extent

aliquantus, -a, -um *adj.* certain, some

aliquātenus *adv.* up to a point

aliquī¹, -qua, -quod *adj.* some; any; not none; certain

aliquī² *adv.* in some way

aliquid *adv.* to some extent

aliquis, -qua, -quid *pron.* someone, something; anyone, anything; *pl.* some people *or* things

aliquō *adv.* to somewhere; in some quarter

aliquot *indecl.adj.* several; *sbst.* more than one, several

aliquotiens *adv.* several times

aliquōvorsum *adv.* in some direction

alis, alis, alid *adj.* see **alius**

aliter *adv.* in another way, otherwise

aliubi (-bī) *adv.* in another place; sometimes

ālium, āl(i)ī *n.* garlic

aliunde *adv.* from another place *or* person

alius¹, -a, -ud *adj.* other; different; **alius ... alius** one ... another

alius², -a, -ud *pron.* another one *or* thing

alivorsum see **aliorsum**

allābor, allapsus 3. *dep.* (+*dat. or* +*ad* +*acc.*) to glide (to); flow towards; creep

allabōrō 1. to toil at; add to with labour

allacrimō 1. to weep at

allapsus, -ūs *m.* gliding towards

allātrō 1. to bark at, rage at

allaudābilis, -is, -e *adj.* praiseworthy

allaudō 1. to praise

allec, -ēcis *n.* fish sauce

allectō 1. to entice

allēgātiō, -ōnis *f.* representation made on another's behalf

allēgātus, -ūs *m.* instigation

allēgō¹ 1. to send as a representative; commission; plead

allegō², -ēgī, -ectum 3. to elect, select

allevāmentum, -ī *n.* relief, alleviation

allevātiō, -ōnis *f.* alleviating, assuaging

allevō 1. to raise; alleviate; comfort; remove

allicefaciō, -fēcī, -factum 3. to allure, entice

alliciō, allexī, allectum 3. to attract; entice, lure; win over

allīdō, -sī, -sum 3. (+*dat. or* +*ad* +*acc.*) to dash against; shipwreck

alligō 1. to bind; bond; impede; bind by oath; bandage

allinō, allēvī, allitum 3. (+*dat.*) to spread over

allocūtiō, -ōnis *f.* address; exhortation

alloquium, -iī *n.* talk, conversation; encouragement

alloquor, -cūtus 3. *dep.* to address; harangue; invoke; comfort

allubescō 3. to please, gratify

allūceō, -uxī 2. (+*dat.*) to shine (for); light (for)

allūdiō 1. to play

allūdō, -sī, -sum 3. (+*dat. or* +*ad* +*acc.*) to frolic beside; play against; jest, playfully allude (to); (+*acc.*) play with

alluō, -uī 3. to flow near, wash against; wet

alluviēs, -ēī *f.* flooded land

alluviō, -ōnis *f.* addition to one's land from alluvial deposition

almus, -a, -um *adj.* nourishing, nurturing; kindly

alnus, -ī *f.* alder; object of alder-wood; ship

alō, aluī, al(i)tum 3. to nurse, nourish; feed; nurture; strengthen

aloē, -ēs *f.* bitterness

alogia, -ae *f.* nonsense

alpha *indecl.n.* first letter of the Greek alphabet, *alpha*; first of a group

alsius, -a, -um *adj.* cold, chilly

alsus, -a, -um *adj.* cool

altāria, -ium *n.pl.* section of altar for burnt offerings; high altar; burnt offerings

altē *adv.* on high, highly; deeply; thickly; remotely

alter¹, -era, -erum *adj.* one (*of two*), other (*of two*); second (*of two*); contrary

alter², -era, -erum *pron.* the other (*of two*); another; the second (*of two*)

alterās *adv.* at another time

altercātiō, -ōnis *f.* dispute; legal wrangle; debate

altercor 1. *dep.* to dispute, debate

alterinsecus see **altrinsecus**

alternātus, -a, -um *adj.* alternate; alternating

alternīs *adv.* alternately

alternō 1. to alternate; vacillate

alternus, -a, -um *adj.* alternate; interchanging; reciprocal; **pedēs alternī** elegiac verse

alteruter¹, -tra, -trum *adj.* either

alteruter², -tra, -trum *pron.* one *or* the other (*of two*), either

altilis, -is, -e *adj.* fattened; rich; *f.sbst.* fattened fowl

altisonus, -a, -um *adj.* high-sounding; sublime

altitonans, -ntis *adj.* high-thundering

altitūdō, -inis *f.* height; eminence; depth; sagacity; nobility; secrecy

altiusculus, -a, -um *adj.* rather too high

altivolans, -ntis *adj.* high-flying

altor, -ōris *m.* one who nourishes, foster-father

altrinsecus *adv.* on the other side

altrix, -īcis *f.* female nourisher, foster-mother; homeland

altrovorsum *adv.* on the other hand

altum, -ī *n.* the deep; the sea; high point; remote place

altus, -a, -um *adj.* high; deep; thick; loud; profound; noble

ālūcinātiō, -ōnis *f.* mental delusion

ālūcinor 1. *dep.* to wander in mind, talk idly

alumentum see **alimentum**

alumna, -ae *f.* female nursling; foster-daughter; pupil

alumnulus, -ī *m.* little foster-son

alumnus¹, -a, -um *adj.* (+*gen.*) fostered (by), reared (by)

alumnus², -ī *m.* male nursling; foster-son; pupil; sapling

alūta, -ae *f.* soft leather; leather purse; leather shoe; flaccid penis

alvārium, -(i)ī *n.* beehive

alveolus, -ī *m.* trough-shaped dish; gabion; gaming-board

alveus, -ī *m.* channel; trough; bath-tub; hull; boat; gaming-board

alvus, -ī *f./m.* belly, stomach; womb; bowels; hollow

amābilis, -is, -e *adj.* lovable; delightful

amābilitās, -ātis *f.* lovableness

amābiliter *adv.* in a loving mannner

āmandātiō, -ōnis *f.* banishment

āmandō 1. to banish, relegate

amans¹, -ntis *adj.* loving, affectionate

amans², -ntis *m./f.* one who loves, lover

amanter *adv.* lovingly

āmanuensis, -is *m.* secretary

amāracinum, -ī *n.* perfume of marjoram

amāracus, -ī *m.* marjoram

amarantus, -ī *m.* amaranth

amārē *adv.* bitterly

amāritiēs, -ēī *f.* bitterness

amāritūdō, -inis *f.* bitterness; harshness

amāror, -ōris *m.* bitter taste

amārus, -a, -um *adj.* bitter, pungent; shrill; caustic, acrimonious; distressing

amāsius, -(i)ī *m.* lover

amāta, -ae *f.* loved one

amātiō, -ōnis *f.* love-making, intrigue

amātor, -ōris *m.* lover, paramour; admirer; devotee

amātorculus, -ī *m.* little lover

amātōriē *adv.* lovingly

amātōrium, -īī *n.* love-charm

amātōrius, -a, -um *adj.* of love, amatory; love-inducing

amātrix, -īcis *f.* female lover

ambactus, -ī *m.* servant, dependant

ambāgēs, -um *f.pl.* roundabout route; wandering to and fro; circumlocution

ambedō, -esse, -ēdī, -ēsum *v.irreg.* to eat at; consume

ambestrix, -īcis *f.* female consumer, gluttoness

ambigō 3. to quarrel; be in doubt; argue about

ambiguē *adv.* ambiguously; indecisively; unreliably

ambiguitās, -ātis *f.* ambiguity

ambiguum, -ī *n.* ambiguity, uncertainty

ambiguus, -a, -um *adj.* doubtful; undecided; unreliable; hybrid

ambiō, -īre, -iī (-īvī), -itum 4. to go round, orbit; surround; embrace; canvass

ambitiō, -ōnis *f.* canvassing; candidature; self-advancement; ostentation; favouritism

ambitiōsē *adv.* ingratiatingly; ambitiously; ostentatiously; by canvassing

ambitiōsus, -a, -um *adj.* winding; eager for favour; ambitious; earnest; ostentatious

ambitus, -ūs *m.* winding route; revolution; circumference; circumlocution; canvassing; ambition; contention; bribery; flattery; ostentation; **verbōrum ambitus** well-balanced sentence

ambō, -ae, -ō *pl.adj.* both, two together; *pron.* both people *or* things

ambrosia, -ae *f.* ambrosia, the food of the gods; mythical healing plant

ambrosius, -a, -um *adj.* ambrosial, divine

ambūbāia, -ae *f.* female (Syrian) musician

ambulācrum, -ī *n.* promenade, avenue

ambulātiō, -ōnis *f.* walking; stroll; promenade, portico

ambulātiuncula, -ae *f.* small walk; little portico

ambulātor, -ōris *m.* wandering tradesman, pedlar

ambulō 1. to walk; strut; go; continue; **in iūs ambulāre** to go to court

ambūrō, -ussī, -ustum 3. to burn around, char, scorch; burn wholly; cremate

ambustulātus, -a, -um *adj.* scorched around

amellus, -ī *m.* star-wort

āmens, -ntis *adj.* demented; frantic, panic-stricken

āmentia, -ae *f.* dementia; reckless folly; frenzy

āmentō 1. to furnish with a throwing-strap; hurl

āmentum, -ī *n.* throwing-strap for a javelin

ames, amitis *m.* pole that supports bird nets

amethystinātus, -a, -um *adj.* wearing an amethyst-coloured dress

amethystinus, -a, -um *adj.* decorated with amethysts; amethyst-coloured

amethystus, -ī *f.* amethyst

amīca, -ae *f.* female friend; mistress

amīcē *adv.* in a friendly manner

amiciō, -xī, -ctum 4. to clothe, surround

amīciter *adv.* in a friendly manner

amīcitia, -ae or **-iēs, -ēī** *f.* friendship, friendly relations; friend; accord

amīcō 1. to propitiate

amictorium, -ī *n.* light scarf

amictus, -ūs *m.* manner of dressing, clothing; cloak; drapery, vesture

amīcula, -ae *f.* little mistress

amiculum, -ī *n.* cloak, mantle; clothing

amīculus, -ī *m.* dear friend

amīcus¹, -a, -um *adj.* friendly, loving; favourable; dear

amīcus², -ī *m.* friend; lover

āmigrō 1. to go away

āmissiō, -ōnis *f.* loss, deprivation

āmissus, -ūs *m.* act of losing, loss

amita, -ae *f.* paternal aunt; **magna amita** great-aunt

āmittō, āmīsī, āmissum 3. to send away; release, let slip; lose; abandon

amm- see **ām-**

amnicola, -ae *f.adj.* growing beside a river

amniculus, -ī *m.* small river, rivulet

amnis, -is *m./f.* river, stream; water

amō 1. to love; be fond of, like; make love to; (+*inf.*) be accustomed *or* wont (to); **amābō (tē)** please

amoenē *adv.* agreeably, pleasantly

amoenitās, -ātis *f.* pleasantness, charm; pleasant place; luxury

amoenus, -a, -um *adj.* pleasant, delightful; attractive

āmōlior 4. *dep.* to remove, erase; rebut

amōmum (-on), -ī *n.* eastern spice-plant; its spice *or* balsam

amor, amōris *m.* love, sexual passion; Cupid; love affair; loved one; fondness; eagerness

āmōtiō, -ōnis *f.* removal

āmoveō, āmōvī, āmōtum 2. (+*ab* +*abl.* or +*abl.*) to take away (from), remove (from); dispel; discard; keep away (from)

amphibolia, -ae *f.* double meaning, ambiguity

amphisbaena, -ae *f.* fictitious Libyan serpent with a head at either end of its body

amphitheātrālis, -is, -e *adj.* of *or* relating to the amphitheatre

amphitheātrum, -ī *n.* amphitheatre

amphora, -ae *f.* large two-handled jar (*esp. for wine*); measure of this size

ampla, -ae *f.* handhold, opportunity

amplē *adv.* generously; richly

amplector, -xus 3. *dep.* or **-ō** 3. to embrace; encircle; cling to; seize; welcome; consider

amplexor 1. *dep.* or **-ō** 1. to embrace; cling to; cherish; welcome

amplexus, -ūs *m.* embrace; encircling; circumference

amplificātiō, -ōnis *f.* increasing; amplification

amplificātor, -ōris *m.* enlarger, extender

amplificē *adv.* splendidly

amplificō 1. to increase, augment; magnify; exalt

ampliō 1. to increase; postpone; glorify

ampliter *adv.* abundantly; deeply; generously

amplitūdō, -inis *f.* size, abundance; eminence; amplification

amplius *adv.* more; further; longer

ampliusculē *adv.* rather more

amplus, -a, -um *adj.* large, ample; full; great; distinguished; important; generous

ampulla, -ae *f.* pear-shaped flask, used esp. for oil; *pl.* bombastic expressions

ampullārius, -(i)ī *m.* trader of *ampullae*

ampullor 1. *dep.* to speak bombastically

amputātiō, -ōnis *f.* pruning

amputō 1. to cut off; remove, exclude; prune, cut down

amurca, -ae *f.* watery fluid from a pressed olive

amygdalum, -ī *n.* almond

amystis, -idis *f.* emptying of a cup with one draft, downing

an *part.* or, either; (+*question*) whether

anabathrum, -ī *n.* raised seating

anadēma, -atis *n.* hair-band

anaglypta, -ōrum *n.pl.* work carved with low relief

anagnostēs, -ae *m.* educated slave who read aloud

analecta, -ae *m.* slave who gathered up crumbs from a meal

analemptris, -idis *f.* bandage for the shoulders

analogia, -ae *f.* reasoning based upon parallel example, analogy

anancaeum, -ī *n.* large drinking cup whose contents had to be drunk in one draught

anapaestum, -ī *n.* anapaestic line

anapaestus, -a, -um *adj.* anapaestic; *m. sbst.* anapaestic foot; anapaestic metre

anas, anatis *f.* duck

anaticula, -ae *f.* duckling; darling

anatīnus, -a, -um *adj.* of a duck

anatocismus, -ī *m.* compound interest

anceps, ancipitis *adj.* two-faced, two-edged; double; dangerous; undecided; wavering; ambiguous

ancīle, -is *n.* small-waisted shield

ancilla, -ae *f.* maidservant, slave girl

ancillāriolus, -ī *m.* lover of slave girls

ancillāris, -is, -e *adj.* worthy of a slave girl

ancillula, -ae *f.* young *or* mere slave girl

ancīsus, -a, -um *adj.* cut all over

anc(h)ora, -ae *f.* anchor; grappling hook

ancorāle, -is *n.* anchor cable

ancorārius, -a, -um *adj.* pertaining to anchors

andabata, -ae *m.* gladiator who fought blindfolded

androgynus, -ī *m.* hermaphrodite

andrōn, -ōnis *m.* corridor

ānellus, -ī *m.* small ring

anēthum, -ī *n.* dill, anise

anfractus, -ūs *m.* curvature; winding course; circular motion; circumlocution

angellus, -ī *m.* very small angle

angina, -ae *f.* throat infection, quinsy

angiportum, -ī *n.* or **angiportus, -ī** *m.* narrow passage, alley

angō, anxī, anctum 3. to strangle; distress; be distressed

angor, -ōris *m.* strangling; distress, anxiety

anguicomus, -a, -um *adj.* snake-haired

anguiculus, -ī *m.* small snake

anguifer, -era, -erum *adj.* snake-bearing; occupied by snakes

anguigenae, -ārum *m.pl.adj.* born of a serpent (*epithet of the Thebans*)

anguilla, -ae *f.* eel

anguimanus, -a, -um *adj.* snake-handed

anguīnus, -a, -um *adj.* of snakes

anguipēs, -pedis *adj.* snake-footed, *m.sbst.* giant

anguis, -is *m./f.* snake, serpent

angulātus, -a, -um *adj.* having corners

angulus, -ī *m.* angle; corner; small secluded place, retreat

angustē *adv.* narrowly; sparingly; exactly

angustia, -ae *f.* narrowness; crowdedness; narrow space; limitation; straits

angusticlāvius, -a, -um *adj.* wearing a thin purple band, equestrian

angustō 1. to narrow, limit; crowd

angustum, -ī *n.* small space; circumscription; straits

angustus, -a, -um *adj.* narrow, tight; thin; limited; poor

anhēlitus, -ūs *m.* breath; gasping, panting

anhēlō 1. to gasp, pant; exhale; emit vapour

anhēlus, -a, -um *adj.* gasping; causing breathlessness; steaming

anicula, -ae *adj.* little old woman

anīlis, -is, -e *adj.* of an old woman, anile

anīlitās, -ātis *f.* old age of women

anīliter *adv.* in the manner of an old woman

anima, -ae *f.* breath; soul, life; air

animadversiō, -ōnis *f.* attention; punishment

animadversor, -ōris *m.* observer

animadvertō, -tī, -sum 3. to turn the mind towards; heed; notice; punish

animal, -ālis *n.* animal, living thing; monster

animālis, -is, -e *adj.* of the air; animate; of a living thing

animans[1]**, -ntis** *adj.* living

animans[2]**, -ntis** *m.* living creature

animātiō, -ōnis *f.* living thing

animātus, -a, -um *adj.* animated; living; having a certain attitude

animō 1. to bring to life; rouse; endow with a certain disposition

animōsē *adv.* courageously; nobly; keenly

animōsus, -a, -um *adj.* spirited, brave; noble; boisterous

animula, -ae *f.* little life

animulus, -ī *m.* heart, darling

animus, -ī *m.* spirit; mind; desire; attitude; character; pride; courage; anger; air; **ūnō animō** unanimously; **bonō animō esse** to be of good cheer

annālis¹, -is *m.* book of annals, chronicles; tale

annālis², -is, -e *adj.* annual; **lex annālis** law prescribing the minimum ages for various offices

anniculus, -a, -um *adj.* one year old

anniversārius, -a, -um *adj.* annual; used yearly

annōna, -ae *f.* annual output; corn supply; price of corn; corn

annōsus, -a, -um *adj.* long-lived, immemorial

annōtinus, -a, -um *adj.* one year old

annus, -ī *m.* year; age; year's produce

annuum, -ī *n.* annual stipend

annuus, -a, -um *adj.* annual; year-long; for a year

anquīrō, -sīvī, -sītum 3. to seek after; enquire into; hold a judicial enquiry; bring a charge

ansa, -ae *f.* handle; loop; hook; opportunity

ansātus, -a, -um *adj.* with handles

anser, -eris *m.* goose

ante¹ *prep.* (+*acc.*) in front of; before; above

ante² *adv.* in front; forwards; before

anteā *adv.* previously

anteactus, -a, -um *adj.* past; *n.pl.sbst.* past deeds

anteambulō, -ōnis *m.* one who walks ahead to clear the way

antecapiō, -cēpī, -ceptum 3. to grasp beforehand; act in advance

antecēdens, -ntis *adj.* previous; foregoing

antecēdō, -cessī, -cessum 3. (+*acc./dat.*) to precede; be in front of; anticipate; surpass

antecellō 3. (+*dat./acc.*) to surpass, be superior (to)

antecessiō, -ōnis *f.* going before; antecedent

antecessor, -ōris *m.* military scout

antecessus, -ūs *m.* advance; **in antecessum** in advance

antecursōrēs, -um *m.pl.* leading troops

anteeō, -īre, -īī (-īvī), -itum 4. to go ahead, precede; surpass; forestall

anteferō, -ferre, -tulī, -lātum *v.irreg.* (+*dat.*) to carry in front (of); bring in advance; prefer (to), rank higher (than)

antefixa, -ōrum *n.pl.* ornamental roof fixtures

antefixus, -a, -um *adj.* (+*dat.*) fixed in front of

antegredior, -ssus 3. *dep.* to precede; occur before

antehabeō 2. (+*dat.*) to prefer (to)

antehāc *adv.* previously; up till now

antelogium, -(i)ī *n.* prologue, preamble

antelūcānum, -ī *n.* early hours of the night before dawn

antelūcānus, -a, -um *adj.* occurring in the hours before dawn

antemerīdiānus, -a, -um *adj.* occurring before midday

antemna (-nna), -ae *f.* sailyard; sail

anteoccupātiō, -ōnis *f.* anticipation of an opponent's arguments

antepartum (-pertum), -ī *n.* property obtained in the past

antepēs, -pedis *m.* forefoot

antepīlānī, -ōrum *m.pl.* front lines of soldiers in the Roman army

antepōnō, -posuī, -positum 3. (+*dat.*) to place before; prefer (to); appoint

antepotens, -ntis *adj.* excelling

antequam *conj.* before

antēs, -ium *m.pl.* rows (*of vines*)

antesignānī, -ōrum *m.pl.* soldiers at the front of a legion; *sg.* leader

antestō see **antistō**

antestor 1. *dep.* to call as witness

anteveniō, -vēnī, -ventum 4. to go ahead of, arrive before; (+*dat.*) surpass; anticipate

antevertō, -tī 3. or **-or** 3. *dep.* (+*dat.*) to go ahead of; anticipate; give priority to

antevolō 1. to fly ahead of

antevortō see **antevertō**

anticessus see **antecessus**

anticipātiō, -ōnis *f.* preconception

anticipō 1. to occupy beforehand;

anticipate; hold a preconception; **viam anticipāre** to lead a race

antideā sèe **anteā**

antideō, -īre 4. to excel, surpass

antidhāc see **antehāc**

antidotum, -ī *n.* antidote

antipodes, -um *m.pl.* inhabitants of the other (i.e. southern) side of the earth

antīquāria, -ae *f.* female student of antiquity

antīquārius, -īī *m.* student of antiquity

antīquē *adv.* in an ancient manner

antīquī, -ōrum *m.pl.* men of old, the ancients

antīquitās, -ātis *f.* oldness; antiquity; men of old; ancient practice; reverence

antīquitus *adv.* long ago; from long ago

antīquō 1. to vote to reject, reject

antīquum, -ī *n.* ancient practice; **ex antīquō** in the old-fashioned manner

antīquus, -a, -um *adj.* former; ancient; time-honoured; venerable; situated before

antisophistēs, -ae *m.* opponent in debate

antistes, -itis *m./f.* high-priest *or* priestess; patron; master, teacher

antistita, -ae *f.* high-priestess

antistō, -itī 1. to excel, surpass

antitheton, -ī *n.* antithesis

antlia, -ae *f.* mechanism for drawing water with the foot

antrum, -ī *n.* cave, den; tomb; cavity

ānulārius[1], -(i)ī *m.* ring-maker

ānulārius[2], -a, -um *adj.* of *or* relating to ring-makers

ānulātus, -a, -um *adj.* decorated with a ring

ānulus, -ī *m.* ring, signet-ring; ringlet; link of chain

ānus[1], ānī *m.* ring; anus

anus[2], anūs *f.* old woman; *f.adj.* old

anxiē *adv.* anxiously; meticulously

anxietās, -ātis *f.* anxiety; over-carefulness

anxifer, -era, -erum *adj.* causing anguish

anxitūdō, -inis *f.* anxiety

anxius, -a, -um *adj.* anxious; causing anxiety; involving distress; meticulous

apage *imper.* get away!; nonsense!

aper, aprī *m.* wild boar

aperiō, -uī, -tum 4. to open; cut open; uncover; make clear; disclose

apertē *adv.* openly; frankly; clearly

apertō 1. to expose

apertum, -ī *n.* open space; *pl.* clear facts; **ex apertō** openly

apertus, -a, -um *adj.* open; accessible; uncovered; manifest; frank

apex, apicis *m.* top of helmet; diadem, mitre; mountain top; tree top; tip of flame

aphractum, -ī *n.* or **aphractus, -ī** *f.* ship without a deck

aphronitrum, -ī *n.* sodium carbonate, washing soda

apiastrum, -ī *n.* balm

apicātus, -a, -um *adj.* wearing a priest's cap

apicula, -ae *f.* little bee

apinae, -ārum *f.pl.* trifles, worthless things

apis, apis *f.* bee

apiscor, aptus 3. *dep.* to grasp; (+*acc./gen.*) obtain; win

apium, ap(i)ī *n.* celery

aplūda, -ae *f.* chaff

aplustre, -is or **-um, -ī** *n.* decorated stern of a ship

apodytērium, -(i)ī *n.* undressing room

apolactizō 1. to kick away, reject

apologō 1. to reject, spurn

apologus, -ī *m.* tale, fable

apophorēta, -ōrum *n.pl.* gifts to be taken away by guests; book of epigrams by Martial

apoproegmena, -ōrum *n.pl.* things which are to be rejected

aposphrāgisma, -atis *n.* image on a signet-ring

apothēca, -ae *f.* store-room, warehouse

apparātē *adv.* sumptuously

apparātiō, -ōnis *f.* preparation

apparātus[1], -a, -um *adj.* prepared; sumptuous

apparātus[2], -ūs *m.* preparation; provision; apparatus; armaments; trappings; sumptuousness

appārens, -ntis *adj.* visible, apparent

appāreō 2. to appear; be visible, perceptible; be manifest; (+*dat.*) serve

appariō 3. to acquire

appāritiō, -ōnis *f.* preparation; service; servants

appāritor, -ōris *m.* public servant, attendant

apparō 1. to prepare; provide; organize; (+*inf.*) prepare (to)

appellātiō, -ōnis *f.* name; title; appeal

appellātor, -ōris *m.* one who appeals

appellitō 1. to call often

appellō[1] 1. to address; call; call upon; entreat; solicit; mention; pronounce

appellō[2], **appulī, appulsum** 3. (+*dat.* or +*ad/in* +*acc.*) to drive (to); bring (to); put into shore; turn (to)

appendicula, -ae *f.* small addition

appendix, -icis *f.* appendage, adjunct

appendō, -dī, -sum 3. to hang; weigh out

appetens, -ntis *adj.* (+*gen.*) greedy, eager (for); covetous

appetenter *adv.* greedily

appetentia, -ae *f.* appetite, desire

appetītiō, -ōnis *f.* grasping after; desire

appetītus, -ūs *m.* appetite, desire

appetō, -īvī (-iī), -ītum 3. to reach after; desire; seek out; attempt; attack

applaudō, -sī, -sum 3. to slap; applaud

applausus, -ūs *m.* beating (*of wings*)

applicātiō, -ōnis *f.* joining, attaching

applicātus, -a, -um *adj.* (+*ad* +*acc.*) devoted (to); (+*dat.*) situated (by)

applicitus, -a, -um *adj.* (+*dat.*) adjacent (to)

applicō, -āvī or **-uī, -ātum** 1. (+*dat.* or +*ad* +*acc.*) to bring (to); place (near); attach (to); apply (to)

applōrō 1. (+*dat.*) to weep (at)

appōnō, apposuī, appositum 3. (+*dat.* or +*ad* +*acc.*) to place near; set down; serve; apply; add; appoint

apporrectus, -a, -um *adj.* stretched out beside

apportō 1. (+*dat.*) to bring (to)

apposcō 3. to demand in addition

appositē *adv.* suitably

appositus, -a, -um *adj.* (+*dat.* or +*ad* +*acc.*) situated near; at hand; alike; suitable (for)

appōtus, -a, -um *adj.* drunk

apprecor 1. *dep.* to pray to, beseech

appre(he)ndō, -dī, -sum 3. to grasp; gain; take up

apprīmē *adv.* extremely, very

apprimō, appressī, appressum 3. (+*dat.* or +*ad* +*acc.*) to press to; clench

approbātiō, -ōnis *f.* assent, approbation; confirmation; decision

approbātor, -ōris *m.* one who approves

approbō 1. to approve; make acceptable; prove; confirm

apprōmittō 3. to promise in addition

approperō 1. to hasten; speed up

appropinquātiō, -ōnis *f.* approach

appropinquō 1. to approach; be nigh

appugnō 1. to attack

appulsus, -ūs *m.* approach; landing; influence

aprīcātiō, -ōnis *f.* basking in the sun

aprīcor 1. *dep.* to bask in the sunshine

aprīcum, -ī *n.* sunshine

aprīcus, -a, -um *adj.* sunny; basking in the sun

aprugnus, -a, -um *adj.* of the wild boar

aps see **ab**

apsinthium see **absinthium**

apsis, -dis *f.* segment of a circle

aptē *adv.* closely; fittingly; suitably

aptō 1. (+*dat.* or +*ad* +*acc.*) to fit on; add (to); apply (to); prepare; adapt

aptus, -a, -um *adj.* fastened; connected; (+*abl.*) provided (with); (+*dat.* or +*ad* +*acc.*) ready (for); suitable (for), apt

apud *prep.* (+*acc.*) near, beside; at the house of; among; in the hands of; in the view of

apȳrīnus, -a, -um *adj.* (*of fruit*) without a kernel; *n.sbst.* pomegranate

aqua, -ae *f.* water; sea; rain; *pl.* baths

aquāliculus, -ī *m.* pot-belly

aquālis, -is *m.* water-basin

aquārius[1], **-a, -um** *adj.* of or relating to water; **provincia aquāria** oversight of public waterworks

aquārius[2], **-iī** *m.* water-bearer

aquāticus, -a, -um *adj.* aquatic; rainy

aquātilis, -is, -e *adj.* aquatic

aquātiō, -ōnis *f.* drawing of water

aquātor, -ōris *m.* water-carrier

aquātus, -a, -um *adj.* watered down

aquila, -ae *f.* eagle; Roman military standard; pediment

aquilex, -egis *m.* water-diviner

aquilifer, -erī *m.* standard-bearer of a Roman legion

aquilīnus, -a, -um *adj.* of an eagle

aquilō, -ōnis *m.* north wind, Boreas; the north

aquilōnius, -a, -um *adj.* northern; of Boreas

aquilus, -a, -um *adj.* dark-coloured, swarthy

aquola, -ae *f.* small amount of water; little stream

aquor 1. *dep.* to fetch water

aquōsus, -a, -um *adj.* of water; watery; rainy; well-watered; crystal-clear

āra, ārae *f.* altar; refuge; protector

arabarchēs,-ae *m.* Egyptian tax officer

arānea, -ae *f.* spider's web; spider

arāneola, -ae *f.* spider

arāneōsus, -a, -um *adj.* full of spider's webs

arāneus, -ī *m.* spider

arātiō, -ōnis *f.* estate of arable land

arātiuncula, -ae *f.* small estate of arable land

arātor, -ōris *m.* ploughman; farmer of arable land; *adj.* ploughing

arātrum, -ī *n.* plough

arbiter, -trī *m.* witness; legal umpire, judge; ruler; fulfiller

arbitra, -ae *f.* female witness; judge

arbitrāriō *adv.* doubtfully

arbitrārius, -a, -um *adj.* discretionary

arbitrātus, -ūs *m.* choice; jurisdiction; **arbitrātū** (+*gen. or meo etc.*) at the discretion of; as much as (one) wishes

arbitrium, -(i)ī *n.* decision; legal sentence; authority; witnessing; desire

arbitrō 1. to judge; consider

arbitror 1. *dep.* to witness; judge; think

arbor, -oris *f.* tree; trunk; mast; oar; spear

arboreus, -a, -um *adj.* of trees; like a tree

arbōs see **arbor**

arbuscula, -ae *f.* small tree

arbustum, -ī *n.* plantation of trees *or* bushes

arbustus, -a, -um *adj.* planted with trees

arbuteus, -a, -um *adj.* of the strawberry tree; of its wood

arbutum, -ī *n.* strawberry; leaves of the strawberry tree

arbutus, -ī *f.* strawberry tree, arbutus

arca, -ae *f.* box; coffin, cell; treasury; wealth

arcānō *adv.* secretly

arcānus, -a, -um *adj.* secret; private; mysterious; secretive; *n.sbst.* secret, mystery; secret place

arceō 2. to confine; control; keep away;

protect; (+*abl. or +ab +abl.*) prevent (from)

arcersō see **arcessō**

arcessītus, -ūs *m.* calling, summons

arcessō, -īvī, -ītum 3. to send for, fetch; summon; bring about; drag in

archetypum, -ī *n.* original, model

archetypus, -a, -um *adj.* original; autograph; real-life; genuine

archimagīrus, -ī *m.* chief cook, head chef

archimīmus, -ī *m.* leader of a group of mime artists

archipīrāta, -ae *m.* pirate leader

architectō 1. to design

architechtōn, -ōnis *m.* architect

architector 1. *dep.* to plan

architectūra, -ae *f.* architecture

architectus, -ī *m.* architect; deviser

archōn, -ontis *m.* one of the highest Athenian magistrates

arcitenens see **arquitenens**

arcuātus, -a, -um *adj.* bow-shaped; hooded

arcula, -ae *f.* small box, casket

arculārius, -(i)ī *m.* maker of boxes

arcus, -ūs *m.* bow; rainbow; arch; curve

ardaliō, -ōnis *m.* busy-body

ardea, -ae *f.* heron

ardens, -ntis *adj.* burning; shining; passionate; enthusiastic

ardenter *adv.* with a burning sensation; ardently; enthusiastically

ardeō, arsī 2. to burn, blaze; gleam; rage; be in love

ardescō 3. to catch fire; flare up; grow fierce

ardor, -ōris *m.* fire; heat; gleam, flash; fervour; love

arduum, -ī *n.* high *or* steep place; difficult task

arduus, -a, -um *adj.* high; elevated; sublime; steep; difficult

ārea, -ae *f.* open space; forecourt; threshing floor; site; plane; bald patch

ārefaciō, -fēcī, -factum 3. to make dry

arēna see **(h)arēna**

ārens, -ntis *adj.* dry; dried; parching

āreō 2. to be dry; be thirsty; be unwatered

āreola, -ae *f.* small courtyard

ārescō, āruī 3. to become dry; run dry

aretālogus, -ī *m.* professional recounter of tales

argentāria, -ae *f.* banking house; banking

argentārius¹, -a, -um *adj.* monetary; of *or* relating to bankers

argentārius², -(i)ī *m.* banker

argentātus, -a, -um *adj.* decorated with silver; monetary

argenteolus, -a, -um *adj.* of silver

argenteus, -a, -um *adj.* of silver; silvery; monetary; *m.sbst.* silver coin

argentum, -ī *n.* silver; work of silver; money

argilla, -ae *f.* potter's clay

argūmentātiō, -ōnis *f.* argumentation; proof

argūmentor 1. *dep.* to argue; prove; conclude

argūmentum, -ī *n.* argument; proof; deduction; motive; subject; tale

arguō, -uī, -ūtum 3. to assert; accuse; prove; convict; confute; criticize

argūtātiō, -ōnis *f.* creaking

argūtē *adv.* sagaciously; acutely

argūtiae, -ārum *f.pl.* verbal cleverness, sophistry; pleasantries

argūtō 1. to babble

argūtor 1. *dep.* to babble, prattle

argūtulus, -a, -um *adj.* rather shrewd, clever

argūtus, -a, -um *adj.* clear-sounding; tuneful; eloquent; garrulous; shrewd

argyraspides, -um *m.pl.* silver-shielded corps of soldiers in the army of Alexander the Great

āridulus, -a, -um *adj.* somewhat parched

āridum, -ī *n.* dry land

āridus, -a, -um *adj.* dry, parched; dried up; miserly; austere; grating

ariēs, -etis *m.* ram; battering ram; buttress

arietātiō, -ōnis *f.* collision, butting

arietō 1. to butt; batter; strike together; stumble

arista, -ae *f.* awn of grain; ear of corn; grain crop; stalk

aristolochia, ae *f.* birthwort, medicinal plant

arithmēticum, -ī *n.* arithmetic

āritūdō, -inis *f.* dryness, aridity

arma, -ōrum *n.pl.* weapons, defensive arms; military force; battle

armāmenta, -ōrum *n.pl.* sailing gear; rigging

armāmentārium, -(i)ī *n.* arsenal, armoury

armāriolum, -ī *n.* small chest, cabinet

armārium, -(i)ī *n.* cabinet, book-case

armātūra, -ae *f.* armament; **levis armātūra** lightly armed troops

armātus¹, -a, -um *adj.* armed; of weapons

armātus², -ī *m.* armed man, soldier

armātus³, -ūs *m.* arms; **gravis armātus** heavily armed troops

armentālis, -is, -e *adj.* of herds

armentārius, -(i)ī *m.* herdsman

armentum, -ī *n.* herd; cattle; horse

armifer, -era, -erum *adj.* bearing arms; martial; producing armed men

armiger¹, -era, -erum *adj.* bearing arms; producing armed men

armiger², -erī *m.* armour-bearer; **Iovis armiger** eagle

armigera, -ae *f.* female armour-bearer; **Iovis armigera** eagle

armilla, -ae *f.* bracelet, arm-band

armillātus, -a, -um *adj.* wearing a bracelet *or* bracelets

armipotens, -ntis *adj.* powerful in war; *m.sg.sbst.* Mars

armisonus, -a, -um *adj.* resounding with the clash of arms

armō 1. (+*abl.*) to arm (with), equip (with); rouse to war; mobilize; rig

armus, -ī *m.* shoulder; flank

arō 1. to plough, cultivate; wrinkle

arquātus, -a, -um *adj.* jaundiced

arquitenens, -ntis *adj.* bow-bearing; *m.sg. sbst.* Apollo

arrabō, -ōnis *m.* token payment, pledge

arrectus, -a, -um *adj.* steep

arrēpō, -epsī 3. (+*dat. or +ad +acc.*) to creep up to; move gently towards

arrīdeō, -sī, -sum 2. to smile at *or* upon; (+*dat.*) please

arrigō, arrexī, arrectum 3. to stand upright; become erect; arouse

arripiō, -ipuī, -eptum 3. to snatch; lay hold of; arrest; assume; assail; attack

arrīsor, -ōris *m.* one who smiles

arrōdō, -sī, -sum 3. to gnaw at; erode

arrogans, -ntis *adj.* arrogant, insolent; presumptuous

arroganter *adv.* arrogantly; presumptuously

arrogantia, -ae *f.* arrogance; presumptuousness

arrogō 1. to ask in addition; lay claim to; adopt; assign; appoint in addition

arrōsor, -ōris *m.* one who gnaws (at)

ars, artis *f.* skill, art; work of art; profession; characteristic; theory; artifice

artē *adv.* tightly, compactly; strictly; deeply

artēria, -ae *f.* or **artērium, -(i)ī** *n.* trachea; artery

arthrīticus, -a, -um *adj.* rheumatic, arthritic

articulāris, -is, -e *adj.* of the joints; **articulāris morbus** arthritis

articulātim *adv.* limb by limb; note by note; point by point

articulō 1. to divide up individually

artic(u)lus, -ī *m.* joint; finger; point of time; clause

artifex¹, -icis *m.* artist, craftsman; actor; professional; schemer

artifex², -icis *adj.* artistic, creative; expert; skilfully made; cunning

artificiōsē *adv.* artistically; technically; artificially

artificiōsus, -a, -um *adj.* artistic; ingenious; technical; artificial

artificium, -(i)ī *n.* artistic skill, craft; work of art; theory; cunning

artō 1. to tighten; crowd; cramp; restrict; abridge

artocreas *n.* bread and meat distributed freely

artolaganus, -ī *m.* fatty cake

artopta, -ae *f.* bread-pan

artum, -ī *n.* confined space; narrow sphere; strait(s); short supply

artus¹, -a, -um *adj.* tight; close; thick; narrow; strict; restricted; critical

artus², -ūs *m.* joint; limb, member

artūtus, -a, -um *adj.* large-limbed

ārula, -ae *f.* small altar

arvīna, -ae *f.* lard, fat

arvum, -ī *n.* arable field; country; countryside; *pl.* lowlands

arvus, -a, -um *adj.* ploughed

arx, arcis *f.* citadel, fortress; city; peak; refuge

as, assis *m.* copper coin of the smallest value; one pound (*in weight*)

asarōta, -ōrum *n.pl.* unswept areas

ascaulēs, -is *m.* bagpiper

ascendō, -dī, -sum 3. to climb, mount; embark; rise; reach

ascensiō, -ōnis *f.* ascent; advancement

ascensus, -ūs *m.* ascent; way up; step; height

asciō 4. to admit, associate

asciscō, ascīvī, ascītum 3. to admit, adopt; assume

ascopa, -ae *f.* leather bag

ascrībō, ascripsī, ascriptum 3. (+*dat.* or +*ad* +*acc.*) to add in writing (to); enrol; assign (to); number among

ascriptīcius, -a, -um *adj.* enrolled in addition

ascriptiō, -ōnis *f.* addition in writing, addendum

ascriptīvus, -a, -um *adj.* enrolled as a supernumerary

ascriptor, -ōris *m.* one who signs a document in approval; supporter

asella, -ae *f.* female ass

asellus, -ī *m.* donkey, ass; prized fish (*perhaps* the hake)

asīlus, -ī *m.* gadfly

asinārius, -(i)ī *m.* donkey-driver

asinus, -ī *m.* donkey, ass; fool

asōtus, -ī *m.* debauchee

asparagus, -ī *m.* asparagus

aspectābilis, -is, -e *adj.* visible

aspectō 1. to observe; face; respect; attend

aspectus, -ūs *m.* seeing; sight; vision; gaze; appearance

aspellō 3. to drive away, banish

asper, -era, -erum *adj.* rough, shaggy, rugged; sharp; harsh; savage; severe; difficult; adverse

asperē *adv.* roughly; harshly; strictly; drastically

aspergō¹, -sī, -sum 3. (+*dat.*) to sprinkle upon; splash; add in small amount (to); inflict

aspergō², -inis *f.* sprinkling; spray

asperitās, -ātis *f.* roughness; jaggedness; relief; harshness; savagery; severity; difficulty

aspernātiō, -ōnis *f.* (+*gen.*) rejection (of), spurning (of)

aspernor 1. *dep.* to repel; reject; decline; (+*inf.*) refuse (to)

asperō 1. to make rough; sharpen; enrage; aggravate

aspersiō, -ōnis *f.* sprinkling

aspiciō, aspexī, aspectum 3. to notice, behold; face; visit; perceive; consider

aspīrātiō, -ōnis *f.* breathing; exhalation; aspiration in speech

aspīrō 1. (+*dat. or +ad +acc.*) to breathe *or* blow upon; infuse; favour; aspire to; approach

aspis, -idis *f.* venomous African snake, asp

asportātiō, -ōnis *f.* removal

asportō 1. to remove, carry away

asprētum, -ī *n.* area of rough ground

assa¹, -ae *f.* nurse

assa², -ōrum *n.pl.* sweating bath, sudatorium

assectātiō, -ōnis *f.* respectful attendance

assectātor, -ōris *m.* attendant; devotee

assector 1. *dep.* to attend; support

assecula, -ae *m.* attendant; lackey

assensiō, -ōnis *f.* approval; agreement; Stoic belief in sensible impulses

assensor, -ōris *m.* one who agrees

assensus, -ūs *m.* approval, assent

assentātiō, -ōnis *f.* adulation, flattery

assentātiuncula, -ae *f.* trivial flattery

assentātor, -ōris *m.* flatterer

assentātōriē *adv.* in a flattering manner

assentātrix, -īcis *f.* female flatterer

assentiō, -sī, -sum 4. or **assentior, -sus** 4. *dep.* to assent, approve; (+*dat.*) agree (with)

assentor 1. *dep.* to assent; (+*dat.*) flatter

assequor, -cūtus 3. *dep.* to follow; catch up, overtake; attain; achieve; understand

asser, -eris *m.* wooden beam; pole of a litter

asserō¹, -uī, -tum 3. to claim; arrogate; declare; defend; liberate

asserō², assēvī, assitum 3. (+*dat.*) to sow near

assertiō, -ōnis *f.* declaration of a slave's freedom

assertor, -ōris *m.* claimant; defendant

asserviō 4. (+*dat.*) to apply oneself (to)

asservō 1. to observe; guard; retain

assessiō, -ōnis *f.* sitting beside

assessor, -ōris *m.* counsellor, assessor

assessus, -ūs *m.* sitting beside

assevēranter *adv.* emphatically, earnestly

assevērātiō, -ōnis *f.* earnestness; emphasis; assertion

assevērō 1. to be earnest; assert; proclaim

assībilō 1. (+*dat.*) to hiss (upon)

assiccō 1. to make dry; dry up

assideō, assēdī, assessum 2. (+*dat.*) to sit by; sit in council; camp near; besiege; dwell near; attend upon; devote onself to; resemble

assīdō, assēdī 3. to sit down; perch; (+*dat.*) sit near (to)

assiduē *adv.* continually, incessantly

assiduitās, -ātis *f.* constant attendance; application; persistency

assiduō *adv.* continually

assiduus, -a, -um *adj.* constantly present; incessant; persistent; regular; landowning

assignātiō, -ōnis *f.* distribution of land; allotment

assignō 1. (+*dat.*) to allot (to); confer; ascribe (to); seal

assiliō, -uī 4. (+*dat.*) to leap up (to); attack; rush (at *or* into)

assimilis, -is, -e *adj.* (+*dat./gen.*) similar (to), like

assimiliter *adv.* in the same manner

assimulātiō, -ōnis *f.* comparison

assimulō 1. to feign, pretend; simulate; (+*dat.*) make resemble; compare (to); assimilate

assis see **axis²**

assistō, astitī 3. (+*dat.*) to stand by; attend; support; take up position; halt

associō 1. to associate with

assoleō 2. to be accustomed with, be usual

assonō 1. to answer with sound

assūdescō 3. to begin to sweat

assuēfaciō, -fēcī, -factum 3. (+*abl./dat. or* +*ad +acc.*) to make accustomed (to)

assuescō, -ēvī, -ētum 3. (+*abl./dat. or +ad +acc. or +inf.*) to become accustomed (to); (+*abl.*) make accustomed (to)

assuētūdō, -inis *f.* habit; intimacy

assuētus, -a, -um *adj.* (+*dat./abl./inf.*) accustomed (to); customary

assūgō, assuxī, assuctum 3. to suck towards

assula, -ae *f.* splinter, (*wooden or stone*) chip

assulātim *adv.* into splinters

assultō 1. to leap towards; rush at; (+*acc./ dat.*) attack

assultus, -ūs *m.* assault, charge

assūmō, -umpsī, -umptum 3. (+*dat. or* +*ad +acc.*) to take in addition (to); add (to); assume; appropriate; claim; borrow

assumptiō, -ōnis f. adoption; introduction; minor premiss

assumptīvus, -a, -um adj. based upon extrinsic reasoning

assuō, -uī, -ūtum 3. to sew on

assurgō, -rrexī, -rrectum 3. to stand up; rise; be elevated

assus, -a, -um adj. baked; dry

ast conj. but if, and if; whereas; thereupon

asternō, astrāvī, astrātum 3. (+dat.) to lie (on); pass. prostrate oneself

asticus, -a, -um adj. urban

astipulātor, -ōris m. legal associate; adherent

astipulor 1. dep. (+dat.) to support

astituō, -uī, -ūtum 3. to place before

astō, astitī 1. (+dat.) to stand by; attend; stand up; stand still

astrepō, -uī 3. (+dat.) to shout in support (of); (+acc.) rail at

astrictē adv. strictly; concisely

astrictus, -a, -um adj. bound; busy; brief; compact; parsimonious

astrīdeō 2. to hiss

astrifer, -era, -erum adj. starry

astriger, -era, -erum adj. star-bearing

astringō, -nxī, -ctum 3. to bind; tighten; contract; (+abl.) restrain (with), restrict (by)

astrologia, -ae f. astronomy

astrologus, -ī m. astronomer, astrologer

astronomia, -ae f. astronomy

astrum, -ī n. star; constellation; heavenly body; pl. heavens

astruō, -xī, -ctum 3. (+dat.) to build on; heap on; contribute (to), add (to)

astu indecl.n. the city (Athens)

astupeō 2. (+dat.) to be amazed (at)

astus, -ūs m. cunning; trick

astūtē adv. cunningly, astutely

astūtia, -ae f. cunning; trick

astūtus, -a, -um adj. cunning, astute

asȳlum, -ī n. refuge, asylum

asymbolus, -a, -um adj. without paying an entrance fee

at conj. but, yet; but then; yes, and; nevertheless

atavus (-os), -ī m. great-great-great-grandfather; remote ancestor

āter, ātra, ātrum adj. black; dark; smoky; ill-omened; deadly

āthlēta, -ae m. athlete; wrestler; pl. athletic contest

āthlēticē adv. like an athlete

atomus (-os), -ī f. smallest, indivisible part of matter, atom

atque or **ac** conj. and; and then; and also; and even; than

atquī conj. but; nevertheless; and yet

ātrāmentum, -ī n. black colouring, ink

ātrātus, -a, -um adj. dressed in black (esp. for mourning)

ātricolor, -ōris adj. black, dark-coloured

ātriēnsis, -is m. household steward; house-servant

ātriolum, -ī n. small ante-room

ātritās, -ātis f. blackness

ātrium, -(i)ī n. hall; pl. palace

atrōcitās, -ātis f. dreadfulness; savagery; severity

atrōciter adv. violently; bitterly; savagely; severely

atrox, -ōcis adj. terrible; violent; bitter; savage; severe; shocking

attactus, -ūs m. contact, touch

attagēn, -ēnis m. or **attagēna, -ae** f. partridge-like bird

attamen conj. but yet

attat(ae) interj. expression of surprise or fear

attegia, -ae f. hut

attemperātē adv. opportunely

attemptō 1. to attack; make an attempt on; essay

attendō, -dī, -tum 3. (+dat. or +ad +acc.) to pay attention (to); (+acc.) study, watch; note, observe; deal with; exert oneself; **animum attendere** to concentrate

attentē adv. attentively, with concentration

attentiō, -ōnis f. attention, concentration

attentō see **attemptō**

attentus, -a, -um adj. attentive; concentrated; careful

attenuātē adv. plainly, simply

attenuātus, -a, -um adj. plain, simple

attenuō 1. to make thin; reduce; simplify; impoverish; weaken

atterō, attrīvī, attrītum 3. to wear, rub; wear away; waste; weaken

attexō, -uī, -tum 3. to weave on; add on

attigō see **attingō**

attineō, attinuī, attentum 2. to hold; restrain; detain; (+*ad*+*acc.*) concern; avail

attingō, attigī, attactum 3. to touch; adjoin; reach; assail; affect; touch upon; take up; concern

attollō 3. to lift up, raise; carry; erect; set up; exalt

attondeō, -dī, -sum 2. to shear, crop close; fleece (*of money*); thrash

attonitus, -a, -um *adj.* struck by lightning; dumbstruck; terrified; frantic; (+*ad* +*acc.*) intent on

attonō, -uī, -itum 1. to strike with lightning; make frenzied

attorqueō 2. to whirl at

attractō see **attrectō**

attractus, -a, -um *adj.* drawn together

attrahō, -xī, -ctum 3. to draw towards; attract; drag forcibly; compel; inhale

attrectō 1. to touch; appropriate; assault; touch upon

attremō 3. (+*dat.*) to tremble (at)

attrepidō 1. to rouse oneself

attribuō, -uī, -ūtum 3. (+*dat. or* +*ad*+*acc.*) to assign (to); appoint; add (to); ascribe (to)

attribūtiō, -ōnis *f.* assignment of debt; grammatical attribute

attrītus¹, -a, -um *adj.* worn, smoothed; hardenened; attenuated

attrītus², -ūs *m.* wear; abrasion

au *interj.* ah! (*expression of surprise or distress*)

auceps, aucupis *m.* bird-catcher; bird-seller; eavesdropper

auctārium, -(i)ī *n.* augmentation, addition

auctifer, -era, -erum *adj.* productive, fertile

auctificus, -a, -um *adj.* increasing, enlarging

auctiō, -ōnis *f.* auction; goods on sale at auction

auctiōnārius, -a, -um *adj.* of a public auction

auctiōnor 1. *dep.* to put up for sale, auction

auctitō 1. to keep increasing

auctō 1. to make grow; (+*abl.*) thrive (with)

auctor, -ōris *m./f.* creator; founder; inventor; author; cause; leader; authority; supporter, approver, champion; bail; vendor

auctōrāmentum, -ī *n.* contract; pay; reward

auctōrātus, -ī *m.* hired gladiator

auctōritās, -ātis *f.* leadership; authority; repute; sanction; informal approval (*esp. of the senate*); precedent

auctōrō 1. *refl./pass.* to hire oneself out

auctus¹, -a, -um *adj.* augmented, enlarged; intensified; empowered

auctus², -ūs *m.* augmentation; growth; advancement; abundance

aucupium, -(i)ī *n.* bird-catching; game fowl; hunting after

aucupor 1. *dep.* or **aucupō** 1. to hunt birds; seek after; snatch at; eavesdrop

audācia, -ae *f.* daring, boldness; impudence, audacious behaviour

audāc(i)ter *adv.* boldly; audaciously

audax, -ācis *adj.* daring, bold; impudent, audacious

audens, -ntis *adj.* daring, bold

audenter *adv.* boldly; audaciously

audentia, -ae *f.* daring, boldness

audeō, ausus sum 2. *semi-dep.* to be bold; intend; venture upon; (+*inf.*) dare (to)

audientia, -ae *f.* listening, attention; **audientiam facere** to gain a hearing

audiō 4. to hear; listen; attend; learn; grant; obey

audītiō, -ōnis *f.* hearing; listening; report; rumour

auditō 1. to hear often

audītor, -ōris *m.* listener; (+*gen.*) pupil (of)

audītōrium, -iī *n.* lecture hall; audience

audītus, -ūs *m.* hearing; hearsay

auferō, auferre, abstulī, ablātum *v.irreg.* (+*ab* +*abl. or* +*dat.*) to carry away (from), remove (from); obtain; steal (from); kill; mislead; cease (from)

aufugiō, aufūgī 3. (+*ab* +*abl.*) to flee (from); disappear; shun

augeō, auxī, auctum 2. to increase; enlarge; raise; equip; magnify

augescō, auxī 3. to increase; grow; rise; prosper

augmen, -inis *n.* addition, increase; bulk

augur, -uris *m./f.* interpreter of birds, augur; prophet

augurāle, -is *n.* headquarters of a Roman camp; augur's staff

augurālis, -is, -e *adj.* of augurs; **cēna**

augurālis banquet held for augur taking office

augurātiō, -ōnis *f.* divining by augury

augurātō *adv.* after taking auguries

augurātus[1]**, -a, -um** *adj.* founded after taking auguries

augurātus[2]**, -ūs** *m.* office of augur; augury

augurium, -(i)ī *n.* augury; prediction; surmise; portent

augurius, -a, -um *adj.* of *or* relating to augury

augurō 1. or **auguror** 1. *dep.* to practise augury; prophesy; surmise

augustē *adv.* solemnly, reverently

augustus, -a, -um *adj.* solemn; venerable; dignified

aula[1]**, -ae** *f.* courtyard; entrance hall; palace, royal court; temple

aula[2]**, -ae** *f.* see **olla**

aulaeum, -ī *n.* theatre curtain; *pl.* curtains, drapes

aulicus, -a, -um *adj.* of the royal court; *m.sbst.* courtier

auloedus, -ī *m.* one who sings to the flute

aura, -ae *f.* air; breeze; breath, exhalation; aroma

aurāria, -ae *f.* gold mine

aurārius, -a, -um *adj.* of *or* relating to gold

aurāta, -ae *f.* the gilthead (a prized fish)

aurātus, -a, -um *adj.* adorned with gold, gilded; golden; containing gold

aureolus[1]**, -a, -um** *adj.* golden; gold-coloured; excellent

aureolus[2]**, -ī** *m.* golden coin

aureus, -a, -um *adj.* golden; gilded; gold-coloured; beautiful; **aurea aetās** Golden Age; *n.sbst.* golden coin

aurichalcum see **orichalcum**

auricomus, -a, -um *adj.* golden-leaved

auricula, -ae *f.* ear; hearing

aurifer, -era, -erum *adj.* gold-bearing

aurifex, -icis *m.* goldsmith

aurīga, -ae *m.* charioteer; helmsman; groom

aurīgārius, -(i)ī *m.* owner of a racing chariot

aurīgātiō, -ōnis *f.* charioteering

aurigena, -ae *m.adj.* gold-born

auriger, -era, -erum *adj.* gold-bearing

aurīgō 1. to drive a chariot

auris, -is *f.* ear; hearing; earth-board (*of a plough*)

auriscalpium, -(i)ī *n.* ear-pick

aurītus, -a, -um *adj.* having large *or* long ears; attentive

aurōra, -ae *f.* dawn; goddess of the dawn; the east; eastern people

aurum, -ī *n.* gold; gold object; gleam of gold

ausculor see **osculor**

auscultātiō, -ōnis *f.* eavesdropping; obeying

auscultātor, -ōris *m.* listener

auscultō 1. to listen (to); listen secretly (to); (+*dat.*) obey

auspex, -icis *m.* interpreter of birds, augur; wedding official; patron

auspicātō *adv.* after taking auspices; auspiciously

auspicātus, -a, -um *adj.* consecrated by auguries; auspicious

auspicium, -(i)ī *n.* divination by birds, auspices; omen; augural rights; inauguration; authority

auspicor 1. *dep.* or **auspicō** 1. to take auspices; inaugurate; begin

auster, -trī *m.* south wind; *pl.* the south

austērē *adv.* austerely

austēritās, -ātis *f.* bitterness; severity

austērus, -a, -um *adj.* bitter; austere; severe

austrālis, -is, -e *adj.* of the south wind; southern

austrīnus, -a, -um *adj.* of the south wind

austrum see **ostrum**

ausum, -ī *n.* act of daring; outrage

aut *conj.* or; **aut ... aut** either ... or

autem *part.* but; however; moreover; on the contrary

authepsa, -ae *f.* self-cooker

autographus, -a, -um *adj.* written with one's own hand

automatum, -ī *n.* automaton

autumnālis, -is, -e *adj.* of autumn, autumnal

autumnus, -ī *m.* autumn; harvest

autumō 1. to affirm; mention; judge

auxiliāris, -is, -e or **-ius, -ia, -ium** *adj.* helpful; auxiliary; *m.pl.sbst.* auxiliary troops

auxiliātor, -ōris *m.* helper

auxiliātus, -ūs *m.* help

auxilior 1. *dep.* to help; heal; be of use

auxilium, -(i)ī *n.* help, aid; remedy; garrison; *pl.* auxiliary troops

avārē *adv.* greedily; stingily

avāriter *adv.* greedily

avāritia, -ae or **-ēs, -ēī** *f.* greed, avarice; stinginess

avārus, -a, -um *adj.* greedy, avaricious; stingy

avē *interj.* greetings!, hello; farewell; **avēre iubēre** (+*dat.*) to offer greetings (to)

āvehō, -xī, -ctum 3. to drag away; *pass.* ride away, depart

āvellō, āvellī or **āvolsī, āvolsum** 3. to pluck off; tear away; extort

avēna, -ae *f.* oat; wind pipe; *pl.* pan-pipes

avēnāceus, -a, -um *adj.* made of oats

aveō 2. to crave, be eager for; (+*inf.*) desire (to)

āverrō, -ī 3. to sweep away

āverruncō 1. to ward off

āversābilis, -is, -e *adj.* abominable, repulsive

āversātiō, -ōnis *f.* aversion, dislike

āversiō, -ōnis *f.* dislike

āversor[1] 1. *dep.* to turn away; show aversion (to); shun; reject

āversor[2]**, -ōris** *m.* pilferer, embezzler

āversus, -a, -um *adj.* facing away; reversed; at the back; remote; hostile; *n.pl.sbst.* rear parts

āvertō, -tī, -sum 3. (+*ab* +*abl.*) to turn away (from); carry away; divert *or* avert (from); put to flight; estrange (from)

avia[1]**, -ae** *f.* grandmother

āvia[2]**, -ōrum** *n.pl.* wilderness, wasteland

aviārium, -(i)ī *n.* aviary; abode of wild birds

avicula, -ae *f.* small bird

avidē *adv.* greedily, avariciously; eagerly

aviditās, -ātis *f.* cupidity; gluttony; vehement desire

avidus, -a, -um *adj.* greedy, avaricious; eager; insatiable; passionate

avis, avis *f.* bird; bird omen

avītus, -a, -um *adj.* of a grandfather; ancestral

āvius, -a, -um *adj.* pathless; remote, inaccessible; straying from course

āvocāmentum, -ī *n.* diversion, distraction

āvocātiō, -ōnis *f.* distraction

āvocō 1. to call away; divert; deter; distract; take over

āvolō 1. to fly away; flee

āvollō see **āvellō**

avunculus (avo-), -ī *m.* maternal uncle; **avunculus magnus** maternal great-uncle

avus, avī *m.* grandfather; forefather

axilla, -ae *f.* small wing

axis[1]**, axis** *m.* axle; axis; chariot; north pole; heavens

axis[2]**, axis** *m.* plank, board

axitia, -ae *f.* unidentified cosmetic article

B

babae *interj.* incredible!, wonderful!
bāca (bacca), -ae *f.* berry; pearl
bācātus, -a, -um *adj.* decorated with pearls
baccar, -aris *n.* plant (with aromatic root)
bacchātiō, -ōnis *f.* revel, orgy
bacchor 1. *dep.* to celebrate the festival of Dionysus; revel, rave, rage
baceolus, -a, -um *adj.* stupid
bācifer, -era, -erum *adj.* bearing berries, laden with berries
bacillum, -ī *n.* small stick; lictor's rod
baculum, -ī *n.* or **-us, -ī** *m.* stick, staff
bādizō 1. to walk, march
baeticātus, -a, -um *adj.* wearing wool from Baetica
bāiulō 1. to carry a load, heft
bāiulus, -ī *m.* porter, carrier
bālaena, -ae *f.* whale
balanātus, -a, -um *adj.* perfumed in balsam
balanus, -ī *f.* balsam-nut; shellfish
balatrō, -ōnis *m.* joker, clown
bālātus, -ūs *m.* bleating
balbus, -a, -um *adj.* stammering, stuttering
balbutiō 4. to stammer, stutter, speak unclearly
ballaena see **bālaena**
balin- see **baln-**
ballista, -ae *f.* large military engine (*for firing stones or other missiles*)
ballistārium, -īī *n.* emplacement for catapult
balneae, -ārum *f.pl.* public baths
balneāria, -ōrum *n.pl.* bathing-rooms
balneātor, -ōris *m.* bath-attendant
balneolum, -ī *n.* bathroom
balneum, -ī *n.* bath
bālō 1. to bleat
balsamum, -ī *n.* balsam tree, balm
balteus, -ī *m.* belt, sword-belt; girdle

balux, -ūcis *f.* gold-dust
baptistērium, -īī *n.* plunge-bath
barathrum, -ī *n.* abyss, chasm
barba, -ae *f.* beard
barbara, -ae *f.* barbarian woman
barbarē *adv.* like a foreigner, roughly, cruelly
barbaria, -ae or **-iēs, -ēī** *f.* foreign country; lack of sophistication; savageness, barbarism
barbaricus, -a, -um *adj.* barbarous, foreign
barbariēs see **barbaria**
barbarismus, -ī *m.* barbarism
barbarus¹, -a, -um *adj.* barbarous, foreign; uncivilized, cruel; *n.sbst.* barbarism
barbarus², -ī *m.* barbarian, foreigner
barbātulus, -a, -um *adj.* with a little beard
barbātus, -a, -um *adj.* bearded; adult; *m.sbst.* ancient Roman; philosopher
barbiger, -era, -erum *adj.* bearded
barbitos, -ī *m/f.* lyre
barbula, -ae *f.* small beard
bardocucullus, -ī *m.* heavy Gallic cloak
bardus, -a, -um *adj.* stupid, dull
bāris, -idos *f.* flat-bottomed Nile boat
bārō, -ōnis *m.* idiot, fool
barrītus, -ūs *m.* war-cry
barrus, -ī *m.* elephant
bascauda, -ae *f.* dishpan
bāsiātiō, -ōnis *f.* kiss, kissing
bāsiātor, -ōris *m.* kisser
basilica, -ae *f.* basilica, public building
basilicē *adv.* royally
basilicus, -a, -um *adj.* royal, princely; best throw (*in game of dice*)
basiliscus, -ī *m.* kind of snake, basilisk
bāsiō 1. to kiss
basis, -is *f.* base; pedestal; foundation
bāsium, -(i)ī *n.* kiss

batioca, -ae *f.* drinking cup
battuō 3. to beat, strike; fence
baubor 1. *dep.* to bark
baxea, -ae *f.* kind of sandal
beātē *adv.* happily; prosperously
beātitās, -ātis *f.* happiness, blessedness
beātitūdō, -inis *f.* happiness, blessedness
beātulus, -a, -um *adj.* rather blessed
beātus, -a, -um *adj.* happy, blessed; prosperous; abundant
bellāria, -ōrum *n.pl.* fruit, dessert
bellātor, -ōris *m.* warrior; *adj.* warlike, martial
bellātōrius, -a, -um *adj.* warlike, martial
bellātrix, -īcis *f.adj.* warlike
bellax, -ācis *adj.* warlike
bellē *adv.* well, nicely, neatly
belliātulus, -a, -um *adj.* rather beautiful
belliātus, -a, -um *adj.* beautiful
bellicōsus, -a, -um *adj.* warlike, martial
bellicum, -ī *n.* signal for attack
bellicus, -a, -um *adj.* of *or* relating to war; warlike, martial
belliger, -era, -erum *adj.* warlike, martial
belligerō 1. to wage war, fight
bellipotens, -ntis *adj.* mighty in war
bellō 1. *or* **bellor** 1. *dep.* to wage war, fight
bellulus, -a, -um *adj.* rather nice, elegant
bellum, -ī *n.* war, combat
bellus, -a, -um *adj.* pretty; charming; smart; excellent, fine
bēlua, -ae *f.* wild animal, monster, brute
bēluātus, -a, -um *adj.* covered with figures of monsters
bēluōsus, -a, -um *adj.* full of monsters
bene *adv.* well, properly, thoroughly
benedicē *adv.* with friendly words
benedīcō, -dixī, -dictum 3. to speak nicely to; (+*dat.*) praise
benefaciō, -fēcī, -factum 3. to do a service (for), do a good deed (to)
benefactum, -ī *n.* good deed, service
beneficentia, -ae *f.* kindness
beneficiārius¹, -a, -um *adj.* given out of kindness, as a favour
beneficiārius², -(i)ī *m.* privileged soldier (exempt from certain arduous duties)
beneficium, -(i)ī *n.* benefit, service, kindness, favour
beneficus, -a, -um *adj.* kind, generous
benevolē *adv.* in a kindly manner, as a friend

benevolens, -ntis *adj.* kind, benevolent
benevolentia, -ae *f.* kindness, benevolence, goodwill
benevolus, -a, -um *adj.* kind, benevolent, well-disposed
benignē *adv.* kindly, readily, generously
benignitās, -ātis *f.* kindness, courtesy, generosity
benignus, -a, -um *adj.* kind, friendly; generous, favourable; abundant
beō 1. to bless, make happy
bēryllus, -ī *m.* beryl, precious stone
bēs, bessis (bēsis) *m.* two thirds
bēsālis, -is, -e *adj.* of two thirds (*of a pound*), i.e. of eight ounces
bestia, -ae *f.* beast, wild animal
bestiārius, -a, -um *adj.* of *or* relating to wild animals; *m.sbst.* one who fights wild animals
bestiola, -ae *f.* small animal
bēta¹, -ae *f.* beet, vegetable
bēta² *indecl.n.* second letter of the Greek alphabet, *beta*; second in order
bētāceus, -ī *m.* beet
bētizō 1. to be like beet, i.e. be weak
biberārius, -ī *m.* drink-seller
bibliopōla, -ae *m.* bookseller
bibliothēca, -ae *or* **-ē, -ēs** *f.* collection of books, library
biblus, -ī *f.* papyrus
bibō, bibī 3. to drink, imbibe; swallow, suck, absorb
bibulus, -a, -um *adj.* fond of drinking; absorbent; sodden
biceps, bicipitis *adj.* two-headed, with twin peaks
biclīnium, -(i)ī *n.* couch for two diners
bicolor, -ōris *adj.* of two colours
bicornis, -is, -e *adj.* two-horned, with two points
bicorpor, -oris *adj.* with two bodies
bidens, -ntis *adj.* with two teeth *or* prongs; *m.sbst.* two-pronged hoe; *f.sbst.* sacrificial animal, sheep
bidental, -ālis *n.* place struck by lightning
bīduum, -ī *n.* period of two days
biennium, -(i)ī *n.* period of two years
bifāriam *adv.* in two parts; in two ways
bifer, -era, -erum *adj.* bearing fruit twice a year
bifidus, -a, -um *adj.* divided into two parts

biforis, -is, -e *adj.* with two openings, double-doored

biformātus, -a, -um *adj.* with two forms

biformis, -is, -e *adj.* with two forms

bifrons, -ntis *adj.* with two faces

bifurcus, -a, -um *adj.* with two prongs *or* forks

bīga, -ae *f.* (*usu. pl*) pair of horses, two-horse chariot

bīgātus, -a, -um *adj.* bearing the image of a two-horse chariot; *m.pl.sbst.* coins bearing image of a two-horse chariot

biiugis, -is, -e *or* **-us, -a, -um** *adj.* yoked together; *m.pl.* two-horse chariot

bilībris, -is, -e *adj.* weighing two pounds; holding two pints

bilinguis, -is, -e *adj.* with two tongues; bilingual; double-tongued, deceitful

bīlis, -is *f.* bile; anger; in madness; **bīlem movēre** (+*dat.*) to provoke anger (in)

bilix, -īcis *adj.* double-stitched

bilustris, -is, -e *adj.* lasting ten years

bimaris, -is, -e *adj.* overlooking *or* between two seas

bimarītus, -ī *m.* bigamist

bimāter, -tris *adj.* having two mothers

bimembris, -is, -e *adj.* part-man part-beast; *m.pl.sbst.* Centaurs

bime(n)stris, -is, -e *adj.* of *or* relating to two months; two months old

bīmulus, -a, -um *adj.* (only) two years old

bīmus, -a, -um *adj.* two years old; lasting two years

bīnī, -ae, -a *pl.adj.* two each; two at a time; a pair, two

binoctium, -(i)ī *n.* period of two nights

binōminis, -is, -e *adj.* having two names

bipalmis, -is, -e *adj.* two palms in length *or* breadth

bipart- see **bipert-**

bipatens, -ntis *adj.* with doors on two sides; wide open

bipedālis, -is, -e *adj.* two feet wide *or* broad

bipennifer, -era, -erum *adj.* wielding a double-edged axe

bipennis, -is, -e *adj.* double-edged; *f.sbst.* double-edged axe

bipertītō *adv.* in two parts

bipertītus, -a, -um *adj.* in two parts, bipartite

bipēs, bipedis *adj.* two-footed

birēmis, -is, -e *adj.* with two oars, with two banks of oars; *f.sbst.* ship with two banks of oars

bis *adv.* twice; doubly

bisōn, -ontis *m.* bison

bisulcis, -is, -e *or* **-us, -a, -um** *adj.* cloven, forked

bītō 3. to go

bitūmen, -inis *n.* pitch, bitumen

bitūmineus, -a, -um *adj.* consisting of pitch/bitumen

bivertex, -icis *adj.* with twin peaks

bivium, -(i)ī *n.* place where two roads meet; fork in the road

bivius, -a, -um *adj.* accessible from two directions

blaesus, -a, -um *adj.* stammering, slurred

blandē *adv.* flatteringly, seductively, charmingly

blandidicus, -a, -um *adj.* speaking flatteringly, sweet-talking

blandiloquentulus, -a, -um *adj.* rather flattering in speech

blandiloquus, -a, -um *adj.* speaking flatteringly, sweet-talking

blandīmentum, -ī *n.* flattering words, blandishment, flattery; charm, delight

blandior 4. *dep.* to flatter; fawn upon; coax, soothe, fondle

blanditer *adv.* charmingly

blanditia, -ae *f.* (*usu. pl.*) flattery, sweet-talk; charm, delight

blandus, -a, -um *adj.* smooth-tongued, flattering, charming, seductive, fawning

blaterō 1. to babble

blatiō 4. to say in a babble

blatta, -ae *f.* cockroach, bookworm; moth

blattārius, -a, -um *adj.* appropriate for moths

blennus, -ī *m.* fool, blockhead

bliteus, -a, -um *adj.* tasteless, insipid; *n.sbst.* useless rubbish

blitum, -ī *n.* spinach

boārius, -a, -um *adj.* of *or* relating to cattle; **forum boārium** cattle market at Rome

bōia, -ae *f.* collar

bōlētar, -āris *n.* mushroom jar

bōlētus, -ī *m.* mushroom

bolus, -ī *m.* throw (*of dice*); haul (*of a fishing net*); gain, profit

bombax *interj.* incredible!, wonderful!

bombus, -ī *m.* deep sound, humming, buzzing

bombȳcinus, -a, -um *adj.* of silk, silken; *n.pl.sbst.* silken clothes

bombyx, -ȳcis *m.* silk-worm; silk

bonitās, -ātis *f.* goodness, excellence, virtue; kindness

bonum, -ī *n.* good, profit, benefit; *pl.* property, possessions; good fortune

bonus, -a, -um *adj.* good, fine, virtuous; favourable, fortunate; *m.pl.sbst.* conservatives, loyalists

boō 1. to cry out, shout, roar

bōs, bovis *m./f.* ox, bull, cow; *pl.* cattle; **bōs Lūca** elephant

botellus, -ī *m.* small sausage

botulārius, -īī *m.* sausage-seller

botulus, -ī *m.* black pudding

botyrō, -ōnis *m.* grape cluster

bovārius see **boārius**

bovillus, -a, -um *adj.* consisting of cattle

brabeuta, -ae *m.* umpire

brācae, -ārum *f.pl.* trousers, breeches

brācātus, -a, -um *adj.* wearing trousers *or* breeches

brac(c)hiālis, -is, -e *adj.* of *or* relating to the arm

brac(c)hiolum, -ī *n.* small arm

brac(c)hium, -(i)ī *n.* arm, forearm; claw; branch; yard-arm (*of a ship*); spur (*of land*); rampart

brassica, -ae *f.* cabbage

brattea, -ae *f.* gold leaf

bratteātus, -a, -um *adj.* gilded, superficially coated

bratteola, -ae *f.* thin gold leaf

brevī *adv.* shortly; in a few words

breviārium, -īī *n.* summary, brief report

breviculus, -a, -um *adj.* rather short

breviloquens, -ntis *adj.* brief, sparing of words

breviloquentia, -ae *f.* conciseness of speech

brevis, -is, -e *adj.* short, narrow, small; shallow; brief, concise; *n.pl.sbst.* shallows

brevitās, -ātis *f.* shortness; brevity, conciseness

breviter *adv.* shortly; in a few words

brūma, -ae *f.* the shortest day, winter solstice; winter

brūmālis, -is, -e *adj.* of *or* relating to the winter solstice; of winter, hibernal

brūtus, -a, -um *adj.* heavy, inert; unfeeling, insensitive, brutish

būbalus, -ī *m.* buffalo

būbile, -is *n.* cow-shed

būbō, -ōnis *m./f.* owl, horned owl

būbula, -ae *f.* beef

bubulcitor 1. *dep.* to drive cattle

bubulcus, -ī *m.* herdsman, ploughman

būbulus, -a, -um *adj.* of *or* relating to cattle *or* oxen

būcaeda, -ae *m.* ox-butcher

bucca, -ae *f.* cheek; mouth; mouthful; trumpeter; puffed-up orator

buccella, -ae *f.* small mouthful of food

buccō, -ōnis *m.* fool, blockhead

buccula, -ae *f.* cheek; cheekpiece (*of a helmet*)

bucculentus, -a, -um *adj.* with full cheeks

būcerus, -a, -um *adj.* with cows' horns, horned

būcētum, -ī *n.* grazing ground for cattle

būcina, -ae *f.* trumpet, horn

būcinātor, -ōris *m.* trumpeter

būcolicus, -a, -um *adj.* bucolic, pastoral; *n.pl.sbst.* pastoral poetry

būcula, -ae *f.* heifer, young cow

būfō, -ōnis *m.* toad

bulbus, -ī *m.* bulb; onion

būlē, -ēs *f.* Greek council

būleuta, -ae *m.* Greek councillor

bulla, -ae *f.* bubble; knob, boss; amulet worn around neck by Roman children

bullātus, -a, -um *adj.* wearing the *bulla* of childhood

bulliō 4. to make bubbles

būmastus, -ī *f.* vine bearing large grapes

būris, -is *f.* plough-beam, curved timber holding the ploughshare

bustirapus, -ī *m.* grave-robber

bustuārius, -a, -um *adj.* connected to place of burial *or* cremation; **bustuārius gladiātor** gladiator who fought in front of the tomb as part of funeral rites for the departed

bustum, -ī *n.* funeral-pyre, grave, tomb; corpse

būthysia, -ae *f.* sacrifice of oxen

buxētum, -ī *n.* boxwood plantation

buxeus, -a, -um *adj.* of the colour of boxwood

buxifer, -era, -erum *adj.* bearing box-trees

buxus, -ī *f.* or **buxum, -ī** *n.* box-tree; boxwood; boxwood object (e.g. spinning-top, tablet, comb, flute, pipe)

C

caballīnus, -a, -um *adj.* of a horse
caballus, -ī *m.* horse, cart-horse
cacāturiō 4. to feel the urge to defecate
caccabus, -ī *m.* cooking pot
cachinnābilis, -is, -e *adj.* uproarious
cachinnātiō, -ōnis *f.* loud laugh
cachinnō 1. to laugh loudly
cachinnus, -ī *m.* wild laughter; crash of waves
cacō 1. to defecate; cover with excrement
cacoēthes, -is *n.* terrible urge
cacozēlia, -ae *f.* bad *or* tasteless imitation
cacozēlus, -ī *m.* bad *or* tasteless imitator
cacula, -ae *m.* soldier's slave, batman
cacūmen, -inis *n.* point, peak; tip, extremity
cacūminō 1. to make pointed *or* peaked
cadāver, -eris *n.* corpse, dead body
cadāverōsus, -a, -um *adj.* like a corpse
cadō, cecidī, cāsum 3. to fall; sink, drop; die, fail; (+*dat.*) occur, happen (to); (+*in* +*acc.*) terminate (in)
cādūceātor, -ōris *m.* staff-carrying herald sent to negotiate terms of peace
cādūceus, -ī *m.* herald's staff, signifying peace; staff of Mercury
cādūcifer, -erī *m.* bearer of the staff; Mercury
cadūcus, -a, -um *adj.* falling, fallen; likely to fall, ready to fall; destined to die; frail, futile; **cadūca bona** *n.pl.sbst.* an inheritance that is not transferred to the designated heir
cadurcum, -ī *n.* quilt for a bed; bed
cadus, -ī *m.* wine-jar; storage vessel; urn
caecigenus, -a, -um *adj.* born blind
caecitās, -ātis *f.* blindness
caecō 1. to blind, make blind; darken
caecus, -a, -um *adj.* blind; dark, hidden, dim, uncertain

caedēs, -is *f.* cutting down; killing, massacre; bloodshed (*from fighting*); corpses, victims
caedō, cecīdī, caesum 3. to strike, cut; carve; wound; cut down, kill
caeduus, -a, -um *adj.* ready for felling
caelāmen, -inis *n.* engraved work, engraving
caelātor, -ōris *m.* engraver, carver
caelātūra, -ae *f.* engraved work, engraving
caelebs, -libis *m./f.adj.* unmarried, single; *m.sbst.* bachelor; widower
caeles, -itis *adj.* heavenly, celestial; *m.sbst.* god
caelestis, -is, -e *adj.* heavenly, celestial, from the sky, divine; *m./f.sbst.* god; *n.pl.* heavenly matters *or* bodies
caelibātus, -ūs *m.* celibacy
caelicolae, -(ār)um *m./f.pl.* inhabitants of heaven, gods, goddesses
caelifer, -era, -erum *adj.* supporting the heavens
caelipotens, -ntis *adj.* powerful in heaven
caelō 1. to engrave, carve; adorn
caelum¹, -ī *n.* sky, heaven; atmosphere, climate
caelum², -ī *n.* chisel, instrument for engraving
caementum, -ī *n.* stone chippings, rubble; aggregate
caenōsus, -a, -um *adj.* muddy
caenum, -ī *n.* mud, dirt, filth
caepe, -is *n.* onion
caerimōnia, -ae *f.* sanctity; veneration; religious ceremony, sacred rites
caerula, -ōrum *n.pl.* blue sea; blue sky
caeruleus, -a, -um *adj.* blue, blue-green; dark, gloomy
caesariātus, -a, -um *adj.* with long hair
caesariēs, -ēī *f.* head of hair, long hair

caesim *adv.* by cutting *or* slashing; in short clauses

caesius, -a, -um *adj.* bright-eyed, bright-blue

caespes, -itis *m.* turf; mound, rampart; altar; grass

caestus, -ūs *m.* boxing-glove

caetra, -ae *f.* short leather shield

caetrātus, -a, -um *adj.* armed with a *caetra*; *m.sbst.* soldier armed with a *caetra*

caiō 1. to beat

calamārius, -a, -um *adj.* containing writing implements

calamister, -trī *m.* or **calamistrum, -ī** *n.* curling-iron

calamistrātus, -a, -um *adj.* with curled *or* permed hair; curled

calamitās, -ātis *f.* damage, ruin; defeat; disaster

calamitōsē *adv.* unhappily

calamitōsus, -a, -um *adj.* ruinous, disastrous; suffering misfortune, unhappy

calamus, -ī *m.* reed, cane; stalk; pen; fishing rod; arrow; musical pipe, pan-pipes; lime-twig for catching birds

calathiscus, -ī *m.* small basket

calathus, -ī *m.* basket; cup

calātor, -ōris *m.* servant; attendant of priest

calcar, -āris *n.* spur, stimulus

calceāmentum, -ī *n.* shoe

calceārium, -iī *n.* money for the purchase of shoes

calceātus, -ūs *m.* shoes

calceō 1. to put on shoes; shoe

calceolārius, -(i)ī *m.* shoemaker

calceolus, -ī *m.* small shoe

calceus, -ī *m.* shoe

calciā- see **calceā-**

calcitrō¹ 1. to kick; be stubborn

calcitrō², -ōnis *m.* one who lashes out with the feet

calcō 1. to tread under foot; crush; spurn

calculātor, -ōris *m.* teacher of arithmetic

calculus, -ī *m.* pebble, small stone used for counting, gaming or voting; calculation

cald- see **calid-**

cal(e)faciō (calficiō), -fēcī, -factum 3. to heat, make warm

calefactō 1. to heat, make warm

calida, -ae *f.* warm water

calidārium, -iī *n.* hot bath

calidē *adv.* promptly

calidum, -ī *n.* heat; hot drink

calidus, -a, -um *adj.* hot, fiery; hot-headed, hasty

caliendrum, -ī *n.* woman's wig

caliga, -ae *f.* soldier's boot

caligātus, -a, -um *adj.* wearing soldier's boots

cālīginōsus, -a, -um *adj.* dark; misty, foggy

cālīgō¹, -inis *f.* darkness, mist; fog

cālīgō² 1. to be dark, misty; make dark; be blind, dizzy

calix, -icis *m.* cup; dish

callaïnus, -a, -um *adj.* turquoise

calleō 2. to be thick-skinned, hard; have experience of, be skilled at; (+*inf.*) know how (to)

callidē *adv.* skilfully, cunningly

calliditās, -ātis *f.* skill, cunning

callidus, -a, -um *adj.* skilled, experienced; clever, cunning

callis, -is *m./f.* track, pathway; *pl.* pasture-land

callōsus, -a, -um *adj.* thick-skinned, hardened

callum, -ī *n.* thick skin

cālō, -ōnis *m.* soldier's servant, batman

calor, -ōris *m.* heat; summer; heat of passion, love

calt(h)a, -ae *f.* marigold

caltula, -ae *f.* yellow tunic

columnia, -ae *f.* false accusation, misrepresentation; trickery, pretence

columniātor, -ōris *m.* one who makes false accusations

columnior 1. *dep.* to make a false accusation, misrepresent; find fault with

calva, -ae *f.* bald head, scalp

calvitiēs, -ēī *f.* baldness

calvitium, -(i)ī *n.* baldness

calvor 3. *dep.* to deceive

calvus, -a, -um *adj.* bald

calx¹, -cis *m.* heel, hoof

calx², -cis *f./m.* limestone; small stone used for gaming; finishing line, end point

camara see **camera**

camella, -ae *f.* cup

camēlus, -ī *m.* camel

camera, -ae *f.* vault, arch; boat with arched awning

camīnus, -ī *m.* furnace, forge; fire

cammarus, -ī *m.* crustacean, small crab

campester, -tris, -tre *adj.* flat, level; of the field *or* plain; of the Campus Martius

campestre, -is *n.* short leather skirt worn by wrestlers

campestria, -ium *n.pl.* level ground, plain

campus, -ī *m.* plain, field; level surface; battlefield

camur, -ra, -rum *adj.* curved, crooked

canālis, -is *m.* waterpipe, channel, canal

cancellī, -ōrum *m.pl.* barrier, railings; limits

cancer, -crī *m.* crab; sign of the zodiac; the south; seering heat; cancerous tumour

candēla, -ae *f.* candle of wax *or* tallow; wax-coated cord

candēlābrum, -ī *n.* candlestick, chandelier

candeō 2. to be white, shine, glisten; be hot, glow

candescō, -duī 3. to become white, begin to shine *or* glow; grow hot

candidātōrius, -a, -um *adj.* of a candidate

candidātus, -a, -um *adj.* dressed in white; *m.sbst.* candidate for political office

candidē *adv.* in white

candidulus, -a, -um *adj.* gleaming white

candidus, -a, -um *adj.* white, shining white; bright; splendid; dressed in white; pure; sincere; happy

candor, -ōris *m.* shining whiteness; brightness; splendour; purity; sincerity; openness

cāneō 2. to be white; be hoary; be old

cānescō 3. to whiten, become hoary; grow old

cānī, -ōrum *m.pl.* grey hairs

canīcula, -ae *f.* little dog; the Dog-star, Sirius; worst throw (*in game of dice*)

canīnus, -a, -um *adj.* of *or* relating to a dog, canine

canis (-ēs), -is *m./f.* dog; ferocious person; shameless person; follower, hanger-on; worst throw of the dice

canistra, -ōrum *n.pl.* baskets (*esp. for bread, fruit or flowers*)

cānitiēs, -ēī or **-a, -ae** *f.* whiteness *or* greyness (*of hair*); white *or* grey hair; old age

canna, -ae *f.* reed, cane; pipe; reed boat

canō, cecinī, cantum 3. to sing (of),

celebrate in song; play an instrument; sound (*a battle signal*); prophesy

canor, -ōris *m.* sound, song

canōrus, -a, -um *adj.* resonant, tuneful, musical

cantāmen, -inis *n.* incantation

cantātor, -ōris *m.* singer

cantharis, -idis *f.* poisonous fly

cantharus, -ī *m.* large cup with handles; type of fish

canthērius, -(i)ī *m.* horse; gelding

canthus, -ī *m.* iron track around wheel; wheel

canticum, -ī *n.* song from Roman comedy set to music and performed on stage; song; singing tone

cantilēna, -ae *f.* old song; tittle-tattle

cantiō, -ōnis *f.* song; spell

cantitō 1. to sing repeatedly

cantiuncula, -ae *f.* little song; ditty

cantō 1. to sing, sing of; compose; charm; sound, play on an instrument; play a part; predict; keep on about

cantor, -ōris *m.* singer; performer; eulogist

cantrix, -īcis *f.* female singer

cantus, -ūs *m.* singing, music, poetry, incantation

cānus, -a, -um *adj.* white, grey, hoary; old, ancient

canusīnātus, -a, -um *adj.* dressed in Canusian wool

capācitās, -ātis *f.* capacity, size

capax, -ācis *adj.* capacious, large; (*+gen.*) big enough (for); receptive; capable

capēduncula, -ae *f.* small vessel used at sacrifices

capella, -ae *f.* she-goat

caper, caprī *m.* he-goat; body-odour

caperrō 1. to be wrinkled

capessō, -īvī (-iī), -ītum 3. to seize, take up; go (towards), make for; undertake

capillāmentum, -ī *n.* wig; plant fibres

capillāre, -is *n.* oil for the hair

capillātus, -a, -um *adj.* hairy; with long hair

capillus, -ī *m.* hair (*of the head or beard*); strand of hair

capiō, cēpī, captum 3. to take, catch, arrest; take up, undertake; arrive at; hold, contain; receive, obtain; choose, select; attack, injure; captivate, deceive

capis, -idis *f.* cup (*for ritual use*)

capistrō 1. to fasten with a halter, muzzle

capistrum, -ī *n.* halter, muzzle

capital (-āle), -ālis *n.* capital crime

capitālis, -is, -e *adj.* of *or* relating to the head *or* life; punishable by death; deadly, dangerous; distinguished

capitāliter *adv.* with lethal intent

capitō, -ōnis *m.adj.* big-headed

capitulātim *adv.* briefly

capitulum, -ī *n.* small head; man

cāpō, -ōnis *m.* castrated cock, capon

capparis, -is *f.* caper

capra, -ae *f.* she-goat; goatish body odour

caprea, -ae *f.* small deer, roe-deer

capreāginus, -a, -um *adj.* like a roe-deer

capreolus, -ī *m.* roe-deer; rafter, prop

caprifīcus, -ī *f.* wild fig-tree; wild fig

caprigenus, -a, -um *adj.* of goats; born from goats

caprimulgus, -ī *m.* one who milks goats; yokel

caprīnus, -a, -um *adj.* of goats

capripēs, -pedis *adj.* goat-footed

capsa, -ae *f.* case for books; box

capsārius, -iī *m.* slave who carried boy's school-books

capsella, -ae or **capsula, -ae** *f.* small box

captātiō, -ōnis *f.* (+*gen.*) act of aiming at; eagerness to take hold (of)

captātor, -ōris *m.* (+*gen.*) one eager to take hold (of); legacy hunter

captiō, -ōnis *f.* trick, deception; fallacy; loss

captiōse *adv.* in a deceitful *or* misleading way

captiōsus, -a, -um *adj.* deceitful; misleading, fallacious; harmful

captiuncula, -ae *f.* small deception; verbal snare

captīva, -ae *f.* female captive

captīvitās, -ātis *f.* captivity; capture

captīvus¹, -a, -um *adj.* captured (*in war*), taken, caught

captīvus², -ī *m.* captive

captō 1. to catch; strive to obtain; seek, pursue; snatch at; entice

captūra, -ae *f.* booty, catch; profit, wages

captus, -ūs *m.* taking, seizing; capacity, ability

capūdō, -inis *f.* cup (*for ritual use*)

capulāris, -is, -e *adj.* at death's door; ready for the grave

capulus, -ī *m.* handle, sword hilt; coffin

caput, -itis *n.* head; summit; source; life; individual, leader; essence, first part; principal sum of money; **poena capitis** capital punishment; **capitis accūsāre** to accuse of a capital crime

carbaseus, -a, -um *adj.* made of fine linen

carbasus¹, -ī *f.* (*n.pl.* **carbasa, -ōrum**) fine linen; linen clothing; curtain; sail

carbasus², -a, -um *adj.* made of fine linen

carbō, -ōnis *m.* charcoal; burning charcoal

carbōnārius, -(i)ī *m.* charcoal-burner

carbunculus, -ī *m.* small piece of (burning) charcoal

carcer, -eris *m.* prison; prisoners; (*usu. pl.*) starting gates at race-course

carcerārius, -a, -um *adj.* of *or* relating to a prison

carchēsium, -(i)ī *n.* drinking-cup; mast-head of ship

carcinōma, -atis *n.* ulcer, cancer

cardiacus, -a, -um *adj.* having a stomach complaint *or* heart condition; *m.sbst.* person with such symptoms

cardō, -inis *m.* hinge; pole (*of the earth*); limit; pivotal moment, turning point; **extrēmus cardō** end point of life

carduus, -ī *m.* thistle

cārē *adv.* dearly, at a great price

cārectum, -ī *n.* place where rushes grow

careō 2. (+*abl.*/*acc.*) to lack, be without, be free (from); abstain (from); be deprived (of)

cārex, -icis *f.* sedge, rush

cariēs, [-ēī] *f.* (*only nom.*/*acc.*/*abl.sg.*) decay, rot

carīna, -ae *f.* keel of ship; ship

carinārius, -(i)ī *m.* one who dyes (*garments*) brown

carinus, -a, -um *adj.* nut-brown in colour

cariōsus, -a, -um *adj.* decayed, rotten

cāritās, -ātis *f.* high price, costliness; high regard, affection, love

carmen, -inis *n.* spell, incantation, oracle; poem, poetry; song, tune

carnārium, -(i)ī *n.* meat-rack, meat-hook; larder

carnārius, -(i)ī *m.* flesh-lover

carnifex, -ficis *m.* executioner; murderer, torturer; scoundrel

carnificīna, -ae *f.* torture, execution; role of executioner

carnificius, -a, -um *adj.* of an executioner
carnificō 1. to execute, cut to pieces
carnu- see **carni-**
carō[1]**, carnis** *f.* flesh, meat
carō[2] 3. to card *or* comb (*wool*)
carpatinus, -a, -um *adj.* made of hide
carpentum, -ī *n.* two-wheeled carriage
carpō, -psī, -ptum 3. to gather, pluck, seize; (*of flocks*) graze; shear; tear, divide; card *or* comb (*wool*); find fault with, carp at; diminish, weaken; wear away, consume
carptim *adv.* separately, in parts; in different places; at different times
carptor, -ōris *m.* carver of food
carrūca, -ae *f.* four-wheeled carriage
carrus, -ī *m.* waggon, cart
carta see **charta**
caruncula, -ae *f.* little piece of flesh
cārus, -a, -um *adj.* dear, costly, precious, beloved
caryōta, -ae *or* **-is, -idis** *f.* date (*the fruit*)
casa, -ae *f.* hut, cottage
cascus, -a, -um *adj.* old, ancient
cāseolus, -ī *m.* small cheese
cāseus, -ī *m.* cheese
casia, -ae *f.* cinnamon-like bark; sweet-smelling plant
cassida see **cassis**[1]
cassis[1]**, -idis** *f.* helmet
cassis[2]**, -is** *m.* (*usu. pl.*) hunter's net; snare; spider's web
cassō 1. to shake, totter
cassus, -a, -um *adj.* empty; (*+abl.*) devoid (of); worthless; *n.pl.sbst.* vain things; **in cassum** *or* **incassum** *adv.* in vain
castanea, -ae *f.* chestnut-tree; chestnut
castē *adv.* purely; innocently; honestly; virtuously, piously
castellānus, -a, -um *adj.* of a castle *or* fortress; *m.pl.sbst.* occupants of a fortress
castellātim *adv.* by *castella*
castellum, -ī *n.* castle, fortress, stronghold
castēria, -ae *f.* rest-room on ship for rowers
castificus, -a, -um *adj.* chaste, pure
castīgābilis, -is, -e *adj.* reprehensible; worthy of punishment
castīgātē *adv.* in a restrained manner
castīgātiō, -ōnis *f.* chastisement, correction; punishment
castīgātor, -ōris *m.* one who chastises *or* corrects

castīgātōrius, -a, -um *adj.* of *or* relating to chastisement
castīgātus, -a, -um *adj.* restrained, taut; neat
castīgō 1. to chastise, correct; punish
castimōnia, -ae *f.* chastity; religious purity
castitās, -ātis *f.* chastity, purity
castor (*acc.* **-orem** *or* **-ora**), **-oris** *m.* beaver
castoreum, -ī *n.* pungent, bitter-tasting liquid extracted from beavers for medicinal use
castra, -ōrum *n.pl.* camp, encampment; war; area of operations; day's march
castrensis, -is, -e *adj.* of *or* relating to war; military
castrō 1. to castrate, geld, emasculate
castrum, -ī *n.* castle, fortress, stronghold
castus, -a, -um *adj.* chaste, pure; virtuous; (*+abl.*) free (from)
casula, -ae *f.* small hut *or* cottage
cāsus, -ūs *m.* fall, falling; happening, incident; accident, chance; misfortune; downfall; outcome, end; risk; grammatical case; **cāsū** by chance, accidentally
catadromus, -ī *m.* rope-suspended catwalk
cataf- see **cataph-**
catagraphus, -a, -um *adj.* painted, coloured
cataphracta, -ae *m.* armour
cataphractus, -a, -um *adj.* wearing armour; *m.sbst.* soldier wearing full armour
cataplexis, -is *f.* cause of wonder *or* amazement
cataplūs, [-ū] *m.* arrival of ship into harbour
catapulta, -ae *f.* catapult, engine used to project missiles
catapultārius, -a, -um *adj.* pertaining to a catapult
cataracta, -ae *f.* waterfall; portcullis
cataractria, -ae *f.* made-up spice
catasta, -ae *f.* stage on which slaves were exhibited for sale
catē *adv.* skilfully, ingeniously; thoroughly
cateia, -ae *f.* kind of missile
catella[1]**, -ae** *f.* or **catellus, -ī** *m.* small dog, young puppy
catella[2]**, -ae** *f.* small chain, bracelet
catēna, -ae *f.* chain, shackle

catēnātus, -a, -um *adj.* chained, bound by a chain, connected

caterva, -ae *f.* crowd, company, troop, band; squadron (*of soldiers*)

catervārius, -a, -um *adj.* of *or* relating to a squadron

catervātim *adv.* in troops *or* companies; in crowds

cathedra, -ae *f.* chair; cushioned seat; sedan chair; professorial chair

cathedrārius, -a, -um *adj.* seated in a professorial chair

catillō 1. to lick plates; feed greedily

catillus, -ī *m.* small bowl, dish, plate

catīnus, -ī *m.* large dish *or* bowl

catōmum *adv.* over the shoulders

catta, -ae *f.* kind of bird

catula, -ae *f.* puppy, young bitch

catulus, -ī *m.* puppy, young dog; young animal, cub

catus, -a, -um *adj.* cunning, shrewd, wise

cauda, -ae *f.* tail, appendage; penis; **caudam trahere** to wear the tail, i.e. suffer mockery

caudeus, -a, -um *adj.* made of wicker *or* rushes

caudex, -icis *m.* tree trunk; book consisting of wooden tablets; account book, ledger; blockhead, idiot

caudicālis, -is, -e *adj.* of *or* relating to wood *or* logs

caudicārius, -a, -um *adj.* fashioned from tree-trunks

caula, -ae *f.* sheepfold; opening, hole

caulis, -is *m.* stalk, stem; cabbage

caullātor see **cavillātor**

caupō, -ōnis *m.* innkeeper

caupōna, -ae *f.* inn, tavern

caupōnius, -a, -um *adj.* of an inn *or* tavern

caupōnula, -ae *f.* small inn

caurus, -ī *m.* north-west wind

causa, -ae *f.* cause, reason, motive; excuse; legal case, trial; faction, side; situation; bond of friendship; **causā** (*+gen.*) for the sake of, because of; **meā** (*etc.*) **causā** for my part

causārius, -a, -um *adj.* sick, diseased; *m. sbst.* discharged soldier

causea, -ae *f.* broad-brimmed hat

causidicus, -ī *m.* advocate, barrister

caus(ific)or 1. *dep.* to allege as a reason, pretend

causula, -ae *f.* trivial legal case; trifling excuse

cautē *adv.* cautiously, warily, carefully; safely

cautēla, -ae *f.* caution, care

cautēs, -is *f.* rock, cliff, crag

cautim *adv.* cautiously, warily

cautiō, -ōnis *f.* caution, precaution, care; obligation, security, bail

cautor, -ōris *m.* one who is wary *or* on his guard; one who stands bail for someone

cautus, -a, -um *adj.* cautious, wry, careful; sly, cunning; safe, secured

cavea, -ae *f.* hollow place, cavity; cave; cage; beehive; auditorium; seats; theatre; spectators

caveō, cāvī, cautum 2. to take care, beware; avoid; look out for; provide, pledge; give *or* obtain guarantee

caverna, -ae *f.* hollow, cavity, cave; ship's hold; arched roof (*of the sky*)

cavilla, -ae *f.* joke, jest; jeer

cavillātiō, -ōnis *f.* witty conversation, banter; mockery; cleverness with words, sophistry

cavillātor, -ōris *m.* wag, wit; sophist

cavillor 1. *dep.* to joke, jest; jeer, mock; be clever with words, employ sophistry

cavō 1. to hollow out, make hollow; excavate, cut through

cavum, -ī *n.* or **cavus, -ī** *m.* hollow, cavity, hole

cavus, -a, -um *adj.* hollow, concave; hollowed out, deep-channelled

cēdō[1], cessī, cessum 3. to go; (*+dat.*) give way (to), yield (to); submit (to), obey; (*+ab +abl.* or *+abl.*) withdraw (from), depart (from); renounce, resign; pass away, come to an end; (*+adv.*) turn out (in such a way), result; (*+in +acc.*) pass into the possession of; turn (into), become; (*+dat./abl.*) be inferior (to); be equivalent (to)

cedō[2] (*pl.* **cette**) *imper.* give *or* bring (*sthg*) here!; tell us!, out with it!; come now!; (*+si*) what if?

cedrus, -ī *f.* cedar; cedar-wood; cedar-oil

cēlātor, -ōris *m.* (*+gen*) one who conceals

celeber (-bris), -bris, -bre *adj.* much frequented, busy, crowded; renowned, famous; frequent, numerous

celebrātiō, -ōnis *f.* crowd; festival; celebration

celebrātor, -ōris *m.* one who celebrates *or* praises

celebrātus, -a, -um *adj.* much frequented, crowded; renowned, famous, well-known

celebritās, -ātis *f.* crowd, assembly of people; festivity, celebration; renown, fame; frequency

celebrō 1. to crowd, fill; frequent; celebrate, make known, proclaim; praise; establish; perform, engage in

celer, -ris, -re *adj.* swift, quick, hasty

celere *adv.* swiftly, quickly

celeripēs, -pedis *adj.* swift-footed

celeritās, -ātis *f.* swiftness, quickness, haste

celeriter *adv.* swiftly, quickly, hastily

celerō 1. to be swift, go quickly, make haste, hurry

celeuma, -atis *n.* coxswain's call (*by which rowers keep in time*)

cella, -ae *f.* store-room, chamber; small room; cell (*of a beehive*); room within temple containing statue of deity

cellārius, -a, -um *adj.* of a store-room; *m. sbst.* storekeeper, steward

cellula, -ae *f.* small room *or* chamber

cēlō 1. to hide, conceal, keep secret

celox, -ōcis *f.* yacht, fast boat

celsus, -a, -um *adj.* high, tall, elevated, lofty

cēna, -ae *f.* main meal of the day, dinner; supper; course of food; company of diners

cēnāculum, -ī *n.* upper storey of house, attic, garret

cēnāticus, -a, -um *adj.* of *or* relating to a dinner

cēnātiō, -ōnis *f.* dining-room

cēnātiuncula, -ae *f.* small dining-room

cēnātōria, -ōrum *n.pl.* clothes for dinner, evening wear

cēnāturiō 4. to want to dine

cēnātus, -a, -um *adj.* having eaten dinner, had supper

cenchris, -is *m.* kind of snake

cēnitō 1. to have dinner regularly

cēnō 1. to have dinner; dine on, eat

censeō, -uī, -um 2. (+*acc.*+*inf.*) to think (that), suppose (that); imagine (that); decree, resolve (that); recommend (that); assess, register

censiō, -ōnis *f.* assessment; punishment

censor, -ōris *m.* one of two magistrates responsible for census roll of citizens; critic, judge

censōrius, -a, -um *adj.* of *or* relating to a censor; requiring intervention of a censor; with title *or* former title of censor; censorious, strict

censūra, -ae *f.* office of a censor, censorship; assessment, judgement

census, -ūs *m.* registration and assessment of citizens, census; register of citizens, citizen roll; property class *or* qualification; property, wealth

centaurēum, -ī *or* **centaurium, -iī** *n.* centaury, a pungent plant

centēnus, -a, -um *adj.* (*usu. pl.*) one hundred each; one hundred

centensimus (-tēs-), -a, -um *adj.* hundredth, hundredth part

centēsima, -ae *f.* one hundredth part; one percent tax

centiceps, -cipitis *adj.* with a hundred heads

centiens (-ēs) *adv.* one hundred times; 100,000 sesterces

centimanus, -a, -um *adj.* with one hundred hands

centō, -ōnis *m.* patchwork garment *or* blanket

centum *indecl.adj.* one hundred

centumgeminus, -a, -um *adj.* hundredfold

centumplex, -icis *adj.* hundredfold

centumpondium, -(i)ī *n.* hundred-pound weight

centumvirālis, -is, -e *adj.* of *or* relating to the *centumviri*

centumvirī, -ōrum *m.pl.* the *centumviri*, panel of judges (*for civil cases*)

centunculus, -ī *m.* small *or* meagre; patchwork blanket

centuria, -ae *f.* century, unit of one hundred soldiers *or* citizens

centuriātim *adv.* by centuries; by hundreds

centuriātus[1], -a, -um *adj.* of or relating to *centuriae*; **comitia centuriāta** Roman assembly which voted upon capital issues and elected primary magistrates

centuriātus[2], -ūs *m.* division into centuries; office of centurion

centuriō[1] 1. to divide into centuries

centuriō[2], **-ōnis** *m.* centurion, officer in charge of century

centuriōnātus, -ūs *m.* office of centurion; election of centurions

centussis, -is *m.* one hundred *asses*

cēnula, -ae *f.* light dinner

cēpa, -ae *f.* onion

cēpolendrum, -ī *n.* made-up condiment

cēra, -ae *f.* wax; wax-coated writing tablet; page; seal; wax figure, portrait bust; *pl.* honeycomb

cērārium, -(i)ī *n.* fee for sealing document

cerastēs, -ae *m.* horned snake

cerasus, -ī *f.* cherry tree; cherry wood; cherry

cērātum, -ī *n.* wax-based ointment

cērātus, -a, -um *adj.* wax-coated

cercopithēcus (-os), -ī *m.* long-tailed monkey

cercūrus (-ȳrus), -ī *m.* boat, light sailing vessel; sea-fish

cerdō, -ōnis *m.* huckster, profiteer

cerebellum, -ī *n.* brain

cerebrōsus, -a, -um *adj.* passionate, hot-headed

cerebrum, -ī *n.* brain; sense, understanding; anger

cēreus[1], **-a, -um** *adj.* waxen, of wax; wax-coloured; malleable

cēreus[2], **-ī** *m.* wax taper

ceriāria, -ae *f.* kind of female labourer

cērintha, -ae *f.* plant loved by bees, bee-bread

cērinum, -ī *n.* wax-coloured tunic

cernō, crēvī, crētum 3. to sift, separate, distinguish; decide, judge; discern, examine, look at; resolve, determine, fight; **hērēditātem cernere** to accept an inheritance

cernulō 1. to send headlong

cernuus, -a, -um *adj.* headlong

cērōma, -atis *n.* oily mud used by wrestlers; wrestling place

cērōmaticus, -a, -um *adj.* covered in *ceroma*

cerrītus, -a, -um *adj.* fanatic, frenzied, raving

certāmen, -inis *n.* contest, competition, fight, argument

certātim *adv.* competitively, eagerly

certātiō, -ōnis *f.* or **certātus, -ūs** *m.* contest, competition, fight

certē *adv.* certainly, undoubtedly; yet surely, at least

certō[1] 1. to contend, vie, strive, fight, struggle

certō[2] *adv.* certainly, undoubtedly; **certō scīre** to know for a fact

certum, -ī *n.* that which is fixed *or* certain; **prō certō** for a certainty

certus, -a, -um *adj.* certain, fixed; decided, resolved; constant, dependable, sure; **certiōrem tē facere** to inform you

cērula, -ae *f.* wax crayon

cērussa, -ae *f.* white lead; face paint

cērussātus, -a, -um *adj.* daubed with *cerussa*

cerva, -ae *f.* hind, deer

cervīcal, -ālis *n.* pillow

cervīcula, -ae *f.* neck

cervīnus, -a, -um *adj.* of a stag *or* deer

cervix, -īcis *f.* (*usu. pl.*) neck, nape

cervus, -ī *m.* stag, deer; *pl.* pallisades, forked stakes

ceryx, -ȳcis *m.* herald

cesp- see **caesp-**

cessātiō, -ōnis *f.* delay; inactivity

cessātor, -ōris *m.* lazy *or* unproductive person, 'slow-coach'

cessim *adv.* backwards

cessiō, -ōnis *f.* surrender, capitulation

cessō 1. to cease, stop; fail, be idle, delay; be neglected, lie fallow

cestrosphendonē, -ēs *f.* sling machine for firing missiles

cestus (-os), -ī *m.* leather support for breasts

cētārium, -(i)ī *n.* fish-pond

cētārius, -(i)ī *m.* fishmonger

cētē see **cētus**

cēterā *adv.* as for the rest; furthermore

cēterōquī *adv.* otherwise

cēterum *adv.* as for the rest; furthermore; otherwise, but, on the other hand

cēterus, -a, -um *adj.* the other, the remainder, the rest; **et cētera** and so on

cētus, -ī *m.* (*n.pl.* **cētē**) sea-monster; whale, shark

ceu *part.* in the same way as, like; as if

cēveō 2. to thrust one's hips, mince

chaere *interj.* greetings!

chalcaspides, -um *m.pl.* soldiers with bronze shields

chalybēius, -a, -um *adj.* of steel

chalybs, -ybis *m.* steel

chamaeleōn, -ontis *m.* chameleon

channē, -ae *f.* fish, perch

chaos, -ī *n.* shapeless material out of which the world came into being; abyss, empty space; underworld

chara, -ae *f.* edible root

charactērismos, -ī *m.* characterization

charmidō 1. to turn into Charmides

charta, -ae *f.* papyrus; page, sheet; writing

chartula, -ae *f.* small sheet of papyrus

chelidōn, -onis *f.* female genitalia

chelydrus, -ī *m.* water-snake

chelys, -yos *f.* tortoiseshell lyre

cheragra, -ae *f.* gout *or* arthritis in the hand

chersos, -ī *f.* land tortoise

chersydros, -ī *m.* amphibious serpent

chīliarchus, -ī *m.* commander of one thousand men

chīrographum, -ī *n.* handwriting; hand-written document, written promise

chīronomōn, -ontis or **-us, -ī** *m./f.* one who gesticulates *or* moves the hands

chīrurgia, -ae *f.* surgery

chīrurgus, -ī *m.* surgeon

chlamydātus, -a, -um *adj.* dressed in a cloak

chlamys, -ydis *f.* cloak (*commonly worn by soldiers*)

chorāgium, -(i)ī *n.* theatrical props

chorāgus, -ī *m.* stage-manager, theatrical outfitter

choraulēs, -ae *m.* pipe-player

chorda, -ae *f.* string of musical instrument

chorēa (-ea), -ae *f.* dance, dance in a circle

chorēus (-īus), -ī *m.* metrical foot, trochee

chorocitharistēs, -ae *m.* cithara player who accompanies chorus

chors see **cohors**

chorus, -ī *m.* choral dance; troop of dancers, chorus; band, company, crowd

chrīa, -ae *f.* moralizing statement used as starting point for rhetorical exercise

chrӯsendetus, -a, -um *adj.* inlaid with gold

chrӯsizōn, -ontos *adj.* golden

chrӯsocolla, -ae *f.* copper-carbonate, malachite

chrӯsolithos, -ī *m.* chrysolite, topaz

chrӯsos, -ī *m.* gold

cibāria, -ōrum *n.pl.* food, rations, provisions

cibārius, -a, -um *adj.* of *or* relating to food; of common *or* simple nature

cibātus, -ūs *m.* food, fodder

cibō 1. to feed

cibōrium, -(i)ī *n.* large drinking cup

cibus, -ī *m.* food, meal; nourishment, sustenance

cicāda, -ae *f.* cicada

cicātrīcōsus, -a, -um *adj.* covered with scars

cicātrix, -īcis *f.* scar

ciccum, -ī *n.* worthless object; **ciccum nōn interduim** I couldn't give a damn

cicer, -ris *n.* chick-pea

cichorēum, -ī *n.* chicory

cicimalindrum, -ī *n.* made-up name for condiment

cicindēla, -ae *f.* glow-worm; candle

cicōnia, -ae *f.* stork

cicur, -ris *adj.* tame

cicūta, -ae *f.* hemlock; hemlock stalk, pipe

cieō, cīvī, citum 2. to move, stir, rouse; summon (*to help*), invoke; provoke; produce, cause

cilicium, -(i)ī *n.* goats'-hair blanket

cīmex, -icis *m.* bug, pest

cinaedicus, -a, -um *adj.* debauched, effeminate

cinaedus, -a, -um *adj.* debauched, effeminate; *m.sbst.* passive sex object, rent-boy

cincinnātus, -a, -um *adj.* with hair in curls *or* ringlets

cincinnus, -ī *m.* curl of hair, ringlet; rhetorical flourish

cincticulus, -ī *m.* small belt *or* girdle

cinctūra, -ae *f.* belt, girdle

cinctus, -ūs *m.* way of gathering up clothes around the waist; belt, girdle

cinctūtus, -a, -um *adj.* wearing a belt *or* girdle, girt

cinefactus, -a, -um *adj.* reduced to ashes

cinerārius, -(i)ī *m.* hairdresser

cingō, cinxī, cinctum 3. to gird, tie up; (+*abl.*) equip (with); surround, encircle; escort, accompany

cingula see **cingulum**

cingulum, -ī *n.* belt, band, girdle

cingulus see **cingulum**

ciniflō, -ōnis *m.* hairdresser

cinis, -eris *m./f.* ashes, embers, cinders

cinnamon (-um), -ī *n.* cinnamon

cinnus, -ī *m.* grimace

ciō 4. see **cieō**

cippus, -ī *m.* sharp stake; grave marker

circā *adv.* around, round about; *prep.* (+*acc.*) around, round about; (*of time*) about; with, near; concerning, with regard to

circāmoerium, -(i)ī *n.* area to either side of wall

circensis, -is, -e *adj.* of *or* relating to the Circus Maximus; *m.pl.sbst.* games held in the Circus Maximus

circinō 1. to take a circular course through

circinus, -ī *m.* pair of compasses

circiter *adv.* about, nearly; *prep.* (+*acc.*) about, near

circitō 1. to go around on patrol

circius, -(i)ī *m.* north-west wind

circlus see **circulus**

circueō see **circumeō**

circuitiō, -ōnis *f.* patrolling; verbal wandering, periphrasis

circuitus, -ūs *m.* rotation, cycle; periodic sentence; boundary, circumference; roundabout way of moving *or* speaking

circulātim *adv.* in circles

circulātor, -ōris *m.* pedlar; travelling performer

circulātrix, -īcis *f.adj.* of a pedlar *or* travelling performer

circulor 1. *dep.* to form a group; gather together; gather people around one (*for a performance*)

circulus, -ī *m.* circle, ring, orbit

circum *adv.* round, round about; *prep.* (+*acc.*) around, round about, near

circumactus, -ūs *m.* revolution

circumagō, -ēgī, -actum 3. to drive round, turn; revolve; change; *pass.* be spent, pass away

circumarō 1. to plough round

circumaspiciō 3. to ponder

circumcaesūra, -ae *f.* outline, contour

circumcīdō, -dī, -sum 3. to cut around, prune; circumcise; curtail, cut off

circumcircā *adv.* all around, in every direction

circumcīsus, -a, -um *adj.* steep, sheer; concise

circumclūdō, -sī, -sum 3. to surround, enclose

circumcolō 3. to live near to

circumcursō 1. to run round

circumdō, -dedī, -datum 1. to put round, surround

circumdūcō, -duxī, -ductum 3. to lead *or* move round; encircle; deceive

circumductiō, -ōnis *f.* cheating

circumeō, -īre, -iī, -itum 4. to go around, surround; visit; pass by, skirt; deceive

circumequitō 1. to ride around

circumerrō 1. to wander round

circumferō, -ferre, -tulī, -lātum *v.irreg.* to carry *or* take round; turn round; circulate, spread

circumflectō, -xī, -xum 3. to bend *or* turn round

circumflō 1. to blow round, buffet

circumfluō, -xī 3. to flow round, overflow; (+*abl.*) abound (in)

circumfluus, -a, -um *adj.* flowing round; surrounded

circumfodiō, -ssum 3. to dig round

circumforāneus, -a, -um *adj.* around the forum; market-trading

circumfremō 3. to make noise on every side (of)

circumfundō, -fūdī, -fūsum 3. to pour round, surround, place around

circumgemō 3. to roar on every side of

circumgestō 1. to carry round

circumgredior, -ssus 3. *dep.* to go round behind

circumiaceō 2. (+*dat.*) to lie near *or* round about

circumiciō, -iēcī, -iectum 3. to throw round, put round, surround

circumiectus[1], -a, -um *adj.* surrounding; surrounded

circumiectus[2], -ūs *m.* surrounding

circumitiō see **circuitiō**

circumitus see **circuitus**

circumligō 1. to tie round, encircle; (+*dat.*) fasten (to)

circumlinō, -lēvī, -litum 3. to smear (on), cover

circumlitiō, -ōnis *f.* covering

circumluō 3. to wash *or* flow all round

circumlustrō 1. to range around

circumluviō, -ōnis *f.* island formed by alluvial deposition

circummittō, -mīsī, -missum 3. to send round

circummoeniō see **circummūniō**

circummūgiō 4. to low around

circummūniō 4. to fortify, encircle with a wall

circummūnītiō, -ōnis f. fortifying, encircling with a wall

circumpadānus, -a, -um adj. near the river Po

circumplaudō 3. to surround with applause

circumplector, -ctus 3. dep. or **circumplectō** 3. to surround, embrace

circumplicō 1. to wind round

circumpōnō, -posuī, -positum 3. to place round

circumpōtātiō, -ōnis f. symposium

circumpulsō 1. to assail from all sides

circumrētiō 4. to surround with a net, ensnare

circumrōdō, -sī, -sum 3. to gnaw or nibble at

circumsaepiō, -psī, -ptum 4. to fence round, enclose

circumscindō 3. to tear (clothing)

circumscrībō, -scripsī, -scriptum 3. to draw a line round; limit, confine; restrict; exclude; cheat, deceive, circumvent

circumscriptē adv. with precision, concisely; in periods

circumscriptiō, -ōnis f. circle, circumference; limit; cheating, deception; rhetorical amplification

circumscriptor, -ōris m. cheat, deceiver

circumscriptus, -a, -um adj. precise, concise; periodic

circumsecō 1. to cut around; circumcise

circumsedeō, -sēdī, -sessum 2. to surround, besiege

circumsessiō, -ōnis f. act of besieging, siege

circumsideō see **circumsedeō**

circumsīdō 3. to surround, besiege

circumsiliō 4. to jump or hop around

circumsistō 3. to stand round, surround

circumsonō 1. to echo all round, resonate; make to resonate; surround (with sound)

circumsonus, -a, -um adj. echoing all round

circumspectātrix, -īcis f. female spy

circumspectē adv. cautiously, warily; carefully, deliberately

circumspectiō, -ōnis f. caution, circumspection

circumspectō 1. to look round, survey, examine; search for

circumspectus¹, -a, -um adj. cautious, wary; careful, deliberate

circumspectus², -ūs m. survey; contemplation

circumspiciō, -spexī , -spectum 3. to look round, survey, examine; search for

circumstō, -stetī 1. to stand round, surround; besiege

circumstrepō, -uī, -itum 3. to make noise around, shout around

circumstruō, -xī, -ctum 3. to build round

circumtentus, -a, -um adj. covered, enclosed

circumterō 3. to jostle from every side, crowd round

circumtextus, -a, -um adj. woven all round

circumtonō 1. to thunder or make a loud noise on all sides of

circumtonsus, -a, -um adj. shorn or clipped all round

circumvādō, -sī 3. to surround, attack on every side

circumvagus, -a, -um adj. flowing around

circumvallō 1. to surround with a wall, blockade

circumvectiō, -ōnis f. transportation of merchandise; circuit, revolution

circumvector 1. dep. to travel round; describe

circumvehor, -vectus 3. dep. to travel round; describe

circumvēlō 1. to veil round, cover

circumveniō, -vēnī, -ventum 4. to surround (with hostile intent); assail, beset; cheat, deceive

circumversor 1. dep. to turn about repeatedly

circumvertor 3. to turn round, revolve

circumvinciō, -nctum 4. to bind or tie round

circumvīsō 3. to look round at

circumvolitō 1. to fly around; wander this way and that

circumvolō 1. to fly around

circumvolvor 3. *dep*. to revolve, roll through

circumvortor see **circumvertor**

circus, -ī *m*. circle, ring, orbit; circus, racecourse

cīris, -is *f*. mythical bird

cirrātus, -a, -um *adj*. having curly hair

cirrus, -ī *m*. curl

cis *prep*. (+*acc*.) on this side of; to this side of; within

cisalpīnus, -a, -um *adj*. cisalpine, on this (*i.e. the Roman*) side of the Alps

cisium, -(i)ī *n*. two-wheeled vehicle

cista, -ae *f*. box, chest

cistell(ul)a, -ae *f*. little box, casket

cistellātrix, -īcis *f*. female slave responsible for mistress's cabinet

cisterna, -ae *f*. cistern, underground pool of water

cistophorus, -ī *m*. Asiatic coin (bearing image of Dionysiac celebrant carrying sacred chest)

cistula, -ae *f*. little box, casket

citātus¹, -a, -um *adj*. urged on, stirred up; quick, rapid

citātus², -ūs *m*. impulse

citerior, -or, -us *compar.adj*. on this (*i.e. the Roman*) side; nearer

cithara, -ae *f*. stringed instrument, cithara, lyre

citharista, -ae *m*. lyre-player

citharistria, -ae *f*. female lyre-player

citharizō 1. to play the lyre

citharoedicus, -a, -um *adj*. of *or* relating to a lyre-player

citharoedus, -ī *m*. one who plays lyre and sings

citimus, -a, -um *superl.adj*. nearest

citius *compar.adv*. sooner

cito¹ *adv*. quickly, soon, easily

citō² 1. to rouse, set in motion; summon, call (on); cite, mention

citrā *adv*. on this side; *prep*. (+*acc*.) on this side of; this side of; within; without, stopping short of; before

citreus, -a, -um *adj*. made of citrus wood

citrō *adv*. **citrō ultrō** backwards and forwards, to and fro; mutually, reciprocally

citrum, -ī *n*. citrus wood

citrus, -ī *f*. citron tree

citus, -a, -um *adj*. quick, rapid

cīvica, -ae *f*. civic crown

cīvicus, -a, -um *adj*. of *or* relating to citizens, civic, civil

cīvīlis, -is, -e *adj*. of *or* relating to citizens *or* the state, civic, civil; unassuming, moderate

cīvīlitās, -ātis *f*. lack of pretension, straightforwardness, moderation

cīvīliter *adv*. like a citizen, according to citizen rights, civilly, moderately

cīvis, -is *m./f*. citizen, countryman

cīvitās, -ātis *f*. body of citizens, city, state; citizenship, citizen rights

cīvitātula, -ae *f*. citizenship of a small city

clādēs, -is *f*. disaster, defeat, destruction, slaughter; cause of disaster

clam *adv*. secretly, in secret; *prep*. (+*acc./ abl*.) unknown to; without the knowledge of

clāmātor, -ōris *m*. shouter, bawler, din-maker

clāmitātiō, -ōnis *f*. shouting, bawling

clāmitō 1. to shout repeatedly, cry aloud

clāmō 1. to shout, cry aloud, call by name, proclaim

clāmor, -ōris *m*. shout, cry, noise, roar

clāmōsus, -a, -um *adj*. noisy, bawling

clanculārius, -a, -um *adj*. clandestine, nameless

clanculum *adv*. secretly, in secret; *prep*. (+*acc*.) unknown to; without the knowledge of

clandestīnō *adv*. secretly

clandestīnus, -a, -um *adj*. secret, hidden, unknown, clandestine

clangō 3. (*of a trumpet*) to sound, resound

clangōr, -ōris *m*. sound of trumpet; noise, clanging

clārē *adv*. clearly, distinctly; brightly; illustriously

clāreō 2. to be clear; shine, be bright; be illustrious

clārescō, -ruī 3. to become clear; become bright; become illustrious

clārigātiō, -ōnis *f*. demand for satisfaction; fine for transgression

clārisonus, -a, -um *adj*. clear-sounding

clāritās, -ātis *f*. clarity; brightness; fame

clāritūdō, -inis *f*. brightness, fame

clārō 1. to make clear; illuminate; make famous

clārus, -a, -um *adj*. clear, distinct; bright, illustrious; loud

classiārius, -a, -um *adj.* of *or* relating to a fleet; *m.pl.sbst.* marines, sailors, naval force

classicula, -ae *f.* flotilla

classicum, -ī *n.* battle-signal; trumpet-call

classicus, -a, -um *adj.* of *or* relating to a fleet; *m.sbst.* marine, sailor

classis, -is *f.* fleet; (social) class

clātrātus, -a, -um *adj.* grated, barred

clātrī, -ōrum *m.pl.* bars, railings

claudeō, -sum 2. to limp, be lame; be deficient, fail

claudicātiō, -ōnis *f.* limping, lameness

claudicō 1. to limp, be lame; be deficient, fail; incline

claudō¹, -sī, -sum 3. to shut, close; enclose, conceal; confine, suppress; conclude; **agmen claudere** to bring up the rear

claudō² see **claudeō**

claudus, -a, -um *adj.* limping, lame; wavering, disabled

claustrum, -ī *n.* (*usu. pl.*) bolt, bar, lock; confines; barrier; strategic key

clausula, -ae *f.* end, ending, conclusion

clausum, -ī *n.* confined space, enclosure

clāva, -ae *f.* club, cudgel; wooden sword

clāvārium, -iī *n.* money supplied to soldiers for hob-nails

clāvātor, -ōris *m.* one who wields a club *or* cudgel

clāvīcula, -ae *f.* vine tendril

clāviger¹, -era, -erum *adj.* club-carrying

clāviger², -era, -erum *adj.* key-bearing

clāvis, -is *f.* key; stick (*used with a trochus*)

clāvus, -ī *m.* nail; rudder; purple stripe

clēmens, -ntis *adj.* mild, gentle, merciful

clēmenter *adv.* mildly, gently, with mercy

clēmentia, -ae *f.* mildness, clemency, mercy

clepō, -psī, -ptum 3. to steal; *refl.* hide

clepsydra, -ae *f.* water-clock

clepta, -ae *m.* thief

cliens, -ntis *m.* client, dependant (*under protection of patronus*)

clienta, -ae *f.* female client *or* dependant

clientēla, -ae *f.* relationship between client and patron; clientship, patronage

clientulus, -ī *m.* mere client

clīmactēricus, -a, -um *adj.* climacteric, critical, fatal

clīnāmen, -inis *n.* swerve

clīnātus, -a, -um *adj.* inclined, bent

clīnicus, -ī *m.* clinician, bed-side doctor

clīnopalē, -ēs *f.* physical exertion in bed, 'sexercise'

clipeātus, -a, -um *adj.* armed with shield; *m.pl.sbst.* soldiers armed with shields

clipeus, -ī *m.* or **clipeum, -ī** *n.* round shield made of bronze; disk of sun

clītellae, -ārum *f.pl.* pack-saddle, panniers

clītellārius, -a, -um *adj.* fitted with a pack-saddle

clīvōsus, -a, -um *adj.* steep, hilly

clīvus, -ī *m.* slope, ascent, hill

cloāca, -ae *f.* sewer, covered drain

clūdō see **claudō¹**

clueō 2. to be named, be famous; exist

clūnis, -is *m./f.* (*usu. pl.*) buttocks, haunches

clūrīnus, -a, -um *adj.* of apes

clystēr, -ēris *m.* syringe, enema

coacervātiō, -ōnis *f.* heaping together, amassing

coacervō 1. to heap together, amass

coacēscō, coacuī 3. to grow sour

coactiō, -ōnis *f.* collection (*of money*)

coactō 1. to force

coactor, -ōris *m.* collector (*of money*); one who chivvies people along; **coactōrēs agminis** rear-guard

coactus, -ūs *m.* force, constraint

coaedificō 1. to build (on)

coaequō 1. to level; treat as equal

coagmentātiō, -ōnis *f.* fastening together, connection

coagmentō 1. to fasten together, connect, cement

coagmentum, -ī *n.* fastening, joint

coāgulum, -ī *n.* rennet (*used to make milk curdle*); curdled milk

coalēscō, -luī, -litum 3. to grow together, unite; take root, become established

coangustō 1. to narrow, confine, limit

coarguō 3. to prove, demonstrate; prove guilty *or* wrong, convict

coartātiō, -ōnis *f.* crowding together

coartō 1. to compress, confine

coaxō 1. to croak

coccinātus, -a, -um *adj.* clothed in scarlet

coccineus, -a, um *adj.* dyed scarlet

coccinus, -a, -um *adj.* scarlet; *n.pl.sbst.* scarlet clothes

coccum, -ī *n.* berry used to produce scarlet dye; scarlet dye; scarlet clothing

coc(h)lea, -ae *f.* snail; snail-shell

cocleāre, -is *n.* spoon

cocta, -ae *f.* cooled boiled water

coctilis, -is, -e *adj.* made of fired bricks

coctum, -ī *n.* cooked food

coctūra, -ae *f.* heating

coctus, -a, -um *adj.* cooked, baked, roasted, boiled; ripe

cocus see **coquus**

cōda see **cauda**

cōdex see **caudex**

cōdicarius see **caudicārius**

cōdicillī, -ōrum *m.pl.* writing-tablets; letter; petition; codicil

coemō, coēmī, coemptum 3. to purchase, buy up

coemptiō, -ōnis *f.* form of marriage involving giving of bride and groom to one another

coeō, coīre, coīvī (coiī), coitum 4. (+*cum* +*abl.* or +*in* +*acc.* or +*dat.*) to come or go together (with); assemble, meet (with); unite; have sex (with); thicken (with)

coepī, coeptum (*pf. only*) 3. (+*inf.*) to have begun or commenced (to)

coeptō 1. to begin

coeptum, -ī *n.* or **coeptus, -ūs** *m.* beginning, undertaking, attempt

coepulōnus, -ī *m.* fellow diner

coerceō 2. to confine, restrain; check, curb; punish

coercitiō, -ōnis *f.* confinement, restraint, punishment

coetus, -ūs *m.* meeting, assembly, crowd; gang

cōgitābilis, -is, -e *adj.* imaginable, conceivable

cōgitāta, -ōrum *n.pl.* thoughts, intentions; considered opinion

cōgitātē *adv.* carefully, considerately, thoughtfully

cōgitātiō, -ōnis *f.* thinking, thought; consideration, deliberation; purpose

cōgitō 1. to think, consider, meditate

cognāta, -ae *f.* female relative

cognātiō, -ōnis *f.* relation by blood, kinship, kinship group

cognātus¹, -a, -um *adj.* (+*dat.*) related (by blood), kindred (to); akin (to)

cognātus², -ī *m.* male relative

cognitiō, -ōnis *f.* acquisition or possession of knowledge; idea; investigation; recognition

cognitor, -ōris *m.* guarantor (*of identity*); advocate, supporter

cognitus¹, -a, -um *adj.* known, ascertained, recognized

cognitus², -ūs *m.* getting to know, becoming acquainted (with)

cognōmen, -inis or **cognōmentum, -ī** *n.* surname; name

cognōminis, -is, -e *adj.* with the same name

cognōminō 1. to surname, name, nickname

cognōscō, -nōvī, -nitum 3. to get to know, know; learn, find out, discover, investigate; recognize, acknowledge, understand

cōgō, coēgī, coactum 3. to drive or bring together, collect, gather; (+*inf.*) compel (to), force (to); constrain, compress; thicken; conclude; **agmen cōgere** bring up the rear

cohaerentia, -ae *f.* coherency

cohaereō, -sī, -sum 2. (+*dat.*) to stick together (to), adhere (to); hold together; be coherent

cohaerescō 3. to stick together, cohere

coherceō see **coerceō**

cohērēs, -ēdis *m.* co-heir

cohibeō 2. to hold, contain, confine; check, stop, hold back

cohonestō 1. to honour, do honour to

cohorrescō, -rruī 3. to tremble, shiver, shudder

cohors, -rtis *f.* enclosure for animals, coop; division of soldiers; group of men, crew; staff, entourage

cohortātiō, -ōnis *f.* encouragement, exhortation

cohortor 1. *dep.* to encourage, exhort

cōiciō see **cōniciō**

cōiector see **coniector**

cōiectūra see **coniectūra**

coitiō, -ōnis *f.* meeting, assembly; political faction; conspiracy

coitus, -ūs *m.* joining together, meeting, union; sexual intercourse

colaphus, -ī *m.* punch, blow, slap

cōleī, -ōrum *m.pl.* testicles

cōliculus, -ī *m.* cabbage-sprout

collabascō 3. to totter, waver

collabefactō 1. to make to fall

collabefīō, -fierī, -factus *v.irreg.* to be made to fall, break up; be overthrown

collābor, -lapsus 3. *dep.* to fall down, collapse; give way, sink, fail

collacerātus, -a, -um *adj.* mutilated, cut up

collacrimātiō, -ōnis *f.* weeping, lamentation

collacrimō 1. to accompany in weeping; weep for, lament

collāre, -is *n.* collar

collātiō, -ōnis *f.* bringing together, combination; collection; contribution; comparison

collātīvus, -a, -um *adj.* well-supplied *or* stocked

collātor, -ōris *m.* contributor

collaudātiō, -ōnis *f.* praise, commendation

collaudō 1. to praise, commend

collaxō 1. to loosen, slacken

collecta, -ae *f.* contribution, collection

collectāneus, -a, -um or **collectīcius, -a, -um** *adj.* gathered together, collected

collectiō, -ōnis *f.* bringing together, collection; swelling; summary; inference

collectus, -ūs *m.* pile, mass

collēga, -ae *m.* colleague, partner in office

collēgium, -(i)ī *n.* college, club; society, guild; body *or* board of men; colleagueship

collēvō 1. to make smooth

collībertus, -ī *m.* fellow freedman

collibuit, -itum (*pf. only*) 2. *impers.* (*+dat. +inf.*) it pleases (one) (to), is agreeable (to)

collīdō, -sī, -sum 3. to strike together, crush, break; bring into collision

colligātiō, -ōnis *f.* connection, bond

colligō[1] 1. to bind together, tie up; connect, unite

colligō[2] **, -lēgī, -lectum** 3. to gather together, collect, assemble; compress, gather in; gather oneself together; acquire, obtain; conclude, infer; add up

collīniō 1. to aim, direct to a mark; hit the mark

collinō, -lēvī, -litum 3. to daub, annoint; defile

colliquefactus, -a, -um *adj.* melted, dissolved

collis, -is *m.* hill, elevated ground

collocātiō, -ōnis *f.* arrangement, positioning; giving in marriage

collocō 1. to place, arrange, position, station; expend; give in marriage

collocuplētō 1. to enrich

collocūtiō, -ōnis *f.* conversation, discussion, conference

colloquium, -(i)ī *n.* conversation, discussion, conference

colloquor, -locutus 3. *dep.* (*+cum +abl. or +dat.*) to converse (with); discuss; confer

collūceō, -luxī 2. to shine brightly, glitter

colluctor 1. *dep.* to struggle; (*+cum +abl.*) wrestle (with)

collūdō , -sī, -sum 3. (*+dat.*) to play together, play (with); (*+cum +abl.*) act collusively (with)

collum, -ī *n.* or **collus, -ī** *m.* neck; ridge

colluō, -uī, -ūtum 3. to wash

collūsiō, -ōnis *f.* collusion, intrigue

collūsor, -ōris *m.* playmate, fellow-gambler

collustrō 1. to brighten, illuminate; survey, look around

collutulentō 1. to defile, pollute

colluviēs, -ēī or **-iō, -ōnis** *f.* filth, dirt; rabble; jumble, hodge-podge

collȳbus, -ī *m.* cost of exchange

collȳra, -ae *f.* kind of pasta

collȳricus, -a, -um *adj.* made of *collyra*

collȳrium, -(i)ī *n.* eye-salve

colō, coluī, cultum 3. to cultivate; foster; inhabit; respect, worship, honour; study

colocāsia, -ōrum *n.pl.* Egyptian bean

colocyntha, -ae *f.* gourd

cōloephium see **cōlȳphium**

colōna, -ae *f.* country-woman

colōnia, -ae *f.* colony, settlement

colōnicus, -a, -um *adj.* of *or* relating to a colony, colonial

colōnus, -ī *m.* farmer, countryman, rustic; colonist; inhabitant

color, -ōris *m.* colour, tint, pigment; complexion; appearance

colōrō 1. to colour, tan

colōs see **color**

colossēus, -a, -um *adj.* colossal

colossus, -ī *m.* larger than life statue

colostra see **colustra**

coluber, -brī *m.* or **colubra, -ae** *f.* snake, serpent

colubrifer, -era, -erum *adj.* with snaky hair

colubrīnus, -a, -um *adj.* snake-like, cunning

cōlum, -ī *n.* colander, sieve

columba, -ae *f.* dove, pigeon

columbar, -āris *n.* punitive collar

columbīnus, -a, -um *adj.* of *or* relating to a dove *or* pigeon

columbor 1. *dep.* to kiss like doves, coo

columbula, -ae *f.* little dove

columbus, -ī *m.* dove, pigeon

columella, -ae *f.* small column

columen, -inis *n.* peak, summit; roof; main-stay, corner-stone

columna, -ae *f.* column, pillar; prop; spout

columnārium, -(i)ī *n.* tax on columns

columnātus, -a, -um *adj.* propped up with pillars

colurnus, -a, -um *adj.* of hazel wood

colus, -ī or **-ūs** *m./f.* distaff, destiny

colustra, -ae *f.* or **colustra, -ōrum** *n.pl.* colostrum, first milk produced by mother after giving birth

cōlÿphium, -(i)ī *n.* choice cut of meat

coma, -ae *f.* hair (*of the head*), lock of hair; mane; foliage, leaves

comans, -ntis *adj.* with long *or* flowing hair; hairy

cōmarchus, -ī *m.* village chief

comātus, -a, -um *adj.* with long *or* flowing hair

combardus, -a, -um *adj.* very stupid, dim-witted

combibō¹ 3. to drink (up), imbibe; absorb; take in

combibō², -ōnis *m.* fellow-drinker

combūrō, -ussī, -ustum 3. to burn utterly, destroy with fire

comedō, -esse, -ēdī, -ēsum (-essum or **-estum)** *v.irreg.* to eat, eat up, consume; waste, squander

comes, -itis *m./f.* companion, friend, associate; attendant, assistant; follower

comētēs, -ae *m.* comet

cōmicē *adv.* in a comic manner

cōmicus¹, -a, -um *adj.* of *or* relating to comedy, comical

cōmicus², -ī *m.* comic actor; comic writer

cōminus see **comminus**

cōmis, -is, -e *adj.* gentle, kind, mild; good-humoured, obliging; elegant

cōmis(s)ābundus, -a, -um *adj.* revelling

cōmis(s)ātiō, -ōnis *f.* revel

cōmis(s)ātor, -ōris *m.* reveller

cōmis(s)or 1. *dep.* to revel

cōmitās, -ātis *f.* kindness, courtesy; generosity; elegance

comitātus¹, -a, -um *adj.* accompanied, attended

comitātus², -ūs *m.* company of attendants, retinue, troop

cōmiter *adv.* kindly, courteously; politely, obligingly

comitiālis, -is, -e *adj.* of *or* relating to the *comitia*

comitiātus, -ūs *m.* assembly of the people

comitium, -(i)ī *n.* area of Roman forum where *comitia* were held; *pl.* public meeting, assembly, election

comitō 1. to accompany, attend

comitor 1. *dep.* to accompany, attend, go along with, follow

commaculō 1. to stain, pollute, sully

commanipulāris, -is *m.* fellow-soldier, comrade

commarītus, -ī *m.* fellow-husband

commeātus, -ūs *m.* coming and going, free passage; convoy; cargo, supplies, provisions; leave of absence, furlough

commeditor 1. *dep.* to imitate

commeiō, -inxī, -ictum 3. to urinate on; defile

commeminī (*pf. only*) 3. to remember, recollect

commemorābilis, -is, -e *adj.* memorable, worthy of being remembered

commemorātiō, -ōnis *f.* reminder, recollection, mention

commemorō 1. to mention, call to mind, recall; recount, relate

commendābilis, -is, -e *adj.* commendable, praiseworthy

commendātīcius, -a, -um *adj.* supplying recommendation

commendātiō, -ōnis *f.* commendation, praise, recommendation; esteem

commendātrix, -īcis *f.* female who commends *or* praises

commendō 1. (+*dat.* or +*ad* +*acc.*) to commit *or* entrust (to); commend (to), make attractive (to), recommend (to)

commentāriolum, -ī *n.* short commentary

commentārius, -(i)ī *m.* or **commentār-**
ium, -(i)ī *n.* journal, notebook; commentary, notes

commentātiō, -ōnis *f.* consideration,
meditation

commentīcius, -a, -um *adj.* invented,
fictitious, imaginary

commentor[1] 1. *dep.* to consider, meditate,
think about; practise, prepare; compose,
write

commentor[2], **-ōris** *m.* inventor, deviser

commentum, -ī *n.* invention, fiction,
contrivance

commentus, -a, -um *adj.* feigned, fictitious

commeō 1. to come and go, travel

commercium, -(i)ī *n.* commerce,
exchange, trade; bartering; communication

commercor 1. *dep.* to purchase, buy up

commereō 2. or **commeror** 2. *dep.* to
merit, deserve; commit

commers, -rcis *f.* friendly exchange

commētior, -mensus 4. *dep.* to measure;
compare

commētō 1. to go frequently

commigrō 1. to migrate, move house

commīlitium, -(i)ī *n.* fellowship in war,
comradeship

commīlitō, -ōnis *m.* fellow-soldier, comrade

comminātiō, -ōnis *f.* threat, menace

commingō see **commeiō**

comminiscor, -mentus 3. *dep.* to devise,
invent; contrive, feign

comminor 1. *dep.* to threaten

comminuō 3. to break into pieces, crush;
lessen, diminish

comminus *adv.* at close quarters, close at
hand; in close combat, hand to hand

commisceō, -scuī, -xtum 2. to mix
together, blend, confuse

commiserātiō, -ōnis *f.* pity, pathos; part of
speech intended to arouse pity

commiserescō 3. to pity, have compassion

commiseror 1. *dep.* to pity, have compassion; arouse pity

commissiō, -ōnis *f.* commencement,
contest

commissum, -ī *n.* undertaking; crime,
offence; secret, trust

commissūra, -ae *f.* joint, connection

commītigō 1. to make soft

committō, -mīsī, -missum 3. (+*dat.* or
+*in*/*ad* +*acc.*) to join together (with),
connect (to); entrust (to); engage (with);
impart (to); begin, commence; commit,
do

commodē *adv.* fittingly, aptly, to the
purpose; helpfully; readily; pleasantly

commoditās, -ātis *f.* aptness; opportunity; convenience; indulgence

commodō 1. to lend, hire; give; help

commodum[1], **-ī** *n.* advantage, reward;
provision

commodum[2] *adv.* just now, at that very
moment

commodus, -a, -um *adj.* convenient,
appropriate, suitable; agreeable; favourable

commōlior 4. *dep.* to set in motion

commonefaciō, -fēcī, -factum 3. to
remind, warn; call to mind

commoneō 2. to remind, warn; call to
mind

commonstrō 1. to show, point out

commorātiō, -ōnis *f.* delay, lingering,
dwelling

commorior, -mortuus 3. *dep.* (+*dat.*) to
die together, die along (with)

commoror 1. *dep.* to delay; remain, stay

commōtiō, -ōnis *f.* agitation, disturbance

commōtiuncula, -ae *f.* slight disturbance

commōtus, -a, -um *adj.* excited, nervous;
vexed

commoveō, -mōvī, -mōtum 2. to move,
stir; shake up, disturb

commūne, -is *n.* (*usu. pl.*) public property;
commonwealth, state; **in commūne** in
the public interest, for common use,
generally

commūnicātiō, -ōnis *f.* sharing, impart-
ing, communicating

commūnicō 1. (+*cum* +*abl.*) to share
(with); communicate (with); confer
(with); unite (with)

commūniō[1] 4. to fortify on all sides,
secure, strengthen

commūniō[2], **-ōnis** *f.* equal enjoyment of
the same thing, sharing, association

commūnis, -is, -e *adj.* shared, common,
universal, public

commūnitās, -ātis *f.* community, common right, fellowship; affability

commūniter *adv.* in common, alike, together, generally, without discrimination

commūnītiō, -ōnis *f.* building up, fortification

commurmuror 1. *dep.* to mutter, murmur

commūtābilis, -is, -e *adj.* changeable, adaptable

commūtātiō, -ōnis *f.* change, reversal, alteration

commūtātus, -ūs *m.* change, alteration

cōmō, compsī, comptum 3. to arrange, adorn, dress, embellish

cōmoedia, -ae *f.* comedy

cōmoedicē *adv.* in a comedic fashion

cōmoedus[1], -ī *m.* comedian

cōmoedus[2], -a, -um *adj.* comic

compaciscor, -pectus 3. *dep.* to make an agreement

compactiō, -ōnis *f.* fitting *or* joining together

compactō *adv.* by agreement

compactum, -ī *n.* agreement, compact

compactus, -a, -um *adj.* fastened together; compact, well-set

compāgēs, -is *f.* joining together; connection, joint, seam; framework, structure

compāgō, -inis *f.* joining together, fastening; framework, structure

compār, -paris *adj.* (+*dat.*) equal (to), alike, well-matched; *m./f.sbst.* companion, partner; husband, wife

comparābilis, -is, -e *adj.* comparable, similar

comparātē *adv.* comparatively

comparātiō[1], -ōnis *f.* preparation, provision, agreement

comparātiō[2], -ōnis *f.* comparison, relationship

comparātīvus, -a, -um *adj.* comparative

comparcō, -rsī, -rsum 3. to scrape together, save up; refrain from

compāreō 2. to appear, be evident; exist, be present

comparō[1] 1. to prepare, arrange; acquire, obtain, procure, buy; establish, settle

comparō[2] 1. to compare, match, pair, couple together

compascō 3. to graze cattle on common land

compascuus, -a, -um *adj.* for common grazing

compect- see **compact-**

compedio 4. to shackle, fetter

compellātiō, -ōnis *f.* reproaching, chiding

compellō[1], -pulsī, -pulsum 3. to drive together, collect; force, compel

compellō[2] 1. to call by name, address, accost

compendiāria, -ae *f.* or **compendiārium, -(i)ī** *n.* short-cut

compendium, -(i)ī *n.* gain, profit, advantage; saving; (*usu. pl.*) short-cut; abbreviation, shortening

compensātiō, -ōnis *f.* balancing (*of accounts*), weighing up

compensō 1. to balance, weigh together; match, counterbalance, offset, make up for

compercō see **comparcō**

comperendinātiō, -ōnis *f.* or **comperendinātus, -ūs** *m.* two-day adjournment of legal trial

comperendinō 1. to adjourn legal trial for two days

comperiō, -perī, -pertum 4. or **comperior, -pertus** 4. *dep.* to find out, discover, learn, ascertain, be informed

compertus, -a, -um *adj.* known, proved, certain; convicted; **prō compertō** for certain

compes, -edis *f.* (*usu. pl.*) fetters, chain for feet

compescō, -uī 3. to restrain, curb, check, confine, repress

competītor, -ōris *m.* candidate, rival, competitor

competītrix, -īcis *f.* female candidate *or* rival

competō, -īvī (-iī), -ītum 3. to come together; coincide, happen, occur; be sufficient, competent

compīlātiō, -ōnis *f.* plundering, theft

compīlō 1. to rob, plunder, steal from

compingō, -pēgī, -pactum 3. to fasten together, construct; confine, conceal

compitum, -ī *n.* (*usu. pl.*) cross-roads

complaceō, -placuī 2. or **-placitus sum** 2. *semi-dep.* (+*dat.*) to please greatly

complānō 1. to level, flatten, make smooth; pull down

complector, -plexus 3. *dep.* to embrace,

welcome, hug, grasp; comprehend,
encircle, surround, include

complēmentum, -ī *n.* that which completes *or* perfects a thing, complement

compleō, -ēvī, -ētum 2. (+*abl.*) to fill (up)
(with); fill with men; finish, complete,
perfect

complexiō, -ōnis *f.* combination, connection, group; period, sentence; summary; conclusion of argument *or*
syllogism; dilemma

complexus, -ūs *m.* embrace, encircling,
grasp, grip

complicō, -āvī (-uī), -ātum (-itum) 1. to
fold together, fold up

complōrātiō, -ōnis *f.* or **complōrātus, -ūs**
m. weeping, lamentation

complōrō 1. to weep, lament

complūrēs, -ēs, -a *pl.adj.* several, many,
very many

complūriens (-ēs) *adv.* many times

complusculī, -ae, -a *pl.adj.* several, some

compluvium, -(i)ī *n.* open space above
central area of house, through which
rainwater was channelled into the
impluvium below

compōnō, -posuī, -positum 3. to place,
place together; match, compare; arrange,
order, settle, calm; construct, devise,
plan, contrive, feign, adapt; compose,
compile, write

comportō 1. to carry, bring together, collect

compos, compotis *adj.* (+*gen /abl.*) in
possession of, controlling; sharing in,
enjoying; **compos vōtī** having obtained
one's wish

compositē *adv.* deliberately, neatly, in
order

compositiō, -ōnis *f.* agreement, arrangement, mixture, pairing

compositō *adv.* (*oft. preceded by* ex) on
purpose, *deliberately*

compositor, -ōris *m.* arranger, maker,
author

compositūra, -ae *f.* connection, structure

compositus, -a, -um *adj.* orderly, wellarranged; calm, peaceful

compōtātiō, -ōnis *f.* drinking party, symposium

compotiō 4. (+*abl.*) to put into possession
of, make master of

compōtor, -ōris *m.* drinking companion

compōtrix, -īcis *f.* female drinking companion

compransor, -ōris *m.* fellow diner, dinner
guest

comprecātiō, -ōnis *f.* supplication, solemn prayer

comprecor 1. *dep.* to pray to, call upon,
supplicate

comprehendibilis, -is, -e *adj.* comprehensible

compre(he)ndō, -dī, -sum 3. to take hold
of, catch, embrace; apprehend, grasp,
perceive, discover, comprehend; include,
comprise, count; describe

compr(eh)ensiō, -ōnis *f.* taking hold of,
arresting; comprehension, understanding, perception; period, sentence

compressē *adv.* briefly, succinctly

compressiō, -ōnis *f.* pressing together,
compression; embrace; conciseness

compressū *m.abl.sg.* by pressing together,
embracing

comprimō, -pressī, -pressum 3. to press,
squeeze together, constrict, compress,
pack closely; hold back, check, restrain,
curb, repress, silence; copulate with

comprobātiō, -ōnis *f.* approval

comprobātor, -ōris *m.* approver

comprobō 1. to approve, prove, confirm,
verify

comprōmissum, -ī *n.* compromise,
mutual agreement

comprōmittō, -mīsī, -missum 3. to
compromise

comptē *adv.* neatly, elegantly

comptiōnālis, -is, -e *adj.* of *or* relating to
the *coemptio*; worthless

comptulus, -a, -um *adj.* rather neat, elegant

comptus¹, -a, -um *adj.* rather neat, elegant, ornamented, smart, trim

comptus², -ūs *m.* union; adornment (*of
hair*)

compungō, -punxī, -punctum 3. to
prick, puncture, mark with spots

computātiō, -ōnis *f.* reckoning, calculation

computātor, -ōris *m.* reckoner, calculator

computō 1. to reckon, calculate

computrescō, -truī 3. to putrefy, rot

cōnāmen, -inis *n.* attempt, effort

concitāte

cōnātum, -ī *n.* endeavour, undertaking

cōnātus, -ūs *m.* attempt, effort, undertaking

conb– see **comb–**

conca see **concha**

concacō 1. to defile, soil

concaedēs, -ium *f.pl.* timber barricade

concal(e)faciō, -fēcī, -factum 3. to warm, make warm

concaleō 2. to be warm

concalescō, -luī 3. to become warm, be warmed

concallescō, -lluī 3. to become hard *or* insensitive; be well practised

concamarō 1. to arch over, cover with an arch

concastīgō 1. to chastise thoroughly

concavō 1. to hollow out, make hollow

concavus, -a, -um *adj.* hollow, concave

concēdō, -cessī, -cessum 3. to depart, withdraw, retire; yield; (*+dat.*) give place (to); concede, allow

concelebrō 1. to frequent, fill, populate; celebrate together, make public

concēnātiō, -ōnis *f.* dinner-party, banquet

concentiō, -ōnis *f.* singing together

concenturiō 1. to assemble in centuries, gather together

concentus, -ūs *m.* singing together, music, harmony; concord, agreement

conceptiō, -ōnis *f.* conception, pregnancy; drawing up of a legal formula

conceptum, -ī *n.* foetus

conceptus, -ūs *m.* taking, capturing; conception, pregnancy

concerpō, -psī, -ptum 3. to pull *or* tear to pieces, attack

concertātiō, -ōnis *f.* dispute, conflict, debate, strife

concertātor, -ōris *m.* rival

concertātōrius, -a, -um *adj.* controversial

concertō 1. to strive eagerly, contest, dispute, debate

concessiō, -ōnis *f.* yielding, allowing; concession, admission

concessō 1. to desist, leave off

concessū *m.abl.sg.* (*+gen.*) by permission (of)

concha, -ae *f.* shellfish, seashell; oyster, murex (purple-fish); pearl; shell-shaped jar; conch; female genitals

conchis, -is *f.* bean

conchīta, -ae *m.* gatherer of shellfish

conchȳliātus, -a, -um *adj.* dyed with purple; clothed in purple

conchȳlium, -(i)ī *n.* shellfish; murex (purple-fish); purple dye; purple clothing

concidō¹, -dī 3. to fall down, collapse, die, fail, droop, subside

concīdō², -dī, -sum 3. to cut up, kill, cut down; beat, break up, destroy

concieō, -ēre (-īre), -īvī (-iī), -itum (-ītum) 2./4. to stir up, rouse, excite, provoke; call together, assemble

conciliābulum, -ī *n.* place of assembly

conciliātiō, -ōnis *f.* joining together, union, winning over, acquisition, inclination, attraction

conciliātor, -ōris *m.* conciliator, mediator, instigator

conciliātrīcula, -ae *f.* recommender

conciliātrix, -trīcis *f.* female who unites *or* brings together, match-maker, go-between

conciliātūra, -ae *f.* match-making

conciliātus, -ūs *m.* joining together, union

conciliō 1. to join together, unite; win over, endear, make acceptable; obtain, procure; cause, bring about

concilium, -(i)ī *n.* union, assembly, meeting, council

concinnē *adv.* elegantly, neatly, finely

concinnitās, -ātis or **-tūdō, -inis** *f.* elegance, neatness, careful arrangement

concinnō 1. to make neat, arrange carefully, put together; cause, make

concinnus, -a, -um *adj.* elegant, neat, carefully adjusted; pleasing, tasteful, appropriate

concinō, -uī 3. to sing, sing together, chant; sound together; be in harmony, agree; celebrate, praise

conciō see **concieō**

concipilō 1. to seize

concipiō, -cēpī, -ceptum 3. to receive, take in, absorb; catch, take; conceive, produce, devise; understand, comprehend, imagine; express (*in a prescribed form of words*)

concīsiō, -ōnis *f.* division, cutting up

concīsūra, -ae *f.* division, distribution

concīsus, -a, -um *adj.* brief, short, concise

concitātē *adj.* vehemently

concitātiō, -ōnis f. violent movement, sudden excitement, agitation, tumult

concitātor, -ōris m. one who excites or stirs up, agitator

concitātus, -a, -um adj. excited, agitated; swift, rapid, violent

concitō 1. to move or set in motion, excite, agitate, stir up; hurl, throw with force; call together, assemble; cause, produce

concitor, -ōris m. one who excites or stirs up, agitator

concitus, -a, -um adj. stirred up, excited, swift, rapid, impetuous

conclāmātiō, -ōnis f. collective shout or cry, acclamation

conclāmitō 1. to cry out (together)

conclāmō 1. to cry out (together); call together; call upon, invoke; lament; **conclāmātum est** there is no hope

conclāve, -is n. room, apartment; enclosed space; public convenience

conclūdō, -sī, -sum 3. to shut up, enclose, confine, limit; complete, round off; conclude, infer

conclūsē adv. in periods

conclūsiō, -ōnis f. closing, shutting up, blockade; end, close, conclusion; period, consequence

conclūsiuncula, -ae f. silly inference or syllogism

concolor, -ōris adj. of the same colour, matching

concomitātus, -a, -um adj. accompanied, attended

concoquō, -coxī, -coctum 3. to boil, cook together; digest; ripen; consider, deliberate; endure, tolerate

concordia, -ae f. agreement, union, harmony, concord

concorditer adv. harmoniously, by one consent

concordō 1. to agree, accord

concors, -cordis adj. of one mind, unanimous, agreeable, harmonious

concrēdō, -didī, -ditum 3. to confide, entrust

concremō 1. to burn, consume by fire

concrepō, -uī 1. to make a noise, crash, clash, rattle, creak, rustle

concrescō, -crēvī, cretum 3. to grow together, thicken, curdle, solidify, freeze; contract

concrētiō, -ōnis f. growing together, congealing, solidification; solidity

concrētus, -a, -um adj. hard, solid; dense; constructed, composed

concrīminor 1. dep. to accuse, blame

concruciō 1. to afflict, distress, torture

concubīna, -ae f. concubine

concubīnātus, -ūs m. concubinage

concubīnus, -ī m. male concubine, younger man in same-sex relationship

concubitus, -ūs m. lying together, copulation

concubius, -a, -um adj. **concubiā nocte** at bed-time, at dead of night; n.sbst. bed-time, dead of night

conculcō 1. to tread down, trample underfoot; despise, treat badly

concumbō, -cubuī, -cubitum 3. (+dat. or +cum +abl.) to lie together, sleep with

concupiscō, -īvī, -ītum 3. to desire greatly, long for

concūrō 1. to take care of

concurrō, -cu(cu)rrī, -cursum 3. to run together, meet, flock; fight, clash; occur simultaneously, agree

concursātiō, -ōnis f. running together or to and fro, combination; skirmish

concursātor, -ōris m.adj. skirmishing

concursiō, -ōnis f. running together, meeting, conjunction; combination of words

concursō 1. to run together or to and fro, meet; go round, go to visit; skirmish

concursus, -ūs m. running together or to and fro; meeting, encounter, collision, attack; conjunction, combination

concussus, -ūs m. striking together, collision

concustōdiō 4. to keep guard over

concutiō, -ssī, -ssum 3. to shake, agitate, cause to tremble; hurl, brandish; weaken, impair, trouble, excite, stir up

condalium, -(i)ī n. ring

condecet 2. impers. it is proper, suitable, fitting

condecorō 1. to decorate, adorn

condemnātiō, -ōnis f. condemnation

condemnātor, -ōris m. accuser

condemnō 1. (+gen./abl.) to condemn, cause to be condemned, convict; blame, disapprove

condenseō 2. to compress

condensō 1. to make thick, condense, crowd

condensus, -a, -um *adj.* thick, dense, crowded, close

condiciō, -ōnis *f.* agreement, declaration, contract; proposal, condition, option; position, status, nature, circumstance, situation

condīcō, -dixī, -dictum 3. to agree to *or* upon, appoint

condignē *adv.* (+*abl.*) suitably, in a manner worthy (of)

condignus, -a, -um *adj.* (+*abl.*) worthy, deserving (of)

condīmentum, -ī *n.* seasoning, condiment, sauce, spice

condiō 4. to season, pickle, preserve, embalm; soften, allay

condiscipula, -ae *f.* female fellow-pupil

condiscipulātus, -ūs *m.* fellowship in learning

condiscipulus, -ī *m.* fellow-pupil

condiscō, -didicī 3. to learn thoroughly

condītiō, -ōnis *f.* seasoning, salting, pickling

conditor¹, -ōris *m.* founder, maker, inventor, author, contriver

condītor², -ōris *m.* (+*gen.*) one who seasons

conditōrium, -(i)ī *n.* coffin, tomb

condītūra, -ae *f.* method of seasoning *or* preserving

conditus¹, -a, -um *adj.* stored, hoarded, hidden, concealed

condītus², -a, -um *adj.* seasoned, preserved

condō, condidī, conditum 3. to store, hoard, hide, conceal; (+*in* +*acc./abl.*) bury, sheathe, plunge, place *or* throw (in); found, establish, institute, compose; pass *or* spend (*time*)

condocefaciō, -fēcī, -factum 3. to instruct, teach, train

condoceō, -doctum 2. to teach, instruct

condolescō, -luī 3. to be in pain, be distressed, ache

condōnātiō, -ōnis *f.* giving away

condōnō 1. to give away, present; deliver up, sacrifice; grant (*pardon*); excuse, forgive

condormiō 4. to sleep, go to sleep

condormiscō, -īvī (-iī) 3. to sleep, go to sleep

condūcibilis, -is, -e *adj.* profitable, expedient, advantageous

condūcō, -duxī, -ductum 3. to bring together, assemble, collect; unite, coagulate, curdle; hire, employ, rent, take on a contract, farm; *impers.* (+*dat.*) it is profitable, advantageous, *or* fitting (for)

conductīcius, -a, -um *adj.* hired, mercenary

conductiō, -ōnis *f.* bringing together of argument; hiring, farming

conductor, -ōris *m.* hirer, tenant; contractor

conductum, -ī *n.* rented accommodation

conductus, -a, -um *adj.* hired; *m.pl.sbst.* hired men, mercenaries

conduplicātiō, -ōnis *f.* doubling; repetition

conduplicō 1. to double

condūrō 1. to harden

condus, -ī *m.* steward

cōnectō, -xuī, -xum 3. to fasten, join together, unite, connect

cōnexiō, -ōnis *f.* sequence

cōnexus, -ūs *m.* connection

confābulor 1. *dep.* to talk together; discuss

confarreō 1. to marry (through ceremony of *confarreatio* in which an offering of bread is made)

confātālis, -is, -e *adj.* bound by the same fate, co-fated

confectiō, -ōnis *f.* making, composing; consuming, chewing, finishing, completing

confector, -ōris *m.* one who makes, conducts, concludes *or* destroys

conferciō, -rsī, -rtum 4. to cram together, stuff, compress

conferō, conferre, contulī, collātum *v. irreg.* to bring together, collect, gather; contribute, pay; compare; oppose, engage, fight; apply *or* devote (oneself); go, resort (to); change; remove, transfer; discuss; refer, assign, ascribe, direct; **signa conferre** to engage in battle; **pedem conferre** to fight at close quarters

confertim *adv.* compactly, in close array

confertus, -a, -um *adj.* crammed together, stuffed, full, crowded

confervēfaciō, -fēcī, -factum 3. to heat, melt

confervēscō, -ferbuī 3. to grow hot, become heated

confessiō, -ōnis f. confession, acknowledgement, admission

confessus, -a, -um adj. evident, certain, undoubted

confestim adv. immediately, without delay

conficiens, -ntis adj. efficient, effective

conficiō, -fēcī, -fectum 3. to make, accomplish; cause, get, produce, provide; compose, record; write; finish, conclude, complete; kill, destroy; consume, use up; wear out

confictiō, -ōnis f. fabrication, counterfeit

confīdens, -ntis adj. confident, bold, daring, rash

confīdenter adv. confidently, boldly, daringly, rashly

confīdentia, -ae f. confidence, boldness, assurance, audacity

confīdentiloquus, -a, -um adj. speaking rashly

confīdō, -fīsus sum 3. semi-dep. (+dat./ abl.) to trust, put confidence in, rely upon; (+acc.+inf.) be confident (that)

configō, -fixī, -fixum 3. to fix or fasten together; pierce, transfix, run through

confīne, -is n. boundary

confingō, -finxī, -fictum 3. to make, form, construct; invent, counterfeit, pretend

confīnis¹, -is, -e adj. (+dat.) bordering up, next to, adjoining; similar, closely connected

confīnis², -is m. neighbour

confīnium, -(i)ī n. common boundary, limit, frontier; proximity

confīō, -fierī, -factus v.irreg. to be done, be made or produced, be brought about or effected

confirmātiō, -ōnis f. confirming, making secure, establishing; confirmation, proof, assertion; encouragement, consolation

confirmātor, -ōris m. surety, security; guarantor

confirmō 1. to confirm, strengthen, establish; encourage, console, support; prove, affirm

confiscō 1. to confiscate; store up

confīsiō, -ōnis f. confidence, assurance

confiteor, -fessus 2. dep. to confess, acknowledge, reveal

conflagrātiō, -ōnis f. burning, conflagration

conflagrō 1. to be on fire, be in flames; be destroyed (by fire)

conflictiō, -ōnis f. clash, disagreement

conflictō 1. (usu. pass.) to strike together; trouble, harass; (usu. dep.) struggle, be in conflict

conflictus, -ūs m. clashing, collision

conflīgō, -flixī, -flictum 3. to strike together, clash, collide; struggle, be in conflict

conflō 1. to blow together, blow upon; kindle, ignite; melt, melt down, fuse; forge, fabricate; compose; cause, occasion; raise, collect

confluens, -ntis m. confluence, point where rivers flow together

confluō, -fluxī 3. to flow together, meet; flock or crowd together

confodiō, -fōdī, -fossum 3. to dig; wound, pierce, stab, run through

confore (future inf. of [**consum**]) to be about to happen

conformātiō, -ōnis f. form, shape; arrangement, manner; notion, idea; figure of speech

conformō 1. to mould, shape; harmonize; teach

confrag(ōs)us, -a, -um adj. rough, rugged, uneven

confremō, -uī 3. to make a loud noise, roar, murmur, resound

confricō 1. to rub vigorously, massage

confringō, -frēgī, -fractum 3. to break to pieces, shatter; destroy, cripple, weaken

confugiō, -fūgī 3. to flee, take refuge with, have recourse to

confugium, -(i)ī n. refuge, shelter, retreat

confulgeō, -fulsī 2. to shine, glisten, glitter

confultus, -a, -um adj. pressed together

confundō, -fūdī, -fūsum 3. to pour out together, mingle, mix, blend; unite; confuse, obscure, disorder; move, disturb

confūsē adv. confusedly, without order or method

confūsīcius, -a, -um adj. mixed together, confused

confūsiō, -ōnis f. mixing, mixture, confusion, disturbance; blush

confūsus, -a, -um adj. mixed together, confused, disordered, troubled

confūtō 1. to restrain, repress, check, silence; prove wrong, refute

confutuō, -uī, -ūtum 3. to have sex with, fuck

congelō 1. to congeal, freeze, grow hard; become inert

congeminātiō, -ōnis f. making double, duplication

congeminō 1. to double, redouble; strike repeatedly, repeat

congemō, -uī, -itum 3. to groan, wail, lament

conger, -grī m. conger, sea-eel

congeriēs, -ēī f. mass, heap, pile, hoard

congerō, -gessī, -gestum 3. to bring together, heap up, amass, accumulate; hurl, throw, shower

congerrō, -ōnis m. jovial companion

congestīcius, -a, -um adj. heaped or piled up

congestus, -ūs m. gathering together, heaping up; pile, heap

congiālis, -is, -e adj. containing a congius

congiārium, -(i)ī n. gift of wine, oil or money

congius, -(i)ī m. measure for liquid

conglaciō 1. to freeze, turn to ice

congliscō 3. to grow, be kindled

conglobātiō, -ōnis f. coming together (into the shape of a ball), crowding together

conglobō 1. to come together (into the shape of a ball), crowd together

conglomerō 1. to form into the shape of a ball, conglomerate

conglūtinātiō, -ōnis f. gluing together, cementing

conglūtinō 1. to glue together, cement, confirm

congraecō 1. to use like a Greek

congrātulor 1. dep. to congratulate, wish joy to

congredior, -gressus 3. dep. (+acc./dat. or +cum +abl.) to meet, go up to, approach; fight, accost

congregābilis, -is, -e adj. sociable

congregātiō, -ōnis f. gathering together, assembly

congregō 1. to gather together (into a flock), assemble

congressiō, -ōnis f. coming together, meeting; sexual intercourse

congressus, -ūs m. coming together, meeting; conflict, encounter, engagement

congruens, -ntis adj. (+dat. or +cum +abl.) agreeing, in accord (with); suitable, fit, proper, consistent, agreeable, harmonious

congruenter adv. (+dat.) agreeably, suitably (for)

congruentia, -ae f. likeness, conformity

congruō, -uī 3. to come together, meet, combine; (+dat. or +cum +abl.) correspond, agree (with); fit, be appropriate

congruus, -a, -um adj. agreeing, in accord, suitable, fit

cōniciō, -iēcī, -iectum 3. to throw together, conjecture, guess; infer; interpret; throw, hurl, aim; drive, thrust; force, impel; spend, waste

coniectiō, -ōnis f. throwing, hurling; interpretation

coniectō 1. to conjecture, guess, infer, interpret

coniector, -ōris m. interpreter of dreams

coniectrix, -īcis f. female interpreter of dreams

coniectūra, -ae f. conjecture, guess, inference; divination, interpretation of dreams

coniectūrālis, -is, -e adj. conjectural, based on inference

coniectus, -ūs m. throwing together, casting; motion, glance; reach; heap, pile, collection

cōnifer, -era, -erum adj. bearing cones

cōniger, -era, -erum adj. bearing cones

cōnītor, cōnixus (cōnīsus) 3. dep. to strive, endeavour, struggle; give birth

coniugālis, -is, -e adj. of or relating to marriage, conjugal

coniugātiō, -ōnis f. verbal connection

coniugātor, -ōris m. one who joins or unites together

coniugiālis, -is, -e adj. of or relating to marriage, conjugal

coniugium, -(i)ī n. joining together, union, marriage; husband, wife

coniugō 1. to join together, unite, connect

coniunctē *adv.* jointly, together; closely, intimately

coniunctim *adv.* jointly, together

coniunctiō, -ōnis *f.* joining together, union, connection, conjunction; agreement, alliance; affinity

coniungō, -nxī, -nctum 3. to join together, unite, connect, associate; form; undertake together; include

coniunx, -ugis *m./f.* husband, wife, spouse, partner

coniūrātī, -ōrum *m.pl.* conspirators

coniūrātiō, -ōnis *f.* conspiracy, plot; confederacy, sworn alliance

coniūrātus, -a, -um *adj.* sworn, bound by oath

coniūrō 1. to swear together, take an oath; conspire, plot

cōnīveō, -vī 2. to be shut, close; blink, wink; take no notice of, overlook; go to sleep, sleep

conl- see **coll-**

conm- see **comm**

conn- see **cōn-**

cōnōpēum, -ī or **-ium, -(i)ī** *n.* canopy, mosquito-net

cōnor 1. *dep.* (+*inf.*) to try (to), attempt (to), strive (to)

conp- see **comp-**

conquassātiō, -ōnis *f.* shaking, disturbance

conquassō 1. to shake, shatter, disturb

conqueror, -questus 3. *dep.* to complain; lament, bewail

conquestiō, -ōnis *f.* complaint, lamentation

conquestus see **conquestiō**

conquiēscō, -quiēvī, -quiētum 3. to rest, be at rest; take rest; halt, come to a stop

conquiniscō 3. to stoop, sit, squat

conquīrō, -quīsīvī (-siī), -quīsitum 3. to seek, search for, collect

conquīsītiō, -ōnis *f.* search, inquiry; conscription, collection

conquīsītor, -ōris *m.* recruiting officer; spy

conquīsītus, -a, -um *adj.* carefully sought out, choicest, most exquisite

conr- see **corr-**

consaepiō, -psī, -ptum 4. to enclose, fence in, hedge in

consaeptum, -ī *n.* enclosure, fenced-off area

consalūtātiō, -ōnis *f.* greeting (*of one another*)

consalūtō 1. to greet, salute one another

consānescō, -nuī 3. to become healthy

consanguineus, -a, -um *adj.* related by blood, of the same blood, kindred; of a brother *or* sister; *m.sbst.* brother; *f.sbst.* sister; *pl.* relations, relatives

consanguinitās, -ātis *f.* blood-relationship

consauciō 1. to wound *or* hurt severely

conscelerātus, -a, -um *adj.* wicked, villainous, depraved

conscelerō 1. to pollute, defile, stain with crime

conscendō, -dī, -sum 3. to ascend, climb (up to *or* on to), mount; embark, board ship

conscensiō, -ōnis *f.* embarking

conscientia, -ae *f.* collective knowledge, consciousness; conscience (good or bad)

conscindō, -scidī, -scissum 3. to cut *or* tear into pieces

consciō 4. to be conscious of some fault, feel guilty

consciscō, -scīvī (-sciī), -scītum 3. to determine, resolve, decree; (*usu.* +*sibi etc.*) bring upon oneself

conscius, -a, -um *adj.* (+*gen.*) conscious, aware; privy to; *m.sbst.* accomplice

conscreor 1. *dep.* to clear one's throat noisily, hawk

conscribillō 1. to scribble upon, mark all over

conscrībō, -scripsī, -scriptum 3. to enlist, raise, levy, enroll; write, compose; mark

conscriptiō, -ōnis *f.* or **conscriptum, -ī** *n.* written document

consecō, -uī, -tum 1. to cut, cut up, cut in pieces

consecrātiō, -ōnis *f.* consecration, dedication, deification

consecrō 1. to consecrate, dedicate, devote; make holy, deify; immortalize; curse

consectārius, -a, -um *adj.* following as a logical consequence

consectātiō, -ōnis *f.* pursuit, hunt, search

consectātrix, -īcis *f.* one who pursues *or* searches

consector 1. *dep.* to pursue, go after, follow; seek; imitate

consecūtiō, -ōnis *f.* consequence, logical arrangement

consenescō, -nuī 3. to grow old, become weak; fall into disuse; decay

consensiō, -ōnis *f.* or **consensus, -ūs** *m.* agreement, consent, unanimity, harmony; plot, conspiracy

consentāneus, -a, -um *adj.* agreeable; suitable, reasonable; (+*dat.* or +*cum* +*abl.*) appropriate (for)

consentiens, -ntis *adj.* agreeing, of the same opinion, unanimous

consentiō, -sensī, -sensum 4. (+*dat.* or +*cum* +*abl.*) to agree (with), accord (with), be of the same opinion, be in harmony; share in feeling, sympathize (with); plot together, conspire

consequens, -ntis *adj.* following, coming after, ensuing; agreeable; reasonable, appropriate; *n.sbst.* inference, consequence

consequentia, -ae *f.* consequence, succession

consequor, -secūtus 3. *dep.* to follow, come or go after, pursue; come upon, reach, overtake; result from, follow as a consequence; imitate, equal; acquire, obtain, gain; understand, comprehend, find out

conserō¹, -sēvī, -situm 3. to sow, plant, set

conserō², -uī, -tum 3. to join together, connect; **certāmen/manum/pugnam/ proelium conserere** to join battle, fight hand to hand, engage in close combat; **ex iūre manum conserere** to engage in a property dispute; **sermōnem conserere** to converse

consertē *adv.* closely, connectedly

consertus, -a, -um *adj.* interwoven, knitted together, tightly packed

conserva, -ae *f.* female fellow-slave

conservātiō, -ōnis *f.* keeping, maintaining, preservation

conservātor, -ōris *m.* preserver, protector, saviour

conservātrix, -īcis *f.* preserver, protector

conservitium, -(i)ī *n.* shared state of servitude

conservō 1. to preserve, defend; take care of; maintain, observe

conservus, -ī *m.* fellow-slave

consessor, -ōris *m.* fellow-spectator, neighbour, fellow-juror

consessus, -ūs *m.* assembly, gathering; crowd, audience

consīderātē *adv.* with consideration, thoughtfully

consīderātiō, -ōnis *f.* consideration, regard, contemplation

consīderātus, -a, -um *adj.* considered, thought out; cautious, circumspect

consīderō 1. to consider, deliberate, reflect upon; inspect, study, examine

consīdō, -sēdī 3. to sit down (together), sit in judgement; pitch, settle; stop, stay, delay; sink, give way, fall (in); subside, abate, allay; finish, close

consignō 1. to seal, record, register, authenticate

consilescō, -luī 3. to become silent

consiliārius¹, -a, -um *adj.* counselling, advising

consiliārius², -(i)ī *m.* counsellor, adviser

consiliātor, -ōris *m.* counsellor

consiliō *adv.* on purpose, deliberately

consilior 1. *dep.* to counsel, advise, deliberate

consilium, -(i)ī *n.* counsel, advice, deliberation; plan, scheme, purpose, decision, resolution; judgement, prudence, understanding; body of advisers, council

consimilis, -is, -e *adj.* (+*gen./dat.*) similar (to), like

consistō, constitī 3. to stop, halt, stand, stand still; stand firm, make a stand; settle, reside; exist, endure; (+*ex/in* +*abl.*) consist of, be based upon

consitiō, -ōnis *f.* planting, sowing

consitor, -ōris *m.* planter, sower

consitūra, -ae *f.* planting, sowing

consōbrīna, -ae *f.* female cousin

consōbrīnus, -ī *m.* mother's sister's son; cousin

consocer, -erī *m.* father-in-law

consociātiō, -ōnis *f.* association, union

consociātus, -a, -um *adj.* united, closely linked

consociō 1. to associate, unite, join together, connect; share

consōlābilis, -is, -e *adj.* consolable

consōlātiō, -ōnis *f.* consolation, comfort, solace

consōlātor, -ōris *m.* one who consoles, comforter

consōlātōrius, -a, -um *adj.* consolatory

consōlor 1. *dep.* to console, comfort, solace; alleviate, relieve; encourage

consonō, -uī 1. to sound together, resound, re-echo; agree, accord; utter together

consonus, -a, -um *adj.* sounding together, concordant, in tune; agreeable, fit, suitable

consōpiō 4. to lull to sleep

consors, -rtis *adj.* (*+gen.*) having an equal share (in), partaking (of); brotherly, sisterly; shared; *m./f.sbst.* partner, sharer (*esp. of inheritance*); brother, sister

consortiō, -ōnis *f.* partnership, association

consortium see **consortiō**

conspectus¹, -a, -um *adj.* visible; conspicuous, worthy of notice; distinguished

conspectus², -ūs *m.* sight, view, appearance; mental view; inspection

conspergō, -rsī, -rsum 3. to sprinkle (*with water*); scatter, strew

conspiciendus, -a, -um *adj.* conspicuous, worthy of attention, distinguished

conspiciō, -spexī, -spectum 3. to catch sight of, see, behold; perceive; observe, look at intently

conspicor see **conspiciō**

conspicuus, -a, -um *adj.* conspicuous, clear, visible; illustrious, distinguished, remarkable

conspīrātiō, -ōnis *f.* agreement, consent, harmony, concord; plot, conspiracy

conspīrātus, -ī *m.* conspirator

conspīrō 1. to agree, unite; blow *or* sound together; plot, conspire

consponsor, -ōris *m.* joint surety

conspuō, -uī, -ūtum 3. to spit upon

conspurcō 1. to defile, pollute, befoul

conspūtō 1. to spit upon

constabiliō 4. to establish, make firm, secure

constans, -ntis *adj.* standing together, firm, steady; consistent, uniform; resolved, determined; constant, unchanging

constanter *adv.* firmly, steadily; consistently, uniformly; constantly

constantia, -ae *f.* firmness, steadiness; consistency, uniformity; constancy, perseverance

consternātiō, -ōnis *f.* consternation, dismay, fear, alarm, astonishment; disturbance; mutiny

consternō¹ 1. to alarm, terrify, throw into confusion; excite *or* drive (into action)

consternō², -strāvī, -strātum 3. to cover, strew, pave; bring down, bring to the ground

constīpō 1. to press *or* crowd together

constituō, -uī, -ūtum 3. to set up, establish; put, place, station, settle, halt; create, appoint; decide, resolve, fix, determine

constitūtiō, -ōnis *f.* arrangement, disposition; constitution, condition; structure, system; definition

constitūtum, -ī *n.* appointment, private agreement; **ad constitūtum** at the appointed time

constitūtus, -a, -um *adj.* set up, arranged, appointed, established

constō, -stitī 1. to stand together, stand still, exist; persist, remain, continue; (*+cum +abl. or +dat.*) agree (with), be consistent (with), correspond (to); rest, depend, lie; (*+ex/de +abl.*) be composed of, made up of; cost, be valued at; **constat** (*+acc.+inf.*) it is agreed (that), well-known (that)

constrātum, -ī *n.* decking, platform

constringō, -nxī, -ctum 3. to bind together, tie fast; confine, compress; curb, restrain

constructiō, -ōnis *f.* construction, arrangement, making, fashioning

construō, -xī, -ctum 3. to heap *or* pile up; hoard, amass; construct, put together, build

constuprātor, -ōris *m.* rapist, debaucher

constuprō 1. to rape, ravish, violate, debauch

consuādeō, -sī, -sum 2. to advise strongly; (*+dat.*) persuade

consuāsor, -ōris *m.* counsellor, adviser

consūcidus, -a, -um *adj.* juicy, succulent

consūdō 1. to sweat

consuēfaciō, -fēcī, -factum 3. to accustom, train by practice, habituate

consuescō, -suēvī, -suētum 3. (*+ad +acc. or +dat./inf.*) to become accustomed *or* used to; *pf.* be accustomed to, be in the habit of; be familiar *or* intimate with; accustom, habituate

consuētiō, -ōnis *f.* familiarity, intimacy

consuētūdō, -inis *f.* custom, usage, habit, practice, convention; familiarity, intimacy

consuētus, -a, -um *adj.* accustomed, usual, ordinary

consul, -lis *m.* consul; one of the two supreme magistrates of the Roman Republic

consulāris, -is, -e *adj.* consular, of *or* belonging to a consul; *m.sbst.* ex-consul; governor of consular rank

consulāriter *adv.* in a manner appropriate to a consul

consulātus, -ūs *m.* consulate, consulship, office of consul

consulō, -luī, -ltum 3. to consult, deliberate; decide, resolve; (*+dat.*) look after, pay attention to

consultātiō, -ōnis *f.* consultation, deliberation, consideration; asking of advice

consultē *adv.* prudently, advisedly

consultō[1] *adv.* on purpose, deliberately

consultō[2] 1. to consult, deliberate, ask advice; take care, provide

consultor, -ōris *m.* counsellor, adviser; one who asks for advice, client

consultrix, -īcis *f.* (*+gen.*) she that provides *or* cares (for)

consultum, -ī *n.* decree, statute, ordinance; plan, resolution; oracular response

consultus[1], -a, -um *adj.* discussed, considered; prudent, advised; practised, skilful

consultus[2], -ī *m.* lawyer

consummābilis, -is, -e *adj.* that may be perfected

consummātiō, -ōnis *f.* perfection, completion

consummātus, -a, -um *adj.* perfect

consummō 1. to add together; achieve, accomplish, complete, perfect

consūmō, -sumpsī, -sumptum 3. to consume, devour, swallow up; destroy, kill; reduce, exhaust, use up, expend; waste, squander

consumptiō, -ōnis *f.* consumption; wasting, squandering

consumptor, -ōris *m.* consumer; waster, squanderer

consuō, -suī, -sūtum 3. to sew together, stitch up; devise, plan

consurgō, -surrexī, -surrectum 3. to rise, stand up, get up; spring up; reach up

consurrectiō, -ōnis *f.* rising, standing up

consusurrō 1. to whisper together

contābēfaciō, -fēcī, -factum 3. to consume, waste

contābescō, -buī 3. to waste away, pine, droop

contabulātiō, -ōnis *f.* flooring, planking, decking

contabulō 1. to cover with boards, plank *or* floor with boards; bridge with wood

contactus[1], -a, -um *adj.* defiled, polluted, infected

contactus[2], -ūs *m.* touch, contact; infection, contagion, contamination

contāgēs see **contactus[2]**

contāgiō, -ōnis *f.* or **contāgium, -(i)ī** *n.* touch, contact; infection, contagion, contamination; moral pollution; sympathetic affection

contāminō 1. to pollute, defile, desecrate; spoil, stain

contechnor 1. *dep.* to devise, plot

contegō, -xī, -ctum 3. to cover, bury; hide, conceal; protect

contemerō 1. to pollute, defile, violate

contemnō, -mpsī, -mptum 3. to despise, hold in contempt, slight, insult; disdain

contemplātiō, -ōnis *f.* viewing, surveying; contemplation, consideration

contemplātīvus, -a, -um *adj.* speculative, theoretical

contemplātor, -ōris *m.* observer, one who studies

contemplātus, -ūs *m.* contemplation, consideration

contemplō 1. or **contemplor** 1. *dep.* to view, survey; contemplate, consider

contemptim *adv.* with contempt, scornfully

contemptiō, -ōnis *f.* contempt, scorn, disdain

contemptor, -ōris *m.* despiser, insultor

contemptrix, -īcis *f.* female who despises *or* scorns

contemptus[1], -a, -um *adj.* contemptible, despicable, abject

contemptus[2], -ūs *m.* see **contemptiō**

contendō, -dī, -tum 3. to strain, stretch, exert; throw, shoot; strive, struggle, labour, exert oneself; contend, contest, compete, fight, engage; compare, contrast, set together; maintain, assert, insist upon, demand; hurry, advance quickly

contentē *adv.* with great force *or* vigour, vehemently

contentiō, -ōnis *f.* straining, effort, exertion; endeavour, force, vehemence; contest, competition, struggle, dispute, debate, disagreement; comparison, contrast

contentiōsus, -a, -um *adj.* quarrelsome

contentus, -a, -um *adj.* strained, stretched, drawn tight; energetic, vehement; content, satisfied

conterminus, -a, -um *adj.* neighbouring, adjacent, bordering; *n.sbst.* adjacent region

conterō, -trīvī, -trītum 3. to grind, pound, bruise; wear out, rub away; use up, consume, exhaust; blot out, erase; treat with contempt

conterreō 2. to terrify, frighten greatly

contestor 1. *dep.* to call to witness, invoke; **lītem contestārī** to begin an action, bring a law suit

contexō, -xuī, -xtum 3. to weave, weave together, entwine; unite, connnect, join together; compose; devise

contextē *adv.* by means of close connection

contextus¹, -a, -um *adj.* woven, woven together; joined together, connected; continuous

contextus², -ūs *m.* weaving together; connection, arrangement; structure; scheme, plan; continuation

conticescō, -cuī 3. to fall silent, become quiet; cease, abate

conticinnum, -ī *n.* night-time, dead of night

contignātiō, -ōnis *f.* flooring, floor, rafters

contignō 1. to join together with beams, furnish with joists

contiguus, -a, -um *adj.* neighbouring, adjacent, near; within range

continens, -ntis *adj.* (*+dat.*) adjoining, adjacent, next (to); continual, uninterrupted, unbroken, in succession; restrained, self-controlled; *f.sbst.* main-

land, continent; *n.sbst.* main point; **in/ex continentī** immediately, at once

continenter *adv.* without a break, successively; moderately, with restraint

continentia, -ae *f.* moderation, self-control, abstinence

contineō, -tinuī, -tentum 2. to contain, hold, comprise; keep together, join, connect; enclose, confine, limit; detain, restrain; hold tight, retain; be made of, consist in; keep from; maintain, sustain, support; preserve; be the main point; *pass.* (*+abl.*) depend on

contingō, -tigī, -tactum 3. to touch, come in contact with; be in contact with, border on; reach, arrive at; take hold of, seize; sprinkle, anoint; infect, pollute, contaminate; concern, affect; happen, come to pass

continuātiō, -ōnis *f.* continuation, unbroken sequence; period

continuātus, -a, -um *adj.* continuous, unbroken, uninterrupted; adjoining, contiguous

continuō¹ *adv.* immediately, at once, right away; consequently, necessarily

continuō² 1. to join, connect, make continuous; continue, keep on (doing), prolong

continuus, -a, -um *adj.* continuous, without interruption, incessant; following in close succession, next

contiō, -ōnis *f.* public meeting, assembly; audience; public speech; speaker's platform

contiōnābundus, -a, -um *adj.* speaking in public

contiōnalis, -is, -e or **contiōnārius, -a, -um** *adj.* of *or* relating to public meetings; demagogic

contiōnātor, -ōris *m.* public speaker, demagogue

contiōnor 1. *dep.* to speak in public; attend a public meeting

contiuncula, -ae *f.* small public meeting; short speech

contollō 3. **gradum contollere** to step forward

contonat 1. *impers.* it thunders violently

contorqueō, -rsī, -rtum 2. to twist, turn, whirl; throw, hurl, cast; turn, steer; influence, guide

contortē *adv.* intricately

contortiō, -ōnis *f.* twisting; intricate arrangement

contortiplicātus, -a, -um *adj.* intricate, involved

contortor, -ōris *m.* perverter

contortulus, -a, -um *adj.* somewhat forced, overly complicated

contrā¹ *adv.* opposite, face to face; in opposition; in reply, in return; on the other hand, on the contrary; otherwise

contrā² *prep.* (+*acc.*) against, facing, in the direction of; opposite; in response to; in opposition to, contrary to

contractābiliter *adv.* softly, gently

contractiō, -ōnis *f.* contraction, drawing together, shrinking; compression, abbreviation

contractiuncula, -ae *f.* mild despondency

contractō see **contrectō**

contractus, -a, -um *adj.* drawn together, restricted; narrow; diminished, confined, condensed; restrained, frugal

contrādīcō, -dixī, -dictum 3. to speak against, contradict, oppose, thwart

contrādictiō, -ōnis *f.* speaking against, contradiction

contrahō, -xī, -ctum 3. to draw together; contract, draw in; narrow, shorten, reduce; restrict, diminish; assemble, unite, collect; bring about, cause; incur; enter into, have dealings with; transact business with

contrāriē *adv.* in the opposite direction; contrariwise

contrārium, -(i)ī *n.* the opposite; **ē(x) contrāriō** on the other side; on the contrary, on the other hand

contrārius, -a, -um *adj.* (+*dat.*) opposite, contrary (to), contradictory; at variance (with); hostile (to), adverse (to), harmful (to)

contrectātiō, -ōnis *f.* touching, handling, fondling

contrectō 1. to touch, handle; fondle, grope; have sex with

contremescō (-miscō), -muī 3. to tremble violently; be afraid of

contremō 3. to tremble violently

contribuō, -uī, -ūtum 3. (+*dat.*) to join (to), add (to); incorporate, unite (with); contribute (to), give (to), bestow (upon)

contristō 1. to make sad, dishearten; make gloomy

contrītus, -a, -um *adj.* worn, wasted; trite, stale

contrōversia, -ae *f.* controversy, debate, dispute

contrōversiōsus, -a, -um *adj.* disputed, questionable

contrōversor 1. *dep.* to debate, dispute

contrōversus, -a, -um *adj.* disputed, questionable, controversial

contrucīdō 1. to kill, slay, butcher

contrūdō, -sī, -sum 3. to crowd together, thrust

contruncō 1. to kill, slay, cut to pieces

contubernālis, -is *m./f.* one who shares the same tent *or* occupies the same quarters; comrade

contubernium, -(i)ī *n.* tent shared by soldiers, quarters, house; comradeship, fellowship; concubinage, cohabitation

contueor 2. *dep.* to stare at intently, behold; view, survey

contuitus, -ūs *m.* intent stare; sight

contumācia, -ae *f.* stubbornness, obstinacy; firmness

contumāciter *adv.* stubbornly, obstinately

contumax, -ācis *adj.* stubborn, obstinate

contumēlia, -ae *f.* insult, reproach, outrage, affront

contumēliōsē *adv.* insolently, outrageously, abusively

contumēliōsus, -a, -um *adj.* insolent, outrageous, abusive

contumulō 1. to bury, inter

contundō, -tudī, -tūsum 3. to pound, batter, knock, bruise; break, crush

contuor see **contueor**

conturbātiō, -ōnis *f.* disorder, confusion

conturbātor, -ōris *m.adj.* expensive enough to ruin one

conturbō 1. to trouble greatly, disturb, disorder, confuse; suffer financial ruin, become bankrupt

contus, -ī *m.* long pole, punt pole; spear, pike

contūtus see **contuitus**

cōnūbiālis, -is, -e *adj.* of *or* relating to marriage, conjugal

cōnūbium, -(i)ī *n.* marriage, intermarriage

cōnus, -ī *m.* cone, crest of helmet

convador 1. *dep.* to extract a guarantee that one will appear in court

convalescō, -luī 3. to grow strong, acquire strength; recover (*from an illness*)

convallis, -is *f.* enclosed valley

convāsō 1. to pack up baggage

convectō 1. to collect, gather together

convector, -ōris *m.* fellow passenger

convehō, -vexī, -vectum 3. to bring together, collect; convey

convellō, -vellī, -vulsum 3. to tear apart, rend, tear away; shake; dislocate, remove, overturn; weaken, impair

convenae, -ārum *m.pl.* assembled crowd of strangers, refugees

conveniens, -ntis *adj.* (+*dat.*) suitable (for), appropriate (for), convenient (for); agreeable (to); unanimous, harmonious

convenienter *adv.* suitably, aptly, conveniently; agreeably; consistently

convenientia, -ae *f.* accord, agreement, harmony

conveniō, -vēnī, -ventum 4. to come together, meet, assemble; visit, approach, go up to, speak to; (+*dat.*) agree (with), be agreed upon; *impers.* (+*dat.+inf.*) it is appropriate *or* agreed (for one) (to)

conventīcium, -(i)ī *n.* payment for attending assembly

conventīcius, -a, -um *adj.* (*perhaps*) met by chance

conventiculum, -ī *n.* assembly, small meeting; meeting place

conventiō, -ōnis *f.* or **conventum, -ī** *n.* agreement, contract

conventus, -ūs *m.* coming together, union; meeting, assembly; provincial assembly, provincial meeting of law-courts, assizes

converberō 1. to strike, beat, buffet

converrō, -rrī, -rsum 3. to sweep up

conversātiō, -ōnis *f.* familiarity, acquaintance

conversiō, -ōnis *f.* turning round, revolution, circuit; change, alteration, inversion; rhetorical period

conversō 1. to turn, turn round

conversor 1. *dep.* (+*dat.* or +*cum* +*abl.*) to associate (with)

convertō, -tī, -sum 3. to turn, turn about, turn back; face, turn towards, direct; change, transform; turn aside,

divert, distract; **sē/terga convertere** to retreat; **in fugam convertere** to put to flight

convestiō 4. to clothe, cover

convexus, -a, -um *adj.* convex, vaulted, arched; sloping, curved, inclined

convīciātor, -ōris *m.* one who taunts *or* rails at

convīcior 1. *dep.* to taunt, reproach, rail at

convīcium, -(i)ī *n.* loud noise, uproar, persistent noise; verbal insult, abuse, reproach

convictiō, -ōnis *f.* living together, familiarity, intimacy

convictor, -ōris *m.* close companion, familiar acquaintance, intimate

convictus, -ūs *m.* living together, familiarity, intimacy; feast, banquet; circle of friends

convincō, -vīcī, -victum 3. to convict; refute; prove clearly

convīsō, -sī, -sum 3. to go to see, visit; view, survey

convīva, -ae *m.* guest, table-companion

convīvālis, -is, -e *adj.* of a feast, festal, convivial

convīvātor, -ōris *m.* host

convīvium, -(i)ī *n.* feast, banquet, entertainment; guests

convīvō, -vixī, -victum 3. to live with, live together; dine together

convīvor 1. *dep.* to feast, banquet

convocātiō, -ōnis *f.* convocation, calling together, assembly

convocō 1. to call together, assemble, summon

convolnerō see **convulnerō**

convolō 1. to fly *or* flock together, meet together

convolsus see **convellō**

convolvō, -vī, -ūtum 3. to roll together, roll round; enfold, envelop, wrap up; intertwine

convolūtor 1. *dep.* to wallow

convomō, -uī, -itum 3. to vomit upon

convortō see **convertō**

convulnerō 1. to wound severely

cooperiō, -ruī, -rtum 4. to cover over, envelop, overwhelm

cooptātiō, -ōnis *f.* co-option, election (*to fill vacant position*)

cooptō 1. to choose, elect

coorior, coortus 4. *dep.* to arise, spring up; be born; break out

coortus, -ūs *m.* rising, springing up

cōpa, -ae *f.* dancing-girl (*at drinking establishments*)

cophinus, -ī *m.* basket

cōpia, -ae *f.* (+*gen.*) abundance (of), plenty; quantity (of); *pl.* supplies, provisions; troops, forces

cōpiōsē *adv.* abundantly, plentifully, copiously

cōpiōsus, -a, -um *adj.* rich, well-endowed; abundant, plentiful, copious

cōpis, -is, -e *adj.* rich, well-endowed

cōpō see **caupō**

coprea, -ae *m.* low-life buffoon, stinking clown

copta, -ae *f.* hard biscuit

cōpula, -ae *f.* rope, fastening, leash, bond

cōpulātiō, -ōnis *f.* union, coming together

cōp(u)lātus, -a, -um *adj.* united, joined, related

cōpulō 1. to unite, join, connect

coqua, -ae *f.* female cook

coquinō 1. to cook

coquīnus, -a, -um *adj.* of *or* associated with cooking

coquō, coxī, coctum 3. to cook, bake, boil; cook up; ripen; digest; stir up

coquus, -ī *m.* cook, chef

cor, cordis *n.* heart, spirit; mind; **cordī esse** (+*dat.*) to be dear (to)

coracīnus, -ī *m.* Egyptian fish

cōram[1] *adv.* openly, in person

cōram[2] *prep.* (+*abl.*) in the presence of

corbis, -is *f.* basket

corbīta, -ae *f.* heavily-laden boat, slow-moving merchant ship

corbula, -ae *f.* small basket

corcodīlus see **crocodīlus**

corcōta see **crocōta**

corcōtārius, -a, -um *adj.* of *or* relating to saffron-coloured clothing

corculum, -ī *n.* little heart, dear heart

corda see **chorda**

cordātē *adv.* wisely, cleverly

cordātus, -a, -um *adj.* wise, clever

cordolium, -(i)ī *n.* heartache, grief

cordȳla, -ae *f.* immature tunny-fish

coriandrum, -ī *n.* coriander

corium, -(i)ī *n.* or **corius, -(i)ī** *m.* skin, hide

corneolus, -a, -um *adj.* horny

corneus[1]**, -a, -um** *adj.* of horn

corneus[2]**, -a, -um** *adj.* of cornel trees, of cornel-wood

cornicen, -inis *m.* horn-player, trumpeter

cornīcor 1. *dep.* to caw, say in a hoarse voice

cornīcula, -ae *f.* little crow

corniculārius, -(i)ī *m.* adjutant

corniger, -era, -erum *adj.* horned

cornipēs, -pedis *adj.* hooved

cornix, -īcis *f.* crow

cornū, -ūs *n.* horn; trumpet; bow; lantern; funnel; hoof; beak; extremity, tip; headland; crest of helmet; wing of an army

cornum[1]**, -ī** *n.* cornelian cherry; cornel-wood spear

cornum[2]**, -ūs** *n.* see **cornū**

cornus, -ī or **-ūs** *f.* cornel tree; cornel wood; cornel-wood spear

corolla, -ae *f.* small garland *or* floral wreath

corollārium, -(i)ī *n.* present, gratuity

corōna, -ae *f.* garland, floral wreath, crown; halo; constellation; ring of spectators; cordon of soldiers; **sub corōnā vendere** to sell into slavery

corōnārius, -a, -um *adj.* used for making crowns

corōnis, -idis *f.* symbol *or* device placed at end of book

corōnō 1. to crown, wreathe, surround

corporālis, -is, -e *adj.* of *or* associated with the body, corporeal

corporātus, -a, -um *adj.* corporeal, tangible

corporeus, -a, -um *adj.* of *or* associated with the body, corporeal; fleshy

corpulentus, -a, -um *adj.* heavily-built, corpulent

corpus, -oris *n.* body, flesh, trunk; person; corpse; substance, particle

corpusculum, -ī *n.* small body, particle, atom

corrādō, -sī, -sum 3. to scrape together

correctiō, -ōnis *f.* amendment, correction, improvement

corrector, -ōris *m.* amender, corrector, improver

correpō, -repsī, -reptum 3. to creep, crawl, slink

correptē *adv.* shortly, with a short syllable

corrīdeō 2. to laugh together

corrigia, -ae f. shoe-lace, strap

corrigō, -rexī, -rectum 3. to make straight; amend, correct, improve

corripiō, -ripuī, -reptum 3. to snatch up, seize, take hold of; carry away; attack; blame, accuse; shorten; **viam/gradum corripere** to hurry on one's way

corrōborō 1. to strengthen, fortify

corrōdō, -sī, -sum 3. to gnaw, chew to pieces

corrogō 1. to gather together, collect (by request)

corrotundō 1. to make round

corrūgō 1. to wrinkle, scrunch up

corrumpō, -rūpī, -ruptum 3. to destroy, ruin; damage, harm, spoil; falsify; corrupt, seduce, bribe

corruō, -ruī 3. to fall, collapse; be ruined; overthrow; gather up

corruptē adv. incorrectly; in a corrupt manner

corruptēla, -ae f. corruption, perversion; bribery, seduction; corrupter

corruptiō, -ōnis f. corruption; bribery, seduction

corruptor, -ōris m. corrupter, seducer

corruptrix, -īcis f.adj. corrupting

corruptus, -a, -um adj. corrupt, decayed; decadent; depraved, improper

cors see **cohors**

cortex, -icis m./f. bark, rind; shell; cork

cortīna, -ae f. cauldron, round-bottomed pot (spec. the vessel that sat on Apollo's tripod at Delphi)

corulus see **corylus**

cōrus see **caurus**

coruscō 1. to shake, brandish; flit, flutter; tremble; gleam, flash

coruscus, -a, -um adj. shaking, trembling; gleaming, flashing

corvus, -ī m. raven

cōrycus, -ī m. punchbag

corylētum, -ī n. plantation of hazel trees, hazel copse

corylus, -ī f. hazel tree

corymbifer, -era, -erum adj. carrying clusters of ivy berries

corymbus, -ī m. cluster of ivy berries or other fruit/flowers

coryphaeus, -ī m. leader, head

cōrytos (-us), -ī m. quiver

cōs, cōtis f. hard stone, flint; whetstone

cosmētēs, -ae m. slave in charge of mistress's clothing and make-up

cosmicos, -ē, -on adj. fashionable, worldly

costa, -ae f. rib; side, back

costum, -ī n. or **costos, -ī** f. aromatic plant

cōtēs see **cautēs**

cothu- see **cotu-**

cōti- see **cotti-**

cottabus, -ī m. drinking game (in which dregs of wine are projected at target); clap, stroke

cottana, -ōrum n.pl. Syrian figs

cottīdiānō adv. every day, daily

cottīdiānus, -a, -um adj. daily, everyday

cottīdiē adv. every day

cottona see **cottana**

cotula, -ae f. small measure of liquid

coturnātus, -a, -um adj. wearing coturni; tragic, elevated

coturnix, -īcis f. quail

coturnus, -ī m. (usu. pl.) boot worn by actors in tragedies; hunting boot; tragedy, tragic style

covinnārius, -(i)ī m. one who fights from a covinnus

covinnus, -ī m. war chariot; carriage

coxa, -ae f. hip; hip-joint

coxendix, -īcis f. hip

crābrō, -ōnis m. hornet

crambē, -ēs f. cabbage

crāpula, -ae f. hangover, drunkenness

crāpulārius, -a, -um adj. for the prevention or relief of drunkenness

crās adv. tomorrow

crassē adv. coarsely; confusedly

crassitūdō, -inis f. thickness, density

crassus, -a, -um adj. thick, dense; heavy, coarse; stupid

crastinus, -a, -um adj. of tomorrow; n.sbst. tomorrow, the morrow

crātēr, -ēris m. or **crātēra, -ae** f. large mixing bowl (esp. for wine)

crātīcula, -ae f. small gridiron

crātis, -is f. wickerwork used as frame; basket; inner part of shield; harrow, fascine

creātiō, -ōnis f. election

creātor, -ōris m. creator, founder, father

creātrix, -īcis f. creator, founder, mother

crēber, -bra, -brum adj. thick, crowded

together; frequent, numerous, repeated; (+*abl.*) full (of), packed (with)

crēbrescō, -bruī 3. to increase, grow in strength

crēbritās, -ātis *f.* frequency

crēbrō *adv.* thickly; frequently, repeatedly, often

crēdibilis, -is, -e *adj.* credible, plausible, convincing, likely

crēdibiliter *adv.* credibly

crēditor, -ōris *m.* creditor

crēditum, -ī *n.* loan

crēdō, -didī, -ditum 3. (+*dat.*) to entrust (to), loan (to); (+*acc.*) have confidence in, trust, believe; (+*acc.*+*inf.*) believe *or* think (that)

crēdulitās, -ātis *f.* credulity

crēdulus, -a, -um *adj.* credulous, trusting

cremō 1. to burn, consume by fire, cremate

cremor, -ōris *m.* thick broth *or* juice

creō 1. to make, produce, beget; elect; cause

creper, -era, -erum *adj.* dark, obscure, uncertain

crepida, -ae *f.* (*usu. pl.*) thick-soled sandal

crepidātus, -a, -um *adj.* wearing *crepidae*

crepīdō, -inis *f.* elevated platform; high projection; embankment, edge, pier

crepidula, -ae *f.* small sandal

crepitācillum, -ī *n.* small rattle for child

crepitō 1. to rattle, clatter, creak, crackle, rustle

crepitus, -ūs *m.* rattling, clattering, creaking

crepō, -uī, -itum 1. to rattle, clatter, creak; crackle, rustle; fart; snap (*fingers*); prattle

crepundia, -ōrum *n.pl.* child's rattle

crepusculum, -ī *n.* dusk, twilight; darkness

crescō, crēvī, crētum 3. to be born, come forth, arise; grow (up), increase; advance

crēta, -ae *f.* white clay, chalk (*used as cosmetic, for cleaning clothes, for making auspicious marks with etc.*)

crētātus, -a, -um *adj.* whitened with chalk; clothed in white

crēterra, -ae *f.* large mixing bowl (*for wine*)

crēteus, -a, -um *adj.* made of chalk *or* clay

crētiō, -ōnis *f.* declaration made by heir on accepting inheritance

crētōsus, -a, -um *adj.* rich in chalk *or* clay

crētula, -ae *f.* clay

crētus, -a, -um *adj.* (+*abl. or* +*ab/de* +*abl.*) descended from, born of

crībrum, -ī *n.* sieve

crīmen, -inis *n.* charge, accusation, reproach; fault, crime; cause of crime

crīminātiō, -ōnis *f.* charge, accusation

crīminātor, -ōris *m.* accuser

crīminor 1. *dep.* or **crīminō** 1. to bring a charge, accuse; slander; complain of

crīminōsē *adv.* in an accusatory manner, slanderously

crīminōsus, -a, -um *adj.* accusatory, slanderous

crīnālis, -is, -e *adj.* of *or* relating to the hair; *n.sbst.* hairgrip

crīniger, -era, -erum *adj.* with long hair

crīniō 4. to cover with hair

crīnis, -is *m.* hair; tail of comet

crīnītus, -a, -um *adj.* with long hair

crisis (*acc.sg.* **crisin**) *f.* crisis-point, critical stage

crīsō 1. (*of women*) to thrust one's hips

crispō 1. to curl; wave, shake, brandish

crispulus, -a, -um *adj.* curly, curly-haired

crispus, -a, -um *adj.* curly, curly-haired; trembling, quivering

crista, -ae *f.* crest, plume

cristātus, -a, -um *adj.* crested, plumed

criticus, -ī *m.* critic

crocciō 4. to croak

croceus, -a, -um *adj.* of saffron; saffron-coloured, yellow

crocinus, -a, -um *adj.* saffron-coloured, yellow; *n.sbst.* saffron oil

crocodīlus, -ī *m.* crocodile

crocōta, -ae *f.* saffron-coloured dress

crocōtula, -ae *f.* (small) saffron-coloured dress

crocum, -ī *n.* or **crocus, -ī** *m.* saffron; colour of saffron

crotalistria, -ae *f.* castanet dancer

crotalum, -ī *n.* castanet

cruciābilitās, -ātis *f.* torment

cruciābiliter *adv.* with torture

cruciāmentum, -ī *n.* torture

cruciātus, -ūs *m.* torture, torment

cruciō 1. to torture, torment

crūdēlis, -is, -e *adj.* cruel, savage, harsh, inhuman

crūdēlitās, -ātis *f.* cruelty, inhumanity

crūdēliter *adv.* cruelly, inhumanely

crūdescō, -duī 3. to become rough, savage

crūditās, -ātis f. indigestion

crūdus, -a, -um adj. raw, uncooked; bleeding; rough, coarse; unripe, immature; cruel, inhumane; undigested, dyspeptic

cruentē adv. bloodthirstily

cruentō 1. to stain with blood, make bloody, wound

cruentus, -a, -um adj. bloody; bloodthirsty; blood-coloured

crumilla, -ae f. small purse

crumīna, -ae f. purse, money

cruor, -ōris m. blood, gore; bloodshed

cruppellārius, -(i)ī m. fully armed Gallic fighter

crūricrepida, -ae m. one whose legs clank in chains

crūrifragius, -i(ī) m. one whose legs are broken

crūs, crūris n. leg, shin

crusculum, -ī n. small leg

crusma, -atis n. tune

crusta, -ae f. crust, shell, rind, casing; embossed work

crustō 1. to encrust, cover

crustulārius, -(i)ī m. seller of crustula

crustulum, -ī n. small cake

crustum, -ī n. cake

crux, crucis f. cross; crucifixion; thing of torment

crypta, -ae f. covered passage, underground gallery

crystallinus, -a, -um adj. of crystal; n.pl. sbst. crystal vases

crystallum, -ī n. or crystallus, -ī m. crystal; crystal cup

cubiculāris, -is, -e adj. of or relating to the bedroom

cubiculārius, -(i)ī m. chamber-slave

cubiculum, -ī n. bedroom, chamber; theatre box

cubīle, -is n. bed, couch; lair, den, nest

cubital, -ālis n. cushion for elbow

cubitālis, -is, -e adj. one cubit in breadth or length

cubitō 1. to lie, sleep

cubitum, -ī n. elbow; cubit

cubitūra, -ae f. lying down

cubitus¹, -ūs m. lying down, reclining

cubitus², -ī m. see cubitum

cubō, -uī, -itum 1. to lie down, recline; cubitum īre to go to bed

cubus, -ī m. cube

cucullus, -ī m. hood

cucūlus, -ī m. cuckoo

cucuma, -ae f. cooking pot

cucumis, -eris m. cucumber

cucurbita, -ae f. gourd; cupping-glass

cūdō 3. to beat, strike, mint

cūiās, -ātis adj. from where?, from what country?

cūius, -a, -um adj. whose?; (rel.) whose

culcita, -ae f. mattress, bolster, pillow

culcitula, -ae f. small mattress

cūleus see culleus

culex, -icis m./f. gnat, midge

culillus, -ī m. drinking-cup

culīna, -ae f. kitchen; cooking

culix see culex

culleus, -ī m. leather bag or sack; liquid measure

culmen, -inis n. top, summit; roof, ridgepole; height

culmus, -ī m. stem, stalk, straw

culpa, -ae f. blame, fault

culpābilis, -is, -e adj. at fault, to blame

culpitō 1. to find fault with

culpō 1. to blame, find fault with

culta, -ōrum n.pl. farmland

cultē adv. in a refined manner

cultellus, -ī m. small knife

culter, -trī m. knife

cultiō, -ōnis f. cultivation

cultor, -ōris m. cultivator, farmer; keeper; supporter, worshipper; inhabitant

cultrārius, -(i)ī m. sacrificial priest who wielded knife

cultrix, -īcis f. inhabitant; cultivator

cultūra, -ae f. cultivation, agriculture, culture

cultus¹, -a, -um adj. cultivated; refined; smart

cultus², -ūs m. cultivation (of land); education; maintenance, support, worship; adornment, refinement, style; habitation

cūlus, -ī m. anus

cum¹ prep. (+abl.) with, together with; cum eō quod/ut... on the condition that; cum prīmīs especially

cum² conj.

1. cum + subjunctive

a) since, although, whereas

cum aeger essem, Romam profectus sum
although I was ill, I set out for Rome
b) when (in historic sequence: imperfect,
pluperfect, perfect without have)
cum puer essem, in horto ludebam when I
was a boy, I used to play in the garden

2. **cum** + *indicative*
a) whenever (with future perfect, perfect,
pluperfect)
cum te viderant, laetus eras whenever
they saw you, you were happy
b) when (inverted time clause)
cum Caesar interfectus est, pluebat when
Caesar died, it was raining
c) when (in primary sequence: present,
future, perfect with have, future perfect)
cum insulam invenit gaudet when he
finds the island, he rejoices

cūmātilis, -is, -e *adj.* the colour of waves
cumba, -ae *f.* boat, skiff
cumera, -ae *f.* box, receptacle
cumīnum, -ī *n.* cumin
cumulātē *adv.* abundantly, copiously,
fully
cumulātus, -a, -um *adj.* abundant; (+*dat./
gen.*) abounding (in)
cumulō 1. to heap up, pile up, amass; fill,
overload; increase, add; perfect, crown
cumulus, -ī *m.* heap, pile, mass; increase,
addition; culmination, pinnacle
cūnābula, -ōrum *n.pl.* cradle
cūnae, -ārum *f.pl.* cradle
cunctābundus, -a, -um *adj.* hesitant,
tardy
cunctans, -ntis *adj.* hesitating, delaying
cunctanter *adv.* hesitantly, slowly
cunctātiō, -ōnis *f.* (+*gen.*) hesitation,
delaying (over)
cunctātor, -ōris *m.* (+*gen.*) one who hesi-
tates *or* delays (over)
cunctor 1. *dep.* or **cunctō 1.** to hesitate,
delay; linger, loiter, dawdle
cunctus, -a, -um *adj.* all, the whole
cuneātim *adv.* in a wedge shape
cuneātus, -a, -um *adj.* wedge-shaped
cuneō 1. to wedge
cuneolus, -ī *m.* small wedge
cuneus, -ī *m.* wedge
cunīculōsus, -a, -um *adj.* full of rabbits

cunīculus, -ī *m.* rabbit; burrow, tunnel;
mine
cunīla, -ae *f.* plant
cunnilingus, -ī *m.* one who engages in
cunnilingus, cunt-licker
cunnus, -ī *m.* vagina, cunt
cūpa, -ae *f.* barrel, cask
cupidē *adv.* eagerly, keenly, hastily
cupiditās, -ātis *f.* desire, longing; passion,
lust; greed; ambition
cupīdō, -inis *f./m.* desire, longing; passion,
lust; greed; ambition
cupidus, -a, -um *adj.* desirous, keen, eager;
passionate; greedy; ambitious
cupiens, -ntis *adj.* (+*gen.*) desiring, keen
(for)
cupienter *adv.* eagerly, keenly
cupiō 4. to desire, want, long for; (+*dat.*)
favour, wish well
cupītor, -ōris *m.* one who desires
cuppēdia[1], -ae *f.* passion for delicacies
cuppēdia[2], -ōrum *n.pl.* delicacies, tit-bits
cuppēdinārius, -(i)ī *m.* confectioner
cuppēdō see **cupīdō**
cuppēs, -ēdis *adj.* passionate about delicacies
cupressētum, -ī *n.* cypress grove
cupresseus, -a, -um *adj.* made of cypress-
wood
cupressifer, -era, -erum *adj.* cypress-
bearing
cupressus, -ī *or* **-ūs** *f.* cypress
cūr *adv.* why?
cūra, -ae *f.* care; careful attention, trouble,
pains; worry, concern; anxiety, distress;
administration, management; treatment,
cure; object of care, love; work, study;
cūrae esse (+*dat. of person*) to be dear (to)
cūrābilis, -is, -e *adj.* needing medical
treatment
cūralium, -(i)ī *n.* coral
cūrātē *adv.* carefully
cūrātiō, -ōnis *f.* care, management; treatment
cūrātor, -ōris *m.* curator, superintendent
cūrātūra, -ae *f.* care, management; treatment
curculiō, -ōnis *m.* corn-weevil
curculiunculus, -ī *m.* little corn-weevil
cūria, -ae *f.* senate house, senate (*original
name given to the thirty separate divisions of
the Roman electorate*)

cūriālis, -is, -e *adj.* of the same *curia*; *m. sbst.* member of the same *curia*

cūriātim *adv.* by *curiae*

cūriātus, -a, -um *adj.* of *or* relating to the *curiae*; **comitia cūriāta** assembly of the *curiae*

cūriō, -ōnis *m.* priest connected to *curia*; herald; **cūriō maximus** chief priest of the *curiae*

cūriōsē *adv.* carefully, attentively; inquisitively

cūriōsitās, -ātis *f.* curiosity, inquisitiveness

cūriōsus, -a, -um *adj.* careful, attentive; curious, inquisitive, interfering; careworn

curis, -is *f.* spear

cūrō 1. to care for, take care of, attend to; (+*ut/ne* +*subj.*) undertake, see to; administer, manage; treat, cure; take trouble; (+*acc.+inf.*) worry (that)

curriculum, -ī *n.* running; race; lap, circuit, course; race-track; chariot; **curriculō** at a run

currō, cucurrī, cursum 3. to run; hurry, speed (on), fly; **currentem incitāre** to spur on a willing horse

currus, -ūs *m.* chariot; team of horses; triumph; ship; plough

cursim *adv.* at a run, quickly

cursitō 1. to run about

cursō 1. to run about habitually

cursor, -ōris *m.* runner; courier; footman

cursūra, -ae *f.* running

cursus, -ūs *m.* running, charge; rapid movement, speed; course, direction; journey, march; progress; **cursū** at a run

curtō 1. to shorten, diminish

curtus, -a, -um *adj.* shortened, diminished, curtailed; mutilated, castrated

curūlis, -is, -e *adj.* of *or* relating to the office of the curule magistrate, curule

curvāmen, -inis *n.* curve, bend, arc

curvātūra, -ae *f.* curve, bend, arc

curvō 1. to curve, bend; make to yield

curvus, -a, -um *adj.* curved, bent, bowed

cuspis, -idis *f.* point, tip; spear; stake

custōdēla, -ae *f.* guarding, custody, care

custōdia, -ae *f.* guard, custody; care, watch; garrison, picket; guard-house; confinement, prison; prisoners

custōdiō 4. to guard, keep watch over; keep safe, protect; keep, preserve

custōs, -ōdis *m./f.* guard, watchman, sentry; doorkeeper

cutīcula, -ae *f.* skin

cutis, -is *f.* skin

cyathissō 1. to ladle out wine

cyathus, -ī *m.* wine ladle; liquid measure, one-twelfth of a *sextarius*

cybaea, -ae *f.* merchant ship

cybium, -(i)ī *n.* young tunny fish

cycladātus, -a, -um *adj.* wearing a *cyclas*

cyclas, -adis *f.* woman's outer garment with decorative border

cyclicus, -a, -um *adj.* cyclic; of the epic cycle

cycnēus, -a, -um *adj.* of a swan

cycnus (cygnus), -ī *m.* swan

cydōnium, -ī *n.* quince

cylindrus, -ī *m.* cylinder, roller

cymbalum (-on), -ī *n.* cymbal

cymbium, -(i)ī *n.* small cup

cynicē *adv.* in the way of the Cynics

cynicus, -a, -um *adj.* Cynic; *m.sbst.* Cynic philosopher

cynocephalus, -ī *m.* dog-faced baboon

cyparissus, -ī *f.* cypress

cytisus, -ī *f.* or **cytisum, -ī** *n.* the plant treemedick, trefoil

dactylicus, -a, -um *adj.* consisting of dactyls, dactylic

dactyliothēca, -ae *f.* box for rings

dactylus, -ī *m.* metrical foot, dactyl

daedalus, -a, -um *adj.* skilful; wrought with skill

dāmiurgus (dēm-), -ī *m.* highest magistrate in certain Greek states

damma, -ae *f./m.* deer, antelope; venison

damnātiō, -ōnis *f.* condemnation in court

damnātōrius, -a, -um *adj.* of *or* relating to condemnation

damnātus, -a, -um *adj.* condemned

damnificus, -a, -um *adj.* causing loss *or* harm

damnigerulus, -a, -um *adj.* bringing injury, pernicious

damnō 1. to condemn, sentence; disapprove of; (+*dat.*) assign (to); (+*inf.*) bind (to)

damnōsē *adv.* ruinously

damnōsus, -a, -um *adj.* causing loss, ruinous; prodigal

damnum, -ī *n.* loss, damage; penalty fine

danista, -ae *m.* money-lender

danisticus, -a, -um *adj.* of *or* relating to money-lenders

daphnōn, -ōnos *m.* grove of laurels

dapinō 1. to pay the cost of

daps, dapis *f.* sacrificial feast; banquet, meal

dapsile *adv.* plentifully

dapsilis, -is, -e *adj.* plentiful; (+*abl.*) abundant (in)

datārius, -a, -um *adj.* to be given away; relating to giving away

datātim *adv.* by giving from hand to hand

datiō, -ōnis *f.* handing over, payment; assignation

datō 1. to give out of habit

dator, -ōris *m.* giver, donor

datum, -ī *n.* gift; debit

datus, -ūs *m.* giving

dē *prep.* (+*abl.*) down from, away from, from; out of; concerning; on account of; after

dea, deae *f.* goddess

dealbō 1. to whitewash, plaster

deambulātiō, -ōnis *f.* walking

deambulō 1. to take a walk

deamō 1. to love passionately

dearmō 1. to strip of arms

deartuō 1. to tear limb from limb

deasciō 1. to smooth off; get the better of

dēbacchor 1. *dep.* to rave, revel

dēbellātor, -ōris *m.* conqueror, subduer

dēbellō 1. to wage war to the end, fight to the finish; conquer, subdue

dēbeō 2. to owe, be indebted; be under obligation; (+*inf.*) be bound (to)

dēbilis, -is, -e *adj.* enfeebled, weak; maimed

dēbilitās, -ātis *f.* physical infirmity; feebleness

dēbilitātiō, -ōnis *f.* enfeeblement

dēbilitō 1. to deprive of strength, weaken; remove power from

dēbitiō, -ōnis *f.* owing, debt

dēbitor, -ōris *m.* one who owes, debtor

dēbitum, -ī *n.* that which is owed, debt

dēblaterō 1. to babble foolishly

dēcantō 1. to chant repeatedly; reel off

dēcēdō, dēcessī, dēcessum 3. to move away, withdraw; deviate; desert; die; (+*dat.*) yield (to)

decem *indecl.adj.* ten; *n.sbst.* the number ten; ten men

decempeda, -ae *f.* measuring rod ten feet in length

decempedātor, -ōris *m.* land-surveyor

decemplex, -icis *adj.* ten-fold

decemprīmus, -a, -um *adj.* one of the ten chief members in the senate of a *colonia* or a *municipium*

decemscalmus, -a, -um *adj.* having ten rowlocks

decemvir, -rī *m.* one of ten members of a committee

decemvirālis, -is, -e *adj.* of *or* relating to a *decemvir*

decemvirātus, -ūs *m.* office of a *decemvir*

decennis, -is, -e *adj.* lasting for ten years; ten years old

decens, -ntis *adj.* proper, fitting; attractive, graceful

decenter *adv.* fittingly, becomingly; gracefully

decentia, -ae *f.* propriety, decency

dēceptor, -ōris *m.* one who deceives, deceiver

dēcernō, dēcrēvī, dēcrētum 3. to decide (*a matter*), determine; decree; propose

dēcerpō, -sī, -tum 3. to pluck, pick off; catch, snatch; remove

dēcertātiō, -ōnis *f.* fighting out (*of a dispute*)

dēcertō 1. to fight (*a matter*) to the end; argue it out; vie for

dēcessiō, -ōnis *f.* departure; abatement; decrease

dēcessor, -ōris *m.* magistrate retiring from his administrative post

dēcessus, -ūs *m.* departure; retirement (*from an administrative post*); death; diminution

decet 2. to add grace to, become; be proper, fitting; *impers.* (+*acc. of person* +*inf.*) it is right (to), becomes (one) (to)

dēcidō¹, -ī 3. to fall down; fall over, wilt; fall into a worse condition; die

dēcīdō², -dī, -sum 3. to cut off *or* down; decide; (+*abl.*) agree on

deciens (-ēs) *adv.* ten times

decima, decimānus see **decuma, decumānus**

decimō 1. to punish one man in ten (chosen by lot)

decimum *adv.* for the tenth time

decimus, -a, -um *adj.* tenth

dēcipiō, dēcēpī, dēceptum 3. to deceive, elude; cheat, beguile

dēcīsiō, -ōnis *f.* agreement, decision

dēclāmātiō, -ōnis *f.* practice of a set speech; artificial practice speech; loud and violent speech

dēclāmātor, -ōris *m.* one who delivers speeches for oratorical practice

dēclāmātōrius, -a, -um *adj.* of *or* relating to declamation, rhetorical

dēclāmitō 1. to declaim repeatedly *or* habitually

dēclāmō 1. to make practice speeches; declaim; speak violently (against)

dēclārātiō, -ōnis *f.* the act of declaring, revelation

dēclārātor, -ōris *m.* announcer

dēclārō 1. to make known, declare; indicate, show; (*of words*) mean

dēclīnātiō, -ōnis *f.* deviation, inclination; avoidance; digression

dēclīnis, -is, -e *adj.* moving down, drooping; turning aside

dēclīnō 1. to divert, deflect; avoid; droop; change direction, digress

dēclīve, -is *n.* downward sloping surface

dēclīvis, -is, -e *adj.* with a downward sloping surface, moving downwards

dēclīvitās, -ātis *f.* downwards slope, declivity

dēcocta, -ae *f.* drink brought to the boil and then cooled in snow

dēcoctor, -ōris *m.* insolvent person, bankrupt

dēcoctus, -a, -um *adj.* (*of speech*) rich; mature

decollō 1. to behead

dēcōlō 1. to trickle *or* ooze away

dēcolor, -ōris *adj.* discoloured; darkskinned; base, depraved

dēcolōrātiō, -ōnis *f.* discoloration

dēcolōrō 1. to discolour, stain

dēcoquō, -xī, -ctum 3. to boil down *or* away; stew; melt down; consume; squander; become bankrupt

decor, -ōris *m.* beauty, grace; charm; adornment; propriety

decorē *adv.* beautifully, gracefully; properly

decoris, -is, -e *adj.* beautiful

decorō 1. to adorn, beautify; glorify, do credit to

decōrus, -a, -um *adj.* beautiful, handsome; graceful; glorious; seemly, becoming

dēcrepitus, -a, -um *adj.* infirm from age, decrepit

dēcrescō, dēcrēvī, dēcrētum 3. to decrease in size; become less; weaken, decline

dēcrētōrius, -a, -um *adj.* decisive, crucial

dēcrētum, -ī *n.* resolve, decision; decree; dogma, principle

dēculcō 1. to tread down

decum- see **decim-** (other than below)

decuma, -ae *f.* tenth part, tithe; tax *or* offering of a tithe; tenth hour of day

decumānus¹, -a, -um *adj.* of *or* relating to the tenth; concerning *or* subject to the tax of a tenth; **porta decumāna** rear gate of the Roman camp

decumānus², -ī *m.* soldier of the tenth legion; tithe-collector

decumātēs, -um *m.pl.adj.* subject to tithes

dēcumbō, dēcubuī 3. to lie down, recline; lie ill; fall in battle

decuria, -ae *f.* group of ten men; division (*esp. of jurors*); party, club

decuriātiō, -ōnis *f.* the act of dividing (*Roman tribes*) into groups of ten for voting

decuriō¹ 1. to divide into bodies of ten (*esp. of cavalry*); array in military fashion

decuriō², -ōnis *m.* officer commanding ten men (*esp. of cavalry*); foreman in charge of slaves; member of a municipal senate, councillor

dēcurrō, dē(cu)currī, dēcursum 3. to run down; run a race; charge for; run through (*a drill*); pass over; have recourse (to); (*of ships*) come to land

dēcursiō, -ōnis *f.* mock military exercise for training *or* display

dēcursus, -ūs *m.* downhill running, descent; course of a race; channel (*for water*); military manoeuvre

dēcurtātus, -a, -um *adj.* with limbs lopped off; truncated

decus, -oris *n.* glory, honour; virtue, distinction; beauty; adornment

decussis, -is *m.* coin worth ten *asses*

decussō 1. to divide into a cross shape

dēcutiō, -ssī, -ssum 3. to shake down *or* off; overturn

dēdecet, -uit 2. to be unbecoming (to), dishonour; *impers.* (*+acc. of person +inf.*) it is unbecoming (to)

dēdecor, -oris *adj.* unseemly, shameful

dēdecorō 1. to dishonour, disfigure

dēdecorus, -a, -um *adj.* dishonourable

dēdecus, -oris *n.* dishonour, shame; disgraceful act; repulsive appearance

dēdicātiō, -ōnis *f.* consecration, dedication

dēdicō 1. (*+dat.*) to dedicate (to); devote (to); declare

dēdignātiō, -ōnis *f.* contempt, disdain

dēdignor 1. *dep.* to reject with contempt, spurn; (*+inf.*) refuse scornfully (to)

dēdiscō, dēdicī 3. to unlearn, forget; (*+inf.*) forget (how to)

dēditīcius, -a, -um *adj.* having surrendered

dēditiō, -ōnis *f.* surrender, capitulation

dēditus, -a, -um *adj.* (*+dat. or +in +acc.*) devoted (to); fond (of)

dēdō, -idī, -itum 3. to give up, surrender; (*+dat.*) consign (to); allot (to)

dēdoceō, -uī, -tum 2. to unteach, cause to forget

dēdoleō 2. to bring an end to one's grief

dēdolō 1. to cut down to shape

dēdūcō, dēduxī, dēductum 3. to lead away; bring down; avert; withdraw; escort; bring home (*a bride*); settle (*a colony*); compose (*a literary work*); reduce; deduce; deduct

dēductiō, -ōnis *f.* drawing off; settling (*of colonies*); deduction; reduction

dēductor, -ōris *m.* escort

dēductus, -a, -um *adj.* (*of the face*) bent downwards; (*of literature*) fine-spun; (*of the voice*) soft

de(e)rrō 1. to wander astray; make a mistake

dēfaecō 1. to remove the impurities from, purify

dēfaenerō 1. to bring to insolvency by debt collection

dēfatīgātiō, -ōnis *f.* exhaustion, weariness

dēfatīgō 1. to wear out, exhaust; *pass.* lose heart

dēfectiō, -ōnis *f.* deficiency, weakness; defection; eclipse

dēfector, -ōris *m.* rebel, defector; (*+abl.*) one who revolts (from)

dēfectus¹, -a, -um *adj.* enfeebled, exhausted

défectus², **-ūs** *m*. deficiency, weakness; diminution; eclipse

défendō, -dī, -sum 3. to ward off, repulse; defend; make a defence for (*esp. in court*); maintain (*a proposition*)

défensiō, -ōnis *f*. the act of defending; defence (*esp. in court*); excuse

défensitō 1. to make defences habitually

défensō 1. to defend, protect continually; ward off

défensor, -ōris *m*. one who averts; one who defends, protector; legal defendant; apologist, champion

défenstrix, -īcis *f*. female defender

déferō, déferre, détulī, délātum *v.irreg*. to bring down *or* away; carry; transfer; report against; award

défervescō, -vī 3. to cease boiling, cool off; calm down

défervō 3. to rage furiously

défetiscor, défessus 3. *dep*. to become exhausted; lose heart; (*+inf.*) become worn out (with)

déficiō, défēcī, défectum 3. to fall short, fail; weaken; falter; die; revolt; let down; abandon

défīgō, défīxī, défīxum 3. to thrust down, plant firmly; affix; make motionless; bewitch

défingō, -nxī 3. to mould into shape

défīniō 4. to set the limits of; restrict, confine; put an end to; define; assert; settle

défīnītē *adv*. definitely, precisely; expressly

défīnītiō, -ōnis *f*. definition; classification; speech based upon verbal definition

défīnītīvus, -a, -um *adj*. of *or* relating to definition

défīnītus, -a, -um *adj*. finite, delimited; precise; concerning particulars

défīō, défierī, défectus *v.irreg*. to be in short supply, fail

défīxus, -a, -um *adj*. motionless

déflagrātiō, -ōnis *f*. destruction by fire

déflagrō 1. to burn down, destroy by fire; be burnt down; lose ardour, cool down

déflectō, -xī, -xum 3. to bend downwards; turn aside, divert; distract; modify; deviate, digress

défleō, -ēvī, -ētum 2. to weep greatly for; bewail; deplore; cry bitterly

défloccō 1. to fleece, strip of possessions

déflōrescō, -ruī 3. to lose bloom; fade away, decline

défluō, -xī, -xum 3. to flow *or* float down; fall down, sink; flow away, disappear; (*+ab +abl.*) originate (from)

défluus, -a, -um *adj*. flowing down

défodiō, défōdī, défossum 3. to bury, plant firmly; dig out, excavate

déformātiō, -ōnis *f*. disfigurement, deformation

déformis, -is, -e *adj*. misshapen, ugly; disfigured; shapeless; unbecoming, shameful

déformitās, -ātis *f*. deformity, ugliness; disfigurement; shapelessness; shame, disgrace

déformiter *adv*. disgracefully, shamefully

déformō 1. to arrange, sketch out; disfigure, spoil; disgrace

défraudō 1. to defraud, cheat; (*+abl.*) rob (of)

défremō, -uī 3. to cease shouting

défrēnatus, -a, -um *adj*. unbridled

défricō 1. to rub thoroughly, rub down

défringō, défrēgī, défractum 3. to break off

défrustror 1. *dep*. to foil completely

défrutum (-ūtum), -ī *n*. drink of boiled-down grape juice

défugiō, défūgī 3. to flee from, avoid; make one's escape

défunctus, -a, -um *adj*. dead; *m./f.sbst.* dead person

défundō, défūdī, défūsum 3. to pour, discharge; pour out (*a vessel*)

défungor, -nctus 3. *dep*. to bring to the end, settle; (*+abl.*) come to the end of, finish with

défutūtus, -a, -um *adj*. fucked out

dégener, -ris *adj*. low-born, of inferior birth; unworthy of one's forebears, degenerate; ignoble; weak; (*+gen.*) untrue (to)

dégenerō 1. to fall away from one's race in behaviour, degenerate; (*+ab +abl.*) fall away from; be unworthy of

dégerō, -ssī 3. to carry away, remove

déglūbō, -upsī, -uptum 3. to flay, skin

dégō 3. to pass (*time*); live, continue on

dégrandinat 1. *impers*. it continues hailing

dēgrassor 1. *dep.* to rush upon

dēgravō 1. to weigh down upon, press down; overwhelm

dēgredior, -ssus 3. *dep.* to go down, descend; depart, divert

dēgustō 1. to take a taste of; have a slight experience of; form an opinion about

dehinc *adv.* from now on, thereafter; next, then

dehiscō 3. to split open, gape; leave a space

dehonestāmentum, -ī *n.* source of disgrace; disfigurement

dehonestō 1. to dishonour, disgrace

dehortor 1. *dep.* to dissuade, discourage; deter

dēiciō, dēiēcī, dēiectum 3. to throw *or* pour down; fell, overthrow; kill; evict, drive out; lower (*the eyes*)

dēiectiō, -ōnis *f.* ejection; bout of diarrhoea

dēiectus¹, -a, -um *adj.* downcast, dispirited

dēiectus², -ūs *m.* throwing down, felling; declivity

dēierō 1. (+*acc.*+*inf.*) to swear an oath (that)

dein see **deinde**

deinceps *adv.* successively, one after the other; next, then; henceforth, thereafter

deinde *adv.* afterwards, next; thereafter, henceforth; from that place

dēiungō, -xī, -ctum 3. to unyoke; (+*ab* +*abl.*) release (from)

dēiūrō see **dēierō**

dēiuvō 1. to refuse to aid

dēlābor, dēlapsus 3. *dep.* to fall down, descend, sink; lose strength; lapse

dēlacerō 1. to tear to pieces

dēlambō 3. to lick up and down

dēlāmentor 1. *dep.* to mourn completely

dēlassō 1. to tire out, exhaust

dēlātiō, -ōnis *f.* denunciation, accusation

dēlātor, -ōris *m.* bearer; accuser, informer

dēlēbilis, -is, -e *adj.* capable of being destroyed, delible

dēlectābilis, -is, -e *adj.* delicious

dēlectāmentum, -ī *n.* instrument of pleasure

dēlectātiō, -ōnis *f.* delight, pleasure; source of pleasure

dēlectō 1. to delight, charm; be pleasing to; *impers.* (+*acc.*+*inf.*) it pleases (one) (to)

dēlectus, -a, -um *adj.* specially selected; *m. pl.sbst.* picked men, the élite

dēlēgātiō, -ōnis *f.* assignation of debt to a third party

dēlēgō 1. (+*dat.* or +*ad* +*acc.*) to assign (to), entrust (to), refer (to)

dēlēnificus, -a, -um *adj.* mollifying, cajoling

dēlēnīmentum, -ī *n.* blandishment; soothing act

dēlēniō (dēlīniō) 4. to mollify, soothe; weaken

dēlēnītor, -ōris *m.* one who soothes, appeaser

dēleō, -ēvī, -ētum 2. to expunge, delete; wipe out, destroy; abolish; annihilate

dēlētrix, -īcis *f.adj.* (+*gen.*) causing the destruction (of)

dēlīberābundus, -a, -um *adj.* deep in deliberation

dēlīberātiō, -ōnis *f.* deliberation; speech of a deliberative nature

dēlīberātīvus, -a, -um *adj.* deliberative

dēlīberātor, -ōris *m.* one who deliberates

dēlīberātus, -a, -um *adj.* determined, resolved

dēlīberō 1. to deliberate; think over; consult; *pf.* have decided

dēlībō 1. to remove (*part of*), deplete; diminish, spoil; have a taste of

dēlībrō 1. to strip the bark from

dēlībūtus, -a, -um *adj.* (+*abl.*) thickly smeared (with), steeped (in)

dēlicātē *adv.* comfortably, luxuriously; gently; carefully

dēlicātus, -a, -um *adj.* luxurious; frivolous; spoiled; fastidious; elegant; dainty, delicate

dēlicia, -ae *f.* (*usu. pl.*) pleasurable thing *or* act; delicacies; luxuries; darling, pet; affected mannerisms

dēliciolae, -ārum *f.pl.* or **dēliciolum, -ī** *n.* little darling

dēlicō 1. to reveal, disclose

dēlictum, -ī *n.* unworthy act, misdeed; defect

dēlicuus, -a, -um *adj.* wanting, missing

dēligō¹ 1. to bind fast, tie up

dēligō², dēlēgī, dēlectum 3. to pick off; pick out, select; enrol (*soldiers*)

dēlingō 3. to lick

dēlinō, -tum 3. to smudge out

dēlinquō, dēlīquī, dēlictum 3. to be lacking; act unworthily, do wrong

dēliquescō, -cuī 3. to melt away; fade away

dēliquiō, -ōnis f. lack, failure

dēlīrāmentum, -ī n. delusion, nonsense

dēlīrātiō, -ōnis f. madness, lunacy

dēlīrō 1. to be mad; rave deliriously

dēlīrus, -a, -um adj. deranged, insane; senseless

dēlītigō 1. to dispute earnestly

dēlitiscō (-escō), -tuī 3. to go into hiding, withdraw; become invisible; take refuge

delphīnus, -ī or **delphīn, -nis** m. dolphin

dēlūbrum, -ī n. shrine, temple

dēlūctō 1. or **dēluctor** 1. dep. to wrestle, fight

dēlūdificō 1. or **dēlūdificor** 1. dep. to make a complete fool of

dēlūdō, -sī, -sum 3. to deceive, cheat

dēlumbis, -is, -e adj. weak, nerveless

dēlumbō 1. to weaken, make lame

dēmandō 1. (+dat.) to entrust (to)

dēmānō 1. to drip down, percolate

dēmarchus, -ī m. chief magistrate of an Attic deme

dēmens, -ntis adj. insane, frenzied

dēmenter adv. insanely, madly

dēmentia, -ae f. insanity, madness; folly

dēmentiō 4. to lose one's wits, become mad

dēmereō 2. to earn; win the favour of, please

dēmergō, -sī, -sum 3. to submerge, immerse; cause to sink; bury

dēmēt- see **dīmēt-**

dēmetō, -ssuī, -ssum 3. to mow, reap; pluck; cut off

dēmigrātiō, -ōnis f. emigration (of colonists)

dēmigrō 1. to go away, depart; emigrate

dēminuō, -uī, -ūtum 3. to lessen in size, diminish; impair, weaken; deduct, detract

dēminūtiō, -ōnis f. diminution; abatement; deduction, right to transfer property

dēmīror 1. dep. to be utterly astonished at

dēmissē adv. at a low altitude; dejectedly, modestly

dēmissīcius, -a, -um adj. flowing to the ground

dēmissiō, -ōnis f. lowering; dejection

dēmissus, -a, -um adj. having a low altitude, low; hanging down; dejected; modest, mean

dēmītigō 1. to calm down, soothe

dēmittō, dēmīsī, dēmissum 3. to let fall, shed; thrust down; send down; lower; bring to land (a ship); demote; dispirit

dēmō, dempsī, demptum 3. to take away or off, remove; subtract

dēmōlior 4. dep. to throw off; pull down, demolish

dēmōlītiō, -ōnis f. pulling down, demolition

dēmonstrātiō, -ōnis f. pointing out; description; explanation; demonstrative oratory

dēmonstrātīvus, -a, -um adj. demonstrative

dēmonstrātor, -ōris m. one who points out, demonstrator

dēmonstrō 1. to point out, demonstrate by gestures; indicate; explain; describe; recommend

dēmordeō, -sum 2. to bite off

dēmorior, -tuus 3. dep. to die, become extinct; be dying to have

dēmoror 1. dep. to detain, delay; hold off; linger, tarry

dēmoveō, dēmōvī, dēmōtum 2. to remove, dislodge, depose; banish; turn aside

dēmūgītus, -a, -um adj. filled with the sound of lowing

dēmulceō, -sī, -sum 2. to rub soothingly, stroke

dēmum adv. at last, not till; only, alone; in the end, in fine

dēmurmurō 1. to murmur over

dēmūtō 1. to alter, change; change one's mind

dēnārius, -(i)ī m. Roman coin of silver worth ten, later sixteen, asses

dēnarrō 1. to relate in full

dēnāsō 1. to remove the nose (from a face)

dēnatō 1. to swim downstream

dēnegō 1. to deny; (+acc.+inf.) say that … not; refuse

dēnī, -ae, -a pl.adj. ten each; ten together

dēnicālis, -is, -e adj. fēriae dēnicālēs funeral ceremony in which the family of the dead were purified

dēnique *adv.* at last, in the end; finally; to sum up; even, at worst

dēnōminō 1. to give a name to

dēnormō 1. to make misshapen

dēnotō 1. to apply (*colours*); indicate, imply; censure

dens, dentis *m.* tooth, tusk; ivory

densē *adv.* thickly; frequently

denseō 2. to thicken; press together, make thick and fast

densitās, -ātis *f.* thickness; multitude

densō 1. to thicken; press together

densus, -a, -um *adj.* dense, thick; closely packed; (+*abl.*) crowded (with); frequent; loud, harsh

dentālia, -ium *n.pl.* share-beam (*of a plough*)

dentātus, -a, -um *adj.* furnished with teeth; (*of tools*) toothed; polished with ivory

dentifrangibulus, -a, -um *adj.* tooth-breaking

dentifricium, -(i)ī *n.* tooth-powder, dentifrice

dentilegus, -ī *m.* one who picks up his teeth (*that have been knocked out*)

dentiō 4. (*of teeth*) to grow

dentiscalpium, -iī *n.* toothpick

dēnūbō, dēnupsī, dēnuptum 3. to marry away (*a bride*)

dēnūdō 1. to strip, lay bare; despoil; expose; disclose

dēnumerō 1. to pay in full

dēnuntiātiō, -ōnis *f.* announcement, declaration; threat

dēnuntiō 1. to give notice of, announce; (+*acc.*+*inf.*) declare (that); threaten; (+*inf.*) enjoin (to); summon (*to court*)

dēnuō *adv.* afresh; for a second time; again

deonerō 1. to unburden

deorsum (-us) *adv.* downwards, down; below

deosculor 1. *dep.* to kiss lovingly

dēpangō, -actum 3. to drive down

dēparcus, -a, -um *adj.* very stingy

dēpascō, dēpāvī, dēpastum 3. or **dēpascor** 3. *dep.* to eat up, feed off; graze (*cattle*) on; consume

dēpeciscor, -ctus 3. to bargain for; make a bargain, agree

dēpectō, -xum 3. to comb out *or* off

dēpeculātor, -ōris *m.* one who embezzles

dēpeculātus, -ūs *m.* embezzlement, defrauding

dēpeculor 1. *dep.* to embezzle, steal

dēpellō, dēpulī, dēpulsum 3. to drive away; avert; expel; force down

dēpendeō, -ī 2. (+*abl.*/*dat.*) to hang down (from); depend on; derive from

dēpendō, -dī, -sum 3. to pay, pay down; expend

dēperdō, -idī, -itum 3. to lose; *pass.* be ruined, be destroyed

dēpereō, -īre, -iī 4. to perish, die; be destroyed; be desperately in love with

dēpilātus, -a, -um *adj.* with plucked plumage

dēpingō, -nxī, -ctum 3. to depict in painting; colour; embroider; describe

dēplangō, -nxī 3. to bewail by beating the breast

dēplector, -exus 3. *dep.* to pull into one's grasp

dēpleō, -ēvī, -ētum 2. to drain off

dēplōrābundus, -a, -um *adj.* lamenting bitterly

dēplōrātiō, -ōnis *f.* lamentation

dēplōrātus, -a, -um *adj.* incurable

dēplōrō 1. to lament, deplore; despair of

dēpluō, -uī 3. to rain down

dēpōnō, dēposuī (-osīvī), dēpositum 3. to put down *or* off; deposit, entrust; abandon

dēpopulātiō, -ōnis *f.* pillaging, plundering

dēpopulātor, -ōris *m.* one who sacks, plunderer

dēpopulor 1. *dep.* or **dēpopulō** 1. to plunder; ravage, lay waste to

dēportō 1. to bring, carry along; convey; bring back (*esp. to Rome*)

dēposcō, dēpoposcī 3. to demand, ask for; demand (*for punishment*)

dēpositum, -ī *n.* deposit, trust (*esp. of money*)

dēpositus, -a, -um *adj.* despaired of, hopeless

dēprāvātē *adv.* perversely

dēprāvātiō, -ōnis *f.* perversity, distortion; deformity

dēprāvō 1. to make crooked, disfigure; distort, misrepresent; pervert, corrupt

dēprecābundus, -a, -um *adj.* entreating earnestly

dēprecātiō, -ōnis *f.* entreaty, plea; deprecation; invocation

dēprecātor, -ōris *m.* one who deprecates,
intercessor; (+*gen.*) one who pleads (for)

dēprecor 1. *dep.* to try to avert by prayer,
deprecate; beg mercy from; entreat;
intercede for

dēpre(he)ndō, -dī, -sum 3. to catch,
intercept; overtake; catch unawares; light
upon; detect

dēprehensiō, -ōnis *f.* detection

dēpressus, -a, -um *adj.* low-lying, deep
down; low-pitched; base

dēprimō, dēpressī, dēpressum 3. to
press down; weigh down; sink; bring
down, lower

dēproelior 1. *dep.* to fight violently

dēprōmō, -ompsī, -omptum 3. to bring
out, produce; utter

dēproperō 1. to hasten to finish

depsō, -uī, -tum 3. to have sex with, fuck

dēpudescō, -duī 3. to lose all sense of
shame

dēpūgis, -is, -e *adj.* with insubstantial
buttocks

dēpugnō 1. to fight to the end, battle
against

dēpulsiō, -ōnis *f.* thrusting down; repulsion; rebuttal

dēpulsō 1. to thrust away

dēpulsor, -ōris *m.* one who repels, averter

dēpungō 3. to mark down

dēputō 1. to define, classify

dēqueror, -stus 3. *dep.* to bewail, complain about

dērect- see **dīrect-**

dērelictiō, -ōnis *f.* neglect, desertion

dērelictus, -a, -um *adj.* derelict, abandoned; *n.sbst.* that which has been
abandoned

dērelinquō, -līquī, -lictum 3. to leave
behind, abandon

dērepente *adv.* suddenly

dērēpō, dērepsī 3. to crawl down

dērīdeō, -sī, -sum 2. to mock, laugh at

dērīdiculum, -ī *n.* ridiculous thing,
absurdity

dērīdiculus, -a, -um *adj.* ridiculous,
absurd

dērigescō, -guī 3. to become rigid, stiffen

dērigō see **dīrigō**

dēripiō, -ipuī, -eptum 3. (+*abl./dat.*) to
snatch (off); seize (from); pull down

dērīsor, -ōris *m.* one who mocks, derider

dērīsus, -ūs *m.* mockery, derision

dērīvātiō, -ōnis *f.* diversion, leading aside

dērīvō 1. to divert, lead aside; (+*abl.*) derive
(from)

dērōdō, -sum 3. to nibble away at

dērogō 1. to propose, modify; subtract;
(+*dat.*) take away (from)

dēruncinō 1. to plane off; fleece, cheat

dēruō, -uī, -utum 3. to cast down, cause to
fall

dēruptus, -a, -um *adj.* precipitous, steep

dēsacrō 1. to consecrate, dedicate

dēsaeviō 4. to rage violently, vent one's
fury

dēsaltō 1. to dance through

dēscendō, -dī, -sum 3. to come *or* go
down, descend; march down; dismount;
sink; lower oneself; (+*inf.*) stoop (to); be a
descendant

dēscensiō, -ōnis *f.* going down; low-lying
bath

dēscensus, -ūs *m.* going down, descent

dēscīscō, dēscīvī (-iī), dēscītum 3. to
desert, revolt from; fall away from

dēscrībō, dēscrīpsī, dēscrīptum 3. to
draw, mark out; write down; transcribe;
describe; prescribe, establish

dēscrīptē *adv.* clearly described

dēscrīptiō, -ōnis *f.* drawing out; transcript; description

dēscrīptus, -a, -um *adj.* marked out,
organized

dēsecō, -uī, -tum 1. to cut down, reap; cut
off

dēsenescō, -nuī 3. to die away with time

dēserō, -uī, -tum 3. to leave, abandon;
give up; fail

dēserpō 3. (+*dat.*) to creep over

dēsertor, -ōris *m.* one who abandons,
deserter (*esp. of a duty*)

dēsertus, -a, -um *adj.* alone, solitary;
deserted, uninhabited; *n.pl.sbst.* unfrequented places

dēserviō 4. (+*dat.*) to devote oneself (to),
engage (in)

dēses, -idis *adj.* idle, sluggish

dēsiccō 1. to dry thoroughly

dēsideō, dēsēdī 2. to sit; loiter, be slothful

dēsīderābilis, -is, -e *adj.* desirable; missed, longed for

dēsīderium, -(i)ī *n.* (+*gen.*) desire, longing (for); need; request; darling, favourite

dēsīderō 1. to desire, long for; need; request; miss, feel the lack of; lose (*esp. soldiers*)

dēsidia, -ae *f.* idleness, sluggishness; leisure

dēsidiābulum, -ī *n.* place for loitering

dēsidiōsē *adv.* idly, sluggishly

dēsidiōsus, -a, -um *adj.* idle, sluggish

dēsīdō, dēsēdī 3. to subside, settle down

dēsignātiō, -ōnis *f.* mention; arrangement; appointment (*to office*)

dēsignō 1. to mark out; point out; (*of words etc.*) denote, indicate; assign; appoint; plan

dēsiliō, -uī 4. to jump down, dismount

dēsinō, -īvī (-iī), -itum 3. (+*abl./gen.*) to leave off (from), finish; come to an end; cease from; (+*inf.*) cease (to)

dēsipiens, -ntis *adj.* witless, foolish

dēsipientia, -ae *f.* loss of wits, foolishness

dēsipiō 3. to lose one's wits, be foolish

dēsistō, dēstitī 3. to leave off, cease; (+*abl.*) cease (from); (+*inf.*) cease (to); *refl.* (+*abl.*) separate oneself (from)

dēsōlō 1. to abandon, forsake; leave empty

dēspectō 1. to look down at, overlook; look down upon, despise

dēspectus[1], -a, -um *adj.* contemptuous, despicable

dēspectus[2], -ūs *m.* view downwards; contempt

dēspēranter *adv.* despairingly

dēspērātiō, -ōnis *f.* despair, hopelessness; desperate state of illness

dēspērātus, -a, -um *adj.* desperate, hopeless; desperately ill; reckless

dēspērō 1. to despair of, give up hope for; despair

dēspicātiō, -ōnis *f.* contempt

dēspicātus[1], -a, -um *adj.* contemptuous, despicable

dēspicātus[2], -ūs *m.* contempt

dēspiciens, -ntis *adj.* (+*gen.*) contemptuous (of)

dēspicientia, -ae *f.* contempt; (+*gen.*) disregard (for)

dēspiciō, dēspēxī, dēspectum 3. to look down on *or* over; despise

dēspicor 1. *dep.* to despise

dēspoliātor, -ōris *m.* plunderer

dēspoliō 1. (+*abl.*) to plunder, despoil (of); strip

dēspondeō, -dī, -sum 2. to betroth (*a woman*); promise, pledge; **animum (-ōs) dēspondēre** to give up hope

dēsponsō 1. to betroth

dēspūmō 1. to remove foam from, skim; shed foam; settle down

dēspuō 3. to spit out, reject; spit on the ground

dēsquāmō 1. to remove the scales from

dēstertō, -uī 3. to snore off

dēstillātiō, -ōnis *f.* rheum, catarrh

dēstillō 1. to drip down; (+*abl.*) be dripping (with)

dēstimulō 1. to goad excessively

dēstinātiō, -ōnis *f.* designation; specification; intention

dēstinātō *adv.* designedly

dēstinātum, -ī *n.* objective; intention; **ex dēstinātō** designedly

dēstinātus, -a, -um *adj.* obstinate, firm

dēstinō 1. to fasten down; fix upon; intend; settle upon; appoint, destine

dēstituō, -uī, -ūtum 3. to set up, place; forsake, abandon; fail

dēstitūtiō, -ōnis *f.* desertion; betrayal

dēstitūtus, -a, -um *adj.* (+*gen.*) destitute (of); childless

dēstrictus, -a, -um *adj.* strict, severe

dēstringō, -nxī, -ctum 3. to strip off; scrape down; graze, touch slightly; censure, injure; unsheathe

dēstructiō, -ōnis *f.* pulling down, destruction

dēstruō, -xī, -ctum 3. to demolish; destroy

dēsubitō *adv.* suddenly

dēsūdascō 3. to sweat away

dēsūdō 1. to sweat copiously; exert oneself

dēsuēfīō, -fierī, -factus *v.irreg.* to be disaccustomed

dēsuescō, dēsuēvī, dēsuētum 3. to become disaccustomed, unlearn

dēsuētūdō, -inis *f.* desuetude, disuse

dēsuētus, -a, -um *adj.* disaccustomed; obsolete, unfamiliar

dēsultor, -ōris *m.* circus performer who jumps from horse to horse

dēsultōrius, -a, -um *adj*. of *or* belonging to a *desultor*

dēsultūra, -ae *f*. jumping down

dēsum, deesse, dēfuī *v.irreg*. to be lacking; (+*dat*.) fall short (of), fail

dēsūmō, dēsumpsī, dēsumptum 3. to select, pick out

dēsuper *adv*. from above; (+*acc*.) above

dēsurgō, -rrexī, -rrectum 3. to get up and leave

dētegō, -xī, -ctum 3. to unroof; uncover, expose; reveal, disclose

dētendō, -dī, -sum 3. to unstretch, loosen; strike (*a tent*)

dētergeō, -sī, -sum 2. to wipe off *or* away; clean; shear off

dēterior, -or, -us *compar.adj*. worse, inferior, poorer; more unpleasant; more wicked; more serious; more harmful

dēterius *compar.adv*. worse, less desirably; more wickedly

dēterminātiō, -ōnis *f*. boundary; conclusion

dēterminō 1. to delimit, bound; define; conclude (*a sentence*)

dēterō, dētrīvī, dētrītum 3. to wear down; rub off; impair

dēterreō 2. to discourage, deter

dētestābilis, -is, -e *adj*. detestable, abominable; under a solemn curse

dētestātiō, -ōnis *f*. execration, cursing; aversion

dētestor 1. *dep*. to execrate, curse; avert by entreaty; detest, loathe

dētexō, -uī, -tum 3. to weave completely; finish

dētineō, -inuī, -entum 2. to detain, hold back; keep occupied; delay

dētondeō, -dī, -sum 2. to shear, crop; cut off

dētonō, -uī 1. to cease thundering; thunder out

dētorqueō, -sī, -tum 2. to turn aside, deflect; divert; distort; misrepresent

dētractiō, -ōnis *f*. removal; deduction

dētractō see **dētrectō**

dētractor, -ōris *m*. one who detracts, disparager

dētrahō, -xī, -ctum 3. to pull off, remove; force down; bring; detract (*from*); diminish; subtract

dētrectātiō, -ōnis *f*. refusal, renunciation

dētrectātor, -ōris *m*. one who detracts, disparager

dētrectō 1. to decline, shirk; detract from, disparage

dētrīmentōsus, -a, -um *adj*. harmful

dētrīmentum, -ī *n*. reduction; injury, damage, loss

dētrūdō, -sī, -sum 3. to thrust away, drive off; dislodge; force; postpone

dētruncō 1. to cut to pieces, remove the branches of; lop off

dētumēscō, -muī 3. to become less swollen; die down

dēturbō 1. to dash down, force away; dislodge

dēturpō 1. to disfigure

deunx, -ncis *m*. eleven-twelfths

deūrō, deussī, deustum 3. to burn thoroughly, burn up

deus, deī *m*. god; divine being; statue of a god

deūtor 3. *dep*. (+*abl*.) to use wrongly, misuse

dēvastō 1. to lay waste to, devastate; slaughter

dēvehō, -xī, -ctum 3. to carry, convey (*esp. by sea*); *pass*. travel by sea

dēvellō, -ellī, -olsum 3. to pluck (*hair or plumage*); pluck out

dēvēlō 1. to unveil

dēveneror 1. *dep*. to avert by prayer

dēveniō, dēvēnī, dēventum 4. (+*in/ad* +*acc*.) to arrive, come to; visit; turn to; fall into

dēverberō 1. to flog thoroughly

dēverbium, -iī *n*. spoken part of a play

dēversor¹ 1. *dep*. to lodge as a guest, stay

dēversor², -ōris *m*. lodger, guest

dēversōriolum, -ī *n*. small lodging

dēversōrium, -(i)ī *n*. lodging, inn

dēversōrius, -a, -um *adj*. **taberna deversōria** inn with lodgings

dēverticulum, -ī *n*. byway; way round; digression; lodging

dēvertō, -tī, -sum 3. to turn away, divert; make a detour, digress

dēvēscor 3. *dep*. to devour

dēvexitās, -ātis *f*. downward slope

dēvexus, -a, -um *adj*. downward sloping; downhill moving, sinking; *n.sg.sbst*. slope

dēvinciō, -nxī, -nctum 4. to bind, tie fast; subjugate; oblige, constrain

dēvincō, dēvīcī, dēvictum 3. to defeat utterly, subdue

dēvinctus, -a, -um *adj.* (*+dat.*) bound (to), attached (to)

dēvītātiō, -ōnis *f.* avoidance

dēvītō 1. to avoid

dēvius, -a, -um *adj.* remote, sequestered straying, erratic; *n.pl.sbst.* remote parts;

dēvocō 1. to call down; call away, divert

dēvolō 1. to fly down, hurry down

dēvolvō, -vī, -ūtum 3. to roll off *or* down; *pass.* (*+in +acc.*) fall (into)

dēvor- see **dēver-** (other than below)

dēvorō 1. to devour, gulp down; absorb; use up; put up with

dēvōtiō, -ōnis *f.* consecration, devotion; execration

dēvōtō 1. to enchant, bewitch

dēvōtus, -a, -um *adj.* accursed; (*+dat.*) devoted (to), attached (to)

dēvoveō, dēvōvī, dēvōtum 2. to consecrate; (*+dat.*) devote (to); destine; curse; enchant

dextans, -ntis *m.* five-sixths

dextella, -ae *f.* little right hand

dexter, -(e)ra, -(e)rum *adj.* right, on the right hand; favourable; dexterous, skilful

dext(e)ra¹, -ae *f.* the right hand; right-hand side; contract

**dext(e)rā² *adv.* (*+gen.*) on the right-hand side (of)

dexterē *adv.* skilfully

dexteritās, -ātis *f.* readiness to help

dextr(ōv)orsum *adv.* towards the right-hand side

diabathrārius, -(i)ī *m.* slipper-maker

diadēma, -atis *n.* ornamental headdress, diadem, crown; royal power

diadēmātus, -a, -um *adj.* wearing a diadem, crowned

diadūmenos, -ī *m.* one engaged in tying up one's hair in a band

diaeta, -ae *f.* regimen; room, cabin

dialecticē *adv.* dialectically

dialecticus, -a (-ē), -um *adj.* of *or* relating to rational discussion, dialectical, logical; *m.sbst.* dialectician; *f.sg.sbst.* the art of reasoning, dialectics

dialectos, -ī *f.* form of speech, dialect

dialogus, -ī *m.* discussion; literary dialogue

diapasma, -atis *n.* scented powder (*for sprinkling on the body*)

diāria, -ōrum *n.pl.* daily ration of food

diatrēta, -ōrum *n.pl.* vessels with pierced decoration

dibaphus, -a, -um *adj.* twice dyed; *f.sbst.* robe of a Roman magistrate

dica, -ae *f.* lawsuit

dicācitās, -ātis *f.* sarcasm, biting wit

dicāculus, -a, -um *adj.* talkative, ready of speech

dicātiō, -ōnis *f.* settling as a citizen in another state

dicax, -ācis *adj.* with a ready tongue, witty, sarcastic

dichorēus, -ī *m.* double trochee

diciō, -ōnis *f.* power, authority; sovereignty

dicis *f.gen.sg.* **dicis causā** for the sake of appearance

dicō¹ 1. to show; (*+dat.*) dedicate (to); deify; devote, assign (to)

dīcō², dixī, dictum 3. to say, tell, speak; assert; speak of; mean; declare; name, designate

dicrotum, -ī *n.* ship with two banks of oars

dictamnus, -ī *f.* or **dictamnum, -ī** *n.* the plant dittany

dictāta, -ōrum *n.pl.* dictated lessons *or* exercises

dictātor, -ōris *m.* magistrate granted absolute power at Rome in times of emergency, dictator

dictātōrius, -a, -um *adj.* of *or* relating to a dictator

dictātrix, -īcis *f.* female dictator

dictātūra, -ae *f.* dictatorship

dictērium, -iī *n.* joke, witty comment

dictiō, -ōnis *f.* speaking, utterance; style of speaking; speech

dictitō 1. to say continually, repeat; plead (*cases*) habitually; call habitually

dictō 1. to say repeatedly, recite; dictate (*for writing*); prescribe, order

dictum, -ī *n.* that which is said, utterance; saying; witticism; order; pledge

dictus, -ūs *m.* speaking, talking

dīdō, -idī, -itum 3. to deal out; spread, diffuse

dīdūcō, dīduxī, dīductum 3. to draw apart, separate; split; divide; scatter

dīductiō, -ōnis f. separation, distribution

diēcula, -ae f. little day, short time

dīērectē adv. adverbial expression conveying disdain

dīērectus, -a, -um adj. (perhaps) worthless, good-for-nothing

diēs, diēī m./f. day, daylight; period of twenty-four hours; (usu. f.) appointed day; time

diffāmō 1. to spread news of, popularize; slander

differentia, -ae f. difference, distinction; distinctive feature

differitās, -ātis f. difference

differō, differre, distulī, dīlātum v.irreg. to carry away, disperse, separate; defer; spread about; slander; bewilder; differ, disagree

differtus, -a, -um adj. crammed, stuffed full

diffībulō 1. to unbuckle

difficilis, -is, -e adj. difficult, troublesome; obdurate, intractable

difficiliter adv. with difficulty; unwillingly

difficultās, -ātis f. difficulty, trouble; intractability

difficulter see **difficiliter**

diffīdēns, -ntis adj. lacking in confidence, distrustful

diffīdenter adv. without confidence

diffīdentia, -ae f. lack of confidence, distrust

diffīdō, -sus sum 3. semi-dep. to lack confidence; (+dat.) have no trust or faith (in)

diffindō, -fidī, -fissum 3. to split, cleave; **diem diffindere** to defer the day (esp. of a trial)

diffingō 3. to mould into a different shape

diffiteor 2. dep. to deny, disavow

difflāgitō 1. to importune greatly

difflō 1. to disperse by blowing

diffluō, -xī, -xum 3. to flow away; be diffuse; waste away, dissolve

diffringō, -frēgī, -fractum 3. to break apart, shatter

diffugiō, diffūgī 3. to run apart, disperse

diffugium, -iī n. dispersion in flight

diffunditō 1. to squander, dissipate

diffundō, diffūdī, diffūsum 3. to spread about, diffuse; expand; squander; cheer, relax

diffūsē adv. copiously, amply

diffūsilis, -is, -e adj. diffusive

diffūsus, -a, -um adj. spread out, extensive; diffuse

diffutūtus, -a, -um adj. fucked-out

dīgerō, -ssī, -stum 3. to move in all directions, disperse; lay out, arrange

dīgestiō, -ōnis f. arrangement, organization

dīgestus, -ūs m. administration

digitulus, -ī m. small finger

digitus, -ī m. finger; toe; finger's breadth, inch

dīgladior 1. dep. to fight in a gladitorial contest

dignātiō, -ōnis f. (+gen.) respect, regard (for); repute; rank

dignē adv. worthily, fittingly

dignitās, -ātis f. suitability; worthiness; excellence, dignity; rank; political office

dignō 1. or **dignor** 1. dep. to consider worthy; (+inf.) think fit (to), deign (to)

dignus, -a, -um adj. (+abl./gen.) worthy, suitable, deserving (of); n.sbst. worth, merit

dīgredior, -ssus 3. dep. to go away, leave, part; digress

dīgressiō, -ōnis f. departure, separation; digression

dīgressus, -ūs m. departure, separation

dīi- see **disi-** (other than below)

dīiūdicātiō, -ōnis f. decision (between two things)

dīiūdicō 1. to decide, settle; distinguish

dīiunctē adv. disjunctively

dīlābor, dīlapsus 3. dep. to flow apart, spread; run or melt away; disperse; disintegrate, decay

dīlacerō 1. to tear to pieces

dīlaniō 1. to tear to pieces

dīlapidō 1. to demolish

dīlargior 4. dep. to give away freely, lavish

dīlātātus, -a, -um adj. spread out, dilated

dīlātiō, -ōnis f. delay, adjournment

dīlātō 1. to spread, dilate; expand; state more fully; exaggerate

dīlātor, -ōris m. one who defers, procrastinator

dīlaudō 1. to praise greatly

dīlectus¹, -a, -um adj. dear, beloved

dīlectus², -ūs *m.* choosing, selection; discrimination; recruitment (*of troops*), levy

dīlibūtus see **dēlibūtus**

dīlīdō 3. to beat to pieces

dīligens, -ntis *adj.* (+*gen.*) fond of; attentive, diligent; thrifty

dīligenter *adv.* attentively; thoroughly

dīligentia, -ae *f.* (+*gen.*) attentiveness, assiduity (to); thriftiness

dīligō, dīlexī, dīlectum 3. to love, be fond of, esteem

dīlōrīcō 1. to tear open

dīlūceō 2. to be evident, be apparent

dīlūcescō, dīluxī 3. to become light, dawn

dīlūcidē *adv.* clearly, lucidly

dīlūcidus, -a, -um *adj.* clear, lucid

dīlūculum, -ī *n.* dawn, daybreak

dīlūdium, -(i)ī *n.* interval between games

dīluō, -uī, -ūtum 3. to wash away, dissolve; bathe; dilute; explain away

dīluviēs, -ēī *f.* flood

dīluviō 1. to flood

dīluvium, -iī *n.* flood

dīmadescō, -duī 3. to melt away

dīmensiō, -ōnis *f.* measuring

dīmensus, -a, -um *adj.* measured, regular

dīmētior, dīmensus 4. *dep.* to measure out, weigh out

dīmētor 1. *dep.* to measure out

dīmicātiō, -ōnis *f.* fighting, battle; struggle

dīmicō, -āvī (-uī), -ātum 1. to fight, battle; struggle

dīmidia, -ae *f.* half

dīmidiātus, -a, -um *adj.* halved, half

dīmidium, -(i)ī *n.* half

dīmidius, -a, -um *adj.* half; incomplete

dīmissiō, -ōnis *f.* sending forth, dismissal

dīmittō, dīmīsī, dīmissum 3. to send away; dismiss; disband; dispatch; let go, lay down; give up

dimminuō, -uī, -ūtum 3. to break in pieces, shatter

dīmoveō, dīmōvī, dīmōtum 2. to move apart, divide; disperse; remove; (+*abl.*) divert (from)

dīnoscō 3. to know apart; (+*abl.*) distinguish (from); discern

dīnotō 1. to mark distinctively

dīnumerātiō, -ōnis *f.* counting; enumeration (*in a speech*)

dīnumerō 1. to count; pay out

diōbolāris, -is, -e *adj.* worth two obols, dirt cheap

dioecēsis, -is *f.* district of a Roman province

dioecētēs, -ae *m.* treasurer

diōta, -ae *f.* two-handled wine-jar

diplōma, -atis *n.* letter of introduction given to travellers to aid their journey

dipsas, -adis *f.* venomous snake, whose bite aroused thirst in the victim

dipyrus, -a, -um *adj.* twice burnt

dīrae, -ārum *f.pl.* bad omens, curses

dīrectē *adv.* in a straight line, directly

dīrectō *adv.* in a straight line; immediately

dīrectus, -a, -um *adj.* straight; straightforward; upright; simple

dīremptus, -ūs *m.* separation

dīreptiō, -ōnis *f.* pillaging, plundering; scramble

dīreptor, -ōris *m.* pillager, plunderer

diribitiō, -ōnis *f.* sorting (*of votes*)

diribitor, -ōris *m.* sorter (*of votes*)

diribitōrium, -iī *n.* building in Rome used for the sorting of votes and the distribution of soldiers' pay

dīrigō, -exī, -ectum 3. to put in line, arrange; straighten; steer; aim, direct; regulate

dirimō, -ēmī, -emptum 3. to part, divide; separate, break up; interrupt

dīripiō, -ipuī, -eptum 3. to tear to pieces; snatch away; plunder, steal; scramble for

dīritās, -ātis *f.* fierceness, frightfulness; calamity, disaster

dīrumpō, dīrūpī, dīru(m)ptum 3. to break apart, split

dīruō, -uī, -utum 3. to pull to pieces, demolish

dīrus, -a, -um *adj.* awful, dire; frightful, dreadful

dīs see **dīves**

discalciātus, -a, -um *adj.* barefoot

discēdō, -cessī, -cessum 3. to separate, disperse; come apart, diverge; depart, move away; (+*ab* +*abl.*) cease (from)

discens, -ntis *m.* trainee, apprentice

disceptātiō, -ōnis *f.* dispute, debate; judgement

disceptātor, -ōris *m.* arbitrator, judge

disceptātrix, -īcis *f.* arbitress

disceptō 1. to dispute, debate; judge

discernō, -crēvī, -crētum 3. to divide, separate; distinguish; settle

discerpō, -psī, -ptum 3. to tear to pieces

discessiō, -ōnis f. withdrawal; (+*gen.*) division, separation (from)

discessus, -ūs m. separation, parting; departure

discidium, -(i)ī n. splitting, division; divorce; discord

discīdō, -dī, -sum 3. to cut to pieces; beat to pieces

discinctus, -a, -um adj. without a girdle *or* belt; easy-going, dissolute

discindō, discidī, discissum 3. to cut in two, divide

discingō, -xī, -ctum 3. to remove the girdle *or* belt from

discip(u)līna, -ae f. teaching, training; branch of study, school; system; orderliness, discipline

discipula, -ae f. female pupil

discipulus, -ī m. pupil, trainee

disclūdō, -sī, -sum 3. (+*abl.*) to keep apart (from), shut off (from); divide

discō, didicī 3. to learn; hear of, ascertain; get to know

discolor, -ōris adj. of a different colour; of different colours, variegated, multicoloured

discondūcō 3. (+*dat.*) to be harmful to

disconveniō 4. to be different, inconsistent

discoquō, -xī, -ctum 3. to distribute by cooking

discordābilis, -is, -e adj. discordant

discordia, -ae f. discord, dissension

discordiōsus, -a, -um adj. full of discord

discordō 1. to disagree, quarrel; differ

discors, -rdis adj. disagreeing, discordant; different

discrepantia, -ae f. difference, discrepancy

discrepitō 1. to be discordant, be different

discrepō 1. to be out of tune, be discordant; (+*ab* +*abl.*) be different (from), disagree (with)

discrētus, -a, -um adj. separate, set apart

discrībō, discripsī, discriptum 3. to distribute, allot; arrange; divide up

discrīmen, -inis n. dividing line, partition; difference; discrimination; critical point, crisis

discrīminō 1. to divide up, separate; differentiate

discriptē adv. in an orderly fashion

discriptiō, -ōnis f. dividing up, distribution; disposition

discruciō 1. to torture, vex

discumbō, -cubuī, -cubitum 3. to lie down to sleep; recline at a dinner table

discupiō 3. (+*inf.*) to desire ardently (to)

discurrō, -(cu)rrī, -rsum 3. to run in different directions, run about; branch out

discursus, -ūs m. running apart, dispersal; running about; bustling activity

discus, -ī m. discus

discutiō, -ssī, -ssum 3. to shake to pieces, shatter; shake out; scatter, dispel

disertē adv. clearly; eloquently

disertim adv. clearly

disertus, -a, -um adj. eloquent, skilfully written

disiciō, -iēcī, -iectum 3. to break up *or* apart; scatter, disperse; dispel; squander

disiectō 1. to throw about, scatter

disiectus¹, -a, -um adj. scattered, dispersed

disiectus², -ūs m. dispersal, scattering

disiunctiō (dīi-), -ōnis f. separation; disjunctive proposition; synonym

disiunctus (dīi-), -a, -um adj. separated, set apart; distinct, different

disiungō (dīi-), -xī, -ctum 3. to unyoke; break off; (+*ab* +*abl.*) separate (from); distinguish

dismarītus, -ī m. husband of two wives

dispālescō 3. to be spread about

dispālor 1. dep. to wander off *or* apart

dispandō, -nsum 3. to spread out *or* apart

dispār, -aris adj. unequal, different

disparātus, -a, -um adj. negatively opposite

disparilis, -is, -e adj. different, dissimilar

disparō 1. to separate, divide; be different

dispart- see **dispert-**

dispectus, -ūs m. discernment, consideration

dispellō, -pulī, -pulsum 3. to drive away; divide

dispendium, -(i)ī n. cost, expenditure; loss, damage

dispēnsātiō, -ōnis f. administration, management; stewardship

dispensātor, -ōris *m.* administrator, steward

dispensō 1. to pay out, apportion; administer, arrange

dispercutiō 3. to smash to pieces

disperdō, -idī, -itum 3. to destroy utterly, ruin

dispereō, -īre, -iī 4. to perish, die; be ruined

dispergō, -sī, -sum 3. to spread about, disperse; extend out; (+*abl.*) sprinkle (with)

dispersē or **dispersim** *adv.* sporadically

dispersus¹, -a, -um *adj.* scattered, dispersed

dispersus², -ūs *m.* dispersal

dispertiō 4. or **dispertior** 4. *dep.* to separate, distribute

dispertītiō, -ōnis *f.* distribution

dispiciō, dispexī, dispectum 3. to look about for; see clearly; discern; perceive; examine, consider

displiceō 2. (+*dat.*) to displease, offend

displōdō, -sī, -sum 3. to burst apart

dispōnō, -posuī, -positum 3. to place about, distribute; lay out, arrange; manage; assign, post; ordain

dispositē *adv.* orderly, methodically

dispositiō, -ōnis *f.* layout, arrangement

dispositūra, -ae *f.* layout, arrangement

dispositus¹, -a, -um *adj.* properly laid out, orderly

dispositus², -ūs *m.* administration, management

dispudet 2. *impers.* (+*acc.*) it shames utterly

dispungō, -nxī, -nctum 3. to mark off, check

disputābilis, -is, -e *adj.* disputable, controversial

disputātiō, -ōnis *f.* discussion, dispute; essay written in the form of a debate

disputātiuncula, -ae *f.* little discussion

disputātor, -ōris *m.* one who argues, disputant

disputō 1. to argue one's case, debate; discuss, argue

disquīrō 3. to investigate, examine

disquīsītiō, -ōnis *f.* investigation, examination

dissaeptiō, -psī, -ptum 4. to separate off; break down

dissaeptum, -ī *n.* partition, wall

dissecō, -uī, -tum 1. to cut to pieces

dissēminō 1. to distribute widely, disseminate

dissensiō, -ōnis *f.* disagreement, dissension; discrepancy

dissensus, -ūs *m.* disagreement, dissent

dissentāneus, -a, -um *adj.* disagreeing, dissenting

dissentiō, -sī, -sum 4. (+*ab/de* +*abl.*) to disagree, dissent (from); differ (from)

disserēnō 1. to become clear

disserō¹, -eruī, -itum 3. to sow about, plant out; scatter

disserō², -uī, -tum 3. to lay out in words, discuss

disserpō 3. to spread apart

dissertō 1. to discuss, treat in words

dissideō, -sēdī 2. to sit apart, be separated; be out of place; differ, disagree

dissignātiō, -ōnis *f.* arrangement

dissignātor, -ōris *m.* managing official, master of ceremonies

dissiliō, -uī 4. to leap apart; burst apart

dissimilis, -is, -e *adj.* unlike, different

dissimiliter *adv.* differently

dissimilitūdō, -inis *f.* difference, dissimilarity; contrast

dissimulābiliter *adv.* secretly, furtively

dissimulanter *adv.* dissemblingly, disingenuously

dissimulantia, -ae *f.* dissemblance

dissimulātiō, -ōnis *f.* dissimulation, dissemblance; feigned ignorance, Socratic irony

dissimulātor, -ōris *m.* dissembler; one who claims false ignorance

dissimulō 1. to disguise, conceal; pretend (*a thing*) is otherwise; ignore, overlook

dissipābilis, -is, -e *adj.* able to be scattered *or* dispersed

dissipātiō, -ōnis *f.* scattering, distribution; dissolution

dissipātus, -a, -um *adj.* scattered, dispersed; disordered

dissipō 1. to scatter, disperse; spread; shatter, destroy completely; squander

dissociābilis, -is, -e *adj.* incompatible, irreconcilable

dissociātiō, -ōnis *f.* separation, dissociation

dissociātus, -a, -um *adj.* (+*ab* +*abl.*) separated; alien (to)

dissociō 1. to separate, break apart; dissolve, dissociate

dissolūbilis, -is, -e *adj.* destructible, dissoluble

dissolūtē *adv.* disjointedly; laxly

dissolūtiō, -ōnis *f.* breaking up, dissolution; loss of strength; disconnection; refutation

dissolūtus, -a, -um *adj.* loose, disjointed; lax, dissolute

dissolvō, -vī, -ūtum 3. to break up; dissolve, melt; set free; pay; weaken; refute

dissonus, -a, -um *adj.* (+*dat.*) dissonant, disharmonious (from); confused in sound; (+*dat.*) inconsistent (with); heterogenous, diverse

dissors, -rtis *adj.* (+*ab* +*abl.*) having no share in

dissuādeō, -sī, -sum 2. to advise against; (+*inf.*) advise not (to)

dissuāsiō, -ōnis *f.* (+*gen.*) speech advising against (*a proposal*)

dissuāsor, -ōris *m.* discourager; speaker against

dissultō 1. to leap apart, bounce off; burst about

dissuō, -uī, -ūtum 3. to rip apart, unsew

dissup- see **dissip-**

distaedet 2. *impers.* (+*acc.*) it tires, it wearies

distantia, -ae *f.* distance; difference

distendō, -dī, -tum 3. to stretch out, extend; cause to swell, fill out; distract

distentus¹, -a, -um *adj.* (+*abl.*) swollen (with)

distentus², -a, -um *adj.* (+*abl.*) busy (with), preoccupied (with)

disterminō 1. to divide apart; (+*ab* +*abl.*) separate (from)

distichon, -ī *n.* poem of two lines, couplet

distinctē *adv.* clearly, distinctively

distinctiō, -ōnis *f.* separation, distinction; discrimination; distinctive quality; definition

distinctus¹, -a, -um *adj.* separated; distinct, different; definite, clear

distinctus², -ūs *m.* distinguishing; distinctive quality

distineō, -inuī, -entum 2. to hold apart; keep off; divide; distract, perplex, hinder

distinguō, -xī, -ctum 3. to separate, keep apart; (+*ab* +*abl.*) distinguish (from), regard as different (from); define; decorate; interrupt

distō 1. (+*abl.*/*dat.*) to stand apart, be distant (from); be different (from)

distorqueō, -sī, -tum 2. to twist about; deform, torture

distortiō, -ōnis *f.* twisting, distortion

distortus, -a, -um *adj.* misshapen, distorted; perverse

distractiō, -ōnis *f.* tearing apart, severance; dissociation

distractus, -a, -um *adj.* rarefied; distracted, perplexed

distrahō, -xī, -ctum 3. to pull apart *or* away; separate; dissociate; disrupt; distract

distribuō, -uī, -ūtum 3. to divide up, allot; distribute, arrange

distribūtē *adv.* methodically, with proper distribution

distribūtiō, -ōnis *f.* division into parts; sharing out, distribution; arrangement; classification

districtus, -a, -um *adj.* distracted, busy

distringō, -nxī, -ctum 3. to stretch apart; distract; (*of emotions*) pull in different directions

distruncō 1. to chop up

disturbātiō, -ōnis *f.* destruction

disturbō 1. to disturb, demolish; upset, break up (*an activity*)

dītescō 3. to become rich

dithyrambicus, -a, -um *adj.* written in dithyrambic form

dithyrambus, -ī *m.* form of verse (*esp. for choral singing*), dithyramb

dītiae see **dīvitiae**

dītō 1. to enrich

diū¹ (diŭ) *adv.* for a long time; taking a long time

**diū(s)² ** *adv.* by day

dīum *n.* open sky; **sub dīō** in the open air

diurnum, -ī *n.* daily ration; daily accounts book

diurnus, -a, -um *adj.* of *or* relating to the day, diurnal; daily

dīus, dīa, dīum *adj.* lit by day; divine; divinely inspired

diūtinē *adv.* for a long time

diūtinus (diu-), -a, -um *adj.* lasting for a long time, prolonged; long-standing

diuturnitās, -ātis *f.* long period of time; long duration, permanence; longevity

diuturnus, -a, -um *adj.* lasting for a long time; permanent, lasting; long-standing

dīva, -ae *f.* goddess

dīvāricō 1. to cause to sit astraddle

dīvellō, -ellī (-ulsī), -ulsum 3. to tear apart; (+*ab*+*abl.* or +*abl.*) break up, sunder (from); force away (from)

dīvendō, -didī, -ditum 3. to put up for sale in lots

dīverberō 1. to beat apart, split

dīversē *adv.* in different directions; in various places; differently

dīversitās, -ātis *f.* separateness; difference, diversity; disagreement, inconsistency

dīversus, -a, -um *adj.* facing in different directions; situated apart, distant; separate; different; hostile; **ex dīversō** on the other hand, on the opposite side

dīvertō, -tī, -sum 3. (+*ab*+*abl.*) to separate from; diverge

dīves, -itis *adj.* rich, wealthy; fertile; valuable; (+*gen.*/*abl.*) abundant (in), well-endowed (with)

dīvexō 1. to ravage; vex, harass

dīvidia, -ae *f.* vexation; **dīvidiae esse** (+*dat.*) to be vexing (to)

dīvidō, dīvīsī, dīvīsum 3. to divide, split; separate; divide into parts; share out, distribute; classify

dīviduus, -a, -um *adj.* divided, parted; shared out

dīvīnātiō, -ōnis *f.* prophecy, prognostication; guess, intuition

dīvīnē *adv.* by divine inspiration; divinely

dīvīnitās, -ātis *f.* divinity, divineness; divine being

dīvīnitus *adv.* by divine inspiration; divinely

dīvīnō 1. to foresee, guess, divine; practise divination, make a guess

dīvīnus, -a, -um *adj.* of or relating to the gods, divine, sacred; heaven-sent; god-like, excellent; prognostic

dīvīsiō, -ōnis *f.* division into parts; separation; distribution; classification

dīvīsor, -ōris *m.* one who divides into shares, distributor; agent who distributes bribes

dīvīsus[1], -a, -um *adj.* divided

dīvīsus[2], -ūs *m.* division

dīvitiae, -ārum *f.pl.* riches, wealth

dīvors- see **dīvers-**

dīvortium, -(i)ī *n.* parting, divergence; divorce; dividing point, barrier

dīvulgātus, -a, -um *adj.* widely accessible, commonly available

dīvulgō 1. to make public, divulge; make common property, publish

dīvulsiō, -ōnis *f.* wrenching apart

dīvum, -ī *n.* open sky; **sub dīvō** in the open air

dīvus, -ī *m.* god

dō, dare, dedī, datum 1. to give; grant; permit; furnish; offer; lend; ascribe; tell of; cause; produce

doceō, -uī, -tum 2. to inform; instruct; show; teach; (+*inf.*) to teach (to)

dochmius, -lī *m.* the dochmiac foot

docilis, -is, -e *adj.* keen to learn, attentive; skilful; teachable; tractable

docilitās, -ātis *f.* ability to learn

doctē *adv.* cleverly; skilfully; in a learned manner

doctor, -ōris *m.* teacher, instructor

doctrīna, -ae *f.* teaching, training; that which is taught; learning, science

doctus, -a, -um *adj.* learned, clever; expert

documen, -inis *n.* warning, caution

documentum, -ī *n.* example, lesson, warning

dōdrans, -ntis *m.* three-quarters

dōdrantārius, -a, -um *adj.* of or relating to three-quarters

dogma, -atis *n.* doctrine, tenet

dolābra, -ae *f.* pick-axe, mattock

dolens, -ntis *adj.* causing sorrow

dolenter *adv.* sorrowfully

doleō 2. to be in pain; grieve; feel pain at; cause grief

dōliāris, -is, -e *adj.* shaped like a *dolium*, barrel-shaped

dōliolum, -ī *n.* small jar

dōlium, -ī *n.* large earthenware jar

dolō[1] 1. to cut into shape; beat

dolō[2], -ōnis *m.* iron-pointed staff, pike; topsail

dolor, -ōris *m.* pain; grief, distress; indignation

dolōsē *adv.* using trickery or fraud

dolōsus, -a, -um *adj.* artful, deceitful; deceptive

dolus, -ī *m.* deliberate wrongdoing, evil intent; trickery; plot, stratagem

domābilis, -is, -e *adj.* able to be tamed

domesticātim *adv.* by the use of one's domestic staff

domesticī, -ōrum *m.pl.* members of a household; entourage

domesticus, -a, -um *adj.* of *or* concerning a household, domestic; familial; personal, private; native; familiar

domicēnium, -iī *n.* meal taken at home

domicilium, -(i)ī *n.* dwelling-place, habitation

domina, -ae *f.* female head of a household, mistress; female ruler

dominans, -ntis *adj.* ruling; (*of words*) proper

dominātiō, -ōnis *f.* authority of the head of a family; absolute power, dominion

dominātor, -ōris *m.* absolute ruler, lord

dominātrix, -īcis *f.* female ruler

dominātus, -ūs *m.* absolute power, dominion; ownership

dominicus, -a, -um *adj.* of *or* relating to a ruler *or* emperor

dominium, -(i)ī *n.* dominion; ownership; banquet

dominor 1. *dep.* to be the head of a household; hold absolute sway; dominate, rule

dominus, -ī *m.* head of a household, master; lord, ruler; manager

domiporta, -ae *f.* house-carrier (*of a snail*)

domitō 1. to tame, subdue

domitor, -ōris *m.* one who tames, trainer (*of animals*); subduer; conqueror

domitrix, -īcis *f.* female tamer

domitus[1], -ūs *m.* taming (*of animals*)

domītus[2], -a, -um *adj.* house-bound

domō, -uī, -itum 1. to tame, break in; subdue, conquer; overcome

domus, -ūs *f.* house, home; (*of animals or birds*) dwelling-place, nest; household; home town *or* land; **domī** at home

dōnābilis, -is, -e *adj.* (+*abl.*) worthy to be the receiver (of)

dōnārium, -(i)ī *n.* part of a temple where voting offerings were made and kept

dōnātiō, -ōnis *f.* donation, gift

dōnātīvum, -ī *n.* donation of money given

to soldiers by the emperor on celebrated occasions

dōnātor, -ōris *m.* one who gives, donor

dōnec *conj.* until, as long as

dōnicum *conj.* until

dōnique see **dōnec**

dōnō 1. (+*abl.*) to present with, endow with; give, grant (to); (+*inf.*) grant power (to); forgive; give up, consign (to)

dōnum, -ī *n.* gift, present, reward; offering; bounty, favour

dorcas, -adis *f.* gazelle

dormiō 4. to be asleep, sleep; be idle, do nothing

dormītātor, -ōris *m.* (*perhaps*) daydreamer *or* night-prowler

dormītō 1. to be sleepy, doze off

dormītor, -ōris *m.* sleeper

dormītōrius, -a, -um *adj.* used for sleeping

dorsum, -ī *n.* or **-us, -ī** *m.* back, hinder part; hump, ridge (*esp. of hills*)

doryphoros, -ī *m.* spear-bearer

dōs, dōtis *f.* dowry; endowment; virtue, talent

dōtālis, -is, -e *adj.* forming part of a dowry

dōtātus, -a, -um *adj.* with a rich dowry, well endowed

dōtō 1. to provide a dowry for; (+*abl.*) endow (with)

drachma (-uma), -ae *f.* Greek silver coin

drachumissō 1. to work for a drachma a day

dracō, -ōnis *m.* snake; water heater shaped like a snake

dracōnigenus, -a, -um *adj.* descended from a snake

drāpeta, -ae *m.* runaway, fugitive

draucus, -ī *m.* athlete

dromas, -ados *adj.* fast-running

dromos, -ī *m.* open space (*for running etc.*)

drōpax, -acis *m.* ointment to remove hair, depilatory

druidae, -ārum or **-ēs, -um** *m.pl.* druids

dryas, -adis *f.* wood-nymph, dryad

dubiē *adv.* hesitatingly; doubtfully

dubitābilis, -is, -e *adj.* open to doubt

dubitanter *adv.* hesitating

dubitātiō, -ōnis *f.* doubt, uncertainty; hesitation

dubitō 1. to be uncertain; doubt; hesitate over

dubius, -a, -um *adj.* uncertain, hesitant; doubtful; fickle, variable; suspect; dangerous

ducātus, -ūs *m.* leadership

ducēnārius, -a, -um *adj.* having 200,000 sesterces

ducēnī, -ae, -a *pl.adj.* two hundred each; two hundred at once

ducentēsimus, -a, -um *adj.* two-hundredth; *f.sbst.* tax of half a percent

ducentī, -ae, -a *pl.adj.* two hundred

ducentiens *adv.* two hundred times

dūcō, duxī, ductum 3. to lead, bring; lead off *or* away; marry; conduct, command; draw; fashion; believe

ductilis, -is, -e *adj.* that is led along in a channel

ductim *adv.* in draughts

ductitō 1. to lead off *or* take home habitually

ductō 1. to conduct, lead; take home; draw; allure

ductor, -ōris *m.* commander, leader

ductus, -ūs *m.* command, leadership; conveyance; controlled movement; line

dūdum a short while ago; for a long time up to now; **iam dūdum** now at last

duell- see **bell-**

dulcēdō, -inis *f.* sweetness (*of taste*); pleasantness, charm

dulcescō 3. to become sweet; lose salt (*of sea water*)

dulciārius, -a, -um *adj.* of *or* relating to confectionery

dulciculus, -a, -um *adj.* sweet little

dulcifer, -era, -erum *adj.* sweet

dulcis, -is, -e *adj.* sweet; (*of water*) fresh, without salt; sweet-sounding; sweet-smelling; delightful; dear, charming

dulciter *adv.* melodiously; delightfully

dulcitūdō, -inis *f.* sweetness

dūlicē *adv.* in the manner of a slave

dum¹ *conj.*

1. **dum** + *indicative*
a) while, during the time that (usu. present tense)
   dum haec aguntur, consules bellum gerebant while these things were going on, the consuls were waging war
b) so long as, all the time that (any tense)

dum memoria manebit, laudabitur so long as the memory remains, he shall be praised

c) until, up until the time that (with simple emphasis on time: any tense)
   dum Marcus rediit, silentium fuit until Marcus returned, there was silence

2. **dum** + *subjunctive*
a) provided that
   oderint dum(modo) metuant let them hate provided that they fear
b) until (with implication of purpose: present or imperfect)
   Aeneas pervagatus est, dum urbem conderet Aeneas wandered around until he could establish a city

dum² *adv.* in the meantime

dūmētum, -ī *n.* (*usu. pl.*) thorn bush, thicket

dummodo *conj.* (+*subj.*) provided that, as long as

dūmōsus, -a, -um *adj.* rife with thorn bushes

dumtaxat *adv.* up to, at most; no more than; at any rate; provided that

dūmus, -ī *m.* thorn bush

duo, duae, duo *adj.* two; a pair of; *sbst.* the number two; a pair

duodeciens (-ēs) *adv.* twelve times

duodecim *indecl.adj.* twelve; **tabulae duodecim** the Twelve Tables and their laws

duodecimus, -a, -um *adj.* twelfth

duodēnī, -ae, -a *pl.adj.* twelve each; twelve at once

duodēquadrāgēsimus, -a, -um *adj.* thirty-eighth

duodēquadrāgintā *indecl.adj.* thirty-eight

duodēquinquāgēsimus, -a, -um *adj.* forty-eighth

duodētrīciens *adv.* twenty-eight times

duodētrīgintā *indecl.adj.* twenty-eight

duodēvīcēnī, -ae, -a *pl.adj.* eighteen each

duodēvīcēsimus, -a, -um *adj.* eighteenth

duodēvīgintī *indecl.adj.* eighteen

duoetvīcensimānī, -ōrum *m.pl.* soldiers of the twenty-second legion

duoetvīcensimus, -a, -um *adj.* twenty-second

duplex, -icis *adj.* doubled over; double, twice as large; twofold; dual; two-faced

duplicārius, -iī *m.* soldier who receives double rations as a reward

duplicātiō, -ōnis *f.* doubling

dupliciter *adv.* doubly, in two ways

duplicō 1. to double over; double

duplus, -a, -um *adj.* double; *n.sg.sbst.* double the amount; **in duplum** for twice as much

dupondius, -(i)ī *m.* the sum of two *asses*

dūrābilis, -is, -e *adj.* durable, long-lasting

dūracinus, -a, -um *adj.* having a hard berry

dūrāmen, -inis *n.* that which hardens

dūrāmentum, -ī *n.* firmness

dūrateus, -a, -um *adj.* wooden

dūrē *adv.* heavily, clumsily; harshly; unsympathetically; unpleasantly

dūrescō, dūruī 3. to become hard, solidify

dureta, -ae *f.* wooden bathing tub

dūritās, -ātis *f.* harshness

dūriter *adv.* harshly, severely

dūritia, -ae or **-ēs, -ēī** *f.* hardness; toughness; absence of feeling; severity, harshness

dūriusculus, -a, -um *adj.* somewhat harsh

dūrō 1. to harden, solidify; inure; become hard; hold out, endure; continue, last

dūrus, -a, -um *adj.* hard; tough, robust; stubborn, brazen; heavy, solid; oppressive, difficult; harsh (*in taste*); pitiless, severe

duumvir, -rī *m.* one of two officials appointed for various functions; *pl.* pair of these officials

duumvirātus, -ūs *m.* the office of a *duumvir*

dux, dūcis *m.* leader, guide; driver; chief; commander, general

dynastēs, -ae *m.* ruler, prince

ē see **ex**

eā *adv.* that way; there

eādem *adv.* by the same way; simultaneously

eam, eās etc. (*present subj. of* **eō**)

eātenus *adv.* so far, to such an extent

eben- see **heben-**

ēbibō, -ī, -itum 3. to drink up, swallow down; absorb

ēbītō 3. to go out

ēblandior 4. *dep.* to obtain by flattery, coax out; provide delight

ēborātus, -a, -um *adj.* decorated with ivory

ēbrietās, -ātis *f.* drunkenness, insobriety

ēbriolus, -a, -um *adj.* somewhat drunk, tipsy

ēbriōsitās, -ātis *f.* addiction to drink

ēbriōsus, -a, -um *adj.* addicted to drink

ēbrius, -a, -um *adj.* drunk, inebriated; drunken; (+*abl.*) teeming (in)

ēbulliō 4. to rant about; **animam ēbullīre** to give up the ghost, die

ebulum, -ī *n.* danewort

ebur, eboris *n.* ivory; ivory object; elephant's tusk; elephant

eburneolus, -a, -um *adj.* made of ivory

eburn(e)us, -a, -um *adj.* made of ivory; ivory-white

ēcastor (ec-) *interj.* by Castor!

ecca *interj.* here they are!

eccam *interj.* here she is!

eccās *interj.* (*of women*) here they are!

ecce *adv.* look!, see!

eccere (-rē) *adj.* look!, see!

eccillum, -am, -ud *interj.* there he/she/it is!

eccistam *interj.* there she is!

ecclēsia, -ae *f.* popular assembly

eccōs *interj.* (*of men*) here they are!

eccum *interj.* here he is!

ecdicus, -ī *m.* public prosecutor

ecf- see **eff-**

echenāis, -idis *f.* remora

echidna, -ae *f.* adder, viper

echīnus, -ī *m.* sea-urchin; item of kitchenware

ēchō, -ūs *f.* echo; repetition

ecloga, -ae *f.* short poem, eclogue

ecquandō *adv.* ever?, at any time?

ecquī¹ *adj.* is there any ... that?; *pron.* is there anyone who?

ecquī² *adv.* is there any way in which?

ecquid *adv.* at all?; (*in indir. questions*) whether

ecquis, ecquis, ecquid *pron.* is there anyone who?, is there anything that?; *adj.* is there any ... that?

ecquisnam, ecquisnam, ecquidnam *pron.* is there anyone at all who?

ecquō *adv.* to any place?

eculeus, -ī *m.* young horse, foal; torture rack

edācitās, -ātis *f.* greed, gluttony

edax, edācis *adj.* greedy, gluttonous; consuming, devouring

ēdentō 1. to knock the teeth out of

ēdentulus, -ā, -um *adj.* toothless

edepol *interj.* by Pollux!

edera see **hedera**

ēdīcō, ēdixī, ēdictum 3. to declare, proclaim; ordain, decree

ēdictiō, -ōnis *f.* decree, edict

ēdictō 1. to declare, proclaim

ēdictum, -ī *n.* decree, proclamation, edict

ēdiscō, ēdidicī 3. to learn thoroughly, learn by heart

ēdisserō, -uī, -tum 3. to set forth fully, relate at length

ēdissertō 1. to set forth fully, relate at length

ēditīcius, -a, -um *adj.* nominated by a plaintiff

ēditiō, -ōnis *f.* assertion, statement; publication; nomination by a plaintiff

ēditor, -ōris *m.* (+*gen.*) one that emits

ēditus, -a, -um *adj.* high, lofty; outstanding; *n.sbst.* high point; decree

ēdō¹, ēdidī, ēditum 3. to emit, eject; produce; perform; exhibit; declare, proclaim; publish; lift

edō², esse, ēdī, ēsum (essum) *v.irreg.* to eat; consume, eat away

ēdoceō, -uī, -tum 2. to teach thoroughly

ēdolō 1. to hew out

ēdomō 1. to tame fully, bring under control

ēdormiō 4. to sleep off (*esp. wine*); spend (*time*) in sleep

ēdormiscō 3. to sleep off (*esp. wine*); sleep through

ēducātiō, -ōnis *f.* rearing, nurturing

ēducātor, -ōris *m.* one who nurtures, foster-father

ēducātrix, -īcis *f.* female who nurtures, foster-mother

ēducō¹ 1. to rear, nurture

ēdūcō², ēduxī, ēductum 3. to lead out; rescue; extract; summon; produce; rear, nurture

edūlis, -is, -e *adj.* edible; *n.pl.sbst.* edibles

ēdūrō 1. to endure, last

ēdūrus, -a, -um *adj.* very hard

effātum, -ī *n.* prognostication; proposition

effectē *adv.* in an accomplished manner

effectiō, -ōnis *f.* accomplishment; efficient cause

effector, -ōris *m.* (+*gen.*) one who causes, originator (of)

effectrix, -īcis *f.* (+*gen.*) female originator (of)

effectum, -ī *n.* effect

effectus, -ūs *m.* enacting, performing; completion; outcome, effect; success

effēminātē *adv.* in an effeminate manner

effēminātus, -a, -um *adj.* effeminate, unmanly

effēminō 1. to make feminine, emasculate; enervate

efferātus, -a, -um *adj.* bestial, brutal

efferciō, effertum 4. to fill full, cram

efferitās, -ātis *f.* savagery

efferō¹ 1. to make wild; enfuriate, madden

efferō², efferre, extūlī, ēlātum *v.irreg.* to carry out *or* away; produce; spread abroad; publish; raise; exalt; carry away (*with emotion*)

effertus, -a, -um *adj.* (+*abl.*) crammed full (of)

efferus, -a, -um *adj.* bestial, wild; ferocious, furious

effervō 3. to boil up, boil over

effervescō, -vī 3. to boil up, boil over; become enraged

effētus, -a, -um *adj.* exhausted, worn out, weak

efficācitās, -ātis *f.* efficiency, effectiveness

efficāciter *adv.* effectually

efficax, -ācis *adj.* effective, efficient

efficiens, -ntis *adj.* effective, causative

efficienter *adv.* efficiently

efficientia, -ae *f.* efficiency, influence

efficiō, effēcī, effectum 3. to make, form; constitute; produce; bring about, cause; perform, complete; deduce

effigiēs, -ēī or **-a, -ae** *f.* likeness, effigy, imitation; ghost, spectre; guise

effingō, -nxī, -ctum 3. to mould, fashion; portray, reproduce, imitate

efflāgitātiō, -ōnis *f.* urgent demand

efflāgitātus, -ūs *m.* urgent demand

efflāgitō 1. to demand urgently, insist

efflictim *adv.* passionately, 'to death'

efflictō 1. to strike dead

efflīgō, -ixī, -ictum 3. to strike dead, kill

efflō 1. to blow out, exhale, emit

efflōrescō, -ruī 3. to bloom, flourish

effluō, -uxī 3. to flow out *or* away, dissolve; escape

effluvium, -iī *n.* outlet (*of a lake*)

effodiō, effōdī, effossum 3. to dig up *or* out; hollow out

effor 1. *dep.* to utter, say; declare as consecrated

effractārius, -iī *m.* burglar

effrēnātē *adv.* unrestrainedly

effrēnātiō, -ōnis *f.* lack of restraint, unbridledness

effrēnātus, -a, -um *adj.* unrestrained, unbridled

effrēnō 1. to slacken the reins of

effrēnus, -a, -um *adj.* unrestrained, unbridled, unruly

effricō 1. to rub away

effringō, effrēgī, effractum 3. to break open

effugiō, effūgī 3. to flee, escape; escape from; avoid; baffle

effugium, -(i)ī *n.* means of escape, escape

effulgeō, effulsī 2. or **effulgō** 3. to shine forth, flash; be outstanding

effulgurō 1. to sparkle

effultus, -a, -um *adj.* (+*abl.*) supported (by), resting (on)

effundō, effūdī, effūsum 3. to pour forth, pour out; bring to the ground; shed, emit; produce; utter; give vent to; waste

effūsē *adv.* extensively; in disarray; lavishly, unrestrainedly

effūsiō, -ōnis *f.* pouring forth; discharge; lavish expenditure

effūsus, -a, -um *adj.* widespread; disorderly; unrestrained; (*of speech*) flowing

effūtiō 4. to babble, blurt out

effutuō, -uī, -ūtum 3. to wear out by fucking

ēgelidus, -a, -um *adj.* rather chilly; lukewarm, tepid

egens, egentis *adj.* needy, poverty-stricken; *m.pl.sbst.* the needy

egēnus, -a, -um *adj.* needy, poverty-stricken; (+*gen./abl.*) deprived (of), in need (of)

egeō, eguī 2. (+*abl./gen.*) to need, want, lack

ēgerō, ēgessī, ēgestum 3. to carry out; extract, remove; discharge, emit; expend; express

egestās, -ātis *f.* poverty, destitution; dearth; craving

ēgestiō, -ōnis *f.* removal; wasting

ēgestus, -ūs *m.* excavation

ēgignō 3. to bring forth, produce

egō (ego) (*acc.* **mē**, *gen.* **meī**, *dat.* **mihī (mihi)**, *abl.* **mē**) *pron.* I (me)

ēgredior, ēgressus 3. *dep.* to go out *or* away; march out; ascend; digress; leave behind, pass

ēgregiē *adv.* outstandingly, remarkably, excellently

ēgregius, -a, -um *adj.* outstanding, remarkable, eminent, excellent

ēgressus, -ūs *m.* going out *or* away, departure; digression; egress

ēgurgitō 1. to pour forth in abundance

ehem *interj.* oh! (*exclam. of surprise*)

ēheu *interj.* alas!, ah!

eho *interj.* hey!, oi! (*exclam. to attract another's attention*)

ei *interj.* ah! (*exclam. of anguish*)

eia see **heia**

ēiaculor 1. *dep.* to hurl out, emit

ēiciō, ēiēcī, ēiectum 3. to cast out, discard; emit; extract, remove; expel; divert

ēiectāmentum, -ī *n.* something thrown up

ēiectiō, -ōnis *f.* expulsion, banishment

ēiectō 1. to throw off, emit

ēiectus, -ūs *m.* expulsion

ēierō see **ēiūrō**

ēiulātiō, -ōnis *f.* wailing, lamentation

ēiulātus, -ūs *m.* wailing, lamentation

ēiulō 1. to wail, lament; bewail

ēiūrō 1. to resign upon oath; resign; disown, renounce

ēlābor, ēlapsus 3. *dep.* to slip away, drop off; slip off, escape

ēlabōrātus, -a, -um *adj.* well-wrought, elaborate

ēlabōrō 1. to bestow care upon, perfect; endeavour, strive

ēlāmentābilis, -is, -e *adj.* very sorrowful

ēlanguescō, -guī 3. to grow faint, languish

ēlargior 4. *dep.* (+*dat.*) to bestow lavishly (upon)

ēlātē *adv.* proudly; (*of speech*) loftily, grandly

ēlātiō, -ōnis *f.* glorification, exalting; exalted state of mind, elation

ēlātrō 1. to bark out

ēlātus, -a, -um *adj.* elevated, raised; exalted, grand

ēlavō, ēlāvī, ēlautum (ēlōtum) 1. to wash away; wipe out (*one's fortune*)

ēlecebra, -ae *f.* means of coaxing (*sthg*) out

ēlectē *adv.* in a well-chosen manner

ēlectilis, -is, -e *adj.* excellent, choice

ēlectiō, -ōnis *f.* choice, selection

ēlectō 1. to coax out, tease out

ēlectrum, -ī *n.* amber; alloy of gold and silver

ēlectus¹, -a, -um *adj.* excellent, choice

ēlectus², -ūs *m.* choice

ēlegans, -ntis *adj.* tasteful, refined; fastidious; elegant; excellent, choice

ēleganter *adv.* with good judgement, tastefully; elegantly, neatly

ēlegantia, -ae *f.* taste, propriety, refinement; fastidiousness; elegance, neatness

elegēum, -ī *n.* elegiac poem

elegī, -ōrum *m.pl.* elegiac verses

elegīa (-īā), -ae *f.* elegy

elegīdion, -(i)ī *n.* short elegiac poem

elementārius, -a, -um *adj.* at the elementary stages of learning

elementum, -ī *n.* one of the four elements; atom; letter of the alphabet; *pl.* basic principles

elenchus, -ī *m.* pearl pendant

elephantus, -ī or **elephans, -ntis** *m./f.* elephant; ivory

eleutheria, -ōrum *n.pl.* festival of Liberty

ēlevō 1. to lift up, raise; diminish, allay; trivialize

ēliciō, -cuī, -citum 3. to coax out, entice out; summon; draw forth, elicit; excite

ēlīdō, -sī, -sum 3. to crush, smash, squeeze; eliminate, eject; emit

ēligō, ēlēgī, ēlectum 3. to pluck out; select, choose

ēlīminō 1. to put out of doors; let out, blab

ēlīmō 1. to produce by filing; polish (*speeches etc.*)

ēlinguis, -is, -e *adj.* voiceless, speechless; uneloquent

ēlinguō 1. to tear the tongue from

ēliquō 1. to purify by straining

ēlīsiō, -ōnis *f.* forcing out, emission

ēlix, ēlicis *m.* drainage furrow

ēlixus, -a, -um *adj.* boiled

ellam *interj.* there she is!

elleborōsus, -a, -um *adj.* full of hellebore, insane

elleborus, -ī *m.* or **-um, -ī** *n.* hellebore

ellum *interj.* there he is!

ēlocō 1. to lease out, let

ēlocūtiō, -ōnis *f.* expression, elocution

ēlogium, -(i)ī *n.* epitaph; codicil; record (*of a legal case*); elegiac distich

ēloquens, -ntis *adj.* eloquent, articulate

ēloquenter *adv.* eloquently

ēloquentia, -ae *f.* eloquence, articulateness

ēloquium, -(i)ī utterance; eloquence

ēloquor, ēlocūtus 3. *dep.* to utter, state; divulge, tell; speak

ēlūceō, ēluxī 2. to shine out; be outstanding

ēluctor 1. *dep.* to force a way out of, break free from; break free

ēlūcubrō 1. or **ēlūcubror** 1. *dep.* to work at nocturnally

ēlūdō, -sī, -sum 3. to foil, evade; trick; mock; behave licentiously

ēlūgeō, ēluxī 2. to bewail; mourn

ēlumbis, -is, -e *adj.* dislocated, feeble

ēluō, ēluī, ēlūtum 3. to wash off; wash clean; wipe out (*one's fortune*)

ēlūtus, -a, -um *adj.* watery, washed out

ēluviēs, -ēī *f.* flood, inundation; floodwater

ēluviō, -ōnis *f.* flood, inundation

em *interj.* here!, look!

ēmācitās, -ātis *f.* craze for purchasing

ēmadescō, ēmaduī 3. to become damp

ēmancipātiō, -ōnis *f.* legal transference of property

ēmancipō 1. to release from one's legal ownership; (+*dat.*) make subservient (to)

ēmaneō, ēmansī, ēmansum 2. to stay away

ēmānō 1. to flow forth; arise, emanate; leak out, become known

ēmarcescō, -cuī 3. to wither away

ēmātūrescō, -ruī 3. to become soft, relent

emax, emācis *adj.* (excessively) fond of purchasing

emblēma, -ātis *n.* internal relief (*of bowls etc.*)

embolium, -(i)ī *n.* interposition; interlude

ēmendābilis, -is, -e *adj.* able to be emended

ēmendātē *adv.* correctly, flawlessly

ēmendātiō, -ōnis *f.* correction, emendation

ēmendātor, -ōris *m.* one who emends; textual critic, rigorous scholar

ēmendātrix, -īcis *f.* female corrector

ēmendātus, -a, -um *adj.* correct, flawless

ēmendīcō 1. to obtain by begging

ēmendō 1. to free from faults, correct, improve, amend

ēmentior 4. *dep.* to misrepresent, falsify; invent, fabricate

ēmercor 1. *dep.* to buy up

ēmereō 2. or **ēmereor** 2. *dep.* to complete (*one's service, duty etc.*); earn, deserve; conciliate

ēmergō, -rsī, -rsum 3. to emerge, come forth; come to light; extricate oneself

ēmētior, ēmensus 4. *dep.* to measure out; traverse, cover; complete

ēmetō 3. to reap away

ēmicō 1. to dash forth, spring up; flash forth; be outstanding

ēmigrō 1. to move out

ēminātiō, -ōnis *f.* threatening

ēminens, -ntis *adj.* prominent, projecting; eminent, outstanding

ēminentia, -ae *f.* projecting part; eminence

ēmineō, -nuī 2. to stand out, project; be evident; be eminent

ēminor 1. *dep.* to threaten

ēminus *adv.* at long-range; from afar

ēmīror 1. *dep.* to gaze at in wonder

ēmissārium, -(i)ī *n.* effluent, drain

ēmissārius, -(i)ī *m.* agent, emissary

ēmissīcius, -a, -um *adj.* sent out as an agent

ēmissiō, -ōnis *f.* discharge, emission

ēmissus, -ūs *m.* discharge, emission

ēmittō, ēmīsī, ēmissum 3. to send forth, dispatch; discharge, emit; let fly; publish

emō, ēmī, emptum 3. to purchase, buy; procure; win over, bribe

ēmoderor 1. *dep.* to restrain, check

ēmodulor 1. *dep.* to set to a rhythm

ēmōlior 4. *dep.* to carry out, achieve; heave up

ēmolliō 4. to soften, soothe; enervate

ēmolō 3. to grind thoroughly

ēmolumentum, -ī *n.* advantage, gain

ēmoneō 2. to exhort thoroughly

ēmorior, ēmortuus 3. *dep.* to die off, perish

ēmortuālis, -is, -e *adj.* of *or* relating to death

ēmoveō, ēmōvī, ēmōtum 2. to expel, remove; protrude

empīricus, -ī *m.* empirical doctor

emporium, -(i)ī *n.* market, market-town

emptiō, -ōnis *f.* purchasing; purchase

emptitō 1. to purchase habitually

emptor, -ōris *m.* purchaser; briber

emptum, -ī *n.* purchase

ēmulgeō, -lsī, -lsum 2. to drain out

ēmundō 1. to clean thoroughly

ēmungō, -nxī, -nctum 3. to wipe the nose of; defraud, swindle

ēmūniō 4. to fortify, secure; pile up

ēmussitātus, -a, -um *adj.* made to perfection

ēn *interj.* look!, here!; **ēn umquam** at any time at all?

ēnarrābilis, -is, -e *adj.* describable, explicable

ēnarrātiō, -ōnis *f.* description, exposition

ēnarrō 1. to describe in full

ēnascor, ēnātus 3. *dep.* to spring forth, sprout

ēnatō 1. to escape by swimming

ēnāvigō 1. to sail forth, sail out; sail across

encaustus, -a, -um *adj.* burnt in

endo *prep.* (+*abl.*) in

endromis, -idos *f.* heavy cloak worn by athletes after exercise

ēnecō, -cuī, -ctum 1. to kill off, destroy

ēnervātus, -a, -um *adj.* feeble, languid

ēnervis, -is, -e *adj.* feeble, languid, weak

ēnervō 1. to make feeble, enervate

ēnicō see **ēnecō**

enim *part.* for, for instance; yes, for; truly; namely; well!

enimvērō *part.* yes indeed, truly; and what's more

ēniteō 2. to shine forth; be outstanding

ēnitescō, -tuī 3. to begin to shine forth; be outstanding

ēnītor, ēnīsus or **ēnixus** 3. *dep.* to force a way up *or* out; strive; struggle over; give birth to

ēnixē *adv.* assiduously, earnestly

ēnixus, -a, -um *adj.* assiduous, earnest

enlychnium, -iī *n.* lamp-wick

ēnō 1. to swim out, glide forth

ēnōdātē *adv.* in a clear manner

ēnōdātiō, -ōnis *f.* elucidation

ēnōdis, -is, -e *adj.* free from knots, smooth

ēnōdō 1. to free from knots; unravel, elucidate

ēnormis, -is, -e *adj.* shapeless, irregular; extravagant; huge

ēnōtescō, -tuī 3. to become well known

ēnotō 1. to note down

ensiculus, -ī *m.* small (toy) sword

ensifer, -era, -erum *adj.* carrying a sword

ensiger, -era, -erum *adj.* carrying a sword

ensis, -is *m.* sword

enterocēlē, -ēs *f.* intestinal hernia

enterocēlicus, -a, -um *adj.* suffering from intestinal hernia

entheātus, -a, -um *adj.* possessed by a god, frenzied

entheus, -a, -um *adj.* possessed by a god, frenzied; causing divine frenzy

enthȳmēma, -atis *n.* kind of syllogism involving suppression *or* assumption of premises

ēnūbō, ēnupsī, ēnuptum 3. to marry outside one's home; marry outside one's rank

ēnucleātē *adv.* with precision, accurately

ēnucleātus, -a, -um *adj.* free from obscurity, precise

ēnucleō 1. to free from obscurity, examine minutely

ēnumerātiō, -ōnis *f.* enumeration; recapitulation; argument by elimination

ēnumerō 1. to reckon up, count; enumerate; pay out; recapitulate

ēnuntiātiō, -ōnis *f.* announcing; assertion

ēnuntiātīvus, -a, -um *adj.* assertive, predicative

ēnuntiātum, -ī *n.* assertion, proposition

ēnuntiō 1. to disclose, make known; assert, express

ēnuptiō, -ōnis *f.* (+*gen.*) right (*of women*) to marry (outside)

ēnūtriō 4. to rear, nurture

eō[1] (*3rd pl.* **eunt**), **īre**, **īvī (iī)**, **itum** 4. to go; march; (*of time*) pass; turn out

eō[2] *adv.* to there; up to that point; such an extent

eō[3] *adv.* therefore; so much; **eō locī** there

eōdem *adv.* to the same place; up to the same point; for the same purpose

epaphaeresis, -is *f.* second removal (*of hair*)

ephēbus, -ī *m.* boy (*usu. Greek*) aged between 18 and 20

ephēmeris, -idos *f.* daily record, account book; calendar

ephippiātus, -a, -um *adj.* riding with a cloth saddle

ephippium, -(i)ī *n.* cloth saddle

ephorus, -ī *m.* one of five Spartan magistrates, ephor

epicēdīon, -īī *n.* funeral ode

epichysis, -is *f.* kind of wine-ladle

epicōpus, -a, -um *adj.* propelled by oars

epicrocum, -ī *n.* fine yellow garment

epicus, -a, -um *adj.* epic

epidicticus, -a, -um *adj.* epideictic

epidīpnis, -idis *f.* savoury dessert course

epigramma, -ātis (-os) *n.* epitaph; epigram

epilogus, -ī *m.* peroration, epilogue

epimēnia, -ōrum *n.pl.* monthly ration

epinīcion, -īī *n.* victory song

epirēdium, -(i)ī *n.* horse-drawn coach

epistola see **epistula**

epistolium, -(i)ī *n.* short letter

epistula, -ae *f.* letter, dispatch; preface

epistulāris, -is, -e *adj.* of *or* relating to letters

epitaphios, -(i)ī *m.* funeral oration

epithalamium, -īī *n.* nuptial song

epitomē, -ēs *f.* abridgement, epitome

epitȳrum, -ī *n.* preserve made from olives

epochē, -ēs *f.* suspension of judgement

epops, epopis *m.* hoopoe

epos (*nom. and acc.sg. only*) *n.* epic poetry

ēpōtō 1. to drink down; swallow, absorb

epulae, -ārum *f.pl.* banquet; delicacies, sumptuous food

epulāris, -is, -e *adj.* of *or* relating to a banquet

epulātiō, -ōnis *f.* banqueting

epulō, -ōnis *m.* diner at a banquet; priest who oversaw public religious feasts

epulor 1. *dep.* to banquet; feast upon

epulum, -ī *n.* banquet, feast

equa, -ae *f.* mare

eques, -itis *m.* horseman; cavalryman; member of a Roman order between the populace and senate in distinction, knight

equester, -tris, -tre *adj.* of *or* relating to an *eques*, equestrian

equidem *part.* I for my part; indeed

equīle, -is *n.* horse stable

equīnus, -a, -um *adj.* of *or* relating to horses

equitātus, -ūs *m.* cavalry; equestrian order of Rome

equitō 1. to ride, travel on horseback

equuleus see **eculeus**

equus, -ī *m.* horse, stallion

era, erae *f.* mistress (*esp. of the house*)

ērādīcō 1. to destroy utterly, annihilate

ērādō, -sī, -sum 3. to scrape off; scrape clean; erase

erciscor 3. *dep.* to apportion

erctum, -ī *n.* inheritance; **erctum ciēre** to divide an inheritance

ērectē *adv.* assuredly, boldly

ērectus, -a, -um *adj.* upright, erect; alert; assured, bold

ērēpō, ērepsī, ēreptum 3. to crawl out; crawl up; crawl across

ēreptiō, -ōnis *f.* plunder, robbery

ēreptor, -ōris *m.* plunderer, robber

erga *prep.* (+*acc.*) towards, for; in respect of, in relation to; next to

ergastulum, -ī *n.* prison workhouse; slaves at such a workhouse

ergō[1] **(-o)** *part.* therefore; then; well then

ergō[2] *prep.* (+*gen.*) on account of, for the sake of

ēricius, -(i)ī *m.* spiked barricade

erifuga, -ae *m.* runaway

ērigō, ērexī, ērectum 3. to raise, elevate; set up, erect; excite

erīlis, -is, -e *adj.* of *or* relating to the master of the house

ēripiō, ēripuī, ēreptum 3. to tear *or* snatch away; carry off, seize; rescue

ērōdō, -sī, -sum 3. to gnaw at, erode

ērogātiō, -ōnis *f.* request for payment

ērogitō 1. to ask repeatedly

ērogō 1. to expend, pay out

errābundus, -a, -um *adj.* wandering about, vagrant

errāticus, -a, -um *adj.* wandering, erratic

errātiō, -ōnis *f.* wandering, deviation

errātum, -ī *n.* error, mistake

errō[1] 1. to wander, rove; digress; waver; err

errō[2], **-ōnis** *m.* truant, absentee

error, -ōris *m.* wandering; digression; wavering; error, mistake

ērubescō, -buī 3. to redden, blush; be ashamed

ērūca, -ae *f.* the herb rocket

ēructō 1. to belch up, disgorge

ērudiō 4. to teach, instruct

ērudītē *adv.* learnedly, eruditely

ērudītiō, -ōnis *f.* teaching, instruction; erudition

ērudītulus, -ī *m.* somewhat learned

ērudītus, -a, -um *adj.* learned, erudite; accomplished

ērumpō, ērūpī, ēruptum 3. to burst forth, break out; break in

ēruō, ēruī, ērutum 3. to dig up; unearth; destroy completely

ēruptiō, -ōnis *f.* bursting out, discharge; onrush, sally

erus, erī *m.* master (*esp. of the house*)

ervum, -ī *n.* kind of vetch

esca, -ae *f.* food; bait

escārius, -a, -um *adj.* of *or* relating to food; *n.pl.sbst.* bait

escendō, -dī, -sum 3. to go up, ascend; mount (*a speaker's platform*)

escensiō, -ōnis *f.* inland military incursion

escensus, -ūs *m.* ascent

esculentus, -a, -um *adj.* edible; *n.pl.sbst.* edibles

ēsitō 1. to eat habitually

essedārius, -(i)ī *m.* one who fights from a war-chariot

essedum, -ī *n.* kind of war-chariot

ēsuriālis, -is, -e *adj.* of *or* relating to famine

ēsuriō[1] 4. to be hungry, ravenous; hunger after

ēsuriō[2], **-ōnis** *m.* hungry man

ēsurītiō, -ōnis *f.* state of hunger

ēsurītor, -ōris *m.* hungry man

ēsus, ēsūs *m.* eating, consuming

et *conj.* and; yes, in fact; than, as; *adv.* also; even

etenim *conj.* and indeed, as a matter of fact

etēsiae, -ārum *f.pl.* annual north-westerly winds, Etesian winds

etēsius, -a, -um *adj.* annual

ēthologia, -ae *f.* characterization

ēthologus, -ī *m.* one who mimics others by gestures

etiam *conj.* also, too; even; even now; indeed

etiamdum *adv.* yet; already

etiamnum (-nunc) *adv.* even now, still; yet again

etiamsī *conj.* even if, although

etiamtum (-tunc) *adv.* still, yet

etsī *conj.* even if, although

eu *interj.* splendid!, excellent!

euans see **euhans**

euax *interj.* hooray!

eucharisticon *n.* thanksgiving

eug(a)e *interj.* excellent!

eugepae *interj.* excellent!

euhans, -ntis *adj.* uttering Bacchic cries

euhoe *interj.* euhoe! (*ritual cry of Bacchantes*)

eunūchus, -ī *m.* eunuch

euoe see **euhoe**

euphōnus, -a, -um *adj.* sonorous, resonant

eurīpus, -ī *m.* narrow channel, waterway

euröus, -a, -um *adj.* eastern

eurus, -ī *m.* east wind; the east

euschēmē *adv.* gracefully, becomingly

ēvādō, -sī, -sum 3. to go away; escape; climb up; turn out, result; pass; escape from

ēvagātiō, -ōnis *f.* deviation

ēvagor 1. *dep.* to stray, wander off; overflow; deviate from

ēvalescō, -luī 3. to become strong, develop; *pf.* have enough strength

ēvalidus, -a, -um *adj.* very strong, mighty

ēvānescō, -nuī 3. to vanish, disappear; fade away, die out

ēvānidus, -a, -um *adj.* vanishing, disappearing; perishing

ēvastō 1. to devastate, destroy utterly

ēvehō, -xī, -ctum 3. to carry out *or* away; ascend; exalt; *pass.* ride away, sail out

ēvellō, ēvellī, ēvolsum (ēvul-) 3. to tear out, uproot; get rid of

ēveniō, ēvēnī, ēventum 4. to come out, issue; (+*dat.*) happen (to); be allotted (to)

ēventum, -ī *n.* outcome; occurrence, event

ēventus, -ūs *m.* outcome; occurrence, event; success

ēverberō 1. to beat violently

ēverriculum, -ī *n.* drag-net

ēverrō, -rrī, -rsum 3. to sweep out

ēversiō, -ōnis *f.* overthrowing, destruction

ēversor, -ōris *m.* one who overthrows, destroyer

ēvertō, -rtī, -rsum 3. to turn up; overturn; overthrow, upset; (+*abl.*) expel (from)

ēvidens, -ntis *adj.* obvious, manifest

ēvidenter *adv.* obviously, manifestly

ēvidentia, -ae *f.* obviousness

ēvigilō 1. to wake up; be vigilant; compose carefully

ēvīlescō, -luī 3. to become worthless

ēvinciō, -nxī, -nctum 4. to bind round

ēvincō, ēvīcī, ēvictum 3. to conquer utterly, overcome fully; persuade

ēvirō 1. to unman, make effeminate

ēviscerō 1. to disembowel, eviscerate

ēvītābilis, -is, -e *adj.* avoidable

ēvītō 1. to avoid, shun

ēvocātor, -ōris *m.* summoner of troops

ēvocātus, -ī *m.* veteran soldier called back into service

ēvocō 1. to call out, summon; provoke; entice

ēvolgō see **ēvulgō**

ēvolō 1. to fly out *or* away; hurry out, flee; fly up

ēvolsiō, -ōnis *f.* tearing out, extraction

ēvolūtiō, -ōnis *f.* reading through (*of a book*)

ēvolvō, -vī, -ūtum 3. to roll out; unroll, unfurl; disentangle; disclose

ēvomō, -uī, -itum 3. to spew forth, vomit out

ēvulgō 1. to make public, divulge

ex *or* **ē** *prep.* (+*abl.*) out of, from; after; according to; as a result of

exacerbō 1. to aggravate; irritate, enrage

exactiō, -ōnis *f.* expulsion; exaction (*of tax etc.*)

exactor, -ōris *m.* one who expels; exactor (*of taxes*); supervisor

exactus, -a, -um *adj.* precise, exact

exacuō, -uī, -ūtum 3. to sharpen; stimulate

exadversum (-us) *prep.* (+*acc.*) opposite, against; *adv.* opposite

exaedificātiō, -ōnis *f.* completion of a building project

exaedificō 1. to complete the building of; turn out of doors

exaequātiō, -ōnis *f.* making equal

exaequō 1. to make equal, level; match; (+*abl.*) compensate (for)

exaeresimus, -a, -um *adj.* that can be removed

exaestuō 1. to boil up, seethe, rage

exaggerātiō, -ōnis *f.* exaltation

exaggerō 1. to pile up; amplify, exaggerate

exagitō 1. to rouse, stir; harass, vex; agitate; drive away

exagmen see **exāmen**

exagōga, -ae *f.* exportation

exalbescō, -buī 3. to turn pale

exāmen, -inis *n.* swarm, multitude; balance (*for weighing*)

exāminō 1. to weigh, balance; examine, ponder

examussim *adv.* exactly, perfectly

exanclō 1. to draw off, exhaust; endure

exanimālis, -is, -e *adj.* dead; deadly

exanimātiō, -ōnis *f.* paralysis (*from fear*)

exanimis, -is, -e *adj.* dead, lifeless;

unconscious; paralysed (*with fear*), breathless

exanimō 1. to kill; paralyse (*with fear*); exhaust; deflate

exanimus, -a, -um *adj*. dead, lifeless; unconscious

exardescō, -rsī, -rsum 3. to catch fire, blaze up; become hot, inflamed; break out

exārescō, -ruī 3. to dry up; disappear

exarmō 1. to disarm, dismantle; weaken

exarō 1. to plough, dig up; produce by ploughing; write (*on wax*)

exasceātus, -a, -um *adj*. hewn out

exasperō 1. to make rough; irritate, vex; make worse

exauctōrō 1. to dismiss from military service

exaudiō 4. to hear; pay heed to, listen to

exaugeō 2. to amplify, augment

exaugurātiō, -ōnis *f*. deconsecration, profanation

exaugurō 1. to deconsecrate, make profane

exauspicō 1. to receive a good augury

exb- see **ēb-** (other than below)

exballistō 1. to batter down the defences of

exc- see **exsc-** (other than below)

excaecō 1. to blind; stop up

excalceō (-iō) 1. to remove the shoes from

excandescentia, -ae *f*. blazing up (*in anger*)

excandescō, -duī 3. to grow hot, flare up

excantō 1. to charm out

excarnificō (-nuf-) 1. to punish with torture, torment

excavō 1. to hollow out, excavate

excēdō, excessī, excessum 3. to depart, retire; extend; exceed, go beyond

excellens, -ntis *adj*. outstanding, excellent

excellenter *adv*. outstandingly, excellently

excellentia, -ae *f*. pre-eminence, excellence

excellō 3. to be pre-eminent, excel

excelsē *adv*. loftily, sublimely

excelsitās, -ātis *f*. loftiness, sublimity

excelsum, -ī *n*. high altitude, height; loftiness, eminence

excelsus, -a, -um *adj*. high, lofty; sublime, elevated; of high status

exceptiō, -ōnis *f*. reservation, proviso; exception, counterplea

exceptiuncula, -ae *f*. minor reservation, proviso

exceptō 1. to take up, pick out

excernō, excrēvī, excrētum 3. to sift out, sort out

excerpō, -psī, -ptum 3. to pick out, select; take away

excessus, -ūs *m*. departure; digression; death

excetra, -ae *f*. water-snake; spiteful woman

excidium, -(i)ī *n*. destruction, overthrow

excidō[1], -dī 3. to fall out; be lost, perish; escape; lose one's senses

excīdō[2], -dī, -sum 3. to cut down; cut out; hollow out; destroy, raze

exciō 4. or **excieō** 2. to rouse, stir; evoke; summon

excipiō, excēpī, exceptum 3. to take out; pick up; take, receive; welcome; exempt; intercept; succeed

excīsiō, -ōnis *f*. destruction, razing

excitātus, -a, -um *adj*. lively, vigorous; shrill

excitō 1. to rouse; stir; summon; raise; excite

exclāmātiō, -ōnis *f*. exclamation; utterance

exclāmō 1. to cry out, declare aloud; shout the name of

exclūdō, -sī, -sum 3. to exclude, prevent; keep off; cut off; hatch

exclūsiō, -ōnis *f*. exclusion

excōgitātiō, -ōnis *f*. thinking out, devising

excōgitō 1. to think out, devise

excolō, excoluī, excultum 3. to cultivate; improve, refine; honour

excoquō, -xī, -ctum 3. to boil off; boil thoroughly, melt down; dry out

excors, -rdis *adj*. unintelligent, stupid

excrēmentum, -ī *n*. outgrowth

excrescō, excrēvī, excrētum 3. to grow up, grow out

excruciābilis, -is, -e *adj*. deserving of torture

excruciō 1. to torture, torment

excubiae, -ārum *f.pl.* vigil, keeping watch; lookout

excubitor, -ōris *m.* sentinel, lookout

excubō, -uī, -itum 1. to sleep outdoors; be vigilant, keep watch

excūdō, -dī, -sum 3. to hammer out, forge; hatch out

exculcō 1. to tread down; knock out

excūrō 1. to take good care of

excurrō, ex(cu)currī, excursum 3. to run out; extend; digress; exceed

excursiō, -ōnis *f.* running out, sally; expedition

excursō 1. to run out, sally

excursor, -ōris *m.* emissary, scout

excursus, -ūs *m.* sally, raid; expedition; digression

excūsābilis, -is, -e *adj.* pardonable, excusable

excūsātē *adv.* pardonably, excusably

excūsātiō, -ōnis *f.* justification, excuse, plea

excūsātus, -a, -um *adj.* exempt from blame, excused

excūsō 1. to excuse, justify; exempt

excussus, -a, -um *adj.* vigorous, powerful

excutiō, -ssī, -ssum 3. to shake off *or* out; throw out, discharge; rouse; examine

exd- see **ēd-** (other than below)

exdorsuō 1. to remove the spine from

exec- see **exsec-**

exedō, exesse, exēdī, exēsum *v.irreg.* to eat up, devour; eat away, consume

exedra, -ae *f.* recess for seating

exedrium, -(i)ī *n.* small recess for seating

exemplar, -āris *n.* specimen, archetype, exemplar; copy

exemplāris, -is *m.* copy, transcript

exemplum, -ī *n.* specimen, example; precedent, parallel; pattern; copy

exenterō 1. to disembowel, eviscerate

exeō, exīre, exiī (exīvī), exitum 4. to go out *or* away; result, issue; spring up, rise; extend; expire

exeq- see **exseq-**

exerceō 2. to exercise, train; employ, practise; harass; levy (*tax*)

exercitātē *adv.* in a skilled manner

exercitātiō, -ōnis *f.* exercise, work; practice; skill

exercitātus, -a, -um *adj.* skilled, practised; harassed

exercitium, -iī *n.* exercise, practice

exercitō 1. to exercise, train; harass, trouble

exercitor, -ōris *m.* physical trainer

exercitus¹, -a, -um *adj.* skilled, practised; harassed, troubled

exercitus², -ūs *m.* army; exercise

exerrō 1. to wander off course

exēsor, -ōris *m.* (+*gen.*) that which eats away (at)

exf- see **eff-**

exhālātiō, -ōnis *f.* vapour, exhalation

exhālō 1. to breathe out, exhale; **animam exhālāre** to die

exhauriō, -sī, -stum 4. to draw off, drain; exhaust, finish; remove; see through (*tasks etc.*)

exhērēdō 1. to disinherit

exhērēs, -dis *adj.* disinherited

exhibeō 2. to produce, hold out; exhibit, show; provide; cause

exhilarō 1. to cheer

exhorrescō, -rruī 3. to shudder; shudder at

exhortātiō, -ōnis *f.* encouragement, exhortation

exhortor 1. *dep.* to encourage, incite

exigō, exēgī, exactum 3. to drive out, force out; demand; enforce, exact; finish; pass (*time*); consider, examine

exiguē *adv.* scantily, sparingly; briefly

exiguitās, -ātis *f.* scantiness; smallness

exiguum, -ī *n.* small amount; small space

exiguus, -a, -um *adj.* small; scant, meagre; brief; trivial

exīlis, -is, -e *adj.* thin, slender; scanty, meagre; plain, dry; trivial

exīlitās, -ātis *f.* thinness, slenderness; plainness, dryness

exīliter *adv.* thinly; briefly; sparingly

exilium, -(i)ī *n.* exile

exim see **exinde**

eximiē *adv.* outstandingly, excellently

eximius, -a, -um *adj.* exempt, excepted; outstanding, excellent

eximō, exēmī, exemptum 3. to take out, extract; take away, remove; relieve, exempt

exin see **exinde**

exināniō 4. to drain, dry up; lay bare, strip

exinde *adv.* thereafter, next; therefore; **exinde ut** according as

existimātiō, -ōnis *f.* judging, forming an opinion; judgement, opinion; reputation

existimātor, -ōris *m.* judge, critic

existimō (-stumō) 1. to form an opinion about, judge; (+*gen./abl.*) value (at); suppose, think

exitiābilis, -is, -e *adj.* causing death, lethal

exitiālis, -is, -e *adj.* causing death, lethal

exitiō, -ōnis *f.* going out; (+*acc.*) avoiding

exitiōsus, -a, -um *adj.* causing death, lethal

exitium, -(i)ī *n.* death; destruction, ruin

exitus, -ūs *m.* going out, exit; means of exit; result, outcome; conclusion, end

exl- see **ēl-** (other than below)

exlex, exlēgis *adj.* exempt from the law

exm- see **ēm-**

exn- see **ēn-**

exobsecrō 1. to entreat earnestly

exoculō 1. to remove the eyes from

exodium, -(i)ī *n.* short dramatic afterpiece

exolescō, -lēvī, -lētum 3. to grow up; fade away, die out

exolētus, -ī *m.* male prostitute

exonerō 1. to unload, disburden; (+*abl.*) relieve (of)

exoptābilis, -is, -e *adj.* desirable

exoptō 1. to desire, wish for

exōrābilis, -is, -e *adj.* open to entreaty, sympathetic

exōrābula, -ōrum *n.pl.* entreaties

exōrātor, -ōris *m.* one who entreats successfully

exordior, exorsus 4. *dep.* to begin weaving; begin, start

exordium, -(i)ī *n.* beginning, start; preface

exorior, exortus 4. *dep.* to come into view, appear; come into being; arise, come about

exornātiō, -ōnis *f.* adornment, embellishment

exornātor, -ōris *m.* adorner, embellisher

exornātulus, -a, -um *adj.* rather prettily dressed

exornō 1. to kit out, equip; adorn, embellish, glorify

exōrō 1. to prevail upon; obtain by entreaty

exorsus, -ūs *m.* beginning

exortus, -ūs *m.* rising (*esp. sunrise*), appearance

exos, exossis *adj.* boneless

exosculor 1. *dep.* to kiss eagerly

exossō 1. to remove the bones from

exostra, -ae *f.* theatrical machine revealing interior scenes

exōsus, -a, -um *adj.* (+*acc.*) hating, loathing

exōticus, -a, -um *adj.* foreign, imported

exp- see **exsp-** (other than below)

expallescō, -lluī 3. to turn pale

expallidus, -a, -um *adj.* very pale

expalliō 1. to remove the cloak from

expalpō 1. to obtain by coaxing

expandō, -dī, -sum 3. to spread out, expand; expound

expatrō 1. to squander, waste

expavescō, expāvī 3. to become frightened; take fright at

expediō 4. to disentangle, untie, extricate; settle, solve; supply; prepare; be of use

expedītē *adv.* freely, without restraint; clearly; speedily

expedītiō, -ōnis *f.* military expedition, raid

expedītus, -a, -um *adj.* free, unencumbered; agile, nimble; ready, at hand; easy; **in expedītō** without hindrance

expellō, expulī, expulsum 3. to drive out, expel, eject; banish

expendō, -dī, -sum 3. to weigh; pay (*money, a penalty*); ponder, estimate

expensum, -ī *n.* expenditure

expergēfaciō, -fēcī, -factum 3. to awaken, rouse; arouse

expergiscor, experrectus 3. *dep.* to wake up, rouse oneself

expergō, -ī, -itum 3. to awaken, rouse

experiens, -ntis *adj.* active, enterprising

experientia, -ae *f.* trial, test; experience

experīmentum, -ī *n.* trial, test; proof; experience

experior, expertus 4. *dep.* to try, test; (+*inf.* or +*ut* +*subj.*) try (to); experience

experrectus, -a, -um *adj.* vigilant, attentive

expers, -rtis *adj.* (+*gen./abl.*) having no part (in), devoid (of), inexperienced (in)

expertus, -a, -um *adj.* tested; (+*gen.*) well-proved (in)

expetessō 3. to seek earnestly

expetibilis, -is, -e *adj.* that which is desirable but not desired

expetō, -īvī (-iī), -ītum 3. to ask for, demand; seek after, desire; occur

expiātiō, -ōnis f. expiation, purification; averting of omens by expiation

expīlātiō, -ōnis f. plundering, pillaging

expīlātor, -ōris m. plunderer, pillager

expīlō 1. to plunder, pillage

expingō, -nxī, -ctum 3. to put paint on; depict

expiō 1. to purify; make amends for, expiate; avert by expiation; propitiate

expiscor 1. dep. to search out, angle for

explānātē adv. clearly, plainly

explānātiō, -ōnis f. clear exposition

explānātor, -ōris m. one who explains, expositor

explānō 1. to make clean, explain; enunciate clearly; make flat

explēmentum, -ī n. filling, stuffing

expleō, explēvī, explētum 2. to fill up, stuff; carry through, accomplish; satisfy

explētiō, -ōnis f. satisfaction, fulfilment

explicātē adv. clearly, plainly

explicātiō, -ōnis f. unravelling, solution; description, exposition

explicātor, -ōris m. one who expounds, expositor

explicātrix, -īcis f.adj. unravelling, revealing

explicātus¹, -a, -um adj. clear, uncomplicated

explicātus², -ūs m. explanation

explicitus, -a, -um adj. free from problems, easy

explicō, -āvī (-uī), -ātum 1. to unravel, disentangle, extricate; carry through, accomplish; expand; expound

explōdō, -dī, -sum 3. to drive off the stage; reject

explōrātē adv. with certainty, surely

explōrātiō, -ōnis f. searching out, investigation

explōrātor, -ōris m. investigator; scout

explōrātōrius, -a, -um adj. of or relating to scouts

explōrātus, -a, -um adj. certain, sure, proven; (+ab +abl.) free (from)

explōrō 1. to search out, investigate; try out; inquire

explōsiō, -ōnis f. driving off the stage

expoliō 4. to smooth, polish; perfect; adorn, refine

expolītiō, -ōnis f. polishing; polish, refinement

expolītus, -a, -um adj. smooth, polished

expōnō, exposuī, expositum 3. to put out, set forth; lay out; (+dat.) expose (to); relate, explain

expor(ri)gō, -rrexī, -rrectum 3. to spread out, smooth

exportātiō, -ōnis f. exportation

exportō 1. to carry out, take away; export

exposcō, expoposcī 3. to ask for, demand, require

expositīcius, -a, -um adj. (of children) exposed

expositiō, -ōnis f. exposition, description

expositus, -a, -um adj. frank, plain; commonplace

expostulātiō, -ōnis f. complaint, protest

expostulō 1. to demand; complain about; remonstrate

expressē adv. with precision, distinctly

expressus, -a, -um adj. clear, distinct

exprimō, expressī, expressum 3. to squeeze, press; squeeze out, elicit; express, relate; copy, reproduce

exprobrātiō, -ōnis f. (+gen.) reproach (arising from)

exprobrō 1. (+dat.) to use as a reproach (against)

exprōmō, -ompsī, -omptum 3. to put out, put to use; express; reveal

expugnābilis, -is, -e adj. assailable, open to attack

expugnātiō, -ōnis f. capture by assault

expugnātor, -ōris m. one who takes by storm, capturer

expugnax, -ācis adj. effective in attack

expugnō 1. to take by storm, capture; plunder; overcome, break down

expulsiō, -ōnis f. expulsion

expulsō 1. to drive away

expulsor, -ōris m. one who drives out

expultrix, -īcis f. female who drives out

expungō, -nxī, -nctum 3. to cross off, check; prick thoroughly

expurgō (-ūrigō) 1. to cleanse, purge; excuse, justify

expūrigātiō, -ōnis f. excuse, justification

expūtescō 3. to rot away

exputō 1. to examine thoroughly; come to a conclusion

exquīrō, exquīsīvī, exquīsītum 3. to inquire into; seek out, look for; discover

exquīsītē *adv.* precisely, meticulously

exquīsītus, -a, -um *adj.* precise, meticulous

exrādīcitus *adv.* utterly, completely

exsaeviō 4. to lose fury

exsanguis, -is, -e *adj.* bloodless; pale; feeble, unspirited

exsaniō 1. to drain

exsarciō, -sī, -tum 4. to patch up, fix

exsatiō 1. to sate, satisfy

exsaturābilis, -is, -e *adj.* that can be sated

exsaturō 1. to sate, satisfy

exsce- see **esce-**

exscindō, -idī, -issum 3. to destroy, exterminate

exscreō 1. to cough out, expectorate

exscrībō, exscripsī, exscriptum 3. to write out, copy; resemble

exsculpō, -psī, -ptum 3. to carve, chisel out; dig out

exsecō, -uī, -tum 1. to cut out, remove; cut; castrate

exsecrābilis, -is, -e *adj.* accursed, execrable; of *or* relating to cursing

exsecrātiō, -ōnis *f.* cursing, execration; curse invoked for a broken promise

exsecrātus, -a, -um *adj.* accursed, execrable

exsecror 1. *dep.* to curse; detest

exsectiō, -ōnis *f.* cutting out, excision

exsecūtiō, -ōnis *f.* enactment; discussion, treatment

exsecūtor, -ōris *m.* avenger

exsequiae, -ārum *f.pl.* funeral procession, obsequies

exsequiālis, -is, -e *adj.* funereal; *n.pl.sbst.* funeral rites

exsequium, -iī *n.* funeral rites

exsequor, exsecūtus 3. *dep.* to follow; pursue, strive after; execute; persist at

exserō, -uī, -tum 3. to stretch out, thrust out; lay bare, reveal; exercise

exsertō 1. to stretch out; lay bare

exsertus, -a, -um *adj.* protruding, stretched out

exsībilō 1. to hiss off the stage

exsiccō 1. to make dry; drain; drain off

exsicō see **exsecō**

exsignō 1. to certify with a seal

exsiliō, -uī (-īvī) 4. to spring forth, leap out

exsilium see **exilium**

exsistō, exstitī, exstitum 3. to step forth, come forward; appear, emerge, arise

exsolvō, -vī (-uī), -ūtum 3. to unfasten, loose; release; pay; do away with

exsomnis, -is, -e *adj.* sleepless, vigilant

exsorbeō 2. to absorb, swallow; drain

exsors, -rtis *adj.* (+*gen.*) having no share (in), exempt (from); without lottery, personally assigned

exspatior 1. *dep.* to stretch out, extend

exspectātiō, -ōnis *f.* expectation, longing for

exspectātus, -a, -um *adj.* expected, longed for

exspectō 1. to expect, wait for; long for; wait expectantly

exspergō, -sī, -sum 3. to scatter abroad

exspēs (*nom.sg. only*) *adj.* without hope

exspīrātiō, -ōnis *f.* exhalation

exspīrō 1. to breathe out, exhale; expire, die; be exhaled

exsplendescō, -duī 3. to become conspicuous

exspoliō 1. to despoil, plunder; (+*abl.*) deprive (of)

exspuō, -uī, -ūtum 3. to spit out; emit

exstans, -ntis *adj.* prominent

exsternō 1. to make frantic, panic

exstillō 1. to drip, run

exstimulātor, -ōris *m.* inciter, instigator

exstimulō 1. to stir up, incite

exstinctiō, -ōnis *f.* extinction

exstinctor, -ōris *m.* one who extinguishes, annihilator

exstinguō, -nxī, -nctum 3. to extinguish, quench; kill, destroy, annihilate

exstirpō 1. to tear out by the roots, eradicate

exstō, exstitī 1. to stand out, protrude; be prominent; exist

exstructiō, -ōnis *f.* construction; structure

exstruō, -xī, -ctum 3. to heap *or* pile up; construct, build; arrange

exsuctus, -a, -um *adj.* dried up, without juice

exsūdō 1. to sweat over; ooze out

exsūgō, -uxī, -uctum 3. to suck out; draw matter from

exsul(-) see **exul(-)**

exsultanter *adv.* elatedly, boisterously

exsultātiō, -ōnis *f.* leaping; elation, exultation

exsultim *adv.* with leaping

exsultō 1. to leap up, dance; act unrestrainedly, run riot; exult

exsuperābilis, -is, -e *adj.* able to be overcome

exsuperantia, -ae *f.* pre-eminence, superiority

exsuperō 1. to surmount; overcome; exceed, outdo; excel, prevail

exsurdō 1. to make deaf; dull

exsurgō, -rrexī 3. to get up, arise; come into being; swell, extend

exsuscitō 1. to awaken; kindle; rouse

ext- see **exst-** (other than below)

exta, -ōrum *n.pl.* chief internal organs

extābescō, -buī 3. to waste away

extāris, -is, -e *adj.* for cooking the chief internal organs

extemplō *adv.* at once, immediately; directly

extemporālis, -is, -e *adj.* extempore, unplanned

extemporālitās, -ātis *f.* ability to compose extempore

extempulō see **extemplō**

extendō, -dī, -sum (-tum) 3. to stretch out, extend; increase, enlarge; prolong; smooth

extentō 1. to stretch; exert fully

extentus, -a, -um *adj.* level, even

extenuātiō, -ōnis *f.* rhetorical lessening

extenuō 1. to narrow, rarefy; diminish, belittle

exter, -ra, -rum *adj.* external; foreign, strange

exterebrō 1. to bore out, extort

extergeō, -rsī, -rsum 2. to rub clean, scour

exterior, -or, -us *compar.adj.* outer, exterior

exterius *compar.adv.* externally

exterminō 1. to expel, banish

externus, -a, -um *adj.* external; foreign; *m.sbst.* foreigner; *n.pl.sbst.* foreign things

exterō, extrīvī, extrītum 3. to tread down, crush; wear down, rub away

exterreō 2. to terrify, scare; (+*abl.*) frighten (out of)

extersus, -ūs *m.* wiping off

extexō, -uī, -tum 3. to unweave

extimescō, -muī 3. to take fright, be afraid; dread, fear

extimus, -a, -um *superl.adj.* outermost, farthest

extispex, -spicis *m.* one who divines by examining sacrificial entrails

extispicium, -(i)ī *n.* examination of sacrificial entrails for divination

extollō 3. to raise, lift up; praise, extol; defer; embellish, adorn

extorqueō, -rsī, -rtum 2. to twist out, wrest away; extort; sprain; torture

extorris, -is, -e *adj.* banished, exiled

extortor, -ōris *m.* one who extorts

extrā *prep.* (+*acc.*) outside; as well as; without; *adv.* outside; from outside; outwards

extrahō, -xī, -ctum 3. to draw out, extract; fetch out; protract; extricate

extrāneus, -a, -um *adj.* external, foreign (*esp. to a household*); *m.pl.sbst.* strangers

extraordinārius, -a, -um *adj.* special, additional; exceptional, irregular

extrārius, -a, -um *adj.* external (*esp. to a household*)

extrēmitās, -ātis *f.* border, extremity, end

extrēmō *adv.* at last, finally

extrēmum, -ī *n.* limit, end; ultimate degree

extrēmus, -a, -um *adj.* outermost; lowest; hindmost; final, last; extreme, desperate

extrīcō 1. to loose, set free

extrinsecus *adv.* externally, from without

extrūdō, -sī, -sum 3. to thrust out, expel; push back, repel

extumeō 2. to swell up

extundō, -udī, -ūsum 3. to hammer out; extort; expel

exturbō 1. to drive out, eject; banish; divorce; throw into chaos

exūberō 1. to gush up, surge forth; abound, be plentiful

exul, -lis *m./f.* exile

exulcerō 1. to make sore, hurt; aggravate

exulō 1. to be banished, be in exile

exululō 1. to howl; call upon by howling

exundātiō, -ōnis *f.* flooding, welling up

exundō 1. to gush up, rise in flood; (+*abl.*) overflow (with), abound (in); be washed up

exunguor, -nctus 3. *dep.* to waste money on unguents

exuō, exuī, exūtum 3. to take off, throw off; lay bare, strip; release

exurgeō 2. to squeeze out

exūrō, exussī, exustum 3. to burn up, destroy by fire; make dry, parch

exustiō, -ōnis *f.* consumption by fire, burning

exuviae, -ārum *f.pl.* spoils, plundered armour; animal skin

exuvium, -(i)ī *n.* spoils

F

faba, -ae *f.* bean; bean-plant
fabālis, -is, -e *adj.* of *or* relating to beans
fābella, -ae *f.* short story, anecdote; dramatic play
faber¹, fabrī *m.* craftsman, artisan; engineer; the fish dory
faber², fabra, fabrum *adj.* of *or* relating to a craftsman
fabrē *adj.* skilfully, artfully
fabrēfactus, -a, -um *adj.* skilfully crafted
fabrica, -ae *f.* craft, art; manufacture, construction; workshop
fabricātiō, -ōnis *f.* manufacture, construction
fabricātor, -ōris *m.* artificer, fashioner
fabricō 1. *or* **fabricor 1.** *dep.* to fashion, craft, construct; devise
fabrīlis, -is, -e *adj.* of *or* relating to a craftsman; skilled
fābula, -ae *f.* talk, gossip; story, tale, fable; dramatic play
fābulāris, -is, -e *adj.* of *or* relating to tales, mythological
fābulātor, -ōris *m.* story-teller
fābulor 1. *dep.* to talk, chat
fābulōsus, -a, -um *adj.* fictitious, fabulous; famous, fabled
fabulus, -ī *m.* bean
facessō, -īvī (-iī), -ītum 3. to perform, accomplish; depart, leave; **perīculum facessere** (+*dat.*) to bring a case (against)
facētē *adv.* wittily; cleverly
facētiae, -ārum *f.pl.* wit; cleverness; *sg.* joke
facētus, -a, -um *adj.* witty, humorous; clever, adept
faciēs, -ēī *f.* shape, form; appearance, guise; character; beauty
facile *adv.* easily; readily, willingly; carelessly; **nōn/haud facile** rarely

facilis, -is, -e *adj.* easy; ready, willing; favourable, affable; agile
facilitās, -ātis *f.* easiness, facility; readiness, willingness; affability
facinerōsus (-nor-), -a, -um *adj.* wicked, criminal
facinus, -oris (-eris) *n.* act, deed; crime, bad deed; criminal
faciō, fēcī, factum 3. to make, produce; do, perform; produce; provide; imagine; act
facteon *indecl.adj.* one must do
factiō, -ōnis *f.* making, producing; group, band; clique, faction
factiōsus, -a, -um *adj.* partisan, factious; busy
factitō 1. to make habitually; do habitually
factor, -ōris *m.* player
factum, -ī *n.* deed, act, exploit
factus, -a, -um *adj.* elaborate, finished; done, formed
facula, -ae *f.* small torch
facultās, -ātis *f.* capacity, faculty; power; means, resource; opportunity
fācundē *adv.* eloquently
fācundia, -ae *f.* eloquence, fluency
fācunditās, -ātis *f.* eloquence
fācundus, -a, -um *adj.* eloquent, fluent
faeceus, -a, -um *adj.* resembling dregs, impure
faecula, -ae *f.* lees of wine, tartar
faenebris, -is, -e *adj.* of *or* relating to usury; lent on interest
faenerātiō, -ōnis *f.* usury, lending on interest
faenerātō *adv.* with interest
faenerātor, -ōris *m.* usurer, money-lender
faenerō 1. *or* **faeneror 1.** *dep.* to lend on interest; invest
faeneus, -a, -um *adj.* of *or* made of hay

faeniculārius, -a, -um *adj.* containing fennel

faeniculum, -ī *n.* fennel

faenīlia, -ium *n.pl.* hay-barn

faeniseca, -ae *m.* hay-cutter, mower

faenum, -ī *n.* hay

faenus, -oris *n.* interest; gain, capital; debt

faenusculum, -ī *n.* small amount of interest

faex, faecis *f.* lees of wine, dregs; sediment

fāgin(e)us, -a, -um *adj.* of *or* made of beech

fāgus, -ī *f.* beech tree; beech wood

fala, -ae *f.* mobile siege-tower

falārica, -ae *f.* pitch-covered missile

falcārius, -(i)ī *m.* scythe-maker

falcātus, -a, -um *adj.* armed with scythes; sickle-shaped

falcifer, -era, -erum *adj.* bearing a scythe

fallācia, -ae *f.* deceit, trick

fallāciloquus, -a, -um *adj.* speaking deceitfully

fallāciter *adv.* deceitfully

fallax, -ācis *adj.* deceitful, deceptive; fake, false

fallō, fefellī, falsum 3. to deceive, trick; cause to err; disguise; escape the notice of, elude

falsārius, -iī *m.* forger

falsē *adv.* falsely

falsidicus, -a, -um *adj.* lying

falsificus, -a, -um *adj.* acting deceitfully

falsiiūrius, -a, -um *adj.* swearing falsely

falsiloquus, -a, -um *adj.* speaking deceitfully

falsimōnia, -ae *f.* deceit, trick

falsiparens, -ntis *adj.* having a putative father

falsō *adv.* falsely, deceitfully; erroneously, mistakenly

falsum, -ī *n.* lie, falsehood; deceit

falsus, -a, -um *adj.* false, deceitful; erroneous, wrong; fake, spurious

falx, falcis *f.* scythe, pruning-hook, curved blade

fāma, -ae *f.* report, news; talk, hearsay; reputation; renown; notoriety

famēlicus, -a, -um *adj.* hungry, famished

famēs, -is *f.* hunger, famine, starvation; desire, craving; poverty of expression

fāmigerātiō, -ōnis *f.* gossip, rumour

fāmigerātor, -ōris *m.* gossip, rumour-monger

familia, -ae *f.* household, estate; band of slaves (*of a household*); family; sect

familiāris, -is, -e *adj.* of *or* relating to a household; private; familiar; friendly; *m. sbst.* slave (*of a household*)

familiāritās, -ātis *f.* familiarity, intimacy; friend

familiāriter *adv.* familiarly, intimately

fāmōsus, -a, -um *adj.* renowned, famous; notorious; defamatory

famul see **famulus**[1]

famula, -ae *f.* maid, female servant

famulāris, -is, -e *adj.* of *or* relating to a servant

famulātus, -ūs *m.* slavery, servitude

famulor 1. *dep.* (+*dat.*) to be a slave (to), serve

famulus[1]**, -ī** *m.* servant, slave

famulus[2]**, -a, -um** *adj.* servile; enslaved, subject

fānāticus, -a, -um *adj.* of *or* relating to a temple; inspired, frenzied

fandus, -a, -um *adj.* that can be spoken of, lawful, proper

fānor 1. *dep.* to be frenzied

fānum, -ī *n.* temple, shrine

far, farris *n.* grain, spelt, meal

farciō, farsī, fartum 4. to stuff, fill full; (+*in* +*abl.*) cram (into)

farferum, -ī *n.* the plant coltsfoot

farīna, -ae *f.* flour, meal

farrāgō, -inis *m.* mixed fodder; medley, hotchpotch

farrātus, -a, -um *adj.* containing porridge; *n.pl.sbst.* porridge

fartim *f.acc.sg.* stuffing

fartor, -ōris *m.* one who fattens fowls

fās *indecl.n.* that which is ordained by divine law, that which is right *or* proper

fascia, -ae *f.* ribbon, band; bandage; girdle

fasciculus, -ī *m.* bundle of books; posy of flowers

fascinō 1. to bewitch, enchant

fascinum, -ī *n.* or **fascinus, -ī** *m.* penis

fasciō 1. to bandage

fasciola, -ae *f.* ribbon, band (*worn about the legs*)

fascis, -is *m.* bundle, load; *pl.* bundle of rods carried by lictors before Roman magistrates; magistracy

fastīdiō 4. to treat with disdain, scorn, dislike; be disdainful

fastīdiōsē *adv.* disdainfully; fussily

fastīdiōsus, -a, -um *adj.* disdainful, scornful; disgusting, nauseating; fussy, particular

fastīdium, -(i)ī *n.* disgust, repulsion, dislike; disdain, scorn; nausea; fussiness, fastidiousness

fastīgātē *adv.* at a slanted angle

fastīgium, -(i)ī *n.* pediment; roof; peak, apex; height, depth; slope; dignity, eminence

fastīgō 1. to taper, make narrow; make sloping

fastōsus, -a, -um *adj.* disdainful, haughty

fastus¹, -ūs *m.* haughtiness, pride

fastus², -a, -um *adj.* (*of days*) on which business can be carried out; *m.pl.sbst.* days on which business can be carried out; list of festivals, calendar; list of consuls

fātālis, -is, -e *adj.* of *or* relating to fate; destined, fated; deadly, fatal

fātāliter *adv.* according to fate

fateor, fassus 2. *dep.* to confess, own; concede; reveal

fāticanus (-cinus), -a, -um *adj.* prophetic

fātidicus, -a, -um *adj.* prophetic; *m.sbst.* prophet

fātifer, -era, -erum *adj.* bringing death, fatal

fatīgātiō, -ōnis *f.* weariness, fatigue

fatīgō 1. to weary, exhaust; worry, harass; overcome

fātilegus, -a, -um *adj.* collecting death

fātiloquus, -a, -um *adj.* prophetic

fatīscō 3. or **fatīscor** 3. *dep.* to split apart, crack; grow weary, flag

fatuē *adv.* foolishly

fatuitās, -ātis *f.* foolishness, idiocy

fātum, -ī *n.* decree of fate, prophecy; destiny, fate; outcome; death, ruin

fatuor 1. *dep.* to play the fool

fatuus, -a, -um *adj.* foolish, idiotic; tasteless, insipid; *m./f.sbst.* jester

fauce *f.abl.sg.* see **faucēs**

faucēs, -ium *f.pl.* throat, gullet; gulf; narrow entrance; pass, strait

faustē *adv.* auspiciously

faustitās, -ātis *f.* prosperity

faustus, -a, -um *adj.* auspicious, favourable; fortunate, lucky

fautor, -ōris *m.* promoter, supporter, patron

fautrix, -īcis *f.* female promoter, patroness

faveō, fāvī, fautum 2. (+*dat.*) to favour, support, be propitious (to); be of good omen

favilla, -ae *f.* ashes, cinders; hot ash, spark

favor, -ōris *m.* favour, goodwill; partiality; support; applause, acclamation

favōrābilis, -is, -e *adj.* favoured, popular; designed to win favour

favōrābiliter *adv.* so as to win favour

favus, -ī *m.* honeycomb

fax, facis *f.* torch, firebrand; flame, light; ray, beam; instigator

febrīcitō 1. to have a fever

febrīcula, -ae *f.* slight fever

febrīculōsus, -a, -um *adj.* prone to fevers, feverish

febris, -is *f.* fever

februa, -ōrum *n.pl.* expiatory offerings

fēcunditās, -ātis *f.* fertility, productivity

fēcundō 1. to make fruitful, fertilize

fēcundus, -a, -um *adj.* fertile, fruitful, productive

fel, fellis *n.* bile, gall; gall-bladder; venom, bitterness

fēles (-is), -is *f.* wild cat

fēlīcitās, -ātis *f.* happiness, success, felicitousness

fēlīciter *adv.* happily, successfully, felicitously

fēlix, -īcis *adj.* fertile, productive; favourable; happy, successful, felicitous; wealthy

fellātor, -ōris *m.* one who engages in fellatio

fēllō 1. to engage in fellatio

fēmella, -ae *f.* young woman, girl

fēmina, -ae *f.* woman, female

feminālia, -ium *n.pl.* thigh-coverings

fēmineus, -a, -um *adj.* of *or* relating to a woman, feminine; effeminate

femur, -inis or **-oris** *n.* thigh

fēn- see **faen-**

fenestra, -ae *f.* window; breach, loophole

fera, -ae *f.* wild animal, beast

ferāciter *adv.* fruitfully

fērālis, -is, -e *adj.* of *or* relating to the dead, funerary; fatal

ferax, -ācis *adj.* fruitful, fertile, productive

ferculum, -ī *n.* carrying frame, tray, litter; course (*of a meal*), dish

ferē *adv.* almost, virtually; approximately; generally, usually

ferentārius, -(i)ī *m.* light-armed soldier who used only missiles

feretrum, -ī *n.* litter, bier

fēriae, -ārum *f.pl.* holy days; holiday, leisure

fēriātus, -a, -um *adj.* on holiday; idle, unused; **diēs fēriātus** holiday

ferīna, -ae *f.* flesh of wild animals, game

ferīnus, -a, -um *adj.* of *or* relating to wild animals; bestial, wild

feriō 4. to strike, hit; knock dead, kill; pierce; trick

feritās, -ātis *f.* wildness; brutality, ferocity

fermē see **ferē**

fermentum, -ī *n.* means of fermentation, yeast; ferment

ferō (*2nd sg.* **fers**, *3rd sg.* **fert**), **ferre, tulī, lātum** *v.irreg.* to bear, carry; bring, fetch; lift; carry off; produce, yield; endure, suffer; allow; talk about; allege; (+*adv.*) react (in a certain way)

ferōcia, -ae *f.* ferocity; aggressiveness, courage; arrogance

ferōcitās, -ātis *f.* ferocity; aggressiveness; arrogance

ferōciter *adv.* ferociously; arrogantly

ferox, -ōcis *adj.* wild, fierce, ferocious; defiant, unbridled; arrogant

ferrāmentum, -ī *n.* (*usu. pl.*) iron tool

ferrārius, -a, -um *adj.* of *or* relating to iron; *f.sbst.* iron-mine

ferrātilis, -is, -e *adj.* bound in iron

ferrātus, -a, -um *adj.* covered with iron, iron-clad

ferreus, -a, -um *adj.* made of *or* resembling iron; unyielding; stern, cruel

ferricrepinus, -a, -um *adj.* clinking with iron

ferriterium, -(i)ī *n.* place in which one chafes on iron, workshop

ferriterus, -a, -um *adj.* wearing out fetters

ferritrībax, -ācis *adj.* wearing out fetters

ferrūgin(e)us, -a, -um *adj.* rust-coloured

ferrūgō, -inis *f.* the colour of rust; envy

ferrum, -ī *n.* iron, steel; sword, weapon

fertilis, -is, -e *adj.* fertile, productive; fertilizing; (+*dat.*) productive (for)

fertilitās, -ātis *f.* fertility, productivity

fertum, -ī *n.* sacrificial cake

ferula, -ae *f.* rod, stick

ferus¹, -a, -um *adj.* wild, untamed, barbarous; fierce, savage; cruel; dangerous

ferus², -ī *m.* wild animal, beast

fervefaciō, -fēcī, -factum 3. to make very hot, boil

fervens, -ntis *adj.* very hot, boiling; seething, ardent; inflamed

ferveō, ferbuī 2. to be very hot, boil; seethe, be ardent; be enraged, be impassioned

fervescō 3. to become hot; begin to seethe

fervidus, -a, -um *adj.* very hot, boiling; seething, ardent; enraged, impassioned

fervō 3. see **ferveō**

fervor, -ōris *m.* intense heat; fever; seething; passion, ardour

fessus, -a, -um *adj.* tired, wearied; weakened, enfeebled

festīnanter *adv.* hurriedly, speedily

festīnātiō, -ōnis *f.* hurrying, haste, speed

festīnātō *adv.* hurriedly, speedily

festīnō 1. to hurry, hasten; do in haste, do without delay

festīnus, -a, -um *adj.* hurried, speedy; premature

festīvē *adv.* festively, cheerfully; amusingly; charmingly

festīvitās, -ātis *f.* festivity, good cheer; humour, wit; charm, delight

festīvus, -a, -um *adj.* cheerful, good humoured; witty; fine, excellent

festūca, -ae *f.* rod used in ceremonies of manumission; pile-driver

festum, -ī *n.* festival, holiday

festus, -a, -um *adj.* of *or* relating to holidays; on holiday; festive, merry; **diēs festus** holiday

fēta, -ae *f.* pregnant *or* recently pregnant female animal

fēteō, fētidus, fētor see **foeteō, foetidus, foetor**

fētiālis¹, -is, -e *adj.* of *or* relating to the priests who served as Roman diplomats

fētiālis², -is *m.* one of the priests who served as Roman diplomats

fētūra, -ae *f.* breeding; offspring, brood

fētus¹, -a, -um *adj.* pregnant *or* recently pregnant; fertile, productive

fētus², **-ūs** *m.* giving birth; breeding; offspring, brood; crop

fibra, -ae *f.* fibre, fibril; lobe; *pl.* entrails

fībula, -ae *f.* bolt, bar; clasp, buckle

fīcēdula (fīce-), -ae *f.* the bird beccafico

fīcētum, -ī *n.* plantation of fig trees

fīcōsus, -a, -um *adj.* afflicted with piles

fictē *adv.* falsely, untruthfully

fictilis, -is, -e *adj.* made of clay, earthenware; *n.sbst.* earthenware vessel

fictor, -ōris *m.* sculptor; one who makes; attendant of a priest

fictrix, -īcis *f.* that which fashions

fictum, -ī *n.* falsehood, untruth

fictūra, -ae *f.* fashioning, forming

fictus, -a, -um *adj.* false, untrue

fīcula, -ae *f.* small fig

fīculnus, -a, -um *adj.* of *or* relating to a fig tree

fīcus, -ī or **-ūs** *f./m.* fig tree; fig; piles

fīdē *adv.* faithfully

fidēlia, -ae *f.* pot, bucket

fidēlis, -is, -e *adj.* faithful, loyal; sincere; reliable

fidēlitās, -ātis *f.* faithfulness, loyalty

fidēliter *adv.* faithfully, loyally; reliably; securely

fīdens, -ntis *adj.* bold, self-assured; (*+gen.*) confident (in)

fīdenter *adv.* boldly, self-assuredly

fīdentia, -ae *f.* boldness, self-assurance

fidēs¹, -ēī *f.* trust, reliance; fidelity, loyalty; sincerity; self-assurance; conviction; guarantee

fidēs², -is *f.* (*usu. pl.*) lyre; lyre string

fidicen, -inis *m.* lyre-player; lyric poet

fidicina, -ae *f.* female lyre-player

fidicinius, -a, -um *adj.* lyre-playing

fidicula, -ae *f.* small lyre; *pl.* instrument of torture

fīdō, fīsus sum 3. *semi-dep.* (*+abl./dat.*) to trust, rely (on)

fīdūcia, -ae *f.* trust, reliance; confidence, assurance

fīdūciārius, -a, -um *adj.* held on trust; of *or* relating to a trustee

fīdus, -a, -um *adj.* faithful, loyal; reliable; sincere

fīgō, fixī, fixum 3. to fix, fasten; drive in, implant; attach

figulāris, -is, -e *adj.* of *or* relating to a potter

figulus, -ī *m.* potter

figūra, -ae *f.* shape, form; appearance; arrangement; image; figure

figūrō 1. to form, fashion

fīlātim *adv.* thread by thread

fīlia, -ae (*dat./abl.pl.* **fīliābus**) *f.* daughter

filicātus, -a, -um *adj.* adorned with fern patterns

fīliola, -ae *f.* little daughter

fīliolus, -ī *m.* little son

fīlius, -(i)ī *m.* son

filix, -icis *f.* fern, bracken

fīlum, -ī *n.* thread, cord; (*of speech*) texture

fimbriae, -ārum *f.pl.* fringe(s)

fimbriātus, -a, -um *adj.* having a fringe

fimum, -ī *n.* dung, excrement

findō, fidī, fissum 3. to cleave, split, divide

fingō, finxī, fictum 3. to form, fashion; represent; feign, fabricate; compose

fīniō 4. to limit, demarcate; define, prescribe; bring to an end, stop; finish

fīnis, -is *m./f.* boundary, border; limit; goal; end, finish; death; *pl.* territory

fīnītē *adv.* to a limited extent

fīnitimus (-tumus), -a, -um *adj.* bordering, neighbouring; similar, kindred; *m.pl. sbst.* neighbours; *n.pl.sbst.* neighbouring lands

fīnītiō, -ōnis *f.* boundary, border; definition; limit, extremity

fīnītor, -ōris *m.* one who determines boundaries, surveyor; one who sets a limit

fīnītus, -a, -um *adj.* definite, determinate; finite; well-rounded

fīō, fierī, factus *v.irreg.* to arise, come about, happen; become; be made; be done

firmāmen, -inis *n.* support, prop

firmāmentum, -ī *n.* support, prop; central point (*of an argument*)

firmātor, -ōris *m.* one who makes firm, confirmer

firmē *adv.* firmly; steadfastly

firmitās, -ātis *f.* firmness, stability; steadfastness; reliability

firmiter *adv.* firmly, securely

firmitūdō, -inis *f.* firmness, stability; steadfastness; reliability

firmō 1. to make firm, strengthen; make

stable, support; confirm, establish; affirm; encourage, animate

firmus, -a, -um *adj.* firm, strong; in good health, sound; valid; steadfast; reliable

fiscālis, -is, -e *adj.* of *or* relating to the state treasury

fiscella, -ae *f.* small basket

fiscina, -ae *f.* woven basket

fiscus, -ī *m.* money-bag, purse; state treasury

fissilis, -is, -e *adj.* that may be split; split, cleft

fissiō, -ōnis *f.* splitting, cleaving

fissum, -ī *n.* split, cleft

fistūca see **festūca**

fistula, -ae *f.* pipe, tube; reed-pipe

fistulātor, -ōris *m.* piper

fistulātus, -a, -um *adj.* fitted with pipes

fistulōsus, -a, -um *adj.* full of holes, porous

fixus, -a, -um *adj.* fixed, immutable; (*+abl.*) fitted (with)

flābellifera, -ae *f.* female servant who fans her mistress

flābellulum, -ī *n.* small fan

flābellum, -ī *n.* fan

flābilis, -is, -e *adj.* of *or* resembling wind, airy

flābra, -ōrum *n.pl.* blasts of wind, gusts

flacceō 2. to flag, languish

flaccescō 3. to droop, languish

flaccidus, -a, -um *adj.* drooping, languid

flaccus, -a, -um *adj.* flap-eared

flagellō 1. to whip, lash; keep up (*prices*)

flagellum, -ī *n.* whip, lash; arm, tentacle; sprout, shoot (*of a vine*)

flāgitātiō, -ōnis *f.* demand, entreaty

flāgitātor, -ōris *m.* one who earnestly demands

flāgitiōsē *adv.* outrageously, shamelessly

flāgitiōsus, -a, -um *adj.* outrageous, shameless; infamous

flāgitium, -(i)ī *n.* disgraceful action, outrage; scandal; disgrace, infamy; public demand

flāgitō 1. to entreat earnestly; demand, clamour for; summon (*to court*)

flagrans, -ntis *adj.* blazing, burning; impassioned, ardent; flagrant

flagranter *adv.* passionately, ardently

flagrantia, -ae *f.* blaze, glow

flagritriba, -ae *m.* one who wears out a whip (*by constantly being flogged*)

flagrō 1. to burn, blaze; glow, shine; be impassioned, ardent

flagrum, -ī *n.* whip, lash; flogging

flāmen¹, -inis *m.* priest of a given deity

flāmen², -inis *n.* blast of wind, gust; wind

flāminica, -ae *f.* wife of a *flamen*

flamma, -ae *f.* flame, fire; firebrand, torch; heat; gleam; passion

flammans, -ntis *adj.* burning, flaming

flammāris, -is, -e *adj.* flame-coloured

flammārius, -(i)ī *m.* one who dyes clothes flame-coloured

flammātus, -a, -um *adj.* burning, flaming; thirsty

flammeolum, -ī *n.* small (flame-coloured) bridal veil

flammescō 3. to become inflamed

flammeum, -ī *n.* (flame-coloured) bridal veil

flammeus, -a, -um *adj.* blazing, fiery; hot; flame-coloured; passionate, ardent

flammifer, -era, -erum *adj.* bearing flames, fiery

flammiger, -era, -erum *adj.* bearing flames, fiery

flammō 1. to set fire to, kindle, inflame

flammula, -ae *f.* small flame

flāmōnium, -(i)ī *n.* office of a *flamen*

flātus, -ūs *m.* blast of wind, gust; breathing; arrogance, pride

flāvens, -ntis *adj.* yellow, golden-yellow

flāveō 2. to be yellow

flāvescō 3. to become yellow, become golden

flāvus, -a, -um *adj.* yellow, golden yellow, blonde

flēbilis, -is, -e *adj.* to be wept over, lamentable; causing tears; tearful, weeping

flēbiliter *adv.* tearfully

flectō, flexī, flexum 3. to bend, curve; turn, divert; modulate; change, influence

flēmina, -um *n.pl.* swelling of the ankles

fleō, flēvī, flētum 2. to cry, weep; lament, bewail

flētus, -ūs *m.* crying, lamentation

flexanimus, -a, -um *adj.* persuasive, moving

flexibilis, -is, -e *adj.* flexible, pliant, supple

flexilis, -is, -e *adj.* flexible, pliant

flexiloquus, -a, -um *adj.* ambiguously expressed, riddling

flexiō, -ōnis *f.* bending; modulation; circuitous route

flexipēs, -pedis *adj.* having crooked shoots

flexuōsus, -a, -um *adj.* full of turns, sinuous

flexūra, -ae *f.* bending, turning

flexus[1], -a, -um *adj.* bent, twisted; riddling

flexus[2], -ūs *m.* bending, turning; bend, curve

flictus, -ūs *m.* collision, impact

flō 1. to blow; breathe; blow on *or* into; cast (*coins etc.*)

floccus, -ī *m.* tuft of wool; **(nōn) floccī facere** (+*acc.*) to think unimportant

flōreō 2. to blossom, flower; (+*abl.*) shine (with); be prosperous, famous; be at one's prime

flōrescō 3. to come into flower, blossom

flōreus, -a, -um *adj.* consisting of flowers, flowery

flōridulus, -a, -um *adj.* somewhat flowery

flōridus, -a, -um *adj.* covered in flowers, flowery; fresh, blooming; bright, attractive

flōrifer, -era, -erum *adj.* bearing flowers; flowery

flōrilegus, -a, -um *adj.* culling flowers

flōs, flōris *m.* flower, bloom; aroma; prime, zenith; youthful beauty

flosculus, -ī *m.* small flower; prime example

fluctifragus, -a, -um *adj.* that breaks the waves

fluctiger, -era, -erum *adj.* carried by the waves

fluctisonus, -a, -um *adj.* resounding with waves

fluctivagus, -a, -um *adj.* that wanders the waves

fluctuātiō, -ōnis *f.* moving to and fro, swaying

fluctuō 1. or **fluctuor** 1. *dep.* to billow, undulate; be wave-tossed; waver, fluctuate

fluctuōsus, -a, -um *adj.* full of waves, billowy

fluctus, -ūs *m.* wave, billow; flood; disturbance, commotion

fluens, -ntis *adj.* flowing, fluent

fluenter *adv.* in a flowing manner

fluentisonus, -a, -um *adj.* resounding with waves

fluentum, -ī *n.* stream, flood

fluidus, -a, -um *adj.* flowing, fluid; unstable; soft, flabby

fluitō 1. to flow, run; float, drift; be unsteady

flūmen, -inis *n.* river, stream; current

flūmineus, -a, -um *adj.* of *or* relating to rivers

fluō, fluxī, fluxum 3. to flow, run; stream, pour; (+*abl.*) flow (with); spread; droop, sink; decay; (+*ab/ex* +*abl.*) proceed (from)

flūtō see **fluitō**

fluviā(ti)lis, -is, -e *adj.* of *or* relating to rivers

fluvidus see **fluidus**

fluvitō see **fluitō**

fluvius, -(i)ī *m.* river, stream; river-god

fluxus, -a, -um *adj.* flowing; unstable, wavering; soft, flabby; dissolute

fōcāle, -is *n.* neck-scarf

focilō 1. to revive; foster

foculum, -ī *n.* vessel for warming something

foculus, -ī *m.* small stove, brazier

focus, -ī *m.* hearth, fireplace; home

fodicō 1. to prod, prick

fodiō, fōdī, fossum 3. to dig; dig out; prod, prick

foedē *adv.* foully, horribly; shamefully

foederātus, -a, -um *adj.* allied, federated

foedifragus, -a, -um *adj.* treaty-breaking, treacherous

foeditās, -ātis *f.* foulness, unpleasantness; shame, disgrace

foedō 1. to befoul, defile; mangle, disfigure; shame, disgrace

foedus[1], -a, -um *adj.* foul, unpleasant, horrible; shameful, disgraceful

foedus[2], -eris *n.* league, treaty, bond; law

foeteō 2. to stink, reek

foetidus, -a, -um *adj.* stinking, foul-smelling

foetor, -ōris *m.* stench, foul smell

foliātum, -ī *n.* ointment made from spikenard leaves

folium, -(i)ī *n.* leaf, petal

folliculus, -ī *m.* small bag; chrysalis; inflated ball

follis, -is *m.* bag, purse; inflated ball; scrotum; *pl.* bellows

follītus, -a, -um *adj.* imprisoned in a sack

fōmentum, -ī *n.* poultice, fomentation; solace, remedy

fōmes, -itis *m.* tinderwood

fons, fontis *m.* spring, fount; spring-god; source, origin

fontānus, -a, -um *adj.* of *or* relating to a spring

fonticulus, -ī *m.* small spring

for, fārī, fātus 1. *dep.* to speak; say

forābilis, -is, -e *adj.* that may be pierced

forāmen, -inis *n.* aperture, hole

forās *adv.* to the outside, outdoors; out, forth

forceps, -cipis *f.* tongs, tweezers; shears

forda, -ae *f.adj.* pregnant (*of animals*)

fore *inf.* (*used as alternative future infinitive of* **sum**)

forem *subj.* (*used as alternative imperfect subjunctive of* **sum**)

forensis, -is, -e *adj.* of *or* relating to the marketplace; of *or* relating to law-courts; public; *n.pl.sbst.* public dress

forfex, -icis *f.* shears, clippers

forica, -ae *f.* public toilet

foris¹, -is *f.* door; entrance; *pl.* double door

forīs² *adv.* outside; away from Rome; from outside

forma, -ae *f.* form, shape; appearance; beauty; image, likeness; mould; diagram; outline; class, type

formālis, -is, -e *adj.* having a set pattern

formāmentum, -ī *n.* arrangement, conformation

formātor, -ōris *m.* one who forms, fashioner

formātūra, -ae *f.* forming, shaping; form

formīca, -ae *f.* ant

formīcīnus, -a, -um *adj.* moving like an ant

formīdābilis, -is, -e *adj.* terrifying, frightening

formīdō¹, -inis *f.* terror, dread; object of terror

formīdō² 1. to fear, dread

formīdulōsē (-dol-) *adv.* in a terrifying manner

formīdulōsus (-dol-), -a, -um *adj.* terrifying, frightening; frightened

formō 1. to shape, fashion, mould; represent; compose; regulate, order

formōsē *adv.* beautifully

formōsitās, -ātis *f.* beauty

formōsus, -a, -um *adj.* beautiful, handsome, pretty

formula, -ae *f.* formula; covenant; charter; rule; beauty

fornācālis, -is, -e *adj.* of *or* relating to ovens

fornācula, -ae *f.* small furnace

fornax, -ācis *f.* furnace, oven

fornicātiō, -ōnis *f.* arch, vaulting

fornicātus, -a, -um *adj.* arched, vaulted

fornix, -icis *m.* arch, vault; cellar; brothel

fornus *see* **furnus**

forō 1. to pierce, perforate

forpex, -icis *f.* tongs

fors, fortis *f.* chance, luck; accident; destiny

fors(it)(an) *adv.* (+*indic./subj.*) perhaps, perchance

fortasse(an) *adv.* (+*indic./subj.*) perhaps, possibly

fortassis *adv.* (+*indic./subj.*) perhaps, possibly, it may be (that)

forte *adv.* by chance; accidentally; perhaps

forticulus, -a, -um *adj.* rather brave

fortis, -is, -e *adj.* strong, powerful; brave, valiant; bold

fortiter *adv.* strongly, powerfully; bravely; boldly; energetically

fortitūdō, -inis *f.* strength; bravery; boldness; *pl.* deeds of bravery

fortuitō (-ītō) *adv.* by chance, accidentally; at random

fortuitus (-ītus), -a, -um *adj.* happening by chance, accidental; haphazard; *n.sbst.* chance event

fortūna, -ae *f.* chance, fortune; lot, destiny; good fortune; misfortune; status; *pl.* property

fortūnātē *adv.* with good fortune, prosperously

fortūnātus, -a, -um *adj.* fortunate, lucky; blessed; rich, prosperous

fortūnō 1. to make fortunate, bless

forulus, -ī *m.* bookshelf

forum, -ī *n.* public space, square; market, forum (*esp. at Rome*); court of law; **forum cēdere** to go bankrupt

forus, -ī *m.* gangway; *pl.* benches for spectators

fossa, -ae *f.* ditch, trench, moat

fossiō, -ōnis *f.* digging, excavation

fossor, -ōris *m.* one who digs, miner

fossūra, -ae *f.* digging, excavation

fovea, -ae *f.* pit; pitfall, trap

foveō, fōvī, fōtum 2. to make warm, heat; keep warm, foment; encourage; cherish; soothe

fractus, -a, -um *adj.* broken, rough; ruined, crushed; effeminate

frāga, -ōrum *n.pl.* strawberries

fragilis, -is, -e *adj.* brittle, fragile; weak, flimsy; uncertain, impermanent; crackling

fragilitās, -ātis *f.* uncertainty, impermanence

fragmen, -inis *n.* fragment, chip

fragmentum, -ī *n.* fragment, chip

fragor, -ōris *m.* crash, din; breaking up

fragōsus, -a, -um *adj.* brittle, fragile; broken, rough

fragrō 1. to smell strongly

framea, -ae *f.* German spear

frangō, frēgī, fractum 3. to break, smash, crush; break down, weaken; tame, subdue

frāter, -tris *m.* brother; cousin

frāterculus, -ī *m.* little brother

frāternē *adv.* in a brotherly manner

frāternitās, -ātis *f.* brotherhood, fraternity

frāternus, -a, -um *adj.* of *or* relating to brothers (*or* cousins), fraternal

frātricīda, -ae *m.* one who murders one's brother, fratricide

fraudātiō, -ōnis *f.* swindling, fraud

fraudātor, -ōris *m.* swindler, defrauder

fraudō 1. (+*abl.*) to swindle, defraud (of); embezzle

fraudulentia, -ae *f.* deceitfulness

fraudulentus, -a, -um *adj.* deceitful, fraudulent

fraus, -dis *f.* deceit, fraud; crime, offence; damage, harm; liability to punishment, guilt

fraxin(e)us, -a, -um *adj.* made of ash wood, ashen

fraxinus, -ī *f.* ash tree; ash; ashen spear

fremibundus (-meb-), -a, -um *adj.* roaring, rumbling

fremitus, -ūs *m.* roar, rumble; muttering, mumbling

fremō, -uī, -itum 3. to roar, rumble; mutter, mumble; complain noisily; demand noisily

fremor, -ōris *m.* roar, rumble

frēnātor, -ōris *m.* one who equips a horse with a bridle

frendō, frēsum 3. to gnash the teeth; grind up

frēniger, -era, -erum *adj.* having a bridle

frēnō 1. to equip with a bridle; restrain, check

frēnum, -ī (*pl.* -a or -ī) *n.* (*usu. pl.*) bridle, bit; restraint

frequens, -ntis *adj.* condensed, crowded; numerous; common, frequent

frequentātiō, -ōnis *f.* concentration, crowding

frequenter *adv.* in crowds; commonly, frequently

frequentia, -ae *f.* closely packed group, throng; abundance, multitude; frequency

frequentō 1. to make crowded, throng; assemble; frequent, haunt; do often; observe, attend

fretensis, -is, -e *adj.* of or relating to straits

fretum, -ī *n.* or **fretus, -ūs** *m.* strait, channel; (*usu. pl.*) sea, waters

frētus, -a, -um *adj.* (+*abl./dat.*) relying (on), confident (of)

fricō, -uī, -(ā)tum 1. to rub, rub down

frīgefactō 1. to make cold

frīgeō 2. to be cold; be inactive, be lifeless; fall flat, be coldly received

frīgerō 1. to make cold

frīgescō 3. to become cold, cool

frīgida, -ae *f.* cold water

frīgidārius, -a, -um *adj.* of or relating to cooling

frīgidē *adv.* without effect, flatly

frīgidulus, -a, -um *adj.* somewhat cold, chilly

frīgidus, -a, -um *adj.* cold, cool; lifeless, dull; chilling; flat, torpid

frīgō, frixī, frictum 3. to roast

frīgus, -oris *n.* cold, chilliness; lifelessness, dullness; flatness

friguttiō 4. to stammer, stutter

fringillus, -ī *m.* chaffinch

friō 1. to break into pieces, crumble

fritillus, -ī *m.* dice-box

frīvolus, -a, -um *adj.* worthless, trifling

frondātor, -ōris *m.* one who prunes trees

frondeō 2. to be in leaf, be leafy

frondescō 3. to become leafy

frondeus, -a, -um *adj.* covered with leaves, leafy

frondifer, -era, -erum *adj.* bearing leaves, leafy

frondōsus, -a, -um *adj.* abounding in leaves, leafy

frons¹, -ndis *f.* foliage, leaves

frons², -ntis *f./m.* forehead, brow; front side; outer face

frontālia, -ium *n.pl.* frontlet (*of an elephant's trappings*)

frontō, -ōnis *m.* one with a large forehead

fructifer, -era, -erum *adj.* bearing fruit, fruitful

fructuārius, -a, -um *adj.* fruitful, productive

fructuōsus, -a, -um *adj.* full of fruit, fruitful, productive; profitable

fructus, -ūs *m.* enjoyment; pleasure; fruit; profit

frūgālis, -is, -e *adj.* temperate, frugal

frūgālitās, -ātis *f.* temperance, frugality

frūgāliter *adv.* temperately, frugally

frūgī *indecl.adj.* temperate, frugal; honest

frūgifer, -era, -erum *adj.* fruit-bearing, fruitful

frūgiferens, -ntis *adj.* bringing fruit, fruitful

frūgilegus, -a, -um *adj.* grain-gathering

frūgiparus, -a, -um *adj.* grain-producing

frūmentārius, -a, -um *adj.* of *or* relating to corn *or* its distribution; *m.sbst.* corntrader

frūmentātiō, -ōnis *f.* foraging for provisions

frūmentātor, -ōris *m.* one who procures corn, forager

frūmentor 1. *dep.* to gather corn, forage

frūmentum, -ī *n.* corn, grain; cereal; *pl.* crops

frūniscor, frūnītus 3. *dep.* to enjoy

fruor, fructus or **fruitus** 3. *dep.* (*+abl./ acc.*) to enjoy, delight in; profit from

frustillātim *adv.* bit by bit

frustrā *adv.* in vain, to no effect; in error, mistakenly

frustrāmen, -inis *n.* error, deception

frustrātiō, -ōnis *f.* trick, deception

frustrātus, -ūs *m.* trick, deception

frustror 1. *dep.* or **frustrō** 1. to trick, deceive; frustrate, disappoint

frustulentus, -a, -um *adj.* full of crumbs

frustum, -ī *n.* crumb, morsel

frutex, -icis *m.* shrub, bush; blockhead, fool

fruticētum, -ī *n.* thicket of shrubs

fruticō 1. or **fruticor** 1. *dep.* to shoot out, become bushy

fruticōsus, -a, -um *adj.* full of shrubs; like a shrub, bushy

frux, frūgis *f.* (*usu. pl.*) fruit, crop; fruition; success, reward; morality, virtue

fūcātus, -a, -um *adj.* not genuine, fake

fūcō 1. to dye, colour; make up

fūcōsus, -a, -um *adj.* counterfeit, sham

fūcus¹, -ī *m.* seaweed; dye; disguise, sham

fūcus², -ī *m.* drone; bee-glue

fuga, -ae *f.* fleeing, flight; swift movement; avoidance; banishment; means of escape

fugāciter *adv.* evasively

fugax, -ācis *adj.* likely to flee, evasive; fleeting, swift

fugiens, -ntis *adj.* (*+gen.*) averse (to)

fugiō, fūgī 3. to flee, fly; escape; go into exile; vanish; flee from; avoid; escape the notice of

fugitans, -ntis *adj.* (*+gen.*) averse (to)

fugitō 1. to flee from; avoid; flee

fugitor, -ōris *m.* one who runs away, fugitive

fugō 1. to cause to flee, rout; drive into exile; dismiss, dispel

fulcīmen, -inis *n.* support, prop

fulciō, fulsī, fultum 4. to support, prop up; fortify, strengthen; oppress

fulcrum, -ī *n.* headrest (*of a couch*)

fulgeō, fulsī 2. or **fulgō** 3. to shine brightly, gleam; be bright, be distinguished; *impers.* it lightens, there is lightning

fulgidus, -a, -um *adj.* shining, bright

fulgor, -ōris *m.* flash of lightning; brightness, radiance; bright object; glory, splendour

fulgur, -uris *n.* flash of lightning; brightness

fulgurālis, -is, -e *adj.* of *or* relating to lightning

fulgurātor, -ōris *m.* one who interprets omens from lightning

fulgurītus, -a, -um *adj.* lightning-struck

fulgurō 1. to shine, gleam; *impers.* it lightens, there is lightning

fulica, -ae *f.* coot

fūlīgō, -inis *f.* soot

fulix, -icis *f.* coot

fullō, -ōnis *m.* fuller (*of clothes*)

fullōnia, -ae *f.* trade of clothes-fulling

fullōnius, -a, -um *adj.* of *or* relating to fulling

fulmen, -inis *n.* lightning, thunderbolt; sudden disaster, calamitous news

fulmenta, -ae *f.* support, prop

fulmineus, -a, -um *adj.* of *or* relating to lightning; like lightning, lightning-quick

fulminō 1. to cause lightning; strike with lightning; strike like lightning; *impers.* it lightens, there is lightning

fultūra, -ae *f.* support, prop

fulvus, -a, -um *adj.* deep yellow, tawny

fūmārium, -īī *n.* smoke-room (*for the maturation of wine*)

fūmeus, -a, -um *adj.* full of smoke, smoky

fūmidus, -a, -um *adj.* full of smoke, smoky; steaming

fūmifer, -era, -erum *adj.* producing smoke

fūmificō 1. to make smoke

fūmificus, -a, -um *adj.* making smoke

fūmō 1. to emit fumes, smoke, be smoky; give off steam

fūmōsus, -a, -um *adj.* full of smoke, smoky; smoked

fūmus, -ī *m.* smoke, fumes; steam; nothingness

fūnāle, -is *n.* wax torch; chandelier

fūnālis, -is, -e *adj.* made of rope; **equus fūnālis** trace-horse

fūnambulus, -ī *m.* rope-walker

functiō, -ōnis *f.* performance, execution

functus, -a, -um *adj.* dead; *m.pl.sbst.* the dead

funda, -ae *f.* sling; casting-net

fundāmen, -inis *n.* foundation

fundāmentum, -ī *n.* foundation, basis

fundātor, -ōris *m.* founder

fundātus, -a, -um *adj.* firmly founded

funditō 1. to pour out; attack with slings

funditor, -ōris *m.* slingsman, slinger

funditus *adv.* from the foundations; at the bottom; completely, wholly

fundō¹ 1. to lay the foundations of, base; institute, found

fundō², fūdī, fūsum 3. to pour; pour out; cast (*metals*); emit, stream; spread, scatter; put to flight; squander

fundus, -ī *m.* bottom, base; foundation, basis; farm, estate; **fundō** wholly

fūnebris, -is, -e *adj.* of *or* relating to a funeral, funereal; fatal, deadly; *n.pl.sbst.* funeral rites

fūnereus, -a, -um *adj.* of *or* suitable for a funeral, funerary; fatal, deadly

fūnerō 1. to carry out the funeral of, bury; consign to the grave, kill

fūnestō 1. to defile with murder; make mournful

fūnestus, -a, -um *adj.* of *or* suitable for a funeral, funereal; defiled by murder; deadly, fatal; grievous, lamentable

fungīnus, -a, -um *adj.* of *or* like a mushroom

fungor, functus 3. *dep.* (+*abl./acc.*) to perform, discharge; undergo, suffer; serve, act

fungus, -ī *m.* fungus, mushroom; blockhead, fool

fūniculus, -ī *m.* thin rope, cord

fūnis, -is *m.* rope, cable

fūnus, -eris *n.* funeral, funeral rites; death; dead body, corpse

fūr, fūris *m./f.* thief, robber

fūrācitās, -ātis *f.* thievishness

fūrāciter *adv.* in the manner of a thief

fūrax, -ācis *adj.* prone to stealing, thievish

furca, -ae *f.* two-pronged fork, pitch-fork; fork-shaped prop; fork-shaped rack of torture

furcifer, -rī *m.* one punished on the *furca*, gallows-bird

furcilla, -ae *f.* pitchfork

furcillō 1. to punish with a pitchfork

furcula, -ae *f.* small fork

furens, -ntis *adj.* mad, frenzied

furenter *adv.* madly, furiously

furfurēs, -um *m.pl.* bran

furia, -ae *f.* (*usu. pl.*) madness, frenzy; tormenting spirit; *pl.* goddesses of vengeance, Furies

furiālis, -is, -e *adj.* of *or* relating to the

Furies, avenging; Fury-like; maddening; mad, frenzied

furiāliter *adv.* like a Fury

furibundus, -a, -um *adj.* maddened, frenzied; enraged, furious

fūrīnus, -a, -um *adj.* of *or* relating to thieves

furiō 1. to madden, enrage

furiōsē *adv.* madly, furiously

furiōsus, -a, -um *adj.* full of madness, frenzied, wild

furnāria, -ae *f.* trade of a baker

furnus, -ī *m.* oven, bakehouse

furō 3. to be mad, frenzied, wild; rage, storm

fūror¹ 1. *dep.* to steal, thieve; withdraw stealthily

furor², -ōris *m.* madness, insanity; inspiration, ecstasy; rage, fury; frenzied action; passionate desire; object of passion

furtificus, -a, -um *adj.* thievish

furtim *adv.* stealthily, secretly; imperceptibly

furtīvē *adv.* stealthily, secretly

furtīvus, -a, -um *adj.* stolen, pilfered; stealthy, secret

furtō *adv.* stealthily, secretly

furtum, -ī *n.* stealing, theft; stolen property; deception, trick; secret deed

fūrunculus, -ī *m.* petty thief

furvus, -a, -um *adj.* dark-coloured, swarthy, dusky

fuscātor, -ōris *m.* one who makes dark

fuscina, -ae *f.* three-pronged fork, trident

fuscō 1. to make dark, darken; become dark

fuscus, -a, -um *adj.* dark-coloured, dusky; dark; hoarse, indistinct

fūsē *adv.* widely, loosely; fully, at length

fūsilis, -is, -e *adj.* fusible; liquid, molten

fūsiō, -ōnis *f.* pouring; effusion

fustis, -is *m.* stick, cudgel, club

fustitudinus, -a, -um *adj.* stick-beating

fustuārium, -(i)ī *n.* cudgelling to death

fūsus¹, -a, -um *adj.* widespread; loose, expansive

fūsus², -ī *m.* spindle

fūtil- see **futtil-**

futtile *adv.* in vain, to no effect

futtilis, -is, -e *adj.* vain, futile; ineffective; fragile, brittle

futtilitās, -ātis *f.* vanity, futility

futuō, -uī, -ūtum 3. to have sex with, fuck

futūrum, -ī *n.* the future; *pl.* future events

futūrus, -a, -um *adj.* that is to be, future; imminent, impending

futūtiō, -ōnis *f.* sex

futūtor, -ōris *m.* man who has sex

futūtrix, -īcis *f.adj.* having sex, fucking

G

gabata, -ae f. unknown dish

gaesum, -ī n. Gallic spear

gāïolus, -ī m. kind of sweet delicacy

galbaneus, -a, -um adj. of or relating to galbanum

galbanum, -ī m. resin from a Syrian plant, galbanum

galbeus, -ī m. ornamental armband

galbinātus, -a, -um adj. wearing greenish-yellow

galbinus, -a, -um adj. greenish-yellow; n.pl.sbst. greenish-yellow garments

galea, -ae f. helmet

galeātus, -a, -um adj. wearing a helmet

galēriculum, -ī n. cap, wig

galērītus, -a, -um adj. wearing a skin cap

galērus, -ī m. skin cap, wig; ceremonial religious cap

galla, -ae f. gall-nut

galliambos, -ī m. metre used in the worship of Cybele

gallica, -ae f. sandal worn by the Gauls

gallīna, -ae f. hen

gallīnāceus, -a, -um adj. of or relating to hens or poultry

gallīnārius, -(i)ī m. one who keeps poultry

gallīnula, -ae f. chick

gallus, -ī m. cockerel

gānea, -ae f. or **gāneum, -ī** n. vulgar eating house, cook-shop; gluttony

gāneō, -ōnis m. glutton, debauchee

ganniō 4. to snarl; speak menacingly

gannītus, -ūs m. snarling; menacing speech; murmuring

garriō 4. to chatter, jabber; talk nonsense

garrulitās, -ātis f. talkativeness, garrulity

garrulus, -a, -um adj. talkative, garrulous; babbling

garum, -ī n. rich fish sauce

gaudeō, gāvīsus sum 2. semi-dep. (+abl.) to be glad (about), rejoice (in), be pleased (with); (+acc.+inf.) rejoice (that); (+acc.) be glad at

gaudium, -(i)ī n. delight, joy; source of joy

gaulus, -ī m. bucket

gausapa, -ae f. or **gausape, -is** n. woollen cloth; woollen cloak

gausapātus, -a, -um adj. wearing a gausapa

gausapinus, -a, -um adj. made of woollen cloth; f.sbst. cloak of this material

gāza, -ae f. treasure, riches

gelasīnus, -ī m. dimple

gelida, -ae f. ice-cold water

gelidē adv. unenthusiastically, coldly

gelidus, -a, -um adj. cold, icy, frozen

gelō 1. to cause to freeze, chill; congeal

gelū, -ūs or **gelum, -ī** n. frost, ice; cold, chilliness

gemebundus, -a, -um adj. full of groaning

gemellipara, -ae f.adj. twin-bearing

gemellus, -a, -um adj. twin-born; double; alike

geminātiō, -ōnis f. doubling

geminō 1. to double, duplicate; become double; pair, unite

geminus, -a, -um adj. twin-born; double, twofold; alike; sbst. twin, pair

gemitus, -ūs m. groaning, moaning

gemma, -ae f. jewel, gem; crystal; signet; bud

gemmans, -ntis adj. bejewelled; glittering, decorated

gemmātus, -a, -um adj. bejewelled

gemmeus, -a, -um adj. made of precious stone; bejewelled

gemmifer, -era, -erum adj. containing jewels; bejewelled

gemmō 1. to come into bud

gemō 3. to groan, moan; grieve for

gena, -ae f. cheek; eyelid; pl. the eyes

geneālogus, -ī m. genealogist

gener, -rī m. son-in-law

generālis, -is, -e adj. generic; relating to character; general

generāliter adv. generally, unspecifically

generascō 3. to come into being

generātim adv. by classes or species; separately; generally

generātor, -ōris m. generator, father

generō 1. to beget, create, produce

generōsē adv. nobly

generōsitās, -ātis f. nobility of breeding

generōsus, -a, -um adj. high-born, of good stock; noble

genesis, -is f. horoscope, nativity

genethliacon, -ī n. birthday poem

genetīvus, -a, -um adj. of or relating to birth; genitive

genetrix, -īcis f. mother, foundress

geniālis, -is, -e adj. of or relating to marriage; festive, merry

geniāliter adv. with good cheer

geniculātus, -a, -um adj. having nodes

genista, -ae f. broom-plant, greenweed

genitābilis, -is, -e adj. causing growth

genitālia, -ium n.pl. genitals

genitālis, -is, -e adj. creative, reproductive; **diēs genitālis** birthday

genitāliter adv. reproductively

genitor, -ōris m. creator, father

genitūra, -ae f. horoscope

genius, -(i)ī m. divine spirit of a gens, genius; talent

genō 3. to create, engender

gens, gentis f. race, nation; Roman clan, family

genticus, -a, -um adj. of or relating to a nation

gentīlicius, -a, -um adj. of or relating to a Roman gens

gentīlis, -is, -e adj. of or relating to a Roman gens; tribal, native; m.sbst. member of the same gens

gentīlitās, -ātis f. relationship between members of the same gens

genū, -ūs n. knee

genuālia, -ium n.pl. ornamental kneebands

genuīnus, -a, -um adj. natural, innate; m.sbst. molar tooth

genus[1], -eris n. birth, origin; descendants; race; kind, class; method

genus[2] see **genū**

geōgraphia, -ae f. geographical work

geōmetrēs, -ae m. geometrician

geōmetri(c)a, -ae f. geometry

geōmetricus, -a, -um adj. of or relating to geometry; n.pl.sbst. geometry

germāna, -ae f. (blood) sister

germānitās, -ātis f. relationship between siblings; germaneness

germānus[1], -a, -um adj. born of the same parents; genuine, proper

germānus[2], -ī m. (blood) brother

germen, -inis n. sprout, bud

germinō 1. to sprout, bud; grow

gerō, gessī, gestum 3. to bear, carry; produce; exhibit; administer, perform; treat

gerrae interj. nonsense!

gerrēs, -is m.(?) unknown fish of little esteem

gerrō, -ōnis m. blockhead, buffoon

gerulifigulus, -ī m. comic word for lay worker

gerulus, -ī m. porter, carrier

gerūsia, -ae f. building housing a council of elders

gesta, -ōrum n.pl. deeds, business

gestāmen, -inis n. something worn on the body

gestātiō, -ōnis f. riding, carrying; walkway

gestātor, -ōris m. rider, carrier

gestātōrius, -a, -um adj. for carrying

gesticulātiō, -ōnis f. gesticulation

gesticulor 1. dep. to perform by mime

gestiō[1] 4. to exult; desire, long

gestiō[2], -ōnis f. performance, action

gestitō 1. to carry continually

gestō 1. to carry about, wear; take for a ride

gestor, -ōris m. carrier

gestus, -ūs m. bodily movement, gesture; attitude

geuma, -atis n. taster, little bit

gibba, -ae f. hump

gibber, -era, -erum adj. hump-backed

gibberōsus, -a, -um adj. hump-backed

gibbus, -ī m. bodily lump, protuberance

gignentia, -ium n.pl. vegetation, greenery

gignō, genuī, genitum 3. to create, bear; produce

gilvus, -a, -um adj. pale yellow

gingīva, -ae *f.* gum (*of the mouth*)
glaber, -bra, -brum *adj.* hairless, shorn; *m.sbst.* effeminate slave
glabrāria, -ae *f.* shorn sheep
glaciālis, -is, -e *adj.* icy, frozen
glaciēs, -ēī *f.* ice
glaciō 1. to freeze, turn to ice
gladiātor, -ōris *m.* gladiator; assassin; *pl.* gladiatorial show
gladiātōrium, -iī *n.* gladiator's wage
gladiātōrius, -a, -um *adj.* of *or* relating to gladiators, gladiatorial
gladiātūra, -ae *f.* gladiatorial profession
gladius, -(i)ī *m.* sword
glandifer, -era, -erum *adj.* acorn-bearing
glandiōnida, -ae *m.* 'son of tenderloins'
glandium, -(i)ī *n.* tenderloin
glandulae, -ārum *f.pl.* pig's testicles
glans, -ndis *f.* acorn, beechmast; missile of a sling
glārea, -ae *f.* gravel
glāreōsus, -a, -um *adj.* full of gravel
glaucina, -ōrum *n.pl.* unguent
glaucūma, -ae *f.* cataract
glaucus, -a, -um *adj.* grey-blue, grey-green
glēba, -ae *f.* clod (*of earth*); soil; mass, lump; *pl.* land
glēbula, -ae *f.* small piece of land
glēsum, -ī *n.* amber
glīs, glīris *m.* dormouse
gliscō 3. to swell, fill out; grow in force
globōsus, -a, -um *adj.* round, spherical
globus, -ī *m.* spherical mass, sphere; dense mass (*esp. of men*); clique
glomerāmen, -inis *n.* mass, aggregation
glomerō 1. to gather into a ball; mass together, collect; race across
glomus, -eris *n.* spherical mass
glōria, -ae *f.* glory, honour; vainglory; glorious deed *or* object
glōriātiō, -ōnis *f.* boasting
glōriola, -ae *f.* small glory
glōrior 1. *dep.* to boast; glory in
glōriōsē *adv.* gloriously; boastingly
glōriōsus, -a, -um *adj.* glorious; boastful; ambitious
glūbō 3. to peel
glūten, -inis *n.* glue
glūtinātor, -ōris *m.* one who glues papyrus strips to form a roll
glūtinō 1. to glue
gluttiō 4. to swallow down

gluttus, -ūs *m.* swallowing, gulp
gnāritās, -ātis *f.* knowledge
gnāruris, -is, -e *adj.* knowledgeable
gnārus, -a, -um *adj.* (+*gen.*) knowledgeable (in); well-known
gnāt- see **nāt-**
gnāv- see **nāv-**
gōbius, -iī *or* **gōbiō, -ōnis** *m.* small fish, gudgeon
gonger see **conger**
gōrȳtos, -ī *m.* quiver
grabātus, -ī *m.* low couch, camp-bed
gracilis, -is, -e *adj.* slim, slender; narrow; light
gracilitās, -ātis *f.* slimness, slenderness
grāculus, -ī *m.* jackdaw
gradārius, -a, -um *adj.* steadily paced
gradātim *adv.* by steps, progressively
gradātiō, -ōnis *f.* gradation
gradātus, -a, -um *adj.* gradated, in steps
gradior, gressus 3. *dep.* to proceed, walk
gradus, -ūs *m.* step, stride; position; rank; degree; *pl.* steps, stairs
graecissō 1. to act like the Greeks
graecor 1. *dep.* to act like the Greeks
grallātor, -ōris *m.* stilt-walker
grāmen, -inis *n.* grass; herb
grāmineus, -a, -um *adj.* grassy; consisting of grass
grammatica, -ae *or* **-ē, -ēs** *f.* philology, grammar
grammaticus¹, -a, -um *adj.* of *or* relating to grammar
grammaticus², -ī *m.* scholar of grammar, grammarian
grānārium, -(i)ī *n.* granary
grandaevus, -a, -um *adj.* of a great age, elderly
grandescō 3. to grow in size, swell
grandiculus, -a, -um *adj.* quite large, biggish
grandifer, -era, -erum *adj.* bearing large crops
grandiloquus, -a, -um *adj.* loftily *or* arrogantly speaking
grandinat 1. *impers.* it is hailing
grandiō 4. to increase, make large
grandis, -is, -e *adj.* full-grown, large; immense; important; grand
grandiscāpius, -a, -um *adj.* (*of trees*) having a wide trunk

granditās, -ātis *f.* grandeur, grandiloquence

grandō, -inis *f.* hail; missile

grānifer, -era, -erum *adj.* grain-carrying

grānum, -ī *n.* grain, seed, pip

graphiārius, -a, -um *adj.* of *or* relating to a stylus; *n.sbst.* case for a stylus

graphicē *adv.* perfectly, properly

graphicus, -a, -um *adj.* perfect, exquisite

graphium, -ī *n.* pointed writing instrument, stylus

grassātor, -ōris *m.* street-robber

grassātūra, -ae *f.* street-robbery

grassor 1. *dep.* to advance, wander; prowl; run riot

grātē *adv.* gratefully, gladly

grātēs, -ium *f.pl.* thanks, thanksgivings; **grātēs agere** to give thanks

grātia, -ae *f.* favour, regard; kindness; thanks, gratitude; requital; charm; motive; **grātiās (-am) agere** to give thanks

grātificātiō, -ōnis *f.* complaisance, favour

grātificor 1. *dep.* to gratify, oblige; (+*acc.*) bestow

grātiōsus, -a, -um *adj.* popular, influential; friendly

grātor 1. *dep.* to congratulate

grātuitō (-uītō) *adv.* without payment, freely

grātuitus (-uītus), -a, -um *adj.* free of charge, gratuitous; unprofitable; unprovoked

grātulābundus, -a, -um *adj.* full of congratulations

grātulātiō, -ōnis *f.* thanksgiving; congratulation; rejoicing

grātulātor, -ōris *m.* one who congratulates

grātulor 1. *dep.* (+*dat.*) to congratulate, give thanks to; rejoice

grātus, -a, -um *adj.* grateful; deserving thanks; popular; pleasant

gravātē (-im) *adv.* reluctantly

gravēdinōsus (-vīd-), -a, -um *adj.* prone to catarrh

gravēdō (-vīdō), -inis *f.* catarrh, cold

graveolens, -ntis *adj.* reeking, foul-smelling

gravescō 3. to become weighed down; worsen, strengthen

graviditās, -ātis *f.* pregnancy

gravidō 1. to make pregnant

gravidus, -a, -um *adj.* full, laden; swollen; pregnant

gravis, -is, -e *adj.* heavy, burdensome; pregnant; low in pitch; unpleasant; serious, stern; important

gravitās, -ātis *f.* weight, heaviness; oppressiveness; seriousness, sternness; importance

graviter *adv.* heavily; with low pitch; unpleasantly; seriously; intensely

gravō 1. to weigh down, oppress; aggravate

gregālis, -is, -e *adj.* common, rank and file; *m.sbst.* crony (*of a party*), comrade

gregārius, -a, -um *adj.* common, belonging to the rank and file; *m.sbst.* common soldier

gregātim *adv.* in herds *or* flocks

gregō 1. to herd together

gremium, -(i)ī *n.* lap, bosom; female genitals; inner depths

gressus, -ūs *m.* stepping, walking

grex, -gis *m./f.* herd, flock; company, clique

grundītus, -ūs *m.* grunting

grūs, gruis *f.* crane (the bird)

gryps, grȳpos *m.* griffin

gubernābilis, -is, -e *adj.* controllable

gubernāc(u)lum, -ī *n.* steering oar, helm

gubernātiō, -ōnis *f.* steering, control

gubernātor, -ōris *m.* helmsman, controller

gubernātrix, -īcis *f.* female controller

gubernō 1. to steer, control; govern

gubernum, -ī *n.* steering oar

gula, -ae *f.* throat, gullet; appetite

gulōsus, -a, -um *adj.* fond of dainty food, luxurious; *m.sbst.* lover of dainty food

gurges, -itis *m.* whirlpool, eddy; river, waters

gurguliō, -ōnis *m.* throat, gullet

gurgustium, -(i)ī *n.* drinking hovel

gustātōrium, -iī *n.* tray for hors d'oeuvres

gustātus, -ūs *m.* tasting, taste

gustō 1. to taste, sip; have a little experience of

gustus, -ūs *m.* tasting, taste; hors d'oeuvre

gutta, -ae *f.* drop; speck

guttātim *adv.* drop by drop

guttātus, -a, -um *adj.* speckled

guttula, -ae *f.* tiny drop

guttur, -uris *n./m.* throat

guttus (gūtus), -ī *m.* narrow flask

gymnas, -adis *f.* athletic match

gymnasiarchus, -ī *m.* overseer of a gymnasium

gym(i)nasium, -(i)ī *n.* centre for athletic practice, gymnasium

gymnasticus, -a, -um *adj.* gymnastic

gymnicus, -a, -um *adj.* of *or* relating to the gymnasium, gymnastic

gynaecīum (-ēum), -(ī)ī *n.* women's quarters (in a Greek house)

gynaecōnītis see **gynaecīum**

gypsātus, -a, -um *adj.* whitened with gypsum

gypsō 1. to whiten with gypsum

gypsum, -ī *n.* gypsum, plaster

gȳrus, -ī *m.* race circuit; orbit; circle

habēna, -ae *f.* rein; strap, cord
habeō 2. to have, possess; retain; know; (+*adv.*) be disposed (in such a way)
habilis, -is, -e *adj.* easy to handle, tractable
habilitās, -ātis *f.* aptitude
habitābilis, -is, -e *adj.* inhabitable
habitātiō, -ōnis *f.* residence, habitation; rent
habitātor, -ōris *m.* inhabitant
habitō 1. to inhabit; dwell, live
habitūdō, -inis *f.* physical appearance
habituriō 4. to be eager to have
habitus¹, -ūs *m.* condition; physical appearance; character, demeanour; style of dress
habitus², -a, -um *adj.* in good condition
habrotonum, -ī *n.* or **-us, -ī** *m.* aromatic plant
hāc *adv.* by this way, thus; on this side
hāctenus *adv.* thus far, this much; until now
haedilia, -ae *f.* small female kid
haedillus, -ī *m.* small kid
haedīnus, -a, -um *adj.* of *or* relating to a kid
haedulus, -ī *m.* small kid
haedus, -ī *m.* kid, young goat
haemorrhois, -idos *f.* snake whose bite caused bodily bleeding
haereō, -sī, -sum 2. (+*dat.*) to cling (to), stick (to); be motionless; be in difficulty
haerescō 3. to stick together
haeresis, -is *f.* philosophical school
haesitābundus, -a, -um *adj.* full of hesitation
haesitantia, -ae *f.* hesitancy
haesitātiō, -ōnis *f.* hesitation, faltering
haesitātor, -ōris *m.* hesitater
haesitō 1. to stick; hesitate, falter
ha(ha)hae *interj.* haha! (*cry of amusement*)

haliāetos, -ī *m.* osprey
halica see **alica**
hālitus, -ūs *m.* exhalation, breath; vapour
hallec see **allec**
hālō 1. to exhale; give off a scent
halōs, -ō *f.* halo
halōsis, -is *f.* capture
halter, -ēris *m.* handheld weight to aid jumping athletes
(h)ama, -ae *f.* water-bucket
hāmātilis, -is, -e *adj.* using hooks
hāmātus, -a, -um *adj.* hooked, barbed; crooked
hāmiōta, -ae *m.* fisherman
hammodytēs, -ae *m.* sand-viper
hāmulus, -ī *m.* small hook
hāmus, -ī *m.* hook; barb
haphē, -ēs *f.* sand sprinkled on wrestlers
hara, -ae *f.* sty, pen
(h)arēna, -ae *f.* sand; desert; arena of amphitheatre
harēnāria, -ae *f.* sand-pit
harēnivagus, -a, -um *adj.* sand-wandering
(h)arēnōsus, -a, -um *adj.* sandy; sand-like
hariola, -ae *f.* prophetess
(h)ariolor 1. *dep.* to prophesy, divine
hariolus, -ī *m.* prophet, diviner
harmonia, -ae *f.* melody; concord, harmony
harpagō¹, -ōnis *m.* grappling hook; rapacious person
harpagō² 1. to steal, seize
harpastum, -ī *n.* handball
harpē, -ēs *f.* scimitar
harundifer, -era, -erum *adj.* reed-bearing
harundinētum, -ī *n.* reed-bed
harundineus, -a, -um *adj.* made of reed; full of reeds
harundinōsus, -a, -um *adj.* full of reeds

(h)arundō, -inis f. reed; fishing rod; pastoral pipe

(h)aruspex, -icis m. diviner who inspects entrails, prophet

haruspica, -ae f. female *haruspex*

haruspicīnus, -a, -um adj. of or relating to the practice of *haruspices*; **f.sg.sbst.** divination by a *haruspex*

(h)aruspicium, -(i)ī n. divination from inspecting entrails

hasta, -ae f. spear, javelin

hastātus¹, -a, -um adj. armed with spears

hastātus², -ī m. spearman; pl. front-line soldiers of the Roman army

hastīle, -is n. spear shaft; spear

hastula, -ae f. stem, shoot

haud (haut) part. not, by no means

hauddum adv. not yet

hau(d)quāquam adv. by no means, not at all

hauriō, -sī, -stum 4. to draw (up); drink; absorb; draw (*blood*); devour, exhaust

haustor, -ōris m. drinker

haustrum, -ī n. scoop (*of a water wheel*)

haustus, -ūs m. drawing (up); drinking, swallowing; absorption

hebdomas, -ados f. fever occurring every seventh day

hebenus, -ī m. ebony

hebeō 2. to be blunt; be inactive; grow dim

hebes, -etis adj. blunt; sluggish; stupid; dim, faint

hebescō 3. to grow blunt; become sluggish; grow faint

hebetātiō, -ōnis f. blunting

hebetō 1. to make blunt; make sluggish; make faint, dull

hecatombē, -ēs f. sacrifice of one hundred animals

hedera, -ae f. ivy

hederiger, -era, -erum adj. ivy-bearing

hederōsus, -a, -um adj. ivy-covered

hēdycrum, -ī n. fragrant ointment

(h)eia interj. ah! (*exclam. of desperation, deprecation, surprise*); come on!

helciārius, -iī m. one who drags boats with a tow-rope

helica, -ae f. spiral

hellebor- see **ellebor-**

helluātiō, -ōnis f. debauch

helluō, -ōnis m. debauchee, glutton

helluor 1. dep. to gourmandize, squander

hem interj. well!; alas!; what's that?

hēmerodromos, -ī m. courier

hēmicyclium, -(i)ī n. semicircular seat

hēmīna, -ae f. measure of capacity, half a *sextarius*

hēmitritaeus, -a, -um adj. suffering from a semitertian fever; **m.sbst.** semitertian fever

hendecasyllabus, -ī m. verse of eleven syllables (*esp. Phalaecean hendecasyllabic*)

hēpatiārius, -a, -um adj. of or relating to the liver

heptēris, -is f. ship with seven banks of oars

hera see **era**

herba, -ae f. herb, weed; grass

herbescō 3. to grow into blades, shoot

herbeus, -a, -um adj. grass-green

herbidus, -a, -um adj. full of grass, grassy

herbifer, -era, -erum adj. bearing herbs; grassy

herbigradus, -a, -um adj. going over grass

herbōsus, -a, -um adj. full of grass, grassy

herbula, -ae f. small herb

herc(u)le interj. by God! (*exclam. of strong feeling*)

hērēditārius, -a, -um adj. of or relating to inheritance; hereditary

hērēditās, -ātis f. hereditary succession; inheritance

hērēdium, -iī n. hereditary estate

hērēs, -ēdis m. heir, successor

heri (-ī) adv. yesterday

hērōicus, -a, -um adj. of or relating to the heroes, heroic

hērōīnē, -ēs or **-a, -ae** f. heroine

hērōis, -idos f. heroine

hērōs, -ōos m. hero (*mythical or real*)

hērōus, -a, -um adj. heroic; of or relating to epic verse; **m.pl.sbst.** dactylic hexameter verse

herus see **erus**

hesternus, -a, -um adj. of or relating to yesterday

hetaeria, -ae f. fraternity, society

heu interj. alas!, woe!

heus interj. hello there!, hallo!

hexaclīnon, -ī n. couch for six diners

hexameter, -tra, -trum adj. having six metrical feet

hexaphorum, -ī n. litter carried by six men

hexēris, -is f. ship with six banks of oars

hiātus, -ūs *m.* gaping; fissure, chasm; prosodic hiatus

hīberna, -ōrum *n.pl.* winter quarters; time spent wintering there

hībernāculum, -ī *n.* winter apartment

hībernō 1. to spend the winter

hībernus, -a, -um *adj.* of *or* relating to winter; wintry

hibiscum, -ī *n.* marshmallow

hīc¹, haec, hoc *pron.* this one *or* thing, he, she, it; *adj.* this; **ille ... hīc** the former ... the latter

hīc² *adv.* here, in this place; at this point

hiemālis, -is, -e *adj.* of *or* relating to the winter; wintry

hiemō 1. to be wintry; spend the winter

hiem(p)s, -mis *f.* winter; extreme cold; stormy weather

hieronīca, -ae *m.* victor in the games

hietō 1. to gape

hilarē (-e) *adv.* cheerfully

hilariculus, -a, -um *adj.* rather cheerful

hilaris, -is, -e *adj.* cheerful, light-hearted, buoyant

hilaritās, -ātis *f.* cheerfulness

hilaritūdō, -inis *f.* cheerfulness

hilarō 1. to cheer, gladden

hilarulus, -a, -um *adj.* rather cheerful

hilarus see **hilaris**

hilla, -ae *f.* intestine stuffed with meat

hīlum, -ī *n.* smallest bit, minimal part

hinc *adv.* from this place, hence, next

hinniō 4. to whinny

hinnītus, -ūs *m.* whinnying

hīnuleus see **īnuleus**

hiō 1. to gape; be greedy (for); be in hiatus

hippagōgos, -ī *f.* ship for transporting cavalry

hippocentaurus, -ī *m.* centaur

hippodromus, -ī *m.* hippodrome

hippomanes, -is *n.* mucous discharge from mares in heat

hippopērae, -ārum *f.pl.* saddle-bags

hippotoxota, -ae *m.* archer on horseback

hīra, -ae *f.* intestine

hircīnus (-quīnus), -a, -um *adj.* made of goatskin; like a goat

hircōsus, -a, -um *adj.* smelling like a goat

hircus, -ī *m.* he-goat

hirnea¹, -ae *f.* hernea, rupture

hirnea², -ae *f.* jug, can

hirsūtus, -a, -um *adj.* hairy, shaggy; covered with foliage

hirtus, -a, -um *adj.* hairy, shaggy; rough

hirūdō, -inis *f.* leech

hirundinīnus, -a, -um *adj.* of *or* relating to a swallow

hirundō, -inis *f.* swallow

hiscō 3. to gape; utter

hispidus, -a, -um *adj.* hairy, shaggy; rough

historia, -ae *f.* inquiry; learning; history; narrative

historicē *adv.* in historiographical fashion

historicus¹, -a, -um *adj.* of *or* relating to historiography

historicus², -ī *m.* researcher, historian

histriō, -ōnis *m.* actor, pantomimer

histriōnālis, -is, -e *adj.* of *or* relating to actors

histriōnia, -ae *f.* acting

hiulcē *adv.* disjointedly

hiulcō 1. to split open

hiulcus, -a, -um *adj.* open-mouthed, gaping; causing hiatus

hōc *adv.* to this place, hither

hōcusque *adv.* to this degree

hodiē *adv.* today, now

hodiernus, -a, -um *adj.* of *or* relating to today

holitor, -ōris *m.* vegetable-grower

holitōrius, -a, -um *adj.* of *or* relating to vegetables

(h)olus, -eris *n.* vegetable

holuscula, -ōrum *n.pl.* mere vegetables

homicīda, -ae *m.* murderer

homicīdium, -iī *n.* homicide, murder

homō, -inis *m.* man, person, human

homoeomerīa, -ae *f.* similarity of parts

homullus see **homunciō**

homunciō, -ōnis *m.* mere man, mortal; puny man

homunculus see **homunciō**

honestāmentum, -ī *n.* ornament

honestās, -ātis *f.* honour; integrity

honestē *adv.* honourably; decently

honestō 1. to honour, make honourable; adorn

honestum, -ī *n.* virtue, morality

honestus, -a, -um *adj.* honourable, respectable; well-born; handsome

honor (-ōs), -ōris *m.* honour, respect; public office; grace; Honour, personified as a god

honōrābilis, -is, -e *adj.* bringing honour

honōrārius, -a, -um *adj.* given voluntarily, complimentary

honōrātus, -a, -um *adj.* honoured (*esp. by public office*)

honōrificē *adv.* with honour, respectfully

honōrificus, -a, -um *adj.* conferring honour

honōrō 1. to honour

honōrus, -a, -um *adj.* conferring honour

(h)oplomachus, -ī *m.* heavily armed gladiator

hōra, -ae *f.* hour; season

hōraeus, -a, -um *adj.* seasonable

hordeāceus, -a, -um *adj.* of barley

hordeia, -ae *f.* kind of fish

hordeum, -ī *n.* barley

hōr(e)ia, -ae *f.* fishing boat

hōriola, -ae *f.* small fishing boat

hornō *adv.* this year

hornōtinus, -a, -um *adj.* of this year's production

hornus, -a, -um *adj.* of *or* relating to this year

hōrologium, -(i)ī *n.* sundial, water-clock

hōroscopus, -ī *m.* horoscope

horrendus, -a, -um *adj.* fearful, terrible

horreō 2. to stand erect, bristle; be rough; shudder (at)

horrescō 3. to become erect, bristle; shudder (at)

horreum, -ī *n.* granary

horribilis, -is, -e *adj.* fearful

horridē *adv.* roughly; harshly

horridulus, -a, -um *adj.* rather rough; shivering; somewhat erect

horridus, -a, -um *adj.* rough; harsh; shivering; unpolished

horrifer, -era, -erum *adj.* frightening; chilling

horrificē *adv.* in a frightening manner

horrificō 1. to make rough; terrify

horrificus, -a, -um *adj.* frightening

horrisonus, -a, -um *adj.* making a dreadful sound

horror, -ōris *m.* bristling, shuddering; roughness; fear; object of terror

horsum *adv.* hither

hortāmen, -inis *n.* encouragement, incentive

hortāmentum, -ī *n.* encouragement, incentive

hortātiō, -ōnis *f.* exhortation

hortātor, -ōris *m.* inciter, encourager

hortātrix, -īcis *f.* female inciter

hortātus, -ūs *m.* exhortation

hortor 1. *dep.* to incite, encourage

hortulus, -ī *m.* small garden *or* park

hortus, -ī *m.* garden, plot, park

hospes¹, -itis *m.* host; guest; stranger

hospes², -itis *adj.* acting as a host; foreign

hospita¹, -ae *f.* hostess; female guest; stranger

hospita², -ae *f.adj.* providing hospitality; acting as a guest; foreign

hospitālis, -is, -e *adj.* of *or* relating to hospitality; hospitable

hospitālitās, -ātis *f.* hospitality

hospitāliter *adv.* in a hospitable manner

hospitium, -(i)ī *n.* hospitality; accommodation

hospitor 1. *dep.* to put up as a guest

hostia, -ae *f.* sacrificial victim

hostiātus, -a, -um *adj.* provided with a sacrificial victim

hosticum, -ī *n.* enemy territory

hosticus, -a, -um *adj.* of the enemy; foreign

hostificus, -a, -um *adj.* hostile

hostīlis, -is, -e *adj.* of the enemy; hostile

hostīliter *adv.* in a hostile manner

hostīmentum, -ī *n.* compensation

hostiō 4. to recompense

hostis, -is *m./f.* stranger; (personal) enemy

hūc *adv.* to this place, hither

hūcusque *adv.* thus far

hui *interj.* ha! (*exclam. of surprise*)

hūmānē *adv.* reasonably; courteously

hūmānitās, -ātis *f.* human nature; civility; kindness

hūmāniter *adv.* reasonably; courteously

hūmānitus *adv.* humanly; humanely

hūmānus, -a, -um *adj.* human; humane, refined

humātiō, -ōnis *f.* burial

humātor, -ōris *m.* burier

humerus see **umerus**

hūmidus see **ūmidus**

humilis, -is, -e *adj.* low; lowly, humble; mean

humilitās, -ātis *f.* lowness; humbleness; humility

humiliter *adv.* at a low level; abjectly

humō 1. to bury, perform funeral rites for

hūmor see **ūmor**

humus, -ī *f.* earth, ground, soil

hyacinthinus, -a, -um *adj.* of hyacinth; hyacinth-coloured

hyacinthus, -ī *m.* flower (*perhaps* the iris)

hyaena, -ae *f.* hyena

hyalus, -ī *m.* glass

hybrida, -ae *m.* half-bred creature

hydra, -ae *f.* the monster Hydra; the Echidna; snake

hydraula, -ae *m.* player of the water-organ

hydraulicus, -a, -um *adj.* powered by piped water

hydraulus, -ī *m.* water-organ

hydria, -ae *f.* water-jug

hydrocēlē, -ēs *f.* scrotal swelling

hydrōpicus, -a, -um *adj.* suffering from dropsy

hydrops, -ōpis *m.* dropsy

hydrus, -ī *m.* water-snake

hyperbaton, -ī *n.* transposition of words

hyperbolē, -ēs *f.* exaggeration

hypocauston, -ī *n.* underground heating system of air channels

hypocrita, -ae *m.* actor

hypodidasculus, -ī *m.* assistant teacher

hypomnēma, -atis *n.* aide-memoire

hypothēca, -ae *f.* security for a loan

hystericus, -a, -um *adj.* suffering pain in the womb

iaceō, -uī, -tum 2. to lie, rest; recline; lie dead; lie in ruins; be idle

iaciō, iēcī, iactum 3. to throw; throw down *or* away; emit; utter

iactans, -ntis *adj.* arrogant, proud

iactanter *adv.* arrogantly

iactantia, -ae *f.* boasting; ostentation

iactātiō, -ōnis *f.* tossing, flinging; boasting; flaunting

iactātor, -ōris *m.* (+*gen.*) one who boasts (of)

iactātus, -ūs *m.* tossing, flinging

iactitō 1. to throw; boast of

iactō 1. to throw, toss; throw away; brandish; utter forcibly; brag about; flaunt; *refl.* boast, show off

iactūra, -ae *f.* throwing away; loss; cost

iactus, -ūs *m.* throwing; tossing away; emission; range (*of missiles*)

iaculābilis, -is, -e *adj.* able to be thrown

iaculātor, -ōris *m.* one who throws; spear-thrower

iaculātrix, -īcis *f.* female spear-thrower

iaculor 1. *dep.* to throw a spear; throw; strike with a spear

iaculum, -ī *n.* spear, javelin; casting net

iaculus, -a, -um *adj.* used for casting; *m.sbst.* snake that leaps onto its prey

iālūnitās see **iēiūnitās**

iam *adv.* now, already

iambēus, -a, -um *adj.* iambic

iambicus, -a, -um *adj.* iambic

iambus, -ī *m.* foot of a short then a long syllable, iamb; iambic trimeter; *pl.* iambic verse

iamprīdem *adv.* long ago

iānitor, -ōris *m.* door-keeper, porter

iānitrix, -īcis *f.* female door-keeper

iantāculum, -ī *n.* breakfast

ianthinus, -a, -um *adj.* violet-coloured; *n.pl.sbst.* violet-coloured garments

iantō 1. to have breakfast

iānua, -ae *f.* door, doorway

iānus, -ī *m.* gateway, archway

iaspis, -idis *f.* jasper

iātraliptēs, -ae *m.* masseur

ibī (ibi) *adv.* there; thereupon

ibīdem (ibidem) *adv.* in that very place; in the same place; there and then

ībis, ībidis (ībis) *f.* ibis, the sacred bird of Egypt

ichneumōn, -ōnis *m.* ichneumon

īciō (īcō), īcī, ictum 3. to strike, smite; **foedus īcere** to seal a treaty

īconicus, -a, -um *adj.* having an exact likeness

īconismus, -ī *m.* distinguishing features (*of a person*)

ictericus, -a, -um *adj.* suffering from jaundice

ictus, -ūs *m.* blow, stroke; musical beat

idcircō *adv.* therefore, for that reason

idea, -ae *f.* Platonic Form, blueprint

īdem, eadem, idem *pron.* the same person *or* thing; *adj.* the same

identidem *adv.* again and again

ideō *adv.* for the reason (that); therefore

idiōta, -ae *m.* layman, amateur

īdōlon, -ī *n.* ghost, image

idōneē *adv.* suitably

idōneus, -a, -um *adj.* suitable, adequate; financially able

īdos *n.* form, aspect

īdūs, īduum *f.pl.* 13th day of the month (15th day of March, May, July and October)

īdyllium, -iī *n.* pastoral poem, idyll

iecur, iec(in)oris *n.* liver

iecusculum, -ī *n.* small liver**

iēiūnē *adv.* scantily

iēiūniōsus, -a, -um *adj.* full of hunger

iēiūnitās, -ātis *f.* fasting; lack; meagreness (*of literary style*)

iēiūnium, -(i)ī *n.* fasting, fast; starvation

iēiūnus, -a, -um *adj.* hungry, fasting; (+*abl.*) barren (of), devoid (of)

iens, euntis (*present participle of* eō)

ientāculum see **iantāculum**

igitur *conj.* therefore; accordingly; well then

ignārus, -a, -um *adj.* (+*gen.*) ignorant (of), unacquainted (with); unknown

ignāvē *adv.* feebly, without spirit

ignāvia, -ae *f.* indolence; lack of spirit

ignāvus, -a, -um *adj.* indolent, lazy; spiritless; useless; ignoble

ignescō 3. to catch fire, become inflamed; redden

igneus, -a, -um *adj.* consisting of fire, burning; fiery

ignicolōrius, -a, -um *adj.* fire-coloured

igniculus, -ī *m.* small fire; spark

ignifer, -era, -erum *adj.* fire-bearing, burning

ignigena, -ae *m.* one born from fire

ignipēs, -edis *adj.* fiery-footed

ignipotens, -ntis *adj.* controlling fire; *m. sg.sbst.* the god Vulcan

ignis, -is *m.* fire; lightning; gleam; fever; rage

igniscō see **ignescō**

ignōbilis, -is, -e *adj.* unknown; unimportant, inglorious; of low birth

ignōbilitās, -ātis *f.* obscurity; low birth

ignōminia, -ae *f.* degradation by a censor, disqualification; disgrace, ignominy

ignōminiōsus, -a, -um *adj.* suffering *ignominia*, disgraced; disgraceful

ignōrābilis, -is, -e *adj.* unknown

ignōrantia, -ae *f.* ignorance

ignōrātiō, -ōnis *f.* ignorance

ignōrātus, -a, -um *adj.* done in ignorance

ignōrō 1. to be ignorant; be unfamiliar with; ignore

ignoscens, -ntis *adj.* forgiving, pardoning

ignoscō, ignōvī, ignōtum 3. (+*acc. of offence* +*dat. of person*) to forgive (*one for sthg*); (+*dat. of offence*) to forgive

ignōtus, -a, -um *adj.* unknown, unfamiliar; obscure; ignorant

īlex, īlicis *f.* holm-oak, ilex; wood *or* fruit of the holm-oak

īlia, īlium *n.pl.* groin

īlicet *adv.* straightaway; be off with you!; we're done for!

īlicētum, -ī *n.* grove of holm-oaks

īliceus, -a, -um *adj.* made of holm-oak

īlicō (-o) *adv.* just there; there and then

īlignus, -a, -um *adj.* of *or* made from the holm-oak

illā *adv.* by that way; there

illabefactus, -a, -um *adj.* unshaken

illābor, illapsus 3. *dep.* (+*acc./dat.*) to glide, flow (into); sink (into)

illabōrātus, -a, -um *adj.* untilled, unworked

illabōrō 1. (+*dat.*) to work at

illāc *adv.* by that way

illacessītus, -a, -um *adj.* unattacked

illacrimābilis, -is, -e *adj.* unwept; remorseless

illacrimō 1. or **illacrimor** 1. *dep.* (+*dat.*) to shed tears (for *or* at)

illaesus, -a, -um *adj.* unharmed, unimpaired

illaetābilis, -is, -e *adj.* joyless, unhappy

illaqueō 1. to ensnare, entangle

illātrō 1. (+*dat.*) to bark (at)

illaudābilis, -is, -e *adj.* not praiseworthy

illaudātus, -a, -um *adj.* unpraised

illautus see **illōtus**

ille, illa, illud *pron.* that person *or* thing, he, she, it; *adj.* that; the former; the well-known

illecebra, -ae *f.* (+*gen.*) allurement, enticement (to)

illecebrōsus, -a, -um *adj.* alluring, enticing

illectus¹, -ūs *m.* allurement

illectus², -a, -um *adj.* unread

illepidē *adv.* without refinement *or* wit

illepidus, -a, -um *adj.* unrefined

illex¹, -ēgis *adj.* lawless

illex², -icis *m./f.* one who allures *or* entices

illī *adv.* there

illibātus, -a, -um *adj.* undiminished, unimpaired

illīberālis, -is, -e *adj.* ignoble, ungenerous; mean, stingy

illīberālitās, -ātis *f.* stinginess, ungenerosity

illīberāliter *adv.* ungenerously, stingily

illic¹, illaec, illuc *pron.* that person *or* thing, he, she, it; *adj.* that

illīc² *adv.* there; in that situation *or* circumstance

illiciō, illexī, illectum 3. to allure, entice

illicitātor, -ōris *m.* one who raises the bidding price artificially at auction

illicitus, -a, -um *adj.* forbidden, illicit, illegal

illicō see **īlicō**

illīdō, -sī, -sum 3. to beat, crush; (+*dat.*) strike (into *or* against)

illigō 1. to tie up, bind; (+*dat.*) to tie (to)

illim *adv.* from there

illīmis, -is, -e *adj.* devoid of slime

illinc *adv.* from there; **hinc ... illinc** on one side ... on the other

illinō, illēvī, illitum 3. (+*dat.*) to smear (onto); (+*abl.*) besmear, anoint (with)

illiquefactus, -a, -um *adj.* melted, liquefied

illitterātus, -a, -um *adj.* uneducated, unlearned

illō(c) *adv.* to there

illocābilis, -is, -e *adj.* unable to be married off

illōtus, -a, -um *adj.* unwashed, dirty; not washed off

illūc *adv.* to there; **hūc ... illūc** this way and that

illūceō 2. (+*dat.*) to shine (on)

illūcescō, illuxī 3. to grow light, dawn; shine out; shine on

illuctor 1. *dep.* (+*dat.*) to struggle against

illūdō, -sī, -sum 3. (+*acc./dat.*) to mock, make fun of; trick; (+*dat.*) use sexually

illūminātē *adv.* luminously, clearly

illūminō 1. to illuminate, brighten; elucidate, reveal

illūnis, -is, -e *adj.* without a moon

illūsiō, -ōnis *f.* ridicule, mockery

illustris, -is, -e *adj.* bright, brilliant; lucid, clear; illustrious, famous

illustrius *compar.adv.* more clearly

illustrō 1. to illuminate, brighten; elucidate, reveal; embellish, glorify

illūtus see **illōtus**

illuviēs, -ēī *f.* dirtiness, uncleanliness; dirt, filth

imāginārius, -a, -um *adj.* unreal, imaginary

imāginātiō, -ōnis *f.* imagination, fantasy

imāginor 1. *dep.* to imagine, picture mentally

imāginōsus, -a, -um *adj.* full of images, reflective

imāgō, -inis *f.* image, likeness; death-mask, bust; reflection; ghost; form; description, simile

imāguncula, -ae *f.* small image, statuette

imbēcillē *adv.* weakly

imbēcillitās, -ātis *f.* weakness, feebleness; impotence

imbēcillus, -a, -um *adj.* weak, feeble; impotent

imbellis, -is, -e *adj.* unwarlike; unsuitable *or* unready for war; free from war

imber, imbris *m.* rainstorm, rain; shower; water

imberbis, -is, -e or **-us, -a, -um** *adj.* beardless

imbibō, -ī, -itum 3. to absorb mentally

imbītō 3. to enter

imbrex, -icis *f.* curved tile; manner of clapping

imbricus, -a, -um *adj.* rainy

imbrifer, -era, -erum *adj.* bringing rain, rainy

imbuō, -uī, -ūtum 3. (+*abl.*) to drench, imbue (with); (+*abl.*) inaugurate, initiate (in)

imitābilis, -is, -e *adj.* capable of being imitated

imitāmen, -inis *n.* imitation, reproduction

imitāmentum, -ī *n.* imitation, reproduction

imitātiō, -ōnis *f.* imitating, mimicking; imitation

imitātor, -ōris *m.* one who copies *or* imitates

imitātrix, -īcis *f.* female copier *or* imitator

imitor 1. *dep.* or **imitō** 1. to imitate, copy; resemble, simulate

immaculātus, -a, -um *adj.* unstained

immadescō, -duī 3. to become wet, moisten

immānis, -is, -e *adj.* huge, vast; frightening; savage

immānitās, -ātis *f.* frightfulness; savagery

immansuētus, -a, -um *adj.* untamed, savage

immātūritās, -ātis *f.* immaturity; prematureness

immātūrus, -a, -um *adj.* immature, unripe; premature; ill-timed

immedicābilis, -is, -e *adj.* incurable

immeiō 3. (+*dat.*) to urinate (into)

immemor, -oris *adj.* (+*gen.*) forgetful (of); heedless

immemorābilis, -is, -e *adj.* inexpressible; unrepeatable; uncommunicative

immemorātus, -a, -um *adj.* (as yet) untold

immensitās, -ātis *f.* immensity, vastness

immensum¹, -ī *n.* infinite space; **in immensum** to an infinite size *or* degree

immensum² *adv.* to an infinite degree

immensus, -a, -um *adj.* infinite, boundless; immeasurable; immense

immerens, -ntis *adj.* undeserving, blameless

immergō, -rsī, -rsum 3. (+*dat.*) to plunge, immerse (into)

immeritō *adv.* undeservedly, unjustly

immeritus, -a, -um *adj.* undeserving; undeserved

immersābilis, -is, -e *adj.* unable to be sunk

immētātus, -a, -um *adj.* unmeasured

immigrō 1. to move (into)

immineō 2. to overhang, be overhead; (+*dat. or* +*in* +*acc.*) be intent (on); threaten; be imminent

imminuō, -uī, -ūtum 3. to reduce, diminish; spoil

imminūtiō, -ōnis *f.* spoiling; disparagement

immisceō, -scuī, -xtum 2. (+*dat.*) to mix (*sthg*) in; mingle; confuse

immiserābilis, -is, -e *adj.* not to be pitied

immisericorditer *adv.* without pity

immisericors, -rdis *adj.* pitiless

immissiō, -ōnis *f.* engrafting, insertion

immītis, -is, -e *adj.* bitter, sour; harsh, pitiless

immittō, immīsī, immissum 3. (+*dat. or* +*in* +*acc.*) to send (to *or* against); introduce; throw (at); allow, admit (into)

immō *part.* rather, particularly

immōbilis, -is, -e *adj.* immovable, unwieldy; motionless; unchanged, steadfast

immoderātē *adv.* without control, immoderately

immoderātiō, -ōnis *f.* lack of moderation

immoderātus, -a, -um *adj.* immoderate; unrestrained

immodestē *adv.* immoderately; impudently

immodestia, -ae *f.* lack of restraint

immodestus, -a, -um *adj.* lacking in restraint

immodicē *adv.* immoderately, unrestrainedly

immodicus, -a, -um *adj.* lacking restraint, immoderate; vast; extravagant

immodulātus, -a, -um *adj.* defective in rhythm

immolātiō, -ōnis *f.* making of a sacrifice

immolātor, -ōris *m.* one who makes a sacrifice

immōlītus, -a, -um *adj.* built, constructed

immolō 1. to offer (*a victim*) in sacrifice

immordeō, -rsum 2. to bite into; spur on

immorior, -rtuus 3. (+*dat.*) to die (in *or* by)

immoror 1. *dep.* to stay; (+*dat.*) linger (upon)

immortālis, -is, -e *adj.* immortal, everlasting; *m.sbst.* god

immortālitās, -ātis *f.* immortality, permanence; divinity

immortāliter *adv.* eternally

immōtus, -a, -um *adj.* motionless; undisturbed, unchanged

immūgiō 4. to bellow, resound

immulgeō 2. (+*dat.*) to milk (into)

immunditia, -ae *f.* uncleanliness, dirtiness

immundus, -a, -um *adj.* unclean, dirty

immūniō 4. to strengthen, fortify

immūnis, -is, -e *adj.* exempt (*esp. from tax*); (+*gen.*) free (from); not performing one's duty

immūnitās, -ātis *f.* exemption from tax; (+*gen.*) immunity (from)

immūnītus, -a, -um *adj.* unfortified; unpaved

immurmurō 1. (+*dat.*) to murmur (to)

immūtābilis¹, -is, -e *adj.* unchangeable, immutable

immūtābilis², -is, -e *adj.* liable to be changed

immūtābilitās, -ātis *f.* immutability

immūtātiō, -ōnis *f.* change, alteration; substitution

immūtātus, -a, -um *adj.* unchanged

immūtescō, -tuī 3. to fall silent

immutilātus, -a, -um *adj.* unmutilated

immūtō 1. to change, alter; substitute

impācātus, -a, -um *adj.* not pacified, restless

impallescō, -lluī 3. (+*dat.*) to turn pale (at)

impār, imparis *adj.* unequal, uneven

imparātus, -a, -um *adj.* unprepared, unready

impariter *adv.* unequally

impastus, -a, -um *adj.* unfed, hungry

impatiens, -ntis *adj.* (+*gen.*) impatient (of); impassive

impatienter *adv.* impatiently

impatientia, -ae *f.* (+*gen.*) intolerance (of); impassivity

impavidē *adj.* without fear

impavidus, -a, -um *adj.* fearless, undaunted

impedīmentum, -ī *n.* obstacle, impediment; *pl.* baggage, equipment

impediō 4. to obstruct, impede; entangle

impedītiō, -ōnis *f.* (+*gen.*) hindrance (of)

impeditō 1. to obstruct

impedītus, -a, -um *adj.* obstructed, hindered, blocked; difficult

impellō, impulī, impulsum 3. to thrust against; set in motion, drive; impel

impendeō, -nsum 2. to hang above; impend, threaten

impendiō *adv.* very much

impendiōsus, -a, -um *adj.* extravagant, lavish

impendium, -(i)ī *n.* expense, payment, cost

impendō, -dī, -sum 3. to pay out, expend; devote

impenetrābilis, -is, -e *adj.* impenetrable

impensa, -ae *f.* expense, cost; building materials

impensē *adv.* immoderately, lavishly

impensus, -a, -um *adj.* immoderate, lavish; worthless

imperātor, -ōris *m.* one who gives orders, general; ruler; Roman emperor

imperātōrius, -a, -um *adj.* of *or* relating to a general; imperial

imperātrix, -īcis *f.* female general

imperātum, -ī *n.* command, order

imperco 3. (+*dat.*) to act sparingly towards

impercussus, -a, -um *adj.* not struck, noiseless

imperditus, -a, -um *adj.* not killed

imperfectus, -a, -um *adj.* imperfect, unfinished

imperfossus, -a, -um *adj.* not pierced

imperiōsus, -a, -um *adj.* commanding, ruling; dictatorial

imperītē *adv.* unskilfully, without experience

imperītia, -ae *f.* lack of skill *or* experience

imperītō 1. to order continually; (+*dat.*) be in command (over)

imperītus, -a, -um *adj.* lacking skill *or* experience; (+*gen.*) unskilled (in)

imperium, -(i)ī *n.* supreme power, dominion, rule; empire

imperiūrātus, -a, -um *adj.* not falsely sworn by

impermissus, -a, -um *adj.* not allowed

imperō 1. (+*dat.*) to command, rule (over); levy

imperpetuus, -a, -um *adj.* not perpetual, short-lived

imperspicuus, -a, -um *adj.* unclear, difficult to comprehend

imperterritus, -a, -um *adj.* fearless

impertiō 4. or **impertior** 4. *dep.* (+*dat.*) to impart (*sthg*) to, share (with); (+*abl.*) to make (*one*) share (in)

imperturbātus, -a, -um *adj.* untroubled, calm

impervius, -a, -um *adj.* impassable

[impes], -etis *m.* onset, attack; extent

impetibilis, -is, -e *adj.* intolerable

impetīgō, -inis *f.* skin disease, impetigo

impetō 3. to attack, assail

impetrābilis, -is, -e *adj.* obtainable; successful in obtaining one's request

impetrātiō, -ōnis *f.* obtaining one's request

impetriō 4. to seek to obtain by favourable omens

impetrō 1. to succeed in one's request, obtain

impetus, -ūs *m.* impulse; vigour, effort; attack; extent

impexus, -a, -um *adj.* uncombed, unkempt

impiē *adv.* impiously

impietās, -ātis *f.* impious, undutiful (*to family, gods etc.*)

impiger, -gra, -grum *adj.* energetic, active

impigrē *adv.* energetically, actively

impigritās, -ātis *f.* energy, activity

impingō, impēgī, impactum 3. (+*dat.*) to dash (against), thrust (upon); fasten (to)

impiō 1. to taint by impious action

impius, -a, -um *adj.* impious, undutiful (*to family, gods etc.*)

implācābilis, -is, -e *adj.* implacable, irreconcilable

implācābiliter *adv.* implacably

implācātus, -a, -um *adj.* implacable, insatiable

implacidus, -a, -um *adj.* restless, turbulent

implectō, -xī, -xum 3. to intertwine, interweave

impleō, -ēvī, -ētum 2. (*+abl./gen.*) to fill (with); make pregnant; fulfil

implicātiō, -ōnis *f.* weaving in; network; complication

implicātus, -a, -um *adj.* intricate, obscure

impliciscō 3. to begin to take hold of

implicitē *adv.* in a complicated manner

implicitus see **implicātus**

implicō, -āvī (-uī), -ātum (-(i)tum) 1. (*+abl.*) to enfold, entwine (with); entangle; involve

implōrātiō, -ōnis *f.* supplication, entreaty

implōrō 1. to make supplication for; invoke, implore

implūmis, -is, -e *adj.* having no feathers

impluō, -ūvī 3. (*+dat.*) to rain (upon)

impluviātus, -a, -um *adj.* resembling an *impluvium*

impluvium, -(i)ī *n.* square pool for collecting rain-water in a Roman *atrium*

impolītē *adv.* inelegantly, rudely

impolītus, -a, -um *adj.* rough; unrefined, inelegant

impollūtus, -a, -um *adj.* unpolluted, unviolated

impōnō, imposuī, impos(i)tum 3. (*+dat.*) to put on, cover; build on; place in control over; impose; deceive

importō 1. to carry in, introduce; cause

importūnitās, -ātis *f.* continual disregard of others, disobligingness

importūnus, -a, -um *adj.* unfavourable, inconvenient; regardless of others, disobliging

importuōsus, -a, -um *adj.* lacking harbours

impos, -otis *adj.* (*+gen.*) lacking control (of)

impotens, -ntis *adj.* powerless; (*+gen.*) lacking control (of); intemperate, violent

impotenter *adv.* ineffectually, weakly; intemperately

impotentia, -ae *f.* weakness; intemperacy, violence

impraesentiārum *adv.* at the present time

impransus, -a, -um *adj.* having not had one's *prandium*

imprecātiō, -ōnis *f.* summoning down of curses

imprecor 1. *dep.* (*+dat.*) to call down (upon), pray (for)

impressiō, -ōnis *f.* thrust, assault; emphasis; impression

imprīmīs *adv.* above all, especially; firstly

imprimō, -ressī, -ressum 3. (*+dat.*) to press (*sthg*) on, apply; thrust in; (*+abl.*) imprint, impress (with)

improbābilis, -is, -e *adj.* unworthy of praise, culpable

improbātiō, -ōnis *f.* rejection (*of sthg*) as unsound

improbē *adv.* wrongly, dishonestly; insolently; immoderately

improbitās, -ātis *f.* dishonesty; insolence; immoderacy

improbō 1. to disapprove (of), reject

improbulus, -a, -um *adj.* somewhat insolent

improbus, -a, -um *adj.* inferior; morally wrong; dishonest; insolent; immoderate

imprōcērus, -a, -um *adj.* of low stature, stunted

imprōdictus, -a, -um *adj.* of which notice has been given in advance

improfessus, -a, -um *adj.* having not registered one's name

impromptus, -a, -um *adj.* unready, slow

imprōperātus, -a, -um *adj.* unhurried, slow

improsperē *adv.* unfortunately

improsperus, -a, -um *adj.* unfortunate, unfavourable

imprōvidē *adv.* without forethought, improvidently

imprōvidus, -a, -um *adj.* without forethought, improvident

imprōvīsō *adv.* unexpectedly

imprōvīsus, -a, -um *adj.* unforeseen, unexpected; **ex/dē imprōvīsō** unexpectedly

imprūdens, -ntis *adj.* (*+gen.*) ignorant

(of), unaware (of); incautious, unthinking

imprūdenter *adv.* thoughtlessly, recklessly; unintentionally

imprūdentia, -ae *f.* ignorance; thoughtlessness; inadvertency; **per imprūdentiam** accidentally

impūbēs (-is), -ēs (-is), -e or **impūbēs, -eris** *adj.* prepubescent; *m.sbst.* prepubescent boy

impudens, -ntis *adj.* impudent, shameless

impudenter *adv.* impudently, shamelessly

impudentia, -ae *f.* impudence, shamelessness

impudīcitia, -ae *f.* unchastity, sexual immorality

impudīcus, -a, -um *adj.* unchaste, sexually immoral; outrageous; foul; **digitus impudīcus** middle finger (*raised as an obscene gesture*)

impugnātiō, -ōnis *f.* armed attack

impugnō 1. to attack with arms, assail; impugn, oppose

impulsiō, -ōnis *f.* thrust, impulse

impulsor, -ōris *m.* one who impels, instigator

impulsus, -ūs *m.* thrust, impulse

impūne *adv.* without punishment; **impūne ferre** or **habēre** to escape punishment

impūnitās, -ātis *f.* freedom from punishment, impunity

impūnītē *adv.* without punishment

impūnītus, -a, -um *adj.* unpunished

impūrātus, -a, -um *adj.* polluted, foul

impūrē *adv.* foully

impūritās, -ātis *f.* impurity, foulness

impūritia, -ae *f.* impurity, foulness

impūrus, -a, -um *adj.* filthy, foul; morally impure

imputātus, -a, -um *adj.* untrimmed, unpruned

imputō 1. to impute (to), charge; reckon

īmulus, -a, -um *adj.* lowest

īmus, īma, īmum *superl.adj.* lowest; innermost, deepest; final

in *prep.* (+*acc.*) to *or* into; against; for; (+*abl.*) in; on; at; amongst

inabruptus, -a, -um *adj.* unbroken

inaccessus, -a, -um *adj.* inaccessible

inacescō, inacuī 3. to become sour, unpleasant

inadustus, -a, -um *adj.* not scorched

inaedificō 1. (+*in* +*abl.*) to build (on *or* in); wall up

inaequābilis, -is, -e *adj.* uneven, unequal

inaequābiliter *adv.* unevenly

inaequālis, -is, -e *adj.* uneven, unequal; inconsistent, irregular

inaequālitās, -ātis *f.* unevenness, inequality; inconsistency

inaequāliter *adv.* unevenly, unequally

inaequō 1. to make level, even

inaestimābilis, -is, -e *adj.* inestimable; inestimably great

inaestuō 1. (+*abl.*) to seethe (in)

inaffectātus, -a, -um *adj.* unaffected

inagitātus, -a, -um *adj.* unperturbed

inamābilis, -is, -e *adj.* unlovable, unpleasant

inamārescō 3. to become bitter

inambitiōsus, -a, -um *adj.* unaspiring, humble

inambulātiō, -ōnis *f.* walking to and fro, pacing

inambulō 1. to walk to and fro, pace

inamoenus, -a, -um *adj.* unpleasant

inānilogista, -ae *m.* talker of nonsense, babbler

inānīmentum, -ī *n.* emptiness

inanimus, -a, -um *adj.* lifeless, inanimate

ināniō 4. to empty

inānis, -is, -e *adj.* empty; hollow; bare; futile; false; foolish; *n.sg.sbst.* empty space, void

inānitās, -ātis *f.* emptiness; futility, inanity

ināniter *adv.* futilely; falsely; groundlessly

inarātus, -a, -um *adj.* unploughed

inardescō, inarsī 3. to kindle; burn, glow

inārescō, ināruī 3. to dry up

inascensus, -a, -um *adj.* unclimbed

inaspectus, -a, -um *adj.* unseen

inassuētus, -a, -um *adj.* unaccustomed

inattenuātus, -a, -um *adj.* undiminished

inaudax, -ācis *adj.* not daring, cowardly

inaudiō 4. to hear of, learn of

inaudītus, -a, -um *adj.* unheard; unheard of

inaugurātō *adv.* with the taking of omens by augury

inaugurō 1. to take omens by augury; consecrate by augury

inaurātus, -a, -um *adj.* gilded

inaurēs, -ium *f.pl.* earrings

inaurō 1. to gild; enrich

inauspicātō *adv.* without the approval of auspices

inauspicātus, -a, -um *adj.* inauspicious, ill-omened

inausus, -a, -um *adj.* undared

inb- see **imb-**

incaeduus, -a, -um *adj.* unfelled

incalescō, -luī 3. to become warm, heat up

incalfaciō, -fēcī, -factum 3. to make hot

incallidē *adv.* unskilfully

incallidus, -a, -um *adj.* unskilful, simple

incandescō, -duī 3. to become very hot

incānescō, -nuī 3. to become white *or* grey

incantō 1. to put a spell on

incānus, -a, -um *adj.* grey, hoary

incassum *adv.* to no purpose, futilely

incastīgātus, -a, -um *adj.* unreproved

incautē *adv.* incautiously, carelessly

incautus, -a, -um *adj.* incautious; unguarded; unforeseen

incēdō, incessī 3. to walk, step; advance; enter; arise

incelebrātus, -a, -um *adj.* unpublicized, unknown

incēnātus, -a, -um *adj.* not having dined

incendiārius, -iī *m.* fire-raiser, incendiary

incendium, -(i)ī *n.* uncontrolled fire, conflagration; meteor

incendō, -dī, -sum 3. to set on fire, kindle; light up; provoke, aggravate

incensiō, -ōnis *f.* setting on fire

incensus[1], -a, -um *adj.* impassioned, incensed

incensus[2], -a, -um *adj.* not registered at a census

inceptiō, -ōnis *f.* beginning; undertaking, venture

inceptō 1. to begin

inceptor, -ōris *m.* one who begins, initiator

inceptum, -ī *n.* undertaking; subject, theme

inceptus, -ūs *m.* beginning

incernō, incrēvī, incrētum 3. (+*abl.*) to sprinkle (with)

incērō 1. to cover with wax

incertē (-ō) *adv.* doubtfully, uncertainly

incertō 1. to make doubtful

incertus, -a, -um *adj.* unfixed, uncertain

incessō, -ī 3. to attack, assail

incessus, -ūs *m.* walking, pacing; attack, advance; approach

incestē *adv.* unholily, unchastely; incestuously

incestificus, -a, -um *adj.* having committed incest

incestō 1. to defile, pollute

incestum, -ī *n.* sexual immorality, unchastity

incestus[1], -a, -um *adj.* unholy, unchaste; incestuous

incestus[2], -ūs *m.* sexual immorality, unchastity

incidō[1], incidī, incāsum 3. (+*dat.* or +*in* +*acc.*) to fall (upon), rush (into); chance upon; befall; occur

incīdō[2], -dī, -sum 3. to cut open; inscribe; sever, break off

incīlō 1. to abuse, rebuke

incinctus, -a, -um *adj.* girt, wrapped

incingō, -nxī, -nctum 3. to wrap round, surround

incinō, -uī 3. to play (*tunes*)

incipiō, incēpī, inceptum 3. to start, begin, undertake; (+*inf.*) begin (to)

incipissō 3. to begin, undertake

incīsē (-im) *adv.* in short phrases

incīsiō, -ōnis *f.* short phrase

incīsum, -ī *n.* short phrase

incitae, -ārum *f.pl.* checkmate (*or sim.*)

incitāmentum, -ī *n.* incentive, goad

incitātē *adv.* rapidly, hurriedly

incitātiō, -ōnis *f.* inciting; impetuosity; ardour

incitātus, -a, -um *adj.* rapid; excited; violent

incitō 1. to spur on, impel; rouse, incite

incitus, -a, -um *adj.* rapid, headlong

incīvīliter *adv.* uncivilly, despotically

inclāmitō 1. to abuse

inclāmō 1. to shout out; call out to; abuse

inclārescō, -ruī 3. to become famous

inclaudicō 1. to be lame

inclēmens, -ntis *adj.* severe, harsh

inclēmenter *adv.* harshly; uncivilly

inclēmentia, -ae *f.* severity, harshness

inclīnābilis, -is, -e *adj.* (+*in* +*acc.*) easily persuaded (to)

inclīnātiō, -ōnis *f.* tilt, inclination, slope; tendency; alteration

inclīnātus, -a, -um *adj.* (favourably) inclined; low in pitch

inclīnō 1. to tilt, incline; turn; lower, droop; affect; decay

inclitus see **inclutus**

inclūdō, -sī, -sum 3. to enclose, shut in; lock away; surround; restrict

inclūsiō, -ōnis f. confinement

inclūsus, -a, -um adj. confined, enclosed; secret

inclutus, -a, -um adj. famous, celebrated

incoactus, -a, -um adj. unforced

incoātus see **inco(h)ātus**

incoctus, -a, -um adj. uncooked, raw

incōgitābilis, -is, -e adj. thoughtless

incōgitans, -ntis adj. thoughtless

incōgitantia, -ae f. thoughtlessness

incōgitātus, -a, -um adj. thoughtless; unexpected, uncomprehended

incōgitō 1. to plan, conceive

incognitus, -a, -um adj. unknown, unfamiliar; untested; unheard (of legal cases)

incognoscō, -nōvī, -nitum 3. to become acquainted with

inco(h)ātus, -a, -um adj. unfinished, imperfect

incohō 1. to begin, initiate, commence

incola, -ae m./f. inhabitant; denizen

incolō, -uī 3. to dwell in, inhabit; dwell

incolumis, -is, -e adj. unharmed, safe, intact

incolumitās, -ātis f. safety

incomitātus, -a, -um adj. unaccompanied

incomitiō 1. to abuse

incommendātus, -a, -um adj. without protection

incommodē adv. inconveniently, annoyingly

incommodesticus, -a, -um adj. troublesome

incommoditās, -ātis f. inconvenience, importunity; disadvantage

incommodō 1. (+dat.) to cause difficulty (for)

incommodum, -ī n. inconvenience; disadvantage

incommodus, -a, -um adj. inconvenient; disadvantageous; disagreeable

incommūtābilis, -is, -e adj. immutable

incompertus, -a, -um adj. unknown, uninvestigated

incompositē adv. in a disorderly fashion

incompositus, -a, -um adj. disordered, irregular; awkward; unaffected

incompre(he)nsibilis, -is, -e adj. that cannot be grasped; incomprehensible

incomptē adv. in a disorderly fashion

incomptus, -a, -um adj. untidy, disordered; rough, unpolished

inconcessus, -a, -um adj. forbidden

inconciliō 1. to obtain by trickery; dupe

inconcinnus, -a, -um adj. awkward, clumsy

inconcussus, -a, -um adj. unshaken, steadfast; untroubled

inconditē adv. crudely; in a disorderly fashion

inconditus, -a, -um adj. crude, rough; disordered; unburied

incongruens, -ntis adj. inconsistent

inconsīderantia, -ae f. inattentiveness; thoughtlessness

inconsīderātē adv. thoughtlessly

inconsīderātus, -a, -um adj. injudicious, thoughtless

inconsōlābilis, -is, -e adj. inconsolable

inconstans, -ntis adj. unsteady; capricious

inconstanter adv. unsteadily; capriciously

inconstantia, -ae f. unsteadiness, uncertainty; fickleness, inconsistency

inconsultē adv. incautiously, inadvisedly

inconsultus¹, -a, -um adj. injudicious, thoughtless; unconsulted

inconsultus², -ūs m. lack of consultation

inconsumptus, -a, um adj. unconsumed

incontāminātus, -a, -um adj. uncontaminated

incontentus, -a, -um adj. not correctly tuned

incontinens, -ntis adj. intemperate, unrestrained

incontinenter adv. intemperately

incontinentia, -ae f. intemperance, self-indulgence

inconveniens, -ntis adj. discordant

incoquō, -xī, -ctum 3. (+abl.) to boil (in); roast

incorpōrālis, -is, -e adj. incorporeal

incorrectus, -a, -um adj. uncorrected

incorruptē adv. without corruption, honestly

incorruptus, -a, -um adj. unspoilt, intact; untainted, uncorrupted; incorruptible

incrēbrescō, -bruī 3. to become more intense

incrēbrō 1. to make frequent

incrēdibilis, -is, -e *adj.* unbelievable, incredible

incrēdibiliter *adv.* unbelievably, incredibly

incrēdulus, -a, -um *adj.* doubting, disbelieving

incrēmentum, -ī *n.* increase, growth; promotion

increpitō 1. to reproach, scold

increpō, -uī, -itum 1. to make a loud noise; strike loudly; protest (about)

increscō, incrēvī 3. to grow; become more intense

incruentātus, -a, -um *adj.* not bloodstained

incruentus, -a, -um *adj.* not bloodstained; without bloodshed

incrustō 1. to daub, coat

incubitō 1. to lie on

incubō, -uī, -itum 3. (+*dat.*) to lie (on), sit (on); brood (over); oversee jealously

incūdō, -dī, -sum 3. to hammer out; emboss

inculcō 1. to force upon; insert; impress

inculpātus, -a, -um *adj.* blameless

incultē *adv.* without refinement, rudely

incultus¹, -a, -um *adj.* uncultivated; untidy; unrefined, unpolished

incultus², -ūs *m.* uncultivated condition; unsophistication; neglect

incumbō, incubuī, incubitum 3. (+*dat.*) to lean (upon *or* towards); incline (towards); press (upon); apply (oneself to)

incūnābula, -ōrum *n.pl.* swaddling clothes; birthplace; infancy

incūrātus, -a, -um *adj.* not treated

incūria, -ae *f.* carelessness, neglect

incūriōsē *adv.* carelessly, negligently

incūriōsus, -a, -um *adj.* careless, negligent; (+*gen.*) indifferent (towards)

incurrō, in(cu)currī, incursum 3. (+*in* +*acc.* *or* +*dat.*) to rush (at), run (into); meet (with); occur

incursiō, -ōnis *f.* assault, incursion

incursitō 1. (+*in* +*acc.*) to bump into continually

incursō 1. to attack, rush (at); (+*dat.*) run into; make incursions into

incursus, -ūs *m.* assault, attack, raid

incurvō 1. to make bent *or* curved; bow, lower

incurvus, -a, -um *adj.* bent, curved; bowed

incūs, -ūdis *f.* anvil

incūsātiō, -ōnis *f.* criticism

incūsō 1. to reproach, criticize; blame

incussus, -ūs *m.* impact, blow

incustōdītus, -a, -um *adj.* unguarded, not overseen; unguarded

incutiō, -ssī, -ssum 3. to strike (on *or* against); instil, inflict

indāgātiō, -ōnis *f.* searching out

indāgātor, -ōris *m.* searcher, tracker

indāgātrix, -īcis *f.* female searcher

indāgō¹ 1. to search out, track down, investigate

indāgō², -inis *f.* ring of hunters (*or* soldiers) surrounding prey (*or* the enemy)

indaudiō see **inaudiō**

inde *adv.* from there; then

indēbitus, -a, -um *adj.* not owed, undue

indecens, -ntis *adj.* unpleasant, unattractive

indecenter *adv.* unbecomingly, uglily

indeceō 2. (+*acc.*) to be unbecoming to

indēclīnābilis, -is, -e *adj.* inflexible, unswerving

indēclīnātus, -a, -um *adj.* unswerving

indecōrē *adv.* unbecomingly, unattractively

indecoris, -is, -e *adj.* shameful, unbecoming

indecorō 1. to dishonour, disgrace

indecōrus, -a, -um *adj.* ugly; inglorious; unbecoming

indēfensus, -a, -um *adj.* defenceless; not (*legally*) defended

indēfessus, -a, -um *adj.* tireless, unwearied

indēflētus, -a, -um *adj.* unlamented

indēflexus, -a, -um *adj.* unchanged, unspoilt

indēiectus, -a, -um *adj.* not overthrown

indēlēbilis, -is, -e *adj.* unable to be blotted out, indelible

indēlībātus, -a, -um *adj.* intact, unharmed

indemnātus, -a, -um *adj.* uncondemned

indemnis, -is, -e *adj.* suffering no (*financial*) loss

indēplōrātus, -a, -um *adj.* unlamented

indēprāvātus, -a, -um *adj.* uncorrupted

indēprensus, -a, -um *adj.* unable to be overtaken; incomprehensible

indēsertus, -a, -um *adj.* not abandoned

indēspectus, -a, -um *adj.* unable to be looked down upon

indēstrictus, -a, -um *adj.* unscratched

indētonsus, -a, -um *adj.* unshorn

indēvītātus, -a, -um *adj.* unavoidable

index, -icis *m./f.* one who points out, informer; sign, indication; book title; list, summary

indicātiō, -ōnis *f.* valuation

indīcens, -ntis *adj.* not speaking

indicium, -(i)ī *n.* information, disclosure, evidence; symbol, sign

indicō¹ 1. to declare, disclose, reveal; value

indīcō², indixī, indictum 3. to proclaim, declare; (+*dat.*) impose (upon) by declaration

indictiō, -ōnis *f.* imposition (*of duties*)

indictus, -a, -um *adj.* unsaid; **indictā causā** without a legal case being heard

indidem *adv.* from the same place; by the same means

indifferens, -ntis *adj.* indifferent

indifferenter *adv.* indifferently

indigena, -ae *m.* native

indigens, -ntis *adj.* needy, dependent upon others

indigentia, -ae *f.* (+*gen.*) need, lack (of)

indigeō 2. (+*abl./gen.*) to need, lack; (+*inf.*) need (to)

indīgestus, -a, -um *adj.* disordered, confused

indignābundus, -a, -um *adj.* indignant

indignans, -ntis *adj.* indignant

indignātiō, -ōnis *f.* indignation, annoyance; indignant outburst

indignātiuncula, -ae *f.* slight indignation

indignē *adv.* undeservedly; shamefully

indignitās, -ātis *f.* unworthiness, shamefulness; indignity, humiliation

indignor 1. *dep.* to be indignant; take offence at, disdain

indignus, -a, -um *adj.* (+*abl./gen.*) unworthy (of), undeserving (of); undeserved; shameful, unbecoming

indigus, -a, -um *adj.* (+*gen./abl.*) needing, devoid (of)

indīligens, -ntis *adj.* negligent, careless

indīligenter *adv.* negligently, carelessly

indīligentia, -ae *f.* negligence, carelessness

indipiscor, indeptus 3. *dep.* or **indipiscō** 3. to acquire, obtain

indīreptus, -a, -um *adj.* not plundered

indiscrētus, -a, -um *adj.* not separated; indistinguishable; indifferent

indisertē *adv.* without skill in speech

indisertus, -a, -um *adj.* unskilled in speech

indispositē *adv.* irregularly

indispositus, -a, -um *adj.* disordered

indissolūbilis, -is, -e *adj.* imperishable

indissolūtus, -a, -um *adj.* imperishable

indistinctus, -a, -um *adj.* disordered; indifferent

indīviduus, -a, -um *adj.* indivisible, inseparable

indīvīsus, -a, -um *adj.* communal, shared

indō, -idī, -itum 3. (+*in* +*acc./abl.*) to place (on), introduce; (+*dat.*) attach (to); instil

indocilis, -is, -e *adj.* unteachable, stubborn; uninstructed, ignorant

indoctē *adv.* ignorantly

indoctus, -a, -um *adj.* unlearned, untrained, ignorant

indolentia, -ae *f.* freedom from pain; insensibility to pain

indolēs, -is *f.* nature, character; innate excellence

indolescō, -luī 3. to grieve, be in pain

indomābilis, -is, -e *adj.* untamable

indomitus, -a, -um *adj.* untamed, unconquered; untamable; unbridled, violent

indormiō 4. (+*dat.*) to sleep (on *or* in); be sleepy (about), forget

indōtātus, -a, -um *adj.* without a dowry

indōtiae see **indūtiae**

indu *prep.* (+*abl.*) in; *adv.* in

indubitābilis, -is, -e *adj.* indubitable

indubitātus, -a, -um *adj.* indubitable

indubitō 1. (+*dat.*) to have doubts (about)

indubius, -a, -um *adj.* not doubted, certain

indūcō, induxī, inductum 3. to lead (into), bring (in *or* on); introduce; put (on); smear (on); erase, cancel

inductiō, -ōnis *f.* bringing in *or* on; application; argument by analogy

inductor, -ōris *m.* one that induces

inductus¹, -ūs *m.* bringing on; inducement

inductus², -a, -um *adj.* alien, strange

indūcula, -ae *f.* female garment

indugredior 3. *dep.* to enter (upon)

indulgens, -ntis *adj.* mild, kind; (+*dat.*) addicted (to)

indulgenter *adv.* mildly, kindly

indulgentia, -ae *f.* mildness, kindness

indulgeō, -lsī, -lsum 2. (+*dat.*) to be mild *or* kind (to); indulge (in); concede

induō, -uī, -ūtum 3. (+*dat.*) to put (on), assume; plunge (into), implant (to); (+*abl.*) dress (in)

indupediō 4. to obstruct, impede

induperātor, -ōris *m.* general, commander; emperor

indūrescō, -ruī 3. to become hard, toughen; become inflexible (*in habits*)

indūrō 1. to make hard; make stubborn

indusiārius, -(i)ī *m.* maker of tunics

indusiātus, -a, -um *adj.* (*of tunics*) of an unknown type

industria, -ae *f.* assiduity, diligence, design

industriē *adv.* assiduously, diligently

industrius, -a, -um *adj.* assiduous, diligent

indūtiae, -ārum *f.pl.* truce, armistice

indūtus, -ūs *m.* putting on

induviae, -ārum *f.pl.* something put on

inēbriō 1. to make drunk

inedia, -ae *f.* fasting, starvation

inēditus, -a, -um *adj.* unpublished

inefficax, -ācis *adj.* ineffectual

inēlegans, -ntis *adj.* ungraceful; unrefined

inēleganter *adv.* in an unrefined manner

inēluctābilis, -is, -e *adj.* inescapable

inēmendābilis, -is, -e *adj.* incorrigible

inēmorior 3. *dep.* (+*dat.*) to die (during)

inemptus, -a, -um *adj.* not bought, unpaid for

inēnarrābilis, -is, -e *adj.* indescribable

ineō, inīre, iniī (inīvī), initum 4. to enter, enter upon; begin; **ratiōnem inīre** to enter a calculation; **consilium inīre** to form a plan

ineptē *adv.* unfittingly, foolishly

ineptia, -ae *f.* foolishness; *pl.* frivolities

ineptiō 4. to be foolish

ineptus, -a, -um *adj.* unfitting, foolish

inermis, -is, -e or **-us, -a, -um** *adj.* unarmed, undefended; peaceful

inerrans, -ntis *adj.* unwandering, fixed

inerrō 1. (+*dat.*) to wander (among)

iners, -rtis *adj.* unskilful; ineffectual; lazy, sluggish

inertia, -ae *f.* unskilfulness; laziness

inērudītus, -a, -um *adj.* uneducated, ignorant

inescō 1. to entice with bait

ineuschēmē *adv.* unbecomingly

inēvītābilis, -is, -e *adj.* unavoidable

inēvolūtus, -a, -um *adj.* not rolled out

inexcitābilis, -is, -e *adj.* unrousable

inexcītus, -a, -um *adj.* unroused; unsummoned

inexcūsābilis, -is, -e *adj.* inexcusable; not valid as an excuse

inexercitātus, -a, -um *adj.* untrained, unpractised

inexhaustus, -a, -um *adj.* inexhausted; limitless

inexōrābilis, -is, -e *adj.* inexorable

inexpectātus see **inex(s)pectātus**

inexperrectus, -a, -um *adj.* not awakened

inexpertus, -a, -um *adj.* inexperienced; untried

inexpiābilis, -is, -e *adj.* inexpiable, implacable

inexplēbilis, -is, -e *adj.* insatiable

inexplētus, -a, -um *adj.* unfilled; insatiable

inexplicābilis, -is, -e *adj.* impassable; complex, baffling

inexplicitus, -a, -um *adj.* unopened; unclear

inexplōrātō *adv.* without prior reconnaissance

inexplōrātus, -a, -um *adj.* unexplored, uninvestigated

inexpugnābilis, -is, -e *adj.* unassailable, impregnable; indestructible

inex(s)pectātus, -a, -um *adj.* unexpected

inex(s)tinctus, -a, -um *adj.* never extinguished

inex(s)uperābilis, -is, -e *adj.* insurmountable, invincible; unsurpassable

inextrīcābilis, -is, -e *adj.* insoluble; pathless

infabrē *adv.* unskilfully

infabricātus, -a, -um *adj.* unfashioned, unworked

infac- see **infic-**

infācundus, -a, -um *adj.* lack of verbal fluency

infāmātus, -a, -um *adj.* infamous

infāmia, -ae *f.* infamy, notoriety; disgrace

infāmis, -is, -e *adj.* infamous, notorious; disgraced, disgraceful

infāmō 1. to bring into dishonour, defame

infandus, -a, -um *adj.* unspeakable, nefarious

infans, -ntis *adj.* unable to speak, inarticulate; newborn, young; *m./f.sbst.* infant, small child

infantāria, -ae *f.* nanny

infantia, -ae *f.* inability to speak, inarticulateness; infancy, childhood

infarciō see **inferciō**

infatīgābilis, -is, -e *adj.* indefatigable

infatuō 1. to make a fool of

infaustus, -a, -um *adj.* ill-starred; accursed

infector, -ōris *m.* one who dyes

infectus, -a, -um *adj.* unfashioned; undone, unfinished

infēcunditās, -ātis *f.* barrenness

infēcundus, -a, -um *adj.* infertile, infecund

infēlīcitās, -ātis *f.* bad luck, misfortune

infēlīciter *adv.* unfortunately; unsuccessfully

infēlīcō 1. to bring bad luck on

infēlix, -īcis *adj.* unlucky, ill-fated; unfortunate; wretched; unproductive

infensē *adv.* hostilely, aggressively

infensō 1. to act hostilely towards

infensus, -a, -um *adj.* hostile, aggressive, savage

inferciō, -sī, -tum 4. to cram in

inferī, -ōrum *m.pl.* inhabitants of the underworld, the dead; the underworld

inferiae, -ārum *f.pl.* rites or offerings for the dead

inferior, -or, -us *compar.adj.* lower, inferior; more recent

inferius *compar.adv.* at a lower level; later

inferne *adv.* below, beneath

infernus, -a, -um *adj.* lower; underground, infernal

inferō, inferre, intulī, inlātum *v.irreg.* (*+in +acc.* or *+dat.*) to carry into; bring forward; inflict (upon); cause, produce; bury

inferveō, -rbuī 2. to come to the boil

inferus, -a, -um *adj.* lower; infernal

infestē *adv.* hostilely, aggressively

infestō 1. to harass, harry; damage; infest

infestus, -a, -um *adj.* hostile, aggressive; dangerous; insecure; (*+abl.*) infested (with)

inficētē *adv.* not smartly

inficētiae, -ārum *f.pl.* clumsiness, crudity

inficētus, -a, -um *adj.* boorish, unwitty

inficiō, infēcī, infectum 3. (*+abl.*) to dye, stain (with); infect; imbue, impregnate

inficiscō 3. (*+abl.*) to imbue (with)

infidēlis, -is, -e *adj.* disloyal, treacherous

infidēlitās, -ātis *f.* disloyalty, faithlessness

infidēliter *adv.* disloyally

infīdus, -a, -um *adj.* disloyal, treacherous

infīgō, infixī, infixum 3. (*+in +acc.*) to drive in, implant; attach

infimātis, -is, -e *adj.* of the lowest rank

infimus, -a, -um *superl.adj.* lowest; deepest; most worthless

infindō, infīdī, infissum 3. to cleave

infīnitās, -ātis *f.* infinity

infīnītē *adv.* infinitely, without limit; unspecifically

infīnītiō, -ōnis *f.* infinitude

infīnītus, -a, -um *adj.* infinite, without limit; unspecific, general

infirmātiō, -ōnis *f.* invalidation, annulment

infirmē *adv.* weakly; ineffectively

infirmitās, -ātis *f.* weakness, ineffectiveness; instability, unreliability

infirmō 1. to weaken; invalidate; refute

infirmus, -a, -um *adj.* weak, fragile; ineffectual; unstable, immature

infit 3. (*+inf.*) he or she begins (to); he or she begins to speak

infitiālis, -is, -e *adj.* containing a denial, negative

infitiās *f.acc.pl.* **infitiās īre** to deny, repudiate

infitiātiō, -ōnis *f.* denial

infitiātor, -ōris *m.* one who denies (*debts etc.*)

infitior 1. *dep.* to deny, repudiate

inflammātiō, -ōnis *f.* kindling, setting on fire

inflammō 1. to kindle, set on fire; rouse, inflame

inflātē *adv.* bombastically

inflātiō, -ōnis *f.* flatulence

inflātus¹, -a, -um *adj.* puffed up, bombastic

inflātus², -ūs *m.* blowing on; inspiration; swelling

inflectō, -xī, -xum 3. to bend, turn; change, alter

inflētus, -a, -um *adj.* unlamented

inflexibilis, -is, -e *adj.* inflexible, stubborn

inflexiō, -ōnis *f.* bending; altering

inflexus, -a, -um *adj.* bent, curved; modulated

inflīgō, -ixī, -ictum 3. (+*dat.*) to strike (against); inflict (upon)

inflō 1. to inflate, blow into; bloat, make swollen; puff up (*with pride etc.*)

influō, -uxī, -uxum 3. (+*in* +*acc.*) to flow in, pour in; sink in (*to the mind*)

infodiō, infōdī, infossum 3. to bury

informātiō, -ōnis *f.* mental conception

informis, -is, -e *adj.* formless; ugly; unbecoming

informō 1. to form, mould; conceive, imagine; sketch

inforō 1. to bore into

infortūnātus, -a, -um *adj.* unfortunate

infortūnium, -(i)ī *n.* misfortune

infrā¹ *prep.* (+*acc.*) lower than; inferior to, beneath

infrā² *adv.* below, beneath; inferiorly

infractiō, -ōnis *f.* breaking

infractus, -a, -um *adj.* broken; humbled; effeminate

infragilis, -is, -e *adj.* indestructible

infremō, -uī 3. to roar, bellow

infrēnātus, -a, -um *adj.* without a bridle

infrendō 3. (+*dat.*) to gnash the teeth (at)

infrēnis see **infrēnus**

infrēnō 1. to harness; restrain

infrēnus, -a, -um *adj.* without a rein; unrestrained

infrequens, -ntis *adj.* not crowded, not fully attended; (*of people*) infrequent, negligent

infrequentia, -ae *f.* lack of people

infringō, infrēgī, infractum 3. to break, shatter; weaken; invalidate

infrons, -ndis *adj.* leafless, bare

infructuōsus, -a, -um *adj.* fruitless, vain

infūcō 1. to cover with paint

infula, -ae *f.* sacrificial headband

infulātus, -a, -um *adj.* wearing an *infula*

infulciō, -lsī, -ltum 3. (+*dat.*) to cram in

infundō, infūdī, infūsum (+*in* +*acc. or* +*dat.*) 3. to pour in *or* on; impart; instil

infuscō 1. to darken; taint, contaminate

ingemescō, -muī 3. to groan

ingeminō 1. to repeat; double

ingemō 3. to groan; groan at

ingenerō 1. to produce, create

ingeniātus, -a, -um *adj.* (+*adv.*) naturally, innately

ingeniōsē *adv.* cleverly

ingeniōsus, -a, -um *adj.* clever; (+*dat. or* +*ad* +*acc.*) naturally suited (to)

ingenitus, -a, -um *adj.* natural, innate

ingenium, -(i)ī *n.* temperament, character; intellect, cleverness; inspiration; *n.pl. sbst.* literary élite

ingens, -ntis *adj.* very great, huge; powerful; proud

ingenuē *adv.* as befits a free-born man; generously

ingenuitās, -ātis *f.* being free-born; free-born character, generosity

ingenuus, -a, -um *adj.* indigenous; free-born; generous, liberal; tender

ingerō, -ssī, -stum 3. to heap on, pour in; throw upon, thrust on; repeat incessantly

[ingignō], ingenuī, ingenitum 3. to implant

inglomerō 1. to mass together

inglōrius, -a, -um *adj.* undistinguished, obscure

ingluviēs, [-ēī] *f.* gullet; gluttony

ingrātē *adv.* ungratefully; unwillingly

ingrāt(i)īs *f.abl.pl.* (+*gen.*) despite; against one's will

ingrātus, -a, -um *adj.* ungrateful; unwelcome; displeasing

ingravescō 3. to become heavier, become more aggravated

ingravō 1. to weigh down, aggravate

ingredior, -ssus 3. *dep.* to enter; embark upon, commence; walk, move forward

ingressiō, -ōnis *f.* entry; advancing

ingressus, -ūs *m.* entry; embarking; walking

ingruō, -uī 3. (+*dat.*) to attack, bear down (on); impend (upon)

inguen, -inis *n.* groin; inguinal swelling

ingurgitō 1. to pour in; drench; glut

ingustātus, -a, -um *adj.* untasted

inhabilis, -is, -e *adj.* unwieldy; ill-suited

inhabitābilis, -is, -e *adj.* uninhabitable

inhabitō 1. to occupy, inhabit
inhaereō, -sī, -sum 2. (+*dat*.) to cling (to), adhere (to); be wholly absorbed (by)
inhaerescō 3. to become fixed
inhālō 1. (+*dat*.) to breathe (upon)
inhibeō 2. to restrain, prevent; (+*dat*.) exert (upon)
inhibitiō, -ōnis f. backing water
inhiō 1. to gape *or* gaze at, long for; (+*dat*.) gape open-mouthed (for), covet
inhonestē *adv*. dishonourably
inhonestō 1. to disgrace
inhonestus, -a, -um *adj*. dishonourable, shameful; ugly
inhonōrābilis, -is, -e *adj*. not bringing honour
inhonōrātus, -a, -um *adj*. unhonoured, undistinguished
inhonōrus, -a, -um *adj*. unhonoured, undistinguished; inglorious
inhorreō 2. (+*abl*.) to bristle (with)
inhorrescō, -ruī 3. to bristle; tremble; shake in fear; become agitated
inhospitālis, -is, -e *adj*. inhospitable
inhospitālitās, -ātis f. inhospitality
inhospitus, -a, -um *adj*. inhospitable
inhūmānē *adv*. insensitively, heartlessly
inhūmānitās, -ātis f. impoliteness, discourtesy; insensitivity
inhūmāniter *adv*. impolitely
inhūmānus, -a, -um *adj*. impolite, uncivilized; insensitive, cruel
inhumātus, -a, -um *adj*. unburied
inibi *adv*. there; nearby
iniciō, iniēcī, iniectum 3. (+*dat*. *or* +*in* +*acc*.) to throw on *or* in; put on; insert, instil (in)
iniectō 1. (+*dat*.) to lay (*hands*) (on)
iniectus, -ūs m. laying on; focusing
iniiciō see **iniciō**
inimīcē *adv*. in an unfriendly manner
inimīcitia, -ae f. unfriendliness, enmity
inimīcō 1. to make unfriendly
inimīcus, -a, -um *adj*. (+*dat*.) unfriendly, hostile (to); harmful (to); *m./f.sbst*. enemy, opponent
inintelligens, -ntis *adj*. without sense
inīquē *adv*. unevenly; unfairly; resentfully
inīquitās, -ātis f. unevenness; unfairness; bias
inīquus, -a, -um *adj*. uneven, unequal; unfair; resentful; prejudicial; *m.sbst*. prejudiced person
initiāmentum, -ī n. rite of initiation
initiātiō, -ōnis f. ritual initiation
initiātus, -ī m. initiate
initiō 1. to initiate with rites
initium, -(i)ī n. beginning, start; source, origin; *pl*. initiatory rites
initus, -ūs m. entry; beginning
iniūcundē *adv*. unpleasantly
iniūcunditās, -ātis f. unpleasantness
iniūcundus, -a, -um *adj*. unpleasant
iniungō, -nxī, -nctum 3. (+*dat*.) to fasten (to); impose (upon)
iniūrātus, -a, -um *adj*. unsworn
iniūria, -ae f. unjust action; injustice; injury; assault
iniūriōsē *adv*. unjustly
iniūriōsus, -a, -um *adj*. unjust; disrespectful
iniūrius, -a, -um *adj*. unjust, unfair
iniūrus, -a, -um *adj*. unjust
iniussū *m.abl.sg*. (+*gen*.) without (one's) leave
iniussus, -a, -um *adj*. unbidden, unordered
iniustē *adv*. unjustly, wrongfully
iniustitia, -ae f. injustice
iniustus, -a, -um *adj*. unjust, unfair; unlawful
inl- see **ill-**
inm- see **imm-**
innābilis, -is, -e *adj*. that cannot be swum in
innascor, innātus 3. *dep*. (+*abl*.) to come into being, be born (in *or* on)
innatō 1. (+*dat*.) to swim in; (+*acc*.) float upon
innātus, -a, -um *adj*. natural, innate
innāvigābilis, -is, -e *adj*. innavigable
innectō, -xuī, -xum 3. (+*dat*.) to fasten, tie (on); (+*abl*.) bind up (with); devise
innītor, -ixus (-īsus) 3. *dep*. (+*dat*.) to lean, rest (on); press (on); rely (on)
innō 1. (+*dat./abl./acc*.) to swim (in), float (on)
innocens, -ntis *adj*. innocent; virtuous, upright; harmless
innocenter *adv*. innocently
innocentia, -ae f. innocence; uprightness
innocuē *adv*. innocently; harmlessly

innocuus, -a, -um *adj.* innocent; harmless; unharmed

innōtescō, -tuī 3. to become famous, well known

innoxiē *adv.* harmlessly

innoxius, -a, -um *adj.* harmless; innocent; unharmed

innuba, -ae *f.adj.* unmarried

innūbilus, -a, -um *adj.* cloudless

innūbis, -is, -e *adj.* cloudless

innūbō, -upsī 3. (+*dat.*) to marry (into)

innumerābilis, -is, -e *adj.* countless

innumerābilitās, -ātis *f.* infinity

innumerābiliter *adv.* countlessly

innumerālis, -is, -e *adj.* countless

innumerus, -a, -um *adj.* countless

innuō, -uī 3. (+*dat.*) to nod (to)

innuptus, -a, -um *adj.* unmarried

innūtriō 4. (+*abl.*) to rear (among)

inoblītus, -a, -um *adj.* unforgetful

inobrutus, -a, -um *adj.* not drowned

inobsequens, -ntis *adj.* (+*dat.*) disobedient (towards)

inobservābilis, -is, -e *adj.* difficult to observe

inobservantia, -ae *f.* lack of observance (*of a routine*)

inobservātus, -a, -um *adj.* unobserved; irregular

inocciduus, -a, -um *adj.* unsetting

inodōrus, -a, -um *adj.* unscented

inoffensē *adv.* without obstruction

inoffensus, -a, -um *adj.* unobstructed; untouched, unharmed

inofficiōsus, -a, -um *adj.* undutiful

inolens, -ntis *adj.* odourless

inolescō, -lēvī 3. (+*dat.*) to grow (in)

inōminātus, -a, -um *adj.* ill-fated

inopia, -ae *f.* poverty, scarcity, deficiency; impotence; defencelessness

inopīnans, -ntis *adj.* unsuspecting

inopīnanter *adv.* unexpectedly

inopīnātō *adv.* unexpectedly

inopīnātus, -a, -um *adj.* unexpected

inopīnus, -a, -um *adj.* unexpected; unsuspecting

inopiōsus, -a, -um *adj.* (+*gen.*) devoid (of)

inops, -pis *adj.* poor, scanty; (+*gen./abl.*) deficient (in); impotent; defenceless

inōrātus, -a, -um *adj.* not pleaded

inordinātus, -a, -um *adj.* disorderly

inornātus, -a, -um *adj.* unadorned, unkempt; unhonoured

inp- see **imp-**

inquam (*only* **inquistī, inquit** *in pf.*) *v. irreg.* to say

inquiēs, -ētis *adj.* restless, unsettled

inquiētō 1. to trouble, disturb

inquiētus, -a, -um *adj.* restless, unsettled; turbulent; worried

inquilīnus, -ī *m.* lodger, tenant

inquinātē *adv.* in a debased style

inquinātus, -a, -um *adj.* morally corrupt, impure; debased

inquinō 1. to befoul, taint; defile, contaminate; defame

inquīrō, -sīvī (-siī), -sītus 3. to search out; investigate; (+*in* +*acc.*) make inquiries (into)

inquīsītiō, -ōnis *f.* searching out; investigation, inquiry

inquīsītor, -ōris *m.* one who searches out; investigator, inspector

inquīsītus, -a, -um *adj.* uninvestigated

inr- see **irr-**

insalūbris, -is, -e *adj.* unhealthy

insalūtātus, -a, -um *adj.* ungreeted

insānābilis, -is, -e *adj.* incurable, irremediable

insānē *adv.* insanely, wildly

insānia, -ae *f.* madness; mania, rage

insāniō 4. to be mad, insane; rave

insānitās, -ātis *f.* mental unsoundness

insānus, -a, -um *adj.* mad, frenzied; raging; maddening; absurd; *n.sg. as adv.* immensely

insapiens see **insipiens**

insatiābilis, -is, -e *adj.* insatiable

insatiābiliter *adv.* insatiably

insatiātus, -a, -um *adj.* unsated

insatietās, -ātis *f.* insatiate passion

insaturābilis, -is, -e *adj.* insatiable

insaturābiliter *adv.* insatiably

inscendō, -dī, -sum 3. to climb up (into); mount, board

inscensiō, -ōnis *f.* boarding (*of a ship*)

insciens, -ntis *adj.* ignorant, unknowing

inscienter *adv.* ignorantly

inscientia, -ae *f.* ignorance, lack of knowledge

inscītē *adv.* ignorantly

inscītia, -ae *f.* ignorance, lack of knowledge

inscītus, -a, -um *adj.* ignorant

inscius, -a, -um *adj.* ignorant, unknowing

inscrībō, inscripsī, inscriptum 3. to inscribe; (+*dat.*) inscribe (to); enter (*a record*) as; entitle

inscriptiō, -ōnis *f.* inscribing; inscription, title

inscriptum, -ī *n.* inscription

insculpō, -psī, -ptum 3. to carve; (+*dat.*) engrave (on)

insecābilis, -is, -e *adj.* indivisible

insecō, -uī, -tum 1. to cut; incise

insectātiō, -ōnis *f.* hostile pursuit; verbal attack

insectātor, -ōris *m.* hostile pursuer

insector 1. *dep.* or **insectō** 1. to pursue in hostility; harry

insēdābiliter *adv.* unassuageably, unquenchably

insegestus, -a, -um *adj.* unsown

insemel *adv.* together, at the same time

insenescō, -nuī 3. (+*dat.*) to grow old (in)

insensilis, -is, -e *adj.* lacking the faculty of sensation

insēparābilis, -is, -e *adj.* inseparable

insepultus, -a, -um *adj.* unburied; unattended by funereal rites

insequens, -ntis *adj.* subsequent, next

insequor, -cūtus 3. *dep.* to follow on; succeed; pursue, hound

inserēnus, -a, -um *adj.* uncalm, stormy

inserō[1], -uī, -tum 3. to insert; (+*dat.*) introduce (into); attach (to)

inserō[2], insēvī, insitum 3. to sow, plant; graft on; implant

insertō 1. (+*dat.*) to insert (into)

inserviō 4. (+*dat./acc.*) to serve, take care of

inservō 1. to notice

insībilō 1. to hiss, whistle

insiccātus, -a, -um *adj.* dried up

insideō, insēdī, insessum 2. (+*dat./acc.*) to sit, rest (on); be situated (in); be burdensome (to)

insidiae, -ārum *f.pl.* ambush, ambuscade; snare; treacherous plot

insidiātor, -ōris *m.* one who lies in ambush; deceiver

insidior 1. *dep.* to lie in ambush; lay traps; (+*dat.*) plot treacherously (against)

insidiōsē *adv.* deceitfully

insidiōsus, -a, -um *adj.* with hidden ambushes, dangerous; deceitful, insidious

insīdō, insēdī, insessum 3. (+*acc./dat.*) to sit upon; settle in, occupy (*by force*); sink in, penetrate

insigne, -is *n.* indication of rank; emblem; characteristic; distinction, honour

insigniō 4. to mark; distinguish; honour

insignis, -is, -e *adj.* manifest, conspicuous; distinguished; remarkable; honourable

insignītē *adv.* signally, markedly

insigniter *adv.* markedly; remarkably

insignītus, -a, -um *adj.* clearly defined, distinctive; remarkable; well-known

insilia, -ium *n.pl.* treadles (*or sim.*) of a loom

insiliō, -uī 4. to jump on, leap on

insimulātiō, -ōnis *f.* allegation

insimulō 1. to accuse, blame; allege

insincērus, -a, -um *adj.* corrupt, impure

insinuātiō, -ōnis *f.* speech designed to win over jury indirectly

insinuō 1. to insinuate, work in; instil

insipiens, -ntis *adj.* unwise, stupid

insipienter *adv.* stupidly

insipientia, -ae *f.* lack of wisdom, stupidity

insistō, institī 3. (+*dat.*) to take one's stand, stand (on); halt, hesitate; set to work (on); pursue; (+*acc.*) stand on; set upon

insitīcius, -a, -um *adj.* foreign, imported

insitiō, -ōnis *f.* grafting (*of trees*)

insitīvus, -a, -um *adj.* produced by grafting; imported

insitor, -ōris *m.* one who grafts trees

insociābilis, -is, -e *adj.* implacable, unsociable; uncommunal

insōlābiliter *adv.* inconsolably

insolens, -ntis *adj.* (+*gen./acc.*) unfamiliar (with); unrestrained; arrogant, insolent

insolenter *adv.* unusually; unrestrainedly; insolently

insolentia, -ae *f.* unfamiliarity, unusualness; immoderacy; insolence

insolescō 3. to become arrogant

insolidus, -a, -um *adj.* not firm, tender

insolitus, -a, -um *adj.* unfamiliar; (+*ad* +*acc.* or +*gen.*) unaccustomed (to)

insomnia, -ae *f.* insomnia

insomnis, -is, -e *adj.* sleepless

insomnium, -(i)ī *n.* insomnia; dream, vision

insonō, -uī 1. to resound; sound out aloud

insons, -ntis *adj.* innocent; harmless

insōpītus, -a, -um *adj.* sleepless

insopor, -ōris *adj.* sleepless

inspectiō, -ōnis *f.* inspection, investigation

inspectō 1. to observe

inspectus, -ūs *m.* observation

inspērans, -ntis *adj.* not hoping

inspērātus, -a, -um *adj.* unhoped for; unforeseen; **ex inspērātō** unexpectedly

inspergō, -rsī, -rsum 3. to sprinkle on

inspiciō, inspexī, inspectum 3. to inspect; watch, observe; investigate, come to know

inspīcō 1. to cleave into the shape of a corn-ear

inspīrō 1. to breathe; (+*acc./dat.*) blow in, infuse; blow on *or* into; infuse; excite

inspoliātus, -a, -um *adj.* not plundered

inspuō, -uī, -ūtum 3. (+*dat.*) to spit (on)

inspurcō 1. to defile

insputō 1. to spit upon

instabilis, -is, -e *adj.* unsteady; unfixed; fickle; unable to be stood upon

instans, -ntis *adj.* urgent, pressing

instanter *adv.* urgently, pressingly

instantia, -ae *f.* impendingness; insistence; concentration

instar *n.* equal, equivalent; (+*gen.*) to the degree (of)

instaurātiō, -ōnis *f.* repetition

instaurātīvus, -a, -um *adj.* repeated

instaurō 1. to repeat; restore; renew, resume

insternō, instrāvī, instrātum 3. (+*dat.*) to spread (on); (+*abl.*) cover (with)

instīgātor, -ōris *m.* instigator

instīgātrix, -īcis *f.* female instigator

instīgō 1. to urge, impel; provoke

instillō 1. to pour in by drops, instil; drip onto

instimulātor, -ōris *m.* provoker, inciter

instimulō 1. to urge, impel

instinctor, -ōris *m.* instigator

instinctus¹, -a, -um *adj.* roused; inspired

instinctus², -ūs *m.* instigation; inspiration

instipulor 1. *dep.* to stipulate for

instita, -ae *f.* ribbon, band

institiō, -ōnis *f.* motionlessness

institor, -ōris *m.* pedlar, retailer

institōrium, -īī *n.* retailing

instituō, -uī, -ūtum 3. to set up, establish; institute; appoint; educate; set to work on

institūtiō, -ōnis *f.* establishment; organization; custom; education; doctrine

institūtum, -ī *n.* plan; custom; *pl.* teachings

instō, -itī 1. (+*dat.*) to stand on *or* over; press (on); threaten; (+*acc.*) set foot on

instrēnuus, -a, -um *adj.* inactive, slothful

instrepō, -uī, -itum 3. to make a loud noise

instringō, -nxī, -ctum 3. to bind

instructē *adv.* elaborately

instructiō, -ōnis *f.* drawing up (*of soldiers*)

instructor, -ōris *m.* one who equips

instructus¹, -a, -um *adj.* (+*abl.*) equipped (with), learned (in); arranged

instructus², -ūs *m.* equipment

instrūmentum, -ī *n.* equipment; instrument, tool

instruō, -xī, -ctum 3. to build; arrange, draw up (*soldiers*); (+*abl.*) equip (with); instruct

insuāvis, -is, -e *adj.* displeasing, disagreeable

insūdō 1. (+*dat.*) to sweat (on *or* at)

insuēfaciō, -fēcī, -factum 3. to accustom

insuescō, insuēvī, insuētum 3. (+*inf./ dat.*) to become accustomed (to); accustom

insuētus, -a, -um *adj.* (+*gen./dat./inf.*) unaccustomed (to); unfamiliar

insula, -ae *f.* island; block of flats

insulānus, -ī *m.* inhabitant of an island, islander

insulsē *adv.* stupidly, boringly

insulsitās, -ātis *f.* stupidity, dullness

insulsus, -a, -um *adj.* stupid, dull

insultō 1. (+*dat.*) to leap on; (+*dat./acc.*) to leap in; mock, jeer

insultūra, -ae *f.* leaping on

insum, inesse, infuī *v.irreg.* (+*in* +*abl. or* +*dat.*) to be in *or* on; be among, involved in

insūmō, -umpsī, -umptum 3. to expend; assume

insuō, -uī, -ūtum 3. to sew on; (+*dat./abl.*) sew up (in)

insuper¹ *adv.* above; furthermore

insuper² *prep.* (+*abl.*) above, besides

insuperābilis, -is, -e *adj.* unconquerable, insurmountable; unsurpassable

insurgō, -rrexī 3. to get up, rise; rise up; rebel

insusurrō 1. to whisper; whisper into someone's ear

intābescō, -buī 3. to melt, waste away

intactilis, -is, -e *adj.* intangible

intactus¹, -a, -um *adj.* untouched, unharmed; unused; virginal; intangible

intactus², -ūs *m.* intangibility

intāminātus, -a, -um *adj.* uncontaminated

intectus, -a, -um *adj.* uncovered, bare; frank

integellus, -a, -um *adj.* unharmed, rather safe

integer, -gra, -grum *adj.* untouched, fresh, intact; unharmed; unused; virginal; upright

integimentum see **integumentum**

integō, -xī, -ctum 3. to cover; roof over

integrascō 3. to break out anew

integrātiō, -ōnis *f.* renewal

integrē *adv.* uprightly, honestly; wholly

integritās, -ātis *f.* wholeness, integrity; uprightness

integrō 1. to renew; resume

integumentum, -ī *n.* covering, wrapping; shield

intellectus, -ūs *m.* recognizing, comprehending; intellect; meaning

intellegens, -ntis *adj.* intelligent, understanding

intellegenter *adv.* intelligently

intellegentia, -ae *f.* comprehending, understanding; intelligence; idea

intellegibilis, -is, -e *adj.* intellectual

intellegō, -exī (-ēgī), -ectum 3. to recognize, comprehend; understand; act intelligently

intellig- see **intelleg-**

intemerātus, -a, -um *adj.* undefiled, unsullied, pure

intemperans, -ntis *adj.* unrestrained; excessive

intemperanter *adv.* unrestrainedly; excessively

intemperantia, -ae *f.* lack of restraint, excessiveness; (+*gen.*) immoderation (in)

intemperātē *adv.* immoderately

intemperātus, -a, -um *adj.* immoderate

intemperiēs, -ēī *f.* or **-ae, -ārum** *f.pl.* immoderateness, intemperateness (*esp. of weather*)

intempestīvē *adv.* unseasonably

intempestīvus, -a, -um *adj.* unseasonable, untimely

intempestus, -a, -um *adj.* unseasonable; stormy; **nox intempesta** dead of night

intemptātus, -a, -um *adj.* untried, unattempted; unassailed

intendō, -dī, -tum 3. to stretch, strain; stretch out; spread out; direct; strive for, make for; accuse

intentē *adv.* intently, attentively

intentiō, -ōnis *f.* tautness; concentration; purpose; accusation

intentō 1. (+*dat.*) to point, direct (at); threaten

intentus¹, -a, -um *adj.* intent; intense; earnest

intentus², -ūs *m.* stretching out

intepeō 2. to be tepid

intepescō, -puī 3. to become warm; become tepid, cool

inter *prep.* (+*acc.*) among, between, amidst

interāmenta, -ōrum *n.pl.* internal fittings

interārescō 3. to dry out

interātim *adv.* meanwhile

interbibō 3. to drink up

interbītō 3. to perish, fail

intercalāris, -is, -e *adj.* inserted into the calendar

intercalārius, -a, -um *adj.* inserted into the calendar

intercalō 1. to insert into the calendar; defer

intercapēdō, -inis *f.* interruption, delay

intercēdō, -cessī, -cessum 3. to intervene; intercede; oppose

interceptiō, -ōnis *f.* interception

interceptor, -ōris *m.* usurper, thief

intercessiō, -ōnis *f.* intercession, veto; going bail

intercessor, -ōris *m.* one who intervenes *or* vetoes; mediator

intercidō¹, -dī 3. to fall between; be lost, perish

intercīdō², -dī, -sum 3. to cut through; interrupt, truncate; tamper with

intercinō 3. to sing between

intercipiō, -cēpī, -ceptum 3. to intercept; interrupt, cut short; seize by force; carry off, thieve

intercīsē *adv.* interruptedly

interclūdō, -sī, -sum 3. to block up, cut off; stifle; prevent, obstruct

interclūsiō, -ōnis *f.* blocking off

intercolumnium, -(i)ī *n.* space between two columns

intercurrō, -rrī, -rsum 3. to run between; intervene

intercursō 1. to run in between

intercursus, -ūs *m.* running between

intercus, -utis *adj.* subcutaneous; **aqua intercus** dropsy

interdīcō, -dixī, -dictum 3. to forbid, prohibit; interdict

interdictiō, -ōnis *f.* (+*gen.*) prohibition (from)

interdictum, -ī *n.* prohibition; interdict

interdictus, -a, -um *adj.* forbidden, prohibited

interdiū (-us) *adv.* by day, diurnally

interdō, -dedī, -datum 1. to put among, interpose

interductus, -ūs *m.* insertion of punctuation

interdum *adv.* now and then, sometimes

intereā *adv.* meanwhile

interemptor, -ōris *m.* killer, murderer

intereō, -īre, -iī, -itum 4. to die, perish; be destroyed, be lost

interequitō 1. to ride among *or* between

interfātiō, -ōnis *f.* interruption in speech

interfector, -ōris *m.* killer, murderer

interfectrix, -īcis *f.* murderess

interficiō, -fēcī, -fectum 3. to kill; destroy, bring to an end

interfīō, -fierī, -factus *v.irreg.* to perish, be destroyed

interfluō, -uxī 3. to flow between *or* among

interfluus, -a, -um *adj.* flowing between

interfodiō, -fōdī, -fossum 3. to penetrate

interfor 1. *dep.* (+*acc./dat.*) to interrupt

interfugiō, -fūgī 3. to escape between

interfulgeō, -lsī 2. (+*dat.*) to shine (amid)

interfurō 3. to rage through

interfūsus, -a, -um *adj.* (+*acc./dat.*) spread out between, interfused

interiaceō 2. to lie between

interiaciō see **intericiō**

interibi *adv.* meanwhile

intericiō, -iēcī, -iectum 3. to insert, introduce

interiectus, -ūs *m.* insertion, interposition

interim *adv.* meanwhile; sometimes

interimō, -ēmī, -emptum 3. to kill, destroy

interior, -or, -us *compar.adj.* inner, interior; deeper; internal; private

interitiō, -ōnis *f.* sudden death

interitus, -ūs *m.* sudden death; destruction

interiungō, -nxī, -nctum 3. to unharness; (+*dat.*) harness (to)

interius *compar.adv.* further in, more deeply; within

interkal- see **intercal-**

interlābor, -lapsus 3. *dep.* to flow between

interlegō, -xī, -ctum 3. to gather here and there

interligō 1. to join together

interlinō, -lēvī, -litum 3. to smear between; falsify (*a document*)

interloquor, -locūtus 3. *dep.* to interrupt

interlūceō, -luxī 2. to shine through *or* between; be clear

interlūnium, -(i)ī *n.* interlunary period

interluō, -uī 3. to flow between

intermaneō, -nsī 2. (+*dat.*) to remain (amidst)

intermenstruus, -a, -um *adj.* interlunar

intermicō 1. to shine temporarily

interminātus, -a, -um *adj.* limitless, infinite

interminor 1. *dep.* (+*dat.*) to threaten; (+*ne* +*subj.*) threaten (that)

intermisceō, -scuī, -xtum 2. (+*dat.*) to intermix (with)

intermissiō, -ōnis *f.* pause, intermission

intermittō, -mīsī, -missum 3. to leave off; leave in between, space out; interrupt

intermorior, -rtuus 3. *dep.* to perish; collapse unconscious

intermundia, -ōrum *n.pl.* interplanetary space

intermūrālis, -is, -e *adj.* placed between two walls

internascor, -nātus 3. *dep.* (+*dat.*) to spring up (amidst)

internecīnus, -a, -um *adj.* murderous

intern-eciō, -ōnis *f.* massacre, destruction

internecīvus, -a, -um *adj.* murderous, lethal

internecō 1. to massacre

internectō 3. to bind together

internic- see **internec-**

internigrans, -ntis adj. interspersed with black

internōdium, -(i)ī n. space between bodily joints

internoscō, -nōvī, -nōtum 3. to know apart, distinguish

internuntia, -ae f. female messenger

internuntiō 1. to send messages between

internuntius, -(i)ī m. messenger, intermediary

internus, -a, -um adj. internal; domestic; private

interō, intrīvī, intrītum 3. to crumble by rubbing

interoscitans, -ntis adj. yawning, half-asleep

interpellātiō, -ōnis f. interruption

interpellātor, -ōris m. one who interrupts

interpellō 1. to interrupt; impede; accost

interplicō 1. to weave between

interpolis, -is, -e adj. renewed, refurbished

interpolō 1. to renew, refurbish

interpōnō, -posuī, -positum 3. to interpose, insert; introduce; interfere

interpositiō, -ōnis f. insertion, introduction

interpositus, -ūs m. interposition

interpres, -etis m./f. intermediary, spokesman; interpreter

interpretātiō, -ōnis f. explanation; interpretation; meaning; translation

interpretor 1. dep. to explain; interpret; translate

interprimō, -pressī, -pressum 3. to strangle

interpunctiō, -ōnis f. interpunctuation (*between words*)

interpunctum, -ī n. pause between words (*or sim.*)

interpungō, -nxī, -nctum 3. to punctuate between, interpose

interquiescō, -quiēvī 3. to pause between; rest temporarily

interregnum, -ī n. period between rulers, interregnum

interrex, -ēgis m. ruling magistrate during an interregnum

interritus, -a, -um adj. unafraid, fearless

interrogātiō, -ōnis f. questioning, question; dialectic

interrogātiuncula, -ae f. petty question

interrogātum, -ī n. question

interrogō 1. to ask, interrogate; consult; indict

interrumpō, -rūpī, -ruptum 3. to break up; interrupt

interruptē adv. discontinuously

intersaepiō, -psī, -ptum 4. to barricade; cut off, divide

interscindō, -scidī, -scissum 3. to sever; cut off

interscrībō, -scripsī, -scriptum 3. to write in

intersecō, -uī, -tum 1. to cut through

intersēpiō see **intersaepiō**

interserō[1], -uī, -tum 3. to insert between, interpose

interserō[2], -sēvī, -situm 3. (+*dat.*) to plant (among)

intersonō, -uī 1. (+*dat.*) to sing (among)

interspīrātiō, -ōnis f. pause for breath

interstinguō, -xī, -ctum 3. to divide up; extinguish temporarily

interstringō, -xī 3. to throttle

intersum, -esse, -fuī v.irreg. (+*inter* +*acc.* or +*dat.*) to lie between, be among; be present (in); differ; **meā** (*etc.*) **interest** it matters to me (*etc.*), is advantageous to me

intertextus, -a, -um adj. interwoven

intertrahō, -xī, -ctum 3. to drag away

intertrīmentum, -ī n. damage from rubbing

interturbō 1. to make trouble by interfering

interutrāsque adv. intermediately, midway

intervallum, -ī n. intervening distance; intermission, interval; difference

intervellō, -ellī, -ulsum 3. to pluck out here and there

interveniō, -vēnī, -ventum 4. to come between, intervene; occur; arrive

interventor, -ōris m. one who intervenes

interventus, -ūs m. intervention; occurrence; arrival

intervertō, -tī, -sum 3. embezzle; cheat; revoke

interviās adv. on the way

intervireō 2. (+*dat.*) to be green (among)

intervīsō, -ī, -um 3. to go to see

intervolitō 1. to fly around amidst

intervolō 1. to fly between

intervomō, -uī, -itum 3. to emit (among)

intervortō see **intervertō**

intestābilis, -is, -e *adj.* forbidden to summon witnesses; shameful, infamous

intestātō *adv.* without having made a will

intestātus, -a, -um *adj.* intestate; unattested, without witness(es)

intestīnum, -ī *n.* alimentary canal; *pl.* intestines

intestīnus, -a, -um *adj.* internal; domestic; private

intexō, -uī, -tum 3. (+*dat.*) to weave (into *or* onto); weave closely; cover by twining

intimē *adv.* profoundly; intimately

intimus, -a, -um *adj.* innermost; most profound; most private; most intimate

intinguō, -nxī, -nctum 3. (+*dat.*) to colour (with)

intolerābilis, -is, -e *adj.* unendurable, insufferable; irresistible

intolerandus, -a, -um *adj.* unendurable, insufferable

intolerans, -ntis *adj.* (+*gen.*) unable to endure; insufferable

intoleranter *adv.* insufferably; impatiently

intolerantia, -ae *f.* intolerant, impatient

intonō, -uī 1. to thunder; thunder forth

intonsus, -a, -um *adj.* uncut, unshorn; not stripped of foliage

intorqueō, -rsī, -rtum 2. to bend round *or* back; twist round; (+*dat.*) launch (at)

intortus, -a, -um *adj.* complicated, intricate

intrā¹ *prep.* (+*acc.*) within, inside

intrā² *adv.* within, inside

intrābilis, -is, -e *adj.* able to be entered

intractābilis, -is, -e *adj.* intractable, unmanageable

intractātus, -a, -um *adj.* untried, unattempted

intremō, -uī 3. to quake, tremble

intrepidē *adv.* fearlessly, bravely

intrepidus, -a, -um *adj.* fearless, brave; unworried

intrīcō 1. to entangle, embarrass

intrinsecus *adv.* internally; inwards

intrītus, -a, -um *adj.* unwearied

intrō¹ 1. to enter; penetrate; begin; study

intrō² *adv.* inside, indoors

intrōdō 1. (*refl.*) to insinuate (oneself)

intrōdūcō, -duxī, -ductum 3. to introduce, insert; bring forward; establish

intrōductiō, -ōnis *f.* introduction

intrōeō, -īre, -iī (-īvī), -itum 4. to enter; invade; assume

intrōferō, -ferre, -tulī, -lātum *v.irreg.* to bring in

intrōgredior, -ssus 3. *dep.* to enter

introitus, -ūs *m.* entrance; invasion; beginning

intrōmittō, -mīsī, -missum 3. to admit, let in; introduce

introrsum (-us) *adv.* inwards; within

intrōrumpō, -rūpī 3. to break in

intrōspectō 1. to gaze in

intrōspiciō, -spexī, -spectum 3. to look into; inspect; regard

intrōsum (-us) see **introrsum (-us)**

intrōvocō 1. to summon in

intubum, -ī *n.* chicory, endive

intueor, -itus 2. *dep.* *or* **intuor** 3. *dep.* to look at, watch; bear in mind; contemplate

intumescō, -muī 3. to swell up, rise; (+*abl.*) swell (*with feelings*)

intumulātus, -a, -um *adj.* unburied

inturbātus, -a, -um *adj.* undisturbed

inturbidus, -a, -um *adj.* undisturbed, quiet

intus *adv.* inside, within; from within; privately

intūtus, -a, -um *adj.* unprotected; unsafe

inula, -ae *f.* elecampane

īnuleus, -ī *m.* young deer, fawn

inultus, -a, -um *adj.* unavenged; unpunished

inumbrō 1. to cast a shadow upon, shade

inundātiō, -ōnis *f.* flooding, inundation

inundō 1. to flood, be flooded; swarm

inunguō, -nxī, -nctum 3. to anoint

inurbānē *adv.* unsophisticatedly

inurbānus, -a, -um *adj.* unrefined, unsophisticated

inurgeō 2. to push

inūrō, inussī, inustum 3. to burn; (+*dat.*) brand (on); curl (*hair*)

inūsitātē *adv.* in an unusual fashion

inūsitātus, -a, -um *adj.* unusual, unfamiliar

inūtilis, -is, -e *adj.* unusable; useless; invalid; inexpedient

inūtilitās, -ātis *f.* uselessness

inūtiliter *adv.* uselessly; inexpediently

invādō, -sī, -sum 3. to attack, set on; seize; (+*in* +*acc.*) set upon; rush in; enter into

invalēscō, -luī 3. to grow strong, more powerful

invalidus, -a, -um *adj.* weak, infirm; ineffectual

invectīcius, -a, -um *adj.* foreign, imported

invectiō, -ōnis *f.* sailing in; importation

invectum, -ī *n.* imported item

invehō, -xī, -ctum 3. to carry in, import; introduce; *pass.* (+*in* +*acc.* or +*dat.*/*acc.*) ride *or* sail in; inveigh (against)

invendibilis, -is, -e *adj.* unable to be sold

inveniō, invēnī, inventum 4. to find, discover; contrive; invent; obtain

inventiō, -ōnis *f.* discovery; contriving; stratagem

inventor, -ōris *m.* discoverer; author

inventrix, -īcis *f.* female discoverer *or* author

inventum, -ī *n.* discovery; plan

inventus, -ūs *m.* discovery, invention

invenustē *adv.* unattractively

invenustus, -a, -um *adj.* unattractive; without love

inverēcundē *adv.* shamelessly

inverēcundia, -ae *f.* shamelessness

inverēcundus, -a, -um *adj.* shameless, impudent

invergō 3. (+*in* +*acc.* or +*dat.*) to pour (upon)

inversiō, -ōnis *f.* ironic usage

invertō, -tī, -sum 3. to invert, reverse; pervert; translate

invesperāscit 3. *impers.* it becomes evening

investīgātiō, -ōnis *f.* (+*gen.*) investigation (into)

investīgātor, -ōris *m.* (+*gen.*) investigator (into)

investīgō 1. to track down, search out, investigate

investiō 4. to clothe, adorn

inveterāscō, -rāvī 3. to become long-standing, chronic

inveterātiō, -ōnis *f.* long-standingness, inveterateness

inveterātus, -a, -um *adj.* long-standing, chronic

inveterō 1. to become entrenched

invicem *adv.* in turn, mutually; alternately; (+*gen.*) in place (of)

invictus, -a, -um *adj.* unconquered; invincible, indestructible; resolute

invidendus, -a, -um *adj.* enviable

invidentia, -ae *f.* envy, jealousy

invideō, invīdī, invīsum 2. (+*acc.*/*dat.*) to envy, be jealous (of); (+*acc.*/*dat.*/*gen.*) grudge

invidia, -ae *f.* envy, jealousy; ill-will, dislike; rousing of envy

invidiōsē *adv.* so as to arouse envy *or* dislike

invidiōsus, -a, -um *adj.* enviable; invidious, hated; envious

invidus, -a, -um *adj.* envious, jealous; hostile, malevolent

invigilō 1. (+*dat.*) to stay awake (for); watch closely (for *or* over)

inviolābilis, -is, -e *adj.* indestructible, inviolable

inviolātē *adv.* without infringement

inviolātus, -a, -um *adj.* unharmed; unviolated

invīsitātus, -a, -um *adj.* unseen; strange, unfamiliar

invīsō, -ī, -um 3. to go to see, visit; watch over

invīsus¹, -a, -um *adj.* odious, detestable

invīsus², -a, -um *adj.* unseen

invītāmentum, -ī *n.* incitement, inducement

invītātiō, -ōnis *f.* invitation

invītātor, -ōris *m.* officer who issued imperial invitations

invītātus, -ūs *m.* invitation

invītē *adv.* unwillingly

invītō 1. to invite; entertain; incite

invītus, -a, -um *adj.* unwilling, reluctant; unwillingly done

invius, -a, -um *adj.* impassable, impenetrable; inaccessible

invocātus, -a, -um *adj.* unsummoned, uninvited

invocō 1. to summon, invoke; pray for

involātus, -ūs *m.* flying into

involitō 1. to float on

involō 1. (+*in* +*acc.* or +*dat.*/*acc.*) to rush (at *or* in), swoop (upon)

involūcrum, -ī *n.* cover, wrapper

involūtus, -a, -um *adj.* concealed, obscure

involvō, -vī, -ūtum 3. to roll, revolve; cover, wrap up; clothe

involvolus, -ī *m.* caterpillar

invortō see **invertō**

invulnerābilis, -is, -e *adj.* invulnerable

invulnerātus, -a, -um *adj.* unwounded

ĭō or **ĭo** *interj.* ritual cry

iocātiō, -ōnis *f.* jesting, joking

iocor 1. *dep.* to jest, joke

iocōsē *adv.* jestingly, jokingly

iocōsus, -a, -um *adj.* jesting, joking; funny

ioculāris, -is, -e *adj.* funny; *n.pl.sbst.* jokes

ioculāriter *adv.* jestingly

ioculārius, -a, -um *adj.* funny

ioculātor, -ōris *m.* jester

ioculor 1. *dep.* to jest, joke

ioculus, -ī *m.* jest, joke

iōcund- see **iūcund-**

iocur see **iecur**

iocus, -ī *m.* or **-a, -ōrum** *n.pl.* joke, jest; laughing-stock; trifle

ĭōta *indecl.n.* the Greek letter *iota*

ipse (-us), -a, -um *pron.* himself, herself, itself; *adj.* the same, the very

ipsissimus, -a, -um *adj.* the very same

īra, īrae *f.* anger, rage; dislike

īrācundē *adv.* irately

īrācundia, -ae *f.* irascibility; anger, resentment

īrācundus, -a, -um *adj.* irascible; angry

īrascor, īrātus 3. *dep.* to become angry, be angry

īre (*present inf. of* **eō**)

īrātus, -a, -um *adj.* angry, furious

īris, īridis *f.* orris

īrōnīa (-ēa), -ae *f.* irony

irradiō 1. to shed light upon

irrāsus, -a, -um *adj.* unshaven

irratiōnālis, -is, -e *adj.* irrational

[irraucescō], irrausī 3. to become hoarse

irredux, -ucis *adj.* from which there is no return

irreligātus, -a, -um *adj.* not bound, untied

irreligiōsē *adj.* impiously, disrespectfully

irreligiōsus, -a, -um *adj.* impious, irreligious

irremeābilis, -is, -e *adj.* that does not allow a return

irremediābilis, -is, -e *adj.* against which there is no remedy

irreparābilis, -is, -e *adj.* irretrievable

irrepertus, -a, -um *adj.* undiscovered

irrēpō, -epsī 3. (+*in* +*acc.*) to creep in; insinuate (into); penetrate, seep into

irreprehensus, -a, -um *adj.* blameless

irreptō 1. (+*dat.*) to creep (over)

irrequiētus, -a, -um *adj.* tireless; unceasing

irresectus, -a, -um *adj.* uncut

irresolūtus, -a, -um *adj.* unloosened

irrētiō 4. to entangle in a net, ensnare

irretortus, -a, -um *adj.* not turned back

irreverens, -ntis *adj.* (+*gen.*) disrespectful (towards)

irreverenter *adv.* disrespectfully

irreverentia, -ae *f.* disrespect

irrevocābilis, -is, -e *adj.* unable to be called back; irreversible, unalterable

irrevocātus, -a, -um *adj.* not called back; unable to be held back

irrīdeō, -sī, -sum 2. to laugh at, make fun of

irrīdiculē *adv.* unamusingly

irrīdiculum, -ī *n.* laughing-stock

irrigātiō, -ōnis *f.* irrigation

irrigō 1. to flood, irrigate; inundate; diffuse

irriguus, -a, -um *adj.* flooded, irrigated; irrigating

irrīsiō, -ōnis *f.* mockery, ridicule

irrīsor, -ōris *m.* mocker

irrīsus, -ūs *m.* mockery, ridicule

irrītābilis, -is, -e *adj.* easily provoked

irrītāmen, -inis *n.* incentive, stir

irrītāmentum, -ī *n.* incentive, stir

irrītātiō, -ōnis *f.* incitement, provocation

irrītātor, -ōris *m.* inciter

irrītō 1. to provoke, annoy; incite, stimulate; aggravate

irritus, -a, -um *adj.* unratified, void; unrealized; ineffectual, useless

irrogātiō, -ōnis *f.* demand; imposition

irrogō 1. to demand; impose

irrōrō 1. to besprinkle; (+*dat.*) sprinkle, rain (on)

irrubescō, -buī 3. to become red

irructō 1. (+*in* +*acc.*) to belch (into)

irrūgō 1. to draw into creases, wrinkle

irrumātiō, -ōnis *f.* receipt of fellatio

irrumātor, -ōris *m.* one who receives fellatio

irrumō 1. to receive fellatio

irrumpō, irrūpī, irruptum 3. to burst into; rush in upon; penetrate

irruō, -uī 3. (+*in* +*acc.*) to rush in; charge (at)

irruptiō, -ōnis f. bursting in; incursion, assault

irruptus, -a, -um adj. unbroken

is, ea, id pron. this one or thing, he, she, it; adj. this; that

īselasticus, -a, -um adj. granting the victor a triumphal return (*of athletic contests*); n.pl.sbst. public allowance granted to a victorious athlete

issula, -ae f. little mistress

istāc adv. that way

istāctenus adv. thus far

iste, ista, istud pron. this one or thing (*of yours*), he, she, it (*of yours*); adj. that (*of yours*)

isthmos (-us), -ī m./f. isthmus

istic[1]**, istaec, istuc** pron. this one or thing (*of yours*), he, she, it (*of yours*); adj. that (*of yours*)

istīc[2] adv. over there (*where you are*)

istim adv. from there (*where you are*)

istinc adv. from there (*where you are*), from your side

istō(c) adv. to there (*where you are*)

istorsum adv. towards you

istūc adv. to there (*where you are*)

ita adv. thus, in this way; so; even so; yes

itaque adv. therefore, accordingly; well then

item adv. similarly; likewise; in turn

iter, itineris n. journey; march; route, road

iterātiō, -ōnis f. reiteration

iterō 1. to repeat, reiterate; renew, rework

iterum adv. (for) a second time, again; contrariwise

itidem adv. similarly, likewise

itiner see **iter**

itiō, -ōnis f. going

itō 1. to go habitually

itus, itūs m. going; leaving

iuba, -ae f. mane; helmet crest

iubar, -aris n. (first) daylight; brightness, light

iubātus, -a, -um adj. having a mane

iubeō, iussī, iussum 2. (+*inf.*) to order (to); (+*ut* +*subj.*) command (to); decree, prescribe; **salvēre iubēre** (+*dat.*) to welcome, greet

iūcundē adv. pleasantly

iūcunditās, -ātis f. pleasantness, agreeableness

iūcundus, -a, -um adj. pleasant, agreeable

iūdex, -icis m./f. judge, juror; critic

iūdicātiō, -ōnis f. reaching a settlement; crucial question

iūdicātum, -ī n. accepted judgement; legal payment of debt

iūdicātus, -ūs m. office of judge

iūdiciālis, -is, -e adj. judicial, forensic

iūdiciārius, -a, -um adj. judicial, forensic

iūdicium, -(i) n. judicial investigation; judgement; decision; opinion; discernment; esteem

iūdicō 1. to judge, adjudge; sentence; decide; appraise; (+*acc.*+*inf.*) consider (that)

iugālis, -is, -e adj. nuptial, matrimonial; m.pl.sbst. team of yoked animals

iugātiō, -ōnis f. trellising (*of vines*)

iūgerum, -ī n. two-thirds of an acre; expanse of land

iuges, [-etis] adj. concerning yoked animals

iūgis, -is, -e adj. continual, ever-flowing

iūglans, -ndis adj. walnut

iugō 1. (+*dat.*) to join (to); marry

iugōsus, -a, -um adj. mountainous

iugulō 1. to slaughter, butcher; destroy

iugulum, -ī n. or **-us, -ī** m. throat; slaughter

iugum, -ī n. yoke; pair (*esp. of yoked animals*); cross-beam; ridge, scar

iūmentum, -ī n. beast of burden

iunceus, -a, -um adj. made of rushes; like a rush

iuncōsus, -a, -um adj. full of rushes

iunctim adv. together; consecutively

iunctiō, -ōnis f. yoking together, association

iunctūra, -ae f. joint; yoking together, juxtaposition

iunctus, -a, -um adj. connected, yoked together; closely associated; complex

iuncus, -ī m. rush

iungō, iunxī, iunctum 3. to yoke; join; combine, unite

iūnior see **iuvenis**

iūniperus, -ī f. juniper tree

iūnix, -īcis f. young cow

iūrātor, -ōris m. sworn witness; tax official

iūrātus, -a, -um *adj.* under oath, sworn in loyalty

iūre *adv.* lawfully, justly; correctly

iurgium, -(i)ī *n.* quarrel; abuse

iurgō 1. to quarrel, wrangle; reproach

iūridiciālis, -is, -e *adj.* concerning the legality (*of actions etc.*)

iūridicus, -ī *m.* judge

iūrigō see **iurgō**

iūrisdictiō, -ōnis *f.* enactment of justice; jurisdiction

iūrō 1. (*+acc.+inf.*) to swear, take an oath (that); conspire

iūs[1], iūris *n.* law; authority; right; convention; **iūs iūrandum** oath

iūs[2], iūris *n.* broth, soup

iussum, -ī *n.* order, command

iussus, -ūs *m.* order, command

iustē *adv.* lawfully, justly

iustificus, -a, -um *adj.* justly dealing

iustitia, -ae *f.* justice, fairness

iustitium, -(i)ī *n.* emergency suspension of judicial activity

iustus, -a, -um *adj.* lawful, just; justified; fair; proper; *n.pl.sbst.* rites, customs

iuvenālis, -is, -e *adj.* youthful, young

iuvenāliter *adv.* in a youthful manner

iuvencus, -a, -um *adj.* young; *m.sbst.* bullock, young ox; *f.sbst.* young cow

iuvenescō 3. to become young; become mature, grow up

iuvenīlis, -is, -e *adj.* youthful

iuvenīliter *adv.* in a youthful manner

iuvenis[1], -is, -e (*compar.* **iūnior, -or, -us**) *adj.* young, youthful

iuvenis[2], -is *m.* young man, youth

iuvenix, -īcis *f.* young cow

iuvenor 1. *dep.* to act youthfully, be irresponsible

iuventa, -ae *f.* being young, youth

iuventās, -ātis *f.* youth

iuventūs, -ūtis *f.* young men, the youth; youthful qualities

iuvō, iūvī, iūtum 1. to help, aid; delight; improve; benefit

iuxtā[1] *prep.* (*+acc.*) beside, next to; according to

iuxtā[2] *adv.* besides, near by; equally

iuxtim *adv.* close by, side by side

K

kalendae (cal-), -ārum *f.pl.* first day of the month, the Kalends

kalendārium, -ī *n.* monthly account-book

labascō 3. to break into pieces; totter, waver

labea see **labia**

lābēcula, -ae *f.* slight disgrace

labefaciō, -fēcī, -factum 3. to cause to totter, shake; weaken; cause to waver

labefactō 1. to loosen, shake; weaken; cause to waver; corrupt

labellum¹, **-ī** *n.* lip

lābellum², **-ī** *n.* small basin

labeōsus, -a, -um *adj.* thick-lipped

lābēs, -is *f.* fall, collapse; ruin; cause of ruin; defect, blemish; disgrace

labia, -ae *f.* lip

labō 1. to totter, be unsteady; waver

lābor¹, **lapsus** 3. *dep.* to slide, glide; flow; slip, fall; decline; err

labor², **-ōris** *m.* work, toil; effort; distress; undertaking; production

labōrifer, -era, -erum *adj.* bringing toil; enduring toil

labōriōsē *adv.* laboriously; painfully

labōriōsus, -a, -um *adj.* full of toil, laborious; painful; hard-working; distressed

labōrō 1. to work, toil; be distressed; be anxious; suffer, be ill; work at

labōs see **labor**²

labrum¹, **-ī** *n.* lip; edge, rim

lābrum², **-ī** *n.* basin, bowl; bathing-place

labrusca, -ae *f.* wild vine

labyrinthēus, -a, -um *adj.* labyrinthine, intricate

labyrinthus, -ī *m.* labyrinth, maze

lac, lactis *n.* milk; milk-like sap

lacer, -era, -erum *adj.* mangled, lacerated, torn

lacerātiō, -ōnis *f.* mangling, lacerating, tearing

lacerna, -ae *f.* mantle, heavy cloak

lacernātus, -a, -um *adj.* wearing a mantle

lacerō 1. to mangle, lacerate, tear; ruin; slander violently

lacerta, -ae *f.* lizard; mackerel

lacertōsus, -a, -um *adj.* muscular, brawny

lacertus¹, **-ī** *m.* upper arm; power, strength

lacertus², **-ī** *m.* see **lacerta**

lacessō, -īvī (-iī), -ītum 3. to provoke, excite; challenge; harass, assail

lachanizō 1. to droop, wilt

lacinia, -ae *f.* fringe, edge

lacrima, -ae *f.* tear; crying; exudation (*from plants*)

lacrimābilis, -is, -e *adj.* mournful, lamentable; tearful, weepy

lacrimābundus, -a, -um *adj.* weeping abundantly

lacrimō 1. to shed tears, weep; bewail; (*of plants*) exude

lacrimōsus, -a, -um *adj.* full of tears, weeping; exciting tears; (*of plants*) exuding juice

lacrimula, -ae *f.* small tear

lactans, -ntis *adj.* sucking milk; milky

lacte see **lac**

lactens, -ntis *adj.* sucking milk; milky; milk-white

lacteolus, -a, -um *adj.* milk-white

lactēs, -ium *f.pl.* small intestines, guts

lactescō 3. to turn to milk

lacteus, -a, -um *adj.* of milk, milky; sucking-milk; milk-white

lactō 1. to allure, entice

lactūca, -ae *f.* lettuce

lactūcula, -ae *f.* small lettuce

lacūna, -ae *f.* hollow, pit; pond; deficiency, gap

lacūnar, -āris *n.* panelled ceiling

lacūnō 1. to work into panels

lacūnōsus, -a, -um *adj.* full of hollows

lacus, -ūs *m*. lake, pond; basin, vat

laedō, -sī, -sum 3. to hurt, injure; damage; violate; offend

laena, -ae *f*. woollen mantle, cloak

laesiō, -ōnis *f*. oratorical attack, injuring

laetābilis, -is, -e *adj*. joyful, gladdening

laetātiō, -ōnis *f*. rejoicing, exultation

laetē *adv*. richly, abundantly; happily, joyfully

laetificans, -ntis *adj*. joyful

laetificō 1. to fertilize, enrich; make joyful

laetificus, -a, -um *adj*. luxuriant, lush; joyful, gladdening

laetitia, -ae *f*. joy, exultation; fertility, lushness; beauty

laetor 1. *dep*. to feel joy, rejoice; (+*abl*./ *acc*.) take delight (in)

laetus, -a, -um *adj*. luxuriant, lush; rich; joyful, cheerful; (+*abl*.) rejoicing (in); fortunate, successful; pleasing; propitious

laeva, -ae *f*. left hand; left side

laevē *adv*. awkwardly

laevus, -a, -um *adj*. left, on the left side; unlucky; harmful; *n.sg. as adv*. on the left side

lagalōpex, -ecis *f*. fennec, hare-fox

laganum, -ī *n*. cake of flour and oil

lagēos, -ēī *f*. kind of vine

lagōis, -idis *f*. kind of bird (*perhaps* a grouse)

lagōna (-ūna), -ae *f*. flask, flaggon

laguncula, -ae *f*. small flask

lalīsiō, -ōnis *m*. young wild ass

lallō 1. to sing a lullaby

lāma, -ae *f*. bog, marsh

lamberō 1. to be victorious over, beat

lambō, -ī 3. to lick, lap; lick up, suck

lāmellulae, -ārum *f.pl*. small sum of money

lāmenta, -ōrum *n.pl*. wailing, lamentation

lāmentābilis, -is, -e *adj*. lamentable; full of sorrow, mournful

lāmentārius, -a, -um *adj*. producing lamentation

lāmentātiō, -ōnis *f*. wailing, lamentation

lāmentor 1. *dep*. to wail, lament; bewail

lamia, -ae *f*. female witch, vampire

lāmina, -ae *f*. thin sheet, strip, lamina

lammina, lamna see **lāmina**

lampas, -adis (-ados) *f*. torch; lantern; light; meteor

lāna, -ae *f*. wool; down

lānārius, -(i)ī *m*. dealer in wool

lānātus, -a, -um *adj*. woolly; downy; *f.pl. sbst*. sheep

lancea, -ae *f*. lance, light spear

lancinō 1. to tear apart, rend; squander

landīca, -ae *f*. clitoris

lāneus, -a, -um *adj*. made of wool, woollen; woolly

languefaciō 3. to make languid, enfeeble

langueō 2. to be languid, enfeebled; wilt; be idle

languescō, -guī 3. to become languid, lose strength; wilt; become idle; calm down

languidē *adv*. feebly, sluggishly

languidulus, -a, -um *adj*. somewhat drowsy; wilting

languidus, -a, -um *adj*. enfeebled, weak; ill; wilting; idle; apathetic

languor, -ōris *m*. feebleness, weakness; illness; idleness, inactivity; apathy

laniātus, -ūs *m*. tearing, lacerating (*of flesh*); flesh wound

laniēna, -ae *f*. butcher's shop

lānificium, -(i)ī *n*. wool-spinning, weaving

lānificus, -a, -um *adj*. wool-spinning, weaving

lāniger, -era, -erum *adj*. wool-bearing, woolly; *m./f.sbst*. sheep

laniō 1. to tear, lacerate, wound; pull to pieces

laniōnius, -a, -um *adj*. of *or* relating to a butcher

lanista, -ae *m*. trainer (*of gladiators, fighting cocks*)

lānitium, -(i)ī *n*. wool

lanius, -(i)ī *m*. butcher

lanterna, -ae *f*. lantern, lamp

lanternārius, -(i)ī *m*. lantern-bearer

lānūgō, -inis *f*. first facial hair, down

lanx, lancis *f*. metal tray, dish, platter

lapathum, -ī *n*. sorrel

lapicīda, -ae *m*. stone-cutter, quarryman

lapicīdīnae, -ārum *f.pl*. stone-quarries

lapidārius, -a, -um *adj*. of *or* relating to stone-cutting

lapidātiō, -ōnis *f*. throwing of stones, stoning

lapidātor, -ōris *m*. thrower of stones

lapideus, -a, -um *adj.* made of stone, stony

lapidō 1. to throw stones at; *impers.* it rains stones

lapidōsus, -a, -um *adj.* full of stones, stony

lapillus, -ī *m.* little stone, pebble; gem

lapis, -dis *m.* stone, pebble; stone, marble; gem

lappa, -ae *f.* burdock

lapsiō, -ōnis *f.* slipping up, erring

lapsō 1. to slip, stumble

lapsus, -ūs *m.* sliding, gliding; slipping, stumbling; falling; erring

laqueāre, -is *n.* panelled ceiling

laqueātus, -a, -um *adj.* panelled; having a panelled ceiling

laqueus, -ī *m.* noose; snare, trap; bond

lardum, -ī *n.* bacon

largē *adv.* generously, liberally; copiously

largificus, -a, -um *adj.* bountiful, liberal

largifluus, -a, -um *adj.* flowing abundantly

largiloquus, -a, -um *adj.* talkative, garrulous

largior 4. *dep.* to give abundantly, lavish; grant, confer; practise bribery; overlook

largitās, -ātis *f.* generosity, liberality; abundance

largiter *adv.* in abundance, copiously; (+*gen.*) with an abundance (of)

largītiō, -ōnis *f.* generosity, largess; bribe

largītor, -ōris *m.* liberal giver, bestower; briber

largus, -a, -um *adj.* lavish, bountiful; (+*abl./gen.*) generous (with); bounteous, plentiful

lāridum see **lardum**

larix, -icis *f.* larch tree

larva (lārua), -ae *f.* ghost, demon; mask

larvālis, -is, -e *adj.* of *or* resembling a ghost, demonic

larvātus, -a, -um *adj.* possessed by a demon, bewitched

lasanum, -ī *n.* chamber-pot

lāsarpīcifer, -era, -erum *adj.* producing asafoetida

lascīvē *adv.* wantonly

lascīvia, -ae *f.* play, frolicking; playfulness, jollity; wantonness, licentiousness

lascīvībundus, -a, -um *adj.* full of frolic, playful

lascīviō 4. to play, frolic; be wanton, run riot

lascīvus, -a, -um *adj.* playful, frolicsome; frivolous; wanton, licentious

lāserpīcium, -(i)ī *n.* asafoetida

lassitūdō, -inis *f.* tiredness, fatigue

lassō 1. to wear out, tire, exhaust; weaken

lassulus, -a, -um *adj.* somewhat weary

lassus, -a, -um *adj.* tired, exhausted; **rēs lassae** trouble, misfortune

lātē *adv.* widely, broadly; extensively

latebra, -ae *f.* (*usu. pl.*) hiding-place, lair; refuge; subterfuge; concealment

latebricola, -ae *m.* one that lives in hiding

latebrōsē *adv.* in hiding, covertly

latebrōsus, -a, -um *adj.* full of hiding-places; hidden, secret; porous

latens, -ntis *adj.* hidden, concealed, secret

latenter *adv.* in secret, privately

lateō 2. to lie hidden, be concealed; keep out of sight; take refuge; be unknown; (+*acc.*) hide (from)

later, lateris *m.* brick, tile; brickwork

laterāmen, -inis *n.* pottery

laterculus see **latericulus**

latericius, -a, -um *adj.* made of brick; *n.sg. sbst.* brickwork

latericulus, -ī *m.* small tile; hard biscuit

latescō 3. to become hidden, vanish

latex, -icis *m.* water; liquid, juice

latibulum, -ī *n.* hiding-place, lair

lāticlāvius, -a, -um *adj.* wearing a broad stripe, senatorial; *m.sbst.* senator

lātifundium, -iī *n.* large estate

lātiō, -ōnis *f.* bringing; proposal

latitō 1. to be in hiding, lie concealed; be obscure

lātitūdō, -inis *f.* breadth, width; broad pronunciation

lātomiae see **lautumiae**

lātor, -ōris *m.* bringer; proposer

lātrātor, -ōris *m.* one who barks

lātrātus, -ūs *m.* barking

lātrīna, -ae *f.* privy, latrine

lātrō[1] 1. to bark, bawl; roar; bark at; clamour at

latrō[2], **-ōnis** *m.* mercenary soldier; robber, bandit; piece in a board game

latrōcinium, -(i)ī *n.* robbery; plunder; horde of robbers

latrōcinor 1. *dep.* to serve as a mercenary soldier; practise robbery

latruncolārius, -a, -um *adj.* of *or* relating to a game involving *latrunculi*

latrunculus, -ī *m.* robber, brigand; piece in a board game

lātūra, -ae *f.* carrying

latus¹, -eris *n.* side, flank

lātus², -a, -um *adj.* broad, wide; expansive; (*of pronunciation*) broad

latusculum, -ī *n.* little side

laudābilis, -is, -e *adj.* praiseworthy, laudable

laudābiliter *adv.* laudably, commendably

laudātiō, -ōnis *f.* commendation, praise; eulogy, encomium; character testimonial

laudātor, -ōris *m.* one who praises, eulogizer; character-witness

laudātrix, -īcis *f.* female praiser

laudātus, -a, -um *adj.* praised, lauded, esteemed

laudō 1. to praise, laud, commend; eulogize; call upon, mention; **laudō** that's fine

laurea, -ae *f.* laurel tree; laurel wreath; victory

laureātus, -a, -um *adj.* crowned with laurel, laureate; *f.pl.sbst.* victory dispatch

laureola, -ae *f.* slight victory

laurētum, -ī *n.* laurel grove

laureus, -a, -um *adj.* of *or* made of laurel

lauricomus, -a, -um *adj.* covered with laurel trees

laurifer, -era, -erum *adj.* laurel-wreathed, laureate

lauriger, -era, -erum *adj.* laurel-wreathed, laureate

laurus, -ī *or* **-us, -ūs** *f.* laurel tree, bay; laurel branch; victory

laus, -dis *f.* praise, commendation, glory, renown, esteem; praiseworthy quality

lautē *adv.* elegantly; luxuriously, sumptuously

lautia, -ōrum *n.pl.* entertainment given in Rome for foreign ambassadors

lautitia, -ae *f.* luxury, sumptuousness; *pl.* luxurious activities

lautumiae, -ārum *f.pl.* stone-quarry; prison

lautus, -a, -um *adj.* washed; neat, elegant; luxurious, sumptuous

lavābrum, -ī *n.* bathtub

lavātiō, -ōnis *f.* washing, bathing

lavō, lāvī, lautum (lōtum) 3. (or 1.) to wash, bathe; wash oneself; wash off; moisten, soak

laxāmentum, -ī *n.* relaxation, mitigation; leisure, respite

laxē *adv.* spaciously; loosely, slackly; lavishly

laxitās, -ātis *f.* spaciousness; relaxation

laxō 1. to widen, spread out; open up; loosen, slacken; relax; reduce

laxus, -a, -um *adj.* wide, spacious; loose, slack; relaxed; lax; far off

lea, leae *f.* lioness

leaena, -ae *f.* lioness

lebēs, -ētis *m.* cauldron

lectīca, -ae *f.* litter, sedan

lectīcāriola, -ae *f.* adulteress of litter-bearers

lectīcārius, -(i)ī *m.* litter-bearer

lectīcula, -ae *f.* small litter, sedan

lectiō, -ōnis *f.* selection, choosing; reading

lectisterniātor, -ōris *m.* one who arranges couches (*for a feast*)

lectisternium, -(i)ī *n.* feast offered to the gods

lectitō 1. to read repeatedly, peruse

lectiuncula, -ae *f.* short reading

lector, -ōris *m.* reader, reciter

lectulus, -ī *m.* small couch, bed

lectus¹, -a, -um *adj.* selected, chosen; outstanding, choice

lectus², -ī *m.* couch, bed; bier; **lectus (geniālis)** marriage-bed

lēgātiō, -ōnis *f.* the office of ambassador; embassy; response of an embassy; lieutenancy

lēgātor, -ōris *m.* one who leaves a legacy

lēgātōrius, -iī *m.* one who receives a legacy

lēgātum, -ī *n.* bequest, legacy

lēgātus, -ī *m.* ambassador, envoy; lieutenant; governor of an imperial province

lēgerupa, -ae *m.* law-breaker

lēgerupiō, -ōnis *f.* breaking of a law

lēgifer, -era, -erum *adj.* law-giving

legiō, -ōnis *f.* legion (4,200–6,000 men); army

legiōnārius, -a, -um *adj.* of *or* relating to a legion; *m.sbst.* legionary

lēgitimē *adv.* legally; properly

lēgitimus, -a, -um *adj.* legal; lawful, legitimate; genuine; proper, fit

legiuncula, -ae *f.* mere legion

lēgō¹ 1. to send as an envoy; appoint as a *legatus*; bequeath

legō², **lēgī**, **lectum** 3. to collect; furl; select; traverse; read, recite

lēguleius, **-ī** *m.* pettifogging lawyer

legūmen, **-inis** *n.* leguminous plant, pulse

lembus, **-ī** *m.* small boat, skiff

lemma, **-atis** *n.* theme; title

lemniscātus, **-a**, **-um** *adj.* adorned with (victory) ribbons

lemniscus, **-ī** *m.* victory ribbon

lemurēs, **-um** *m.pl.* ghosts, spectres

lēna, **-ae** *f.* brothel-keeper

lēnīmen, **-inis** *n.* alleviation, solace

lēnīmentum, **-ī** *n.* alleviation, solace

lēniō 4. to assuage, moderate; placate, mollify; explain away; be calm

lēnis, **-is**, **-e** *adj.* soft, mild, weak; gentle, smooth; lenient, moderate

lēnitās, **-ātis** *f.* softness, mildness; gentleness; leniency, moderation

lēniter *adv.* softly, mildly; gently; moderately

lēnitūdō, **-inis** *f.* mildness, leniency

lēnō, **-ōnis** *m.* brothel-keeper, pimp

lēnōcinium, **-(i)ī** *n.* brothel-keeping, pimping; blandishment; allurement

lēnōcinor 1. *dep.* (+*dat.*) to pander (to), act in the interests (of)

lēnōnius, **-a**, **-um** *adj.* of *or* relating to a brothel-keeper

lens, **lentis** *f.* lentil plant

lentē *adv.* slowly; leisurely; calmly

lentēscō 3. to become sticky; soften, relax

lentiscifer, **-era**, **-erum** *adj.* bearing mastic trees

lentiscus, **-ī** *f.* or **lentiscum**, **-ī** *n.* mastic tree

lentitūdō, **-inis** *f.* sluggishness; apathy

lentō 1. to bend, ply

lentulus, **-a**, **-um** *adj.* somewhat slow

lentus, **-a**, **-um** *adj.* slow, lingering; prolonged; tough, supple; sticky; slow-witted; calm

lēnullus, **-ī** *m.* petty brothel-keeper

lēnunculus¹, **-ī** *m.* small boat, skiff

lēnunculus², **-ī** *m.* petty brothel-keeper

leō, **leōnis** *m.* lion

leōnīnus, **-a**, **-um** *adj.* of *or* relating to a lion

lepas see **lopas**

lepidē *adv.* pleasantly, charmingly; amusingly

lepidus, **-a**, **-um** *adj.* pleasant, charming; amusing

lepōs, **-ōris** *m.* pleasantness, charm; wit; *pl.* witticism

lepus, **-oris** *m.* hare

lepusculus, **-ī** *m.* small hare

lessus, **[-ī]** *m.*(?) mourning

lētālis, **-is**, **-e** *adj.* of *or* relating to death; deadly, lethal

lēthargicus, **-ī** *m.* one suffering from lethargy

lēthargus, **-ī** *m.* lethargy, drowsiness

lētifer, **-era**, **-erum** *adj.* death-bringing, deadly

lētificus, **-a**, **-um** *adj.* causing death, deadly

lētō 1. to kill, murder

lētum, **-ī** *n.* death

leucaspis, **-idis** *f.adj.* armed with white shields

leucophaeātus, **-a**, **-um** *adj.* wearing light-grey clothes

levāmen, **-inis** *n.* alleviation, solace

levāmentum, **-ī** *n.* alleviation, solace; consoling

levātiō, **-ōnis** *f.* alleviation, solace

leviculus, **-a**, **-um** *adj.* light-headed, vain

levidensis, **-is**, **-e** *adj.* thinly spun, poor

levifīdus, **-a**, **-um** *adj.* of little faith, untrustworthy

levipēs, **-pedis** *adj.* light-footed

levis¹, **-is**, **-e** *adj.* light; thin; slight; weak; lightly armed; trivial; fickle

lēvis², **-is**, **-e** *adj.* smooth, even; (*of speeches*) flowing, polished

levisomnus, **-a**, **-um** *adj.* sleeping lightly

levitās¹, **-ātis** *f.* lightness; mildness; fickleness

lēvitās², **-ātis** *f.* smoothness; polish (*of speeches*)

leviter *adv.* lightly, gently; slightly; mildly; with equanimity; groundlessly; in a fickle manner

levō¹ 1. to lift, raise; (+*abl.*) relieve (of); alleviate; make well

lēvō² 1. to smooth, polish; remove hairs from

lēvor, **-ōris** *m.* smoothness, evenness

lex, **lēgis** *f.* law; proposal; rule; right; *pl.* constitution; terms, conditions

lexicographus, **-ī** *m.* writer of dictionaries, harmless drudge

lībāmen, -inis *n.* sacrificial offering, oblation; first-fruits

lībāmentum, -ī *n.* sacrificial offering, oblation; small portion

lībārius, -iī *m.* confectioner

lībātiō, -ōnis *f.* libation

lībella, -ae *f.* silver coin worth a tenth of a *denarius*; plumb-line

libelliō, -ōnis *m.* bookseller

libellus, -ī *m.* small book, pamphlet; programme; dispatch; poster

libens, -ntis *adj.* willing, with readiness; cheerful

libenter *adv.* willingly, readily

libentia, -ae *f.* pleasure, cheerfulness

libeō 2. to be willing, please

liber¹, librī *m.* bark; book; document

līber², -era, -erum *adj.* free, independent; (+*abl./gen.*) free (from); unbound, unrestricted; frank, outspoken; empty; idle

līberālis, -is, -e *adj.* of *or* relating to a free man; noble, gentlemanly; generous, lavish

līberālitās, -ātis *f.* nobility; generosity; donation

līberāliter *adv.* in the manner of a free man; nobly; generously

līberātiō, -ōnis *f.* (+*gen.*) freeing (from); acquittal

līberātor, -ōris *m.* one who sets free, liberator

līberē *adv.* in the manner of a free man; spontaneously; frankly; wantonly

līberī, -(ōr)um *m.pl.* children

līberō 1. to set free, liberate; manumit; acquit; (+*abl.*) deliver (from)

līberta, -ae *f.* freedwoman

lībertās, -ātis *f.* freedom, independence; freedom from restraint; frankness, outspokenness

lībertīna, -ae *f.* freedwoman

lībertīnus¹, -a, -um *adj.* having the status of a freedman; belonging to a freedman

lībertīnus², -ī *m.* freedman; son of a freedman

lībertus, -ī *m.* freedman

libet, -uit 2. *impers.* or **-itum est** 2. *semi-dep. impers.* (+*dat. of person* +*inf.*) it pleases (someone to), is agreeable (to)

libīdinor 1. *dep.* to act in lust

libīdinōsē *adv.* wantonly, arbitrarily

libīdinōsus, -a, -um *adj.* arbitrary, capricious; wanton, lustful

libīdō, -inis *f.* fancy, whim; forceful desire, will; lust, wantonness

libita, -ōrum *n.pl.* desire, pleasure

lībō 1. to offer sacrificially, pour as a libation; taste, nibble; touch lightly; extract; impair

lībra, -ae *f.* balance, scales; Roman weight, equivalent to twelve *unciae*

lībrālis, -is, -e *adj.* weighing a *libra*

lībrāmentum, -ī *n.* counterpoise; geometrical plane

lībrāria, -ae *f.* female secretary

lībrāriolus, -ī *m.* (junior) scribe

lībrārium, -(i)ī *n.* bookcase

lībrārius¹, -a, -um *adj.* of *or* relating to books; *m.sbst.* scribe; bookseller

lībrārius², -a, -um *adj.* weighing a *libra*

lībrātor, -ōris *m.* surveyor

lībrātus, -a, -um *adj.* poised, controlled

lībrīle, -is *n.* slingshot

lībritor, -ōris *m.* one who uses a slingshot

lībrō 1. to poise, balance; aim; ponder

lībum, -ī *n.* sacrificial cake

licens, -ntis *adj.* unrestrained, unbridled

licenter *adv.* freely, without restraint

licentia, -ae *f.* freedom, lack of restraint, licence; outspokenness; wantonness

liceō 2. (+*abl./gen. of price*) to be for sale (at), retail (for)

liceor 2. *dep.* to make a bid for; bid

licet, -uit 2. or **-itum est** 2. *semi-dep. impers.* (+*dat. of person* +*inf.*) it is allowed (for one to), one may

līchēn, -ēnos *m.* ringworm

licitātiō, -ōnis *f.* bidding, proposal of a price

licitātor, -ōris *m.* bidder

licitor 1. *dep.* to make a bid

licitus, -a, -um *adj.* permitted, lawful; *n.pl. sbst.* lawful actions

līcium, -(i)ī *n.* yarn, thread

lictor, -ōris *m.* official attendant upon a magistrate, lictor

līdō 3. to dash, strike

lien, lienis *m.* spleen

lienōsus, -a, -um *adj.* affected by a spleen disorder

ligāmen, -inis *n.* tie, fastening

ligāmentum, -ī *n.* bandage

lignārius, -(i)ī *m.* dealer in timber

lignātiō, -ōnis *f.* collection of firewood

lignātor, -ōris *m.* one who collects firewood

ligneolus, -a, -um *adj.* made of wood, wooden

ligneus, -a, -um *adj.* made of wood, wooden; brawny

lignor 1. *dep.* to collect firewood

lignum, -ī *n.* firewood; wood

ligō¹ 1. to bind, fasten; bandage; (+*dat.* or +*ad* +*acc.*) attach (to); unite

ligō², -ōnis *m.* mattock

ligula see **lingula**

ligurriō (-ūriō) 4. to lick, lick up; long for; sponge off

ligurrītiō (-ūrī-), -ōnis *f.* gluttony, greed

ligustrum, -ī *n.* privet

līlium, -(i)ī *n.* lily; snake-pit (*set as a trap*)

līma, -ae *f.* file; polishing (*of speeches, literature*)

līmātulus, -a, -um *adj.* somewhat polished, refined

līmātus, -a, -um *adj.* polished, refined

līmax, -ācis *f.* slug, snail

limbulārius, -a, -um *adj.* concerned with the production of decorative fringes

limbus, -ī *m.* decorative fringe (*of garments*); girdle

līmen, -inis *n.* doorstep, cross-beam of a door; doorway; threshold; house

līmes, -itis *m.* path, way; trail; boundary; boundary marker

līmō 1. to file, polish; file down *or* off; **caput līmāre** (+*abl.*) to kiss closely

līmōsus, -a, -um *adj.* full of mud, slimy

limpidus, -a, -um *adj.* clear, limpid

līmulus, -a, -um *adj.* (rather) sidelong

līmus¹, -ī *m.* mud, slime; sediment

līmus², -ī *m.* apron worn during sacrifices

līmus³, -a, -um *adj.* oblique, sidelong

līnea, -ae *f.* thread, string; fishing-line, plumb-line; line

līneāmentum, -ī *n.* line; *pl.* outlines, lineaments

līneō 1. to keep straight

līneus, -a, -um *adj.* made of flax, linen

lingō, linxī, linctum 3. to lick

lingua, -ae *f.* tongue; speech; dialect, language; spit of land

lingula, -ae *f.* shoe-flap; spit of land; type of spoon

lingulāca, -ae *f.* chatterbox, gossip

līnia(-) see **līnea(-)**

līniger, -era, -erum *adj.* wearing linen

linō, lēvī, litum 3. (+*abl.*) to smear (with), daub (in); cover (with); befoul (with); erase

linquō, līquī 3. to leave, quit; abandon, leave behind; (+*dat.*) leave (to); *pass.* faint

linteātus, -a, -um *adj.* linen-wearing (*of a Samnite legion*)

linteō, -ōnis *m.* weaver of linen

linteolum, -ī *n.* small piece of linen cloth

linter, -tris *f./m.* small boat, skiff; tank

linteum, -ī *n.* piece of linen cloth; sail; awning; napkin

linteus, -a, -um *adj.* made of linen

līnum, -ī *n.* flax; linen; thread, cord; fishing-line; fishing-net; wick

lippiō 4. to have inflamed eyes, be bleary-eyed

lippitūdō, -inis *f.* inflammation of the eyes

lippus, -a, -um *adj.* having inflamed eyes, bleary-eyed

liquefaciō (liquē-), -fēcī, -factum 3. to make liquid, melt, dissolve

liquens (līq-), -ntis *adj.* liquid, flowing; clear

liqueō, licuī 2. to be clear; be evident, manifest; *impers.* it is evident

liquescō 3. to become liquid, melt; ebb away, decompose

liquidiusculus, -a, -um *adj.* somewhat milder

liquidō *adv.* clearly, plainly, certainly

liquidus (līq-), -a, -um *adj.* liquid, flowing; clear; melodious; plain, evident; undisturbed, pure

liquō 1. to make liquid, melt, dissolve; purify, strain

liquor¹ 3. *dep.* to become liquid, melt; dissolve; flow

liquor², -ōris *m.* liquidity; liquid, fluid

līs, lītis *f.* lawsuit; quarrel, dispute

litāmen, -inis *n.* propitiatory sacrifice

litātiō, -ōnis *f.* receipt of good sacrificial omens

līter- see **litter-**

liticen, -inis *m.* trumpeter

lītigātor, -ōris *m.* litigant

lītigiōsus, -a, -um *adj.* prone to legal disputes, quarrelsome; disputed

lītigium, -(i)ī *n.* quarrel, dispute

lītigō 1. to go to law, litigate; quarrel, dispute

litō 1. to obtain favourable omens; provide favourable omens; (+*dat.*) sacrifice successfully (to); offer as a propitiatory sacrifice

lītorālis, -is, -e *adj.* of *or* relating to the seashore

lītoreus, -a, -um *adj.* of *or* relating to the seashore

littera, -ae *f.* alphabetical letter; *pl.* written letter, document; education, learning; literature

litterārius, -a, -um *adj.* of *or* for reading and writing

litterātē *adv.* literally; eruditely, with learning

litterātor, -ōris *m.* elementary schoolmaster

litterātūra, -ae *f.* alphabet; writing; education

litterātus, -a, -um *adj.* marked with letters, branded; learned, erudite

litterula, -ae *f.* letter, character; *pl.* brief written letter; elementary education; smattering of learning

litūra, -ae *f.* erasure (*on a wax tablet*); smear, blot

lītus, -oris *n.* seashore, coast, beach

lituus, -ī *m.* crooked staff (*of augurs*); curved trumpet, clarion

līvens, -ntis *adj.* black and blue, livid; envious

līveō 2. to be black and blue, livid; (+*dat.*) be envious (towards)

līvescō 3. to become black and blue

līvidulus, -a, -um *adj.* somewhat envious

līvidus, -a, -um *adj.* black and blue, livid; envious

līvor, -ōris *m.* black and blue colour, bruise; envy

lixa, -ae *m.* sutler

locārius, -(i)ī *m.* one who lets out theatre seats

locātiō, -ōnis *f.* letting out, leasing

locātor, -ōris *m.* one who lets out property

locātum, -ī *n.* something let out

locellus, -ī *m.* small box

locitō 1. to let out habitually

locō 1. to place, arrange; (+*dat.*) give (*a girl*) in marriage (to); contract; hire out, let

loculus, -ī *m.* small space; *pl.* box, moneybox, satchel

locuplēs, -ētis *adj.* possessing much land, wealthy; rich, copious; (+*abl.*) well-stocked (with); trusty, sufficient

locuplētō 1. to make rich, enrich

locus, -ī *m.* (*sometimes* **loca, -ōrum** *n.pl.*) place, site, location; post; seat; rank; condition; subject; passage (*of literature*); *n.pl.* region

locusta, -ae *f.* locust; kind of lobster

locūtiō, -ōnis *f.* speaking, speech; pronunciation, diction

lōdīcula, -ae *f.* small blanket

lōdix, -īcis *f.* blanket, rug

logus, -ī *m.* story, tale; *pl.* nonsense!

lolium, -(i)ī *n.* darnel

lollīgō, -inis *f.* squid, cuttle-fish

lollīguncula, -ae *f.* small squid, cuttle-fish

lōmentum, -ī *n.* skin lotion (made from bean-meal)

longaevus, -a, -um *adj.* ancient, old

longē *adv.* over a long distance; far; far off; for a long time; greatly; **longē (ab)esse** to be of no avail

longinquitās, -ātis *f.* length; remoteness, distance; (long) duration

longinquus, -a, -um *adj.* long; far off, remote; from far away; prolonged; *n.sg. as adv.* at length

longitūdō, -inis *f.* length; duration; prolixity; long quantity (*of a syllable*)

longiusculus, -a, -um *adj.* somewhat long

longulē *adv.* at a small distance

longulus, -a, -um *adj.* somewhat lengthy

longum *adv.* from afar; for a long time; lengthily

longurius, -(i)ī *m.* long pole

longus, -a, -um *adj.* long; wide; tall; far off, remote; of long duration; prolix; tedious; long (*of syllabic quantity*)

lopas, -adis *f.* limpet

loquācitās, -ātis *f.* talkativeness, garrulity

loquāciter *adv.* talkatively, verbosely

loquācula, -ae *f.* chatterbox, gossip

loquax, -ācis *adj.* talkative, chattering; expressive

loquēla, -ae *f.* speech, words

loquens, -ntis *adj.* talking, articulate

loquentia, -ae *f.* fluency of speech

loquitor 1. *dep.* to keep talking

loquor, locūtus 3. *dep.* to talk, speak; say; mention

lōrea, lōreola, lōrētum see **laurea, laureola, laurētum**

lōreus, -a, -um *adj.* made of thongs

lōrīca, -ae *f.* cuirass, corselet; parapet

lōrīcātus, -a, -um *adj.* wearing a cuirass

lōripēs, -pedis *adj.* having deformed feet

lōrum, -ī *n.* leather strap, throng; leash; whip

lōtium, -(i)ī *n.* urine

lōtos (-us), -ī *f./m.* African lotus, nettletree; lotus fruit; flute made of lotus wood

lubens, lubet, lubīdō see **libens, libet, libīdō**

lūbricō 1. to make slippery, lubricate

lūbricus, -a, -um *adj.* slippery, lubricated, smooth; flowing; uncertain; hazardous; *n.sbst.* dangerous *or* uncertain situation

lūca bōs, lūcae bovis *f.* elephant

lūcar, -āris *n.* money used for public entertainment

lucellum, -ī *n.* slight gain, minor profit

lūceō, luxī 2. to be light, shine; sparkle; be clear, evident

lucerna, -ae *f.* oil-lamp

lūcescō 3. to begin to shine; *impers.* it dawns

lūcidē *adv.* brightly; clearly, plainly

lūcidus, -a, -um *adj.* full of light, bright, shining; clear, lucid

lūcifer, -era, -erum *adj.* light-bringing; *m.sg.sbst.* morning star, day

lūcifuga, -ae *m.* one who shuns daylight

lūcifugus, -a, -um *adj.* shunning daylight; retiring, private

lūciscō see **lūcescō**

lucrātīvus, -a, -um *adj.* free, bonus

lucrīfaciō see **lucrum**

lucrifer, -era, -erum *adj.* bringing profit, lucrative

lucrificābilis, -is, -e *adj.* profitable, lucrative

lucrificō 1. to gain as profit, win

lucrifuga, -ae *m.* one who shuns profit, spendthrift

lucror 1. *dep.* to gain as profit, win; be spared (*sthg*)

lucrōsus, -a, -um *adj.* full of profit, lucrative

lucrum, -ī *n.* gain, profit; avarice; **lucrī facere** to gain as profit; profit

luctāmen, -inis *n.* wrestling, struggle

luctātiō, -ōnis *f.* wrestling; struggle; controversy

luctātor, -ōris *m.* wrestler

luctifer, -era, -erum *adj.* bringing sorrow, calamitous

luctificābilis, -is, -e *adj.* sorrowing, mournful

luctificus, -a, -um *adj.* causing sorrow, calamitous

luctisonus, -a, -um *adj.* sad-sounding

luctor 1. *dep.* or **luctō** 1. to wrestle; struggle, strain; dispute

luctuōsē *adv.* in a manner causing sorrow

luctuōsus, -a, -um *adj.* full of sorrow, calamitous; sorrowful, mournful

luctus, -ūs *m.* sorrow, mourning, grief, lamentation

lūcubrātiō, -ōnis *f.* working by lamplight, nocturnal work

lūcubrātōrius, -a, -um *adj.* for nocturnal study

lūcubrō 1. to work by lamplight, work at night; work at nocturnally

lūculentē *adv.* brilliantly, excellently

lūculenter *adv.* brilliantly, excellently

lūculentus, -a, -um *adj.* brilliant, splendid, excellent

lucuntulus, -ī *m.* confection of cheese and honey

lūcus, -ī *m.* sacred grove; wood

lūdia, -ae *f.* female gladiatorial slave

lūdibrium, -(i)ī *n.* mockery, derision; laughing-stock; plaything; sham, pretence

lūdibundus, -a, -um *adj.* full of fun, frolicsome; carefree

lūdicer, -cra, -crum *adj.* done in sport, in fun; theatrical

lūdicrum, -ī *n.* amusement, plaything; public show, theatre

lūdificābilis, -is, -e *adj.* that makes one the subject of mockery

lūdificātiō, -ōnis *f.* (+*gen.*) toying (with), trifling (with)

lūdificātor, -ōris *m.* one who toys with another

lūdificātus, -ūs *m.* object of derision, plaything

lūdificor 1. *dep.* or **lūdificō** 1. to toy with, trifle with, mock

lūdiō, -ōnis *m.* stage performer

lūdius, -(i)ī *m.* stage performer

lūdō, lūsī, lūsum 3. to play, sport; frolic, jest; (+*acc./abl.*) play (at); (+*abl.*) amuse oneself (with); toy (with), trifle (with); make love; perform on stage; mock; imitate; deceive

lūdus, -ī *m.* play, game; frivolity, fun; school; public show; *pl.* public games

luella, -ae *f.* atonement

luēs, luis *f.* (*only in sg.*) plague, affliction; moral corruption

lūgeō, luxī, luctum 2. to mourn, lament; bewail, grieve

lūgubris, -is, -e *adj.* of *or* relating to mourning; sorrowful; causing sorrow, calamitous; *n.pl.sbst.* mourning clothes

lumbifragium, -(i)ī *n.* rupture of the loins

lumbrīcus, -ī *m.* earthworm

lumbus, -ī *m.* loins

lūmen, -inis *n.* light; torch, lamp; daylight, day; eye; glory; clarity, understanding

lūminōsus, -a, -um *adj.* full of brilliance

lūna, -ae *f.* moon; moonlight; crescent on the shoes of senators

lūnāris, -is, -e *adj.* of *or* relating to the moon, lunar

lūnātus, -a, -um *adj.* crescent-shaped; having crescent-shaped shields; having senatorial shoes

lūnō 1. to make crescent-shaped

lunter see **linter**

luntriculus *m.* very small boat

lūnula, -ae *f.* crescent-shaped ornament

luō, luī 3. to atone for, expiate; suffer, pay in turn; fulfil

lupa, -ae *f.* she-wolf; prostitute

lupānar, -āris *n.* brothel

lupātus, -a, -um *adj.* toothed; *n.pl.sbst.* toothed bit

lupillus, -ī *m.* lupin seed

lupīnus¹, -ī *m.* lupin; lupin seed

lupīnus², -a, -um *adj.* of *or* relating to a wolf; made of wolf-skin

lupus, -ī *m.* wolf; the fish bass; toothed bit; grappling iron

lurcō, -ōnis *m.* glutton

lūridus, -a, -um *adj.* pale yellow, sallow

lūror, -ōris *m.* pale yellow colour, sallowness

luscinia, -ae *f.* or **luscinius, -(i)ī** *m.* nightingale

lusciniola, -ae *f.* little nightingale

luscītiōsus, -a, -um *adj.* dim-sighted

luscus, -a, -um *adj.* blind in one eye

lūsiō, -ōnis *f.* play, sport

lūsitō 1. to play, sport

lūsor, -ōris *m.* player; trifler, mocker

lūsōrius, -a, -um *adj.* playful, frivolous; *n.pl.sbst.* frivolities

lustra, -ōrum *n.pl.* haunts, lair; brothel, place of debauchery

lustrālis, -is, -e *adj.* of *or* relating to ritual purification; quinquennial

lustrātiō, -ōnis *f.* ritual purification; roaming, circling

lustricus, -a, -um *adj.* of *or* for ritual purification

lustrō 1. to purify, expiate; traverse, circle; survey, review; seek

lustrum, -ī *n.* purificatory ceremony, *esp.* the quinquennial ceremony performed by censors; censor's period of office; five year period; quinquennial festival; period of orbit

lūsus, -ūs *m.* play, sport, game; joke, jest; public show; literary trifle

lūteolus, -a, -um *adj.* yellowish

lūteus¹, -a, -um *adj.* yellow

luteus², -a, -um *adj.* made of mud; full of mud, muddy; worthless

lutitō 1. to bring into contempt

lutō 1. to smear; plaster

lutōsus, -a, -um *adj.* full of mud, muddy

lutulentus, -a, -um *adj.* full of mud, muddy; filthy

lutum¹, -ī *n.* mud, dirt, clay

lūtum², -ī *n.* yellow dye

lux, lūcis *f.* light; daylight; day; eyesight; clarity, illumination; glory, splendour; darling

luxō 1. to sprain, dislocate

luxor 1. *dep.* to run riot

luxuria, -ae or **-iēs, -iēī** *f.* luxuriance, exuberant growth; licentiousness; extravagance, luxury

luxuriō 1. or **luxurior** 1. *dep.* to be luxuriant, grow exuberantly; sport, frisk; be licentious; be extravagant

luxuriōsē *adv.* licentiously; extravagantly

luxuriōsus, -a, -um *adj.* luxuriant, exuberant; licentious; extravagant, luxurious

luxus¹, -ūs *m.* luxury, extravagance; sumptuousness

luxus², -a, -um *adj.* sprained, dislocated

lychnobius, -iī *m.* one who lives by lamplight

lychnūchus, -ī *m.* lamp-stand

lychnus, -ī *m.* lamp

lygdos, -ī *f.* Parian marble

lympha, -ae *f.* water, fresh water; water-nymph

lymphāt(ic)us, -a, -um *adj.* frenzied, frantic

lymphō 1. to drive crazy, make frenzied; *pass.* be in a frenzy

lynx, lyncis *f./m.* lynx; lynx skin

lyra, -ae *f.* lyre; lyric poetry

lyricus, -a, -um *adj.* of *or* relating to the lyre, lyric; *m.sbst.* lyric poet; *n.pl.sbst.* lyric poetry

lyristēs, -ae *m.* lyre-player

M

maccis, -idis f. fabricated name of a spice

macellārius, -(i)ī m. provision-dealer, victualler

macellum, -ī n. or **macellus, -ī** m. provision-market, butcher's stall; provisions purchased from the market

maceō 2. to be thin

macer, macra, macrum adj. thin, lean; poor, scanty

māceria, -ae f. stone wall (esp. around a garden)

mācerō 1. to make wet, soak; weaken, reduce; annoy, torment

macescō 3. to become thin

machaera, -ae f. blade, one-edged sword

machaerophorus, -ī m. swordsman

māchina, -ae f. machine, crane; siege-engine; mill; torture chamber; structure, fabric

māchināmentum, -ī n. machine, instrument; siege-engine

māchinātiō, -ōnis f. machine, instrument; siege-engine; contrivance, machination

māchinātor, -ōris m. maker of machines, engineer; contriver, deviser

māchinor 1. dep. to contrive, devise; plot cunningly

māchinōsus, -a, -um adj. equipped with a machine

maciēs, -ēī f. thinness, leanness; poverty, scantiness

macilentus, -a, -um adj. thin, lean

macrescō 3. to become thin, grow lean

macritūdō, -inis f. thinness, leanness

macrocollum, -ī n. large-sized paper

mactābilis, -is, -e adj. able to slay, lethal

mactātor, -ōris m. slayer, slaughterer

mactātus, -ūs m. sacrificial slaying

macte indecl.adj. well done; (+abl. and usu. *esto*) hurrah (for)!; **macte virtūte** well done, bravo!

mactō 1. to honour, glorify; (+abl.) punish (with); slay sacrificially; kill, butcher

mactus, -a, -um adj. struck, wounded

macula, -ae f. spot, mark; stain, blot; mesh of a net; blemish, stigma, fault

maculō 1. to spot; make variegated; stain, pollute; disgrace, defile

maculōsus, -a, -um adj. covered with spots, dappled, variegated; disgraced, defiled

madefaciō, -fēcī, -factum 3. to make wet, drench, soak

madefactō 1. to make wet, soak

madefīō, -fierī, -factus v.irreg. to become wet, become drenched

madeō 2. to be wet, drenched; be boiled, cooked; be drunk; (+abl.) be steeped (in)

madescō 3. (+abl.) to become wet (with), become drenched (in)

madidē adv. drunkenly

madidus, -a, -um adj. (+abl.) wet (with), drenched (in); moist, damp; boiled, cooked; drunk; (+abl.) steeped (in)

mador, -ōris m. wetness, damp

madulsa, -ae f. drunkenness, inebriation

maena, -ae f. small sea-fish, sprat

maenas, -adis f. female devotee of Bacchus; prophetess

maeniānum, -ī n. balcony, veranda

maereō 2. to be sad, mourn; bewail, mourn over

maeror, -ōris m. sorrow, mourning

maestiter adv. sorrowfully

maestitia, -ae f. sorrow, mourning, grief; dullness

maestitūdō, -inis f. sorrow, mourning

maestus, -a, -um adj. sorrowful, mournful, sad; gloomy; causing sorrow

maga, -ae *f.* witch

māgālia, -ium *n.pl.* tents, huts

mage see **magis**

magicus, -a, -um *adj.* of *or* relating to magic, magical; possessing magic powers

magis or **mage** *adv.* to a greater extent, more; rather, instead; preferably

magister, -trī *m.* master, director; schoolmaster, teacher; keeper; helmsman; driver

magisterium, -(i)ī *n.* master, superintendent; teaching; control, guidance

magistra, -ae *f.* female director, mistress; female teacher

magistrātus, -ūs *m.* office of a magistrate, magistracy; magistrate

magmentārium, -(i)ī *n.* shrine for receiving parts of sacrificial offerings

magnanimitās, -ātis *f.* greatness of spirit, magnanimity

magnanimus, -a, -um *adj.* great in spirit, magnanimous, noble

magnēs, -ētis (-etos) *m.* magnet, loadstone

magnidicus, -a, -um *adj.* big-talking, boastful

magnificē *adv.* splendidly, magnificently; excellently; boastfully

magnificentia, -ae *f.* grandeur in action, nobility; splendour, magnificence; boastfulness

magnificō 1. to set a high price on, esteem

magnificus, -a, -um *adj.* noble, munificent; splendid, magnificent, glorious; boastful

magniloquentia, -ae *f.* grandiloquence; boastfulness

magniloquus, -a, -um *adj.* grandiloquent; boastful

magnitūdō, -inis *f.* size, magnitude; greatness, hugeness; great strength, intensity; great importance; dignity

magnopere *adv.* earnestly; very much, greatly; particularly

magnus, -a, -um *adj.* great, huge, tall; (*of prices*) high, steep; (*of sounds*) loud; noble, grand; powerful, mighty; important; boastful

magus¹, -ī *m.* Persian mystic; magician

magus², -a, -um *adj.* magical, magic

magȳdaris, -is *f.* silphium juice

māiālis, -is *m.* gelded boar, pig (*as term of abuse*)

māiestās, -ātis *f.* majesty, greatness, dignity; sovereignty; high treason

māior, -or, -us *compar.adj.* greater, larger; older; more important

māiusculus, -a, -um *adj.* somewhat greater; somewhat older

māla, -ae *f.* (*usu. pl.*) cheeks; jaws

malacia, -ae *f.* complete calm, tranquillity

malacissō 1. to make soft

malacus, -a, -um *adj.* soft; delicate; pliant, supple

male *adv.* badly; painfully, unpleasantly; wrongly, wickedly; unsuccessfully; **male audīre** to be in disrepute

maledicē *adv.* in an abusive manner, slanderously

maledīcens, -ntis *adj.* abusive, slanderous

maledīcō, -dixī, -dictum 3. (+*dat.*) to abuse, slander

maledictiō, -ōnis *f.* abuse, slander

maledictum, -ī *n.* insult, slander

maledicus, -a, -um *adj.* abusive, slanderous

malefaciō, -fēcī, -factum 3. to act wickedly; (+*dat.*) injure, harm

malefactor, -ōris *m.* wrongdoer

malefactum, -ī *n.* wrongdoing

maleficē *adv.* wickedly

maleficium, -(i)ī *n.* wrongdoing, crime; injury, hurt

maleficus, -a, -um *adj.* evil-doing, wicked; injurious, harmful; *m.sbst.* wrongdoer

malesuādus, -a, -um *adj.* ill-advising

malevolens, -ntis *adj.* ill-disposed, malevolent

malevolentia, -ae *f.* ill-will, malevolence

malevolus, -a, -um *adj.* ill-disposed, malevolent; *m./f.sbst.* ill-wisher

mālifer, -era, -erum *adj.* apple-bearing

malignē *adv.* malignantly, spitefully; stingily, meanly

malignitās, -ātis *f.* ill-will, malice; stinginess, meanness

malignus, -a, -um *adj.* ill-disposed, malignant, spiteful; harmful; stingy, mean; poor, scanty

malitia, -ae *f.* ill-will, malice; fault, vice

malitiōsē *adv.* maliciously

malitiōsus, -a, -um *adj.* full of malice, wicked

malleātor, -ōris *m.* hammerer, beater
malleolus, -ī *m.* fire-missile; mallet-shoot (*for planting*)
malleus, -ī *m.* hammer
mālō, mālle, māluī *v.irreg.* to prefer, wish rather; (+*acc.*+*inf.*) prefer (that)
mālobathrum, -ī *n.* expensive oil from an Indian tree
malum¹, -ī *n.* evil, wickedness; misdeed; woe, pain, distress; illness; harm, damage; scoundrel
mālum², -ī *n.* apple
malus¹, -a, -um *adj.* bad; painful, unpleasant; harmful; wicked, evil; hostile, unfavourable; unsuccessful
mālus², -ī *m.* beam; mast
mālus³, -ī *f.* apple-tree
malva, -ae *f.* mallow
mamilla, -ae *f.* breast, nipple
mamillāre, -is *n.* breast-band
mamma, -ae *f.* breast, teat
mammeātus, -a, -um *adj.* big-breasted
mammicula, -ae *f.* small breast
mammōsus, -a, -um *adj.* big-breasted
mānābilis, -is, -e *adj.* seeping, penetrating
manceps, -cipis *m.* contractor, purchaser, agent
mancipium, -(i)ī *n.* taking in hand under witness, formal acceptance; formal ownership; slave
mancipō 1. to offer for sale under witness, sell formally; give up, surrender
mancup- see **mancip-**
mancus, -a, -um *adj.* crippled, lame; imperfect, defective
mandātum, -ī *n.* order, command
mandātū *m.abl.sg.* by order, by command
mandō¹ 1. (+*dat.*) to hand over (to), entrust (to), commit (to); (+*ut/ne*+*subj.* or +*inf.*) order (to), command (to)
mandō², -dī, -sum 3. to chew, bite
mandra, -ae *f.* train of cattle
mandūcō 1. to chew; eat
mandūcus, -ī *m.* mask of biting jaws (*used in Atellan farces*)
māne *adv.* in the morning; early next morning; *indecl.n.* morning
maneō, mansī, mansum 2. to stay, remain; lodge, stay (*esp. for the night*); abide; persist, continue; be in store, await; wait for
mānēs, -ium *m.pl.* (*usu.* +*dī*) spirits of the dead; ashes, remains, corpse; death; the underworld
mangō, -ōnis *m.* slave-dealer
mangōnicus, -a, -um *adj.* of *or* relating to a slave-dealer
manicae, -ārum *f.pl.* handcuffs; long sleeve(s); glove
manicātus, -a, -um *adj.* with long sleeves
manicula, -ae *f.* small hand
manifestārius, -a, -um *adj.* caught in the act
manifestē *adv.* evidently, manifestly
manifestō¹ 1. to reveal, make manifest
manifestō² *adv.* evidently, manifestly; in the act
manifestus, -a, -um *adj.* evident, manifest; flagrant; caught in the act; unmistakable
manipl- see **manipul-**
manipretium see **manupretium**
manipulāris, -is, -e *adj.* (*of soldiers*) belonging to a company, private; *m.sbst.* common soldier, private; fellow-soldier
manipulātim *adv.* by companies (*of soldiers*)
manipulus, -ī *m.* sheaf, bundle (*of hay etc.*); company of soldiers
mannulus, -ī *m.* (small) pony
mannus, -ī *m.* pony
mānō 1. to run, flow, drip; (+*abl.*) flow (with), drip (with); spread, extend; (+*abl.*) spring (from), emanate (from)
mansiō, -ōnis *f.* staying, remaining; staying place, station
mansitō 1. to lodge, stay the night
mansuēfaciō, -fēcī, -factum 3. to tame; pacify, quieten
mansuēfīō, -fierī, -factus *v.irreg.* to become tame; be pacified
mansuēs, [-ētis] *adj.* tame, gentle
mansuescō, -suēvī, -suētum 3. to become tame; become gentle, soften
mansuētē *adv.* tamely, gently
mansuētūdō, -inis *f.* gentleness, clemency; refinement
mansuētus, -a, -um *adj.* tame; gentle, mild; civilized
mantēle, -is *n.* napkin; tablecloth
mantēlium, -ī *n.* napkin
mantellum, -ī *n.* cloak, covering
mantica, -ae *f.* knapsack
manticinor 1. *dep.* (*perhaps*) to prophesy

mantō 1. to stay, remain; wait for

manuālis, -is, -e *adj.* of a size suitable for the hand

manubiae, -ārum *f.pl.* prize-money, booty (*for a victorious general*); profit, prize

manubiālis, -is, -e *adj.* gained from the sale of booty

manubiārius, -a, -um *adj.* of *or* relating to booty

manubrium, -(i)ī *n.* handle

manuf- see **manif-**

manuleātus, -a, -um *adj.* with long sleeves

manuleus, -ī *m.* long sleeve

manūmissiō, -ōnis *f.* setting free, manumission (*esp. of slaves*)

manūmittō, -mīsī, -missum 3. to set free, manumit, emancipate

manupretium, -(i)ī *n.* workman's pay, labour money; reward

manus, -ūs *f.* hand; paw, trunk; power, jurisdiction; force; workman; band of men, troop; **ad manum** at hand

mapālia, -ium *n.pl.* African huts, hovels

mappa, -ae *f.* napkin

marathus, -ī *m.* fennel

marceō 2. to wither, droop; be weak, flag; be idle

marcescō 3. to become weak; become idle

marcidus, -a, -um *adj.* withered, drooping; weak, enfeebled; idle

marcor, -ōris *m.* idleness, languor

marculus, -ī *m.* small hammer

mare, -is *n.* sea; seawater

margarīta, -ae *f.* pearl

margarītum, -ī *n.* pearl

marginō 1. to give borders to

margō, -inis *m./f.* edge, border, boundary, rim

marīnus, -a, -um *adj.* of the sea, marine; *n. sbst.* sea-creature

marisca, -ae *f.* fig; *pl.* piles

marīta, -ae *f.* wife

marītālis, -is, -e *adj.* of *or* relating to marriage, marital; matrimonial

maritimus, -a, -um *adj.* of *or* relating to the sea, maritime; coastal; seafaring

marītō 1. to marry; wed (*vines*)

marītus¹, -a, -um *adj.* married; of *or* relating to marriage, marital; (*of vines*) wedded

marītus², -ī *m.* husband; mate

marmor, -oris *n.* marble; piece of worked marble; sea (*esp. its whitened surface*)

marmorārius, -iī *m.* marble-mason

marmorātus, -a, -um *adj.* marble-coated

marmoreus, -a, -um *adj.* made of marble; marble-like

marra, -ae *f.* weeding-hook, hoe

marsuppium, -(i)ī *n.* purse, pouch

mās¹, maris *m.* male

mās², maris *adj.* of the male sex, masculine

masculīnus, -a, -um *adj.* of the male sex, masculine

masculus, -a, -um *adj.* masculine; virile, manly; *m.sbst.* male

massa, -ae *f.* lump, mass; large *or* heavy weight

mastīgia, -ae *m.* rascal, scoundrel

mastrūca, -ae *f.* sheepskin coat

mastrūcātus, -a, -um *adj.* wearing sheepskins

matara, -ae or **-is, -is** *f.* Gallic spear

matella, -ae *f.* chamber-pot

matelliō, -ōnis *m.* small pot

māter, mātris *f.* mother; matron; nurse; motherland

mātercula, -ae *f.* dear (little) mother

māterfamiliās, mātrisfamiliās *f.* mistress of a household, matriarch; matron

māteria, -ae *f.* matter, material; timber, wood; natural disposition; means, occasion; subject-matter

māteriārius, -(i)ī *m.* timber-merchant

māteriēs see **māteria**

māteriō 1. to construct with timber

māterior 1. *dep.* to fetch wood

māternus, -a, -um *adj.* of *or* relating to a mother, maternal; like a mother, motherly; relating to pregnancy

mātertera, -ae *f.* maternal aunt

mathēmatica, -ae or **-ē, -ēs** *f.* mathematics; astrology

mathēmaticus, -a, -um *adj.* mathematical; *m.sbst.* mathematician; astrologer; *n.pl.sbst.* mathematics

mātricīda, -ae *m.* killer of one's mother, matricide

mātricīdium, -(i)ī *n.* killing of one's mother, matricide

mātrimōnium, -(i)ī *n.* wedlock, matrimony; marriage

mātrimus, -a, -um *adj.* having a living mother

mātrix, -īcis *f.* parent tree

mātrōna, -ae *f.* married woman, matron

mātrōnālis, -is, -e *adj.* of *or* suitable for a married woman, matronly

mattea, -ae *f.* delicacy, expensive dish

matula, -ae *f.* chamber-pot; blockhead, idiot

mātūrātē *adv.* promptly, swiftly

mātūrē *adv.* at the right time, opportunely; in good time, early; too soon, prematurely; maturely

mātūrescō, -ruī 3. to ripen, mature

mātūritās, -ātis *f.* ripeness, maturity, full development; opportune moment

mātūrō 1. to bring to maturity, ripen; do in good time, anticipate; make quick, accelerate; act hurriedly, hasten; (+*inf.*) hasten (to)

mātūrus, -a, -um *adj.* ripe, mature, developed; grown up, advanced; (+*dat.*) ripe (for); coming quickly, swift; timely, opportune; premature

mātūtīnus, -a, -um *adj.* of *or* belonging to the early morning; *n.sg.sbst.* early morning

mausōlēum, -ī *n.* large tomb, mausoleum (*esp. for Roman emperors*)

maxilla, -ae *f.* (*usu. pl.*) jaw-bone, jaws

maximē *superl.adv.* in the highest degree, most of all; to the greatest extent; especially, particularly; by all means; **cum maximē** exactly when

maximitās, -ātis *f.* greatness in size, immensity

maximus, -a, -um *superl.adj.* greatest in size, largest; greatest in degree, highest; oldest; loudest; most powerful, mightiest; most important

maxum- see **maxim-**

māzonomon, -ī *n.* serving-dish

mē see **ego**

meātus, -ūs *m.* going, motion; course, path, channel

mecastor *interj.* by Castor!

mēchanicus, -ī *m.* engineer

medens, -ntis *m.* doctor, physician

medeor 2. *dep.* (+*dat./acc.*) to heal, cure; comfort, assuage

mediānus, -a, -um *adj.* placed in the middle, central

mediastīnus, -ī *m.* common servant, drudge

mēdica, -ae *f.* clover, lucerne

medicābilis, -is, -e *adj.* that can be healed, curable

medicāmen, -inis *n.* drug, medicine, remedy; cosmetic; dye

medicāmentum, -ī *n.* drug, medicine, remedy; cosmetic

medicātus[1], -a, -um *adj.* healing, curing; drugged

medicātus[2], -ūs *m.* application of drugs

medicīna, -ae *f.* drug, medicine, remedy; application of drugs; medical clinic; (*often +ars*) art of medicine

medicō 1. to heal, cure; give medication to, drug; poison; dye

medicor 1. *dep.* (+*dat./acc.*) to heal, cure

medicus, -a, -um *adj.* healing, curing, medical; *m./f.sbst.* doctor, physician

medīdiēs, -ēī *f.* midday

medietās, -ātis *f.* intermediary part

medimnum, -ī *n.* or **medimnus, -ī** *m.* Greek dry measure

mediocris, -is, -e *adj.* of medium size, moderate; ordinary; middling, fair; trivial

mediocritās, -ātis *f.* moderateness; mediocrity; mean, medium

mediocriter *adv.* moderately; with moderation

medioxumus, -a, -um *adj.* midmost, intermediate

meditāmentum, -ī *n.* training, practice

meditātē *adv.* thoughtfully, designedly

meditātiō, -ōnis *f.* contemplation, meditation; training, practice

mediterrāneus, -a, -um *adj.* inland; coming from inland; *n.sbst.* inland region

meditor 1. *dep.* to think over, contemplate; plan, devise; practise, rehearse; rehearse a speech

meditullium, -(i)ī *n.* inland region

medius, -a, -um *adj.* in the middle, central; intervening; ordinary, middling; neutral; *n.sbst.* the middle, centre; midst; public view; neutrality

medius Fidius *interj.* so help me God!

medix, -icis *m.* chief magistrate in Oscan cities

medulla, -ae *f.* (*usu. pl.*) marrow; medulla; innermost part, heart

medullitus *adv.* from the heart, inwardly

medullula, -ae *f.* inner plumage

mefītis see **mephītis**

megistānes, -um *m.pl.* grandees, magnates (*of eastern countries*)

mēherc(u)le or **mēherculēs** *interj.* by Hercules!

meiō, minxī, mictum 3. to urinate

mel, mellis *n.* honey; pleasantness, sweetness; sweetheart, honey

melancholicus, -a, -um *adj.* having black bile, melancholic

melandrya, -um *n.pl.* salted pieces of dried fish

melanūrus, -ī *m.* small sea-fish

melculum, -ī *n.* sweetheart, honey

melē see **melos**

meleagris, -idis *f.* kind of guinea-fowl

mēlēs, -is *f.* badger

melichrūs *adj.* honey-coloured

melicus, -a, -um *adj.* tuneful, musical; (*of poetry*) lyric; *m.sbst.* lyric poet

melilōtos, -ī *f.* kind of clover

melimēla, -ōrum *n.pl.* kind of sweet apples

melior, -or, -us *compar.adj.* better; more agreeable; nobler; stronger; more favourable

melisphyllum, -ī *n.* balm-gentle

melius *compar.adv.* better; more agreeably; more nobly; more favourably

meliusculē *adv.* slightly better

meliusculus, -a, -um *adj.* slightly better

mella, -ae *f.* honey and water drink

mellifer, -era, -erum *adj.* honey-bearing

mellilla, -ae *f.* sweetheart, honey

mellīna, -ae *f.* badger-skin purse

mellītus, -a, -um *adj.* honeyed; honey-sweet

melos (*pl.* **melē**) *n.* song, melody

membrāna, -ae *f.* skin, membrane; parchment

membrāneus, -a, -um *adj.* made of parchment

membrānula, -ae *f.* thin membrane; piece of parchment

membrātim *adv.* limb by limb; individually, piecemeal

membrum, -ī *n.* limb; penis; part, member; division, section; room; clause (*of a sentence*)

meminī (*pf. only*) 3. (+*gen./acc.*) to remember, recollect; bear in mind, pay heed to; record

memor, -oris *adj.* (+*gen.*) mindful (of), heedful (of); unforgetful; grateful; commemorative

memorābilis, -is, -e *adj.* memorable, remarkable; able to be related

memorātor, -ōris *m.* narrator, story-teller

memorātus¹, -a, -um *adj.* memorable, remarkable, notable

memorātus², -ūs *m.* mentioning

memoria, -ae *f.* memory; recollection; remembrance; tradition, history

memoriālis, -is, -e *adj.* of *or* relating to memory; **libellus memoriālis** notebook

memoriola, -ae *f.* memory

memoriter *adv.* with good memory, accurately

memorō 1. to speak, say; mention; narrate, tell; remind

menda, -ae *f.* blemish; fault, mistake

mendāciloquus, -a, -um *adj.* speaking falsely, lying

mendācium, -(i)ī *n.* lie, falsehood; illusion, deceit

mendāciunculum, -ī *n.* small lie, fib

mendax, -ācis *adj.* prone to lying, untruthful; illusory, deceitful

mendīcābulum, -ī *n.* beggar's instrument

mendīcē *adv.* in a beggarly fashion

mendīcitās, -ātis *f.* beggary

mendīcō 1. or **mendīcor** 1. *dep.* to beg for; be a beggar

mendīculus, -a, -um *adj.* somewhat beggarly

mendīcus, -a, -um *adj.* beggarly, indigent; suitable for a beggar; *m.sbst.* beggar

mendōsē *adv.* faultily; erroneously

mendōsus, -a, -um *adj.* full of faults; erroneous; making a mistake

mendum, -ī *n.* mistake, error

mens, mentis *f.* mind; heart; reason, understanding; judgement; attitude; intention, purpose

mensa, -ae *f.* table; counter (*of a shop etc.*); altar; course of a meal; meal

mensārius, -(i)ī *m.* banker; official of the public treasury

mensiō, -ōnis *f.* measuring

mensis, -is *m.* month; *pl.* menstruation

mensor, -ōris *m.* measurer

menstruālis, -is, -e *adj.* lasting for a month

menstruus, -a, -um *adj.* of *or* relating to a

month; lasting for a month; monthly;
n.sbst. monthly payment; *n.pl.sbst.* menstruation

mensula, -ae *f.* small table

mensūra, -ae *f.* measuring; measurement,
dimension; amount, measure; limit;
yardstick

menta, -ae *f.* mint

mentiens, -ntis *m.* sophistic puzzle

mentiō, -ōnis *f.* mention, allusion

mentior 4. *dep.* to lie; fabricate, invent;
disguise, dissemble; feign, assume

mentula, -ae *f.* penis

mentum, -ī *n.* chin

meō 1. to pass, travel

mephītis, -is *f.* sulphurous exhalation;
goddess who protects against such
exhalations

merāclus, -a, -um *adj.* rather undiluted,
tolerably neat

merācus, -a, -um *adj.* undiluted, neat

mercābilis, -is, -e *adj.* purchasable

mercātor, -ōris *m.* trader, merchant

mercātōrius, -a, -um *adj.* of *or* relating to
trade, mercantile

mercātūra, -ae *f.* trade, commerce

mercātus, -ūs *m.* market, fair

mercēdula, -ae *f.* small wage; low rent

mercennārius, -a, -um *adj.* hired, working
for pay; for hire; *m.sbst.* hired worker;
mercenary soldier

mercēs, -ēdis *f.* wage, payment; income,
rent; bribe

mercimōnium, -(i)ī *n.* merchandise; *pl.*
enterprise, business

mercor 1. *dep.* to purchase; trade, deal

merda, -ae *f.* excrement, dung

merenda, -ae *f.* afternoon meal provided
for workers

mereō 2. or **mereor** 2. *dep.* to deserve,
merit, earn; be worthy of

meretrīciē *adv.* in the manner of a prostitute

meretrīcius, -a, -um *adj.* of *or* like a
prostitute; *n.pl.sbst.* prostitution

meretrīcula, -ae *f.* mere prostitute, courtesan

meretrix, -īcis *f.* prostitute, courtesan

mergae, -ārum *f.pl.* reaping boards

merges, -itis *f.* sheaf of corn

mergō, -sī, -sum 3. to dip, immerse; sink,
overwhelm; flood, engulf; bury

mergus, -ī *m.* seagull (*or sim.*)

merīdiānus, -a, -um *adj.* of *or* occurring at
midday; *m.sbst.* midday gladiator

merīdiātiō, -ōnis *f.* midday nap, siesta

merīdiēs, -ēī *f.* midday, noon; the south

merīdiō 1. to have a siesta

meritō[1] 1. to earn habitually

meritō[2] *adv.* deservedly, rightly

meritōrius, -a, -um *adj.* on hire; *n.pl.sbst.*
rented lodgings

meritum, -ī *n.* due reward; good action,
service

merobibus, -a, -um *adj.* drinking
undiluted wine

merops, -pis *m.* bee-eater

mers see **merx**

mersō 1. to dip, immerse; overwhelm

merula, -ae *f.* blackbird

merum, -ī *n.* undiluted wine

merus, -a, -um *adj.* pure, unmixed,
undiluted; sheer, absolute

merx, mercis *f.* commodity; *pl.* goods;
mala merx (*of people*) bad lot

mesochorus, -ī *m.* chorus leader, who
stands in the middle

messis, -is *f.* harvest; crop; harvest-tide

messor, -ōris *m.* harvester, reaper

messōrius, -a, -um *adj.* of *or* relating to a
harvester

mēta, -ae *f.* cone, pyramid; turning-point;
limit, extremity

metallifer, -era, -erum *adj.* mineral-
bearing

metallum, -ī *n.* quarry, mine; metal,
mineral

mētātor, -ōris *m.* one who measures out

mētior, mensus 4. *dep.* to measure;
measure out, mark off; traverse; weigh up,
estimate

metō, messuī, messum 3. to harvest,
reap; cut down; crop, cut off

metōposcopus, -ī *m.* one who predicts the
future by reading foreheads

mētor 1. *dep.* to measure out, mark off; lay
out; traverse; weigh up

metrēta, -ae *f.* liquid measure of about
nine English gallons; jar of this volume

metrum, -ī *n.* rhythm, metre

metūculōsus, -a, -um *adj.* frightful; fearful, timorous

metuō 3. to be afraid of, fear; (+*ne* +*subj.*)
fear (that); be afraid

metus, -ūs *m.* fear, dread, anxiety; awe, reverence; object of fear

meus, mea, meum *adj.* of *or* belonging to me, my, mine; concerning me; favourable to me; under my control

mia *f.adj.* one

mīca, -ae *f.* crumb, grain

micō, -uī 1. to dart, rush, pulsate; flash, gleam, flicker; play the game *morra*, in which one guesses the number of fingers one's opponent suddenly holds up

micturiō 4. to feel the urge to urinate

migrātiō, -ōnis *f.* change of residence, move

migrō 1. to change residence, move; move on; transport, shift

mīles, -itis *m.* soldier; piece in a board game

mīlia see **mille**

mīliārium, -(i)ī *n.* milestone

mīliārius, -a, -um *adj.* weighing a thousand pounds; a thousand paces long

mīliens (-ēs) *adv.* a thousand times; **mīliens sestertium** 100 million sesterces

mīlitāris, -is, -e *adj.* of *or* relating to the army, military; employed in military service; fit for military service; soldierly; *m.sbst.* soldier

mīlitāriter *adv.* in a soldierly manner

mīlitārius, -a, -um *adj.* soldierly

mīlitia, -ae *f.* military service; military campaign; soldiery

mīlitō 1. to serve as a soldier

milium, -(i)ī *n.* millet

mille (*pl.* **mīlia**) *indecl.n.* thousand; thousand people; *adj.* countless, innumerable; **mille passūs** (or **passuum**) Roman mile

millensimus (-ēsi-), -a, -um *adj.* thousandth; **pars millensima** thousandth

millēsimum *adv.* for the thousandth time

milli- see **mīli-**

mīluīnus, -a, -um *adj.* like a kite; *f.sbst.* hunger as great as a kite's

mīluus or **milvus, -ī** *m.* bird of prey, kite

mīma, -ae *f.* female mimic

mīmiambī, -ōrum *m.pl.* mimes written in choliambics

mīmicē *adv.* in the manner of a comic actor

mīmicus, -a, -um *adj.* of *or* like a comic mime, farcical; typical of a comic actor; fake, sham

mīmula, -ae *f.* small mime

mīmus, -ī *m.* mimic actor, comic; farce; sham, pretence

mina, -ae *f.* (*often* +*argentī*) 100 drachmas' worth of silver; **mina aurī** 100 drachmas' worth of gold

mināciae, -ārum *f.pl.* threats

mināciter *adv.* threateningly, menacingly

minae, -ārum *f.pl.* threats; prognostications, warnings; parapets, battlements

minanter *adv.* threateningly, menacingly

minātiō, -ōnis *f.* threatening

minax, -ācis *adj.* threatening, menacing; jutting out, projecting

mineō 2. to project, overhang

miniātulus, -a, -um *adj.* (somewhat) stained with cinnabar *or* red lead

miniātus, -a, -um *adj.* stained with cinnabar *or* red lead

minimē *superl.adv.* in the least, least; not at all, by no means

minimus, -a, -um *superl.adj.* least, smallest; shortest, lowest; youngest; most trifling; humblest; *n.sbst.* smallest amount

minister[1], -trī *m.* assistant, attendant, servant; subordinate, agent

minister[2], -tra, -trum *adj.* assisting, serving; (+*gen.*) devoted (to)

ministerium, -(i)ī *n.* assistance, attendance, service; duty; (*usu. pl.*) assistant(s), retinue

ministra, -ae *f.* female assistant, attendant, handmaid

ministrātor, -ōris *m.* attendant, servant

ministrātōrius, -a, -um *adj.* used for service at the table

ministrātrix, -īcis *f.* female attendant, handmaid

ministrō 1. (+*dat.*) to attend (to), wait (upon); serve, administer; provide, supply; take care of, govern

minitābundus, -a, -um *adj.* threatening, menacing

minitor 1. *dep.* or **minitō** 1. (+*dat.*) to threaten, menace; (+*inf.*) threaten (to)

minium, -(i)ī *n.* cinnabar

minor[1] 1. *dep.* (+*dat.*) to threaten, menace; (+*inf.*) threaten (to); jut out, project

minor[2], -or, -us *compar.adj.* smaller, lesser; shorter; younger; less important; inferior; *n.sbst.* smaller amount, less

minum- see **minim-**

minuō, -uī, -ūtum 3. to make smaller, reduce; make less; cut into pieces; diminish, weaken

minus *compar.adv.* to a smaller degree, less; fewer; not quite; **sī minus** if not

minusculus, -a, -um *adj.* somewhat smaller, rather less

minūtal, -ālis *n.* mincemeat dish

minūtātim *adv.* little by little, gradually

minūtē *adv.* in small pieces; minutely, meanly

minūtia, -ae *f.* smallness

minūtulus, -a, -um *adj.* rather small, tiny

minūtus, -a, -um *adj.* small, tiny, minute; consisting of small parts; petty, trivial; subtle, fine

mīrābilis, -is, -e *adj.* wonderful, marvellous, amazing

mīrābiliter *adv.* wonderfully, amazingly

mīrābundus, -a, -um *adj.* full of wonder, amazed

mīrāculum, -ī *n.* wonderful sight, marvel; amazing event, miracle; wonder, amazement

mīrāculus, -a, -um *adj.* freakish, bizarre

mīrātiō, -ōnis *f.* wonder, amazement

mīrātor, -ōris *m.* admirer

mīrātrix, -īcis *f.* female admirer

mīrātus, -ūs *m.* wonder, amazement

mīrē *adv.* wonderfully, amazingly

mīrificē *adv.* wonderfully, amazingly

mīrificus, -a, -um *adj.* wonderful, amazing

mīrimodīs *adv.* in a wonderful manner, amazingly

mīror 1. *dep.* to wonder, be amazed; wonder at, marvel at; admire, revere

mīrus, -a, -um *adj.* wonderful, marvellous, amazing

miscellānea, -ōrum *n.pl.* hotchpotch, mishmash

miscellus, -a, -um *adj.* assorted, miscellaneous

misceō, miscuī, mixtum 2. to mix, blend; mix up, concoct; combine, associate; confuse, confound; exchange

misellus, -a, -um *adj.* poor, wretched; pitiful

miser, -era, -erum *adj.* poor, wretched; sick; sad, distressing; pitiful, mean

miserābilis, -is, -e *adj.* pitiable, pathetic; poor, wretched; pitiful, mean

miserābiliter *adv.* pitiably, pathetically

miserātiō, -ōnis *f.* pity, compassion; lamentation, grieving

miserē *adv.* pitiably, pathetically; desperately, violently

misereor 2. *dep.* or **misereō** 2. (+*gen./dat.*) to feel pity (towards); **mē miseret** (+*gen.*) I feel pity (for)

miserescō 3. (+*gen.*) to feel pity (towards); **mē miserescit** (+*gen.*) I feel pity (for)

miseria, -ae *f.* wretchedness, distress, woe

misericordia, -ae *f.* pity, compassion; appeal to pity, pathos

misericors, -rdis *adj.* merciful, compassionate

miseriter *adv.* pitiably, pathetically

miseror 1. *dep.* to pity, show compassion for

missīcius, -a, -um *adj.* (*of soldiers*) discharged; *m.sbst.* discharged soldier

missiculō 1. to send repeatedly

missilis, -is, -e *adj.* that can be thrown; *n. sbst.* missile; *n.pl.sbst.* gifts thrown to a crowd

missiō, -ōnis *f.* discharge, release; sending, dispatch

missitō 1. to send repeatedly

missor, -ōris *m.* hurler, firer (*of missiles*)

missus, -ūs *m.* sending, dispatch; hurling, firing (*of missiles*); distance fired; race

mīte *adv.* mildly, gently

mitellītus, -a, -um *adj.* involving the wearing of silken headdresses

mītescō 3. to become tender, ripen; grow mild, soften

mītificō 1. to soften

mītigātiō, -ōnis *f.* softening, soothing

mītigō 1. to soften; make milder; alleviate, lighten; soothe, assuage

mītis, -is, -e *adj.* tender, ripe; soft, mellow; mild, gentle; merciful, lenient

mitra, -ae *f.* eastern headdress, turban

mitrātus, -a, -um *adj.* wearing a *mitra*, turbaned

mittō, mīsī, missum 3. to send, dispatch; let go, release; give up; throw, hurl; thrust; send away, dismiss; disregard

mītulus, -ī *m.* kind of mussel

mixtim *adv.* in an intermingled fashion

mixtum, -ī *n.* diluted wine

mixtūra, -ae *f.* mixing, mingling; combining, fusing; admixture

mnemosynon, -ī *n.* souvenir, keepsake

mōbilis, -is, -e *adj.* movable, mobile; active, nimble; quick-moving; variable, changeable; fickle

mōbilitās, -ātis *f.* mobility; agility, nimbleness; quickness of movement; variability; fickleness

mōbiliter *adv.* nimbly, quickly; in a fickle manner

mōbilitō 1. to set in quick motion

moderābilis, -is, -e *adj.* controllable, moderate

moderāmen, -inis *n.* means of governing; helm; government

moderanter *adv.* with control

moderātē *adv.* with restraint, moderately

moderātim *adv.* moderately, gradually

moderātiō, -ōnis *f.* restraint, moderation; controlling; self-control, temperateness; checking, curbing

moderātor, -ōris *m.* controller, governor, manager; restrainer; holder, wielder

moderātrix, -īcis *f.* female controller, manageress; restrainer

moderātus, -a, -um *adj.* moderate, restrained; controlled, regulated

moderor 1. *dep.* or **moderō** 1. (+*dat./acc.*) to control, govern, direct; restrain, check; regulate

modestē *adv.* with restraint, temperately; decorously, modestly

modestia, -ae *f.* restraint, temperateness; decency, modesty; discipline, obedience

modestus, -a, -um *adj.* restrained, temperate; decorous, modest; unassuming; disciplined, obedient

modiālis, -is, -e *adj.* containing a *modius*

modicē *adv.* with restraint, temperately; moderately, slightly; poorly, meanly

modicus, -a, -um *adj.* moderate, slight; restrained, temperate; ordinary, mediocre; *n.sg.sbst.* small amount

modificātiō, -ōnis *f.* regulation

modificō 1. to regulate, measure

modius, -(i)ī *m.* Roman dry measure containing 16 *sextarii*; vessel of this size

modo (-ō) *adv.* only, just; just now, recently; **sī modo** if at least

modulātē *adv.* musically, rhythmically

modulātiō, -ōnis *f.* modulation (*of tone*)

modulātor, -ōris *m.* deviser of tunes, musician

modulātus¹, -a, -um *adj.* musical, rhythmical

modulātus², -ūs *m.* creation of tunes, composition

modulor 1. *dep.* to modulate (*in tone etc.*), regulate; set to music; play (*an instrument*)

modulus, -ī *m.* small measure

modus, -ī *m.* measure, quantity; size; bound, limit; restraint, moderation; rhythm, time; method, way; rule; kind, type

moecha, -ae *f.* adulteress

moechissō 1. to commit adultery with

moechor 1. *dep.* to commit adultery

moechus, -ī *m.* adulterer

moen- see **mūn-** (other than below)

moenia, -um *f.* walls (*esp. of a city*); fortified city, citadel

moenis, -is, -e *adj.* indebted, obliged

mola, -ae *f.* sacrificial cake of spelt and salt; millstone; *pl.* mill

molāris, -is, -e *adj.* like a millstone; *m.sbst.* rock the size of a millstone; molar

mōlēs, -is *f.* lump, mass; mass of rock; large building; huge amount; hugeness; might, force; burden, pressure; trouble

molestē *adv.* annoyingly, tiresomely; **molestē ferre** to be annoyed at

molestia, -ae *f.* annoyance, trouble; cause of annoyance, nuisance

molestus, -a, -um *adj.* annoying, tiresome, troublesome

mōlīmen, -inis *n.* exertion, effort; bulk, weight; *pl.* important matters

mōlīmentum, -ī *n.* exertion, effort

mōlior 4. *dep.* to labour at; build, construct; set in motion, hurl; rouse; force; make efforts, strive; proceed with effort

mōlītiō, -ōnis *f.* constructing; demolition

mōlītor, -ōris *m.* constructor, builder; contriver

mōlītrix, -īcis *f.* female contriver

molitus¹, -a, -um *adj.* milled, ground; *n.sbst.* flour

mōlītus², -ūs *m.* exertion, effort

mollescō 3. to become soft; become gentle, effeminate

mollicellus, -a, -um *adj.* rather soft, delicate

molliculus, -a, -um *adj.* rather soft, delicate; effeminate

molliō 4. to soften; weaken, enfeeble;

soothe, tame; make milder; make effeminate

mollipēs, -pedis *adj.* tender-footed

mollis, -is, -e *adj.* soft, yielding; tender, delicate; weak, feeble; pliant, supple; gentle, mild, calm; effeminate; sensitive, impressionable; pleasant

molliter *adv.* softly; delicately; weakly; supplely; gently, mildly; effeminately

mollitia, -ae or **-ēs, -ēī** *f.* softness, tenderness; pliancy, suppleness; gentleness, mildness; effeminacy; sensitivity; luxury

mollitūdō, -inis *f.* softness; weakness; gentleness, mildness

molō, -uī, -itum 3. to grind in a mill

molocinārius, -(i)ī *m.* maker of mallow garments

mōly, -yos *n.* magical plant, moly

mōmen, -inis *n.* movement; impulse; tendency

mōmentum, -ī *n.* movement; impulse, weight; moment; critical point; minute amount; influence, force

monaulos, -ī *m.* single-piped musical instrument

monēdula see **monērula**

moneō 2. to remind; advise, warn, instruct

monēris, -is *m.* ship with one man at each oar

monērula, -ae *f.* jackdaw

monētālis, -is *m.* officer of the mint, coiner

monetrix, -īcis *f.* female adviser

monīle, -is *n.* necklace, collar

monimentum see **monumentum**

monitiō, -ōnis *f.* warning, admonition

monitor, -ōris *m.* adviser, counsellor; prompter, nomenclator

monitus, -ūs *m.* warning, admonition

monobiblos, -ī *m.* book in a single volume (*esp. name of Propertius' first book*)

monogrammus, -a, -um *adj.* incorporeal, shadowy

monopodium, -(i)ī *n.* one-footed table

monopōlium, -īī *n.* commercial monopoly

monotropus, -a, -um *adj.* solitary, alone

mons, montis *m.* mountain, hill; huge rock; mass, pile

monstrābilis, -is, -e *adj.* remarkable, notable

monstrātiō, -ōnis *f.* demonstrating, showing

monstrātor, -ōris *m.* demonstrator; guide

monstrifer, -era, -erum *adj.* producing monsters

monstrō 1. to show, point out; demonstrate; reveal, make known; appoint, ordain; provide directions

monstrōsus see **monstruōsus**

monstrum, -ī *n.* portent, omen; monstrous deed *or* event; monster; wicked person

monstruōsē *adv.* unnaturally

monstruōsus, -a, -um *adj.* ill-omened; monstrous, unnatural

montānus, -a, -um *adj.* of *or* belonging to the mountains; mountainous; *m.sbst.* mountain-dweller; *pl.* inhabitants of the seven hills of Rome

monticola, -ae *m.adj.* mountain-dwelling

montifer, -era, -erum *adj.* bearing a mountain

montivagus, -a, -um *adj.* mountain-wandering

mont(u)ōsus, -a, -um *adj.* full of mountains, mountainous

monumentum, -ī *n.* memorial, monument; statue, tomb; document; book, memoir; *pl.* history

mora¹, -ae *f.* delay; interval, pause; duration; lateness; hindrance, obstacle

mora², -ae *f.* division of the Spartan army

mōrālis, -is, -e *adj.* of *or* relating to morals, ethical; *n.pl.sbst.* ethics

morātor, -ōris *m.* hinderer, delayer; loiterer

mōrātus, -a, -um *adj.* having certain manners; well-mannered, civilized

morbidus, -a, -um *adj.* sick, diseased; causing disease

morbōsus, -a, -um *adj.* debauched

morbus, -ī *m.* sickness, disease, malady; weakness, vice

mordāciter *adv.* bitingly

mordax, -ācis *adj.* biting, snappish; sharp, cutting; stinging, pungent; gnawing; carping

mordeō, momordī (mem-), morsum 2. to bite, nibble; cut; sting; gnaw at, erode; vex, worry; carp at

mordex, -icis *m.* incisor tooth

mordicus *adv.* by biting, with the teeth

mōrē *adv.* foolishly, stupidly

morētum, -ī *n.* cheese and herb dish

moribundus, -a, -um *adj.* dying, moribund; mortal

mōrigeror 1. *dep.* or **mōrigerō** 1. (*+dat.*) to be indulgent (to), gratify

mōrigerus, -a, -um *adj.* (*+dat.*) indulgent (to), compliant (with)

mōriō, -ōnis *m.* jester, fool

morior, mortuus 3. *dep.* to die, perish; die off, come to an end; faint; become obsolete, forgotten

mōrologus, -a, -um *adj.* speaking foolishly

moror 1. *dep.* to delay, hinder, detain; wait, delay, pause; stay behind, loiter; **nīl morārī** to have no care for, ignore

mōrōsē *adv.* captiously

mōrōsitās, -ātis *f.* captiousness, peevishness

mōrōsus, -a, -um *adj.* captious, peevish, pernickety

mors, mortis *f.* death; destruction

morsiuncula, -ae *f.* small bite

morsum, -ī *n.* morsel, piece bitten off

morsus, -ūs *m.* biting; bite; cutting, stinging; corrosion; carping

mortālis, -is, -e *adj.* mortal, perishable; human; *m.sbst.* human being, mortal

mortālitās, -ātis *f.* mortality, perishability; death

mortārium, -(i)ī *n.* grinding mortar

morticīnus, -a, -um *adj.* having died naturally

mortifer, -era, -erum *adj.* death-bringing, lethal

mortiferē *adv.* lethally, fatally

mortuālia, -um *n.pl.* funeral dirges

mortuus, -a, -um *adj.* dead; inanimate; motionless, still; *m.sbst.* corpse

mōrum, -ī *n.* mulberry; blackberry

mōrus[1]**, -ī** *f.* mulberry tree

mōrus[2]**, -a, -um** *adj.* foolish, stupid

mōs, mōris *m.* custom, habit; fashion, style; (*usu. pl.*) character, manners; *pl.* morals, ethics; **mōs mālōrum** tradition; **mōrem gerere** (*+dat.*) to indulge, gratify

mōtiō, -ōnis *f.* movement

mōtiuncula, -ae *f.* slight bout of fever

mōtō 1. to shake, agitate

mōtor, -ōris *m.* one who moves, shaker

mōtus, -ūs *m.* movement; gesture; sensation; emotion; manoeuvre; shift, alter-ation; upset, disturbance; uprising, rebellion

moveō, mōvī, mōtum 2. to set in motion, move; stir, rouse; shift, move; brandish, shake; upset, disturb; affect, influence, move; annoy, provoke; moot; consider, ponder

mox *adv.* soon; next; shortly after

muccus see **mūcus**

mūcidus, -a, -um *adj.* snotty; mouldy

mūcrō, -ōnis *m.* sharp end, point; sword

mūcus, -ī *m.* mucus, snot

mūgilis, -is *m.* grey mullet

mūgīnor 1. *dep.* to dally, shilly-shally

mūgiō 4. to low, moo; roar, bellow

mūgītus, -ūs *m.* lowing, mooing; roaring, bellowing

mūla, -ae *f.* she-mule

mulceō 2. to stroke, caress; soothe, assuage; alleviate; charm

mulcō 1. to beat, thrash, maltreat

mulctra see **mulctrum**

mulctrāria, -um *n.pl.* milking-pails

mulctrum, -ī *n.* milking-pail

mulgeō, mulsī, mulsum 2. to milk

muliebris, -is, -e *adj.* of *or* relating to a woman; womanly, feminine; female; *n.pl.sbst.* female genitalia

muliebriter *adv.* in a womanly manner, effeminately

mulier, -eris *f.* woman; wife, mistress; effeminate

mulierārius, -a, -um *adj.* hired by a woman

muliercula, -ae *f.* little woman, mere woman

mulierōsitās, -ātis *f.* love of women

mulierōsus, -a, -um *adj.* fond of women

mūlīnus, -a, -um *adj.* like a mule

mūliō, -ōnis *m.* mule-driver

mūliōnius, -a, -um *adj.* of *or* belonging to a mule-driver

mullus, -ī *m.* red mullet

mulsum, -ī *n.* wine mixed with honey, oenomel

mulsus, -a, -um *adj.* honey-sweet; *f.sbst.* sweetheart, honey

multa, -ae *f.* fine, penalty (*of cattle or money*)

multangulus, -a, -um *adj.* having many angles

multātīcius, -a, -um *adj.* exacted as a fine

multātiō, -ōnis *f.* imposition of a fine

multēsimus, -a, -um *adj.* very small, minute

multibibus, -a, -um *adj.* drinking much, bibulous

multicavus, -a, -um *adj.* having many holes

multīcia, -ōrum *n.pl.* fine garments

multifāriam *adv.* in many places

multifidus, -a, -um *adj.* divided into many parts

multiformis, -is, -e *adj.* having many forms, varied

multiforus, -a, -um *adj.* having many holes

multigener, -eris *adj.* of many different kinds

multigenus, -a, -um *adj.* of many different kinds

multiiugis, -is, -e or **-us, -a, -um** *adj.* yoked many together; having many parts

multiloquium, -(i)ī *n.* garrulity, loquaciousness

multiloquus, -a, -um *adj.* that talks much

multimodīs *adv.* in many ways

multiplex, -icis *adj.* with many folds; with many turnings; having many parts, complex; manifold; versatile, multifarious

multiplicābilis, -is, -e *adj.* multiple, manifold

multiplicātiō, -ōnis *f.* multiplication

multipliciter *adv.* in many ways

multiplicō 1. to multiply, increase; use often

multipotens, -ntis *adj.* having much power

multisonus, -a, -um *adj.* making much noise

multitūdō, -inis *f.* numerousness, abundance; multitude, crowd; common people, mob

multivagus, -a, -um *adj.* much-wandering, wide-ranging

multivolus, -a, -um *adj.* wanting many (*men*)

multō[1] 1. (+*abl.*) to fine (with); punish (with)

multō[2] *adv.* by far, much

multum, -ī *n.* large amount, much; **multum diēī/noctis** late in the day/night; *pl.* many things; *n.sg.adv.* much, greatly, very; *n.pl.adv.* much

multus, -a, -um *adj.* much, great; *pl.* many; (*of the day/night*) late; regular, zealous; *m.pl.sbst.* many people

mūlus, -ī *m.* mule

mundānus, -a, -um *adj.* of *or* belonging to the world

mundē *adv.* cleanly, neatly

munditer *adv.* neatly

munditia, -ae or **-ēs, -ēī** *f.* cleanliness, neatness; elegance, refinement

mundulus, -a, -um *adj.* rather elegant, dapper

mundus[1]**, -a, -um** *adj.* clean, neat; elegant, refined; **in mundō** at hand, ready

mundus[2]**, -ī** *m.* world; heavens, universe

mundus[3]**, -ī** *m.* female cosmetics, adornment

mūnerārius, -iī *m.* provider of public shows

mūnerigerulus, -ī *m.* bringer of gifts

mūneror 1. *dep.* or **mūnerō** 1. (+*abl.*) to present (with); (+*dat.*) bestow (upon)

mūnia, [-um] *n.pl.* official duties, functions

mūniceps, -cipis *m.* citizen of a *municipium*; fellow-citizen

mūnicipālis, -is, -e *adj.* of *or* belonging to a *municipium*; provincial (*in a derogatory sense*)

mūnicipātim *adv.* by *municipia*

mūnicipium, -(i)ī *n.* autonomous Italian town, municipality

mūnificē *adv.* magnificently, liberally

mūnificentia, -ae *f.* magnificence, liberality

mūnificō 1. (+*abl.*) to enrich (with)

mūnificus, -a, -um *adj.* magnificent, liberal; dutiful

mūnīmen, -inis *n.* fortification, defence

mūnīmentum, -ī *n.* fortification, defence; bulwark, protection

mūniō 4. to fortify, build as a fortification; defend, protect; build

mūnītiō, -ōnis *f.* fortifying; fortification, defence; building

mūnītō 1. to build continually

mūnītor, -ōris *m.* builder of fortifications

mūnītus, -a, -um *adj.* well-fortified, defended; safe, secure

mūnus, -eris *n.* duty, function; office, post; service, favour; public show; gift, present, product

mūnusculum, -ī *n.* small gift, little favour

mūraena see **mūrēna**

mūrālis, -is, -e *adj.* like a wall, turreted; used to attack *or* defend city walls; **corōna mūrālis** crown presented to the first to scale a wall in attack

mūrātus, -a, -um *adj.* walled in

mūrēna, -ae *f.* eel, moray

mūrex, -icis *m.* shellfish that produced purple dye; its spiny shell; its purple dye; sharp rock

muria, -ae *f.* brine, pickle

muriātica, -ōrum *n.pl.* pickled fish

muricidus, -a, -um *adj.* (*perhaps*) cowardly

murmillō see **myrmillō**

murmur, -uris *n.* rumble, roar, growl; mutter, murmur

murmurātiō, -ōnis *f.* grumbling

murmurillum, -ī *n.* quiet mutter

murmurō 1. to rumble, roar; mutter, murmur; grumble

murra¹, -ae *f.* myrrh

murra², -ae *f.* fluorspar

murreus¹, -a, -um *adj.* myrrh-coloured

murreus², -a, -um *adj.* made of fluorspar

murrina, -ae *f.* liqueur wine

murrinus¹, -a, -um *adj.* of *or* belonging to myrrh

murrinus², -a, -um *adj.* made of fluorspar; *n.pl.sbst.* vessels of fluorspar

murt- see **myrt-**

mūrus, -ī *m.* city wall, wall; defence, barrier

mūs, mūris *m.* mouse

musca, -ae *f.* fly

muscārium, -iī *n.* fly-swatter

muscipulum, -ī *n.* mousetrap

muscōsus, -a, -um *adj.* covered in moss, mossy

musculus, -ī *m.* (small) mouse; muscle; siege shelter, mantelet

muscus, -ī *m.* moss

mūsica, -ae or **mūsicē, -ēs** *f.* art of music; music

mūsicē *adv.* elegantly, with refinement

mūsicus, -a, -um *adj.* of *or* relating to the Muses; of *or* relating to music; trained in music; *m.sbst.* musician

mūsīum, -iī *n.* the research institute at Alexandria

mussitō 1. to mutter (continually); be quiet; keep quiet about

mussō 1. to mutter, whisper; be quiet; hesitate, shilly-shally; keep quiet about

mustāceum, -ī *n.* or **mustāceus, -ī** *m.* must-cake baked on laurel

mustēla (-ella), -ae *f.* weasel

mustēlīnus, -a, -um *adj.* of *or* belonging to a weasel

musteus, -a, -um *adj.* juicy, fresh; immature, undeveloped

mustulentus, -a, -um *adj.* abounding in unfermented wine

mustum, -ī *n.* unfermented wine, must

mūtābilis, -is, -e *adj.* changeable; variable, fickle

mūtābilitās, -ātis *f.* liability to change; fickleness

mūtātiō, -ōnis *f.* change, mutation; exchange, substitution

mūtātor, -ōris *m.* changer; exchanger, trader

mutilō 1. to lop off; maim, mutilate

mutilus, -a, -um *adj.* maimed, truncated; (*of cattle*) hornless

mūtō 1. to change, alter, modify; exchange, substitute; shift, move; undergo change; (*+in +acc. or +abl.*) transform (into)

muttiō 4. to mutter, whisper

muttītiō, -ōnis *f.* muttering, whispering

muttō, -ōnis *m.* penis

mūtuātiō, -ōnis *f.* borrowing, receipt of a loan

mūtuē *adv.* reciprocally, mutually

mūtuitor 1. *dep.* to borrow money continually

mutūniātus, -a, -um *adj.* having a large penis

mūtuō *adv.* reciprocally, mutually

mūtuor 1. *dep.* to borrow (*esp. money*)

mūtus, -a, -um *adj.* dumb, mute; speechless; silent

mūtuus, -a, -um *adj.* borrowed, on loan; reciprocal, mutual; shared; *n.sbst.* loan (*esp. of money*)

myoparō, -ōnis *m.* small warship, galley

myrīca, -ae *f.* tamarisk

myrmillō, -ōnis *m.* gladiator with Gallic helmet shaped like a fish

myrobalanum, -ī *n.* oil of the ben-nut

myrobrechēs *adj.* wet with perfume

myropōla, -ae *m.* dealer in perfumes

myropōlium, -(i)ī *n.* perfumer's shop

myrothēcium, -(i)ī *n.* box of unguent *or* perfume

myrrha see **murra**[1]

myrtētum, -ī *n.* myrtle grove

myrteus, -a, -um *adj.* of *or* relating to myrtles; made of myrtle

myrtum, -ī *n.* myrtle-berry

myrtus, -ī or **myrtus, -ūs** *f.* myrtle tree; spear of myrtle wood

mystagōgus, -ī *m.* one who informs visitors, tour-guide

mystērium, -(i)ī *n.* (*usu. pl.*) secret rite, mystery; secret

mystēs, -ae *m.* one initiated into secret rites

mysticus, -a, -um *adj.* of *or* relating to secret mysteries; secret, mysterious

myxa, -ae *f.* wick

nablia, -ium *n.pl.* Phoenician stringed
instrument, harp

naenia see **nēnia**

naevos (-us), -ī *m.* birthmark, mole

nam *part.* for; for example; moreover; well
then

namque *conj.* for; well then; certainly

nanciscor, na(n)ctus 3. *dep.* to get,
obtain; find; arrive at; meet with

nānus, -ī *m.* dwarf

naphtās, -ae *m.* naphtha

narcissus, -ī *m.* narcissus

nardus, -ī *f.* or **nardum, -ī** *n.* nard; balsam
of nard

nāris, -is *f.* nose; *pl.* nostrils, nose

narrābilis, -is, -e *adj.* that can be told

narrātiō, -ōnis *f.* tale, narrative

narrātiuncula, -ae *f.* short tale, anecdote

narrātor, -ōris *m.* narrator

narrātus, -ūs *m.* tale, narrative

narrō 1. to tell, relate; speak about,
describe

narthēcium, -(i)ī *n.* box for perfumes *or*
medicines

nascor, nātus 3. *dep.* to be born, come into
being; rise, grow; originate

nassa, -ae *f.* wickerwork trap for catching
fish

nassiterna, -ae *f.* watering-pot

nasturcium, -(i)ī *n.* cress, water-cress

nāsus, -ī *m.* or **nāsum, -ī** *n.* nose; spout

nāsūtus, -a, -um *adj.* having a big nose;
witty, sharp

nāta, -ae *f.* daughter

nātālicius, -a, -um *adj.* of *or* relating to a
birth *or* birthday; *f.sbst.* birthday

nātālis¹, -is, -e *adj.* of *or* relating to birth,
natal

nātālis², -is *m.* birthday, anniversary;

birth; place of birth; horoscope; *pl.* origin,
parentage

natātor, -ōris *m.* swimmer

natātus, -ūs *m.* swimming

nātiō, -ōnis *f.* birth; race, nation; nation-
ality; set, group

natis, -is *f.* (*usu. pl.*) buttocks

nātīvus, -a, -um *adj.* created, born; natural, innate; native

natō 1. to swim; float; (+*abl.*) abound (in),
overflow (with); sway, waver

natrix, -īcis *f.* water-snake

nātū *m.abl.sg.* by birth; **māior/minor
nātū** older/younger

nātūra, -ae *f.* birth; nature, quality; natural
order; character; **rērum nātūra** Nature

nātūrālis, -is, -e *adj.* natural, native; of
or relating to nature; unartificial,
natural

nātūrāliter *adv.* naturally; spontaneously

nātus, -ī *m.* son; *pl.* children, offspring

nauarchus, -ī *m.* naval commander

nauclēricus, -a, -um *adj.* of *or* relating to a
naval captain

nauclērus, -ī *m.* naval captain

naucula see **nāvicula**

nauculor 1. *dep.* to sail in a small boat

naucum, -ī *n.* trifle, worthless item

naufragium, -(i)ī *n.* shipwreck; ruins

naufragus, -a, -um *adj.* shipwrecked;
causing shipwreck; *m.sbst.* shipwrecked
person

naulum, -ī *n.* fare, passage-money

naumachia, -ae *f.* mock sea-fight; artificial
lake for such fights

naumachiārius, -iī *m.* participator in a
mock sea-fight

nausea, -ae *f.* seasickness, nausea;
disgust

nauseābundus, -a, -um *adj.* seasick, nauseous

nauseātor, -ōris *m.* one liable to seasickness

nauseō 1. to be seasick, suffer from nausea; feel disgust

nauseola, -ae *f.* slight sickness, squeamishness

nausi- see **nause-**

nauta, -ae *m.* sailor, mariner

nautea, -ae *f.* bilge-water, foul liquid

nauticus, -a, -um *adj.* of or relating to a ship, nautical; seafaring; *m.pl.sbst.* sailors, mariners

nāvāle, -is *n.* (*usu. pl.*) shipyard, dockyard

nāvālis, -is, -e *adj.* nautical, naval

nāvē *adv.* diligently, actively

nāvicula, -ae *f.* small boat

nāviculāria, -ae *f.* the shipping business

nāviculārius, -(i)ī *m.* ship-owner

nāvifragus, -a, -um *adj.* causing shipwreck

nāvigābilis, -is, -e *adj.* navigable

nāvigātiō, -ōnis *f.* sailing, voyage

nāviger, -era, -erum *adj.* navigable

nāvigium, -(i)ī *n.* ship, boat

nāvigō 1. to sail, voyage; (+*acc.*) sail over

nāvis, -is *f.* ship, boat

nāvita see **nauta**

nāviter *adv.* diligently, energetically; completely

nāvō 1. to do energetically, carry out diligently

nāvus, -a, -um *adj.* diligent, energetic; carried out diligently

---

nē¹ *conj.*

1. **nē** + *subjunctive*
a) negative of *ut* (purpose clause)
   domum redierunt ne foris dormirent
   they returned home so that they would not sleep outside
b) lest, that (fear clause)
   verebantur ne canes cibum ederent they were afraid that the dogs would eat the food
2. **nē** + *imperative*
do not …!
   ne timete don't be afraid!
3. **nē... quidem** *not even*

---

nē² *part.* indeed, yes

-ne *part.* (*enclitic particle used to introduce questions*)

nebris, -idos *f.* fawn-skin (*worn esp. by Bacchus and Bacchants*)

nebula, -ae *f.* fog, vapour; cloud; film, veneer

nebulō, -ōnis *m.* rascal, good-for-nothing

nebulōsus, -a, -um *adj.* foggy, misty

nec see **neque**

necdum *adv.* not yet; *conj.* and not yet

necessāriō (-ē) *adv.* necessarily, unavoidably

necessārius, -a, -um *adj.* necessary; unavoidable; critical, urgent; closely related; *m./f.sbst.* relation, intimate

necesse *adv.* necessary; unavoidable; indispensable

necessitās, -ātis *f.* necessity; inevitability; need; close relationship; *pl.* requirements, necessaries

necessitūdō, -inis *f.* necessity; inevitability; compulsion; close relationship; intimate relation

necessum (-us) *indecl.adj.* unavoidable; indispensable; enforced; *n.sg.sbst.* compulsion

necne *conj.* or not

necnōn *adv.* also, furthermore

necō 1. to kill, destroy

necopīnans, -ntis *adj.* unsuspecting, unawares

necopīnātō *adv.* unexpectedly

necopīnātus, -a, -um *adj.* unforeseen, unexpected

necopīnus, -a, -um *adj.* unsuspecting; unforeseen

nectar, -aris *n.* nectar, drink of the gods

nectareus, -a, -um *adj.* of or like nectar

nectō, nex(u)ī, nexum 3. to weave, bind together; attach; compose (*literature*); prepare

nēcubi *adv.* lest anywhere; lest at any time

nēcunde *adv.* lest from anywhere

nēdum *conj.* not to speak of, let alone; still less

nefandus, -a, -um *adj.* wicked, heinous

nefāriē *adv.* wickedly, abominably

nefārius, -a, -um *adj.* wicked, abominable, foul

nefās *indecl.n.* wicked act; impious act, sin; horrible thing

nefastum, -ī *n.* wicked act

nefastus, -a, -um *adj.* unholy, impious; abominable
negantia, -ae *f.* denial
negātiō, -ōnis *f.* denial; negation
negitō 1. to deny repeatedly; refuse frequently
neglectiō, -ōnis *f.* neglect
neglectus[1], -a, -um *adj.* neglected
neglectus[2], -ūs *m.* neglect
neglegens, -ntis *adj.* neglectful, careless
neglegenter *adv.* neglectfully, carelessly; indiscriminately
neglegentia, -ae *f.* neglect, carelessness
neglegō, -xī, -ctum 3. to ignore, overlook; neglect; fail to observe
negō 1. to deny; refuse; (*+acc.+inf.*) deny (that), say (that) ... not
negōtiālis, -is, -e *adj.* of *or* relating to business *or* trade
negōtiātiō, -ōnis *f.* business, trade
negōtiātor, -ōris *m.* businessman, trader
negōtiolum, -ī *n.* minor business; small difficulty
negōtior 1. *dep.* to do business, trade
negōtiōsus, -a, -um *adj.* busy, active; **diēs negōtiōsus** workday
negōtium, -(i)ī *n.* business; activity; concern; difficulty, trouble
nēmō, -inis *m./f.* no one, nobody
nemorālis, -is, -e *adj.* of *or* relating to a forest, sylvan
nemorensis, -is, -e *adj.* of *or* relating to the sacred grove of Diana near Aricia; *m.sg. sbst.* this particular area
nemorivagus, -a, -um *adj.* forest-wandering
nemorōsus, -a, -um *adj.* covered in forest, well-wooded
nempe *part.* truly, to be sure; clearly
nemus, -oris *n.* wood, forest; sacred grove
nēnia, -ae *f.* funeral dirge; song; incantation
neō, nēvī, nētum 2. to spin, weave
nepa, -ae *m.* scorpion
nepōs, -ōtis *m.* grandson; descendant; spendthrift
nepōtātus, -ūs *m.* extravagant living
nepōtulus, -ī *m.* little grandson
neptis, -is *f.* granddaughter; female descendant
nēquam (*compar.* **nēquior**, *superl.*

nēquissimus) *indecl.adj.* worthless; useless
nēquāquam *adv.* not at all, by no means
neque or **nec** *conj.* nor, and not; **neque ,..**
neque (nec ... nec) neither ... nor; *adv.* not
nequedum see **necdum**
nequeō, nequīre, nequīvī (nequiī) 4. (*+inf.*) to be unable (to)
nēquior, nēquissimus see **nēquam**
nequīquam *adv.* to no purpose, vainly; groundlessly
nēquiter *adv.* wickedly, badly; worthlessly
nēquitia, -ae or **-iēs, -iēī** *f.* wickedness, villainy; depravity, vice; worthlessness
nervōsē *adv.* vigorously, strongly
nervōsus, -a, -um *adj.* brawny, tough; vigorous
nervulī, -ōrum *m.pl.* vigour, energies
nervus, -ī *m.* sinew, tendon; string; *pl.* vigour, strength, power
nesciō 4. not to know, be ignorant of; **nesciō (-o) an** perhaps; **nesciō (-o) quis** someone or other
nescius, -a, -um *adj.* (*+gen.*) not knowing, ignorant (of); (*+inf.*) unable (to)
neu see **nēve**
neuter, -tra, -trum *adj.* neither; neutral; *pron.* neither one *or* thing
neutiquam *adv.* by no means
neutrō *adv.* in neither direction
neutrubi *adv.* in neither place
nēve or **neu** *conj.* nor, and not; and that ... not
nex, necis *f.* killing, murder; death
nexilis, -is, -e *adj.* woven together, intertwined
nexō 1. to bind, plait
nexum, -ī *n.* arrangement between debtor and creditor
nexus, -ūs *m.* plaiting, binding; bond, restraint
nī *conj.* if ... not, unless; that ... not; *adv.* not
nīcētērion, -iī *n.* victory prize
nictō 1. to wink, flicker
nīdāmenta, -ōrum *n.pl.* material for a nest
nīdificus, -a, -um *adj.* that causes the building of nests
nīdor, -ōris *m.* vapour, fume, scent
nīdulus, -ī *m.* little nest
nīdus, -ī *m.* nest; pigeon-hole; brood

niger, nigra, nigrum *adj.* black, dark; filthy; deadly, evil

nigrans, -ntis *adj.* black, dark

nigrescō, nigruī 3. to become black, darken

nigrō 1. to make black; be black

nigror, -ōris *m.* blackness, darkness

nihil *indecl.n.* nothing; *adv.* not at all

nihilōminus *adv.* nevertheless

nihilum, -ī *n.* nothing; *adv.* not at all

nīl see **nihil**

nīlum see **nihilum**

nimbātus, -a, -um *adj.* frivolous

nimbifer, -era, -erum *adj.* storm-bringing

nimbōsus, -a, -um *adj.* full of rain-clouds, stormy

nimbus, -ī *m.* rain-cloud, cloud; downpour, rainstorm

nīmīrum *part.* certainly, without doubt

nimis *adv.* too much, excessively; *indecl.n.* (+*gen.*) too much (of)

nimium¹, -(i)ī *n.* excessive amount, too much

nimium² *adv.* too much, excessively; very greatly

nimius, -a, -um *adj.* excessive, too much; very great; immoderate, intemperate

ningō, ninxī 3. to snow

ninguis, -is *f.* snowdrift

ninnium, -(i)ī *n.* (*perhaps*) little doll

nisi *conj.* unless, if not; except if

nīsus, -ūs *m.* pressure; straining, effort, striving; thrusting

nītēdula, -ae *f.* dormouse

nītēla, -ae *f.* dormouse

nitens, -ntis *adj.* shining, radiant; glossy; illustrious, brilliant; flourishing

niteō 2. to shine, be radiant; sparkle; be glossy; be illustrious, be brilliant; flourish

nitescō 3. to become bright, begin to shine; become glossy

nitidē *adv.* brightly; brilliantly, elegantly

nitidiusculē *adv.* slightly more smartly

nitidiusculus, -a, -um *adj.* slightly more shiny

nitidus, -a, -um *adj.* shining, bright; sparkling; glossy, blooming; elegant, well-trimmed; polished

nītor¹, nixus or **nīsus** 3. *dep.* (+*abl.*) to lean (upon), rest (on); put one's trust (in); strain, struggle; strive

nitor², -ōris *m.* brightness, splendour; glossiness; illustriousness; elegance

nitrātus, -a, -um *adj.* mixed with natural soda

nitrum, -ī *n.* natural soda, potash

nivālis, -is, -e *adj.* snowy, wintry; snow-covered; snow-white

nivārius, -a, -um *adj.* of *or* relating to snow (*for cooling drinks*)

nivātus, -a, -um *adj.* cooled with snow, ice-cold

nīve *conj.* and not, nor; or if … not

niveus, -a, -um *adj.* consisting of snow, snowy; snow-white; cooled with snow, ice-cold

nivōsus, -a, -um *adj.* full of snow, snowy

nix, nivis *f.* snow; snow-whiteness

nixor 1. *dep.* (+*abl.*) to lean (upon); strive

nixus, -ūs *m.* straining, exertion; *pl.* efforts of childbirth

nō, nāvī 1. to swim; float; (*of eyes*) be unfocused, swim

nōbilis, -is, -e *adj.* well-known, famous; outstanding; remarkable; of noble birth, aristocratic; noble, excellent; *m.sbst.* nobleman

nōbilitās, -ātis *f.* renown, fame; illustriousness; nobility of birth, aristocracy; nobility, excellence

nōbilitō 1. to make known, make renowned *or* notorious; make grander

nocens, -ntis *adj.* harmful, noxious; guilty; *m.sbst.* guilty man, criminal

noceō 2. (+*dat.*) to harm, damage; impair; corrupt

noctifer, -erī *m.* the evening star

noctilūca, -ae *f.adj.* night-shining (*of the moon*)

noctivagus, -a, -um *adj.* wandering by night

noctū *f.abl.sg.* at night, by night

noctua, -ae *f.* owl

noctuīnus, -a, -um *adj.* like that of an owl

nocturnābundus, -a, -um *adj.* operating by night

nocturnus, -a, -um *adj.* of *or* relating to the night, nocturnal; by night

noctuvigilus, -a, -um *adj.* keeping watch by night

nocuus, -a, -um *adj.* harmful, noxious

nōdō 1. to tie in a knot

nōdōsus, -a, -um *adj.* full of knots; gnarled, knotty; difficult to solve

nōdus, -ī *m.* knot; node; bond, obligation; difficulty

noenu *adv.* not

nōlō, nōlle, nōluī *v.irreg.* not to want, be unwilling; **nōlī(te)** (+*inf.*) do not ... !

nōmen, -inis *n.* name; title; reputation, renown; noun; category

nōmenclātor, -ōris *m.* slave who told his master the names of those persons he met; slave who announced meals at a feast

nōminātim *adv.* by name; specifically

nōminātiō, -ōnis *f.* nomination

nōminitō 1. to name, term

nōminō 1. to name; designate, call; mention; nominate; denounce

nomisma, -atis *n.* coin; token

nomos¹, -ī *m.* Egyptian district

nomos², -ī *m.* melody, tune

nōn *adv.* not

nōnae, -ārum *f.pl.* 5th day of the month (7th day of March, May, July and October)

nōnāgēnārius, -a, -um *adj.* ninety years old

nōnāgiens (-ēs) *adv.* ninety times; 9,000,000 sesterces

nōnāgintā *indecl.adj.* ninety

nōnānus, -a, -um *adj.* of the ninth legion; *m.sbst.* soldier of the ninth legion

nōndum *adv.* not yet

nōngentī, -ae, -a *pl.adj.* nine hundred

nōnne *part.* is it not the case that ... ?, surely ... ?

nōnnihil *indecl.n.* a certain amount; *adv.* to a certain degree, somewhat

nōnnullus, -a, -um *adj.* not a little, some; *pl.* not a few, several; *m./f.pl.sbst.* some men/women

nōnnumquam *adv.* sometimes, occasionally

nōnus, -a, -um *adj.* ninth

norma, -ae *f.* carpenter's square; pattern, standard

nōs (*acc.* **nōs**, *gen.* **nostrī** or **nostrum**, *dat./abl.* **nōbīs**) *pron.* we (us)

noscitō 1. to be familiar with, recognize; investigate

noscō, nōvī, nōtum 3. to get to know; investigate; *pf.* know, be familiar with, recognize

noster, -tra, -trum *adj.* our, ours; favourable to us

nostrās, -ātis *adj.* native to our country, indigenous

nota, -ae *f.* mark; marker, sign; brand; sort, quality

notābilis, -is, -e *adj.* noteworthy, remarkable; conspicuous, obvious

notābiliter *adv.* remarkably; conspicuously

notārius, -iī *m.* writer of shorthand

notātiō, -ōnis *f.* marking; noticing; choosing; defining; stigmatizing

nōtescō, nōtuī 3. to become known, become famous

nothus, -a, -um *adj.* illegitimately born, bastard; not genuine

nōtiō, -ōnis *f.* acquaintance; investigation; idea, notion

nōtitia, -ae or **-iēs, -iēī** *f.* acquaintance, familiarity; knowledge; renown, fame; idea, notion

notō 1. to mark, brand; write; mark out; denote; censure; take notice of, observe

nōtor, -ōris *m.* guarantor

nōtus, -a, -um *adj.* known, well-known; familiar; knowing; *m./f.sbst.* acquaintance

novācula, -ae *f.* razor

novāle, -is *n.* or **novālis, -is** *f.* fallow land; field

novātrix, -īcis *f.* female innovator

novē *adv.* in a new manner; fashionably

novellō 1. to plant nurseries

novellus, -a, -um *adj.* new, young; tender

novem *indecl.adj.* nine

novemdiālis (novend-), -is, -e *adj.* lasting nine days; held on the ninth day; *n.sg.sbst.* nine day period

novēnī, -ae, -a *pl.adj.* nine each; nine at a time; *sg.* ninefold

noverca, -ae *f.* stepmother

novercālis, -is, -e *adj.* of *or* relating to a stepmother; like a stepmother

novīcius, -a, -um *adj.* recent, new; (*of slaves*) newly bought; *m.sbst.* newly bought slave

noviens (-ēs) *adv.* nine times

novitās, -ātis *f.* newness, novelty; freshness; unfamiliarity

novō 1. to make new, renew; change, alter; invent

novus, -a, -um *adj.* new, recent; fresh; novel; unfamiliar, strange; **rēs novae** revolution

nox, noctis *f.* night; darkness; **nocte** by night; **nox** by night

noxa, -ae *f.* wrongdoing, injurious conduct; harm, damage

noxia see **noxa**

noxiōsus, -a, -um *adj.* guilty

noxius, -a, -um *adj.* guilty; harmful, noxious

nūbēcula, -ae *f.* small cloud

nūbēs, -is *f.* cloud; swarm; gloom

nūbifer, -era, -erum *adj.* cloud-bringing; cloud-covered

nūbigena, -ae *m.adj.* born *or* originating from clouds

nūbilis, -is, -e *adj.* of an age suitable for marriage, nubile

nūbilus, -a, -um *adj.* cloudy; shadowy; gloomy; confused; *n.sbst.* cloud

nūbis see **nūbēs**

nūbō, nupsī, nuptum 3. (+*dat.*) to get married (to)

nucētum, -ī *n.* grove of nut trees

nucifrangibulum, -ī *n.* nutcracker

nuculeus, -ī *m.* kernel of a nut

nudius tertius *adv.* three days ago

nūdō 1. to make bare, strip; lay bare, expose; plunder; disclose

nūdus, -a, -um *adj.* naked, nude; bare, bald; exposed; destitute; mere, only

nūgae, -ārum *f.pl.* trifles, frivolities; nonsense; rubbish

nūgātor, -ōris *m.* trifler, fool; liar

nūgātōrius, -a, -um *adj.* trifling, frivolous; absurd, futile

nūgigerulus, -ī *m.* peddler of trifles

nūgor 1. *dep.* to speak in a trifling manner; (+*dat.*) lie (to), trick

nullus, -a, -um (*gen.* **-īus** or **-ius**, *dat.* **-ī**) *adj.* not any, none; *sbst.* no one *or* nothing

num *part.*
1. **num?**
surely not? (expects the answer 'no')
num canis fugit? surely the dog hasn't run away?
2. **num**
whether (indirect question)
rogavit num canis fugisset he asked whether the dog had run away
nonne? = surely? (expects the answer 'yes')
nonne canis fugit? surely the dog has run away?

numella, -ae *f.* shackle, fetter

nūmen, -inis *n.* nod; divine influence; divine command; god, deity

numerābilis, -is, -e *adj.* able to be counted

numerātiō, -ōnis *f.* paying out, expenditure

numerātus, -a, -um *adj.* counted out, in ready money; *n.sg.sbst.* ready money, cash

numerō[1] 1. to count; enumerate; count out, pay; reckon (as)

numerō[2] *adv.* prematurely, too soon

numerōsē *adv.* rhythmically

numerōsus, -a, -um *adj.* involving many; numerous; manifold; rhythmical

numerus, -ī *m.* number; total; class; rank; poetic metre; rhythm; *pl.* mathematics; poetry; melody

nummārius, -a, -um *adj.* of *or* relating to coins; able to be bribed, corrupt

nummātus, -a, -um *adj.* rich, well-off

nummāriolus, -ī *m.* petty banker

nummulārius, -iī *m.* money-changer, banker

nummulus, -ī *m.* coin

nummus, -ī *m.* coin, piece of money; sesterce; Roman denarius; silver didrachm

numnam *part.* surely … not?

numquam *adv.* never; under no circumstances

numquid *part.* surely … not?

nunc *adv.* now, at this time; already now; nowadays; but as it is

nunciam *adv.* here and now

nuncupātiō, -ōnis *f.* declaration, pronouncement

nuncupō 1. to declare, pronounce; designate; nominate

nundinae, -ārum *f.pl.* market-day (*held every ninth day*); marketplace; trade

nundinālis, -is, -e *adj.* of *or* relating to market-days

nundinātiō, -ōnis *f.* trading, business

nundinor 1. *dep.* to trade (*at a market*), traffic; buy; swarm in great numbers

nundinum, -ī *n.* **trīnum nundinum** period of three market-days, i.e. 24 days; the third market-day

nunquam see **numquam**

nuntia, -ae *f.* female messenger

nuntiātiō, -ōnis *f.* announcement, notification

nuntiātor, -ōris *m.* informant, notifier

nuntiō 1. to announce, report; notify; warn

nuntius¹, -(i)ī *m.* messenger; message

nuntius², -a, -um *adj.* (+*gen.*) bringing word (of), announcing; *n.sbst.* announcement, message

nūper *adv.* recently, lately; in recent times

nūperus, -a, -um *adj.* recent, fresh

nupta, -ae *f.* wife; **nova nupta** bride

nuptiae, -ārum *f.pl.* marriage; wedding

nuptiālis, -is, -e *adj.* of *or* relating to a marriage *or* wedding, nuptial

nuptus¹, -ī *m.* male bride

nuptus², -ūs *m.* marriage (*to a man*)

nurus, -ūs *f.* daughter-in-law; young married woman

nusquam *adv.* nowhere; on no occasion; in no place

nūtātiō, -ōnis *f.* rocking, swaying

nūtō 1. to nod; rock, sway; waver

nūtrīcātus, -ūs *m.* nourishing, rearing

nūtrīcius, -(i)ī *m.* foster-father, guardian

nūtrīcō 1. to nurse, nourish; rear

nūtrīcula, -ae *f.* wet-nurse, nurse

nūtrīmen, -inis *n.* nourishment

nūtrīmentum, -ī *n.* nourishment; *pl.* nurture, rearing

nūtriō 4. to suckle, nourish; rear; encourage, foster

nūtrītor, -ōris *m.* nourisher; rearer

nūtrix, -īcis *f.* wet-nurse, nurse, nourisher

nūtus, -ūs *m.* nod; command; sinking, gravitation

nux, nucis *f.* nut; nut tree

nympha, -ae or **-ē, -ēs** *f.* nymph; maiden

O

ō(h) *interj.* oh! (*exclam. of joy, surprise, pain etc.*); *also used* (+*voc.*) *in addressing people or things*

ob *prep.* (+*acc.*) in front of, before; because of; in return for; in connection with

obaerātus, -a, -um *adj.* in debt; *m.sbst.* debtor

obambulō 1. to walk (up to); traverse

obardeō, -rsī 2. to flash in one's face

obarmō 1. to equip with weapons

obarō 1. to plough up

obba, -ae *f.* beaker for drinking

obbrūtescō, -tuī 3. to become stupid *or* dull

obc- see **occ-**

obdō, obdidī, obditum 3. (+*dat.*) to place before, interpose; fasten, shut; expose (to)

obdormiō 4. to fall asleep; sleep off (*a hangover*)

obdormiscō 3. to fall asleep; pass away

obdūcō, obduxī, obductum 3. to draw in front, cover; close; obstruct; lead forward; gulp down

obdūrescō, -ruī 3. to become hard; become insensitive

obdūrō 1. to be persistent, hold out; make hard

obeliscus, -ī *m.* obelisk

obeō, obīre, obiī (obīvī), obitum 4. to go to meet, visit; attend; enclose; undertake; (*of heavenly bodies*) set; (*sometimes* +*mortem*) die

obequitō 1. (+*dat.*) to ride up to

oberrō 1. to wander about; (+*dat.*) flit before; (+*abl.*) blunder over

obēsitās, -ātis *f.* fatness, obesity

obēsus, -a, -um *adj.* fat, obese; unrefined, insensitive

ōbex, ōbicis *m./f.* door-bolt, barricade; hindrance, obstacle

obf- see **off-**

obg- see **ogg-**

obhaereō 2. (+*dat.*) to be stuck (to)

obhaerescō, obhaesī 3. (+*in*+*abl. or* +*dat.*) to become stuck (on)

obiaceō 2. (+*dat.*) to lie near; lie in the path of, block

obiciō, obiēcī, obiectum 3. (+*dat.*) to throw in the way (of); interpose, put before; bring upon; expose to; be situated near; lay to (one's) charge; taunt

obiectātiō, -ōnis *f.* taunting

obiectō 1. (+*dat.*) to put before; expose (to); lay to (one's) charge

obiectum, -ī *n.* charge, accusation; object

obiectus, -ūs *m.* placing before, interposition; hindrance, barrier

obiiciō see **obiciō**

obīrascor, obīrātus 3. *dep.* (+*dat.*) to become angry (at)

obiter *adv.* in passing; incidentally, by the way

obitus, -ūs *m.* approach; death; (*of heavenly bodies*) setting

obiurgātiō, -ōnis *f.* rebuking, reproving

obiurgātor, -ōris *m.* one who rebukes, reprover

obiurgātōrius, -a, -um *adj.* reproachful, rebuking

obiurgō 1. to rebuke, reprove; punish, chastise

oblanguescō, -guī 3. to become languid, languish

oblātrātrix, -īcis *f.* nagging female, railer

oblātrō 1. to bark out

oblectāmen, -inis *n.* source of pleasure, delight

oblectāmentum, -ī *n.* source of pleasure, delight

oblectātiō, -ōnis f. act of pleasing, delighting

oblectō 1. to please, delight; while away pleasantly

oblīdō, -sī, -sum 3. to squeeze, crush

obligātiō, -ōnis f. pledging

obligō 1. to tie up, bind; swathe; put under obligation (*religious, legal or personal*), oblige; make guilty

oblīmō 1. to cover with mud, besmear; defile

oblinō, oblīvī, oblitum 3. (+*abl.*) to besmear, daub (with); defile, pollute; blot out

oblīquē adv. at an angle, obliquely; by implication

oblīquitās, -ātis f. slant, obliqueness

oblīquō 1. to set at an angle, turn sideways; utter covertly

oblīquus, -a, -um adj. at an angle, slanted, oblique; sideways; indirect, covert; **in oblīquum** sideways

oblīterō see **oblitterō**

oblitescō, -tuī 3. to become hidden, disappear

oblitterō 1. to blot out of memory, make forgotten

oblīviō, -ōnis f. forgetfulness, oblivion; amnesty

oblīviōsus, -a, -um adj. forgetful; causing forgetfulness

oblīviscor, oblītus 3. dep. to forget; lose sight of; refl. forget oneself

oblīvium, -(i)ī n. forgetfulness, oblivion

oblocūtor, -ōris m. one who interrupts (a speech)

oblongus, -a, -um adj. oblong

obloquor, oblocūtus 3. dep. (+*dat.*) to interrupt, answer back (at); utter in accompaniment

obluctor 1. dep. (+*dat.*) to struggle (against)

oblūdiō 1. to play tricks

obmōlior 4. dep. to block in; block up

obmurmurō 1. (+*dat.*) to murmur (against)

obmūtescō, -tuī 3. to become mute, fall silent

obnātus, -a, -um adj. (+*dat.*) growing (by)

obnītor, obnixus 3. dep. (+*dat.*) to thrust, press (against); take a stand (against), resist

obnixē adv. strenuously, obstinately

obnixus, -a, -um adj. obstinate, resolute

obnoxiē adv. restrictedly; submissively

obnoxiōsē adv. restrictedly

obnoxiōsus, -a, -um adj. submissive, subordinate

obnoxius, -a, -um adj. under obligation, indebted; (+*dat.*) exposed (to), liable (to); submissive (to); guilty (of)

obnūbō 3. to cover (*the head*), veil

obnuntiātiō, -ōnis f. announcement of an unfavourable omen

obnuntiō 1. to announce an unfavourable omen; announce bad news

oboediens, -ntis adj. (+*dat.*) obedient (towards), compliant (with)

oboedienter adv. obediently, compliantly

oboedientia, -ae f. obedience, compliance

oboediō 4. (+*dat.*) to heed, obey; be submissive (to)

oboleō 2. (+*acc.*) to smell (of), reek (of)

obolus, -ī m. Greek coin, obol

oborior, obortus 4. dep. to spring up, rise up; appear, occur

obp- see **opp-**

obrēpō, -epsī, -eptum 3. to creep up, approach stealthily; sneak in; (+*dat.*) visit unexpectedly

obreptō 1. to creep up

obrētiō 4. to catch in a net

obrigescō, -guī 3. (+*dat.*) to become stiff (with); curdle

obrōdō 3. to gnaw at

obrogātiō, -ōnis f. invalidation (*of a law*) by the enactment of a new one

obrogō 1. to invalidate (*a law*) by enacting a new one

obruō, -uī, -utum 3. to cover, bury; (+*abl.*) smother (with); crush, overwhelm; eclipse; collapse

obrussa, -ae f. testing of gold by fire

obsaepiō, -psī, -ptum 4. to obstruct, block up

obsaturō 1. to sate, glut

obscaen- see **obscēn-**

obscaevō 1. (+*dat.*) to be a good (*or* bad) omen (for)

obscēnē adv. obscenely, indecently

obscēnitās, -ātis f. obscenity, indecency

obscēnus, -a, -um adj. inauspicious, ill-omened; filthy, foul; obscene, indecent;

m.sbst. sexual deviant; *n.pl.sbst.* genitals, private parts

obscūrātiō, -ōnis *f.* eclipse; blurring

obscūrē *adv.* obscurely, indistinctly; furtively, secretly

obscūritās, -ātis *f.* darkness, obscurity; lack of clarity; lack of renown, low birth

obscūrō 1. to darken, obscure; conceal, hide; make unknown

obscūrus, -a, -um *adj.* dark, obscure; concealed, hidden; unknown; unclear, indistinct; reserved (*in character*)

obsecrātiō, -ōnis *f.* entreaty, supplication

obsecrō 1. to entreat, beseech

obsecundō 1. (+*dat.*) to act in compliance (with)

obsēpiō see **obsaepiō**

obsequella, -ae *f.* obedience, compliance

obsequens, -ntis *adj.* (+*dat.*) obedient (towards), compliant (with); addicted (to)

obsequenter *adv.* obediently, compliantly

obsequentia, -ae *f.* obedience, compliance

obsequiōsus, -a, -um *adj.* compliant, obsequious

obsequium, -(i)ī *n.* compliance, obedience, subservience

obsequor, obsecūtus 3. *dep.* (+*dat.*) to obey, act in compliance (with), submit (to)

obserō¹ 1. to bolt, bar, block

obserō², obsēvī, obsitum 3. (+*abl.*) to sow, plant (with)

observans, -ntis *adj.* (+*gen.*) attentive (to), respectful (to)

observantia, -ae *f.* attention, respect

observātiō, -ōnis *f.* attention; surveillance; observance (*of customs etc.*); practice, usage

observātor, -ōris *m.* observer

observitō 1. to watch regularly; pay attention to

observō 1. to watch, observe; observe (*customs etc.*); pay regard to, respect

obses, obsidis *m./f.* hostage; guarantee, surety

obsessiō, -ōnis *f.* siege, blockade

obsessor, -ōris *m.* besieger; (+*gen.*) haunter (of), frequenter (of)

obsideō, obsēdī, obsessum 2. to occupy,

throng; frequent; besiege; smother; sit down

obsidiālis, -is, -e *adj.* of *or* relating to a siege

obsidiō, -ōnis *f.* siege, blockade

obsidium¹, -(i)ī *n.* siege, blockade

obsidium², -lī *n.* condition of being a hostage

obsīdō 3. to besiege; occupy

obsignātor, -ōris *m.* sealer (*of documents*)

obsignō 1. to seal (*documents*); imprint

obsipō 1. to besprinkle, scatter

obsistō, obstitī, obstitum 3. (+*dat.*) to block, obstruct; resist, oppose; impede

obsitus, -a, -um *adj.* (+*abl.*) covered (with), smothered (in)

obsolefaciō, -fēcī, -factum 3. to render common, degrade

obsolescō, -lēvī, -lētum 3. to become obsolete, fall into disuse; become degraded

obsolētē *adv.* shabbily

obsolētus, -a, -um *adj.* worn-out, shabby; hackneyed

obsōnātor, -ōris *m.* caterer

obsōnātus, -ūs *m.* obtaining provisions, catering

obsōnium, -(i)ī *m.* provisions (*for a meal*); *pl.* pension

obsōnō¹ 1. or **obsōnor** 1. *dep.* to obtain provisions, cater; obtain (*for a meal*)

obsōnō² 1. (+*dat.*) to interrupt

obsorbeō 2. to swallow, gulp down

obstetrix, -īcis *f.* midwife

obstinātē *adv.* obstinately, stubbornly

obstinātiō, -ōnis *f.* obstinacy, stubbornness; (+*gen.*) stubborn observance (of)

obstinātus, -a, -um *adj.* obstinate, stubborn

obstinō 1. to set one's mind upon

obstipescō see **obstupescō**

obstīpus, -a, -um *adj.* oblique, slanting; bent sideways

obstita, -ōrum *n.pl.* (*perhaps*) places struck by lightning

obstō, obstitī, obstātum 1. (+*dat.*) to stand in the way of, block, impede; resist, oppose; meet

obstrepō, -uī, -itum 3. (+*dat.*) to make a noise (at), clamour (against); protest strongly (at)

obstrigillō 1. to cause obstruction, block

obstringō, -nxī, -ctum 3. to bind, tie fast; confine; place under obligation; implicate, involve

obstructiō, -ōnis *f.* obstruction, hindrance

obstruō, -xī, -ctum 3. to build as a barrier; block up, shut; obstruct

obstupefaciō, -fēcī, -factum 3. to strike dumb, stupefy

obstupescō, -puī 3. to be struck dumb, become stupefied

obstupidus, -a, -um *adj.* dumbstruck, stupefied

obsum, obesse, obfuī *v.irreg.* (+*dat.*) to be a hindrance (to); be prejudiced (against)

obsuō, -uī, -ūtum 3. to sew up

obsurdescō, -duī 3. to become deaf

obtaedescit 3. *impers.* it begins to cause weariness

obtegō, -xī, -ctum 3. to cover; conceal; protect

obtemperātiō, -ōnis *f.* (+*dat.*) compliance (with)

obtemperō 1. (+*dat.*) to comply (with), be submissive (to)

obtendō, -dī, -tum 3. to stretch in front; offer as a pretext; cover

obtentus, -ūs *m.* stretching in front; pretext, excuse; concealing

obterō, obtrīvī, obtrītum 3. to trample upon, crush; destroy; treat with contempt

obtestātiō, -ōnis *f.* solemn invocation; beseeching, entreaty

obtestor 1. *dep.* to invoke (*as a witness*); beseech, entreat; declare under oath

obtexō, -uī, -tum 3. to veil, cover

obticeō 2. to stay silent

obticescō, -cuī 3. to become silent

obtineō, obtinuī, obtentum 2. to keep possession of, occupy; grasp; maintain; obtain, gain; prevail

obtingō, obtigī 3. (+*dat.*) to befall, happen (to)

obtorpescō, -puī 3. to become numb; become stupid

obtorqueō, -rsī, -rtum 2. to tie round; twist round

obtrectātiō (obtrac-), -ōnis *f.* disparagement

obtrectātor (obtrac-), -ōris *m.* disparager, detractor

obtrectō 1. to disparage, belittle

obtrūdō, -sī, -sum 3. (+*dat.*) to thrust (upon); gulp down

obtruncō 1. to cut up, slaughter, behead

obtueor 2. *dep.* or **obtuor** 3. *dep.* to look at, behold

obtundō, obtudī, obtūsum (-unsum) 3. to batter, thump; make blunt; deafen; harass verbally

obtunsus see **obtūsus**

obturbō 1. to throw into confusion, disturb

obturgescō, -rsī 3. to swell up

obtūrō 1. to block up, close

obtūsus, -a, -um *adj.* blunt; dim, obtuse

obtūtus, -ūs *m.* gaze; contemplation

obumbrō 1. to overshadow, darken; conceal, protect

obuncus, -a, -um *adj.* hooked

obustus, -a, -um *adj.* hardened by fire; scorched (*by frost*)

obvāgiō 4. to wail, bleat

obvallō 1. to wall round

obveniō, obvēnī, obventum 4. to meet; (+*dat.*) to befall, happen (to); fall to the lot (of)

obversātiō, -ōnis *f.* moving about in view

obversor 1. *dep.* to move about in view; (+*dat.* or +*ante* +*abl.*) appear (before)

obversus, -a, -um *adj.* (+*in* +*acc.* or +*acc.*) facing, opposite (to)

obvertō, -tī, -sum 3. (+*dat.*) to turn (towards), direct (against)

obviam *adv.* (+*dat.*) in the way (of); at hand; **obviam īre** (+*dat.*) to meet

obvigilō 1. to be vigilant

obvius, -a, -um *adj.* in the way, meeting; (+*dat.*) in opposition (to); exposed; at hand

obvolvō, -vī, -ūtum 3. to wrap up, cover round

occaecō 1. to blind; overcloud; make obscure; conceal

occallescō, -lluī 3. to become callous; become unfeeling

occanō see **occinō**

occantō see **occentō**

occāsiō, -ōnis *f.* opportunity, occasion

occāsiuncula, -ae *f.* critical opportunity

occāsus, -ūs *m.* sinking; decline, destruction; the west

occātiō, -ōnis *f.* harrowing (*of soil*)

occātor, -ōris *m.* harrower (*of soil*)

occēdō, occessī, occessum 3. to go to confront, go towards

occentō 1. to sing at, serenade

occeptō 1. to begin

occidens, -ntis *m.* the west

occīdiō, -ōnis *f.* utter destruction, massacre

occidō[1]**, occidī, occāsum** 3. to fall down, die; (*of heavenly bodies*) sink, set; be ruined

occīdō[2]**, -dī, -sum** 3. to kill, slaughter; bring disaster upon

occiduus, -a, -um *adj.* sinking, setting; declining, coming to an end; western

occillō 1. to smash into pieces

occinō, -nuī 3. to sing *or* sound in interruption

occipiō, occēpī, occeptum 3. to engage in, take up; begin

occipitium, -(i)ī *n.* back of the head

occiput, -pitis *n.* back of the head

occīsiō, -ōnis *f.* killing, murder

occīsor, -ōris *m.* killer, murderer

occlāmitō 1. to shout in interruption

occlūdō, -sī, -sum 3. to shut, close up; restrain

occō 1. to harrow (*soil*)

occubō 1. (+*dat.*) to lie (against); lie dead

occulcō 1. to trample down

occulō, -luī, -ltum 3. to conceal, cover; keep secret

occultātiō, -ōnis *f.* concealment

occultātor, -ōris *m.* one who conceals

occultē *adv.* furtively, secretly; indirectly

occultō 1. to conceal; keep secret

occultus, -a, -um *adj.* concealed, hidden; secret; recondite; secretive, reserved; *n.pl. sbst.* secrets; **per occultum** or **ex occultō** secretly

occumbō, occubuī 3. to meet with (*death*); die

occupātiō, -ōnis *f.* taking possession; preoccupation, employment

occupātus, -a, -um *adj.* occupied, busy

occupō 1. to take possession of, seize; occupy; employ; anticipate

occurrō, -rrī, -rsum 3. to run to meet; come upon; (+*dat.*) attack, confront; check, counteract

occursātiō, -ōnis *f.* running to welcome (*somebody*)

occursō 1. to run to meet; (+*dat.*) obstruct, oppose; occur (*to the mind* or *senses*)

occursus, -ūs *m.* meeting; obstruction; charge, attack

ocellātum, -ī *n.* stone with eye-like markings

ocellus, -ī *m.* (dear) little eye; darling

ōcimum, -ī *n.* basil

ōcior, -or, -us *compar.adj.* quicker, swifter; occurring sooner

ōcissimus, -a, -um *superl.adj.* quickest, swiftest; occurring soonest

ōciter *compar.adv.* more quickly; sooner; more easily; instantly

ocliferius, -a, -um *adj.* eye-catching

ocrea, -ae *f.* greave

ocreātus, -a, -um *adj.* wearing greaves

octaphoros, -os, -on *adj.* carried by eight men; *m.sbst.* litter carried by eight men

octāvum *adv.* for the eighth time

octāvus, -a, -um *adj.* eighth

octiens (-ēs) *adv.* eight times

octingēnī, -ae, -a *pl.adj.* eight hundred each

octingentēsimus, -a, -um *adj.* eight hundredth

octingentī, -ae, -a *pl.adj.* eight hundred

octipēs, -edis *adj.* having eight feet

octiplicō 1. to multiply by eight

octō *indecl.adj.* eight

octōgēnārius, -a, -um *adj.* eighty years old

octōgēnī, -ae, -a *pl.adj.* eighty each

octōgensimus (-gēsi-), -a, -um *adj.* eightieth

octōgiens (-ēs) *adv.* eighty times

octōgintā *indecl.adj.* eighty

octōiugis, -is, -e *adj.* yoked in a team of eight

octōnī, -ae, -a *pl.adj.* eight each; eight at a time

octuplus, -a, -um *adj.* eightfold; *n.sbst.* eightfold penalty

octussis, -is, -e *adj.* sum of eight *asses*

oculātus, -a, -um *adj.* keen-sighted

oculeus, -a, -um *adj.* consisting of eyes

oculissimus, -a, -um *adj.* dearest, most beloved

oculus, -ī *m.* eye; eyesight; bud

ōdēum, -ī *n.* music hall, theatre

ōdī, ōsum (*pf. only*) 3. to hate, detest

odiōsē *adv.* unpleasantly, odiously

odiossicus, -a, -um *adj.* unpleasant, odious

odiōsus (-ossus), -a, -um *adj.* unpleasant, odious; troublesome

odium, od(i)ī *n.* hatred, dislike; object of hatred; unpopularity

odor, odōris *m.* smell, odour; perfume

odōrātiō, -ōnis *f.* sense of smell

odōrātus¹, -a, -um *adj.* scented, sweet-smelling

odōrātus², -ūs *m.* sense of smell; smelling

odōrifer, -era, -erum *adj.* producing perfumes; sweet-smelling

odōrō 1. to make fragrant

odōror 1. *dep.* to smell, inhale; scent, get wind of; acquire a little of

odōrus, -a, -um *adj.* of *or* relating to smell; sweet-smelling; pungent

odōs see **odor**

oeconomicus, -a, -um *adj.* of *or* relating to household management

oenophorum, -ī *n.* large wine-vessel

oenopōlium, -(i)ī *n.* wine-shop

oestrus, -ī *m.* gadfly; frenzy, passion

oesypum, -ī *n.* grease obtained from untreated wool

ofella, -ae *f.* cutlet, morsel

offa, -ae *f.* lump of flour; lump, mass

offātim *adv.* into morsels

offendiculum, -ī *n.* slight hindrance, stumbling-block

offendō, -dī, -sum 3. (+*dat. or* +*ad*+*acc.*) to come upon, meet; annoy, offend; knock (against), dash (against); cause offence (to); err (against)

offensa, -ae *f.* knock, collision; offence; transgression

offensiō, -ōnis *f.* knock, stumbling; set-back; upset; causing *or* taking offence

offensiuncula, -ae *f.* slight set-back; slight taking offence

offensō 1. to knock, collide with

offensus¹, -ūs *m.* knock, collision

offensus², -a, -um *adj.* offended; offensive

offerō, offerre, obtulī, oblātum *v.irreg.* (+*dat.*) to put in (one's) way; expose (to); provide, offer; occasion, bring about

offerūmenta, -ae *f.* ridge

officīna, -ae *f.* workshop, manufactory

officiō, offēcī, offectum 3. (+*dat.*) to get in the way (of), impede, obstruct; (+*acc.*) block

officiōsē *adv.* dutifully, obligingly

officiōsus, -a, -um *adj.* dutiful, obliging

officium, -(i)ī *n.* favour, service; official duty; job, employment; courtesy, respect

offīgō, offīxī, offixum 3. to fasten, fix in

offirmātē *adv.* obstinately, stubbornly

offirmātus, -a, -um *adj.* obstinate, stubborn

offirmō 1. to make obstinate; persevere

offlectō 3. to turn to face

offrēnō 1. to restrain (*with a bridle*)

offūcia, -ae *f.* paint; deceit

offula, -ae *f.* morsel of food

offulgeō, -lsī 2. (+*dat.*) to shine (upon)

offundō, offūdī, offūsum 3. (+*dat.*) to pour (over); (+*abl.*) spread (with), cover (with)

ogganniō 4. to snarl at

oggerō 3. to bring before in abundance

ōh see **ō(h)**

ohē (ōhē) *interj.* whoa!, easy there!

oiei *interj.* ow! (*exclam. of pain*)

ōla see **olla**

olea, -ae *f.* olive; olive tree

oleāginus, -a, -um *adj.* of *or* relating to an olive tree

oleārius, -a, -um *adj.* of *or* relating to olive oil; *m.sbst.* seller of olive oil

oleaster, -trī *m.* oleaster

olefactō 1. to smell, sniff

olens, -ntis *adj.* sweet-smelling; pungent, rank

oleō, oluī 2. (+*acc./abl.*) to smell (of); give off a smell; reek, stink

olētum, -ī *n.* excrement

oleum, -ī *n.* olive-oil; effort

olfaciō, olfēcī, olfactum 3. to smell, scent; detect

olidus, -a, -um *adj.* pungent, stinking

ōlim *adv.* at that time; once upon a time, formerly; for a long time; at times; one day

olīva, -ae *f.* olive; olive tree

olīvētum, -ī *n.* olive plantation

olīvifer, -era, -erum *adj.* olive-bearing

olīvum, -ī *n.* olive-oil

olla, -ae *f.* jar, pot

ollāris, -is, -e *adj.* stored in jars

olle (-us) see **ille**

olō see **oleō**

olor, olōris *m.* swan

olōrifer, -era, -erum *adj.* swan-bearing

olōrīnus, -a, -um *adj.* of *or* relating to a swan

olus see **(h)olus**

omāsum, -ī *n.* tripe of an ox

ōmen, ōminis *n.* omen, augury; good wish

ōmentum, -ī *n.* fatty membrane, caul

ōminātor, -ōris *m.* diviner

ōminor 1. *dep.* to divine, presage, prophesy

ōminōsus, -a, -um *adj.* ominous, foreboding

omissus, -a, -um *adj.* negligent, remiss

omittō, omīsī, omissum 3. to release, let go; give up; leave off; leave out, omit; disregard

omnifer, -era, -erum *adj.* bearing everything

omnigenus, -a, -um *adj.* of every kind

omnimodīs *adv.* in every way

omnīnō *adv.* wholly, entirely; all in all; in general; at all

omniparens, -ntis *adj.* that creates all things

omnipotens, -ntis *adj.* omnipotent, allpowerful; *m.sg.sbst.* Jupiter

omnis, -is, -e *adj.* all, every; whole; of all kinds; each; *n.pl.sbst.* everything

omnituens, -ntis *adj.* all-seeing

omnivagus, -a, -um *adj.* that wanders all over

omnivolus, -a, -um *adj.* that desires all

onager, -grī *m.* wild ass

onerārius, -a, -um *adj.* of *or* for freight; *f. sbst.* freight ship, cargo vessel

onerō 1. to load, burden; fill; overwhelm; oppress; aggravate

onerōsus, -a, -um *adj.* burdensome, weighty; onerous, tiresome

onocrotalus, -ī *m.* pelican

onus, oneris *n.* load, burden; weight; trouble; task

onustus, -a, -um *adj.* laden, freighted; full; oppressed

onyx, onychis *m./f.* onyx; small onyx container

opācitās, -ātis *f.* darkness, shadiness

opācō 1. to overshadow, shade

opācus, -a, -um *adj.* overshadowed, shady; dark; reclusive; *n.pl.sbst.* shady places

opella, -ae *f.* slight effort; trifling business; *pl.* worthwhile effort

opera, -ae *f.* effort, exertion; trouble; service; employment; day's work; workman; *pl.* hired rowdies; (+*dat.*) **operam dare** work hard (at), give attention (to)

operārius, -a, -um *adj.* working for hire; *m./f.sbst.* hired labourer

operātus, -a, -um *adj.* busied, engaged; occupied (*in thought, worship etc.*)

operculum, -ī *n.* lid

operīmentum, -ī *n.* cover, covering

operiō, -ruī, -rtum 4. to cover; bury; conceal; close, shut

operor 1. *dep.* to be at work; worship

operōsē *adv.* laboriously, painstakingly

operōsus, -a, -um *adj.* painstaking, industrious; toilsome; elaborate, studied

opertōrium, -iī *n.* bedcover, blanket

opertum, -ī *n.* secret; secret place; *pl.* riddles

opertus, -a, -um *adj.* covered, concealed; secret

ophītēs, -ae *m.* serpentine

ophthalmicus, -ī *m.* optician, eye-surgeon

opifer, -era, -erum *adj.* bringing help

opifex, -ficis *m.* craftsman, inventor; artisan

opificīna, -ae *f.* workshop

ōpiliō, -ōnis *m.* shepherd, herdsman

opīmē *adv.* richly, splendidly

opīmitās, -ātis *f.* richness, prosperity

opīmus, -a, -um *adj.* rich, fertile; plump; wealthy; **spolia opīma** spoils taken from an enemy general when slain by a victorious Roman general

opīnābilis, -is, -e *adj.* based upon opinion, conjectural

opīnātiō, -ōnis *f.* conjecture, supposition

opīnātor, -ōris *m.* one who (often) conjectures

opīnātus, -ūs *m.* conjecture, supposition

opīniō, -ōnis *f.* opinion; estimation; conjecture; imagination; reputation

opīnor 1. *dep.* or **opīnō** 1. to be of an opinion, conjecture; imagine; opine

opiparē *adv.* richly, sumptuously

opiparus, -a, -um *adj.* rich, sumptuous

opisthographus, -a, -um *adj.* written on the back (*as well as the front*)

opitulor 1. *dep.* (+*dat.*) to help, bring aid (to)

opobalsamum, -ī *n.* resin of the balsam tree

oportet 2. *impers.* (+*acc.*+*inf.*) it is proper, it behoves; it is inevitable (that)

oppangō, oppēgī, oppactum 3. to plant on (*a kiss*)

oppectō 3. to comb through

oppēdō 3. (+*dat.*) to fart in the face (of), mock

opperior, opper(ī)tus 4. *dep.* to wait; await

oppetō, -īvī (-iī), -ītum 3. to meet, encounter; die

oppidānus, -a, -um *adj.* of *or* relating to a town, provincial; *m.sbst.* town-dweller

oppidātim *adv.* by towns

oppidō *adv.* exceedingly, utterly

oppidulum, -ī *n.* small town

oppidum, -ī *n.* town

oppignerō 1. to give as a pledge, mortgage

oppīlō 1. to block up, stop up

oppleō, -lēvī, -lētum 2. to fill up, block; cover

oppōnō, opposuī (-sīvī), oppos(i)tum 3. (+*dat.*) to place (*sthg*) before, put in the way (of); set against, oppose; interpose; contrast; retort; pledge

opportūnē *adv.* conveniently, suitably; opportunely

opportūnitās, -ātis *f.* convenience, suitability; opportuneness; opportunity

opportūnus, -a, -um *adj.* convenient, suitable; at hand; opportune; (+*dat.*) exposed (to)

oppositus¹, -a, -um *adj.* (+*dat.*) situated in front (of); opposing, hostile (to)

oppositus², -ūs *m.* placing in the way, interposal

oppressiō, -ōnis *f.* overpowering, overwhelming; catching unawares

oppressiuncula, -ae *f.* little squeeze

oppressus, -ūs *m.* crushing, squeezing

opprimō, -ressī, -ressum 3. to crush; bury; overwhelm; smother, extinguish; catch unawares

opprobrāmentum, -ī *n.* scandal, disgrace

opprobrium, -(i)ī *n.* scandal, disgrace; cause of disgrace

opprobrō 1. to bring up as a taunt, reproach

oppugnātiō, -ōnis *f.* assault, attack (*esp. upon towns*)

oppugnātor, -ōris *m.* assailant, attacker

oppugnō 1. to assail, attack

ops, opis *f.* power, might; aid; *pl.* influence; resources; wealth

opsōn- see **obsōn-**

optābilis, -is, -e *adj.* desirable

optātiō, -ōnis *f.* wishing, desiring

optātō *adv.* according to one's wish

optātum, -ī *n.* wish

optātus, -a, -um *adj.* wished for, desired

opthalmiās, -ae *m.* kind of fish

optigō see **obtegō**

optimās, -ātis *adj.* aristocratic; *m.pl.sbst.* aristocrats (*esp. the Roman senatorial party of the late Republic*)

optimē *superl.adv.* very well, excellently, in the best manner; most agreeably

optimus, -a, -um *superl.adj.* best, very good, excellent; noblest; most agreeable

optiō, -ōnis *f./m.* choice, option; *m.* military assistant, aide

optīvus, -a, -um *adj.* chosen, selected

optō 1. to wish, desire; choose, select

optum- see **optim-**

opulens, -ntis *adj.* rich, wealthy

opulenter *adv.* richly, splendidly

opulentia, -ae *f.* riches, wealth; splendour

opulentitās, -ātis *f.* richness, wealthiness

opulentō 1. to enrich, make wealthier

opulentus, -a, -um *adj.* rich, wealthy; (+*abl./gen.*) well-stocked (with); splendid

opus, operis *n.* work, labour; employment; deed; effort; finished work; building; *pl.* siege-engines; (+*dat./abl.*) **opus est ...** there is (a) need (for)

opusculum, -ī *n.* small work, trifle

ōra, ōrae *f.* border, margin; coast, bank; region; hawser (*of a ship*)

ōrāc(u)lum, -ī *n.* oracle; oracular utterance

ōrārius, -a, -um *adj.* of *or* relating to the coast, coastal

ōrātiō, -ōnis *f.* speaking, speech; language; statement; oration, discourse; oratory

ōrātiuncula, -ae *f.* small speech

ōrātor, -ōris *m.* orator; spokesman, envoy

ōrātōriē *adj.* in the manner of an orator

ōrātōrius, -a, -um *adj.* of *or* relating to oratory; appropriate for an orator

ōrātrix, -īcis *f.* female suppliant

ōrātum, -ī *n.* request, entreaty

ōrātus, -ūs *m.* request, entreaty

orbātiō, -ōnis *f.* deprivation

orbātor, -ōris *m.* one who causes bereavement

orbis, -is *m.* circle, disc, ring; wheel; sphere; region; rotation, orbit; **terrārum orbis** world

orbita, -ae *f.* wheel-rut, furrow; orbit

orbitās, -ātis *f.* loss of a relative, bereavement; childlessness; orphanhood

orbitōsus, -a, -um *adj.* full of ruts, furrowed

orbō 1. (+*abl.*) to deprive (of), bereave (of)

orbus, -a, -um *adj.* (+*abl./gen.*) deprived (of), bereaved (of), bereft (of); childless; *m./f.sbst.* orphan

orca, -ae *f.* large-bellied jar

orchas, -ados *f.* kind of olive

orchestra, -ae *f.* part of Roman theatre where senators sat; the senate

orcīnus, -a, -um *adj.* appointed in the terms of a will

ordinārius, -a, -um *adj.* regular, normal, ordinary

ordinātim *adv.* regularly, in good order

ordinātiō, -ōnis *f.* arrangement, alignment, setting in order; appointment

ordinātor, -ōris *m.* (+*gen.*) institutor (of)

ordinātus, -a, -um *adj.* well-ordered, regular

ordinō 1. to arrange, set in order, organize; draw up; appoint; govern

ordior, orsus 4. *dep.* to begin, embark upon; begin speaking, speak; (+*ab* +*abl.*) begin (from)

ordō, -inis *m.* line, row; arrangement, order; sequence; pattern; procedure; rank; class

orexis, -is *f.* appetite, desire

organicus, -ī *m.* musician

organum, -ī *n.* musical instrument; water-organ

orgia, -ōrum *n.pl.* secret rites, mysteries (*esp. of Bacchus*)

orichalcum, -ī *n.* copper ore, brass; *pl.* pieces of brassware

ōricilla, -ae *f.* little ear

oriens, -ntis *adj.* rising; *m.sg.sbst.* rising sun, dawn; the east

orīgō, -inis *f.* beginning, origination; source; birth; ancestor, founder

orior, ortus 4. *dep.* to rise; (+*ab* +*abl.*) spring (from); begin; arise, occur

oriundus, -a, -um *adj.* (+*abl.*) sprung (from), originating (from)

ornāmentum, -ī *n.* ornament; distinction; *pl.* equipment, trappings

ornātē *adv.* ornately; elaborately

ornātus¹, -a, -um *adj.* well-equipped; ornate; distinguished; (+*abl.*) furnished (with)

ornātus², -ūs *m.* equipment, attire; adornment, embellishment; distinction

ornō 1. to arrange, prepare; equip, attire; adorn, embellish; distinguish; (+*abl.*) honour (with)

ornus, -ī *f.* mountain-ash

ōrō 1. to supplicate, beseech; plead (*in court*)

orsa, -ōrum *n.pl.* undertakings; utterances

orsus, -ūs *m.* beginning, undertaking

orthographia, -ae *f.* orthography

orthopȳgium, -īī *n.* rump of a bird

ortus, -ūs *m.* rising, sunrise; the east; beginning; birth, origin

oryx, orygis *m.* kind of gazelle

oryza, -ae *f.* rice

ōs¹, ōris *n.* mouth; speech; face; expression; opening

os², ossis *n.* bone; *pl.* very soul

oscen, oscinis *m.* songbird whose cries were taken as omens

oscillum, -ī *n.* small face, mask

oscitanter *adv.* whilst yawning, in a listless fashion

oscitātiō, -ōnis *f.* yawning, yawn

oscitō 1. or **oscitor** 1. *dep.* to gape; yawn

osculābundus, -a, -um *adj.* kissing

osculātiō, -ōnis *f.* kissing

osculor 1. *dep.* to kiss

osculum, -ī *n.* kiss; mouth, lips

ōsor, ōsōris *m.* hater

osseus, -a, -um *adj.* made of bone, bony

ossifraga, -ae *f.* bird of prey

ostendō, -dī, -sum (-tum) 3. to hold out, display, show; reveal; demonstrate

ostentātiō, -ōnis *f.* exhibition, display; showing off, boast; manifestation

ostentātor, -ōris *m.* exhibitionist, show off; (+*gen.*) one who holds out prospects (of)

ostentō 1. to exhibit, display; reveal; demonstrate; show off; hold out (*as a prospect*)

ostentum, -ī *n.* portent, prodigy; *pl.* wonders

ostentus, -ūs *m.* display, mere show; demonstration

ostiārium, -(i)ī *n.* tax upon doors

ostiātim *adv.* from door to door

ostium, -(i)ī *n.* door; entrance, opening; mouth (of a river)

ostreātus, -a, -um *adj.* with stripes like an oyster

ostreōsus, -a, -um *adj.* full of oysters

ostreum, -ī *n.* oyster

ostrifer, -era, -erum *adj.* oyster-bearing

ostrīnus, -a, -um *adj.* purple

ostrum, -ī *n.* purple dye; material dyed purple

ōtior 1. *dep.* to be at leisure, holiday

ōtiōsē *adv.* leisurely, at ease

ōtiōsus, -a, -um *adj.* at leisure, unbusied; undisturbed, peaceful; idle, useless

ōtium, ōt(i)ī *n.* leisure, ease; rest; peace; idleness

ovātus, -a, -um *adj.* triumphal

ovīle, -is *n.* sheepfold, pen; enclosed area on the Campus Martius used for voting

ovīlis, -is, -e *adj.* of *or* relating to sheep

ovillus, -a, -um *adj.* of *or* relating to sheep

ovis, ovis *f.* sheep; wool; simpleton

ovō 1. to celebrate, exult

ōvum, ōvī *n.* egg

oxygarum, -ī *n.* vinegared fish-sauce

oxyporum, -ī *n.* medicine to aid digestion

P

pābulātiō, -ōnis *f.* foraging
pābulātor, -ōris *m.* forager
pābulor 1. *dep.* to forage
pābulum, -ī *n.* fodder, food, nourishment
pācālis, -is, -e *adj.* of peace, peaceful
pācātor, -ōris *m.* peacemaker, pacifier, subduer
pācātus, -a, -um *adj.* peaceful, quiet; *n. sbst.* friendly country, country at peace (*with Rome*)
pācifer, -era, -erum *adj.* peace-bringing
pācificātiō, -ōnis *f.* peacemaking, pacification
pācificātor, -ōris *m.* peacemaker, pacifier
pācificātōrius, -a, -um *adj.* peacemaking
pācificō 1. or **pācificor** 1. *dep.* to make peace; appease
pācificus, -a, -um *adj.* peace-making
paciscō, pactum 3. to secure by negotiation; (+*dat.*) betroth (to)
paciscor, pactus 3. *dep.* to make an agreement, conclude a contract; stipulate for, bargain for; barter, exchange
pactiō, -ōnis *f.* agreement, bargain, contract, treaty; duplicitous agreement; form of words
pactor, -ōris *m.* negotiator
pactus, -a, -um *adj.* agreed, stipulated, settled; betrothed; *f.sbst.* betrothed; *n.sbst.* agreement, bargain, contract, treaty; **nullō pactō** in no way
paeān, -ānis *m.* paean, hymn
paedagōgium, -iī *n.* training school for *paedogogi*
paedagōgus, -ī *m.* slave responsible for children; guide
paedicō[1] 1. to have anal sex with, commit pederasty with
paedīcō[2], **-ōnis** *m.* one who has anal sex, pederast

paedor, -ōris *m.* dirt, filth
paegniārius, -a, -um *adj.* at play
paelex, -icis *f.* mistress, concubine
paelicātus, -ūs *m.* state of being a mistress, concubinage
paene *adv.* almost, nearly
paeninsula, -ae *f.* peninsula
paenitendus, -a, -um *adj.* to be regretted, unsatisfactory
paenitentia, -ae *f.* regret, repentance
paeniteō 2. (*usu. impers.*) (+*acc. of person* +*gen. of cause of regret*) to regret, repent; displease
paenula, -ae *f.* heavy cloak
paenulātus, -a, -um *adj.* cloaked, wearing a *paenula*
paetulus, -a, -um *adj.* with a slight squint
paetus, -a, -um *adj.* with a squint
pāgānicus, -a, -um *adj.* rural; **pila pāgānica** ball filled with feathers
pāgānus, -a, -um *adj.* rural; *m.sbst.* peasant, villager; civilian
pāgātim *adv.* by villages
pāgella, -ae *f.* small page
pāgina, -ae *f.* page
pāginula, -ae *f.* small page
pāgus, -ī *m.* village, district
pāla, -ae *f.* shovel, spade; bezel
palaestra, -ae *f.* wrestling school, gymnasium; wrestling; rhetorical exercise *or* training
palaestricus, -a, -um *adj.* of the *palaestra*
palaestrīta, -ae *m.* manager of a *palaestra*
palam *adv.* openly, publicly; *prep.* (+*abl.*) in the presence of
pālāris, -is, -e *adj.* of wooden stakes
palātum, -ī *n.* or **-us, -ī** *m.* palate; taste; judgement; dome
palē, -ēs *f.* wrestling
palea, -ae *f.* chaff; husk

palear, -āris *n.* dewlap; hanging skin

palimpsestum, -ī *n.* palimpsest

paliūrus, -ī *m.* paliurus, Christ's thorn

palla, -ae *f.* robe, mantle, outer garment; curtain

pallaca, -ae *f.* concubine

pallens, -ntis *adj.* pale, pallid; causing paleness

palleō 2. to be pale; grow pale; be anxious *or* fearful

pallescō, palluī 3. to grow pale, turn pale

palliātus, -a, -um *adj.* wearing a *pallium*

pallidulus, -a, -um *adj.* rather pale, pallid

pallidus, -a, -um *adj.* pale, pallid

palliolātim *adv.* in a *pallium*

palliolātus, -a, -um *adj.* wearing a *pallium*

palliolum, -ī *n.* small *pallium*

pallium, -(i)ī *n.* outer garment, Greek cloak; throw, bed-cover

pallor, -ōris *m.* paleness, pallor; dimness

pallula, -ae *f.* small *palla*

palma, -ae *f.* palm, hand; oar blade; palm tree; fruit of date-palm, date; palm broom; palm branch; victory, honour, prize, reward

palmāris, -is, -e *adj.* deserving of the prize, excellent

palmārium, -(i)ī *n.* that which deserves the prize, masterpiece

palmātus, -a, -um *adj.* with palm-leaf motif

palmes, -itis *m.* vine shoot; vine; branch

palmētum, -ī *n.* palm grove

palmifer, -era, -erum *adj.* palm-bearing

palmōsus, -a, -um *adj.* abounding in palms

palmula, -ae *f.* oar blade; date

pālor 1. *dep.* to wander about, be dispersed, stray, scatter

palpātiō, -ōnis *f.* stroking, caress

palpātor, -ōris *m.* coaxer

palpebra, -ae *f.* eyelid

palpitātiō, -ōnis *f.* throbbing, quivering, trembling

palpitō 1. to throb, quiver, pulsate, tremble

palpō 1. *or* **palpor** 1. *dep.* to stroke, caress, coax

palpus, -ī *m.* coaxing

palūdāmentum, -ī *n.* palm of hand

palūdātus, -a, -um *adj.* wearing a military cloak

palūdōsus, -a, -um *adj.* marshy, swampy, boggy

palumbēs, -is or **-us, -ī** *m./f.* wood pigeon

pālus¹, -ī *m.* stake, post, peg

palūs², -ūdis *f.* marsh, swamp, bog

paluster, -tris, -tre *adj.* marshy, boggy

pampineus, -a, -um *adj.* consisting of vine tendrils *or* leaves

pampinus, -ī *m.* vine tendril *or* leaf

panaca, -ae *f.* drinking vessel

panacēa, -ae *f.* or **panacēs, -is** *m.* plant with healing qualities

pānāriolum, -ī *n.* small bread-basket

pānārium, -iī *n.* bread-basket

panchrestos, -os, -on *adj.* good for everything

pancraticē *adv.* like a competitor in *pancratium*

pancratium, -iī *n.* combination of boxing and wrestling

pandiculor 1. *dep.* to gape, yawn

pandō¹ 1. to bend, curve, bow

pandō², pandī, passum or **pansum** 3. to spread out, stretch out, extend; open, uncover, reveal

pandus, -a, -um *adj.* curved, bent, bowed

panēgyricus, -ī *m.* eulogy on Athens, composed by Isocrates

pangō, pepigī or **pēgī, pactum** 3. to fix, plant, drive in; settle, arrange, agree upon; compose, write

pānicum, -ī *n.* panic-grass, Italian millet

pānificium, -(i)ī *n.* (*pl.*) loaves, cakes

pānis, -is *m.* or **-e, -is** *n.* bread, loaf, food

panniculus, -ī *m.* small piece of cloth, rag

pannōsus, -a, -um *adj.* ragged, tattered

pannūceus (-ius), -a, -um *adj.* wrinkled, shrivelled

pannus, -ī *m.* piece of cloth; 'racing silk'; *pl.* rags

pansa, -ae *m.adj.* with broad, flat feet, splay-footed

pantex, -icis *m.* (*usu. pl.*) guts, bowels

panthēra, -ae *f.* leopard, spotted wild-cat

panthērīnus, -a, -um *adj.* of a leopard

pantomīmicus, -a, -um *adj.* pantomimic, relating to the pantomime

pantomīmus, -ī *m.* pantomimic

pantopōlium, -(i)ī *n.* market

papae *interj.* exclamation of amazement, joy *or* alarm

pāpās *m. paedagogus* (*child's speak*)

papāver, -ris *n./m.* poppy; poppy-seed
papāvereus, -a, -um *adj.* of poppies
pāpiliō, -ōnis *m.* butterfly, moth
papilla, -ae *f.* nipple, teat; breast
pappō 1. to eat
pappus, -ī *m.* woolly *or* hairy seed
papula, -ae *f.* pimple, pustule, boil
papȳrifer, -era, -erum *adj.* papyrus-bearing
papȳrus, -ī *m.* papyrus
pār¹, paris *adj.* equal, matching, comparable
pār², paris *m./f.* equal, partner, opponent
pār³, paris *n.* pair
parābilis, -is, -e *adj.* easy to procure *or* obtain
parabola, -ae *f.* comparison
paradoxa, -ōrum *n.pl.* paradoxes
paraeneticē, -ēs *f.* moral, educative philosophy
paralysis, -is *f.* paralysis, apoplexy
parasīta, -ae *f.* female parasite
parasītaster, -trī *m.* despicable parasite
parasītātiō, -ōnis *f.* action of a parasite, parasitism
parasīticus, -a, -um *adj.* of a parasite
parasītor 1. *dep.* to play the parasite, sponge
parasītus, -ī *m.* guest, parasite, sponger
parātē *adv.* readily, promptly
parātiō, -ōnis *f.* getting, procuring
paratragoedō 1. to exclaim tragically, rant
parātus¹, -a, -um *adj.* prepared, ready, equipped
parātus², -ūs *m.* preparation, provision; apparatus, equipment; garb, attire
parazōnium, -iī *n.* belt with a sword
parcē *adv.* sparingly, frugally, thriftily
parcēprōmus, -ī *m.* parsimonious person, curmudgeon
parcitās, -ātis *f.* sparingness, parsimony
parcō, pepercī or **parsī** 3. (+*dat.*) to spare, be sparing, refrain from, leave off; (+*inf.*) forbear (to)
parcus, -a, -um *adj.* sparing, frugal, economical, stingy, parsimonious
pardus, -ī *m.* panther
pārens¹, -ntis *adj.* obedient, subservient
parens², -ntis *m./f.* parent, mother *or* father; *pl.* ancestors, relations; progenitor, founder, origin, author

parentālia, -ium *n.pl.* festival in honour of deceased family members (February 13–21)
parentālis, -is, -e *adj.* parental
parenticīda, -ae *m.* parent killer
parentō 1. to perform family funeral rites; appease, satisfy, revenge
pāreō 2. to appear, be seen; be manifest, be clear; (+*dat.*) obey, be subject to, be ruled by, give way, yield to
pariās, -ae *m.* snake
pariēs, -etis *m.* wall (of house *or* other building)
parietinae, -ārum *f.pl.* ruined walls
parīlia, -ium *n.pl.* festival of Pales (April 21)
parilis, -is, -e *adj.* equal, like
pariō, peperī, partum 3. to bear (*offspring*), produce, bring forth, create
pariter *adv.* equally, in like manner; together, at the same time
paritō 1. to prepare, get ready
parma, -ae *f.* small round shield
parmātus, -a, -um *adj.* armed with a *parma*
parmula, -ae *f.* small *parma*
parmulārius, -iī *m.* supporter of those armed with *parmae*
parō 1. to prepare, make ready, provide; procure, acquire, obtain, buy; intend, plan
parochus, -ī *m.* one responsible for provision of supplies to travelling officials
parōn, -ōnis *m.* kind of boat
paropsis, -idis *f.* dish, plate
parra, -ae *f.* kind of inauspicious bird
parricīda, -ae *m.* parricide, murderer (of close family members), assassin; traitor
parricīdium, -(i)ī *n.* parricide, murder, assassination; treachery, treason
pars, -tis *f.* part, portion, piece, share
parsimōnia, -ae *f.* frugality, thrift, parsimony
parthenicē, -ēs *f.* kind of camomile
particeps, -ipis *adj.* (+*gen.*) partaking (of), having a share (in); *m./f.sbst.* partner, companion, associate
participō 1. to participate in, share; (+*gen.*) give a share (of), acquaint (with)
particula, -ae *f.* small part, particle
particulātim *adv.* bit by bit, part after part, piecemeal

partim *adv.* partly, in part; some, some part

partiō[1] 4. to divide, share, distribute

partiō[2], **-ōnis** *f.* bringing forth young, giving birth

partītē *adv.* methodically, with division into proper parts

partītiō, -ōnis *f.* dividing, distributing, sharing; division of speech into sections

partitūdō, -inis *f.* bringing forth young, giving birth

parturiō 4. to be in labour, bring forth; be about to give birth; be pregnant with, full of

partus, -ūs *m.* birth, bringing forth; young, offspring

parum *indecl.n.* and *adv.* too little, not enough

parumloquium, -(i)ī *n.* talking too little

parumper *adv.* for a short time, a while

parvitās, -ātis *f.* smallness, littleness

parvulus (-volus), -a, -um *adj.* very small, very little, very young, tiny; *n.sg. as adv.* very little, puny, insignificant

parvus, -a, -um *adj.* little, small, slight, insignificant

pasceolus, -ī *m.* leather purse *or* bag

pascō, pāvī, pastum 3. to feed, graze, pasture, drive to pasture; nurture, nourish, maintain; feast, entertain

pascuum, -ī *n.* pasture, grazing

pascuus, -a, -um *adj.* fit for pasture *or* grazing

passer, -eris *m.* sparrow

passerculus, -ī *m.* small sparrow

passim *adv.* here and there; everywhere, in every direction; at random, without order

passum, -ī *n.* raisin wine, sweet wine

passus[1], **-a, -um** *adj.* spread out, stretched out, extended, unfolded

passus[2], **-a, -um** *adj.* suffering, having suffered, endured *or* sustained

passus[3], **-ūs** *m.* pace, step, footstep; **mille passūs** mile, **mīlia passuum** miles

pastillus, -ī *m.* pastille

pastiō, -ōnis *f.* feeding, pasturing, grazing; pasture

pastor, -ōris *m.* shepherd, herdsman

pastōrālis, -is, -e *adj.* of a shepherd, rustic, pastoral

pastōr(ic)ius, -a, -um *adj.* of a shepherd, rustic, pastoral

pastus, -ūs *m.* feeding, pasturing, grazing; pasture, food

patagiārius, -(i)ī *m.* manufacturer of decorative fringes for women's tunics

patagiātus, -a, -um *adj.* decorated with a fringe

patefaciō, -fēcī, -factum 3. to open, throw open; disclose, discover, reveal

patefactiō, -ōnis *f.* laying open, disclosing

patella, -ae *f.* dish, plate, pot, pan

patellārius, -a, -um *adj.* of *or* belonging to a *patella*

patens, -ntis *adj.* open, lying open, accessible; evident

patentius *compar.adv.* more openly

pateō 2. to be open, lie open, be accessible; extend, stretch; be subject to; be clear, plain, evident

pater, patris *m.* father, sire; *pl.* parents, forefathers, senators

patera, -ae *f.* dish *or* saucer used for making libations

paternus, -a, -um *adj.* of *or* belonging to a father; fatherly, paternal; relating to one's country, native

patescō, patuī 3. to be open, spread, extend; be revealed, become clear

pathicus, -a, -um *adj.* passive sexually

patibilis, -is, -e *adj.* tolerable, sufferable; sensitive

patibulātus, -a, -um *adj.* bearing a cross, yoke *or* gibbet

patibulum, -ī *n.* kind of cross *or* gibbet

patiens, -ntis *adj.* (+*gen.*) enduring, suffering, able to bear, capable of enduring, patient

patienter *adv.* patiently, calmly, contentedly

patientia, -ae *f.* patience, endurance, forbearance; submissiveness, subjection

patina, -ae *f.* dish, plate, pot, pan

patinārius, -a, -um *adj.* of *or* relating to a *patina*; *m.sbst.* glutton, bellygod

patior, passus 3. *dep.* to bear, suffer, endure, tolerate; support; permit, allow, let

patrātor, -ōris *m.* accomplisher, causer

patrātus, -ī *m.* **pater patrātus** chief diplomat

patria, -ae *f.* native land, fatherland

patricē *adv.* like a patrician

patriciātus, -ūs *m.* patrician rank *or* status

patricīda, -ae *m.* murderer of father

patricius, -a, -um *adj.* of patrician rank, patrician, noble; *m./f.sbst.* patrician

patrimōnium, -(i)ī *n.* inheritance, personal property, estate

patrimus, -a, -um *adj.* with a father still living

patrissō 1. to resemble *or* take after one's father

patrītus, -a, -um *adj.* of one's father

patrius, -a, -um *adj.* of *or* belonging to a father; fatherly, like a father, paternal

patrō 1. to accomplish, achieve, perform, bring to completion, finish

patrōcinium, -(i)ī *n.* protection, patronage, support

patrōcinor 1. *dep.* to protect, defend, support, patronize

patrōna, -ae *f.* protectress, patroness

patrōnus, -ī *m.* protector, defender, patron, advocate

patruēlis, -is, -e *adj.* of *or* descended from a father's brother; *m.sbst.* cousin

patruus¹, -ī *m.* father's brother, paternal uncle

patruus², -a, -um *adj.* of *or* belonging to a father's brother *or* uncle

patulus, -a, -um *adj.* open, large, wide, ample, spacious, spreading

pauciloquium, -(i)ī *n.* speaking very little

paucitās, -ātis *f.* fewness, scarcity, paucity

pauculī, -ae, -a *pl.adj.* very few

paucus, -a, -um *adj.* few, little

paul(l)ātim *adv.* little by little, gradually, by degrees

paul(l)isper *adv.* for a little while

paul(l)ō *adv.* by a little, somewhat

paul(l)ulō *adv.* a little, a very little

paul(l)ulum, -ī *n.* a little, very little, somewhat; *adv.* to a small extent, somewhat

paul(l)ulus, -a, -um *adj.* little, very little

paul(l)um, -ī *n.* a little, somewhat; *adv.* to a small extent, a little

paul(l)us, -a, -um *adj.* small, little, trifling

pauper, -eris *adj.* poor, needy; *m.sbst.* poor man, beggar, pauper

pauperculus, -a, -um *adj.* poor

pauperiēs, -ēī *f.* poverty

pauperō 1. to make poor, impoverish; (+*abl.*) deprive (of)

paupertās, -ātis *f.* poverty, need

pausārius, -(i)ī *m.* ship's officer in command of rowers

paus(s)a, -ae *f.* pause, stop, intermission

pauxillātim *adv.* little by little

pauxillisper *adv.* little by little

pauxill(ul)us, -a, -um *adj.* very little, very small; *n.sbst.* a very little

pavefactus, -a, -um *adj.* frightened, alarmed

paveō 2. to be afraid, fear, dread

pavescō 3. to begin to be afraid, fear, dread

pavidē *adv.* fearfully, in a panic

pavidus, -a, -um *adj.* afraid, fearful

pavīmentātus, -a, -um *adj.* paved

pavīmentum, -ī *n.* pavement

paviō 4. to beat, strike

pavitō 1. to fear greatly, be very afraid, dread

pāvō, -ōnis *m.* peacock

pāvōnīnus, -a, -um *adj.* of a peacock

pavor, -ōris *m.* fear, dread, alarm, panic, consternation

pax¹, pācis *f.* peace, quiet, concord; tranquillity, serenity; blessing

pax² *interj.* silence!, hush!

peccātum, -ī *n.* fault, error, mistake, offence, sin

peccō 1. to do wrong, make a mistake, transgress, offend, sin

pecorōsus, -a, -um *adj.* abounding in cattle

pecten, -inis *m.* comb, rake; plectrum; shellfish, scallop

pectō, pex(u)ī, pexum 3. to comb, dress (*the hair*); thrash

pectorālis, -is, -e *adj.* of the breast, pectoral

pectus, -oris *n.* breast, chest; heart, soul, mind

pecū *n.* flock, herd, cattle

pecuāria, -ae *f.* cattle-rearing

pecuārius, -a, -um *adj.* of *or* belonging to cattle *or* flocks; *m.sbst.* cattle breeder; *n.pl. sbst.* herds of cattle *or* flocks of sheep

pecūlātor, -ōris *m.* embezzler of public funds

pecūlātus, -ūs *m.* embezzlement of public funds, theft of public property

pecūliāris, -is, -e *adj.* of *or* belonging to one's private property, one's own; particular, specific

pecūliāriter *adv.* particularly, specifically

pecūliō 1. to give a *peculium*

pecūliōsus, -a, -um *adj.* having considerable private property

pecūlium, -(i)ī *n.* private property, small savings

pecūnia, -ae *f.* money, sum of money, property, wealth, riches

pecūniārius, -a, -um *adj.* of *or* belonging to money, pecuniary

pecus¹, -oris *n.* cattle, herd, flock

pecus², -udis *f.* head of cattle, beast, animal

pedālis, -is, -e *adj.* of a foot, a foot long *or* broad

pedārius, -a, -um *adj.* (*of senators*) of inferior rank

pedātus¹, -a, -um *adj.* having feet

pedātus², -ūs *m.* attack, charge

pedes, -itis *m.* on foot; foot-soldier, infantry

pedester (-tris), -tris, -tre *adj.* on foot, going on foot, pedestrian; on land; of the infantry; prosaic

pedetem(p)tim *adv.* little by little, step by step, gradually

pedica, -ae *f.* chain, shackle, fetter, snare

pediculus, -ī *m.* little foot

pēdis, -is *m.* louse

pedisequa, -ae *f.* female attendant, handmaid

pedisequus (-cus), -ī *m.* attendant, footman, lackey

peditastellus, -ī *m.* mere foot-soldier

peditātus, -ūs *m.* infantry

pēditum, -ī *n.* fart

pēdō, pepēdī, pēditum 3. to fart

pedum, -ī *n.* shepherd's crook *or* staff

pēgma, -atis *n.* wooden frame, book-case; scaffold, platform

pēierātiuncula, -ae *f.* little perjury

pei(i)erō (peri-) 1. to violate an oath, be guilty of perjury; (+*acc.*) swear falsely (to)

pēior, -or, -us *compar.adj.* worse, inferior

pēi(i)ūriōsus (peri-), -a, -um *adj.* full of perjury, perjured

pēi(i)ūrium (peri-), -(i)ī *n.* perjury, false oath

pēi(i)ūrus (peri-), -a, -um *adj.* perjured, false, lying

pēius *compar.adv.* worse

pelagus, -ī *n.* sea, open sea

pellācia, -ae *f.* enticing look; deceit, cunning

pellax, -ācis *adj.* enticing, seductive, cunning

pellecebra, -ae *f.* enticement, allurement; (+*gen.*) enticement (to)

pelliciō, -lexī, -lectum 3. to entice, deceive by flattery, allure, seduce

pellicula, -ae *f.* little skin *or* hide

pelliō, -ōnis *m.* tanner, furrier

pellis, -is *f.* skin, hide, pelt

pellītus, -a, -um *adj.* covered with skins

pellō, pepulī, pulsum 3. to beat, strike, knock; move, impel, stimulate, touch; drive *or* chase away, banish

pelta, -ae *f.* light shield, half-moon shield

peltasta, -ae *m.* soldier armed with a *pelta*

peltātus, -a, -um *adj.* armed with a *pelta*

peltifer, -era, -erum *adj.* armed with a *pelta*

pelvis, -is *f.* basin, foot-bath

penārius, -a, -um *adj.* of *or* relating to the provision of food

penātiger, -era, -erum *adj.* carrying the household gods

pendeō, pependī 2. to hang, be suspended; be supported

pendō, pependī, pensum 3. to weigh; pay, render; ponder, deliberate, consider; esteem, value, regard

pendulus, -a, -um *adj.* hanging, pendulous; in suspense, anxious, uncertain

penes *prep.* (+*acc*). in the power of, in one's hands *or* possession, at one's disposal

penetrābilis, -is, -e *adj.* that may be penetrated *or* pierced, penetrable

penetrālis, -is, -e *adj.* interior, internal, innermost; piercing, penetrative; *n.sbst.* recess, innermost part (*of temple, palace etc.*)

penetrō 1. to penetrate, pierce, pass into *or* through

pēnicillus, -ī *m.* painter's brush; sponge

pēniculus, -ī *m.* painter's brush; sponge

pēnis, -is *m.* tail; penis

penitē *adv.* inwardly, deep inside

penitus¹, -a, -um *adj.* interior, innermost

penitus² *adv.* inwardly, within, deeply; thoroughly, utterly

penna, -ae *f.* feather, wing; flight; arrow

pennātus, -a, -um *adj.* having wings, winged

pennipotentēs, -um *m./f.pl.* those with power over their wings, birds

pensilis, -is, -e *adj.* hanging, suspended, pendent, pendulous

pensiō, -ōnis *f.* weighing, weight; payment, instalment, pension, rent

pensitō 1. to weigh; examine, consider; pay

pensō 1. to weigh; ponder, examine, consider; (+*abl.*) compensate, make amends (for)

pensum, -ī *n.* portion of wool assigned to slaves for spinning; task, piece of work

pensus, -a, -um *adj.* weighed; esteemed, prized, valued

penuārius, -a, -um *adj.* of *or* relating to the provision of food

pēnūria, -ae *f.* want, need, scarcity

penus, -ūs *f./m.* or **penum, -ī** *n.* provision of food, sustenance, stores, provisions

peplus, -ī *m.* or **-um, -ī** *n.* woollen robe of Athena (*placed on her statue during the Panatheneia*)

per *prep.* (+*acc.*) through; through the midst of; across, along, all over; throughout, in the course of, during; by means of, by way of; on account of, for the sake of

pēra, -ae *f.* bag, pouch, satchel

perabsurdus, -a, -um *adj.* very absurd, contrary to reason

peraccommodātus, -a, -um *adj.* very convenient

perācer, -cris, -cre *adj.* very sharp, acute, piercing

peracerbus, -a, -um *adj.* very sour, very harsh *or* grievous

peracescō 3. to become very sour

peractiō, -ōnis *f.* completion, finishing, end

peracuō, -uī, -ūtum 3. to make very sharp

peracūtē *adv.* very sharply *or* acutely

peracūtus, -a, -um *adj.* very sharp, keen; acute, shrewd

peradulescens, -ntis *adj.* very young

peraduluscentulus, -ī *m.* very young man

peraequē *adv.* alike, equally

peragitō 1. to stir up repeatedly, agitate

peragō, -ēgī, -actum 3. to drive, agitate, harass; go through, go over, recount; pass through, traverse; run through, pierce, kill; perform, carry out; perfect, finish,

complete, accomplish; cultivate, till; follow through to a conviction, prosecute to the end

peragrātiō, -ōnis *f.* travelling up and down

peragrō 1. to travel through, wander over, traverse, survey

peramans, -ntis *adj.* very fond

peramanter *adv.* very lovingly, very affectionately

perambulō 1. to walk through, travel through *or* over, traverse

peramīcē *adv.* in a very friendly manner, very willingly

peramō 1. to love very much

peramoenus, -a, -um *adj.* very pleasant

peramplus, -a, -um *adj.* very large

perangustē *adv.* very narrowly

perangustus, -a, -um *adj.* very narrow

perantīquus, -a, -um *adj.* very ancient

perappositus, -a, -um *adj.* very suitable *or* apposite

perarduus, -a, -um *adj.* very hard *or* difficult

perargūtus, -a, -um *adj.* very shrill; very sharp *or* witty

perarō 1. to plough, furrow; write

perattentē *adv.* very attentively

perattentus, -a, -um *adj.* very attentive

pērātus, -a, -um *adj.* carrying a *pera*

peraudiō 4. to hear distinctly *or* in full

perbacchor 1. *dep.* to carouse, revel; rage throughout

perbeātus, -a, -um *adj.* very happy *or* fortunate

perbellē *adv.* very well *or* agreeably

perbene *adv.* very well

perbenevolus, -a, -um *adj.* very friendly *or* kind

perbenignē *adv.* very kindly

perbibō, -ī 3. to drink up, imbibe; absorb

perbītō 3. to perish, be ruined

perblandus, -a, -um *adj.* very courteous *or* charming

perbonus, -a, -um *adj.* very good

perbrevī *adv.* very shortly

perbrevis, -is, -e *adj.* very short

perbreviter *adv.* very shortly

perca, -ae *f.* perch

percalefactus, -a, -um *adj.* thoroughly heated

percalescō, -luī 3. to be very warm *or* hot

percallescō, -lluī 3. to become hardened, callous; know well, understand thoroughly

percārus, -a, -um *adj.* very dear

percautus, -a, -um *adj.* very cautious *or* wary

percelebrō 1. to divulge, make public everywhere

perceler, -eris, -ere *adj.* very quick *or* swift

perceleriter *adv.* very quickly *or* swiftly

percellō, -culī, -culsum 3. to strike, hit; strike down, thrust aside, overthrow, overturn; strike with fear, stun, daunt

percenseō, -uī 2. to count, reckon up, survey, examine; travel through

perceptiō, -ōnis *f.* reaping, gathering; understanding, perception

perceptum, -ī *n.* principle, rule

percīdō, -dī, -sum 3. to hit, strike, beat; bugger

percieō, -iī, -itum 2. or **perciō** 3. to set in motion, stir up, move greatly, excite

percipiō, -cēpī, -ceptum 3. to seize, possess, invade, occupy; take, get, obtain, enjoy; perceive, feel; learn, comprehend, understand

percitus, -a, -um *adj.* moved violently, stirred greatly

percīvīlis, -is, -e *adj.* very polite

percognoscō, -nōvī, -nitum 3. to get to know thoroughly

percōlō[1] 1. to filter, strain thoroughly

percōlō[2], **-coluī, -cultum** 3. to respect, honour; adorn, beautify

percōmis, -is, -e *adj.* very kind, affable, courteous

percommodē *adv.* very conveniently, very suitably

percommodus, -a, -um *adj.* very convenient, very suitable

percontātiō, -ōnis *f.* inquiry, interrogation, questioning

percontātor, -ōris *m.* interrogator, inquisitive person

percontor 1. *dep.* to ask, inquire, question, interrogate, demand, examine

percontumax, -ācis *adj.* very stubborn, very obstinate

percōpiōsus, -a, -um *adj.* very copious

percoquō, -xī, -ctum 3. to cook thoroughly, bake, roast, heat; ripen

percrēb(r)escō, -(b)ruī 3. to become known *or* common, be talked of publicly

percrepō 1. to resound, ring

percruciō 1. to torment *or* vex greatly

percupidus, -a, -um *adj.* (+*gen.*) very fond (of)

percupiō 3. to desire greatly

percūriōsus, -a, -um *adj.* very inquisitive, very careful

percūrō 3. to cure thoroughly

percurrō, -(cu)currī, -cursum 3. to run quickly; run through, pass through; run over, pass over

percursātiō, -ōnis *f.* passing through, traversing

percursiō, -ōnis *f.* running through *or* over

percursō 1. to ramble up and down, rove

percussiō, -ōnis *f.* striking, beating, knocking; metrical beat, rhythm

percussor, -ōris *m.* striker, murderer, assassin

percussus, -ūs *m.* striking, beating, knocking

percutiō, -ssī, -ssum 3. to strike, beat, knock, hit, smite, pierce; kill, execute; stamp, coin; deceive; make an impression on

perdecōrus, -a, -um *adj.* very becoming

perdēlīrus, -a, -um *adj.* very silly *or* foolish

perdepsō, -suī, -stum 3. to give a good kneading to

perdifficilis, -is, -e *adj.* very hard *or* difficult

perdifficiliter *adv.* with great difficulty

perdignus, -a, -um *adj.* very worthy

perdīligens, -ntis *adj.* very diligent, very careful

perdīligenter *adv.* very diligently, very carefully

perdiscō, -didicī 3. to learn thoroughly

perdisertē *adv.* very eloquently

perditē *adv.* wickedly, basely; violently, to desperation

perditor, -ōris *m.* destroyer, ruiner

perditus[1], **-a, -um** *adj.* lost, ruined, spoiled, irreparable; profligate, dissolute, desperate

perditus[2], **-ūs** *m.* ruin

perdiū *adv.* for a very long time

perdiuturnus, -a, -um *adj.* lasting a very long time

perdīves, -itis *adj.* very rich

perdix, -īcis *m.* partridge
perdō, -idī, -itum 3. to destroy, ruin; squander, waste, throw away, lose; corrupt, spoil; kill
perdoceō, -uī, -tum 2. to teach thoroughly
perdoctē *adv.* very learnedly
perdoleō 2. to be greatly grieved
perdomō, -uī, -itum 1. to tame, subdue, break, conquer wholly
perdormiscō 3. to sleep right through
perdūcō, -duxī, -ductum 3. to lead, conduct, convey, bring, take; lengthen, extend, prolong; bring round, persuade, induce; coat, anoint, daub
perductō 1. to lead along, guide
perductor, -ōris *m.* guide, leader; pimp, pander, procurer
perdūdum *adv.* long since, a long time ago
perduelliō, -ōnis *f.* treason
perduellis, -is *m.* enemy
perdulcis, -is, -e *adj.* very sweet
perdūrō 1. to last, continue, hold out, endure
peredō, -esse, -ēdī, -ēsum *v.irreg.* to eat up, consume, eat through
peregrē (-ī) *adv.* abroad, away from home; from abroad
peregrīnābundus, -a, -um *adj.* travelling abroad
peregrīnātiō, -ōnis *f.* foreign travel; living abroad
peregrīnātor, -ōris *m.* traveller
peregrīnitās, -ātis *f.* foreign habits *or* manners; state *or* condition of a foreigner
peregrīnor 1. *dep.* to travel abroad; live in foreign countries, be a foreigner
peregrīnus, -a, -um *adj.* foreign, from foreign parts; strange, alien, exotic; inexperienced, ignorant; *m./f.sbst.* stranger, foreigner
perēlegans, -ntis *adj.* very elegant *or* neat
perēleganter *adv.* with great elegance, very elegantly
perēloquens, -ntis *adj.* very eloquent
peremnia, -ium *n.pl.* auspices taken on crossing rivers
peremō see **perimō**
peremptor, -ōris *m.* destroyer, slayer, killer
perendiē *adv.* on the day after tomorrow
perendinus, -a, -um *adj.* after tomorrow

perennis, -is, -e *adj.* lasting throughout the year, continual, perpetual, perennial; durable, never failing
perenniservus, -ī *m.* perpetual slave
perennitās, -ātis *f.* perpetuity, duration
perennō 1. to last, endure, continue
pereō, -īre, -īī (-īvī), -itum 4. to perish, be lost, be ruined, be destroyed, die; vanish, disappear
perequitō 1. to ride through, ride all over
pererrō 1. to wander over, travel over, traverse, explore, examine
perērudītus, -a, -um *adj.* very learned
perexcelsus, -a, -um *adj.* very high
perexiguē *adv.* very meanly
perexiguus, -a, -um *adj.* very small, very little
perexpedītus, -a, -um *adj.* very easy *or* obvious
perfabricō 1. to cheat thoroughly, take in completely
perfacētē *adv.* very wittily
perfacētus, -a, -um *adj.* very witty
perfacile *adv.* very easily; very willingly
perfacilis, -is, -e *adj.* very easy
perfamiliāris, -is, -e *adj.* very familiar, very intimate; *m.sbst.* intimate friend
perfectē *adv.* completely, perfectly, entirely, exactly
perfectiō, -ōnis *f.* making, completing, finishing, perfecting; perfection, completeness, completion
perfector, -ōris *m.* finisher, accomplisher, perfector
perfectus, -a, -um *adj.* finished, completed, perfected, complete
perferō, -ferre, -tulī, -lātum *v.irreg.* to bring *or* carry through; convey, announce; bear, support, put up with, endure; bring to an end, complete, accomplish; carry out, manage
perficiō, -fēcī, -fectum 3. to finish, complete, accomplish, perform; work up, perfect; bring about, cause
perficus, -a, -um *adj.* perfecting
perfidēlis, -is, -e *adj.* very faithful, very trustworthy
perfidia, -ae *f.* treachery, falsehood, perfidy
perfidiōsē *adv.* treacherously, perfidiously
perfidiōsus, -a, -um *adj.* faithless, treacherous

perfidus, -a, -um *adj.* faithless, unfaithful, false, treacherous

perfīgō, -fixī, -fixum 3. to pierce, stab

perflābilis, -is, -e *adj.* that can be blown through

perflāgitiōsus, -a, -um *adj.* very wicked, very shameful

perflātus, -ūs *m.* blowing through; wind, breeze

perflō 1. to blow through *or* over

perfluctuō 1. to flow through, swarm over

perfluō, -xī, -xum 3. to flow through; abound; leak

perfodiō, -fōdī, -fossum 3. to dig through, pierce, penetrate

perforō 1. to bore through, pierce, perforate

perfortiter *adv.* very bravely *or* manfully

perfossor, -ōris *m.* digger; **perfossor parietum** housebreaker

prefrequens, -ntis *adj.* well frequented, very busy

perfricō, -uī, -ātum 1. to rub all over, rub well; **frontem/faciem/ōs perfricāre** to lay aside all sense of shame

perfrīgefaciō 3. to make very cold

perfrīgescō, -ixī, -ictum 3. to become very cold, turn cold, catch cold

perfrīgidus, -a, -um *adj.* very cold

perfringō, -frēgī, -fractum 3. to break, break in pieces, shatter, ruin; break through, break up

perfruor, -fructus 3. *dep.* (+*abl.*) to enjoy fully *or* thoroughly

perfuga, -ae *m.* runaway, fugitive, deserter

perfugiō, -fūgī 3. to flee, take refuge; desert, go over to the enemy

perfugium, -(i)ī *n.* shelter, refuge, sanctuary, asylum

perfunctiō, -ōnis *f.* discharging *or* performing (*of an office*)

perfundō, -fūdī, -fūsum 3. to pour all over, wet, wash, bathe

perfungor, -functus 3. *dep.* (+*abl./acc.*) to discharge, execute, go through with

perfurō 3. to rage furiously, be in a great rage

perfūsōrius, -a, -um *adj.* superficial, slight

pergaudeō 2. to rejoice greatly

pergō, perrexī, perrectum 3. to go, proceed, continue

pergraecor 1. *dep.* to play the Greek, revel like a Greek

pergrandis, -is, -e *adj.* very large *or* great

pergraphicus, -a, -um *adj.* perfect

pergrātus, -a, -um *adj.* very pleasing

pergravis, -is, -e *adj.* very heavy, very weighty, very substantial

pergraviter *adv.* very seriously, very gravely

pergula, -ae *f.* part of house jutting onto street, balcony; shop

perhibeō 2. to say, affirm, assert, hold; give, present

perhīlum *adv.* very little

perhonōrificē *adv.* very honourably, with great respect

perhonōrificus, -a, -um *adj.* very honourable, very respectful

perhorrescō, -rruī 3. to be greatly afraid, shake with fear; shudder at, dread

perhūmāniter *adv.* very kindly, very courteously

perhūmānus, -a, -um *adj.* very kind, very courteous

perīclitātiō, -ōnis *f.* trial, experiment

perīclitor 1. *dep.* to try, prove, make trial of, put to the test; be in danger, run the risk

perīculōsē *adv.* dangerously, with danger

perīculōsus, -a, -um *adj.* dangerous, perilous, hazardous

perīc(u)lum, -ī *n.* danger, peril, risk, hazard; trial, experiment, proof

peridōneus, -a, -um *adj.* very suitable, very fit

perihodos, -ī *f.* grammatical period

perillustris, -is, -e *adj.* very illustrious; very notable

perimbēcillus, -a, -um *adj.* very weak *or* feeble

perimō, -ēmī, -emptum 3. to destroy, extinguish, annihilate, kill; prevent, thwart

perincertus, -a, -um *adj.* very uncertain

perincommodē *adv.* very inconveniently

perincommodus, -a, -um *adj.* very inconvenient

perinde *adv.* similarly, equally; (+*atque/ ac/ut*), just the same (as)

perindignē *adv.* very indignantly, grievously

perindulgens, -ntis *adj.* very indulgent, very kind

perinfāmis, -is, -e *adj.* very infamous

perinfirmus, -a, -um *adj.* very weak, very feeble

peringeniōsus, -a, -um *adj.* very clever

peringrātus, -a, -um *adj.* very ungrateful

perinīquus, -a, -um *adj.* very unjust; very uneasy *or* discontented

perinsignis, -is, -e *adj.* very remarkable

perintempestīvus, -a, -um *adj.* very untimely

perinvīsus, -a, -um *adj.* very hateful, much hated

perinvītus, -a, -um *adj.* very unwilling

peripetasmata, -um *n.pl.* tapestry, hangings, curtains

perīrātus, -a, -um *adj.* very angry

periscelis, -idis *f.* ornament for the leg, garter

peristrōma, -atis or **-mum, -ī** *n.* covering, hanging

peristȳlium, -īī *n.* peristyle, cloister

peristȳlum, -ī *n.* peristyle, cloister

perītē *adv.* skilfully, expertly, in a masterly manner

perītia, -ae *f.* skill, expertise, knowledge

perītus, -a, -um *adj.* (+*gen.*) skilful (in), expert; well-versed (in)

periūcundē *adv.* very pleasantly

periūcundus, -a, -um *adj.* very pleasant, very delightful

periūr- see **pēi(i)ūr-**

perlābor, -lapsus 3. *dep.* to glide along; glide over *or* through

perlaetus, -a, -um *adj.* very happy, full of joy

perlātē *adv.* very widely, very extensively

perlateō 2. to lie hidden, be entirely concealed

perlecebra see **pellecebra**

perlectiō, -ōnis *f.* reading through, perusal

perlegō, -lēgī, -lectum 3. to read through, read over; survey, scan

perlepidē *adv.* very finely, very prettily

perlevis, -is, -e *adj.* very light, very small

perleviter *adv.* very lightly, very slightly

perlibens, -ntis *adj.* very willing

perlibenter *adv.* very willingly

perlīberālis, -is, -e *adj.* very genteel, very well-bred

perlīberāliter *adv.* very generously

perlibet 2. *impers.* (+*dat.*) it is very pleasing *or* agreeable (to)

perlībrō 1. to level; poise, hurl, throw

perlitō 1. to make an auspicious sacrifice

perlongē *adv.* a great way off

perlonginquus, -a, -um *adj.* very long

perlongus, -a, -um *adj.* very long

perlūceō 2. to shine through, be transparent, be seen through; be apparent

perlūcidulus, -a, -um *adj.* transparent

perlūcidus, -a, -um *adj.* clear, transparent, translucent, radiant

perluctuōsus, -a, -um *adj.* very mournful

perluō, -uī, -ūtum 3. to wash *or* bathe all over, wash clean

perlustrō 1. to survey, view all over

permadefaciō, -fēcī, -factum 3. to wet all over, drench

permadescō, -duī 3. to be very wet, be soaked; become very soft

permaestus, -a, -um *adj.* very sad, very dejected

permagnus, -a, -um *adj.* very great, very large; very considerable, very important

permānanter *adv.* by flowing through

permānascō 3. (+*ad* +*acc.*) to flow through (to), penetrate (to)

permaneō, -nsī, -nsum 2. to endure, remain, continue, last, hold out

permānō 1. to flow through, spread; penetrate, enter, reach

permansiō, -ōnis *f.* remaining, abiding, continuing

permarīnus, -a, -um *adj.* that accompanies through the sea

permātūrescō, -ruī 3. to grow fully ripe

permediocris, -is, -e *adj.* very moderate

permeditātus, -a, -um *adj.* thoroughly instructed, well prepared

permeiō, -mi(n)xī, -mi(n)ctum 3. to piss over

permeō 1. to go through *or* over, penetrate, pervade

permereō 2. to serve as a soldier

permētior, -mensus 4. *dep.* to measure; pass over, traverse

permīrus, -a, -um *adj.* very wonderful, very amazing

permisceō 2. to mingle, mix, blend together; throw into confusion, confound

permissiō, -ōnis f. permission, leave, licence; surrender

permissus, -ūs m. permission

permitiālis, -is, -e adj. destructive

permitiēs, [ēī] f. ruin, destruction

permittō, -mīsī, -missum 3. to permit, grant, allow, give leave to; let loose, hurl; give up, yield, concede, surrender

permixtē adv. in a disordered manner, indiscriminately

permixtim adv. in a disordered manner, indiscriminately

permixtiō, -ōnis f. mixture, mixing together, confusion

permixtus, -a, -um adj. mixed together, blended together, confused

permodestus, -a, -um adj. very modest, very discreet

permodicus, -a, -um adj. very small

permolestē adv. very tiresomely; **permolestē ferre** to be greatly displeased by

permolestus, -a, -um adj. very troublesome

permolō 3. to grind thoroughly

permōtiō, -ōnis f. movement, emotion, passion, excitement

permoveō, -mōvī, -mōtum 2. to move greatly, stir up, influence

permulceō, -sī, -sum 2. to stroke, caress, soothe, alleviate; charm

permultus, -a, -um adj. very much, very many

permūniō 4. to fortify strongly, finish fortifying

permūtātiō, -ōnis f. change, alteration; exchange, bartering

permūtō 1. to change, alter, exchange

perna, -ae f. ham

pernecessārius, -a, -um adj. very necessary; very closely connected

pernecesse adv. very necessary

pernegō 1. to deny flatly; refuse altogether

perneō, -ēvī, -ētum 2. to spin to the end, finish

perniciābilis, -is, -e adj. deadly, destructive

perniciēs, -ēī f. death, destruction, ruin, disaster

perniciōsē adv. destructively, hurtfully, perniciously

perniciōsus, -a, -um adj. harmful, hurtful, destructive, deadly

pernīcitās, -ātis f. speed, swiftness, nimbleness

pernīciter adv. speedily, swiftly, nimbly

perniger, -gra, -grum adj. very black

pernimium adv. very much, too much

pernix, -īcis adj. swift, nimble, quick, rapid

pernōbilis, -is, -e adj. very famous

pernoctō 1. to spend the night, remain all night long

pernōnidēs, -ae m. 'son of *perna*'

pernoscō, -nōvī, -nōtum 3. to become thoroughly acquainted with

pernōtescō, -uī 3. to become well-known

pernox, -ctis adj. lasting all night

pernumerō 1. to count out, reckon up

pērō, -ōnis m. rawhide boot

perobscūrus, -a, -um adj. very dark or obscure

perōdī, -sum 3. or **-sus sum** 3. *semi-dep.* (*pf. only*) to hate greatly

perodiōsus, -a, -um adj. very troublesome or grievous

perofficiōsē adv. very respectfully, very courteously

peroleō 2. to smell strongly

pērōnātus, -a, -um adj. wearing rawhide boots

peropportūnē adv. very opportunely or seasonably

peropportūnus, -a, -um adj. very convenient, opportune or seasonable

peroptātō adv. very much to one's wish, very desirably

peropus adv. very necessary

perōrātiō, -ōnis f. peroration, concluding section of a speech

perōrnātus, -a, -um adj. very ornate

perōrnō 1. to adorn or honour greatly

perōrō 1. to conclude a speech, finish; speak against, harangue

perosculor 1. *dep.* to kiss passionately

perpācō 1. to subdue completely

perparcē adv. very sparingly

perparvulus, -a, -um adj. very little or small

perpascō, -pāvī, -pastum 3. to feed well

perpaucī, -ae, -a pl.adj. very few

perpauculī, -ae, -a pl.adj. very few

perpaulum, -ī n. a very little indeed

perpauper, -eris adj. very poor

perpauxillum, -ī *n.* a very little, ever so little

perpavefaciō, -fēcī, -factum 3. to make very afraid, terrify thoroughly

perpellō, -pulī, -pulsum 3. to force, drive; persuade, prevail upon, constrain, oblige

perpendiculum, -ī *n.* plumb-line; **ad perpendiculum** perpendicularly

perpendō, -dī, -sum 3. to weigh carefully *or* exactly, weigh up

perperam *adv.* wrong, amiss, falsely, inadvertently, unadvisedly

perpes, -etis *adj.* continual, uninterrupted; the whole

perpessīcius, -a, -um *adj.* accustomed to hardship, schooled in adversity; *m.sbst.* one who has suffered much

perpessiō, -ōnis *f.* suffering, enduring

perpetior, -ssus 3. *dep.* to suffer, endure, bear, undergo

perpetrō 1. to effect, perform, accomplish, achieve; finish, complete

perpetuārius, -a, -um *adj.* employed in perpetuity

perpetuē *adv.* constantly, continually

perpetuitās, -ātis *f.* perpetuity, continuity, permanence

perpetuō[1] *adv.* continually, uninterruptedly, always

perpetuō[2] 1. to continue, perpetuate, persist in

perpetuus, -a, -um *adj.* perpetual, continual, uninterrupted; complete, entire, universal; **in perpetuum** for ever, always

perplaceō 2. (+*dat.*) to please greatly

perplexābilis, -is, -e *adj.* intricate, entangled, obscure

perplexābiliter *adv.* obscurely, confusingly

perplexē (-xim) *adv.* obscurely, confusingly

perplexor 1. *dep.* to act ambiguously, confuse

perplexus, -a, -um *adj.* intricate, involved, confused

perplicātus, -a, -um *adj.* twisted together

perpluō 3. to let rain through; (*of rain*) come through

perpoliō 4. to polish thoroughly; perfect, finish

perpolītus, -a, -um *adj.* polished, refined, accomplished

perpopulor 1. *dep.* to destroy, ravage

perpōtātiō, -ōnis *f.* drinking continuously, drinking bout

perpōtō 1. to drink continuously; quaff, drink up

perprimō, -prēmī, -pressum 3. to press hard *or* closely

perpropinquus, -ī *m.* very close relative

perprūriscō 3. to itch all over

perpugnax, -ācis *adj.* very pugnacious

perpulcher, -chra, -chrum *adj.* very beautiful

perpurgō (-pūrigō) 1. to make clean, purge thoroughly; deal with fully

perpusillus, -a, -um *adj.* very little

perputō 1. to explain clearly

perquam *adv.* very much, extremely

perquīrō, -sīvī (-siī), -sītum 3. to search for, examine

perquīsītē *adv.* carefully, diligently

perquīsītor, -ōris *m.* hunter *or* seeker out

perrārō *adv.* very seldom *or* rarely

perrārus, -a, -um *adj.* very rare *or* scarce

perreconditus, -a, -um *adj.* very abstruse, obscure *or* recondite

perrepō, -repsī 3. to creep through, crawl over

perreptō 1. to crawl about *or* through

perrīdiculē *adv.* very ridiculously *or* laughably

perrīdiculus, -a, -um *adj.* very ridiculous, foolish, silly, laughable

perrogō 1. to ask in turn

perrumpō, -rūpī, -ruptum 3. to break through, burst through; break into pieces

persaepe *adv.* very often, very frequently

persalsē *adv.* very wittily

persalsus, -a, -um *adj.* very witty

persalūtātiō, -ōnis *f.* greeting of all, assiduous greeting

persalūtō 1. to greet one after another

persanctē *adv.* very devoutly *or* solemnly

persānō 1. to cure thoroughly

persapiens, -ntis *adj.* very wise

persapienter *adv.* very wisely

perscienter *adv.* very skilfully *or* knowingly

perscindō, -scidī, -scissum 3. to cut through, cleave, split

perscītus, -a, -um *adj.* very wise *or* clever

perscrībō, -scripsī, -scriptum 3. to write, write out, write fully

perscriptiō, -ōnis *f.* writing, record; banker's draft

perscriptor, -ōris *m.* writer, scribe, copyist

perscrūtor 1. *dep.* to search thoroughly, investigate

persecō, -uī, -tum 1. to cut through, cut out, dissect

persector 1. *dep.* to pursue; investigate

persedeō, -sēdī 2. to remain *or* continue sitting

persegnis, -is, -e *adj.* very slow, slack *or* sluggish

persentiō, -sī, -sum 4. to perceive *or* feel thoroughly

persentiscō 3. to begin to perceive thoroughly

persequor, -cūtus 3. *dep.* to follow after, pursue, chase; imitate; be a follower of, revenge, take vengeance on; perform, bring about, accomplish; set forth, relate, recount

persevērans, -ntis *adj.* persistent, resolute

persevēranter *adv.* perseveringly, constantly, resolutely

persevērantia, -ae *f.* perseverance, resolve

persevērō 1. to persevere, persist, hold out, continue

persevērus, -a, -um *adj.* very severe *or* harsh

persīdō, -sēdī 3. to sink down, soak through, penetrate

persignō 1. to mark, stamp

persimilis, -is, -e *adj.* (+*gen./dat.*) very like

persimplex, -icis *adj.* very plain, ordinary *or* simple

persolla, -ae *f.* little mask; little fright

persolvō, -vī, -ūtum 3. to pay, pay completely; give, render; unravel, explain

persōna, -ae *f.* mask; character, part; person; standing, rank

persōnālis, -is, -e *adj.* personal

persōnātus, -a, -um *adj.* masked; pretended, counterfeit

personō, -uī 1. to sound loudly; cry out; make to resound

personus, -a, -um *adj.* sounding loudly, resounding

perspectē *adv.* considerately, thoughtfully

perspectō 1. to inspect carefully; look about; watch to the end

perspectus, -a, -um *adj.* observed carefully, fully understood

perspeculor 1. *dep.* to view *or* examine carefully

perspergō, -sī, -sum 3. to sprinkle

perspicax, -ācis *adj.* acute, sharp-sighted, perspicacious

perspicientia, -ae *f.* perfect knowledge, percipience

perspiciō, -spexī, -spectum 3. to see through; see clearly, discern; examine carefully

perspicuē *adv.* clearly, plainly, manifestly

perspicuitās, -ātis *f.* clearness, perspicuity

perspicuus, -a, -um *adj.* clear, transparent, evident

perspissō *adv.* very slowly

persternō, -trāvī, -trātum 3. to pave completely

perstimulō 1. to stir up, excite, incense

perstō, -itī, -ātum 1. to persist, persevere, continue, hold out, endure

perstrepō 3. to make a loud noise, resound

perstringō, -nxī, -ctum 3. to bind tightly; graze, wound slightly; affect deeply; dazzle, daze, stun; censure, blame; touch on briefly, glance at

perstudiōsē *adv.* very carefully *or* attentively

perstudiōsus, -a, -um *adj.* (+*gen.*) very keen on, eager for

persuādeō, -sī, -sum 2. (+*dat.*) to persuade, convince; prevail upon, induce

persuāsiō, -ōnis *f.* persuasion; opinion, belief

persuāstrix, -īcis *f.* female who persuades

persuāsus, -ūs *m.* persuasion

persubtīlis, -is, -e *adj.* very subtle; very fine

persultō 1. to bound, prance; skip over; make inroads, range about

pertaedeō, -sus sum 2. *semi-dep.* to make very weary, disgust

pertegō, -xī, -ctum 3. to cover all over

pertemptō 1. to examine carefully, consider; try out, test, prove

pertendō, -dī 3. to persist, persevere, press on; continue, carry through, bring to a conclusion

pertentō see **pertemptō**

pertenuis, -is, -e *adj.* very thin, very slender, very slight

perterebrō 1. to drill a hole through, bore through, perforate

pertergeō, -sī, -sum 2. to wipe over, brush gently

perterrefaciō, -fēcī, -factum 3. to frighten greatly, terrify

perterreō 2. to frighten greatly, terrify

perterricrepus, -a, -um adj. making terrifying noise

pertexō, -uī, -tum 3. to finish (weaving), complete, accomplish

pertica, -ae f. pole, rod, long staff

perticātus, -a, -um adj. furnished with a staff

pertimescō, -muī 3. to fear greatly, be very afraid

pertinācia, -ae f. obstinacy, stubbornness, pertinacity

pertināciter adv. obstinately, stubbornly, pertinaciously

pertinax, -ācis adj. very tenacious, holding fast, tight-fisted; firm, resolute, persevering; stubborn, obstinate

pertineō 2. to reach, extend, stretch; apply, pertain, relate, concern

pertingō 3. to reach, extend

pertolerō 1. to endure, bear, suffer

pertorqueō 2. to twist, distort

pertractātē adv. tritely

pertractō 1. to handle, touch, fondle; examine, consider thoroughly

pertrahō, -xī, -ctum 3. to drag, draw, lead, conduct, lure

pertrectō see **pertractō**

pertribuō, -uī, -ūtum 3. to give

pertrīcōsus, -a, -um adj. very confused or strange

pertristis, -is, -e adj. very sad; very harsh or severe

pertrītus, -a, -um adj. trite, hackneyed, common

pertumultuōsē adv. in a very agitated or tumultuous manner

pertundō, -udī, -ūsum 3. to bore through, perforate

perturbātē adv. confusedly, in a disturbed manner

perturbātiō, -ōnis f. confusion, disturbance, disorder, agitation; passion, emotion

perturbātrix, -īcis f. one who disturbs

perturbātus, -a, -um adj. confused, disturbed, troubled, agitated

perturbō 1. to throw into confusion, disturb greatly, trouble, perturb, agitate, stir up

perturpis, -is, -e adj. very disgraceful, very indecent

pertūsus (-tussus), -a, -um adj. perforated, pierced

pērula, -ae f. small bag

perung(u)ō, -xī, -ctum 3. to anoint all over, besmear

perurbānus, -a, -um adj. very witty, clever or sophisticated

perūrō, -ussī, -ustum 3. to burn up, scorch; consume; chafe, cut, lacerate

perūtilis, -is, -e adj. very useful or profitable

pervādō, -sī, -sum 3. to go through, pass through, penetrate; spread, pervade; reach, arrive at

pervagātus, -a, -um adj. well-known, widespread, public

pervagor 1. dep. to wander through, rove about, go over; spread over

pervagus, -a, -um adj. wandering or roving about

pervaleō 2. to have great strength

pervariē adv. with much variety, very variously

pervastō 1. to ravage, destroy, lay waste

pervehō, -xī, -ctum 3. to carry along, convey, conduct; pass. travel, sail, sail through, ride

pervellō 3. to pinch, pluck, pull, twitch; blame, disparage; affect, stimulate

perveniō, -vēnī, -ventum 4. to come to, arrive at, reach

pervēnor 1. dep. to hunt through

perversāriō, -ōnis f. gibberish

perversē adv. wrongly, awkwardly, unskilfully, perversely, crossly

perversitās, -ātis f. perversity, awkwardness, peevishness

perversus, -a, -um adj. turned the wrong way, askew, awry; perverse, awkward, peevish

pervertō, -tī, -sum 3. to overthrow, upset, turn upside down, throw down; pervert, corrupt, ruin, destroy

pervesperī adv. very late in the evening

pervestīgātiō, -ōnis f. careful search or investigation

pervestīgō 1. to track down, search carefully for; examine, investigate

pervetus, -eris adj. very old or ancient

pervetustus, -a, -um adj. very old or ancient

pervicācia, -ae f. obstinacy, stubbornness; firmness, persistence

pervicāciter adv. obstinately, stubbornly

pervicax, -ācis adj. obstinate, stubborn, headstrong, wilful; firm, persistent

pervideō, -vīdī, -vīsum 2. to see clearly, perceive, discern

pervigeō 2. to flourish greatly

pervigil, -ilis adj. very watchful, wakeful; awake through the night

pervigilātiō, -ōnis f. staying awake through the night, vigil

pervigilium, -(i)ī n. staying awake through the night, vigil

pervigilō 1. to stay awake through the night, keep watch

pervīlis, -is, -e adj. very cheap

pervincō, -vīcī, -victum 3. to overcome, prevail upon or over; get the better of; gain; prove, demonstrate

pervium, -iī n. passage, way through

pervius, -a, -um adj. accessible, having a way through, passable

pervīvō, -vixī 3. to continue to live, survive

pervolg- see **pervulg-**

pervolitō 1. to fly over or through; flit about

pervolō¹ 1. to fly over or through; fly to, make haste, rush

pervolō², -velle, -voluī v.irreg. to desire or wish greatly

pervolūtō 1. to roll over and over; unroll, read carefully

pervolvō 3. to roll, tumble; unroll, read carefully; *pass.* be conversant or much engaged

pervors- see **pervers-**

pervulgātus, -a, -um adj. common, usual, well-known

pervulgō 1. to make public, divulge, publish, disseminate; wander about, frequent; *refl.* prostitute oneself

pēs, pedis m. foot; rope; metrical foot; measure; **pedem ferre** to go; **pedem**

referre to go back, to return; **pedem conferre** to join battle, fight; **pedem pōnere** to step; **pedibus** on foot, by land; **pedibus merēre** to serve in the infantry; **in sententiam pedibus īre** to support a proposal; **sub pedibus** (+*gen.*) under the control (of)

pessimē (-sumē) superl.adv. very badly, worst; most unfavourably

pessimus (-sumus), -a, -um superl.adj. very bad, worst; most unfavourable

pessulus, -ī m. bar or bolt of door

pessum adv. to the bottom, downwards; **pessum īre** to sink, be ruined or destroyed; **pessum dare** (+*dat.*) to ruin, put an end to

pestifer, -era, -erum adj. destructive, deadly, poisonous, harmful, pernicious, pestilential

pestiferē adv. destructively, injuriously

pestilens, -ntis adj. unhealthy, harmful, deadly, pestilential

pestilentia, -ae f. plague, pestilence, infection, contagion; unhealthy condition or state

pestilitās, -ātis f. plague, pestilence, infection, contagion

pestis, -is f. plague, pestilence, infection, contagion; destruction, ruin; pest, bane, annoyance

petasātus, -a, -um adj. wearing a *petasus*

petasō, -ōnis m. leg of pork

petasunculus, -ī m. small leg of pork

petasus, -ī m. broad-brimmed hat

petaurum, -ī n. springboard

petesso 3. to desire greatly, strive after

petītiō, -ōnis f. petition, demand, request, claim; canvassing for office; thrust, push, attack

petītor, -ōris m. seeker, demander; candidate; plaintiff, claimant

petīturiō 4. to seek after office

petītus, -ūs m. seeking for, inclining towards

petō, -īvī (-iī), -ītum 3. to ask for, seek; beg, entreat, demand; seek office, stand as candidate; aim at, make for, chase; attack, assail, strike; take, fetch, derive

petorritum, -ī n. Gallic carriage or waggon with four wheels

petra, -ae f. rock, crag; stone

petrō, -ōnis m. old male sheep or ram

petulans, -ntis *adj.* impudent, insolent, impertinent, forward; wanton, lascivious

petulanter *adv.* impudently, insolently; wantonly, lasciviously

petulantia, -ae *f.* impudence, insolence; wantonness, lasciviousness

petulcus, -a, -um *adj.* given to butting *or* striking

peucedanon, -ī *n.* plant, sulphur-wort, hog's fennel

pexātus, -a, -um *adj.* wearing a new garment (with the nap still on it)

pexus, -a, -um *adj.* combed

phaecasiātus, -a, -um *adj.* wearing effeminate Greek shoes

phāger, -grī *m.* kind of fish

phalangae, -ārum *f.pl.* rollers

phalangītēs, -ae *m.* soldier belonging to a phalanx

phalanx, -ngis *m.* large body of men drawn up in tight formation, phalanx

phalerae, -ārum *f.pl.* horse trappings; ornaments, finery

phalerātus, -a, -um *adj.* wearing *phalerae*; showy, fine-sounding

phantasma, -atis *n.* apparition

pharetra, -ae *f.* quiver, arrow-case

pharetrātus, -a, -um *adj.* wearing a quiver

pharmacopōla, -ae *m.* medicine-seller, apothecary

phasēlus (-os), -ī *m./f.* small boat, yacht, pinnace; bean (with edible pod)

phāsiāna, -ae *f.* pheasant

phasma, -atis *n.* apparition, phantom, spectre

phengītēs, -ae *m.* white, translucent marble

phiala, -ae *f.* shallow, broad-bottomed cup *or* dish

philēma, -atis *n.* kiss

philītia, -ōrum *n.pl.* communal meals in Sparta

philologia, -ae *f.* study of literature, philology, love of learning

philologus, -ī *m.* scholar, man of letters

philosophia, -ae *f.* philosophy; philosophical system or school

philosophor 1. *dep.* to philosophize, study philosophy

philosophus, -a, -um *adj.* philosophical; *m./f.sbst.* philosopher

philtrum, -ī *n.* love-potion

philyra, -ae *f.* inner bark of the linden tree

phīmus, -ī *m.* dice-box

phōca, -ae *or* **-ē, -ēs** *f.* seal, sea-calf

phoenīcopterus, -ī *m.* flamingo

phoenix, -īcis *m.* phoenix, fabulous bird proverbial for its solitary life and ability to regenerate from its own ashes

phōnascus, -ī *m.* elocution teacher, singing instructor

phrenēsis, -is *f.* madness, frenzy

phrenēticus, -a, -um *adj.* mad, frantic

phrygiō, -ōnis *m.* embroiderer

p(h)thisicus, -a, -um *adj.* consumptive

p(h)thisis, -is *f.* consumption

phȳ *interj.* exclamation of disgust

phȳcis, -idis *f.* kind of fish

phylaca, -ae *f.* prison

phylarchus, -ī *m.* chief of tribe

phȳsēter, -ēris *m.* large fish, whale

physicē *adv.* scientifically, in the manner of natural philosophers

physicus, -a, -um *adj.* physical, natural; *m. sbst.* natural philosopher, natural scientist

physiognōmōn, -onis *m.* physiognomist

physiologia, -ae *f.* natural science

piābilis, -is, -e *adj.* that may be expiated *or* atoned for

piāculāris, -is, -e *adj.* having the power to expiate *or* atone, expiatory; *n.pl.sbst.* expiatory rites

piāculum, -ī *n.* expiation, expiatory sacrifice, atonement; action requiring expiation *or* atonement, wrongdoing

piāmen, -inis *n.* means of expiation *or* atonement

pīca, -ae *f.* magpie, jay

picāria, -ae *f.* place where pitch is produced

picātus, -a, -um *adj.* with the flavour of pitch; *n.sbst.* pitch-flavoured wine

picea, -ae *f.* pitch-pine

piceus, -a, -um *adj.* of pitch; pitchy, black as pitch

picō 1. to pitch, daub with pitch

pictor, -ōris *m.* painter

pictūra, -ae *f.* painting; art of painting; picture; embroidery

pictūrātus, -a, -um *adj.* painted, depicted; embroidered

pictus, -a, -um *adj.* painted, coloured, decorated; embroidered

pīcus, -ī *m.* woodpecker

piē *adv.* piously, dutifully, devoutly, affectionately

pietās, -ātis *f.* piety, respect, duty; veneration, love, affection

piger, pigra, pigrum *adj.* slow, lazy, inactive, dull, sluggish

piget, piguit 2. *impers.* (+*acc. of person* +*gen. of cause of grief*) it grieves, repents *or* pains; it is irksome *or* troublesome

pigmentārius, -(i)ī *m.* dealer in paints *or* cosmetics

pigmentum, -ī *n.* paint, pigment; rhetorical colouring

pignerātor, -ōris *m.* one who takes a pledge, mortgagee

pignerō 1. to pledge, pawn; bind, obligate; *dep.* receive as a pledge, claim as one's own

pignus, -oris *or* **-eris** *n.* pledge, surety, mortgage, security; guarantee, proof; token; wager

pigrē *adv.* slowly, sluggishly, lazily

pigrescō 3. to become slow, slacken

pigritia, -ae *or* **-ēs, -ēī** *f.* slowness, inactivity, laziness

pigrō 1. *or* **pigror** 1. *dep.* to be slow, sluggish

pīla¹, -ae *f.* mortar

pila², -ae *f.* ball, sphere

pīla³, -ae *f.* pillar; pier

pīlānus, -a, -um *adj.* armed with the *pilum*

pīlātus¹, -a, -um *adj.* armed with the *pilum*

pīlātus², -a, -um *adj.* closely packed

pīlentum, -ī *n.* carriage

pilicrepus, -ī *m.* ball-game participant

pilleātus, -a, -um *adj.* wearing the *pilleum*

pilleolus, -ī *m.* small *pilleum*

pilleum, -ī *n.* or **-us, -ī** *m.* felt hat *or* cap

pilō 1. to pluck, make bald

pilōsus, -a, -um *adj.* covered with hair, shaggy

pīlum, -ī *n.* javelin

pilus¹, -ī *m.* strand of hair; jot, whit

pīlus², -ī *m.* division of Roman army; **prīmus pīlus** senior centurion

pīna, -ae *f.* shellfish

pīnētum, -ī *n.* plantation of pine trees, pine wood

pīneus, -a, -um *adj.* of a pine tree, of pine

pingō, pinxī, pictum 3. to paint, draw,
depict, portray; colour, dye; embroider; decorate, embellish, adorn

pingue, -is *n.* fat, grease

pinguescō 3. to grow fat; become fertile *or* fruitful

pinguiārius, -īī *m.* lover of fat

pinguis, -is, -e *adj.* fat, plump; rich, fertile, fruitful; fatty, greasy, oily; dull, heavy, stupid; thick, coarse; comfortable, calm, quite

pīnifer, -era, -erum *adj.* pine-bearing, abounding in pine trees

pīniger, -era, -erum *adj.* pine-bearing

pinna, -ae *f.* feather, wing; fin; arrow; battlement; shellfish

pinnātus, -a, -um *adj.* winged, feathered, plumed

pinniger, -era, -erum *adj.* having wings, winged; having fins, finned

pinnipēs, -edis *adj.* wing-footed

pinnirapus, -ī *m.* crest-snatcher (type of gladiator)

pinnula, -ae *f.* little wing

pīnotērēs, -ae *m.* small crab

pinsitō 1. to pound *or* crush frequently

pī(n)sō, -uī, -itum 3. to pound, crush, bruise, beat

pīnus, -ūs *f.* pine, pine tree; pine torch; ship

piō 1. to propitiate, appease by sacrifice; purge, expiate; atone for

piper, -ris *n.* pepper

piperātus, -a, -um *adj.* seasoned with pepper; crafty

pīpiō 1. to cheep, chirp

pipinna, -ae *f.* little willy

pīpulus, -ī *m.* chirping, cheeping

pīrāta, -ae *m.* pirate

pīrātica, -ae *f.* piracy

pīrāticus, -a, -um *adj.* of pirates, piratical

pirum, -ī *n.* pear

pirus, -ī *f.* pear tree

pīsātiō, -ōnis *f.* pounding

piscārius, -a, -um *adj.* of *or* belonging to fish *or* fishing

piscātor, -ōris *m.* fisherman

piscātōrius, -a, -um *adj.* concerned with fishermen *or* fishing

piscātus, -ūs *m.* fishing; catch of fish

pisciculus, -ī *m.* little fish

piscīna, -ae *f.* fish-pond; swimming-pool

piscīnārius, -(i)ī *m.* lover of fishponds

piscis, -is *m*. fish
piscor 1. *dep*. to fish
piscōsus, -a, -um *adj*. full of fish, abounding in fish
pisculentus, -a, -um *adj*. full of fish, abounding in fish
pistillus, -ī *m*. pestle
pistor, -ōris *m*. miller; bread-maker, baker
pistōrius, -a, -um *adj*. of *or* relating to a baker; **opera pistōria** pastries
pistrilla, -ae *f*. hand-mill
pistrīnensis, -is, -e *adj*. relating to a mill
pistrīnum, -ī *n*. mill, bakery; work-house
pistrix, -īcis *f*. whale, large fish; narrow ship
pithēcium, -(i)ī *n*. little monkey
pītuīta, -ae *f*. phlegm, mucus, catarrh
pītuītōsus, -a, -um *adj*. full of phlegm, mucus *or* catarrh
pityōn, -ōnos *m*. plantation of pine-trees
pius, pia, pium *adj*. pious, holy, devout, dutiful, repectful, loyal, affectionate; honest, just; patriotic; *m.pl.sbst*. the blessed, the dead
pix, picis *f*. pitch
plācābilis, -is, -e *adj*. placable, easily appeased; placatory
plācābilitās, -ātis *f*. placability
plācāmen, -inis *n*. means of appeasing *or* pacifying
plācāmentum, -ī *n*. means of appeasing *or* pacifying
plācātē *adv*. mildly, gently, calmly
plācātiō, -ōnis *f*. appeasing, pacifying
placens, -ntis *adj*. dear, beloved, pleasing
placenta, -ae *f*. cake
placeō, -uī 2. or **-itus sum** 2. *semi-dep*. (+*dat*.) to please, suit, satisfy, delight; *refl*. be pleased with oneself, be proud; *impers*. it seems good, it is agreed *or* resolved
placidē *adv*. quietly, placidly, mildly, gently
placidus, -a, -um *adj*. quiet, placid, calm, mild, gentle, agreeable
placitō 1. to please continually
placitum, -ī *n*. opinion, belief, maxim
placitus, -a, -um *adj*. pleasing, dear
plācō 1. to calm, appease, pacify; (+*dat*.) reconcile (with)
plāga¹, -ae *f*. blow, stroke, lash; wound, cut, laceration
plaga², -ae *f*. tract, region, zone, district

plaga³, -ae *f*. net, trap, snare
plagiārius, -(i)ī *m*. kidnapper; literary thief
plāgiger, -era, -erum *adj*. blow-bearing, much beaten
plāgigerulus, -a, -um *adj*. rather beaten
plāgipatidēs, -ae *m*. descendant of 'Lash-bearer'
plāgōsus, -a, -um *adj*. keen on flogging
plagula, -ae *f*. curtain, hanging, sheet
plagūsia, -ae *f*. kind of fish
planctus, -ūs *m*. loud striking *or* beating; beating (*of breasts*) in mourning; grief, lamentation
plancus, -a, -um *adj*. flat-footed
plānē *adv*. clearly, plainly, evidently, explicitly; absolutely, entirely
plangō, -xī, -ctum 3. to strike *or* beat noisily; beat (*arms or breasts*) in grief; lament, mourn
plangor, -ōris *m*. loud striking *or* beating; beating (*of body*) in mourning; grief, lamentation
plāniloquus, -a, -um *adj*. speaking plainly, openly *or* freely
plānipēs, -edis *m*. bare-foot performer
plānitās, -ātis *f*. clarity, plainness
plānitiēs, -ēī or **-a, -ae** *f*. level ground, plain; flat surface
planta¹, -ae *f*. small twig, shoot; cutting, graft; plant
planta², -ae *f*. sole of the foot
plantāria¹, -ium *n.pl*. young trees, sets, cuttings
plantāria², -ium *n.pl*. sandals
plānum, -ī *n*. flat *or* level ground; **dē plānō** easily
plānus¹, -a, -um *adj*. plain, flat, level, even, smooth; evident, clear, obvious
planus², -ī *m*. imposter, deceiver, cheat, rogue
plasma, -atis *n*. inflection of the voice
platalea, -ae *f*. kind of bird, spoonbill
platanōn, -ōnos *m*. plantation of plane-trees
platanus, -ī *f*. plane tree
platea, -ae *f*. broad street
plaudō, -sī, -sum 3. to make a noise by beating *or* striking; clap hands, applaud, approve
plausibilis, -is, -e *adj*. worthy of applause, acceptable, pleasing

plausor, -ōris *m.* applauder

plaustrum, -ī *n.* wagon, cart

plausus, -ūs *m.* clapping, noisy beating *or* striking, flapping; applause, approval

plēbēcula (-bic-), -ae *f.* common people, mob, rabble

plēbēius, -a, -um *adj.* of the common people, plebeian; common, vulgar; low, sordid

plēbicola, -ae *m.* friend of the people

plēbi(s)scītum, -ī *n.* decree *or* law made by the people

plebs, plēbis *or* **-bēs, -bēī** *f.* the common people, plebeians; masses, lower orders

plectilis, -is, -e *adj.* plaited *or* woven together

plectō¹, -xī, -xum 3. to plait, weave together

plectō² 3. to strike *or* beat; punish

plectrum, -ī *n.* plectrum; lyre, lyric poetry

plēnē *adv.* fully, completely, totally, entirely

plēnus, -a, -um *adj.* (+*gen./abl.*) full (of), filled (with); pregnant; thick, fat, plump; sated, satisfied; rich, wealthy, abounding (in); loaded, laden; full, complete, perfect

plērumque *adv.* for the most part, commonly, generally, often

plērusque, -aque, -umque *adj.* a very great part of, most; *pl.* very many, most, the majority of; *n.sbst.* the greater part; *m. pl.sbst.* the majority

plicō 1. to fold, twine; roll up

plōdō see **plaudō**

plōrābilis, -is, -e *adj.* lamentable

plōrātillus, -a, -um *adj.* tearful, weepy

plōrātor, -ōris *m.* mourner, lamenter

plōrātus, -ūs *m.* weeping, wailing, lamentation

plōrō 1. to weep, wail, cry out; lament, deplore

plostellum, -ī *n.* little cart

plostrum see **plaustrum**

plūma, -ae *f.* soft feather; down

plūmātilis, -is, -e *adj.* feathered

plumbeus, -a, -um *adj.* of lead, leaden, heavy; dull, stupid; worthless

plumbum, -ī *n.* lead; lead bullet; lead pipe

plūmeus, -a, -um *adj.* of feathers; feather-like

plūmipēs, -edis *adj.* feather-footed

plūmō 1. to cover with feathers; embroider

plūmōsus, -a, -um *adj.* feathered, covered with feathers

pluō, plūvī *or* **pluī** 3. to rain

plūrēs, -ēs, -a *pl.adj.* more, very many; **plūribus (verbīs)** at greater length; *m./f. pl.sbst.* the majority, the dead; *n.pl.sbst.* more, more things

plūrifāriam *adv.* in many places *or* parts

plūrimum *superl.adv.* most of all, very much; mostly, for the most part

plūrimus, -a, -um *superl.adj.* very much *or* many, most, the greatest part of

plūs¹, -ris *n.* more; **plūs satis** more than enough; **plūris** at a higher price

plūs² *adv.* more, to a greater degree

plusculum, -ī *n.* a little more; *n.sg.adv.* somewhat more, rather more

plusculus, -a, -um *adj.* a little more, somewhat more

pluteus, -ī *m.* portable military shelter; parapet; (back part of) bed *or* couch; bookcase

pluvia, -ae *f.* rain

pluviālis, -is, -e *or* **pluvius, -a, -um** *adj.* rainy, of rain; produced by rain; rain-like

pōcillum, -ī *n.* little cup

pōc(u)lum, -ī *n.* cup, bowl; drink, draught, potion

podager, -gra, -grum *adj.* gouty

podagra, -ae *f.* gout in the feet

podagricus, -a, -um *adj.* gouty, troubled with gout

podagrōsus, -a, -um *adj.* gouty

pōdex, -icis *m.* anus, fundament

podium, -(i)ī *n.* balcony, parapet

poēma, -atis *n.* poem, piece of poetry

poēmatium, -iī *n.* short poem

poen- see **pūn-** (other than below)

poena, -ae *f.* punishment, penalty; **poenās dare** to be punished

poēsis, -is *f.* poetry, work of a poet; poem

poēta, -ae *m.* poet

poētica, -ae *or* **-ē, -ēs** *f.* poetry, poetic art

poēticē *adv.* poetically, in the manner of a poet

poēticus, -a, -um *adj.* poetic, poetical

poētria, -ae *f.* poetess

poētris, -idos *f.* poetess

pol *interj.* by Pollux!, indeed!, truly!

polenta, -ae *f.* pearl-barley, peeled-barley

polentārius, -a, -um *adj.* of *or* relating to *polenta*

poliō 4. to polish, smooth, make neat, adorn, embellish

polītē *adv.* in a polished manner, elegantly

polītia, -ae *f.* Plato's *Republic*

polīticus, -a, -um *adj.* political, civil

polītūra, -ae *f.* polishing, smoothing

polītus, -a, -um *adj.* polished, smoothed, made neat, refined

pollen, -inis *n.* fine flour; dust, powder

pollens, -ntis *adj.* powerful, strong, potent

pollentia, -ae *f.* power, might, sway

polleō 2. to be able, be very strong *or* powerful; prevail

pollex, -icis *m.* thumb; big toe

polliceor 2. *dep.* to promise, offer

pollicitātiō, -ōnis *f.* promise

pollicitor 1. *dep.* to promise

pollicitum, -ī *n.* promise

pollinārius, -a, -um *adj.* of *or* relating to fine flour

polli(n)ctor, -ōris *m.* one who prepares dead bodies for burial

pollingō, -nxī, -nctum 3. to prepare, wash *or* anoint for burial

pollūceō, -luxī, -luctum 2. to offer in sacrifice; serve up

pollūcibiliter *adv.* sumptuously, magnificently

polluctūra, -ae *f.* serving of a feast

polluō, -uī, -ūtum 3. to pollute, taint, infect, defile, contaminate, corrupt

pollūtus, -a, -um *adj.* polluted, defiled, contaminated

polus, -ī *m.* pole; pole star; sky

polymyxos, -os, -on *adj.* with many wicks

polyphagus, -a, -um *adj.* gluttonous, omnivorous

pōlypōsus, -a, -um *adj.* with a nasal polyp

pōlypus, -ī *m.* polypus, octopus; nasal polyp

pōmārium, -(i)ī *n.* orchard

pōmārius, -īī *m.* fruit-grower

pōmērium, -(i)ī *n.* empty zone on inside and outside of city walls

pōmifer, -era, -erum *adj.* bearing *or* producing fruit, fruitful

pōmōsus, -a, -um *adj.* full of fruit

pompa, -ae *f.* procession, parade; retinue, train; display, ostentation

pompīlus, -ī *m.* pilot-fish

pōmum, -ī *n.* or **pōmus, -ī** *f.* fruit; fruit-tree

ponderō 1. to weigh; weigh up, consider

ponderōsus, -a, -um *adj.* weighty, heavy

pondō *adv.* by weight, in weight

pondus, -eris *n.* weight, mass; load, burden; authority, importance; stability, firmness

pōne *adv.* behind; *prep.* (+*acc.*) behind

pōnō, posuī, positum 3. to put, place, set, lay; set up, erect, build; set out, plant; lay down, stake, wager; loan, invest; serve up, set before; appoint; arrange; propose; lay aside, take off, put down, surrender; bury, inter; ponder, consider; fall, abate; assert, maintain, allege, suppose; set up, dedicate; spend, employ; make, build; *pass.* (+*in* +*abl.*) be based upon, rest *or* depend upon; **castra pōnere** to pitch camp

pons, pontis *m.* bridge; drawbridge; gangway; deck

ponticulus, -ī *m.* little bridge

pontifex, -icis *m.* high priest, chief priest, pontiff

pontificālis, -is, -e *adj.* of *or* relating to a *pontifex*, pontifical

pontificātus, -ūs *m.* office *or* dignity of a *pontifex*

pontificius, -a, -um *adj.* of *or* relating to a *pontifex*, pontifical

pontō, -ōnis *m.* floating bridge, pontoon

pontus, -ī *m.* sea

popa, -ae *m.* priest's assistant (*responsible for the killing of sacrificial victims*); **popa venter** glutton, voracious eater

popellus, -ī *m.* rabble, mob

popīna, -ae *f.* eating-house, tavern, cook-shop; cook-shop fare

popīnō, -ōnis *m.* frequenter of eating-houses, glutton

poples, -itis *m.* knee; hollow of the knee

poppysma, -atis *n.* smacking of the lips (in approval)

populābilis, -is, -e *adj.* that can be destroyed *or* laid waste

populābundus, -a, -um *adj.* ravaging, laying waste

populāris, -is, -e *adj.* of *or* belonging to the people, popular; *m./f.sbst.* fellow-citizen, compatriot, member of the people's party; *m.pl.sbst.* the people's party

populāritās, -ātis *f.* compatriotism; attempt to gain popular support

populāriter *adv.* in the manner of the

people, commonly, vulgarly; so as to court popular favour

populātiō, -ōnis *f.* laying waste, ravaging, pillaging, plundering

populātor, -ōris *m.* ravager, pillager, plunderer

populātrix, -īcis *f.* female ravager

pōpuleus, -a, -um *adj.* of a poplar tree

pōpulifer, -era, -erum *adj.* poplar-bearing

pōpulnus, -a, -um *adj.* of poplar-wood

populor 1. *dep.* or **populō** 1. to ravage, lay waste to, destroy, spoil, plunder, pillage

populus¹, -ī *m.* people, state, nation; the common people, general public; crowd, multitude, throng

pōpulus², -ī *f.* poplar tree

porca, -ae *f.* sow, female pig

porcellus, -ī *m.* young pig, piglet

porcīnārius, -(i)ī *m.* seller of pork

porcīnus, -a, -um *adj.* of *or* relating to pork; *f.sg.sbst.* pork

porculus¹, -ī *m.* young pig, piglet

porculus², -ī *m.* hoop

porcus, -ī *m.* pig, hog, swine

poriciō see **porriciō**

porphyrēticus, -a, -um *adj.* made of porphyry

porphyriō, -ōnis *m.* purple water-fowl

porrectiō, -ōnis *f.* stretching out, extension

porrectus, -a, -um *adj.* stretched out, extended; smoothed, relaxed

porriciō, -ectum 3. to lay out (*entrails of a victim*) on the altar

porrigō¹, -rexī, -rectum 3. to stretch *or* reach out; spread out, extend, lengthen; hold out, offer

porrīgō², -inis *f.* dandruff, scurf

porrō *adv.* forward, further; hereafter; in future; long ago; then, besides, next; furthermore, moreover

porrum, -ī *n.* or **porrus, -ī** *m.* leek

porta, -ae *f.* city gate, gate, door; entrance, outlet

portātiō, -ōnis *f.* carrying, conveyance

portendō, -dī, -tum 3. to portend, foretell, foreshadow, augur, indicate

portentificus, -a, -um *adj.* portentous, prodigious, miraculous

portentōsus, -a, -um *adj.* portentous, prodigious, strange, unnatural, monstrous

portentum, -ī *n.* omen, prodigy, miracle, portent, monstrosity; fiction, fantasy

portentuōsus see **portentōsus**

porthmeus, -eōs *m.* ferryman

porticula, -ae *f.* small portico

porticus, -ūs *f.* portico, colonnade, covered walk

portiō, -ōnis *f.* portion, part, share; proportion, ratio; **prō portiōne** proportionately

portisculus, -ī *m.* instrument used to beat time on rowing boats

portitor, -ōris *m.* custom-house officer; ferryman

portō 1. to carry, bear, convey, conduct; bring

portōrium, -(i)ī *n.* customs duty, toll, tax

portula, -ae *f.* little gate

portuōsus, -a, -um *adj.* with many harbours

portus, -ūs *m.* harbour, port, anchorage; haven, place of refuge

posca, -ae *f.* wine mixed with vinegar

poscō, poposcī 3. to ask, call for; demand; request in marriage

posculentus, -a, -um *adj.* fit to drink

positiō, -ōnis *f.* placing, putting, planting; position, situation

positor, -ōris *m.* builder, founder

positūra, -ae *f.* position, situation; disposition, arrangement

positus, -ūs *m.* position, situation; disposition, arrangement

possessiō, -ōnis *f.* act *or* right of possessing, occupancy; enjoyment; possession, property, estate

possessiuncula, -ae *f.* small property

possessor, -ōris *m.* possessor, owner, occupier

possideō, -sēdī, -sessum 2. to possess, have, hold, occupy, own; enjoy; be master of, dominate

possīdō 3. to take possession of, occupy

possum, posse, potuī *v.irreg.* (+*inf.*) to be able to, have power *or* influence

post¹ or **poste** *adv.* behind; after, after that

post² *prep.* (+*acc.*) behind; after, since

posteā *adv.* afterwards, after that, hereafter, next; later; **quid posteā?** what then?

posteāquam *adv.* after, after that

posterior, -or, -us *compar.adj.* that comes after, later, next; inferior, worse

posteritās, -ātis *f.* posterity, descendants, future generations

posterius *compar.adv.* after, afterwards, later; in aftertimes, in the future

posterus, -a, -um *adj.* coming after, following, next; *m.pl.sbst.* posterity, descendants

postferō -ferre *v.irreg.* to esteem less, regard as less important

postgenitī, -ōrum *m.pl.* posterity, descendants

posthabeō 2. to esteem less, regard as less important; postpone

posthāc *adv.* after this, hereafter; in future

postibi *adv.* afterwards, then

postīculum, -ī *n.* small outhouse

postīcum, -ī *n.* back-door

postīcus, -a, -um *adj.* at the back, behind, posterior

postid(eā) *adv.* afterwards

postilēna, -ae *f.* horse-crupper

postiliō, -ōnis *f.* expiatory sacrifice

postillā(c) *adv.* afterwards, after that

postis, -is *m.* door-post, door-jamb; door, gate

postlīminium, -(i)ī *n.* restoration of rights and property (*on return from exile or other absence*)

postmerīdiānus, -a, -um *adj.* in the afternoon

postmodo (-um) *adv.* presently, shortly, afterwards

postmoerium see **pōmērium**

postpartor, -ōris *m.* successor, heir

postpōnō, -posuī, -positum 3. to esteem less, disregard; postpone

postprincipium, -(i)ī *n.* progress *or* course of a thing after its beginning, sequel

postputō 1. to esteem less, disregard

postquam *conj.* after, after that; when; ever since

postrēmō *superl.adv.* finally, at last, lastly, ultimately

postrēmum *superl.adv.* for the last time, last, finally

postrēmus, -a, -um *superl.adj.* last, hindmost, final; worst, most contemptible

postrīdiē (-uō) *adv.* on the following day, the day after

postscaenium, -(i)ī *n.* secret, thing kept behind the scenes

postscrībō, -scripsī, -scriptum 3. to write after

postulātīcius, -a, -um *adj.* demanded, requested

postulātiō, -ōnis *f.* demand, request; complaint; application for redress in court of law, application to launch a prosecution

postulātor, -ōris *m.* plaintiff, complainant

postulātum, -ī *n.* demand, request

postulātus, -ūs *m.* demand, suit

postulō 1. to demand, ask for; require; (seek leave to) prosecute

postumus, -a, -um *adj.* posthumous, last-born; posthumous *m.sbst.* one born after the writing of a will

pōtātiō, -ōnis *f.* drinking bout, drinking session

pōtātor, -ōris *m.* drinker

potens, -ntis *adj.* (*usu.* +*gen.*) having power (over); master (of), in possession (of) capable (of); strong, potent

potentātus, -ūs *m.* power, dominion, rule

potenter *adv.* powerfully, mightily, strongly; effectively

potentia, -ae *f.* power, force, might; rule, sway, dominion; authority, influence, efficacy

pōtērium, -(i)ī *n.* cup, beaker, drinking-vessel

potesse *etc.* see **possum**

potestās, -ātis *f.* power, control, force; rule, dominion, authority, command; opportunity, ability, liberty, licence, permission

pōtiō[1], -ōnis *f.* drinking, drink; draught, potion

pōtiō[2] 4. (+*gen.*) to place under the control of

pōtiōnātus, -a, -um *adj.* dosed up, poisoned

potior[1] 4. *dep.* (+*acc./gen./abl.*) to gain possession of, become master of, obtain, acquire

potior[2], -or, -us *compar.adj.* better, preferable, more desirable; more powerful; (+*gen.*) with more power over

potis or **pote** *indecl.adj.* (+*inf.*) able (to), capable (of); possible

potissimum *superl.adv.* especially, chiefly, most of all, principally

potissimus, -a, -um *superl.adj.* chief, especial, principal, best, most important

pōtitō 1. to drink often *or* heavily

pōtiuncula, -ae *f.* small drink *or* potion

potius *compar.adv.* rather, more; preferably; instead

pōtō 1. to drink, drink heavily; soak up

pōtor, -ōris *m.* drinker, drunkard

pōtulentus, -a, -um *adj.* drunk, inebriated

pōtus, -ūs *m.* drinking, drink; draught, potion

prae¹ *prep.* (+*abl.*) before, in front of; because of, on account of; compared with; **prae manū** at hand; **prae sē ferre** to show openly, make a show of

prae² *adv.* before, in front; *conj.* **prae ut/ quam** compared with

praeacuō, -uī, -ūtum 3. to make very sharp

praeacūtus, -a, -um *adj.* sharpened at the end; very sharp

praealtus, -a, -um *adj.* very high; very deep

praebeō 2. to offer, present, supply, provide; cause, occasion; *refl.* conduct oneself, behave

praebibō, -ī, -itum 3. to drink to, toast

praebitor, -ōris *m.* provider, supplier, purveyer

praecalidus, -a, -um *adj.* very hot

praecalvus, -a, -um *adj.* very bald

praecantō 1. (+*dat.*) to bewitch

praecantrix, -īcis *f.* sorceress, witch

praecānus, -a, -um *adj.* very grey-haired

praecaveō, -cāvī, -cautum 2. to take care, be on one's guard; guard against

praecēdō, -cessī, -cessum 3. to go before, precede; surpass, excel, be superior to

praeceler, -ris, -re *adj.* very quick *or* swift

praecelerō 1. hurry away before

praecellēns, -ntis *adj.* excelling greatly, surpassing, outstanding

praecellō 3. (+*acc./dat.*) to excel, surpass, exceed

praecelsus, -a, -um *adj.* very high *or* lofty

praecentiō, -ōnis *f.* prelude

praeceps¹, -ipitis *adj.* headlong, head foremost; setting, sinking, declining; downhill, steep, precipitous, sheer; hasty, rash, headstrong; sudden, abrupt; *n.sg. adv.* headlong

praeceps², -ipitis *n.* precipice, sheer drop, brink; **in/per praeceps** headlong

praeceptiō, -ōnis *f.* instruction, precept; precondition; right to receive legacy before the administration of an estate

praeceptīvus, -a, -um *adj.* giving moral rules *or* precepts

praeceptor, -ōris *m.* teacher, instructor

praeceptrix, -īcis *f.* female teacher

praeceptum, -ī *n.* precept, advice, instruction, order, rule, maxim

praecerpō, -psī, -ptum 3. to pluck *or* clip off; gather early; forestall

praecīdō, -dī, -sum 3. to cut *or* chop off, lop; cut out; cut across; cut short, break off

praecinctūra, -ae *f.* girdling

praecingō, -xī, -ctum 3. to gird, surround, encircle, enclose

praecinō, -inuī, -entum 3. (+*dat.*) to sing *or* play in front of; foretell, predict, presage

praecipiō, -cepī, -ceptum 3. to take *or* seize in advance, anticipate, forestall; instruct, teach, direct; suggest, recommend; order

praecipitanter *adv.* with headlong haste, headlong

praecipitātiō, -ōnis *f.* falling headlong

praecipitium, -iī *n.* precipice; headlong fall

praecipitō 1. to throw down, cast headlong; fall headlong, sink; rush headlong; drive headlong; ruin, destroy

praecipuē *adv.* especially, particularly, principally

praecipuus, -a, -um *adj.* particular, special, peculiar; reserved in advance; distinguished, excellent, outstanding

praecīsē *adv.* briefly, succinctly; positively

praecīsus, -a, -um *adj.* cut off, broken off, steep, abrupt

praeclārē *adv.* very clearly, very plainly; successfully, famously, very well

praeclārus, -a, -um *adj.* very clear *or* bright, beautiful; illustrious, remarkable, distinguished, outstanding

praeclūdō, -sī, -sum 3. to shut, bolt, bar; obstruct, impede, stop

praecō, -ōnis *m.* herald, town-crier; auctioneer

praecōgitō 1. to ponder beforehand, premeditate

praecognōscō, -nōvī, -nitum 3. to know in advance, learn beforehand

praecolō, -coluī, -cultum 3. to cultivate early

praecompositus, -a, -um *adj.* prepared beforehand

praecōnium, -(i)ī *n.* office of *praeco*; proclamation, declaration; praise, commendation

praecōnius, -a, -um *adj.* of *or* relating to a *praeco*

praeconsūmō, -sumpsī, -sumptum 3. to spend in advance *or* prematurely

praecontrectō 1. to handle beforehand

praecordia, -ōrum *n.pl.* diaphragm, midriff; bowels, intestines; heart, breast

praecorrumpō, -rūpī, -ruptum 3. to corrupt *or* bribe beforehand

praecox, -ocis (-oquis) *adj.* early, ripe before the usual time, untimely, premature; precocious

praecupidus, -a, -um *adj.* (+*gen.*) very fond (of)

praecurrō, -(cu)currī, -cursum 3. (+*acc./ dat.*) to run in front, precede; outrun, surpass

praecursiō, -ōnis *f.* previous occurrence; skirmish

praecursor, -ōris *m.* forerunner, precursor; scout, spy

praecursōrius, -a, -um *adj.* going in advance, sent beforehand

praecutiō 3. to brandish before

praeda, -ae *f.* booty, spoil, plunder, pillage; prey; profit, gain

praedābundus, -a, -um *adj.* plundering, pillaging

praedamnō 1. to condemn in advance, prejudge

praedātiō, -ōnis *f.* plundering, pillaging

praedātor, -ōris *m.* robber, plunderer, pillager; hunter

praedātōrius, -a, -um *adj.* plundering, pillaging, predatory

praedātrix, -īcis *f.* robber, plunderer, pillager

praedātus, -ūs *m.* plundering, pillaging

praedēlassō 1. to tire *or* weaken beforehand

praediātor, -ōris *m.* official responsible for acquisition of public land

praediātōrius, -a, -um *adj.* of *or* relating to the acquisition of public land

praedicābilis, -is, -e *adj.* laudable, praiseworthy

praedicātiō, -ōnis *f.* public proclamation, announcement; commendation

praedicātor, -ōris *m.* praiser, eulogist

praedicō[1] 1. to proclaim, report, publish; say publicly, declare; praise, commend, celebrate

praedīcō[2] **, -dixī, -dictum** 3. to tell beforehand; foretell, forewarn, predict, prophesy; arrange beforehand; admonish, warn, advise, direct

praedictiō, -ōnis *f.* prediction, prophecy

praedictum, -ī *n.* prediction; order, command; prearrangement

praediolum, -ī *n.* small farm *or* estate

praediscō 3. to learn beforehand

praeditus, -a, -um *adj.* (+*abl.*) having, endowed with, possessed of, furnished with

praedium, -(i)ī *n.* farm, estate

praedīves, -itis *adj.* very rich *or* plentiful

praedīvīnō 1. to divine, presage

praedō, -ōnis *m.* robber, plunderer, pirate

praedoceō, -uī, -tum 2. to teach *or* instruct beforehand

praedoctus, -a, -um *adj.* very learned *or* skilled

praedomō, -uī 1. to subdue beforehand

praedor 1. *dep.* to plunder, pillage, get gain; carry off (as prey)

praedūcō, -duxī, -ductum 3. (+*dat.*) to draw, make *or* put in front (of)

praedulcis, -is, -e *adj.* very sweet, very pleasing

praedūrus, -a, -um *adj.* very hard; very hardy *or* strong

praeeō, -īre, -īvī (-iī) 4. to go ahead, lead the way; precede; guide; dictate, recite, repeat

praefātiō, -ōnis *f.* introduction, opening

praefectūra, -ae *f.* office *or* rank of *praefectus*; command; town *or* area under control of a *praefectus*, prefecture

praefectus, -ī *m.* prefect, commander, governor, superintendent, overseer

praeferō, -ferre, -tulī, -lātum *v.irreg.* to carry in front, carry openly *or* publicly; exhibit, display, show, indicate; anticipate; put forward; (+*dat.*) prefer (to), give preference to; *pass.* go past, ride past

praeferox, -ōcis *adj.* very fierce, very impetuous

praeferrātus, -a, -um *adj.* surrounded with iron, iron-tipped

praefervidus, -a, -um *adj.* very hot

praefestīnō 1. to make too great haste; rush past

praefica, -ae *f.* woman hired to perform funeral lament

praeficiō, -fēcī, -fectum 3.(+*acc. of person* +*dat. of thing ruled*) to set over, put in authority, appoint to the command of

praefīdens, -ntis *adj.* (+*dat.*) trusting too much (in)

praefīgō, -fixī, -fixum 3. to fix *or* fasten in front; (+*dat.*) fix on the end (of); tip, point with; set up in front; pierce, transfix

praefīniō 4. to determine in advance, prescribe, limit

praefiscinī (-fascinē) *adv.* 'allow me to say'; 'let it be said without offence'

praeflōrō 1. to deflower

praefluō 3. to flow in front, flow past

praefōcō 1. to choke, stop up, suffocate

praefodiō, -fōdī, -fossum 3. to dig a trench in front; bury beforehand

praefor 1. *dep.* to say beforehand, preface; invoke, call on; recite

praefractē *adv.* rigidly, resolutely, harshly

praefractus, -a, -um *adj.* abrupt; severe, inflexible, harsh

praefrīgidus, -a, -um *adj.* very cold

praefringō, -frēgī, -fractum 3. to break off at the end

praefulciō, -sī, -tum 4. to support, secure, prop up; use as a prop

praefulgeō, -sī 2. to shine brightly *or* conspicuously, dazzle; (+*dat.*) outshine

praefulgurō 1. to glitter, flash; illuminate

praefurō 3. to rage greatly

praegelidus, -a, -um *adj.* very cold

praegestiō 4. (+*inf.*) to desire greatly (to)

praegnās, -tis (-ans, -ntis) *adj.* pregnant, with child; (+*abl.*) swollen *or* loaded (with), full (of)

praegracilis, -is, -e *adj.* very slender

praegrandis, -is, -e *adj.* very bulky *or* large, huge

praegravis, -is, -e *adj.* very heavy, weighty, unwieldy; wearisome

praegravō 1. to weigh down greatly, be very heavy; oppress; outweigh

praegredior, -ssus 3. *dep.* to go in front, precede; go past

praegressiō, -ōnis *f.* going before, precedence

praegressus, -ūs *m.* precedent

praegustātor, -ōris *m.* taster

praegustō 1. to taste beforehand

praehibeō 2. to provide, supply, offer, present

praeiaceō 2. (+*dat.*) to lie *or* be situated in front (of)

praeiūdicium, -(i)ī *n.* preliminary inquiry; previous judgement; precedent; prejudice

praeiūdicō 1. to judge in advance, prejudge; prejudice

praelābor, -lapsus 3. *dep.* to glide *or* flow in front; pass *or* flow by

praelambō 3. to lick *or* taste first

praelargus, -a, -um *adj.* very bountiful *or* lavish

praelautus, -a, -um *adj.* very sumptuous *or* splendid

praelegō, -lēgī, -lectum 3. to read aloud, lecture on; sail by

praelībō 1. to taste beforehand

praeligō 1. to tie in front, tie up; (+*dat.*) fasten (onto)

praelongus, -a, -um *adj.* very long

praeloquor, -cūtus 3. *dep.* to speak first, speak by way of a preface

praelūceō, -luxī 2. to shine, give light; (+*dat./acc.*) carry a light in front (of); (+*dat.*) outshine, surpass

praelūdō, -sī, -sum 3. to perform beforehand

praelūsiō, -ōnis *f.* prelude

praelustris, -is, -e *adj.* very bright *or* conspicuous

praemandō 1. to order beforehand

praemātūrē *adv.* too early *or* soon, prematurely

praemātūrus, -a, -um *adj.* too early *or* soon, premature

praemedicātus, -a, -um *adj.* furnished with medicine *or* antidote

praemeditātiō, -ōnis *f.* considering beforehand

praemeditor 1. *dep.* to think over, consider beforehand; play as prelude

praemercor 1. *dep.* (+*dat.*) to buy in advance (of)

praemetuenter *adv.* fearfully, cautiously

praemetuō 3. to fear in advance; (+*dat.*) be apprehensive (for)

praemineō 2. to be preeminent *or* superior; surpass

praemior 1. *dep.* to stipulate for a reward

praemittō, -mīsī, -missum 3. to send *or* dispatch in advance; say first

praemium, -(i)ī *n.* reward, prize, recompense; plunder, booty

praemolestia, -ae *f.* fear, apprehension

praemōlior 4. *dep.* to prepare in advance

praemoneō 2. to give advance warning, forewarn; tell previously; predict, foretell

praemonitus, -ūs *m.* warning, forewarning, prediction

praemonstrātor, -ōris *m.* director, guide

praemonstrō 1. to show beforehand, guide; predict, foretell, presage

praemordeō, -sī, -sum 2. to bite, bite off

praemorior, -mortuus 3. *dep.* to die beforehand, die prematurely

praemūniō 4. to fortify in advance, secure, strengthen; build up argument in order to obviate later objections

praemūnītiō, -ōnis *f.* fortifying in advance; preparation, paving the way

praenarrō 1. to tell beforehand

praenatō 1. to swim in front; swim *or* flow by

praenāvigō 1. to sail by *or* past

praeniteō 2. to shine brightly; (+*dat.*) outshine, surpass

praenōmen, -inis *n.* first name

praenoscō, -nōvī 3. to get to know beforehand

praenōtiō, -ōnis *f.* preconception, innate idea, prenotion

praenūbilus, -a, -um *adj.* very cloudy; shady

praenuntiō 1. to foretell, predict, forebode

praenuntius, -a, -um *adj.* foretelling, foreboding; *m./f.sbst.* messenger, harbinger

praeoccupō 1. to seize in advance, preoccupy; anticipate; do before another, anticipate others

praeoleō 2. (+*dat.*) to give out a smell in front of

praeoptō 1. to prefer

praepandō 3. to open out *or* spread out in front; lay open

praeparātiō, -ōnis *f.* preparing, making ready, preparation

praeparō 1. to prepare, get *or* make ready; provide

praepedīmentum, -ī *n.* hindrance, impediment

praepediō 4. to hinder, impede, obstruct; bind, shackle

praependeō 2. to hang down in front

praepes, -etis *adj.* swift of flight, winged, nimble; *f./m.sbst.* bird

praepetō 3. to desire greatly

praepilātus, -a, -um *adj.* tipped with a ball

praepinguis, -is, -e *adj.* very fat; very fertile *or* rich

praepollens, -ntis *adj.* very powerful

praeponderō 1. to outweigh, have more weight *or* influence

praepōnō, -posuī, -positum 3. (+*dat.*) to place first, put *or* set before; set over, appoint, entrust with the command of; prefer, value *or* esteem more

praeportō 1. to carry in front

praepositiō, -ōnis *f.* putting *or* setting in front; preferring; preposition

praepositum, -ī *n.* thing to be preferred (*in Stoic thought*)

praepositus, -ī *m.* army officer, prefect, commander

praeposterē *adv.* without order, confusedly

praeposterus, -a, -um *adj.* confused, out of order, inverted; perverse, awkward

praepotens, -ntis *adj.* very able *or* powerful

praeproperanter *adv.* very hastily *or* speedily

praeproperē *adv.* too hastily *or* speedily

praeproperus, -a, -um *adj.* very hasty *or* speedy; too hasty, overhasty, precipitate

praepūtium, -ī *n.* foreskin

praequam *adv.* compared with; more than that which

praequeror, -stus 3. *dep.* to complain beforehand

praeradiō 1. to outshine

praerapidus, -a, -um *adj.* very swift *or* rapid, precipitate

praerigescō, -guī 3. to become very stiff

praeripiō, -ripuī, -reptum 3. to take *or* snatch away prematurely *or* first; anticipate; do before another, forestall

praerōdō, -sī, -sum 3. to bite *or* nibble off; gnaw at the end *or* top

praerogātīva, -ae *f.* the tribe *or* century to which it fell by lot to vote first; first vote; previous verdict; sure sign, omen

praerogātīvus, -a, -um *adj.* voting first

praerumpō, -rūpī, -ruptum 3. to break off

praeruptus, -a, -um *adj.* steep, craggy, rugged; abrupt, broken off; headstrong, precipitate; violent; *n.sbst.* precipice, broken *or* craggy ground

praes, -dis *m.* one who stands bail for another

praesaep- see **praesēp-**

praesāgātiō, -ōnis *f.* presaging, perceiving in advance

praesāgiō 4. to presage, perceive in advance, augur, forebode

praesāgium, -(i)ī *n.* presage, presentiment, foreboding; prediction

praesāgus, -a, -um *adj.* presaging, foreboding, apprehensive, prophetic

praescīscō, -scīī, -scītum 3. to find out beforehand

praescius, -a, -um *adj.* prescient, prophetic, presaging

praescrībō, -scrīpsī, -scriptum 3. to write first, prefix in writing; order, prescribe, set bounds, limit; dictate; put forward as pretext; outline, trace

praescriptiō, -ōnis *f.* inscription, title; pretext; order, rule, precept; limitation; objection

praescriptum, -ī *n.* order, rule, precept; line, course

praesecō, -uī, -tum 1. to cut off, cut, pare

praesegmen, -inis *n.* cutting, nail-clipping

praesens, -ntis *adj.* present, at hand, here and now; ready, prompt, immediate, instant; resolute, confident, undaunted; propitious, favourable; **in/ad praesens** at the moment, for the present

praesensiō, -ōnis *f.* foresight, prescience, presentiment

praesentāneus, -a, -um *adj.* instant, immediate, operating quickly

praesentārius, -a, -um *adj.* present, at hand, ready

praesentia¹, -ae *f.* presence; effect; **in praesentiā** for the present, at present

praesentia², -ōrum *n.pl.* present state of affairs

praesentiō, -sī, -sum 4. to perceive beforehand, foresee, presage

praesēpe, -is *n.* or **-ēs, -is** *f.* enclosure, stable, stall; crib, manger; bee-hive; brothel

praesēpiō, -sī, -tum 4. to enclose at the front, barricade

praesertim *adv.* especially, particularly

praeserviō 4. (+*dat.*) to serve as a slave (to)

praeses, -idis *m./f.* governor, ruler, prefect; guardian, protector, defender; tutelary deity

praesideō, -sēdī 2. (+*dat./acc.*) to preside over, direct, control, superintend; protect, defend, guard

praesidiārius, -a, -um *adj.* belonging to a garrison, appointed for defence

praesidium, -(i)ī *n.* garrison, guard; escort, convoy; stronghold, fort; protection, defence, security; help, assistance, aid

praesignificō 1. to show beforehand, foretell, predict

praesignis, -is, -e *adj.* illustrious, distinguished, outstanding

praesolidō 1. to make solid beforehand

praesonō, -uī 1. to sound beforehand

praespargō 3. to scatter *or* strew in front

praestābilis, -is, -e *adj.* excellent, distinguished, outstanding

praestans, -ntis *adj.* excellent, distinguished, outstanding

praestantia, -ae *f.* excellence, pre-eminence

praestantissimē *superl.adv.* most excellently

praestātiō, -ōnis *f.* guarantee, warranty; payment

praesternō 3. to scatter in front; prepare

praestes, -itis *m.* guardian, protector

praestinō 1. to buy, purchase

praestituō, -uī, -ūtum 3. to determine beforehand, prescribe

praestō¹ *adv.* present, ready, at hand

praestō², -itī, -ātum or **-itum** 1. to stand in front, surpass, outstrip, excel; make good, maintain, keep; answer *or* vouch for, be accountable *or* surety for; perform, fulfil, discharge; show, prove; give, offer, furnish; be preferable *or* better

praestōlor 1. *dep.* to wait for, expect

praest(r)īgia, -ae *f.* (*usu. pl.*) sleight of hand, trick, deceit

praest(r)īgiātor, -ōris *m.* trickster; juggler

praest(r)īgiātrix, -īcis *f.* female trickster

praestringō, -nxī, -ctum 3. to bind fast *or* hard; blunt, dull; dazzle

praestruō, -xī, -ctum 3. to build in front; stop, block up; build in advance, prepare

praesūdō 1. to work up a sweat beforehand

praesul, -ulis or **praesultātor, -ōris** *m.* leading dancer

praesultō 1. (+*dat.*) to leap or dance in front (of)

praesum, -esse, -fuī *v.irreg.* (+*dat.*) to preside (over), rule (over), be in authority, have command (of)

praesūmō, -sumpsī, -sumptum 3. to take first, anticipate; presume, take for granted

praesumptiō, -ōnis *f.* anticipation, presumption

praesuō, -uī, -ūtum 3. to sew up

praetegō, -xī, -ctum 3. to cover

praetemptō 1. to try beforehand, make a trial of

praetendō, -dī, -tum 3. to stretch *or* hold out; put *or* spread out in front; pretend, give as a pretext

praetepescō, -puī 3. to become very warm; be warm before

praeter *prep.* (+*acc.*) past, along, close by; besides, in addition to; beyond, contrary to; except, save; *adv.* past; except, save

praeteragō 3. to drive past *or* beyond

praeterbītō 3. to pass by *or* beyond

praeterdūcō, -duxī, -ductum 3. to lead past *or* along

praetereā *adv.* besides, moreover; hereafter

praetereō, -īre, -iī (-īvī), -itum 4. to go past *or* beyond, pass by; escape notice; pass over, make no mention of, omit, ignore; surpass, excel, exceed

praeterequitō 1. to ride past

praeterferō, -ferre, -tulī, -lātum *v.irreg.* to carry past *or* beyond

praeterfluō 3. to flow past, run by; flow away

praetergredior, -ssus 3. *dep.* to go past *or* beyond, pass by

praeterhāc *adv.* beyond this, further

praeteritus, -a, -um *adj.* passed, gone by; just past; *n.sg.sbst.* things gone by, the past

praeterlābor, -lapsus 3. *dep.* to flow *or* glide by, pass by

praetermeō 1. to pass by *or* beyond, go past

praetermissiō, -ōnis *f.* passing over, omission

praetermittō, -mīsī, -missum 3. to pass over, let pass, omit, neglect; send *or* transport beyond

praeternāvigō 1. to sail by *or* beyond

praeterō, -trīvī 3. to rub away, wear down in front

praeterquam *conj.* besides, beyond, except

praetervectiō, -ōnis *f.* sailing past

praetervehō, -xī, -ctum 3. to carry past; *pass.* to ride *or* sail past, pass by *or* over, be carried past *or* by

praetervolō 1. to fly past *or* by, pass over; slip by, escape

praetexō, -uī, -tum 3. to weave, fringe, border; adorn; cover, cloak, conceal; give as a pretext, pretend

praetexta, -ae *f.* toga with purple border; tragedy (representing magistrates and other dignitaries)

praetextātus, -a, -um *adj.* wearing the *toga praetexta*; under the age of sixteen; obscene, lewd, corrupt

praetextum, -ī *n.* ornament; pretext, excuse

praetextus¹, -a, -um *adj.* woven, bordered (with purple); wearing the *toga praetexta*

praetextus², -ūs *m.* outward appearance, show; pretence, pretext, cloak

praetimeō 2. to fear beforehand; fear greatly

praetingō, -xī, -ctum 3. to moisten *or* sprinkle beforehand

praetor, -ōris *m.* praetor, commander, general, governor; (chief) magistrate

praetōriānus, -a, -um *adj.* praetorian; of *or* relating to the praetorian cohorts; *m. sbst.* one of the emperor's bodyguards; soldier of praetorian cohorts

praetōricius, -a, -um *adj.* praetorian, of *or* relating to a *praetor*

praetōrium, -(i)ī *n.* general's tent, military headquarters; council of war; governor's residence; palace, grand country house; praetorian guard

praetōrius, -a, -um *adj.* praetorian; of *or* relating to a *praetor or propraetor*; *m.sbst.* ex-praetor; **cohors praetōria** imperial bodyguard; **porta praetōria** main gate of Roman camp

praetorqueō, -sī, -tum 2. to twist *or* wring beforehand

praetractō 1. to examine beforehand

praetrepidō 1. to tremble greatly

praetrepidus, -a, -um *adj.* very anxious *or* disquieted

praetruncō 1. to cut *or* lop off

praetūra, -ae *f.* praetorship, office of *praetor*

praeumbrō 1. to overshadow, eclipse, darken

praeustus, -a, -um *adj.* burnt at the end *or* point; frost-bitten

praeut *conj.* compared with

praevalens, -ntis *adj.* very powerful *or* strong; prevailing

praevaleō, -uī 2. to be stronger *or* more powerful, prevail

praevalidus, -a, -um *adj.* very strong *or* powerful, very robust

praevallō 1. to fortify in front

praevāricātiō, -ōnis *f.* collusion

praevāricātor, -ōris *m.* advocate working in collusion with his opposite number

praevāricor 1. *dep.* to straddle; work in collusion with one's opposite number

praevehor, -ctus 3. *dep.* to be carried forward, go *or* ride past

praeveniō, -vēnī, -ventum 4. to come before, precede; prevent, anticipate

praeverrō 3. to sweep before

praevertō (-vortō), -tī, -sum 3. *or* **-tor, -sus** 3. *dep.* to prefer, take up in preference; do first *or* in preference to anything else, turn to first; outstrip, outrun; anticipate, prevent; prevail over, have more force *or* weight

praevideō, -vīdī, -vīsum 2. to see beforehand, foresee

praevitiō 1. to infect *or* corrupt beforehand

praevius, -a, -um *adj.* going before, leading the way

praevolō 1. to fly in front *or* first

pragmaticus, -a, -um *adj.* skilled in affairs of state; **pragmaticī hominēs** men of the world; *m.sbst.* legal consultant

prandeō, -dī, -sum 2. to eat, dine, take lunch

prandium, -(i)ī *n.* lunch

pransor, -ōris *m.* lunch-guest

prasinus, -a, -um *adj.* leek-green, green

prātensis, -is, -e *adj.* of *or* belonging to a meadow

prātulum, -ī *n.* small meadow

prātum, -ī *n.* meadow; meadow-grass

prāvē *adv.* wrongly, badly, amiss, crookedly

prāvitās, -ātis *f.* deformity, crookedness; perversity, depravity, viciousness, wickedness

prāvus, -a, -um *adj.* crooked, misshapen, deformed; wrong; bad, wicked, vicious, depraved; perverse, obstinate, wilful

precans, -ntis *adj.* praying, begging, suppliant

precāriō *adv.* by entreaty *or* request; uncertainly, precariously

precārius, -a, -um *adj.* obtained by prayer *or* entreaty; uncertain, precarious

precātiō, -ōnis *f.* praying, prayer, entreaty

precātor, -ōris *m.* suppliant, intercessor

precātus, -ūs *m.* prayer, entreaty

preciae, -ārum *f.pl.* kind of vine

precor 1. *dep.* to pray, entreat, supplicate, beg, beseech, request

pre(he)ndō, -dī, -sum 3. to take hold of, grasp, catch, seize, accost; take in, comprehend

prēlum, -ī *n.* press (*for vines, olives or clothes*)

premō, -ssī, -ssum 3. to press, press upon; press *or* weigh down, burden, load; press with one's body; have sex with; press close, strain, squeeze; compress, narrow, block, choke, close, shut; push *or* drive into; sink, depress; diminish, disparage, slander; pursue, chase, press upon; attack;

keep close to, hug; check, subdue, hinder, stop, crush, overwhelm; cover over, hide, overshadow; bury, plant; hold in, constrain

prensātiō, -ōnis *f.* canvassing, soliciting

prensō 1. to clutch at; accost, stop; canvass

pressē *adv.* closely; briefly, concisely; clearly, distinctly; to the point

pressiō, -ōnis *f.* pressing, pressure

pressō 1. to press hard *or* close, squeeze

pressūra, -ae *f.* pressing, squeezing, pressure

pressus¹, -a, -um *adj.* pressed *or* driven in, hard, firm; checked, stifled, subdued, restrained; concise, compressed, compact

pressus², -ūs *m.* pressing, pressure

prester, -ēris *m.* fiery whirlwind, tornado; poisonous snake

pretiōsē *adv.* in a costly manner, richly, splendidly

pretiōsus, -a, -um *adj.* costly, precious, valuable; sumptuous, extravagant

pretium, -(i)ī *n.* price, value, worth; payment, fee, prize, ransom, bribe; **operae pretium esse** to be worthwhile

prex, precis *f.* prayer, entreaty, supplication; curse; good wish

prīdem *adv.* some time since, a while ago; **quam prīdem?** how long is it since?; **iam prīdem** a long time ago; for a long time now

prīdiānus, -a, -um *adj.* of *or* belonging to the day before

prīdiē *adv.* on the day before

prīmaevus, -a, -um *adj.* youthful, flourishing

prīmānī, -ōrum *m.pl.* soldiers of the first legion

prīmārius, -a, -um *adj.* of the first rank *or* importance; chief, principal

prīmē *adv.* chiefly, exceedingly

prīmigenus, -a, -um *adj.* of *or* relating to birth; **diēs prīmigenus** birthday

prīmipīlāris, -is *m.* or **prīmipīlus, -ī** *m.* chief centurion

prīmitus *adv.* at first, first of all, first

prīmō *adv.* at first, first of all, in the first place; firstly

prīmordium, -(i)ī *n.* beginning, origin; **prīmordia rērum** atoms

prīmōris, -is, -e *adj.* first, foremost; tip,

point, extremity of; **m.pl.sbst.** men of the first rank

prīmulum *adv.* first, for the first time

prīmulus, -a, -um *adj.* first

prīmum¹ *adv.* first, in the first place, first of all; **ut/ubi/cum prīmum** as soon as; **quam prīmum** as soon as possible

prīmum², -ī *n.* beginning, first part, front line; *pl.* beginning, first place; first principles *or* elements; **in prīmīs** especially

prīmumdum *adv.* in the first place

prīmus, -a, -um *adj.* first, foremost; the front/end/tip/beginning of; principal, most distinguished *or* excellent; **prīmā nocte** at the beginning of the night

princeps¹, -ipis *adj.* first, foremost, original, chief, most distinguished

princeps², -ipis *m.* leader, head, chief, prince; author, instigator; first citizen, emperor; *pl.* leading men; second line of soldiers

principālis, -is, -e *adj.* principal, chief, first, original; imperial, of *or* relating to the emperor

principāliter *adv.* principally, chiefly, especially; in a princely *or* imperial manner

principātus, -ūs *m.* first place, pre-eminence, supremacy; imperial power, government, rule, dominion; beginning

principiālis, -is, -e *adj.* original, of *or* relating to the beginning

principiō *adv.* first, first of all, in the first place, from the beginning

principium, -(i)ī *n.* beginning, origin, start, opening; *pl.* first principles, elements; front line; general's tent, headquarters

prior, -or, -us *compar.adj.* former, previous, prior, earlier, first; superior, more important; *m.pl.sbst.* ancestors, forefathers

priscē *adv.* in an old-fashioned manner, harshly, severely

priscus, -a, -um *adj.* ancient, old, antique, former, old-fashioned, out of date; *m.pl. sbst.* the ancients

pristinus, -a, -um *adj.* original, first, former; ancient, old; previous

pristis, -is *f.* whale, large fish; narrow ship

prius *compar.adv.* earlier, previously, before, first; sooner

priusquam *conj.* before, sooner, rather

prīvātim *adv.* privately, in private; individually, separately

prīvātiō, -ōnis *f.* taking away, removal, being without

prīvātus, -a, -um *adj.* private, one's own, particular, ordinary; *m.sbst.* private person, individual; *n.sbst.* private property

prīvigna, -ae *f.* stepdaughter

prīvignus, -ī *m.* stepson

prīvilēgium, -(i)ī *n.* law concerning rights of individual; privilege, special right, prerogative

prīvō 1. (+*abl.*) to deprive, bereave (of); free, exempt (from)

prīvus, -a, -um *adj.* individual, one's own, single, particular; (+*gen.*) bereft (of), without

prō¹ *prep.* (+*abl.*) before, in front of, on; for, in favour of, in defence of, on behalf of; in place of, instead of; in exchange, in return for; by virtue of; as, as if, as good as; in proportion to; in relation to; **prō sē quisque** each according to his strength

prō² *interj.* ah!, oh!, heavens!

proāgorus, -ī *m.* chief magistrate

proauctor, -ōris *m.* remote founder, early ancestor

proavia, -ae *f.* great-grandmother

proavītus, -a, -um *adj.* of *or* relating to one's great-grandfather; ancestral, ancient

proavus, -ī *m.* great-grandfather; ancestor

probābilis, -is, -e *adj.* probable, likely; credible, plausible; commendable, acceptable, pleasing

probābilitās, -ātis *f.* probability, likelihood, appearance of truth

probābiliter *adv.* probably, in all likelihood, credibly; commendably

probātiō, -ōnis *f.* proof, demonstration; trial, inspection, examination; approval

probātor, -ōris *m.* approver

probātus, -a, -um *adj.* proved, tried and tested, approved; acceptable

probē *adv.* rightly, properly, excellently; well, thoroughly

probitās, -ātis *f.* honesty, virtue, probity

problēmata, -ōrum *n.pl.* questions, problems

probō 1. to approve (of), commend, value, esteem; examine, inspect, judge; prove,

show, demonstrate; recommend, gain approval for

proboscis, -idis *f.* trunk

probrōsus, -a, -um *adj.* disgraceful, shameful, scandalous

probrum, -ī *n.* shameful action, heinous deed; sexual impropriety; disgrace, dishonour, shame, scandal; abuse, insult, foul language

probus, -a, -um *adj.* good, honest, excellent, virtuous, upright, modest; fit for purpose

procācitās, -ātis *f.* shamelessness, wantonness, forwardness

procāciter *adv.* wantonly, shamelessly, in a forward manner

procax, -ācis *adj.* forward, bold, wanton, shameless, flirtatious

prōcēdō, -cessī, -cessum 3. to proceed, advance, go forward; make progress; continue, go on; go by, pass; turn out, succeed

procella, -ae *f.* storm, tempest, hurricane; commotion, tumult

prōcellō 3. to hurl forward

procellōsus, -a, -um *adj.* stormy, tempestuous

prōcērē *adv.* to a great length, far

procerēs, -um *m.pl.* leading men, nobles

prōcēritās, -ātis *f.* length; height, tallness

prōcērus, -a, -um *adj.* long, tall; high, lofty

prōcessus, -ūs *m.* progress, progression, advance

procī, -ōrum *m.pl.* important class of citizens (*in Servian constitution*)

prōcidō, -ī 3. to fall down flat, fall forward

prōciduus, -a, -um *adj.* fallen down

prōcinctus, -ūs *m.* readiness for battle

prōclāmō 1. to cry out, exclaim; (+*acc.* +*inf.*) proclaim (that)

prōclīnō 1. to incline *or* bend forwards

prōclīve, -is *n.* downward slope

prōclīvī (-e) *adv.* downhill, downwards; easily

prōclīvis, -is, -e *adj.* inclining forwards, sloping down, steep; easy; (+*ad* +*acc.*) prone *or* liable to

prōclīvitās, -ātis *f.* descent, downward slope; inclination, tendency

prōclīviter *adv.* easily, ready

procō 1. to ask, demand, flatter, woo

prōconsul, -lis *m.* proconsul, official with consular authority

prōconsulāris, -is, -e *adj.* proconsular

prōconsulātus, -ūs *m.* office of proconsul, proconsulship

prōcrastinātiō, -ōnis *f.* delaying, putting off from day to day, procrastination

prōcrastinō 1. to put off from day to day, procrastinate, defer, delay

prōcreātiō, -ōnis *f.* begetting, procreation, generation

prōcreātor, -ōris *m.* begetter, parent, creator

prōcreātrix, -īcis *f.* mother

prōcreō 1. to beget, procreate, propagate, generate, produce

prōcrescō 3. to grow up; be produced

prōcubō 1. to lie outstretched, spread over

prōcūdō 3. to hammer *or* beat out, forge, fashion; produce

procul *adv.* far, far off, at *or* from a distance, a great way off; **procul dubiō** without doubt

prōculcātiō, -ōnis *f.* treading *or* trampling on

prōculcō 1. to tread down, trample on

prōcumbō, -cubuī, -cubitum 3. to lean forward, bend towards; lie down *or* along; fall down, sink, go to ruin; prostrate oneself

prōcūrātiō, -ōnis *f.* administration, management, government; office; expiation

prōcūrātiuncula, -ae *f.* small administrative position

prōcūrātor (pro-), -ōris *m.* superintendent, agent, manager, administrator; procurator, governor

prōcūrātrix, -īcis *f.* governess, protectress

prōcūrō (pro-) 1. to take care of, see to, look after; expiate

prōcurrō, -(cu)currī, -cursum 3. to run forward, sally forth; project

prōcursātiō, -ōnis *f.* running forward, sallying forth, skirmishing

prōcursātor, -ōris *m.* skirmisher

prōcursō 1. to run forward, sally forth, skirmish

prōcursus, -ūs *m.* running forward, sallying forth, skirmishing

prōcurvō 1. to bend down, make to stoop

prōcurvus, -a, -um *adj.* curved, crooked

procus, -ī *m.* suitor, wooer

prōdeambulō 1. to go out on a walk

prōdeō, -īre , -iī, -itum 4. to go *or* come forward, advance, proceed; go *or* come out, go outside, appear; stand out, project; spring *or* grow up

prōdīcō, -dixī, -dictum 3. to put off, adjourn; fix, set

prōdigē *adv.* lavishly, extravagantly

prōdigentia, -ae *f.* wastefulness, extravagance

prōdigiālis, -is, -e *adj.* of *or* belonging to prodigies, prodigious

prōdigiāliter *adv.* strangely, monstrously, portentously

prōdigiōsus, -a, -um *adj.* monstrous, marvellous, miraculous, prodigious, portentous

prōdigium, -(i)ī *n.* prodigy, portent, omen; marvel, wonder; monster

prōdigō, -ēgī 3. to consume, waste, lavish, squander

prōdigus, -a, -um *adj.* lavish, extravagant, wasteful, prodigal

prōditiō, -ōnis *f.* treachery, betrayal, treason

prōditor, -ōris *m.* traitor, betrayer

prōdō, -idī, -itum 3. to put forth, produce; declare, disclose, show; betray, forsake; make, elect, appoint; record, hand down, transmit, relate; publish, assert; prolong, delay, put off

prōdoceō 2. to teach openly

prodromus, -ī *m.* forerunner, harbinger

prōdūcō, -duxī, -ductum 3. to bring forward, bring out; bring forward, introduce, make to appear; induce, prevail upon; produce, beget, rear; advance, promote; disclose, reveal; draw out, lengthen, prolong, protract; put off, postpone

prōducta, -ōrum *n.pl.* things to be preferred (*in Stoic thought*)

prōductē *adv.* at length

prōductiō, -ōnis *f.* lengthening, prolonging

prōductō 1. to lengthen, prolong

prōductus, -a, -um *adj.* lengthened, prolonged, drawn out

proēgmena see **prōducta**

proeliāris, -is, -e *adj.* of *or* belonging to battle

proeliātor, -ōris *m.* fighter, warrior, combatant

proelior 1. *dep.* to fight, join battle

proelium, -(i)ī *n.* fight, battle, combat, conflict; *n.pl.sbst.* fighters, warriors

profānō 1. to defile, desecrate, pollute, profane

profānus, -a, -um *adj.* profane, not sacred, secular; uninitiated; impious, irreligious

profātus, -ūs *m.* speaking aloud, pronouncing

profectiō, -ōnis *f.* setting out, departure, journey; source

profectō *adv.* certainly, truly, indeed

prōfectus, -ūs *m.* progress, advancement, profit

prōferō, -ferre, -tulī, -lātum *v.irreg.* to carry *or* bring out; advance, bring forward; show, display, reveal; put forth, produce; publish, display, make known; cite, quote, mention; put off, defer, prolong; enlarge, widen, extend

professiō, -ōnis *f.* declaration, profession, deposition, acknowledgement; occupation

professor, -ōris *m.* professor, public teacher

professōrius, -a, -um *adj.* of *or* belonging to a public teacher

professus, -a, -um *adj.* declared openly, acknowledged; **ex professō** openly, expressly

profestus, -a, -um *adj.* not holy, ordinary

prōficiō, -fēcī, -fectum 3. to make progress, gain ground, profit; be of use, help

proficiscor, -fectus 3. *dep.* or **proficiscō** 3. to set out, depart, proceed; (+*ab/ex* +*abl.*) spring *or* arise from

profiteor, -fessus 2. *dep.* to declare openly, acknowledge, avow, profess; make a return of; enrol, register; promise, volunteer

prōflātus, -ūs *m.* snoring, blast of air

prōflīgātor, -ōris *m.* spendthrift

prōflīgātus, -a, -um *adj.* ruined, abandoned, profligate, corrupt

prōflīgō 1. to throw to the ground, cast down; overwhelm, destroy, ruin; bring almost to an end

prōflō 1. to blow, breathe out

prōfluens, -ntis *adj.* flowing, running; fluent; *f.sbst.* stream, running water

prōfluenter *adv.* flowingly, fluently

prōfluentia, -ae *f.* fluency

prōfluō, -uxī 3. to flow *or* gush out, flow, run; rise, spring from; proceed

prōfluvium, -(i)ī *n.* flowing, gushing

profor 1. *dep.* to speak, speak out; foretell, predict

prōfringō, -frēgī, -fractum 3. to cleave, break up

profugiō, -fūgī 3. to flee, run away, escape, run for help; flee from

profugus, -a, -um *adj.* fleeing, fugitive, exiled; *m/f.sbst.* exile, fugitive, runaway

profundō, -fūdī, -fūsum 3. to pour out *or* forth, shed copiously; spend, lavish, squander; utter; stretch out, prostrate; bring forth, produce

profundum, -ī *n.* depth, profundity; sea, the deep

profundus, -a, -um *adj.* deep, profound; bottomless, boundless; high, lofty

profūsē *adv.* lavishly, extravagantly; riotously

profūsiō, -ōnis *f.* extravagance, wastefulness, profusion

profūsus, -a, -um *adj.* immoderate, excessive, profuse; extravagant, lavish, expensive, wasteful

prōgener, -erī *m.* granddaughter's husband

prōgenerō 1. to beget, produce

prōgeniēs, -ēī *f.* offspring, progeny; descent, lineage, race

prōgenitor, -ōris *m.* ancestor, progenitor

prōgignō, -genuī, -genitum 3. to beget, engender, produce, bring forth

prōgnāriter *adv.* with confidence, expertly

prōgnātus, -a, -um *adj.* (+*ab/ex* +*abl.*) born, descended (from); *m.sbst.* son, child

prognostica, -ōrum *n.pl.* weather signs

prōgredior, -ssus 3. *dep.* to advance, proceed, go forward *or* out

prōgressiō, -ōnis *f.* or **prōgressus, -ūs** *m.* going forward, progress, advancement

progymnastēs, -ae *m.* gymnastics instructor

prohibeō 2. to keep off *or* away; stop, avert, prevent, prohibit; preserve, defend, protect

prohibitiō, -ōnis *f.* prohibition

prōiciō, -iēcī, -iectum 3. to throw *or* fling

forth; throw away, abandon, give up; drive out, eject, expel; pour forth, shed; put or stretch out, extend; *pass.* rush forward

prōiectīcius, -a, -um *adj.* exposed, abandoned

prōiectiō, -ōnis *f.* projection, throwing forth

prōiectus¹, -a, -um *adj.* standing out, jutting, prominent, projecting; excessive, immoderate; abject, despicable, contemptible

prōiectus², -ūs *m.* extent

proin *adv.* accordingly, so then

proinde *adv.* therefore, for that reason; just so, equally; (+*ac/ut/quam*) just as; (+*quasi/ac si*) just as if

prōlābor, -lapsus 3. *dep.* to glide, slip or fall forward; slip, lapse (into); go forward, go on; escape; sink, decline, go to ruin

prōlapsiō, -ōnis *f.* slipping

prōlātiō, -ōnis *f.* bringing forward, mentioning; extending, enlarging; delaying

prōlātō 1. to enlarge, extend; defer, put off, postpone

prōlectō 1. to allure, entice

prōlēs, -is *f.* offspring, progeny; race; descendants; young men; fruit, berries

prōlētārius, -a, -um *adj.* of or relating to the lowest class; *m.sbst.* citizen of the lowest class

prōliciō 3. to allure, entice; induce, excite

prōlixē *adv.* at length; generously, willingly

prōlixus, -a, -um *adj.* long, big, large, extensive; liberal, generous; favourable

prologus, -ī *m.* preface, prologue, proem; speaker of prologue

prōloquor, -cūtus 3. *dep.* to speak out; utter, declare

prōlubium, -(i)ī *n.* whim, inclination, desire

prōlūdō, -sī, -sum 3. to practise, rehearse, serve as a prelude

prōluō, -uī, -ūtum 3. to wash away; wash out; wet, soak, drench

prōlūsiō, -ōnis *f.* prelude, rehearsal

prōluviēs, -ēī *f.* flood, inundation; discharge, excrement

prōmercālis, -is, -e *adj.* that is to be sold, for sale

prōmereō 2. to deserve, merit; win over, conciliate

prōmeritum, -ī *n.* favour, kindness, good turn; just deserts, merit; fault, bad turn

prōminens, -ntis *adj.* standing or jutting out, projecting, prominent

prōmineō 2. to stand or jut out, project; bend, lean or reach out

prōminulus, -a, -um *adj.* jutting out a little

prōmiscam or **prōmisc(u)ē** *adv.* in confusion, at random, without distinction; one with another

prōmisc(u)us, -a, -um *adj.* mingled, confused, indistinct; common, shared

prōmissiō, -ōnis *f.* promising, promise

prōmissor, -ōris *m.* promiser

prōmissum, -ī *n.* promise, pledge, guarantee

prōmittō, -mīsī, -missum 3. to send forward; let grow; promise, pledge, guarantee; give promise of; accept an invitation

prōmō, prompsī, promptum 3. to bring or draw out, bring forth, produce; bring to light, disclose

prōmontūrium see **prōmuntūrium**

prōmōta, -ōrum *n.pl.* things to be preferred (*in Stoic thought*)

prōmoveō, -mōvī, -mōtum 3. to move or push forwards, make to advance; extend, enlarge; promote, advance, prefer; put off, defer

promptārius, -a, -um *adj.* that stores things at hand; **promptāria cella** cellar, storeroom, repository

promptē *adv.* readily, promptly, easily

promptō 1. to bring forth, dispense regularly

promptus¹, -a, -um *adj.* at hand, ready, prepared; easy, practicable; active, ready, prompt, inclined; clear, open, evident, visible

promptus², -ūs *m.* making accessible; **in promptū** at hand, ready; open, obvious, before the eyes; easy

prōmulgātiō, -ōnis *f.* proclaiming, publishing, promulgation

prōmulgō 1. to proclaim, publish, promulgate, divulge

prōmulsis, -idis *f.* hors d'oeuvre, appetizer

prōmuntūrium, -(i)ī *n.* promontory, headland; ridge

prōmus, -ī *m.* steward, butler

prōmūtuus, -a, -um *adj.* paid in advance, loaned

prōnē *adv.* sloping, on a slant

prōnectō 3. to keep on knitting

pronepōs, -ōtis *m.* great-grandson

proneptis, -is *f.* great-granddaughter

pronoea, -ae *f.* providence

prōnuba, -ae *f.* matron of honour; bridal escort

prōnuntiātiō, -ōnis *f.* publication, proclamation, declaration

prōnuntiātor, -ōris *m.* relater

prōnuntiātum, -ī *n.* proposition, axiom

prōnuntiō 1. to pronounce, utter, speak; proclaim, announce; pass sentence, declare officially; nominate, appoint; recite, declaim, deliver; tell, report, relate

prōnūper *adv.* very recently

prōnurus, -ūs *f.* grandson's wife

prōnus, -a, -um *adj.* inclined, leaning *or* bending forward, stooping *or* looking downward; headlong, prone, face-down; sloping, sinking, setting; inclined, well-disposed, favourable; easy, practicable

pro(h)oemium, -(i)ī *n.* preface, introduction, proem, prelude

prooemior 1. *dep.* to begin a speech

propāgātiō, -ōnis *f.* propagation; extension, enlargement

propāgātor, -ōris *m.* extender, enlarger

propāgō¹ (prō-), -inis *f.* layer, slip, shoot; race, stock, offspring, lineage, descent

propāgō² (prō-) 1. to propagate by layers; extend, enlarge; prolong, preserve, maintain

prōpalam *adv.* openly, in public

prōpatulus, -a, -um *adj.* open, uncovered; **in prōpatulō** in the open, in open view, publicly

prope¹ *adv.* near, near by; nearly, almost

prope² *prep.* (+*acc.*) near, close to, not far from

propediem *adv.* in a short time, presently, very soon

prōpellō, -pulī, -pulsum 3. to drive forwards, propel; drive away, keep off, repel; impel, move

propemodum (-o) *adv.* almost, just about

prōpendeō, -dī, -sum 2. to hang down; preponderate; be inclined, have a propensity

prōpensē *adv.* readily, willingly

prōpensiō, -ōnis *f.* inclination, readiness

prōpensus, -a, -um *adj.* hanging down, weighed down; inclined, (well-)disposed, ready, eager

properanter *adv.* quickly, hastily, speedily

properantia, -ae *or* **properātiō, -ōnis** *f.* haste, hurry, speed

properātō *adv.* hastily, speedily

properē *adv.* quickly, hastily, speedily

properipēs, -edis *adj.* swift-footed

properō 1. to make haste, be quick, hurry

properus, -a, -um *adj.* quick, hasty, speedy

prōpexus, -a, -um *adj.* combed *or* hanging down

propin *n.* preprandial drink, apéritif

propīnātiō, -ōnis *f.* drinking to one's health

propīnō 1. to drink one's health, drink to one

propinquē *adv.* at hand, close by

propinquitās, -ātis *f.* nearness, proximity; relationship by blood

propinquō 1. to draw near, approach; hasten; bring near

propinquus, -a, -um *adj.* near, at hand, neighbouring; like, similar, resembling; *m./f.sbst.* relation, kinsman

propior, -or, -us *compar.adj.* nearer, closer; more closely akin; more like; more recent; of closer concern; more intimate

propitiō 1. to propitiate, appease, soothe

propitius, -a, -um *adj.* propitious, favourable, well-disposed

propnigēon, -ī *n.* hot room in bathhouse

prōpōla, -ae *m.* retailer

prōpōnō, -posuī, -positum 3. to set out *or* expose to view, set forth *or* display; proclaim, publish; imagine; tell, explain, relate, point out; state the first premise; determine, appoint, fix; purpose, intend, resolve; propose, suggest, offer, hold out

prōporrō *adv.* moreover, still further; altogether, entirely

prōportiō, -ōnis *f.* proportion, analogy

prōpositiō, -ōnis *f.* displaying, showing; proposal, design, subject, thesis; first proposition of syllogism

prōpositum, -ī *n.* purpose, intention, resolution, design; theme, subject; first proposition of syllogism

prōpraetor, -ōris *m.* propraetor, governor of province (with authority of praetor)

propriē *adv.* as one's own, privately; particularly, in particular; properly, suitably, rightly, correctly

proprietās, -ātis *f.* specific quality *or* nature of a thing, property; ownership

proprītim *adv.* properly, peculiarly

proprius, -a, -um *adj.* one's own, private, personal, particular, special, proper; firm, steady, lasting, permanent

propter[1] *prep.* (+*acc.*) near, close to; on account of, because of

propter[2] *adv.* near, close by

propterā *adv.* therefore, for that reason, on that account

propudiōsus, -a, -um *adj.* shameful, disgraceful, base

propudium, -(i)ī *n.* shameful action; shameful *or* base person

prōpugnāculum, -ī *n.* fort, rampart, bastion, bulwark; defence, protection; grounds of defence

prōpugnātiō, -ōnis *f.* defence, defensive fighting

prōpugnātor, -ōris *m.* defender, champion

prōpugnō 1. to fight in defence of, fight for, defend

prōpulsātiō, -ōnis *f.* keeping *or* warding off

prōpulsō 1. to drive away *or* back, repel, keep *or* ward off

propylaea *n.pl.* gateway to Athenian Acropolis

prōquaestor, -ōris *m.* proquaestor, one invested with power of quaestor

prōquam *adv.* accordingly as, just as

prōra, -ae *f.* prow; ship

prōrēpō, -repsī, -reptum 3. to creep *or* crawl forward; come forward gradually

prōrēta, -ae *or* **prōreus, -eī** *m.* look-out (stationed at prow of ship)

prōripiō, -ripuī, -reptum 3. to snatch away, drag out, take away by force; *refl.* hurry away, rush out

prōrītō 1. to provoke, incite

prōrogātiō, -ōnis *f.* putting off, deferring, adjournment; prolongation

prōrogō 1. to put off, defer, adjourn; prolong

prorsum (-us) *adv.* straight ahead, for-

ward; altogether, entirely; in a word, in short

prōrumpō, -rūpī, -ruptum 3. to burst *or* break forth, break out; send forth

prōruō, -uī, -utum 3. to rush forth; throw *or* pull down, demolish; fall down, collapse

prōsāpia, -ae *f.* race, lineage, stock, family

proscaenium (-scēn-), -(i)ī *n.* stage

proscindō, -scidī, -scissum 3. to split, cut; plough; revile, taunt

proscrībō, -scripsī, -scriptum 3. to post up in writing, advertise; confiscate (*one's property*), proscribe, outlaw

proscriptiō, -ōnis *f.* advertisement of sale; proscription

proscripturiō 4. to desire *or* long to proscribe

proscriptus, -ī *m.* proscribed person, outlaw

prōsecō, -uī, -tum 1. to cut off; plough up

prōsecta, -ōrum *n.pl.* entrails prepared for sacrifice

prōseda, -ae *f.* prostitute

prōsēminō 1. to sow, scatter about, propagate

prōsentiō, -sī 4. to perceive beforehand, foresee

prōsequor, -cūtus 3. *dep.* to follow, accompany, escort, attend; pursue, chase, attack; speak further, continue; honour

prōserō[1]**, -sēvī, -satum** 3. to sow, produce

prōserō[2] 3. to extend, stick out

prōserpō 3. to creep forward, crawl along

proseucha, -ae *f.* synagogue, Jewish place of prayer

prōsiliō, -uī *or* **-īvī** 4. to leap *or* jump forward, spring forth

prōsocer, -erī *m.* wife's grandfather

prospectō 1. to view, gaze upon, behold; look towards; look out for, expect

prospectus, -ūs *m.* view, prospect, sight

prospeculor 1. *dep.* to view, gaze upon; seek out; look out for, await

prosperē *adv.* fortunately, successfully, luckily, prosperously

prosperitās, -ātis *f.* prosperity, good fortune

prosperō 1. to make prosperous, make happy *or* successful

prosperus, -a, -um *adj.* favourable, prosperous; happy, successful, lucky, fortunate

prospicientia, -ae *f.* forethought, prospection

prospiciō, -spexī, -spectum 3. to look forward, look out, watch; command a view *or* prospect of; look to, see to, take care of; (+*dat.*) provide (for), supply, procure; perceive beforehand, foresee

prosternō, -strāvī, -strātum 3. to strike down, throw to the ground, prostrate; defeat, overthrow, ruin

prostibilis, -is *f.* or **prostibulum, -ī** *n.* prostitute

prostituō, -uī, -ūtum 3. to prostitute

prostitūta, -ae *f.* prostitute

prostō, -itī, -itum 1. to be exposed for sale; prostitute onself; project

prōsubigō 3. to dig up; hammer, beat

prōsum¹, -desse, -fuī *v.irreg.* to be useful *or* helpful, advantageous

prōsum² (-us) *adv.* see **prōrsum (-us)**

prōtegō, -xī, -ctum 3. to cover, shelter; hide, conceal; defend, guard, screen, protect

prōtēlō 1. to drive *or* chase away, drive back

prōtēlum, -ī *n.* team of yoked oxen; succession

prōtendō, -dī, -tum 3. to stretch out, hold out, extend

prōterō, -trīvī, -trītum 3. to tread underfoot, trample upon, crush; wear away

prōterreō 2. to frighten, scare *or* chase away

protervē (prō-) *adv.* insolently, impudently; with confidence, boldly

protervitās (prō-), -ātis *f.* insolence, impudence; boldness

protervus (prō-), -a, -um *adj.* insolent, impudent; wayward, untoward, bold; violent

prothymē *adv.* willingly, cheerfully

prothymia, -ae *f.* goodwill, kindness

prōtinus (-tenus) or **protinam** *adv.* forward, further on; immediately, directly; without pause *or* interruption

prōtollō 3. to stretch out, put forward; put off, defer, prolong

prōtopraxia, -ae *f.* priority (over other creditors) in the collection of debts

prōtotomī, -ōrum *m.pl.* first-cuttings, sprouts, early greens

prōtrahō, -xī, -ctum 3. to drag *or* draw out, bring forward; reveal, bring to light; draw out, defer, prolong; compel, induce

prōtrūdō, -sī, -sum 3. to thrust forward, propel, protrude; put off, defer

prōturbō 1. to push off, drive away, repel, send forth

prout *conj.* according as, even as, just as

prōvectus, -a, -um *adj.* advanced

prōvehō, -xī, -ctum 3. to carry forth *or* forward; advance, promote; *pass.* drive, sail *or* ride on

prōveniō, -vēnī, -ventum 4. to come forth, come out, appear; spring up, grow; thrive, prosper; turn out (well *or* badly)

prōventus, -ūs *m.* growth, increase, produce; result, success

prōverbium, -(i)ī *n.* proverb, adage, saying

prōvidens, -ntis *adj.* provident, wise, prudent, careful

prōvidenter *adv.* wisely, prudently, with foresight

prōvidentia, -ae *f.* foresight, forethought, providence

prōvideō, -vīdī, -vīsum 2. to look ahead, see at a distance; foresee; provide *or* guard against; see to, look after; provide, supply

prōvidus, -a, -um *adj.* foreseeing, provident; prudent, careful, considerate

prōvincia, -ae *f.* province, governorship of province; sphere of duty, employment

prōvinciālis, -is, -e *adj.* of *or* belonging to a province, provincial; *m.sbst.* inhabitant of province, provincial

prōvinciātim *adv.* province by province, through the provinces

prōvīsiō, -ōnis *f.* foreseeing, forecasting, foresight; (+*gen.*) provision *or* providing (for)

prōvīsō 3. to come *or* go forth to see, be on the look-out for

prōvīsor, -ōris *m.* foreseer, provider

prōvīsus, -ūs *m.* foreseeing, foresight; (+*gen.*) provision *or* providing (for)

prōvīvō, -vixī 3. to survive, live on

prōvocātiō, -ōnis *f.* challenge; appeal

prōvocātor, -ōris *m.* challenger; type of gladiator

prōvocō 1. to call forth *or* out; provoke, stir up, challenge; appeal

prōvolō 1. to fly out; run *or* rush forward

prōvolvō, -vī, -ūtum 3. to roll *or* tumble forwards, roll along; *refl./pass.* prostrate oneself; *pass.* descend to, be ruined

prōvomō 3. to vomit forth

prōvorsus, -a, -um *adj.* straightforward, direct

prōvulgō 1. to make public, divulge, publish

prox *onomatopoeic* sound of breaking wind

proxenēta, -ae *m.* broker, agent

proximē *superl.adv.* most nearly; by the nearest way; most recently; *prep.* (+*acc.*) nearest to, closest to

proximitās, -ātis *f.* closeness, proximity

proximus, -a, -um *superl.adj.* nearest, closest; most recent; readiest; *m.sbst.* close friend *or* relative; *n.sbst.* close neighbourhood, vicinity

prūdens, -ntis *adj.* possessing foresight, prudent; (+*gen.*) aware (of), foreseeing; clever (in), skilled (in); *m.sbst.* (+*gen.*) expert (in)

prūdenter *adv.* prudently, cautiously; wisely

prūdentia, -ae *f.* providence, foreknowledge; wisdom; proficiency

pruīna, -ae *f.* frost, hoar-frost

pruīnōsus, -a, -um *adj.* frosty, covered with hoar-frost

prūna, -ae *f.* burning *or* live coal

prūniceus, -a, -um *adj.* made of plum-tree wood

prūnum, -ī *n.* plum

prūnus, -ī *f.* plum tree

prūrīgō, -inis *f.* itching, itch; sexual urge

prūriō 4. to itch; feel (sexual) urge

prytanēum, -ēī *n.* town-hall

prytanis, -is *m.* Greek magistrate, prytanis

psallō, -ī 3. to play on a stringed musical instrument

psaltērium, -(i)ī *n.* kind of harp

psaltria, -ae *f.* female player of stringed musical instrument

psellus, -a, -um *adj.* faltering in speech

psēphisma, -atis *n.* decree, resolution

pseudomenos, -ī *m.* conundrum of logic

pseudothyrum, -ī *n.* postern-gate, hidden door

psīlocitharista, -ae *m.* one who plays stringed instrument without singing

psīlothrum, -ī *n.* hair-removing cream

psithius, -a, -um *adj.* psithian (*referring to a type of sweet-grape vine*)

psittacus, -ī *m.* parrot

psȳchomantīum, -ī *n.* place where spirits are raised from the dead

psȳchrolūtēs, -ae *m.* one who bathes in cold water

pūbens, -ntis *adj.* full-grown, in full vigour, exuberant

pūbertās, -ātis *f.* puberty, growth of body hair; maturity

pūbēs¹, -is *f.* puberty, growth of body hair; private parts; youth, men; nation

pūbēs², -eris *adj.* grown-up, mature; downy; *m.pl.sbst.* grown-ups, adult population

pūbescō 3. to reach puberty, grow body hair; become mature

pūblica, -ae *f.* prostitute

pūblicāna, -ae *f.* tax-farmer

pūblicānus, -a, -um *adj.* of *or* relating to the farming of public taxes; *m.sbst.* tax-farmer

pūblicātiō, -ōnis *f.* confiscation

pūblicē or **pūblicitus** *adv.* publicly, by public authority, in the name of the public; at public expense; in the public interest; as one body

pūblicō 1. to confiscate, make public property; make public; prostitute

pūblicum, -ī *n.* public property, public revenues; public place; **in pūblicum/in pūblicō** publicly

pūblicus, -a, -um *adj.* public, belonging to the public, common; universal, general; **rēs pūblica** republic, state

pudendus, -a, -um *adj.* to be ashamed of, shameful, disgraceful

pudens, -ntis *adj.* modest, shamefaced, bashful

pudenter *adv.* modestly, bashfully

pudeō 2. to be ashamed; shame; *impers.* **mē pudet** (+*gen.*) it shames me, I am ashamed of

pudibundus, -a, -um *adj.* shamefaced, bashful, modest

pudīcē *adv.* chastely, modestly, virtuously

pudīcitia, -ae *f.* chastity, modesty, virtue

pudīcus, -a, -um *adj.* chaste, modest, virtuous

pudor, -ōris *m.* sense of shame, bashfulness, modesty, chastity; shame, disgrace; self-respect

puella, -ae *f.* girl; daughter; young woman *or* wife, maiden; mistress, sweetheart

puellāris, -is, -e *adj.* of *or* belonging to a girl, like a girl, girlish

puellāriter *adv.* like a girl

puellula, -ae *f.* little girl

puellus, -ī *m.* little boy

puer, -rī *m.* boy, child; son; servant, slave; young male sex object

puera, -ae *f.* girl

puerascō 3. to grow up to be a boy

puerculus, -ī *m.* little son

puerīlis, -is, -e *adj.* of a boy *or* child, boyish, childish, puerile

puerīlitās, -ātis *f.* boyishness, childishness, puerility

puerīliter *adv.* like a boy, boyishly, childishly

puer(i)tia, -ae *f.* boyhood, childhood

puerpera, -ae *f.* woman in labour

puerperium, -(i)ī *n.* childbirth, delivery

puerperus, -a, -um *adj.* that helps labour

puerulus, -ī *m.* little boy *or* child

pūga, -ae *f.* buttocks

pugil, -ilis *m.* boxer, pugilist

pugilātōrius, -a, -um *adj.* of *or* belonging to a boxer; **follis pugilātōrius** punch bag

pugilātus, -ūs *m.* boxing

pugilicē *adv.* like a boxer

pugillārēs, -ium *m.pl.* or **-ia, -ium** *n.pl.* small (hand-held) wax tablets

pūgiō, -ōnis *m.* dagger, poniard, stiletto

pūgiunculus, -ī *m.* small dagger

pugna, -ae *f.* fight, battle, combat, engagement, contest

pugnācitās, -ātis *f.* eagerness *or* inclination to fight, pugnacity, quarrelsomeness

pugnāciter *adv.* aggressively, violently; argumentatively, obstinately

pugnāculum, -ī *n.* fortress, bulwark

pugnātor, -ōris *m.* fighter, combatant

pugnātōrius, -a, -um *adj.* used in fighting, suitable to fight with

pugnax, -ācis *adj.* fond of fighting, pugnacious, aggressive, ferocious; argumentative, obstinate

pugneus, -a, -um *adj.* of the fist

pugnō 1. to fight, combat; struggle, contend, clash, oppose, be at variance with

pugnus, -ī *m.* fist

pulchellus, -a, -um *adj.* pretty, gorgeous little

pulc(h)er, -c(h)ra, -c(h)rum *adj.* beautiful, handsome, attractive, lovely; excellent, glorious, illustrious; honourable, noble

pulc(h)rē *adv.* beautifully, attractively; excellently, neatly, finely; well, very well; well done!, excellent!

pulc(h)ritūdō, -inis *f.* beauty, attractiveness; excellence

pūlēium, -ī *n.* pennyroyal (pungent-smelling herb with medicinal properties)

pūlex, -icis *m.* flea

pullārius, -(i)ī *m.* feeder of prophetic chickens

pullātus, -a, -um *adj.* wearing dark clothes (*in mourning*); wearing grubby clothes

pullulō 1. to spring *or* sprout up, germinate, grow, increase

pullus¹, -ī *m.* young animal; chicken, pullet; shoot, sprout

pullus², -a, -um *adj.* dark, dusky, blackish; *n.sbst.* dark clothing

pulmentārium, -(i)ī *n.* relish; food

pulmentum, -ī *n.* food

pulmō, -ōnis *m.* lungs

pulmōneus, -a, -um *adj.* of *or* relating to the lungs

pulpa, -ae *f.* flesh; desire of the flesh

pulpāmentum, -ī *n.* slice *or* cut of meat, tit-bit

pulpitum, -ī *n.* stage, raised floor

puls, pultis *f.* thick gruel, pottage

pulsātiō, -ōnis *f.* knocking, beating, pulsation

pulsō 1. to beat repeatedly, strike, knock at, batter; drive forward, impel

pulsus, -ūs *m.* beating, striking; impelling, impulse

pultātiō, -ōnis *f.* beating, knocking

pultiphagus, -ī *m.* pottage-eater

pultō 1. to beat, strike, knock at

pulvereus, -a, -um *adj.* full of dust; dusty, dust-like

pulverulentus, -a, -um *adj.* full of dust, dusty

pulvillus, -ī *m.* small cushion *or* pillow

pulvīnar, -āris *n.* couch with cushions (*reserved for cult statues or dignitaries*); prop for beached ships

pulvīnus, -ī *m.* cushion, pillow

pulvis, -eris *m./f.* dust, powder, ash; arena, place of exercise, field of battle; effort, labour

pulvisculus, -ī *m.* fine dust *or* powder

pūmex, -icis *m.* pumice-stone; soft stone

pūmiceus, -a, -um *adj.* of pumice-stone

pūmicō 1. to polish *or* smooth with pumice stone

pūmiliō, -ōnis or **-ius, -iī** *m./f.* dwarf

pūmilus, -a, -um *adj.* dwarf; *m.sbst.* dwarf

punctim *adv.* with the point of a weapon

punctiuncula, -ae *f.* slight pricking *or* puncture

punctum, -ī *n.* point, prick, puncture; dot, spot; vote; moment, instant; short section

pungō, pupugī (pep-), punctum 3. to prick, puncture; sting; penetrate, pass through; trouble, vex, afflict; goad

pūniceus, -a, -um *adj.* bright red, crimson, purple

pūniō 4. or **pūnior** 4. *dep.* to punish; avenge

pūnītiō, -ōnis *f.* punishment

pūnītor, -ōris *m.* punisher; avenger

pūpa, -ae *f.* young girl; puppet, doll

pūpilla, -ae *f.* young girl; orphan, ward; pupil (of the eye)

pūpillāris, -is, -e *adj.* of *or* belonging to an orphan *or* ward

pūpillus, -ī *m.* orphan, ward

puppis, -is *f.* ship's stern, poop; ship, vessel

pūpula, -ae *f.* pupil (of the eye); eye

pūpulus, -ī *m.* little boy

pūpus, -ī *m.* boy, child

pūrē *adv.* purely, chastely; cleanly, neatly; clearly, plainly

purgāmen, -inis or **purgāmentum, -ī** *n.* filth, dirt, sweepings; means of expiation *or* atonement

purgātiō, -ōnis *f.* scouring, cleansing, purging; excuse, justification

purgō (pūrigō) 1. to make clean, cleanse, purify, purge, clear away; expiate, atone; excuse, justify

pūrificātiō, -ōnis *f.* making clean, purification, expiation

pūrificō 1. to purify, make clean, cleanse, purge; expiate

pūriter *adv.* purely, cleanly

purpura, -ae *f.* purple; purple dye; purple cloth *or* garment (*sign of high rank, mark of royalty etc.*)

purpurascō 3. to become purple

purpurātus, -a, -um *adj.* clothed in purple; *m.sbst.* nobleman, courtier

purpureus, -a, -um *adj.* of purple, purple-coloured, clothed in purple; glowing, shining, bright

purpurissātus, -a, -um *adj.* rouged, painted purple

purpurissum, -ī *n.* purple cosmetic paint, rouge

pūrulentus, -a, -um *adj.* full of pus, purulent

pūrus, -a, -um *adj.* pure, clean, unstained, spotless, chaste; neat, plain, natural, unadorned; unconditional, absolute, entire, complete

pūs, pūris *n.* pus, discharge from sore

pusillus, -a, -um *adj.* very little *or* small, tiny, puny, petty

pūsiō, -ōnis *m.* little boy

pūs(s)ula (pust-), -ae *f.* blister, pustule, pimple

pūsulātus (pust-), -a, -um *adj.* pimpled; refined, purified

putāmen, -inis *n.* husk, shell, covering

putātiō, -ōnis *f.* pruning

putātor, -ōris *m.* pruner

puteal, -ālis *n.* covered structure surrounding well *or* pit

puteālis, -is, -e *adj.* of a well *or* pit

pūteō 2. to stink, have a very bad smell

pūtescō (pūtiscō) 3. to grow rotten, rank *or* fetid, putrefy, stink

puteus, -ī *m.* well; pit

pūtidē *adv.* affectedly, disagreeably, sickeningly

pūtid(iusc)ulus, -a, -um *adj.* rather affected, disgusting *or* sickening

pūtidus, -a, -um *adj.* rotten, putrid, stinking, fetid, foul; affected, tiresome, disagreeable

putillus, -ī *m.* little boy, child

putō 1. to lop, prune; think, suppose,

imagine, believe; reckon, estimate, consider; settle

pūtor, -ōris *m.* stench, fetid smell, stink

putrefaciō (putrēf-), -fēcī, -factum 3. to make rotten, putrefy; disintegrate

putrescō 3. to go rotten, rot, putrefy; disintegrate

putridus, -a, -um *adj.* rotten, putrid, decaying

putris, -is, -e *adj.* rotten, decaying, putrid, fetid, nauseous; disintegrating, crumbling; soft, flabby; languishing

putus, -a, -um *adj.* pure, genuine

pycta (-ēs), -ae *m.* boxer, pugilist

pyelus, -ī *m.* bath

pȳgargus, -ī *m.* kind of antelope

pyra, -ae *f.* funeral pile, pyre

pȳramis, -idis *f.* pyramid

pyrethrum, -ī *n.* medicinal herb

pyrōpus, -ī *m.* gold-bronze; ruby

pyrr(h)ica, -ae *f.* dance in armour

pȳthaulēs, -ae *m.* player of reed instrument

pȳtisma, -atis *n.* wine spat out after tasting

pȳtissō 1. to spit out

pyxis, -idis *f.* small box, casket

Q

quā *adv.* by which route?; how?; (*rel.*) in which, where

quācumque *adv.* by whatever way; wherever; however

quādam ... tenus *adv.* to a certain extent

quadra, -ae *f.* quadrant segment, quarter slice

quadrāgēnārius, -a, -um *adj.* forty years old

quadrāgēnī, -ae, -a *pl.adj.* forty each; forty at a time

quadrāgēsimus (-ens-), -a, -um *adj.* fortieth

quadrāgiens (-ēs) *adv.* forty times

quadrāgintā *indecl.adj.* forty

quadrans, -ntis *m.* quarter; coin worth a quarter of an *as*; quarter of a Roman pound; quarter of a *sextarius*

quadrantal, -ālis *n.* liquid measure the size of a cubic Roman foot

quadrantārius, -a, -um *adj.* of a quarter; costing a quarter of an *as*

quadrātum, -ī *n.* square; cube

quadrātus, -a, -um *adj.* squared, square; cubic; stocky, well-built

quadrīduum, -ī *n.* period of four days

quadriennium, -(i)ī *n.* period of four years

quadrifāriam *adv.* fourfold, in four ways

quadrifidus, -a, -um *adj.* in four parts

quadrīga, -ae *f.* four-horse chariot; team of four chariot-horses

quadrīgārius, -a, -um *adj.* of *or* relating to chariot-racing; *m.sbst.* charioteer

quadrīgātus, -a, -um *adj.* bearing the stamp of a four-horse chariot

quadrīgula, -ae *f.* small four-horse chariot

quadriiugus, -a, -um or **-is, -is, -e** *adj.* yoked four abreast; drawn by four horses; involving four-horse chariots; *m.pl.sbst.* team of four chariot horses

quadrilībris, -is, -e *adj.* containing four pounds' weight

quadrimenstris, -is, -e *adj.* lasting four months

quadrīmulus, -a, -um *adj.* (only) four years old

quadrīmus, -a, -um *adj.* four years old

quadringēnārius, -a, -um *adj.* consisting of four hundred men

quadringēnī, -ae, -a *pl.adj.* four hundred each

quadringentēsimus (-ens-), -a, -um *adj.* four hundredth

quadri(n)gentī, -ae, -a *pl.adj.* four hundred; *n.sbst.* 400,000 sesterces

quadri(n)gentiens (-ēs) *adv.* four hundred times

quadripedans, -ntis *adj.* moving like a galloping horse; *m.pl.sbst.* horses

quadripertītō *adv.* in four parts

quadripertītus, -a, -um *adj.* divided into four, quadripartite

quadripēs, -pedis *adj.* four-legged; going on all fours; *m./f.sbst.* quadruped; horse

quadrirēmis, -is *f.* galley with teams of four rowers

quadrivium, -(i)ī *n.* meeting place of four roads, crossroads

quadrō 1. to make square; quadruple; form a square; (+*ad/in* +*acc.*) fit in (with)

quadrum, -ī *n.* square

quadrupedans see **quadripedans**

quadrupedus, -a, -um *adj.* of *or* relating to galloping

quadrupēs see **quadripēs**

quadruplātor, -ōris *m.* bringer of a criminal investigation

quadruplex, -icis *adj.* fourfold, quadruple

quadruplicō 1. to quadruple

quadruplum, -ī *n.* four times as much
quadruplus, -a, -um *adj.* four times as much *or* many
quadrupulor 1. *dep.* to bring forward a criminal investigation
quaeritō 1. to seek earnestly; ask repeatedly
quaerō, -sīvī (-siī), -sītum 3. to seek, look for; inquire about; investigate; obtain, procure
quaesītiō, -ōnis *f.* search
quaesītor, -ōris *m.* criminal investigator, examining magistrate; (+*gen.*) searcher (for)
quaesītus, -a, -um *adj.* contrived, deliberate; elaborate
quaesō 3. to pray for, ask for; search; **quaesō** please, I ask
quaesticulus, -ī *m.* minor profit
quaestiō, -ōnis *f.* search; inquiry; interrogation; dispute; question, topic
quaestiuncula, -ae *f.* petty problem, trifling puzzle
quaestor, -ōris *m.* quaestor; financial officer
quaestōrium, -(i)ī *n.* headquarters of a quaestor
quaestōrius, -a, -um *adj.* of *or* relating to a quaestor; holding quaestorian rank
quaestuōsus, -a, -um *adj.* profitable, advantageous; financially successful
quaestūra, -ae *f.* office of quaestor, quaestorship
quaestus, -ūs *m.* gain, profit, income; profitable occupation
quālibet *adv.* where you will; somehow
quālis, -is, -e *adj.* of what sort?, of what nature?; (*rel.*) such as, of which sort; (*exclam.*) what a!
quāliscumque, -iscumque, -ecumque *adj.* of whatever kind *or* quality; any kind of
quālislibet, -islibet, -elibet *adj.* of whatever sort you will
quālisnam, -isnam, -enam *adj.* whatever sort of?
quālitās, -ātis *f.* quality, property; essential character, nature
quāliter *adv.* in which manner, just as; (*exclam.*) how!
quālubet see **quālibet**
quālus, -ī *m.* wicker basket

quam *conj.*
a) how, how much
  quam multa how many things!
b) as, as much as
  quam primum as soon as possible
c) than (used in comparisons)
  fides quam quercus fortior est faith is stronger than an oak tree

quamde *adv.* than
quamdiū *adv.* for how long?; (*rel.*) as long as
quamlibet *adv.* however you will
quamobrem *adv.* why?; (*rel.*) for which reason
quamquam *adv.* although, though; notwithstanding that; yet
quamvīs *adv.* as you will, as much as you will; (+*subj.*) however, however much; (+*subj./indic.*) although
quānam *adv.* by what way?
quandō *adv.* at what time?, when?; (*rel.*) when; seeing that, since; (*indef.*) at any time, ever
quandōcumque *adv.* whenever; at any time
quandōque *adv.* whenever; at any time
quandōquidem *adv.* seeing that, since (indeed)
quantillus, -a, -um *adj.* how small?, how little?; *n.sg.sbst.* how little an amount?
quantitās, -ātis *f.* quantity, amount
quantō *adv.* by how much?; (*rel.*) by as much as, according as
quantopere *adv.* how greatly?; (*rel.*) in what degree
quantulum, -ī *n.* how little an amount?; (*rel.*) what small amount; (*exclam.*) how small an amount!
quantulus, -a, -um *adj.* how small?, how little?; (*rel.*) of what size; (*exclam.*) how small!
quantuluscumque, -acumque, -umcumque *adj.* however small; *n.sg. sbst.* however small an amount
quantuluslibet, -alibet, -umlibet *adj.* however small you will
quantum¹, -ī *n.* how much?; (*rel.*) which amount; as far as; (*exclam.*) how much!
quantum² *adv.* how much?; (*rel.*) to what extent; (+*possum etc.*) as much as I can

quantus, -a, -um *adj.* how great?, how much?; (*rel.*) of what size, of what number

quantuscumque, -acumque, -umcumque *adj.* of whatever size; *n.sg.sbst.* however much, whatever

quantuslibet, -alibet, -umlibet *adj.* of whatever size you will; *n.sg.sbst.* as much as you will

quantusquantus, -aquanta, -umquantum *adj.* however great; *n.sg.sbst.* however much

quantusvīs, -avīs, -umvīs *adj.* however great, as great as you wish; *n.sg.sbst.* as much as you wish; (+*adj.*) as ... as you wish

quāpropter *adv.* for what reason?, why?; (*rel.*) because of which

quāquā *adv.* in every place where, wherever

quārē *adv.* for what reason?, why?; how?; (*rel.*) for which reason; whereby; therefore

quarta, -ae *f.* quarter

quartadecimānī, -ōrum *m.pl.* soldiers of the fourteenth legion

quartāna, -ae *f.* quartan fever

quartānus, -a, -um *adj.* quartan; *m.pl.sbst.* soldiers of the fourth legion

quartārius, -(i)ī *m.* small measure, quarter of a *sextarius*

quartō or **quartum** *adv.* for the fourth time

quartus, -a, -um *adj.* fourth; **quartus pater** great-great-great-grandfather; **pars quarta** quarter

quasi *adv.* (+*subj./indic.*) as if, as though; (+*subj.*) on the grounds that; for example; as it were

quasillum, -ī *n.* small wool-basket

quassābilis, -is, -e *adj.* able to be shaken

quassātiō, -ōnis *f.* shaking, vibrating

quassō 1. to shake violently, brandish, wave; batter, weaken

quassus, -a, -um *adj.* battered, shaken; chopped up

quatefaciō, -fēcī, -factum 3. to cause to waver, shake

quātenus *adv.* to what extent?; how long?; (*rel.*) so far as; for as long as; seeing that, since

quater *adv.* four times

quaternī, -ae, -a *pl.adj.* four each; four at a time

quatiō, quassum 3. to shake, wave; brandish; batter, knock; disturb, unbalance; urge on

quatrīduum see **quadrīduum**

quattuor *indecl.adj.* four

quattuordecim *indecl.adj.* fourteen

quattuorvirī, -ōrum *m.pl.* committee of four magistrates in a *municipium*

quāvis *adv.* in whatever way you wish

-que (*enclitic*) and; **-que ... -que** both ... and

quemadmodum *adv.* how?; (*rel.*) in which way, as; (*exclam.*) how!

queō, quīre, quīvī (quiī) 4. (+*inf.*) to be able (to)

querceus, -a, -um *adj.* consisting of oak-leaves

quercus, -ūs *f.* oak; oak-wood; oak-leaf garland

querella (-ēla), -ae *f.* complaint, protest; subject of complaint

queribundus, -a, -um *adj.* full of complaint, plaintive

querimōnia, -ae *f.* complaint, protest

queritor 1. *dep.* to complain bitterly

quernus, -a, -um *adj.* of *or* made of oak; made of oak-leaves

queror, questus 3. *dep.* to express annoyance, complain, lament; protest at; (+*acc.+inf.*) complain (that)

querquētum, -ī *n.* plantation of oaks

querulus, -a, -um *adj.* full of complaints, querulous; mournful

questiō, -ōnis *f.* complaining

questus, -ūs *m.* complaint, protest; wail

quī¹, quae (qua), quod *pron.* who?, what thing?; *adj.* which?, what?; (*rel.*) who, which; that; (+*subj.*) of the sort that; (*exclam.*) what a!; (+*sī/ne*) any

quī² *adv.* in what way?, how?; (*rel.*) whereby; (+*sī/ne*) by any means; (+*subj.*) so that in this way, in order that

quia *conj.* because

quianam *adv.* why ever?

quīcumque, quaecumque, quidcumque *pron.* whoever, whatever; every one who, everything that; *adj.* whichever, whatever, any

quid see **quis¹**

quīdam, quaedam, quoddam *pron.*

someone, something, certain amount; *adj.* a certain, particular, some

quidem *adv.* certainly, in fact, indeed; moreover

quidnī *adv.* why not?, of course

quīdum *adv.* why ever?, how so?

quiēs, -ētis *f.* rest, repose; sleep; inaction; serenity, tranquillity

quiescō, -ēvī, -ētum 3. to rest, repose; sleep; be inactive, abate; be quiet; be at peace

quiētē *adv.* serenely, peacefully

quiētus, -a, -um *adj.* resting, sleeping; inactive; serene, peaceful

quīlibet (-lubet), quaelibet, quodlibet *pron.* whoever *or* whatever you will, anything you will; *adj.* whichever *or* whatever you will, any you will

quīn *adv.* why not?; indeed; and what's more; *conj.* (*+subj.*) so that … not; but that

quīnam, quaenam, quodnam *pron.* who *or* what … I ask?; *adj.* which/what … I ask?

quīnavīcēnārius, -a, -um *adj.* of *or* relating to twenty-five

quinct- see **quint-**

quincunx, -ncis *m.* five-twelfths; five-twelfths of an *as*; five-twelfths of a *sextarius*

quindeciens (-ēs) *adv.* fifteen times

quindecim *indecl.adj.* fifteen

quindecimvir, -rī *m.* one of a committee of fifteen priests overseeing the Sibylline books and their ceremonies

quindecimvirālis, -is, -e *adj.* of *or* relating to the *quindecimviri*

quingēnī, -ae, -a *pl.adj.* five hundred each

quingentēsimus, -a, -um *adj.* five-hundredth

quingentī, -ae, -a *pl.adj.* five hundred

quingentiens (-ēs) *adv.* five hundred times; 50,000,000 sesterces

quīnī, -ae, -a *pl.adj.* five each; five at a time

quinquāgēnī, -ae, -a *pl.adj.* fifty each; fifty at a time

quinquāgēsimus (-ens-), -a, -um *adj.* fiftieth; **(pars) quinquāgēsima** fiftieth part

quinquāgintā *indecl.adj.* fifty

quinquātria see **quinquātrūs**

quinquātrūs, -uum *f.pl.* five-day festival in honour of Minerva in March

quinque *indecl.adj.* five

quinquennālis, -is, -e *adj.* occurring every fifth year, quinquennial; lasting five years

quinquennis, -is, -e *adj.* five years old; quinquennial; lasting five years

quinquennium, -(i)ī *n.* period of five years

quinquepedal, -ālis *n.* five-foot rule

quinquepertītus, -a, -um *adj.* divided into five-parts, fivefold

quinquerēmis, -is, -e *adj.* galley with teams of five rowers

quinquevir, -rī *m.* one of an official committee of five men

quinquevirātus, -ūs *m.* the office of *quinquevir*

quinquiens (-ēs) *adv.* five times; 500,000 sesterces

quinquiplex, -icis *adj.* having five parts, fivefold

quinquiplicō 1. to quintuple

quintadecimānī, -ōrum *m.pl.* soldiers of the fifteenth legion

quintāna, -ae *f.* street in a military camp devoted to trading; the market there

quintānī, -ōrum *m.pl.* of the fifth; *m.pl. sbst.* soldiers of the fifth legion

quintō or **quintum** *adv.* for the fifth time

quintus, -a, -um *adj.* fifth; *f.sbst.* tax of a fifth

quippe *part.* of course, obviously; as one might expect; indeed

quippinī *part.* why not?, of course

quīquomque see **quīcumque**

quirītātiō, -ōnis *f.* public protestation

quirītātus, -ūs *m.* public protestation

quirītō 1. to call to the *Quirites*, protest publicly

quis¹, quis, quid *pron.* who?, what?; *adj.* which?, what?; **quid** why?; what?; how?; (*exclam.*) what!

quis², qua(e), quid *pron.* (*often +si/ne*) anyone, anything; *adj.* a(n), any

quisnam, quaenam, quidnam *pron.* who *or* what, I ask?; which/what …, I ask?

quispiam¹, quaepiam, quippiam *pron.* anybody, somebody; **quippiam** in any degree

quispiam², quaepiam, quodpiam *adj.* some; a certain

quisquam, quisquam, quidquam

(quicquam) *pron.* anyone, anything; *adj.* any

quisque, quaeque, quidque (quicque or **quodque)** *pron.* each one; everybody; whoever, whatever; *adj.* each, every

quisquiliae, -ārum *f.pl.* rubbish, scraps

quisquis, quisquis, quidquid (quicquid) *pron.* whoever, whatever; everyone who; *adj.* each, every

quīvīs¹, quaevīs, quidvīs *pron.* whoever *or* whatever you will, anyone *or* anything

quīvīs², quaevīs, quodvīs *adj.* any you will, no matter what

quīvīscumque, quae-, quod- *adj.* whatever you will, no matter what

quō¹ *adv.* so that, thereby; whereby; (+*subj.*) in order that thereby; (+*eo/hoc*) by that degree

quō² *adv.* to where?; what for?; (*rel.*) to which place; (+*subj.*) in order that ... to that place; (+*si/ne*) to any place

quoad *adv.* how far?; (*rel.*) as far as; until; while

quōcircā *adv.* for which reason, and therefore

quōcumque *adv.* to whatever place

quod *conj.* because; that, in that; as to the fact that; seeing that, since

quōiās see **cūiās**

quōlibet *adv.* to whatever place you will

quom see **cum²**

quōminus *conj.* (+*subj.*) so as to prevent, so that ... not

quōmodo (-ō) *adv.* in what way?, how?; (*rel.*) in the manner in which; as far as; (*exclam.*) how!

quōmodocumque *adv.* in whatever way, however

quōmodonam *adv.* in what way, I ask?

quōnam *adv.* to where, I ask?

quondam *adv.* once, formerly; occasionally; in the future; at times

quoniam *conj.* since, seeing that; because; as soon as

quōpiam *adv.* to somewhere

quōquam *adv.* to any place, in any direction

quoque *adv.* also, too

quōqueversus (-um) *adv.* in every direction

quōquō *adv.* to whatever place, whithersoever; **quōquō versus** in every direction

quor see **cūr**

quorsum (-us) *adv.* to what place?; with what in view?

quot *indecl.adj.* how many?; (*rel.*) as many as; (*exclam.*) how many!

quotannīs *adv.* every year, annually

quotcumque *indecl.adj.* as many as

quotēnī, -ae, -a *pl.adj.* how many each?

quotī- see **cottī-**

quotiens (-ēs) *adv.* how often?, how many times?; (*rel.*) as often; (*exclam.*) how often!

quotienscumque (-ēs-) *adv.* as often as, whenever

quotiensque *adv.* as often as, whenever

quotquot *indecl. adj.* however many, whatever number of

quotumus, -a, -um *adj.* having what position (*in a series*)?, which in order?

quotus, -a, -um *adj.* having what position (*in a series*)?, which in order?; **quotus quisque** how few?

quotuscumque, -acumque, -umcumque *adj.* having whatever proportion, however small

quōusque *adv.* how far?, how much?, how long?; (*rel.*) as much as

quōvīs *adv.* to wherever you will

rabidē *adv.* frenziedly
rabidus, -a, -um *adj.* raging, frenzied, wild
rabiēs, -ēs *f.* frenzy; ferocity; passion
rabiō 3. to be frenzied, rave
rabiōsē *adv.* frenziedly
rabiōsulus, -a, -um *adj.* rather frenzied
rabiōsus, -a, -um *adj.* rabid; frenzied
rabō see **arrabō**
rabula, -ae *m.* noisy wrangler, tub-thumper
racēmifer, -era, -erum *adj.* bearing grape clusters
racēmus, -ī *m.* cluster, bunch (*usu. of grapes*)
radiātus, -a, -um *adj.* radiant, shining
rādīcescō 3. to begin to grow roots, take root
rādīcitus *adv.* by the roots; completely
rādīcula, -ae *f.* little root
radiō 1. or **radior** 1. *dep.* to shine, beam
radius, -(i)ī *m.* ray of light; pointing rod; weaving shuttle; wheel spoke; radius (*of a circle*); type of olive
rādix, -īcis *f.* root; base; origin
rādō, rāsī, rāsum 3. to scratch, scrape; shave; smooth; brush lightly
raeda, -ae *f.* four-wheeled carriage
raedārius, -(i)ī *m.* driver of a *raeda*
rallus, -a, -um *adj.* thin, fine
rāmāle, -is *n.* (*usu. pl.*) branches, brushwood
rāmentum, -ī *n.* or **rāmenta, -ae** *f.* shaving, filing
rāmes see **rāmex**
rāmeus, -a, -um *adj.* of a bough, branch
rāmex, -icis *f.* varicocele, rupture; *pl.* lungs
rāmōsus, -a, -um *adj.* having many branches; ramified
rāmulus, -ī *m.* small branch, twig
rāmus, -ī *m.* branch, twig

rāna, -ae *f.* frog
ranceō 2. to be rotten
rancidulus, -a, -um *adj.* somewhat rancid; rather nauseating
rancidus, -a, -um *adj.* rancid; nauseating
rānunculus, -ī *m.* little frog
rapācida, -ae *m.* 'son of a robber'
rapācitās, -ātis *f.* greed, rapacity
rapax, -ācis *adj.* snatching; greedy
raphanus, -ī *f.* radish
rapidē *adv.* swiftly, hastily
rapiditās, -ātis *f.* swiftness
rapidus, -a, -um *adj.* swift, rapid; fierce; scorching
rapīna, -ae *f.* plunder, abduction; booty
rapiō, -uī, -tum 3. to snatch away, seize; plunder; ravish
raptim *adv.* hastily, hurriedly
raptiō, -ōnis *f.* abduction
raptō 1. to snatch away, drag off; plunder
raptor, -ōris *m.* plunderer; abductor
raptum, -ī *n.* booty, plunder
raptus, -ūs *m.* plunder; abduction
rāpulum, -ī *n.* small turnip
rāpum, -ī *n.* turnip
rārē *adv.* rarely
rārēfaciō, -fēcī, -factum 3. to rarefy
rārēfīō, -fierī, -factus *v.irreg.* to thin out
rārescō 3. to thin out, become less dense
rāritās, -ātis *f.* looseness of structure; infrequency
rārō *adv.* rarely
rārus, -a, -um *adj.* loose-knit; sparse; rare, infrequent
rāsilis, -is, -e *adv.* smoothed, polished
rāsitō 1. to shave (often)
rastellus, -ī *m.* rake, hoe
rastrum, -ī *n.* (**rastrī, -ōrum** *m.pl.*) rake, hoe

ratiō, -ōnis *f.* calculation; account; reason; method, system; theory

ratiōcinātiō, -ōnis *f.* calculation; reasoning

ratiōcinātīvus, -a, -um *adj.* of *or* relating to reason

ratiōcinātor, -ōris *m.* accountant

ratiōcinor 1. *dep.* to keep accounts, calculate; consider

ratiōnālis, -is, -e *adj.* rational; theoretical

ratiōnāliter *adv.* rationally

ratiōnārium, -(i)ī *n.* financial survey

ratis, -is *f.* raft; ship

ratiuncula, -ae *f.* small calculation; trifling syllogism; petty reason

ratus, -a, -um *adj.* authoritative, ratified; fixed

raucisonus, -a, -um *adj.* raucous

raucus, -a, -um *adj.* raucous, hoarse

raudusculum, -ī *n.* small amount of money

ravis, -is *f.* hoarseness

rāvus, -a, -um *adj.* tawny, yellow-grey

rea, reae *f.* female defendant

rēapse *adv.* really, actually

reātus, -ūs *m.* the state of being accused

rebellātiō, -ōnis *f.* revolt, rebellion

rebellātrix, -īcis *f.adj.* rebellious

rebelliō, -ōnis *f.* revolt, rebellion

rebellis, -is, -e *adj.* rebellious; *m.sbst.* rebel

rebellō 1. to revolt, rebel

rebītō 3. to go back

reboō 1. to resound

recalcitrō 1. to kick back

recaleō 2. to become warm again

recalescō 3. to become warm again; become reinvigorated

recalfaciō, -fēcī 3. to make warm again

recalvus, -a, -um *adj.* with balding hair

recandescō 3. to become white, white-hot (again)

recanō see **recinō**

recantō 1. to sign in response; charm away; recant

recēdō, recessī, recessum 3. to draw back, recede; (*+ab +abl.*) depart (from)

recellō 3. to swing back

recens¹, -ntis *adj.* new; recent; fresh

recens² *adv.* recently

recenseō 2. to review, count

recensiō, -ōnis *f.* review by a censor

recensus, -ūs *m.* census

receptāculum, -ī *n.* repository; place of refuge

receptiō, -ōnis *f.* the act of receiving

receptō 1. to take back; receive

receptor, -ōris *m.* one who harbours, shelterer

receptrix, -īcis *f.* female shelterer

receptus, -ūs *m.* withdrawal; means of retreat; place of refuge

recessim *adv.* in retreat

recessus, -ūs *m.* withdrawal; recess; refuge

recharmidō 1. to stop being Charmides

recidīvus, -a, -um *adj.* falling back; reborn

recidō¹, re(c)cidī, recāsum 3. to fall back; relapse; rebound

recīdō², -dī, -sum 3. to cut back, prune

recieō 2. to call back

recingō, -nxī, -nctum 3. to ungird, unfasten

recinō 3. to sing back; call out

reciper- see **recuper-**

recipiō, recēpī, receptum 3. to receive, accept; undertake; recover; *refl.* retreat

reciprocō 1. to move to and fro; move back; reciprocate

reciprocus, -a, -um *adj.* moving to and fro

recitātiō, -ōnis *f.* reading aloud, recital

recitātor, -ōris *m.* one who reads aloud

recitō 1. to recite

reclāmātiō, -ōnis *f.* shout of protest

reclāmitō 1. to shout in protest

reclāmō 1. to shout back; shout in protest

reclīnis, -is, -e *adj.* leaning back

reclīnō 1. to lay or lean back; *refl.* lie back

reclūdō, -sī, -sum 3. to open; lay bare

recōgitō 1. to consider; reflect

recognitiō, -ōnis *f.* review, inspection

recognōscō, -nōvī, -nitum 3. to review, inspect; recognize

recolligō, -lēgī, -lectum 3. to reassemble, recollect

recolō, recoluī, recultum 3. to recultivate; renew; resume

recommentor 1. *dep.* to recollect

recomminiscor 3. *dep.* to recollect

recompōnō, -posuī, -positum 3. to recompose; reharmonize

reconciliātiō, -ōnis *f.* reconciliation

reconciliātor, -ōris *m.* reconciler

reconciliō 1. to reconcile; restore

reconcinnō 1. to repair

reconditus, -a, -um *adj.* hidden; obscure; recondite

recondō, -idī, -itum 3. to put back *or* away; replace

reconflō 1. to rekindle

recoquō, -xī, -ctum 3. to cook up anew; melt down

recordātiō, -ōnis *f.* recollection

recordor 1. *dep.* to call to mind, recollect

recorrigō, -rexī, -rectum 3. to correct

recreō 1. to re-create; restore; revive

recrepō 1. to sound back, resound

recrescō, recrēvī 3. to grow again, grow back

recrūdescō, -duī 3. to become raw again; break out afresh

rectā *adv.* straight, directly

rectē *adv.* rightly; correctly; properly; well

rectiō, -ōnis *f.* governing

rector, -ōris *m.* helmsman; controller; governor

rectrix, -īcis *f.* female controller

rectus, -a, -um *adj.* straight; upright; correct; proper

recubō 1. to lie back, recline

rēcula, -ae *f.* small amount

recumbō, -ubuī 3. to lie back, recline

recuperātiō, -ōnis *f.* recovery

recuperātor, -ōris *m.* one who recovers; assessor

recuperātōrius, -a, -um *adj.* of *or* relating to assessors

recuperō 1. to regain, recover; restore

recūrō 1. to cure; restore

recurrō, -rrī, -rsum 3. to run back; return; revert

recursō 1. to keep running back; recur repeatedly (*in the mind*)

recursus, -ūs *m.* running back; return

recurvō 1. to bend back

recurvus, -a, -um *adj.* bent back *or* round

recūsātiō, -ōnis *f.* objection; counterplea

recūsō 1. to object; oppose; reject; (+*inf.*) decline (to)

recutiō, -ssī, -ssum 3. to make vibrate

recutītus, -a, -um *adj.* having skin removed; circumcised

redambulō 1. to walk back

redamō 1. to love in return

redardescō 3. to blaze again

redarguō, -uī 3. to refute, prove wrong

redauspicō 1. to take auspices again

reddō, -idī, -itum 3. to give back; restore; pay back; hand over; resign; reply; (+*acc. adj./n.*) render

redemptiō, -ōnis *f.* purchasing of a contract *or* legal decision; ransom

redemptō 1. to ransom

redemptor, -ōris *m.* contractor

redemptūra, -ae *f.* undertaking of a public contract

redeō, -īre, -iī, -itum 4. to go back; return; revert (to); recur; become reduced

redhālō 1. to breathe back

redhibeō 2. to take back (to a seller)

redigō, -ēgī, -actum 3. to drive back; restore; reduce; pay in

redimīculum, -ī *n.* headband

redimiō 4. to garland; encircle

redimō, -ēmī, -emptum 3. to buy back; purchase; ransom; make good

redintegrō 1. to refresh; renew

redipiscor 3. *dep.* to regain

reditiō, -ōnis *f.* return

reditus, -ūs *m.* return; revenue

redivīvus, -a, -um *adj.* reused

redoleō 2. to be fragrant; (+*acc.*) smell of

redōnō 1. to give back; forgive

redormiō 4. to go back to sleep

redūcō, -uxī, -uctum 3. to lead back; withdraw; recollect; reduce (to)

reductiō, -ōnis *f.* leading back

reductor, -ōris *m.* one who leads back; restorer

reductus, -a, -um *adj.* set back, recessed

reduncus, -a, -um *adj.* hooked

redundanter *adv.* over-exuberantly

redundō 1. to flow back; overflow, flood out; (+*ad/in* +*acc.*) recoil (upon); (+*abl.*) abound (in)

reduvia, -ae *f.* cuticle

redux (rēdux), -ucis *adj.* that brings home; returning

refectiō, -ōnis *f.* recovery, convalescence

refector, -ōris *m.* repairer

refellō, -ī 3. to refute

referciō, -rsī, -rtum 4. to stuff full, cram

referiō 4. to hit back; reflect

referō, referre, rettulī, relātum *v.irreg.* to bring back; withdraw; revive; propose; recall; repay

rēfert, rēferre, rētulit *v.irreg. impers.* it is important; (+*abl. of pers. pron.*) it matters (to me, you *etc.*)

refertus, -a, -um *adj.* crammed full, loaded
referveō 2. to boil up; blaze
refervescō 3. to boil up
refībulō 1. to unpin
reficiō, refēcī, refectum 3. to restore; revive; reappoint
refīgō, -ixī, -ixum 3. to detach, unfasten
refingō 3. to refashion
reflāgitō 1. to demand repeatedly
reflātus, -ūs *m.* contrary wind
reflectō, -exī, -exum 3. to bend back; turn back; reverse
reflexus, -a, -um *adj.* bent back
reflō 1. to blow back out; blow in a contrary direction; pant
refluō 3. to flow back
refluus, -a, -um *adj.* flowing back
refodiō, refōdī, refossum 3. to dig open
reformātiō, -ōnis *f.* reshaping
reformātor, -ōris *m.* one who reshapes
reformīdātiō, -ōnis *f.* dread, terror
reformīdō 1. to shrink from; dread
reformō 1. to reshape, transform; restore
refoveō, refōvī, refōtum 2. to warm again; revive; reinvigorate
refractāriolus, -a, -um *adj.* somewhat antagonistic, refractory
refractārius, -a, -um *adj.* antagonistic, refractory
refrāgor 1. *dep.* to argue in opposition
refrēnō 1. to hold back, restrain
refricō, -uī, -ātum 1. to make sore again (by rubbing), gall; excite again
refrīgerātiō, -ōnis *f.* cooling
refrīgerō 1. to cool down, chill; calm down
refrīgescō, refrixī 3. to cool down (again); calm down; slow down
refringō, refrēgī, refractum 3. to break back *or* open; repel
refugiō, -ūgī 3. to run away, flee; shrink (from); avoid
refugium, -(i)ī *n.* place of refuge, shelter
refugus, -a, -um *adj.* fleeing back; receding
refulgeō, -lsī 2. to shine brightly, gleam; shine out
refundō, refūdī, refūsum 3. to make flow back; *pass.* flow *or* sink back
refūtātiō, -ōnis *f.* refutation
refūtātus, -ūs *m.* refutation

refūtō 1. to refute; suppress, check
rēgāliolus, -ī *m.* wren
rēgālis, -is, -e *adj.* kingly, regal
rēgāliter *adv.* royally, splendidly
regelō 1. to unfreeze
regemō 3. to groan in return
regens, -ntis *m.* ruler; master
regerō, -ssī, -stum 3. to carry back; restore; throw back; retaliate with
rēgia, -ae *f.* palace; royal house; basilica; **rēgia caelī** the heavens
rēgiē *adv.* royally; despotically
rēgificus, -a, -um *adj.* kingly, splendid
regignō 3. to produce again
rēgillus, -a, -um *adj.* somewhat royal
regimen, -inis *n.* steering (*of a ship*); steering-oar; management; controller
rēgīna, -ae *f.* queen; princess; dominant woman
regiō, -ōnis *f.* direction; (straight) line; boundary; district, region; **ē regiōne** in a straight line
regiōnātim *adv.* by districts
rēgius, -a, -um *adj.* kingly, royal; performed by a king; splendid; despotic
reglūtinō 1. to unglue
regnātor, -ōris *m.* king, lord
regnātrix, -īcis *f.adj.* ruling, reigning
regnō 1. to reign; hold sway; act as king
regnum, -ī *n.* kingship; monarchy; tyranny; dominion, kingdom
regō, rexī, rectum 3. to guide, direct; control; govern
regredior, regressus 3. *dep.* to go back; retreat
regressus, -ūs *m.* return, withdrawal; recourse
rēgula, -ae *f.* measuring rod, rule; rod, bar; principle, standard
rēgulus, -ī *m.* minor king, chieftain; prince
regustō 1. to taste again; experience again
rēiciō, rēiēcī, rēiectum 3. to throw back; drive back; defer; refer for consideration; reject
rēiculus, -a, -um *adj.* rejected as useless
rēiect(āne)a, -ōrum *n.pl.* fit to be rejected
rēiectiō, -ōnis *f.* rejection; refusal
rēiectō 1. to throw back
relābor, relapsus 3. *dep.* to slip back, recede; (*+in +acc.*) relapse (into)
relanguescō, -guī 3. to become faint; slacken off; (*of passions*) cool down

relātiō, -ōnis f. referral (of a matter) to a senate or magistrate; repayment, return

relātus, -ūs m. narration; reply

relaxātiō, -ōnis f. easing off; relaxing

relaxō 1. to loosen, relax; undo; weaken; relieve

relēgātiō, -ōnis f. banishment

relēgō[1] 1. to banish, dismiss

relegō[2], **-ēgī, -ectum** 3. to recover; retrace; read over

relentescō 3. to cool down (of feelings)

relevō 1. to lighten; alleviate; relieve; raise again

relictiō, -ōnis f. abandoning

relictus, -a, -um adj. derelict

relīdō 3. (+in +acc.) to hurl or dash (into)

religātiō, -ōnis f. tying up

rel(l)igiō (rēl-), -ōnis f. supernatural reverence; religious scruple; awe; superstition; religious practice, ritual

religiōsē adv. with religious reverence; conscientiously

religiōsus (rēl-), -a, -um adj. religiously scrupulous; superstitious; taboo; sacred; reverent; conscientious

religō 1. to bind out of the way; bind fast; attach; secure

relinō, relēvī 3. to unseal

relinquō (rēl-), relīquī, relictum 3. to leave; abandon; disregard

reliquiae, -ārum f.pl. remnants, remains; vestiges; survivors

reliquum, -ī n. remainder; financial credit; pl. the future; **in reliquum** henceforth

reliquus, -a, -um adj. remaining, left; owing; future

relūceō, -uxī 2. to shine out, beam

relūcescō, -uxī 3. to become bright again

reluctor 1. dep. to resist, oppose; struggle

remacrescō, -ruī 3. to become thin (again)

remaneō, -nsī 2. to remain, stay; endure

remānō 1. to flow back

remansiō, -ōnis f. remaining behind

remeābilis, -is, -e adj. returning; providing a return

remediābilis, -is, -e adj. curable

remedium, -(i)ī n. remedy, cure

remelīgō, -inis f. hindrance

remeō 1. to go back, return; come round again

remētior, -ensus 4. dep. to measure in return; go back over

rēmex, -igis m. rower; rowing crew

rēmigātiō, -ōnis f. rowing

rēmigium, -(i)ī n. oarage; rowing crew

rēmigō 1. to row

remigrō 1. to move back home; return

reminiscor 3. dep. to recollect, recall to mind

remisceō, -scuī, -xtum 2. to mix in

remissē adv. loosely; unrestrainedly; mildly; placidly

remissiō, -ōnis f. sending back; relaxing; easing off; cancellation

remissus, -a, -um adj. relaxed; subdued; mild; light-hearted

remittō, -īsī, -issum 3. to send back; refer (a matter); release; relax; grant; waive

remōlior 4. dep. to heave back

remollescō 3. to become soft (again); melt; relent

remolliō 4. to make soft, soften

remora, -ae f. hindrance

remordeō, -dī, -sum 2. to bite back; nag

remoror 1. dep. to linger, dally; keep waiting

remōtē adv. far away

remōtiō, -ōnis f. moving back; shifting (of a charge)

remōtus, -a, -um adj. distant; alien; remote; recondite

removeō, remōvī, remōtum 2. to move away; banish; set aside

remūgiō 4. to moo or bellow in return; resound with bellowing

remulceō, -lsī, -lsum 2. to soothe

remulcum, -ī n. tow-rope

remūnerātiō, -ōnis f. paying in return

remūneror 1. dep. to pay back, recompense; requite

remurmurō 1. to murmur back

rēmus, -ī m. oar

renarrō 1. to recount

renascor, renātus 3. dep. to be born again; grow again; be renewed

renāvigō 1. to sail back; traverse again

rēnēs, -(i)um m.pl. kidneys

renīdeō 2. to shine, gleam; smile back (at)

renīdescō 3. to become bright

renītor, -sus 3. dep. to struggle in resistance

renō[1] 1. to swim back

rēnō[2], **-ōnis** m. reindeer skin

renōdō 1. to tie back

renovāmen, -inis *n.* new form
renovātiō, -ōnis *f.* renewal
renovō 1. to renew, restore; revive; resume
renumerō 1. to pay back
renuntiātiō, -ōnis *f.* report; return (*of electoral votes*)
renuntiō 1. to report; announce; call off
renuntius, -(i)ī *m.* reporter
renuō, -uī 3. to toss the head back in disapproval; refuse
renūtō 1. to refuse
renūtus, -ūs *m.* tossing of the head back in disapproval
reor, ratus 2. *dep.* to think, suppose, deem
repāgula, -ōrum *n.pl.* door-bars
repandus, -a, -um *adj.* spread out
reparābilis, -is, -e *adj.* retrievable
reparātor, -ōris *m.* one who restores
reparcō, repersī 3. (+*dat.*) to be sparing (with)
reparō 1. to recover, restore; renew; obtain in exchange (for)
repastinātiō, -ōnis *f.* turning over the soil (again)
repectō, -xī, -xum 3. to comb back
repellō, reppulī, repulsum 3. to drive back; repel; reject; exclude
rependō, -dī, -sum 3. to weigh out in return; pay for; compensate; requite
repens, -ntis *adj.* sudden; new
repente *adv.* suddenly; all at once
repentīnō *adv.* suddenly; all at once
repentīnus, -a, -um *adj.* sudden; suddenly created *or* done
repercō see **reparcō**
repercussus, -ūs *m.* pushing back; reflection; striking
repercutiō, -ssī, -ssum 3. to drive back; reflect; strike
reperiō, repperī, repertum 4. to discover; acquire; devise
repertor, -ōris *m.* inventor, author
repetentia, -ae *f.* power of recollection
repetītiō, -ōnis *f.* repetition
repetītor, -ōris *m.* one who claims back
repetō, -īvī (-iī), -ītum 3. to make for again; recover; repeat; recall; claim back
repleō, -ēvī, -ētum 2. to refill; fill up; restore; sate
replētus, -a, -um *adj.* (+*abl./gen.*) full (of)
replicātiō, -ōnis *f.* rotation in a contrary direction
replicō 1. to bend back; unroll, unwind
replōrō 1. to resound with lamentation
rēpō, repsī 3. to crawl, creep
repōnō, reposuī, repos(i)tum 3. to put back; restore; replace; store away; put to rest
reportō 1. to carry back; plunder; report
reposcō 3. to demand back; demand
repositōrium, -iī *n.* stand for carrying meals to a table
repostor, -ōris *m.* one who re-erects
repōtia, -ōrum *n.pl.* drinking party on the day after a wedding
reppleō see **repleō**
repraesentātiō, -ōnis *f.* instant payment
repraesentō 1. to make immediately available; pay immediately; revive; make manifest; represent (*in art*)
repre(he)ndō, -dī, -sum 3. to seize; reprehend; censure
repre(he)nsiō, -ōnis *f.* censure; refutation
reprehensō 1. to detain
reprehensor, -ōris *m.* one who censures
reprēn- see **repre(he)n-**
repressor, -ōris *m.* one who checks
reprimō, repressī, repressum 3. to check, restrain; repress
reprōmissiō, -ōnis *f.* promise
reprōmittō, -mīsī, -missum 3. to promise; guarantee
reptō 1. to crawl; saunter; crawl over
repudiātiō, -ōnis *f.* refusal, rejection
repudiō 1. to reject, decline; repudiate; divorce
repudiōsus, -a, -um *adj.* liable to be rejected; offensive
repudium, -(i)ī *n.* divorce; breaking of a marriage engagement
repuerascō 3. to become a boy again
repugnans, -ntis *adj.* inconsistent, contradictory
repugnanter *adv.* in antipathy
repugnantia, -ae *f.* antipathy, opposition; inconsistency
repugnō 1. to fight back; (+*dat.*) object (to), clash (with)
repulsa, -ae *f.* electoral defeat; rebuff
repulsō 1. to drive back; reject
repulsus, -ūs *m.* driving back
repungō 3. to goad in return
repurgō 1. to cleanse, make clean
reputātiō, -ōnis *f.* consideration

reputō 1. to calculate; consider

requiēs, -ētis f. rest, respite; pause; recreation; relaxation

requiescō, requiēvī, requiētum 3. to rest; relax; (+ab +abl.) desist (from); cause to rest

requiētus, -a, -um adj. rested; (of fields) fallow

requīritō 1. to demand repeatedly

requīrō, -sīvī (-siī), -sītum 3. to look for; ask for; want; miss; need

rēs, reī (reī or rei) f. thing; matter; property; deed; fact; purpose; lawsuit; **rēs novae** revolution

resacrō see **resecrō**

resaeviō 4. to rage again

resalūtātiō, -ōnis f. returning a greeting

resalūtō 1. to return the greeting of

resānescō, -nuī 3. to be healed

resarciō, -rsī, -rsum 4. to repair

rescindō, -cidī, -cissum 3. to cut away; cut open; revoke, annul

rescīscō, -īvī (-iī), -ītum 3. to get to know of

rescrībō, -ipsī, -iptum 3. to write in response; rewrite; pay back in accounts; enrol in place of another

rescriptum, -ī n. written reply (esp. from emperors)

resecō, -uī, -tum 1. to cut back, prune; sever at the bottom

resecrō 1. to implore again; release from a religious ban

resēminō 1. to reproduce

resequor, -cūtus 3. dep. to follow in reply

reserō 1. to unbar, open; lay bare, uncover

reservō 1. to reserve; preserve; (+dat.) keep (for)

reses, -idis adj. motionless, torpid

resideō, resēdī 2. to sit; remain; persist

resīdō, resīdī 3. to sit down; settle, encamp; sink back; abate

residuus, -a, -um adj. remaining, surviving; still to be done

resignō 1. to unseal; disclose; resign; debit

resiliō, -uī 4. to jump back; rebound; recoil; shrink

resīmus, -a, -um adj. turned up

rēsīna, -ae f. resin

rēsīnātus, -a, -um adj. seasoned with resin; smeared in resin

resipiō 3. (+acc.) taste of, smack of

resipiscō, -īvī (-iī or -uī) 3. to regain consciousness; recover one's reason

resistō, restitī 3. to stop, stand fixed; (+dat.) resist, oppose

resolūtus, -a, -um adj. limp, slack

resolvō, -vī, -ūtum 3. to loosen, unfasten; break up; (+ab +abl.) free (from); finish; pay off (a debt)

resonābilis, -is, -e adj. able to echo sounds

resonāns, -ntis adj. resounding, echoing

resonō 1. to resound, echo

resonus, -a, -um adj. resounding, echoing

resorbeō 2. to absorb; choke back

respectō 1. to keep looking around or behind; keep looking at; await

respectus, -ūs m. looking back; refuge; (+gen.) consideration, concern (for)

respergō, -rsī, -rsum 3. to splash, spatter, sprinkle

respersiō, -ōnis f. splashing (of liquid)

respiciō, -pexī, -pectum 3. to look back or round (at); review; consider; pay heed to

respīrāmen, -inis n. means of breathing

respīrātiō, -ōnis f. recovering one's breath; breathing, exhalation

respīrō 1. to recover one's breath; breathe; have respite

resplendeō 2. to glitter, reflect back

respondeō, -dī, -sum 2. to reply, respond; answer a charge; react; (+dat.) agree (with), correspond (to)

responsiō, -ōnis f. answering; defence

responsitō 1. to answer legal questions habitually

responsō 1. (+dat.) to answer (to); (+dat.) satisfy the needs of

responsor, -ōris m. one who answers

responsum, -ī n. answer, response

rēs pūblica (rēspūblica), reī pūblicae f. state; affairs of state; public good

respuō, -uī 3. to spit out; refuse, reject; repel

restagnō 1. to form a pool by flooding; be covered with flood-water

restaurō 1. to restore, repair

resticula, -ae f. small cord

restinctiō, -ōnis f. quenching (of thirst)

restinguō, -nxī, -nctum 3. to extinguish; quench; suppress, stifle

restiō, -ōnis m. rope seller

restipulātiō, -ōnis f. stipulation (of a counter-guarantee)

restipulor 1. *dep.* to stipulate (*sthg*) as a counter-guarantee

restis, -is *f.* rope, cord

restitō 1. to keep lagging; keep resisting

restituō, -uī, -ūtum 3. to rebuild; revive; restore; reinstate

restitūtiō, -ōnis *f.* rebuilding; renewal; reinstatement

restitūtor, -ōris *m.* restorer; reviver

restō, restitī 1. to stay put, remain; survive; be not yet done; (+*dat.*) resist

restrictē *adv.* grudgingly; selfishly

restrictus, -a, -um *adj.* contracted; strict; grudging

restringō, -inxī, -ictum 3. to fasten *or* tie (behind); repress, check; bare (*esp. teeth*)

resultō 1. to jump back; rebound; echo

resūmō, -umpsī, -umptum 3. to take up again; recover; resume

resuō, -uī, -ūtum 3. to unstitch

resupīnō 1. to lie on one's back; tilt back

resupīnus, -a, -um *adj.* lying on one's back; tilting back; inclined upwards

resurgō, -rrexī, -rrectum 3. to get up again; rise *or* grow again; revive

resuscitō 1. to reawaken (*a passion*)

retardātiō, -ōnis *f.* lingering

retardō 1. to delay, hinder; discourage; linger behind

retaxō 1. to rebuke

rēte, -is *n.* net (*for fishing, hunting etc.*)

retegō, -xī, -ctum 3. to uncover; reveal; make known

retemptō 1. to feel again; try again

retendō, -dī, -tum 3. to unbend

retentiō, -ōnis *f.* restraining; withholding

retentō 1. to hold fast, restrain; retain

reterō, retrīvī, retrītum 3. to wear down (again)

retexō, -xuī, -xtum 3. to unweave, pick apart; retrace; cancel

rētiārius, -iī *m.* gladiator who used a net for ensnaring opponents

reticentia, -ae *f.* silence

reticeō, -uī 2. to keep silent; leave unsaid

rēticulātus, -a, -um *adj.* wearing a hair-net

rēticulum, -ī *n.* small net; hair-net

retināculum, -ī *n.* rope, cable; rein

retinens, -ntis *adj.* (+*gen.*) clinging (to), adhering (to)

retinentia, -ae *f.* ability to retain in the mind

retineō, retinuī, retentum 2. to hold fast; restrain; detain; keep; maintain

retinniō 4. to tinkle back

retonō 1. to thunder back

retorqueō, -rsī, -rtum 2. to twist round *or* back; cast back; deflect

retorridus, -a, -um *adj.* shrivelled

retractātiō, -ōnis *f.* shrinking back; reviewing

retractō 1. to handle again; revise, review; recollect; shrink back; retract

retractus, -a, -um *adj.* lying far back

retrahō, -xī, -ctum 3. to drag back; summon back; withdraw

retribuō, -uī, -ūtum 3. to hand back (*what is owed*)

retrō *adv.* backwards; in the opposite direction; behind

retroagō, -ēgī, -actum 3. to drive back; reverse

retrōcēdō, -cessī, -cessum 3. to move back, retire

retrōdō, -dedī, -datum 1. to cause to move back; return

retroeō, -īre 4. to revert to an inferior state

retrorsum (-us) *adv.* backwards; conversely

retrūdō, -sum 3. to thrust back *or* away

retundō, rettudī, retūsum (-unsum) 3. to make blunt, beat flat; repress, abate

retūsus (-unsus), -a, -um *adj.* blunt; dull

reus, reī *m.* defendant; (+*gen. of crime*) culprit

revalescō, -luī 3. to regain strength

revehō, -xī, -ctum 3. to convey back; *pass.* ride *or* sail back

revellō, -ellī (-ulsī), -ulsum 3. to wrench off; tear up *or* out; remove

revēlō 1. to unveil; reveal

reveniō, revēnī, reventum 4. to come back, return (to)

reverberō 1. to beat back

reverendus, -a, -um *adj.* venerable

reverens, -ntis *adj.* reverent; (+*gen.*) respectful (for)

reverenter *adv.* reverently; respectfully

reverentia, -ae *f.* reverence, awe; shyness

revereor 2. *dep.* to be in awe of; revere

reversiō, -ōnis *f.* return; recurrence

revertor, -tī, -sus 3. *dep.* or **revertō, -tī** 3. to turn back; return (to); recur

revideō, -īsum 2. (+*ad* +*acc.*) to visit again

revinciō, -nxī, -nctum 3. to tie down, bind; gird

revincō, revīcī, revictum 3. to conquer in return; refute; convict

revirescō 3. to become green again; become revived

revīsō 3. to visit again; (+*ad* +*acc.*) pay another visit (to)

revīvescō (-iscō), revixī, revictum 3. to come to life again; grow again; revive

revocābilis, -is, -e *adj.* able to be recalled

revocāmen, -inis *n.* summons back

revocātiō, -ōnis *f.* summoning back; repetition

revocō 1. to summon back; (+*ab* +*abl.*) dissuade (from); annul; reduce

revolūbilis, -is, -e *adj.* rolling back; able to be rolled back

revolvō, -vī, -ūtum 3. to roll back; make to revolve; reenact

revomō, -uī 3. to spew out (again)

revorrō 3. to sweep back

revors-, revort- see **revers-, revert-**

rex, rēgis *m.* king; prince; ruler

rhapsōdia, -ae *f.* recited piece of epic poetry

rhētor, -oris *m.* rhetorician

rhētoricē *adv.* in the manner of a rhetorician

rhētoricus, -a, -um *adj.* of *or* relating to public speaking, rhetorical; *f.sg.sbst.* rhetoric

rhīnocerōs, -ōtis *m.* rhinoceros; oil-flask made from rhinoceros horn

rhō *indecl.n.* the Greek letter *rho*

rhoea, -ae *f.* corn poppy

rhombus, -ī *m.* turbot; musical instrument whirled on a string

rhoncus, -ī *m.* snore, snort

rhythmicus, -ī *m.* expert on rhythm, metrician

rhytion, -iī *n.* drinking horn

rīca, -ae *f.* woman's veil

rictus, -ūs *m.* or **rictum, -ī** *n.* open mouth, gape

rīdeō, rīsī, rīsum 2. to laugh; be cheerful; laugh at, deride

rīdibundus, -a, -um *adj.* full of laughter

rīdiculāria, -ōrum *n.pl.* jokes, jests

rīdiculē *adv.* ridiculously; amusingly

rīdiculus, -a, -um *adj.* ridiculous; amusing

rigens, -ntis *adj.* rigid, stiff; stubborn

rigeō 2. to be stiff, rigid; stand on end

rigescō, riguī 3. to grow stiff *or* rigid; become erect

rigidē *adv.* strictly

rigidō 1. to make rigid

rigidus, -a, -um *adj.* rigid, stiff; erect; stern; stubborn; rugged

rigō 1. to irrigate; soak, wet; convey (*a liquid*) through

rigor, -ōris *m.* rigidity, stiffness; severity; ruggedness

riguus, -a, -um *adj.* irrigating; irrigated

rīma, -ae *f.* crack, chink

rīmor 1. *dep.* to probe, search; look out for; examine closely

rīmōsus, -a, -um *adj.* full of cracks

ringor 3. *dep.* to bare the teeth, snarl

rīpa, -ae *f.* bank (*of a river etc.*)

rīpula, -ae *f.* little bank

riscus, -ī *m.* trunk, chest

rīsiō, -ōnis *f.* laughing

rīsor, -ōris *m.* one who laughs

rīsus, -ūs *m.* laughter; laughing-stock

rīte *adv.* with due rites; properly; rightly

rītuālis, -is, -e *adj.* of *or* relating to ritual ceremonies

rītus, -ūs *m.* (*usu. pl.*) religious rite(s); **rītū** (+*gen.*) in the manner of

rīvālis, -is *m.* rival

rīvālitās, -ātis *f.* rivalry

rīvulus, -ī *m.* small river

rīvus, -ī *m.* river; stream; channel

rixa, -ae *f.* quarrel, dispute

rixor 1. *dep.* to quarrel, brawl; clash (with)

rōbīginōsus, -a, -um *adj.* rusty; envious

rōbīgō, -inis *f.* rust; tartar

rōboreus, -a, -um *adj.* made of oak

rōborō 1. to make strong; reinforce

rōbur, -oris *n.* oak; timber; strength; power; resolve

rōbus, -a, -um *adj.* red

rōbustus, -a, -um *adj.* made of oak; strong; durable; mature

rōdō, rōsī, rōsum 3. to gnaw; erode; carp at

rogālis, -is, -e *adj.* of a funeral pyre

rogātiō, -ōnis *f.* questioning; invitation; proposed law, bill

rogātiuncula, -ae *f.* small question; small bill

rogātor, -ōris *m.* beggar; proposer of laws; voting official

rogātus, -ūs *m.* request
rogitātiō, -ōnis *f.* proposed law, bill
rogitō 1. to ask repeatedly; ask for repeatedly
rogō 1. to ask; request, ask for
rogus, -ī *m.* funeral pyre
rōrārius, -(i)ī *m.* skirmishing soldier
rōridus, -a, -um *adj.* dripping with moisture
rōrifer, -era, -erum *adj.* bringing dew *or* drizzle
rōrō 1. to distil dew; drip with moisture; moisten; sprinkle
rōs, rōris *m.* dew; moisture
rosa, -ae *f.* rose; rose-bush
rosārium, -(i)ī *n.* rose-garden
rosārius, -a, -um *adj.* made from roses
roscidus, -a, -um *adj.* moist with dew, dewy
rosētum, -ī *n.* rose-garden
roseus, -a, -um *adj.* consisting of roses; rose-coloured
rostrātus, -a, -um *adj.* with a beak-shaped prow
rostrum, -ī *n.* snout, beak; beak (*of a ship*); *pl.* speaking platform in Rome
rota, -ae *f.* wheel
rotātor, -ōris *m.* one who makes (*sthg*) whirl
rotātus, -ūs *m.* whirling
rotō 1. to make spin, rotate; swing round; roll forward
rotula, -ae *f.* small wheel
rotundē *adv.* with rounded phrases
rotundō 1. to make round, round off
rotundus, -a, -um *adj.* round, circular; spherical; well-finished
rubefaciō, -fēcī, -factum 3. to make red
rubellus, -a, -um *adj.* reddish
rubens, -ntis *adj.* tinged with red
rubeō 2. to be red
ruber, rubra, rubrum *adj.* red
rubescō, rubuī 3. to become red, blush
rubēta, -ae *f.* toad
rubētum, -ī *n.* bramble thicket
rubicundulus, -a, -um *adj.* somewhat ruddy, rather flushed
rubicundus, -a, -um *adj.* ruddy, flushed; reddish
rubidus, -a, -um *adj.* flushed
rūbīg- see **rōbīg-**

rubor, -ōris *m.* redness; blush, shame; cause of shame
rubrīca, -ae *f.* red ochre; chapter (*of a book*)
rubus, -ī *m.* bramble
ructātrix, -īcis *f.adj.* inducing belches
ructō 1. or **ructor** 1. *dep.* to belch; belch out
ructus, -ūs *m.* belch
rudens, -ntis *adj.* rope (*of a ship*)
rudiārius, -iī *m.* retired gladiator
rudīmentum, -ī *n.* first lessons, training
rudis¹, -is, -e *adj.* crude, unwrought; primitive; immature; (*+gen. or +in +abl.*) ignorant (of)
rudis², -is *f.* blunted sword for mock fights (*usu. given to retiring gladiators*)
rudō (rūdō), -īvī 3. to bellow, roar; bray
rūdus, -eris *n.* piece of bronze
rūfulus, -a, -um *adj.* reddish-haired
rūfus, -a, -um *adj.* red
rūga, -ae *f.* crease; wrinkle; frown
rūgō 1. to become creased
rūgōsus, -a, -um *adj.* creased, wrinkly
ruīna, -ae *f.* headlong fall; forward rush; collapse; debris; *pl.* ruins
ruīnōsus, -a, -um *adj.* near-collapsing; ruined
rumex, -icis *m.* sorrel
rūmiferō 1. to rumour
rūminātiō, -ōnis *f.* chewing over (*of thoughts*)
rūminō 1. to chew repeatedly; chew over, meditate
rūmor, -ōris *m.* rumour; report; esteem; cheer
rumpia, -ae *f.* long Thracian spear
rumpō, rūpī, ruptum 3. to burst, rupture; break open *or* off; violate
rūmusculus, -ī *m.* trivial piece of gossip
runcō 1. to weed
ruō, ruī 3. to rush, hasten; (*+in +acc.*) charge upon; fall headlong; collapse
rūpēs, -is *f.* crag, cliff
ruptor, -ōris *m.* (*+gen.*) one who breaks (*an agreement*)
rūricola, -ae *m./f.* tiller of the land; country-dweller
rūrigena, -ae *m.* one of rustic birth
rūrō 1. to spend time at a country estate
rursus (-um) *or* **rūsus (-um)** *adv.* again; backwards; conversely; in turn; furthermore

rūs, rūris *n.* countryside; country estate; rusticity

ruscus, -ī *f.* butcher's broom

russātus, -a, -um *adj.* dressed in red

russus, -a, -um *adj.* red; red-haired

rusticānus, -a, -um *adj.* living in the country; rustic

rusticātiō, -ōnis *f.* life in the country

rusticē *adv.* like a rustic; boorishly

rusticitās, -ātis *f.* simplicity; boorishness

rusticor 1. *dep.* to reside in the country

rusticula, -ae *f.* kind of game bird

rusticulus, -a, -um *adj.* somewhat rustic; *m.sbst.* peasant

rusticus, -a, -um *adj.* rustic, rural; residing in the country; simple; boorish

rūta, -ae *f.* rue

rutābulum, -ī *n.* oven-rake

rūtātus, -a, -um *adj.* seasoned with rue

rutilō 1. to glow bright red; colour red

rutilus, -a, -um *adj.* red, ruddy

rutrum, -ī *n.* shovel

rūtula, -ae *f.* small piece of rue

rutund- see **rotund-**

S

sabbata, -ōrum *n.pl.* sabbath, day of rest

sabbatāria, -ae *f.* woman who keeps the sabbath, Jew

saburra, -ae *f.* sand, ballast

saburrō 1. to fill with ballast

saccipērium, -(i)ī *n.* pouch for carrying wallet

saccō 1. to strain through a bag, strain, filter

sacculus, -ī *m.* small bag, purse

saccus, -ī *m.* bag, sack

sacellum, -ī *n.* shrine, chapel

sacer, sacra, sacrum *adj.* sacred, holy, consecrated to a divinity; accursed, execrable, detestable

sacerdōs, -ōtis *m./f.* priest; priestess

sacerdōtālis, -is, -e *adj.* priestly, sacerdotal

sacerdōtium, -(i)ī *n.* priesthood, sacerdotal office

sacrāmentum, -ī *n.* oath, solemn obligation *or* engagement; military oath of loyalty

sacrārium, -(i)ī *n.* shrine, chapel

sacrātus, -a, -um *adj.* holy, sacred, hallowed

sacricola, -ae *m.* sacrificing priest *or* worshipper

sacrifer, -era, -erum *adj.* carrying holy objects

sacrificālis, -is, -e *adj.* of *or* belonging to sacrifices, sacrificial

sacrificātiō, -ōnis *f.* sacrificing, sacrifice

sacrificium, -(i)ī *n.* sacrifice

sacrificō 1. to make a sacrifice, sacrifice

sacrificulus, -ī *m.* sacrificing priest

sacrificus, -a, -um *adj.* of *or* belonging to the act of sacrifice, sacrificial

sacrilegium, -(i)ī *n.* theft *or* violation of sacred objects, sacrilege

sacrilegus, -a, -um *adj.* that steals *or* violates sacred objects; *m.sbst.* temple-robber, one who commits sacrilege

sacrō 1. to consecrate, set apart as sacred, devote, hallow; doom to destruction, condemn

sacrōsanctus, -a, -um *adj.* sacred, inviolable, sacrosanct; very sacred

sacrum, -ī *n.* sacred object; sacrificial victim; holy place; sacred rite, religious ceremony, festival; secret, mystery; sanctity; **inter sacrum saxumque stāre** to stand between the victim and the knife, i.e. to be in a difficult situation; **hereditās sine sacrīs** inheritance without expenses for private worship, i.e. profit without trouble

saeculāris, -is, -e *adj.* of *or* belonging to a *saeculum*; **carmen saeculāre** hymn performed at the Saecular Games

saec(u)lum, -ī *n.* lifetime, generation, age; period of a hundred years, century; the age, the times; future age, posterity; race, breed

saepe *adv.* often, many times, frequently

saepenumerō *adv.* often, time and again

saepēs, -is *f.* hedge, fence, enclosure

saepīmentum, -ī *n.* hedge, fence, enclosure

saepiō, -psī, -ptum 4. to surround with a hedge, hedge in, fence in, enclose, surround; cover, envelop

saepissimus, -a, -um *adj.* very frequent

saeptum, -ī *n.* enclosure, hedge, fence, barrier, wall; *pl.* enclosure on Campus Martius (*for voting*)

saeta, -ae *f.* animal hair, bristle; fishing-line

saetiger, -era, -erum *adj.* having coarse hair *or* bristles, bristly; *m.sbst.* wild boar

saetōsus, -a, -um *adj.* bristly, full of coarse hairs

saevē *adv.* fiercely, ferociously, savagely, violently, cruelly

saevidicus, -a, -um *adj.* spoken furiously *or* angrily

saeviō 4. to rage, rave, be furious, savage, violent, cruel, angry

saeviter *adv.* fiercely, ferociously, savagely, violently, cruelly

saevitia, -ae *f.* fierceness, ferocity, savageness, violence, cruelty

saevus, -a, -um *adj.* fierce, ferocious, savage, violent, cruel

sāga, -ae *f.* wise woman, fortune-teller, soothsayer

sagācitās, -ātis *f.* keenness of perception, acuteness, shrewdness, sagacity

sagāciter *adv.* sharply, keenly, with a keen sense of smell; acutely, shrewdly, sagaciously

sagātus, -a, -um *adj.* wearing a *sagum*

sagax, -ācis *adj.* quick, keen, acute, shrewd, sagacious; keen-scented

sagīna, -ae *f.* cramming, stuffing, fattening; food, nourishment

sagīnō 1. to fatten; cram, stuff

sāgiō 4. to perceive quickly *or* keenly

sagitta, -ae *f.* arrow, shaft, bolt; constellation

sagittārius, -a, -um *adj.* armed with arrows; *m.sbst.* archer, bowman

sagittātus, -a, -um *adj.* barbed

sagittifer, -era, -erum *adj.* arrow-bearing; *m.sbst.* archer

sagmen, -inis *n.* clump of earth and grass that gave symbolic protection to Fetial priests

sagulātus, -a, -um *adj.* wearing a *sagulum*

sagulum, -ī *n.* small military cloak

sagum, -ī *n.* coarse woollen cloak, military cloak

sāgus, -a, -um *adj.* presaging, predicting, prophetic

sāl, salis *m./n.* salt; salt-water, sea; wit, shrewdness, sarcasm; *pl.* witticisms, jokes

salacō, -ōnis *m.* swaggerer, braggart

salamandra, -ae *f.* salamander

salapūtium, -(i)ī *n.* diminutive person

salārium, -(i)ī *n.* stipend, allowance, salary, pension

salārius, -a, -um *adj.* of *or* relating to salt; *m.sbst.* dealer in salted fish

salax, -ācis *adj.* lustful, lecherous, salacious, randy; sexually provocative

salebra, -ae *f.* rut, pothole; roughness, ruggedness, unevenness

salebrōsus, -a, -um *adj.* rough, rugged, uneven

saliātus, -ūs *m.* office of a *Salius* (priest of Mars who performs ritual songs and dances)

salictum, -ī *n.* plantation *or* grove of willows

saliens, -ntis *adj.* flowing, gushing, spouting; *f.pl.sbst.* springs, fountains

salignus, -a, -um *adj.* of willow *or* willow-wood,

salillum, -ī *n.* small salt-cellar

salīnae, -ārum *f.pl.* salt-works, salt pits

salīnum, -ī *n.* salt-cellar

saliō, -uī *or* **-iī, -tum** 4. to leap, spring, jump, bound; beat, palpitate; gush, spurt, flow down; mount, cover

saliunca, -ae *f.* wild *or* Celtic nard

salīva, -ae *f.* saliva, spittle; taste, flavour

salix, -icis *f.* willow

salpa, -ae *f.* kind of fish

salpūga, -ae *f.* venomous ant

salsāmentum, -ī *n.* salted *or* pickled fish

salsē *adv.* wittily, acutely

salsipotens, -ntis *adj.* that rules the salt sea

salsūra, -ae *f.* salting, pickling

salsus, -a, -um *adj.* salted; salty, briny; witty, humorous

saltātiō, -ōnis *f.* dancing, dance

saltātor, -ōris *m.* dancer

saltātōrius, -a, -um *adj.* of *or* relating to dancing

saltātrix, -īcis *f.* dancing girl

saltātus, -ūs *m.* dancing, dance

saltem *adv.* at least, at all events, anyhow; **nōn saltem** not even

saltō 1. to dance; perform (*stories*) *or* represent (*characters*) by dancing

saltuōsus, -a, -um *adj.* full of woods *or* forests, well-wooded, woody

saltus¹, -ūs *m.* leap, spring, bound

saltus², -ūs *m.* forest pasture, woodland-pasture, woodland; narrow pass, defile

salūber (-bris), -bris, -bre *adj.* health-giving, wholesome, salubrious; healthy, well; beneficial, advantageous

salūbritās, -ātis f. wholesomeness, salubrity; health, soundness, vigour

salūbriter adv. wholesomely, salubriously; profitably, advantageously

salum, -ī n. sea, open sea, high sea, the deep; stream, current

salūs, -ūtis f. safety, deliverance, help; well-being, health; greeting, salutation

salūtāris, -is, -e adj. of or relating to well-being, wholesome, salutary, beneficial, advantageous; **digitus salūtāris** index finger

salūtāriter adv. profitably, beneficially

salūtātiō, -ōnis f. greeting, salutation; early morning visit by client to patron

salūtātor, -ōris m. one who greets, greeter; client participating in the *salutatio*

salūtātrix, -īcis f.adj. that brings greetings; that participates in the *salutatio*

salūtifer, -era, -erum adj. health-bringing, healing

salūtigerulus, -a, -um adj. that conveys salutations or greetings

salūtō 1. to greet, wish health to, salute; (go to) pay one's respects to, wait upon; bid farewell, take leave

salvē[1] imper. good-day, welcome, hello; how are you? I hope you are well; farewell, goodbye

salvē[2] adv. well, in good health; **satin salvē?** is all well?, all right?

salvus, -a, -um adj. safe, unhurt, uninjured, unharmed, intact, well, sound

sambūca, -ae f. stringed instrument

sambūcistria, -ae f. *sambuca* player

sampsa, -ae f. olive pulp

sānābilis, -is, -e adj. that can be healed, curable, remediable

sānātiō, -ōnis f. healing, curing

sanciō, -xī, -ctum 4. to establish, appoint, decree, ordain; make irrevocable or unalterable; forbid under pain of punishment, enact a penalty against

sanctē adv. solemnly, scupulously, religiously

sanctimōnia, -ae f. sacredness, sanctity, virtuousness

sanctiō, -ōnis f. establishing, ordaining, decreeing as inviolable; decree, ordinance, sanction

sanctitās, -ātis f. inviolability, sacredness, sanctity; virtue, purity, probity, chastity

sanctitūdō, -inis f. sacredness, sanctity

sanctor, -ōris m. establisher, ordainer

sanctus, -a, -um adj. sacred, inviolable, sacrosanct; pure, holy, chaste, virtuous

sandaliārius, -a, -um adj. of or relating to sandals

sandaligerula, -ae f. sandal-carrier

sandalium, -(i)ī n. sandal

sandapila, -ae f. cheap funeral bier

sandyx, -ȳcis m. vermilion, vermilion colour

sānē adv. sensibly, reasonably; well, indeed, truly, certainly, to be sure, right, very; uncommonly, exceedingly

sanguen see **sanguis**

sanguinārius, -a, -um adj. of or relating to blood, blood-

sanguineus, -a, -um adj. of blood, consisting of blood, blood-; blood-coloured, blood-red

sanguinō 1. to be bloodthirsty

sanguinolentus (-nul-), -a, -um adj. full of blood, bloody; blood-red; offensive, injurious

sanguis, -inis m. or **sanguen, -inis** n. blood; blood-line, blood-relation, family; race, stock, offspring, descendant; strength, force, vigour, life-blood

saniēs, [-ēī] f. diseased blood, liquid discharge

sānitās, -ātis f. health, soundness of body; soundness of mind, good sense, discretion, sanity; soundness of style

sanna, -ae f. mocking smile, sneer

sanniō, -ōnis m. buffoon, one who sneers or grimaces in mockery

sānō 1. to heal, cure, restore to health, make sound

sānus, -a, -um adj. sound in body, whole, healthy; sound in mind, in one's right mind, sane, rational, sober

sapa, -ae f. new wine reduced to thickened state

sāperda, -ae m. cheap type of fish

sapiens, -ntis adj. wise, sensible, judicious; m.sbst. wise man, sage, philosopher

sapienter adv. wisely, sensibly, judiciously

sapientia, -ae f. wisdom, good sense, discernment

sapiō, -īvī (-iī) 3. to have sense, be wise;

know, understand; taste of; have good
taste

saplūtus, -a, -um *adj.* exceedingly wealthy

sāpō, -ōnis *m.* hair-dye

sapor, -ōris *m.* taste, flavour, savour

saprophagō 3. to eat putrid food

sapsa *f.pron.* = **ipsa**, see **ipse**

sarcina, -ae *f.* bundle, package, pack; burden, load; *pl.* baggage

sarcinātor, -ōris *m.* mender of old clothes

sarcinātus, -a, -um *adj.* loaded, burdened

sarcinula, -ae *f.* small pack *or* bundle; *pl.*
dowry, belongings

sarciō, sarsī, sartum 4. to mend, patch,
repair, restore; make good, make amends
for

sarcophagus, -ī *m.* sarcophagus, coffin,
grave

sarculum, -ī *m.* small hoe

sardonychātus, -a, -um *adj.* adorned with
a sardonyx

sardonyx, -chis *m./f.* precious stone, sardonyx

sargus, -ī *m.* kind of fish

sāriō, -uī, -tum 4. to hoe, weed

sarīsa, -ae *f.* long Macedonian lance

sarīsophorus, -ī *m.* Macedonian lancer

sariss- see **sarīs-**

sarmentum, -ī *n.pl.* twigs, brushwood

sartāgō, -inis *f.* frying-pan; hotch-potch,
medley

sartor, -ōris *m.* hoer, weeder

sartus, -a, -um *adj.* mended, repaired, put
in order, in good repair

sat see **satis**

sata, -ōrum *n.pl.* crops, standing corn

satagius, -a, -um *adj.* over-anxious

satagō, -ēgī, -actum 3. to have enough to
do, have one's hands full, be in trouble;
bustle about, make a to-do

satelles, -itis *m.* attendant, escort, bodyguard; accomplice, partner in crime

satiās, [-ātis] *f.* sufficiency, abundance,
plentifulness; satisfied desire, satiety;
disgust, distaste

satietās, -ātis *f.* sufficiency, abundance;
state of being glutted *or* sated, satiety

satiō¹ 1. to fill, satisfy, content; sate, saturate; cloy, disgust, weary

satiō², -ōnis *f.* sowing, planting

satira see **satura**

satis *indecl.n.* enough, sufficient, satisfactory; *adv.* enough, sufficiently, tolerably

satisdatiō, -ōnis *f.* giving of bail *or* security

satisdō, -dedī, -datum 1. to give bail or
security

satisfaciō, -fēcī, -factum 3. to give satisfaction, satisfy, content (*by payment or
security*); make amends *or* reparation; ask
pardon, apologize

satisfactiō, -ōnis *f.* satisfaction, amends,
reparation, excuse, apology

sator, -ōris *m.* sower, planter; begetter,
father, creator

satrapēs, -ae *m.* satrap, governor of province (Persian)

satur, -ura, -urum *adj.* well-filled; full,
rich, abundant, fertile

satura, -ae *f.* mixture, medley; satire

satureia, -ōrum *n.pl.* the herb savory

saturitās, -ātis *f.* fullness, satiety; plenty,
abundance

saturō 1. to fill, glut, cloy, satiate; water,
saturate

satus¹, -a, -um *adj.* sprung from; *m.sbst.*
son; *f.sbst.* daughter

satus², -ūs *m.* sowing, planting; begetting,
producing; seed

satyriscus, -ī *m.* little satyr

satyrus, -ī *m.* satyr

sauciātiō, -ōnis *f.* wounding

sauciō 1. to wound, hurt; cut into, plough
up

saucius, -a, -um *adj.* wounded, hurt,
injured, sick; torn; giddy, reeling

sāviolum, -ī *n.* little kiss

sāvior 1. *dep.* to kiss

sāvium, -(i)ī *n.* lips puckered up for kissing; kiss

saxātilis, -is, -e *adj.* dwelling among rocks

saxētum, -ī *n.* rocky place

saxeus, -a, -um *adj.* of rock *or* stone, rocky,
stony

saxificus, -a, -um *adj.* that turns into
stone, petrifying

saxifragus, -a, -um *adj.* stone-breaking,
stone-crushing

saxōsus, -a, -um *adj.* full of rocks *or* stones,
rocky, stony; *n.pl.sbst.* rocky *or* stony
places

saxulum, -ī *n.* small rock

saxum, -ī *n.* rock, stone

scaber, -bra, -brum *adj.* rough, scurfy, scabby, mangy

scabiēs, -ēī *f.* roughness, scurf, scab, mange, itch

scabillum, -ī *n.* foot-operated castanet

scabiōsus, -a, -um *adj.* rough, scurfy, scabby, mangy

scabō, scābī 3. to scratch, scrape

scaena, -ae *f.* stage, backdrop; outward show, pretext

scaenicus, -a, -um *adj.* of *or* relating to the stage, dramatic, theatrical; fictitious, pretended; *m.sbst.* actor, performer

scaeva, -ae *f.* omen

scaevus, -a, -um *adj.* left; unfavourable, unlucky

scālae, -ārum *f.pl.* flight of steps *or* stairs; ladders, scaling ladders

scalmus, -ī *m.* thole pin (on which the oar blade pivoted)

scalpellum, -ī *n.* small surgical knife, scalpel

scalpō, -psī, -ptum 3. to cut, carve, scrape, scratch, engrave

scalprum, -prī *n.* sharp cutting instrument; chisel, chopper, knife

scalptor, -ōris *m.* engraver, sculptor

scalptōrium, -ī *n.* instrument for scratching one's self, back-scratcher

scalptūra, -ae *f.* carving, engraving

scalpurriō 4. to scratch

scambus, -a, -um *adj.* bow-legged, bandy-legged

scamnum, -ī *n.* bench, stool, step, footstool

scamōnea, -ae *f.* convolvulus, scammony

scandō 3. to climb, mount, get up, ascend

scapha, -ae *f.* light boat, skiff

scaphium, -(i)ī *n.* concave vessel in form of boat

scapulae, -ārum *f.pl.* shoulder-blades; shoulders, back

scāpus, -ī *m.* stem, stalk, trunk; shaft

scarus, -ī *m.* kind of sea-fish

scatebra, -ae *f.* bubbling spring

scateō 2. or **scatō** 3. to bubble, gush, spring, flow forth; (*usu. +abl.*) be full of, rich in, crowded with

scaturrīgō, -inis *f.* bubbling spring

scaurus, -a, -um *adj.* with swollen ankles

scazōn, -ontis *m.* iambic trimeter, with spondee in the last foot

scelerātē *adv.* wickedly, impiously, nefariously

scelerātus, -a, -um *adj.* wicked, accursed, impious, infamous; **sēdēs scelerāta** place of punishment in the underworld

scelerō 1. to pollute, defile, contaminate, desecrate

scelerōsus, -a, -um *adj.* full of wickedness, abominable, accursed

scelestē *adv.* wickedly, impiously

scelestus, -a, -um *adj.* wicked, villainous, accursed

scelus, -eris *n.* evil deed, crime, act of wickedness; mishap, calamity; villain, scoundrel

scēma see **schēma**

scēn- see **scaen-**

sceptrifer, -era, -erum *adj.* sceptre-bearing

sceptrum, -ī *n.* royal staff, sceptre; *pl.* kingdom, rule, dominion, authority

sceptūchus, -ī *m.* sceptre-bearer

schēma, -atis *n.* shape, figure, form, fashion, manner; figure of speech, rhetorical figure

schida, -ae *f.* strip of papyrus; piece of paper

schoenicolae, -ārum *f.pl.* prostitutes wearing the scent *schoenus*

schoenobatēs, -ae *m.* rope-dancer

schoenus, -ī *m.* aromatic grass

schola, -ae *f.* place of learning, school; disciples *or* followers of a teacher, school *or* sect; lecture, disputation, dissertation

scholasticus, -a, -um *adj.* of *or* relating to a school, scholastic; *m.sbst.* teacher *or* student of rhetoric, scholar

sciens, -ntis *adj.* knowing, understanding; (*+gen.*) acquainted (with), skilled, expert (in); knowingly, purposely, intentionally

scienter *adv.* knowingly, wisely, skilfully, expertly

scientia, -ae *f.* knowledge, skill, expertise

scīlicet *adv.* it is evident, clear *or* plain; certainly, naturally, evidently; of course, to be sure, doubtless; namely, that is to say

scilla, -ae *f.* sea-onion, sea-leek, squill

scindō, sci(ci)dī, scissum 3. to split, cleave, divide, separate; tear open, tear up, tear apart; cut up, carve

scintilla, -ae *f.* spark; glimmer, faint trace

scintillō 1. to sparkle, glitter, gleam, flash

sciō, scīvī (sciī), scītum 4. to know, understand, perceive; have knowledge of *or* skill in; (+*inf.*) know how (to)

scīpiō, -ōnis *m.* staff, baton

scirpeus, -a, -um *adj.* of rushes, rush-; *f. sbst.* basketwork of rushes

scirpiculus, -ī *m.* basket made of rushes

scirpus, -ī *m.* rush, bulrush; **nōdum in scirpō quaerere** to look for a knot in a bulrush, i.e. to make unnecessary difficulty

sciscitātor, -ōris *m.* investigator, examiner

sciscitor 1. *dep.* or **-ō** 1. to ask, inquire, question, examine, interrogate

sciscō, scīvī, scītum 3. to get to know, learn, ascertain; approve, assent, accept; enact

scītāmenta, -ōrum *n.pl.* dainties, delicacies

scītē *adv.* cleverly, skilfully, shrewdly; elegantly, nicely

scītor 1. *dep.* to seek to know, ask, inquire, consult

scītulus, -a, -um *adj.* elegant, neat, handsome, pretty

scītum, -ī *n.* decree, statute, ordinance

scītus, -a, -um *adj.* knowing, wise, experienced, skilful, shrewd; suitable, judicious, apposite; beautiful, elegant, fine

sciūrus, -ī *m.* squirrel

scloppus, -ī *m.* sound of popping one's cheeks

scobis, -is *f.* powder, dust; saw-dust, scrapings, filings

scomber, -brī *m.* mackerel

scōpae, -ārum *f.pl.* broom, besom

scopulōsus, -a, -um *adj.* full of rocks, rocky, craggy

scopulus[1], -ī *m.* rock, cliff, crag; rock, shelf, ledge (in sea); difficulty, danger, harm

scopulus[2], -ī *m.* target

scordalus, -ī *m.* brawler, trouble-maker

scorpiō, -ōnis *m.* scorpion; military engine for firing darts, stones and other missiles

scorpius (-os), -(i)ī *m.* scorpion; the constellation Scorpio

scorteus, -a, -um *adj.* made of hides *or* leather; *f.sbst.* leather garment

scortillum, -ī *n.* young *or* little prostitute

scortor 1. *dep.* to pay for sex, have sex with a prostitute

scortum, -ī *n.* skin, hide; prostitute

screātor, -ōris *m.* hawker, throat-clearer

screātus, -ūs *m.* hawking, throat-clearing

screō 1. to hawk, clear one's throat

scrība, -ae *m.* public official, clerk, secretary, scribe

scrib(i)līta, -ae *f.* kind of tart

scrībō, -ipsī, -iptum 3. to write, draw; write down, compose, describe, depict; draw up, communicate, announce in writing

scrīnium, -(i)ī *n.* writing-case, letter-case, book-case

scriptiō, -ōnis *f.* writing, composition in writing

scriptitō 1. to write often

scriptor, -ōris *m.* writer, scribe, secretary; author, composer; drawer up, drafter

scriptulum, -ī *n.* marking on board

scriptum, -ī *n.* written composition, writing, treatise, work, script; written ordinance, law; **duodecim scripta** type of board game

scriptūra, -ae *f.* writing, written characters, text; composing, composition; tax paid for using public pastureland

scriptus, -ūs *m.* office of scribe *or* secretary, clerkship, secretaryship

scrīpulum, -ī *n.* smallest division of weight

scrobis, -is *m./f.* ditch, trench, pit

scrōfa, -ae *f.* breeding sow

scrōfipascus, -a, -um *adj.* that keeps sows

scrūpeus, -a, -um *adj.* consisting of pointed *or* sharp rocks; sharp, rough, steep, rugged

scrūpōsus, -a, -um *adj.* full of sharp *or* rough rocks, jagged, rugged

scrūpulōsus, -a, -um *adj.* full of sharp *or* pointed rocks, jagged, rugged; exact, precise, anxious, careful, scrupulous

scrūpulus, -ī *m.* uneasiness, difficulty, trouble, anxiety, doubt, scruple

scrūpus, -ī *m.* uneasiness, anxiety

scrūta, -ōrum *n.pl.* junk, trash, frippery

scrūtātor, -ōris *m.* searcher, examiner, investigator

scrūtor 1. *dep.* to search carefully, examine thoroughly, explore, investigate; find out, search out

sculpō, -psī, -ptum 3. to carve, cut, engrave, chisel

sculpōneae, -ārum *f.pl.* cheap wooden shoes

sculptilis, -is, -e *adj.* formed by carving, engraved

scurra, -ae *m.* dandy, man about town; buffoon, jester

scurrīlis, -is, -e *adj.* buffoon-like, jesting, jeering, scurrilous

scurrīlitās, -ātis *f.* buffoonery, scurrility

scurrīliter *adv.* in a buffoon-like *or* scurrilous manner

scurror 1. *dep.* to play the buffoon *or* jester

scūtāle, -is *n.* thong of a sling

scūtārius, -(i)ī *m.* shield-maker

scūtātus, -a, -um *adj.* armed with a *scutum*

scutella, -ae *f.* salver, shallow pan

scutica, -ae *f.* lash, whip, strap

scūtigerulus, -ī *m.* shield-bearer

scutra, -ae *f.* flat tray, dish *or* platter

scutula¹, -ae *f.* small dish *or* platter; diamond- *or* lozenge-shaped figure

scutula², -ae *f.* wooden roller *or* cylinder

scutulāta, -ōrum *n.pl.* garment with checked patterning

scūtulum, -ī *n.* small shield

scūtum, -ī *n.* (oblong) shield, buckler; protection, safeguard

scymnus, -ī *m.* cub

scyphus, -ī *m.* cup, goblet

scytalē, -ēs *f.* cylindrical snake (of equal thickness throughout)

sē (*gen.* **suī**, *dat.* **sibi (sibī)** *abl.* **sē**) *refl. pron.* himself, herself, itself, themselves; **per sē** by his (*etc.*) own efforts, in itself; **ad/apud sē** to/at his (*etc.*) house

sēbum, -ī *n.* tallow, suet, grease, animal fat

sēcēdō, -essī, -essum 3. to withdraw, retire, separate; revolt, secede; dissent

sēcernō, sēcrēvī, sēcrētum 3. to separate, set apart, divide, sever; distinguish, discern; reject, discard

secespita, -ae *f.* long iron sacrificial knife

sēcessiō, -ōnis *f.* schism, secession, withdrawal

sēcessus, -ūs *m.* withdrawal; (place of) retirement, solitude *or* retreat

sēclūdō, -sī, -sum 3. to shut off, separate; shut up, confine

secō, -uī, -tum 1. to cut, cut off, amputate; cut through, divide, cleave; cut a path

through, travel through, intersect; cut up, carve, slice

sēcrētiō, -ōnis *f.* dividing, separation

sēcrētō *adv.* apart, by itself; secretly, in secret

sēcrētum, -ī *n.* something *or* somewhere secret *or* private; (place of) seclusion, retirement *or* retreat; secret, mystery

sēcrētus, -a, -um *adj.* separate, apart, withdrawn; remote, lonely, solitary; hidden, concealed, secret, private

secta, -ae *f.* path, line; way of life, school (of thought), doctrines, system of ideas

sectārius, -a, -um *adj.* gelded, castrated

sectātor, -ōris *m.* follower, attendant, adherent; *pl.* train, retinue, suite

sectilis, -is, -e *adj.* cut, divided; that may be cut

sectiō, -ōnis *f.* dividing, parcelling out *or* distribution at public auction

sectīvus, -a, -um *adj.* that may be cut

sector¹ 1. *dep.* to follow continually *or* eagerly, accompany; run after, pursue, chase, hunt; strive after, pursue eagerly, seek out; imitate

sector², -ōris *m.* one who cuts, cutter; purchaser of goods at public auction

sectūrae, -ārum *f.pl.* mines, diggings

sēcubitus, -ūs *m.* sleeping *or* lying alone

sēcubō, -uī 1. to sleep *or* lie alone

secundānī, -ōrum *m.pl.* soldiers of the second legion

secundārius, -a, -um *adj.* belonging to the second class, sort *or* quality; second-rate, middling, inferior

secundō¹ 1. to direct favourably; secure a favourable outcome

secundō² *adv.* secondly

secundum¹ *prep.* (+*acc.*) following after, behind; immediately after, next to; in accordance with, according to; in the favour of

secundum² *adv.* after, behind; secondly

secundus, -a, -um *adj.* following, next, second; favourable, fair, propitious, fortunate, encouraging; second-rate, inferior

sēcūrē *adv.* unconcernedly, without fear

sēcūricula, -ae *f.* small axe, hatchet

sēcūrifer, -era, -erum *adj.* axe-bearing

sēcūriger, -era, -erum *adj.* axe-wielding

secūris, -is *f.* axe, hatchet; battle-axe; executioner's axe

secūritās, -ātis *f.* freedom from care, calmness, composure; freedom from danger, safety, security; carelessness, heedlessness, negligence

secūrus, -a, -um *adj.* free from care, untroubled, unconcerned, calm, peaceful; free from danger, safe, secure; careless, reckless, heedless, negligent

secus¹ *n.* sex

secus² *adv.* otherwise, differently, not so; not well, badly; **haud secus** even so, just so; **haud/nōn secus ac** just as

secūtor, -ōris *m.* 'pursuer', gladiator who fought with a *retiarius*

sed *conj.* but; on the contrary, but also, but even, but in fact; **sed enim** but in fact

sēdāmen, -inis *n.* means of allaying, allayment, sedative

sēdātē *adv.* calmly, sedately

sēdātiō, -ōnis *f.* allaying, assuaging, calming

sēdātus, -a, -um *adj.* composed, calm, quiet, tranquil

sēdecim *indecl.adj.* sixteen

sēdēcula, -ae *f.* little seat, low stool

sedens, -ntis *adj.* sitting; squat, low-growing

sedentārius, -a, -um *adj.* sitting, sedentary

sedeō, sēdī, sessum 2. to sit; sit still, remain sitting; sit in council *or* in court; remain encamped; sit idly, be inactive, rest, loiter; sink *or* settle down, subside; sit tight, hold fast, be firm, fixed *or* immovable; be stuck fast; be established

sēdēs, -is *f.* seat; bench, chair, throne; position, place, spot; ground, foundation, bottom; dwelling-place, residence, abode; temple

sedīle, -is *n.* seat, bench, stool, chair

sēditiō, -ōnis *f.* political insurrection, mutiny, sedition; dissension, discord, quarrel, strife

sēditiōsē *adv.* seditiously

sēditiōsus, -a, -um *adj.* mutinous, seditious

sēdō 1. to settle, calm, allay, appease, check, end, stop; become quiet, lull, subside

sēdūcō, -uxī, -uctum 3. to lead aside, lead away, carry off; withdraw; separate, divide

sēductiō, -ōnis *f.* leading *or* drawing aside

sēductus, -a, -um *adj.* remote, distant, separated; retired, living in solitude

sēdulitās, -ātis *f.* zeal, application, assiduity

sēdulō *adv.* diligently, zealously, assiduously

sēdulus, -a, -um *adj.* diligent, zealous, careful, assiduous

seges, -etis *f.* corn-field; standing corn, growing corn; crop, produce; field, ground, soil

segmentum, -ī *n.* (*usu.pl.*) decorative hem, bands, flounces

segne *adv.* slowly, sluggishly, lazily

segnipēs, -edis *adj.* with slow foot

segnis, -is, -e *adj.* slow, tardy, dilatory, sluggish, lazy

segnitās, -ātis *f.* slowness, tardiness, sluggishness

segniter *adv.* slowly, sluggishly, slothfully, lazily

segnitia, -ae or **-ēs, [-ēī]** *f.* slowness, tardiness, sluggishness, inactivity

sēgregō 1. to set apart, lay aside, separate, segregate

sēgrex, [-egis] *adj.* apart, separate

sēiugis, -is *m.* chariot drawn by six horses; *pl.* team of six horses

sēiugō 1. to separate, part

sēiunctim *adv.* separately

sēiunctiō, -ōnis *f.* division, separation

sēiunctus, -a, -um *adj.* separate, distinct

sēiungō, -xī, -ctum 3. to separate, part, disunite; exclude

sēlectiō, -ōnis *f.* choice, selection

sēlectus, -a, -um *adj.* chosen, selected

sēlībra, -ae *f.* half a *libra*

sēligō, sēlēgī, sēlectum 3. to choose, select

sella, -ae *f.* seat, chair, stool

sellāriolus, -a, -um *adj.* for sitting

sellārium, -iī *n.* lavatory

sellārius, -iī *m.* male prostitute

sellisternium, -iī *n.* religious banquet offered to goddesses (corresponding to the *lectisternium* for gods)

sellula, -ae *f.* small chair *or* stool

sellulārius, -a, -um *adj.* sedentary

semel *adv.* once, a single time; at once, in a word, briefly; the first time, first; once, ever, at some time, at any time

sēmen, -inis *n.* seed; element, atom; shoot, cutting, slip; offspring, progeny, posterity; stock, race

sēme(n)stris, -is, -e *adj.* of six months, half-yearly; lasting six months

sēmentis, -is *f.* sowing, seeding; crop

sēmentīvus, -a, -um *adj.* of *or* relating to seed *or* sowing; that occurs at seed-time

sēmēsus, -a, -um *adj.* half-eaten, half-consumed

sēmiadapertus, -a, -um *adj.* half-opened

sēmiambustus, -a, -um *adj.* half-burned, half-consumed

sēmianimis, -is, -e or **-us, -a, -um** *adj.* half-alive, half-dead

sēmiapertus, -a, -um *adj.* half-opened, half-open

sēmibarbarus, -ī *m.* half-barbarian

sēmibōs, -ovis *adj.* half-ox in form

sēmicaper, -prī *m.* half-goat

sēmicinctium, -iī *n.* narrow girdle *or* apron

sēmicremātus, -a, -um *adj.* half-burnt

sēmicremus, -a, -um *adj.* half-burnt

sēmicrūdus, -a, -um *adj.* half-raw; having only partly digested one's food

sēmicubitālis, -is, -e *adj.* half-cubit long

sēmideus, -a, -um *adj.* semi-divine; *m./f. sbst.* demigod/goddess

sēmidoctus, -a, -um *adj.* half-taught, half-educated

sēmiermis, -is, -e or **-us, -a, -um** *adj.* half-armed, poorly armed

sēmifactus, -a, -um *adj.* half-made, half-finished

sēmifer, -era, -erum *adj.* half-man, half-man and half-beast

sēmifultus, -a, -um *adj.* half-propped up

sēmigravis, -is, -e *adj.* half-drunken

sēmigrō 1. to go away

sēmihians, -ntis *adj.* half-opened, half-open

sēmihomo (-ō), -inis *adj.* half-man, half-man and half-beast

sēmihōra, -ae *f.* half an hour, half-hour

sēmilacer, -era, -erum *adj.* half-mangled, half-lacerated

sēmilautus, -a, -um *adj.* half-washed

sēmilīber, -era, -erum *adj.* half-free

sēmilixa, -ae *m.* one little better than a camp-follower

sēmimarīnus, -a, -um *adj.* half in the sea

sēmimās, -aris *adj.* half-male

sēmimortuus, -a, -um *adj.* half-dead

sēminārium, -(i)ī *n.* nursery-garden, nursery

sēminātor, -ōris *m.* originator, producer, author

sēminex, -ecis *adj.* half-dead

sēminium, -(i)ī *n.* procreation; race, stock, breed

sēminō 1. to sow; bring forth, produce

sēminūdus, -a, -um *adj.* half-naked

sēmipāgānus, -a, -um *adj.* half-rustic *or* -yokel

sēmiperfectus, -a, -um *adj.* half-finished

sēmiplēnus, -a, -um *adj.* half-full, half-filled

sēmiplētus, -a, -um *adj.* half-filled

sēmiputātus, -a, -um *adj.* half-pruned

sēmirāsus, -a, -um *adj.* half-shaven

sēmireductus, -a, -um *adj.* half-bent back

sēmirefectus, -a, -um *adj.* half-repaired

sēmirutus, -a, -um *adj.* half-ruined, half-destroyed, half-demolished

sēmis, -issis *m.* one half; half an *as*

sēmisenex, -nis *m.* man old in years, young in mind

sēmisepultus, -a, -um *adj.* half-buried

sēmisomnus, -a, -um *adj.* half-asleep, sleepy, drowsy

sēmisupīnus, -a, -um *adj.* half-bent backward, half-supine

sēmita, -ae *f.* path, lane, track, foot-path, by-way

sēmitālis, -is, -e *adj.* of *or* relating to paths *or* by-ways

sēmitārius, -a, -um *adj.* of *or* relating to paths *or* by-ways

sēmitō 1. to trace across, streak

sēmiustilō 1. to half-burn

sēmiustus, -a, -um *adj.* half-burnt

sēmivir, -rī *adj.* emasculated, unmanly, womanish, effeminate; *m.sbst.* half-man, half-man and half-beast; hermaphrodite

sēmivīvus, -a, -um *adj.* half-alive, half-dead, almost dead

sēmodius, -(i)ī *m.* half a *modius*

sēmōtus, -a, -um *adj.* remote, distant; distinct, familiar

sēmoveō, -ōvī, -ōtum 2. to move apart, separate; exclude

semper *adv.* always, for ever; at all times

sempiternus, -a, -um *adj.* everlasting, eternal, perpetual, continual

sēmuncia, -ae *f.* twenty-fourth part (*of any whole*); twenty-fourth of an *as or libra*; trifle, trifling sum

sēmunciārius, -a, -um *adj.* one twenty-fourth percent per month (*interest*)

senāculum, -ī *n.* senatorial council chamber

sēnāriolus, -ī *m.* insignificant or inconsequential *senarius*

sēnārius, -a, -um *adj.* line consisting of six metrical feet

senātor, -ōris *m.* senator, member of senate

senātōrius, -a, -um *adj.* of or relating to a senator, senatorial

senātus, -ūs *m.* senate, council of elders; meeting of the senate; **senātūs cōnsultum** decree of the senate

senecta, -ae *f.* old age, extreme age, senility

senectūs¹, -ūtis *f.* old age, extreme age, senility

senectus², -a, -um *adj.* aged, very old

seneō 2. to be old

senēscō, senuī 3. to grow old, become aged; grow weak, feeble or powerless; waste away, wane, decline, decay

senex, senis *m.* old man, aged person; *adj.* old-aged, advanced in years

sēnī, -ae, -a *pl.adj.* six each; six at a time

senīlis, -is, -e *adj.* of or relating to old people, old-aged, senile

sēniō, -ōnis *m.* number six (on dice)

senior, -or, -us *compar.adj.* older, more advanced in years; *m.sbst.* man of forty-five years or older

senium, -(i)ī *n.* decline, decay (from old age); old age; moroseness, peevishness, gloom

senius, -(i)ī *m.* old man, old fellow

sensa, -ōrum *n.pl.* thoughts, ideas, opinions

sensibilis, -is, -e *adj.* that can be perceived by the senses, perceptible

sensifer, -era, -erum *adj.* producing sensation

sensilis, -is, -e *adj.* sentient, sensible

sensim *adv.* slowly, gently, gradually

sensus, -ūs *m.* faculty or power of perceiving, perception; sensation, sense; emotion, feeling, sentiment, inclination, state of mind; understanding, reason; idea, meaning, intention; thought expressed in words, sentence

sententia, -ae *f.* way of thinking, opinion, sentiment; purpose, intention, idea; sense, meaning; decision, sentence, judgement, vote; thought expressed in words, sentence; aphorism, maxim

sententiola, -ae *f.* aphorism, maxim

sententiōsē *adv.* sententiously, pithily

sententiōsus, -a, -um *adj.* full of meaning, pithy, sententious

senticētum, -ī *n.* thicket of briers, thornbrake

sentīna, -ae *f.* bilge-water; lowest of the low, dregs, rabble

sentiō, sensī, sensum 4. to perceive, feel; observe, notice, sense; think, deem, judge, imagine, suppose; experience, suffer, undergo; give one's opinion, vote, declare, decide; **tēcum sentiō** I agree with you

sentis, -is *m.* thorn-bush, brier, bramble

sentiscō 3. to perceive, observe

sentus, -a, -um *adj.* thorny, rough, rugged

seorsum (-us) *adv.* separately, apart

sēpār, [-aris] *adj.* separate, different

sēparābilis, -is, -e *adj.* that may be separated, separable

sēparātē *adv.* separately, apart

sēparātim *adv.* apart, separately; generally

sēparātiō, -ōnis *f.* separation, division

sēparātus, -a, -um *adj.* separate, distinct, particular; distant, remote

sēparō 1. to separate, divide; treat or consider separately; except, exclude

sepelībilis, -is, -e *adj.* that may be buried

sepeliō, -elīvī or **-elī, -ultum** 4. to bury, inter; suppress, put an end to

sēpia, -ae *f.* cuttle-fish; ink (derived from cuttle-fish)

sēpōnō, -osuī, -ositum 3. to lay aside; put by, separate; pick out, distinguish; banish, exile

sēpositus, -a, -um *adj.* distant, remote; select, choice

seps, sēpos *m.* venomous serpent (with bite that caused putrefaction)

septem *indecl.adj.* seven

septemdecim *indecl.adj.* seventeen

septemfluus, -a, -um *adj.* sevenfold-flowing

septemgeminus, -a, -um *adj.* sevenfold

septempedālis, -is, -e *adj.* seven feet high

septemplex, -icis *adj.* sevenfold

septemtriōnālis, -is, -e *adj.* of *or* relating to the north, northern, north-

septemtriōnēs, -um *m.pl.* seven stars of the Wain, Ursula Major *or* Ursula Minor; northern regions, north; north wind

septemvir, -rī *m.* one of the *septemviri* (administrative board of seven men)

septemvirālis, -is, -e *adj.* of *or* relating to the *septemviri*, septemviral

septemvirātus, -ūs *m.* office of the *septemviri*, septemvirate

septēnārius, -a, -um *adj.* containing *or* consisting of seven; *m.sbst.* line consisting of seven metrical feet

septēnī, -ae, -a *pl.adj.* seven each; seven; *sg.* sevenfold

septent- see **septemt-**

septiens (-ēs) *adv.* seven times

septimānī, -ōrum *m.pl.* soldiers of the seventh legion

septimontiālis, -is, -e *adj.* of *or* relating to the feast of the Septimontium (held on December 11)

septimum *adv.* for the seventh time

septimus, -a, -um *adj.* seventh

septingentēsimus, -a, -um *adj.* seven hundredth

septingentī, -ae, -a *pl.adj.* seven hundred

septuāgēnī, -ae, -a *pl.adj.* seventy each

septuāgēsimus (-gens-), -a, -um *adj.* seventieth

septuāgiens (-ēs) *adv.* seventy times

septuāgintā *indecl.adj.* seventy

septuennis, -is, -e *adj.* seven years old

septunx, -ncis *m.* seven-twelfths (of a whole)

sepulchr- see **sepulcr-**

sepulcrālis, -is, -e *adj.* of *or* relating to the tomb, sepulchral

sepulcrētum, -ī *n.* burial-place, cemetery

sepulcrum, -ī *n.* burial-place, grave, tomb, sepulchre

sepultūra, -ae *f.* burial, funeral; burial-place

sequax, -ācis *adj.* following *or* seeking

after, pursuing eagerly; yielding, pliable, flexible

sequester, -tra, -trum *or* **-ter, -tris, -tre** *adj.* intermediate; *m./f.sbst.* depositary, trustee; agent, go-between; *n.sbst.* sequestration, trust

sequius *adv.* not well, ill, badly

sequor, secūtus 3. *dep.* to follow, come *or* go after; attend, go with; chase; pursue; strive for, aim at, seek to attain; comply with, accede to, conform to; succeed, result, ensue

sera, -ae *f.* bar (*used to fasten doors*)

serēnitās, -ātis *f.* clear *or* fair weather; fairness, serenity

serēnō 1. to make clear *or* fair; clear up, light up

serēnum, -ī *n.* clear *or* bright sky, fair weather

serēnus, -a, -um *adj.* clear, fair, bright; cheerful, tranquil, favourable

serescō 3. to grow dry

sēria, -ae *f.* large earthen jar

sēricātus, -a, -um *adj.* dressed in silks

seriēs, [-ēī] *f.* row, succession, series, chain; line of descent, lineage

sēriō *adv.* seriously, in earnest

sēriola, -ae *f.* small jar

sērius, -a, -um *adj.* serious, grave, earnest

sermō, -ōnis *m.* talk, conversation, dialogue, discussion; ordinary speech, common talk, rumour; manner of speaking, mode of expression

sermōcinor 1. *dep.* to talk with; converse, hold a conversation

sermunculus, -ī *m.* common talk, tittle-tattle, rumour

serō[1], sēvī, satum 3. to sow, plant; beget, bring forth, produce; sow the seeds of, disseminate, propagate; cause, excite

serō[2], sertum 3. to join *or* bind together, plait, interweave

sērō[3] *adv.* late, at a late hour; too late; **sērius ōcius** later or earlier, i.e. sooner or later

sērōtinus, -a, -um *adj.* that comes *or* happens late

serpens, -ntis *f./m.* snake, serpent

serpentigena, -ae *m.* serpent-born, one sprung from a serpent

serpentipēs, -edis *adj.* serpent-footed

serpō, -psī 3. creep, crawl, move or spread slowly

serpullum, -ī n. thyme, wild thyme

serra, -ae f. saw

serrācum, -ī n. kind of wagon or cart

serrārius, -(i)ī m. saw-maker

serrātus, -a, -um adj. serrated, saw-shaped; m.sbst. coin notched on the edge

serrula, -ae f. small saw

serta¹, -ōrum n.pl. wreaths of flowers, garlands

serta², -ae f. garland, wreath of flowers

serum, -ī n. watery part of curdled milk, whey; semen

sērus, -a, -um adj. late; too late; at a late time, hour

serva, -ae f. female-slave

servābilis, -is, -e adj. that can be saved or rescued

servans, -ntis adj. (+gen.) keeping, observing

servātiō, -ōnis f. observance

servātor, -ōris m. preserver, saviour, deliverer; observer, maintainer

servātrix, -īcis f. preserver, protectress

servīlicolus, -a. -um adj. rather servile or mean

servīlis, -is, -e adj. of or relating to a slave, slavish, servile

servīliter adv. slavishly, servilely

serviō 4. to be a servant or slave, serve, be in service; (+dat.) be subject to, be of use or service to; serve for, be fit or useful for; be subject to a servitude

servitium, -(i)ī n. condition of a slave or servant, slavery, servitude

servitūs, -ūtis f. condition of a slave, slavery, subjection

servō 1. to save, deliver, keep unharmed, preserve, protect; pay attention to, watch, observe

servola (-ula), -ae f. young slave, slave-girl

servolus (-ulus), -ī m. young slave, slave-boy

servus¹, -ī m. slave

servus², -a, -um adj. slavish, servile, subject

sēsama, -ae f. sesame

sescēnārius, -a, -um adj. six hundred strong

sescēnī, -ae, -a pl.adj. six hundred each; six hundred each time

sescentēsimus, -a, -um adj. six-hundredth

sescentī, -ae, -a pl.adj. six hundred

sescentiens (-ēs) adv. six hundred times

sescuncia, -ae f. one and a half unciae

sēsē see **sē**

seselis, -is f. hartwort

sesquī adv. one and a half times

sesquialter, -era, -erum adj. once and a half

sesquihōra, -ae f. one hour and a half

sesquimodius, -(i)ī m. one modius and a half

sesquioctāvus, -a, -um adj. one and an eighth times as much; n.sbst. one and an eighth

sesquiopus, -eris n. one and a half days' work

sesquipedālis, -is, -e adj. of a foot and a half; one foot and a half (in length, breadth or diameter)

sesquipēs, -edis m. one foot and a half (in length, breadth or diameter)

sesquiplāga, -ae f. blow and a half, stroke and a half

sesquiplex, -icis adj. one and a half as much

sesquitertius, -a, -um adj. bearing the ratio of four to three

sessilis, -is, -e adj. of or relating to sitting, fit for sitting on; low, dwarf

sessiō, -ōnis f. sitting; sitting idly, loitering; seat, sitting-place

sessitō 1. to sit much

sessiuncula, -ae f. small group, meeting, company

sessor, -ōris m. one who sits, sitter; horseman, rider; inhabitant, resident

sestertiolum, -ī n. small sesterce

sestertium, -(i)ī n. one hundred thousand sesterces; **deciēs sestertium** a million; **centiēs sestertium** ten millions

sestertius, -a, -um adj. two and a half; m. sbst. sesterce (small silver coin equal to two and a half asses or one fourth of a denarius)

sētius compar.adv. less, less readily; more slowly; **nihilō sētius** nevertheless, just the same

seu see **sīve**

severē adv. sternly, strictly; seriously; austerely, plainly

sevēritās, -ātis f. sternness, severity; seriousness; austerity, plainness

sevēritūdō, -inis f. sternness, severity

sevērus, -a, -um adj. strict, severe; harsh, cruel; serious, important; austere, plain; grim

sēvocō 1. to call aside; withdraw, separate

sex indecl.adj. six

sexāgēnī, -ae, -a pl.adj. sixty each; sixty at a time; sixty

sexāgēsimus (-gens-), -a, -um adj. sixtieth

sexāgiens (-ēs) adv. sixty times; (with or without sestertium) 6,000,000 sesterces

sexāgintā indecl.adj. sixty

sexangulus, -a, -um adj. six-cornered

sexcen- see **sescen-**

sexdecim see **sēdecim**

sexennis, -is, -e adj. six years old

sexennium, -(i)ī n. period of six years

sexiens (-ēs) adv. six times

sextadecimānī, -ōrum m.pl. soldiers of the sixteenth legion

sextans, -ntis m. one-sixth; one-sixth of an as; one-sixth of a sextarius

sextāriolus, -ī m. small jug

sextārius, -(i)ī m. liquid measure (one sixth of a congius, i.e. about a pint)

sextula, -ae f. one sixth of an uncia

sextum adv. for the sixth time

sextus, -a, -um adj. sixth; **sexta (pars)** one sixth

sexus, -ūs m. sex, gender

sī conj. if; **quod sī** but if; **sī minus/nōn** if not

sibi see **sē**

sībilō 1. to hiss, whistle; hiss in contempt; hiss at

sībilus¹, -ī m. hissing, whistling; contemptuous hiss

sībilus², -a, -um adj. hissing

sīc adv. in this way, thus; so; as follows; so much; that is so, yes

sīca, -ae f. dagger

sīcārius, -(i)ī m. murderer, assassin

siccē adv. plainly, dryly

siccitās, -ātis f. dryness; good health; plainness, dryness; pl. dry conditions, drought

siccō 1. to dry, desiccate; drain; staunch; dry up

siccoculus, -a, -um adj. dry-eyed

siccus, -a, -um adj. dry; thirsty, parched; healthy, sound; sober, abstemious; plain, dry; n.sbst. dry land

sicilicissitō 1. to act in a Sicilian fashion

sīcīlicula, -ae f. small sickle

sīcin(e) interrog. is it so (that)?

sīcubi conj. if anywhere

sīcula, -ae f. little dagger, penis

sīcunde conj. if from anywhere

sīcut(ī) conj. just as, as; as indeed; as it were

sīdereus, -a, -um adj. starry; heavenly; sparkling, gleaming

sīdō, -ī 3. to sit down; sink, descend; settle down; (of ships) run aground; subside

sīdus, -eris n. star; heavenly body, planet; constellation; season; pl. heavens

sigillāria, -ium n.pl. small pieces of decorated pottery; market at which such objects were sold; final day of the Saturnalia when such objects were exchanged as gifts

sigillātus, -a, -um adj. decorated with images in relief

sigillum, -ī n. statuette; image in relief; seal

sigma, -atis n. the Greek letter sigma

signātor, -ōris m. witness (esp. to a will)

signātus, -a, -um adj. stamped, coined

signifer¹, -era, -erum adj. holding the constellations; m.sbst. zodiac

signifer², -erī m. standard-bearer; leader

significanter adv. meaningfully, distinctly

significātiō, -ōnis f. making of signs; indication; hint, suggestion; expression of feeling; meaning

significō 1. to indicate, show; make known; signify; make signs

signipotens, -ntis adj. ruling the constellations

signō 1. to mark, impress; stamp; seal; indicate; signify

signum, -ī n. sign, mark; token, seal; signal; warning; command, order; password; military standard, banner; troops; constellation; statue, image

sīlānus, -ī m. fountain, water-spout

silens, -ntis adj. silent, quiet; m.pl.sbst. the dead

silentium, -(i)ī n. silence; inactivity, stillness; speechlessness; obscurity, neglect

sileō, -uī 2. to be silent; be inactive, lie

dormant; say nothing; keep quiet about; leave unsaid

siler, -eris *n.* kind of spindle tree

silescō 3. to fall silent

silex, -icis *m./f.* flint, hard stone; boulder, rock; cliff

silicernium, -(i)ī *n.* 'funeral feast', old codger

silīgineus, -a, -um *adj.* made from *siligo*

silīgō, -inis *f.* soft, white wheat

siliqua, -ae *f.* pod

sillybus see **sittyba**

silūrus, -ī *m.* sheat-fish, catfish

sīlus, -a, -um *adj.* snub-nosed

silva, -ae *f.* wood, forest; foliage (*of a tree*); thicket; grove, park; abundance (*of material*), mass

silvescō 3. to grow thick, bush out

silvestris (-ter), -tris, -tre *adj.* of *or* relating to woods, woodland; living in woodland, wild; rustic, pastoral; savage; covered in trees, wooded; *n.pl.sbst.* woodlands

silvicola, -ae *m.adj.* that inhabits woods

silvicultrix, -īcis *f.adj.* that inhabits woods

silvifragus, -a, -um *adj.* that shatters woods

silvōsus, -a, -um *adj.* covered with woods, well-wooded

sīmia, -ae *f.* monkey, ape

similis, -is, -e *adj.* (+*gen./dat.*) like, similar (to); **vērī similis** plausible, likely; **monstrī similis** incredible; *n.sbst.* comparison, analogue

similiter *adv.* in like manner, similarly

similitūdō, -inis *f.* similarity, likeness; imitation; metaphor, analogy; monotony; **similitūdō vērī** plausibility

sīmiolus, -ī *m.* little monkey

simītū *adv.* at the same time

sīmius, -(i)ī *m.* monkey, ape

simplex, -icis *adj.* simple, plain; single-layered; unconditional; frank, candid; naive

simplicitās, -ātis *f.* singleness; simplicity; frankness, candour; naivety

simpliciter *adv.* simply, plainly; singly; frankly, candidly

simplum, -ī *n.* simple sum (*of money*)

simpulum, -ī *n.* ladle

simpuvium, -iī *n.* ladle

simul *adv.* at the same time; together, at once

simulācrum, -ī *n.* likeness, effigy; ghost; imitation; mock-fight; image; atomic image

simulāmen, -inis *n.* imitation

simulans, -ntis *adj.* (+*gen.*) imitative (of)

simulātē *adv.* feignedly

simulātiō, -ōnis *f.* pretence, simulation; pretext

simulātor, -ōris *m.* feigner, pretender; imitator

simulātrix, -īcis *f.* female producer of forgeries

simulō 1. (+*dat.*) to make similar (to); represent, depict; simulate, feign; counterfeit; pretend

simultās, -ātis *f.* rivalry, feud

simulter *adv.* in the same way

sīmulus, -a, -um *adj.* snub-nosed

sīmus, -a, -um *adj.* snub-nosed; (*of the nose*) flattened

sīn *conj.* but if, if however

sināpis, -is *f.* white mustard

sincērē *adv.* soundly; genuinely, sincerely

sincērus, -a, -um *adj.* whole, sound; pure, unmixed; genuine, uncorrupt

sincipitāmentum, -ī *n.* half-head

sinciput, -pitis *n.* half-head; brain

sindō, -onis *f.* muslin

sine *prep.* (+*abl.*) without

singillātim *adv.* one by one, separately

singlāriter see **singulāriter**

singulāris, -is, -e *adj.* single, individual; singular; special; exceptional, unusual

singulāriter *adv.* one by one; singularly, exceptionally

singulārius, -a, -um *adj.* single, separate

singulātim see **singillātim**

singulī, -ae, -a *pl.adj.* one each; one at a time; single, individual; *m.sbst.* individuals

singultim *adv.* gaspingly, with a stammer

singultiō 4. to throb

singultō 1. to gasp, sob; (+*acc.*) gasp out

singultus, -ūs *m.* gasping, sobbing; hiccup

sinister, -tra, -trum *adj.* on the left, left; adverse, unfavourable; wrong, perverse

sinisteritās, -ātis *f.* social awkwardness

sinistra[1], -ae *f.* left hand; the left

sinistra[2] *adv.* on the left

sinistrē *adv.* adversely; wrongly

sinistrorsum (-us) *adv.* to the left

sinō, sīvī (siī), situm 3. to let be; (+*inf.*) allow (to); (+*acc.*+*inf.* or +*subj.*) grant (that); **sine** very well!

sīnum, -ī *n.* large bowl

sinuō 1. to bend, make curved; fill out (*a sail*)

sinuōsus, -a, -um *adj.* curved, sinuous; full of folds; cavernous

sinus¹, -ūs *m.* curve, bend; bay, gulf; breast, bosom; fold in clothing; pocket; belly of a sail; cavity, hollow

sīnus², -ī *m.* see **sīnum**

sīparium, -(i)ī *n.* curtain concealing part of a stage; mime comedy

sīparum, -ī *n.* topsail

sīphō, -ōnis *m.* tube; jet; device for extinguishing fires

sīp(h)unculus, -ī *m.* small jet (of a fountain)

sīquidem (siq-) *conj.* if indeed; because, since

sīremps(e) *adv.* in the same way

sirpe *n.* asafoetida

sirus, -ī *m.* silo (for corn)

sīs (= sī vīs) please

siser, -eris *m.* rampion

sistō, stetī or **stitī, statum** 3. to cause to stand, set up; fix, position; make appear (*esp. in court*); settle, establish; stop, check; stand; stand firm; come to a halt

sistrātus, -a, -um *adj.* bearing a *sistrum*

sistrum, -ī *n.* rattle (*used in the worship of Isis*)

sisymbrium, -iī *n.* kind of aromatic herb, mint

sitella, -ae *f.* urn from which lots are drawn

sitīculōsus, -a, -um *adj.* dry, parched

sitiens, -ntis *adj.* thirsty; causing thirst; (+*gen.*) desirous (for)

sitienter *adv.* thirstily

sitiō 4. to be thirsty; be parched or dry; thirst for, desire

sitis, -is *f.* thirst; (+*gen.*) desire, thirst (for)

sitītor, -ōris *m.* (+*gen.*) one who thirsts (for)

sittyba, -ae *f.* parchment label attached to a papyrus roll

situla, -ae *f.* water-bucket; urn from which lots are drawn

situs¹, -a, -um *adj.* placed, positioned; deposited; built; (+*in* +*abl.*) dependent (upon)

situs², -ūs *m.* site, position; layout, arrangement; structure

situs³, -ūs *m.* disuse, state of neglect; dirt, decay

sīve (seu) *conj.* or if; **sīve ... sīve ...** whether ... or

smaragdus, -ī *m.* green gem, emerald

smaris, -idis *f.* picarel

smīlax, -acis *f.* bindweed

smyrna, -ae *f.* myrrh

sobolēs see **subolēs**

sōbriē *adv.* soberly; sensibly

sobrīna, -ae *f.* female second cousin

sobrīnus, -ī *m.* second cousin

sōbrius, -a, -um *adj.* not drunk, sober; without wine; moderate, sensible

socculus, -ī *m.* little *soccus*

soccus, -ī *m.* loose Greek slipper (*esp. worn by comic actors*); comedy

socer(us), -erī *m.* father-in-law; grandfather (by marriage)

socia, -ae *f.* female partner or companion; wife

sociābilis, -is, -e *adj.* easily allied, compatible

sociālis, -is, -e *adj.* of or relating to allies; confederate; of or relating to marriages, conjugal

sociālitās, -ātis *f.* sociable nature

sociāliter *adv.* in the manner of an associate, sociably

sociennus, -ī *m.* partner, comrade

societās, -ātis *f.* partnership, companionship; alliance; society, fellowship; affinity

sociō 1. (+*dat.* or +*cum* +*abl.*) to partner (with), unite (with); associate (with); share (with)

sociofraudus, -ī *m.* one who cheats one's partner

socius¹, -a, -um *adj.* acting together, accompanying; allied; shared, joint; of or relating to one's partner

socius², -(i)ī *m.* partner, comrade; political or military ally; husband; brother; (+*gen.*) associate (in)

socordia, -ae *f.* sluggishness; stupidity; negligence

socorditer *adv.* carelessly, negligently

socors, -rdis *adj.* sluggish, slow; stupid, dull; (+*gen.*) careless (about)

socrus, -ūs *f.* mother-in-law

sodālicium, -(i)ī *n.* close bond, association; electioneering faction

sodālis, -is *m.* member of an association *or* club; comrade, companion

sodālitās, -ātis *f.* close bond, association; group, club; electioneering faction

sōdēs = **sī audēs**

sōl, sōlis *m.* sun; sunlight; heat of the sun; day

sōlāciolum, -ī *n.* small comfort

sōlācium, -(i)ī *n.* comfort, solace, consolation

sōlāmen, -inis *n.* comfort, solace

sōlārium, -(i)ī *n.* sundial; place in the sun; terrace, balcony

sōlātium see **sōlācium**

sōlātor, -ōris *m.* comforter

soldurī, -ōrum *m.pl.* small army of experienced warriors attached to a chieftain

soldus see **solidus**

solea, -ae *f.* (*usu. pl.*) sandal; shoe tied onto an animal's hooves; sole (fish)

soleārius, -(i)ī *m.* sandal-maker

soleātus, -a, -um *adj.* wearing sandals

solens, -ntis *adj.* according to one's custom

soleō, -itus sum 2. *semi-dep.* (+*inf.*) to be accustomed (to); be wont (to), tend (to)

solidē *adv.* completely, thoroughly

soliditās, -ātis *f.* firmness, solidity

solidō 1. to make solid; make firm; make complete

solidus, -a, -um *adj.* solid; dense; firm; complete, full; real, enduring; *n.sbst.* solid *or* firm object; (*of money*) full amount

sōlifer, -era, -erum *adj.* bringing the sun

sōliferreum, -ī *n.* javelin made only of iron

sōlistimus, -a, -um *adj.* complete, full

sōlitārius, -a, -um *adj.* alone, solitary; occurring alone; performed alone

sōlitūdō, -inis *f.* solitude, loneliness; state of desertion, emptiness; *usu. pl.* wasteland, desert

solitus, -a, -um *adj.* customary, usual; *n. sbst.* usual activity, custom

solium, -(i)ī *n.* (royal) throne; royal authority; bath-tub; sarcophagus

sōlivagus, -a, -um *adj.* wandering alone, solitary

sollemnis, -is, -e *adj.* religious, solemn; customary, usual, traditional; *n.sbst.* religious ceremony; custom

sollemniter *adv.* religiously, solemnly

sollers, -rtis *adj.* skilled, clever, ingenious

sollerter *adv.* skilfully, cleverly

sollertia, -ae *f.* skill, cleverness

sollicitātiō, -ōnis *f.* anxiety, worry; incitement (*to crime*)

sollicitē *adv.* anxiously; with anxious care

sollicitō 1. to disturb, agitate; trouble, distress; rouse, incite; tempt; try to seduce

sollicitūdō, -inis *f.* agitation, anxiety; anxious care; cause of anxiety

sollicitus, -a, -um *adj.* troubled, agitated, anxious; anxiously careful; disturbed, restless; causing anxiety

sōlō 1. to make deserted

soloecismus, -ī *m.* (grammatical) solecism

sōlor 1. *dep.* to comfort, console; assuage, relieve

solstitiālis, -is, -e *adj.* of *or* relating to the summer solstice; aestival

solstitium, -(i)ī *n.* summer *or* winter solstice; summer, summer-heat

solum¹, -ī *n.* ground, earth; soul; base, foundation; sole (of the foot)

sōlum² *adv.* only, just, alone

sōlus, -a, -um (*gen.* **-īus** or **-ī**) *adj.* alone; lonely; only, sole; unfrequented, deserted

solūtē *adv.* loosely; freely; languidly; fluently; laxly

solūtilis, -is, -e *adj.* easily broken into pieces

solūtiō, -ōnis *f.* loosening; dissolution; payment

solūtum, -ī *n.* payment to discharge debt

solūtus, -a, -um *adj.* free, unbound; loose; languid, limp; independent, free; unrestrained, licentious; fluent, facile; lazy, lax; (+*ab* +*abl.*) free (from)

solvō, -vī (-uī), -ūtum 3. to loosen, untie; free; dissolve, break up; slacken, relax; unfurl (*sails*); acquit, exempt; annul, cancel; pay; discharge, fulfil

somnīculōsē *adv.* sleepily

somnīculōsus, -a, -um *adj.* sleepy, lethargic

somnifer, -era, -erum *adj.* sleep-bringing, soporofic

somniō 1. to dream; day-dream, fantasize; (+*acc.*+*inf.*) dream (that); have delusions about

somnium, -(i)ī *n.* dream; day-dream, fantasy

somnus, -ī *m.* sleep; sleepiness; laziness; sloth

sonābilis, -is, -e *adj.* resonant, sonorous

sonans, -ntis *adj.* noisy; resonant, sonorous

sonipēs, -edis *m.* horse

sonitus, -ūs *m.* sound, noise

sonīvius, -a, -um *adj.* rattling

sonō, -uī, -itum 1. *or* **sonō** 3. to make a sound; be filled with sound, resound; speak; produce as a sound; utter; celebrate, sing of; mean

sonor, -ōris *m.* sound, noise

sonōrus, -a, -um *adj.* resonant, sonorous

sons, sontis *adj.* guilty; *m.*/*f.sbst.* guilty person, criminal

sonticus, -a, -um *adj.* (sufficiently) serious, valid

sonus, -ī *m.* sound, noise; utterance; faculty of speech; tone, style

sophisma, -atis *n.* sophistic argument, sophistry

sophistēs, -ae *m.* sophist; rhetorician

sophos¹, -ī *m.* wise man, sage

sophōs² *interj.* excellent!, wonderful!

sōpiō¹ 4. to make sleep; lull to sleep; stupefy

sōpiō², -ōnis *f.* penis

sopor, -ōris *m.* sleep; stupor; laziness; torpor; sleeping potion

sopōrifer, -era, -erum *adj.* sleep-bringing, soporific

sopōrō 1. to make sleep; instil with soporific force

sopōrus, -a, -um *adj.* sleep-bringing; sleepy

sōracus, -ī *m.* hamper

sorbeō, 2. to suck up, drink up; absorb, soak in; inhale

sorbīlō¹ 1. to sip

sorbīlō² *adv.* sip by sip

sorbitiō, -ōnis *f.* soup, broth

sorbum, -ī *n.* sorb, service-berry

sordeō 2. to be dirty; appear worthless *or* mean

sordēs, -is *f.* dirt, filth; miserliness, greed; vulgarity, baseness; *pl.* shabby clothes (*worn in mourning*)

sordescō 3. to become dirty

sordidātus, -a, -um *adj.* dirtily *or* shabbily dressed; wearing mourning clothes

sordidē *adv.* commonly, vulgarly; meanly, greedily

sordidulus, -a, -um *adj.* somewhat dirty

sordidus, -a, -um *adj.* dirty, filthy; shabby (*from mourning*); poor; miserly, mean; common, base; vile, foul; worthless

sorditūdō, -inis *f.* dirt, filth

sōrex, -icis *m.* shrew-mouse

sōricīnus, -a, -um *adj.* of *or* relating to a shrew-mouse

sōrītēs, -ae *m.* logical trick (in which the conclusion is reached by gradual additions to the proposition)

soror, -ōris *f.* sister; female cousin; close female friend

sororcula, -ae *f.* little sister

sororicīda, -ae *m.* killer of one's sister

sorōrius, -a, -um *adj.* of *or* relating to a sister; sisterly

sors, sortis *f.* lot; casing of lots; share, allotment; official duty; oracular response; fortune, destiny; rank, class; (*of money*) capital

sorsum (-us) see **seorsum (-us)**

sorticula, -ae *f.* ticket (used in a lottery)

sortiger, -erī *m.* provider of oracles

sortilegus, -a, -um *adj.* prophetic; *m.sbst.* prophet, soothsayer

sortior 4. *dep.* or **sortiō 4.** to cast lots; allot, appoint; choose; obtain by lot, receive

sortītiō, -ōnis *f.* casting of lots, lottery

sortītō *adv.* by lot; by fate

sortītor, -ōris *m.* drawer of lots

sortītus, -ūs *m.* casting of lots, lottery; lot

sospes, -itis *adj.* unharmed, safe

sospitālis, -is, -e *adj.* salutary

sospitō 1. to keep safe, defend

spādix, -īcis *m.adj.* chestnut-coloured

spadō, -ōnis *m.* eunuch

spargō, -rsī, -rsum 3. to sprinkle, scatter; shower; moisten; disperse, spread out; make widely known

sparsiō, -ōnis *f.* scattering of presents in a theatre

spartum, -ī *n.* Spanish broom (*used for ropes*)

sparulus, -ī *m.* little sea-bream**

sparus, -ī *m.* hunting-spear

spatha, -ae *f.* weaver's paddle (to beat down woof); broad two-edged sword

spatior 1. *dep.* to walk about, range; spread out, expand

spatiōsē *adv.* amply, extensively; protractedly

spatiōsus, -a, -um *adj.* ample, extensive; protracted, long

spatium, -(i)ī *n.* space, room; distance (between points), extent; race-track, course; open space, area; period of time, interval; metrical time; leisure

speciālis, -is, -e *adj.* of the same species, derivative

speciēs, -ēī *f.* sight, spectacle; appearance, look; glance, look; beauty; show, splendour; vision, apparition; idea, notion; pretext; kind, species

specillum, -ī *n.* medical probe

specimen, -inis *n.* sign, token; pattern, ideal; example, specimen

speciō, -xī, -ctum 3. to look at, observe; observe omens

speciōsē *adv.* attractively; splendidly

speciōsus, -a, -um *adj.* attractive, beautiful; splendid, brilliant; showy; specious, plausible

spectābilis, -is, -e *adj.* that may be observed; worth seeing, remarkable

spectāc(u)lum, -ī *n.* sight, spectacle; show, performance; *pl.* seats in a theatre *or* circus

spectāmen, -inis *n.* distinguishing mark

spectātiō, -ōnis *f.* observation; inspection

spectātor, -ōris *m.* observer, spectator; examiner, critic

spectātrix, -īcis *f.* female observer

spectātus, -a, -um *adj.* manifest, obvious; distinguished, esteemed

spectiō, -ōnis *f.* right to take auspices

spectō 1. to look at, watch; examine, inspect; judge, test; look to; face; consider; look; (*+ad/in +acc.*) face (towards); (*+ad +acc.*) concern

spectrum, -ī *n.* image, apparation

specula¹, -ae *f.* look-out point, watch-tower; observation, keeping look-out; **in speculīs** on look-out

specula², -ae *f.* slight hope

speculābilis, -is, -e *adj.* discernible

speculābundus, -a, -um *adj.* (*+acc.*) engaged in watching

speculāris, -is, -e *adj.* transparent; **lapis speculāris** transparent stone, mica; *n.pl. sbst.* window-panes

speculāria, -ōrum *n.pl.* window-panes

speculātor, -ōris *m.* spy, scout; look-out

speculātōrius, -a, -um *adj.* of *or* relating to a look-out; *f.sbst.* spy-boat

speculātrix, -īcis *f.* female observer

speculoclārus, -a, -um *adj.* shining like a mirror

speculor 1. *dep.* to observe; watch out for; spy out, explore

speculum, -ī *n.* mirror; mirror-image

specus, -ūs *m./n.* cave; pit, tunnel

spēlaeum, -ī *n.* cave, cavern

spēlunca, -ae *f.* cave, cavern

spēra see **spīra**

spērābilis, -is, -e *adj.* that may be hoped for

spernō, sprēvī, sprētum 3. to spurn, disdain, reject; remove

spērō 1. to hope for; expect; (*+acc.+inf.*) hope (that); place one's hope in; anticipate; fear, forebode; entertain hopes, hope

spēs, speī *f.* hope, expectation; prospect; object of one's hope(s); fear, foreboding

sphaera, -ae *f.* globe, sphere; astronomical globe; moving model of the universe

sphaeristērium, -iī *n.* place for ball games

sphaeromachia, -ae *f.* boxing-match with padded gloves

spīca, -ae *f.* ear of corn; **spīca Cilissa** saffron

spīceus, -a, -um *adj.* consisting *or* made of ears of corn

spīcifer, -era, -erum *adj.* bearing ears of corn

spiciō see **speciō**

spīculum, -ī *n.* sharp point; sting; spear, arrow

spīcum see **spīca**

spīna, -ae *f.* thorn, prickle; thorn-bush; backbone, spine; *pl.* thorny problem

spīnētum, -ī *n.* thicket of thorn-bushes

spīneus, -a, -um *adj.* thorny

spīniger, -era, -erum *adj.* bearing thorns, thorny

spīnōsus, -a, -um *adj.* thorny, prickly; covered in thorn-bushes; difficult, thorny

spinter, -ēris n. bracelet
spintria, -ae m. male prostitute
spinturnicium, -(i)ī n. little bird (of
  unknown identity)
spīnus, -ī f. thorn-bush
spīra, -ae f. coil, wreath
spīrābilis, -is, -e adj. that may be breathed,
  respirable
spīrāculum, -ī n. air-hole
spīrāmen, -inis n. air-hole; breathing,
  exhalation
spīrāmentum, -ī n. breathing passage, air-
  hole; brief interval
spīritus, -ūs m. breathing; breath; exhalation; breath of life; divine inspiration;
  spirit; disposition; pride; vigour; wind; air
spīrō 1. to breathe; blow; be alive; exhale;
  (+acc.) breathe out, give off, exhale
spissāmentum, -ī n. stopper, plug
spissē adv. sluggishly, slowly
spissēscō 3. to become thicker, condense
spissigradus, -a, -um adj. stepping slowly
spissō 1. to make thicker, condense; pack
  tightly
spissus, -a, -um adj. dense, compact;
  crowded; sluggish, slow
splēn, -nis m. spleen
splendeō 2. to be bright, shine; be distinguished
splendēscō 3. to become bright, begin to
  shine
splendidē adv. brilliantly, splendidly;
  finely, nobly; with distinction, highly
splendidus, -a, -um adj. bright, shining,
  radiant; clear; splendid; distinguished,
  glorious; showy
splendor, -ōris m. brightness, radiance;
  clarity; parade, splendour; distinction,
  glory
splēniātus, -a, -um adj. covered with a
  plaster
splēnium, -iī n. plaster (for wounds)
spoliārium, -iī n. place in an amphitheatre
  where slain gladiators were stripped of
  their arms
spoliātiō, -ōnis f. plundering, despoiling
spoliātor, -ōris m. plunderer, despoiler
spoliātrix, -īcis f. female plunderer
spoliō 1. to strip, lay bare; despoil (an
  enemy); plunder, pillage; rob
spolium, -(i)ī n. spoils taken from the
  enemy; booty, plunder; skin taken from
  an animal
sponda, -ae f. frame of a bed; bed, couch;
  bier
spondeō, spopondī, sponsum 2. to
  pledge, promise solemnly; act as surety
  for; act as guarantor, go bail
spondēus, -ēī m. spondee
spondylus, -ī m. kind of mussel
spongia (-ea), -ae f. sponge; kind of
  cuirass
[spons], -ntis f. will; **sponte** deliberately;
  sponte (+gen.) by the will of; **sponte
  meā** (etc.) of my (etc.) own accord, willingly; by my (etc.) own agency, alone;
  sponte suā in itself, for its own sake
sponsa, -ae f. fiancée, bride
sponsālia, -ium n.pl. betrothal ceremony
sponsiō, -ōnis f. guarantee, pledge; legal
  wager (that one's party will win the case);
  wager
sponsor, -ōris m. guarantor, surety
sponsus¹, -ī m. bridegroom, fiancé
sponsus², -ūs m. guarantee, pledge
sponte see **[spons]**
sporta, -ae f. basket
sportella, -ae f. small basket
sportula, -ae f. small basket; dole given by
  patrons to clients
sprētor, -ōris m. despiser
spūma, -ae f. foam, froth
spūmātus, -ūs m. froth
spūmēscō 3. to become foamy
spūmeus, -a, -um adj. foaming, frothy
spūmifer, -era, -erum adj. foaming,
  frothy
spūmiger, -era, -erum adj. foaming,
  frothy
spūmō 1. to foam, froth; be covered with
  foam
spūmōsus, -a, -um adj. full of foam, frothy
spuō, spuī, spūtum 3. to spit out
spurcē adv. foully, basely
spurcidicus, -a, -um adj. speaking foully
spurcificus, -a, -um adj. acting foully
spurcitia, -ae or **-ēs, -ēī** f. dirt, filth; moral
  impurity
spurcō 1. to make dirty; deprave
spurcus, -a, -um adj. dirty, filthy; morally
  impure, foul
spūtātilicus, -a, -um adj. worthy of being
  spat at, abominable

spūtātor, -ōris *m.* one who often spits

spūtō 1. to spit out

spūtum, -ī *n.* spittle

squaleō 2. to be rough; be filthy; be dirty from mourning; lie neglected

squālidē *adv.* roughly

squālidus, -a, -um *adj.* rough; dirty, filthy

squālor, -ōris *m.* roughness; dirtiness; dirty state (*from mourning*)

squāma, -ae *f.* scale (of a fish, reptile *etc.*); scale of armour

squāmeus, -a, -um *adj.* scaly

squāmifer, -era, -erum *adj.* scaly

squāmiger, -era, -erum *adj.* scaly; *f.pl. sbst.* fishes

squāmōsus (-ossus), -a, -um *adj.* covered with scales, scaly

squilla, -ae *f.* shrimp, crayfish (*and sim.*)

st *interj.* hush!, sh!

stabilīmentum, -ī *n.* support, prop

stabiliō 4. to make firm, steady; establish firmly

stabilis, -is, -e *adj.* firm, steady, stable; durable; constant

stabilitās, -ātis *f.* stability, firmness; durability

stabiliter *adv.* firmly

stabulō 1. to stable, house; be housed

stabulum, -ī *n.* stable, stall; lair; lodgings for travellers; brothel

stacta, -ae *f.* myrrh

stadium, -(i)ī *n.* running-track; unit of distance, stade

stagnō 1. to form pools; be flooded; cover with flood-water

stagnum¹, -ī *n.* pool of standing water; stretch of water

stagnum², -ī *n.* silver and lead alloy

stalagmium, -(i)ī *n.* ear-drop, pendant

stāmen, -inis *n.* warp; thread, string

stāmineus, -a, -um *adj.* made of thread

statārius, -a, -um *adj.* stationary; calm, steady

statēra, -ae *f.* balance, steelyard

staticulus, -ī *m.* pose

statim *adv.* immediately, at once; straight after; steadfastly; regularly

statiō, -ōnis *f.* standing still; anchorage; station, post; picket; guard-duty

statīvus, -a, -um *adj.* permanent; *n.pl.* permanent camps

stator, -ōris *m.* magistrate's attendant; stayer (cult title of Jupiter)

statua, -ae *f.* statue

statuārius, -(i)ī *m.* sculptor of statues

statūmen, -inis *n.* support, prop

statuō, -uī, -ūtum 3. to set, stand; settle; appoint; stop, halt; (*+acc.+inf.*) declare (that); (*+ut/ne+subj.*) decree (that); (*+inf.*) decide (to)

statūra, -ae *f.* stature

status¹, -ūs *m.* position, standing; condition, state; arrangement; rank

status², -a, -um *adj.* fixed, decided; regular

statūtus, -a, -um *adj.* upstanding, respectable

stega, -ae *f.* deck of a ship

stēliō, -ōnis *m.* gecko

stella, -ae *f.* star; constellation; planet

stellans, -ntis *adj.* starry; glittering like stars

stellātus, -a, -um *adj.* furnished with stars; glittering like stars; arranged in a star shape

stellifer, -era, -erum *adj.* star-bearing

stelliger, -era, -erum *adj.* star-bearing

stemma, -atis *n.* family tree; lineage

stercoreus, -a, -um *adj.* dung-like, filthy

sterculīnum, -ī *n.* manure heap

stercus, -oris *n.* dung, excrement

sterilis, -is, -e *adj.* sterile, infertile, barren; unprofitable, futile

sterilitās, -ātis *f.* sterility, infertility, barrenness

sternax, -ācis *adj.* throwing off its rider

sternō, strāvī, strātum 3. to spread out, stretch out; (*+abl.*) strew (with), pave (with); knock down, lay low; allay

sternūmentum, -ī *n.* sneeze

sternuō, -uī 3. to sneeze

sternūtāmentum, -ī *n.* bout of sneezing

sterquilīnum see **sterculīnum**

stertō 3. to snore

stibadium, -(i)ī *n.* semicircular couch

stigma, -atis *n.* tattoo (*esp. for runaway slaves*); stigma

stigmatiās, -ae *m.* one covered with tattoos

stigmōsus, -a, -um *adj.* covered with tattoos

stilla, -ae *f.* drop

stillicidium, -(i)ī *n.* drop, dripping; drainage water

stillō 1. to drip, trickle; (+*abl.*) drip (with); let drop

stilus, -ī *m.* writing instrument (*on wax*), stylus; literary composition; style

stimulātiō, -ōnis *f.* incitement, spurring on

stimulātrix, -īcis *f.* female who incites

stimuleus, -a, -um *adj.* involving the goad

stimulō 1. to goad on, spur; incite, rouse; torment

stimulus, -ī *m.* goad, spur; stake (used as a military trap); torment

stinguō 3. to extinguish; destroy

stīpātiō, -ōnis *f.* crowding together; retinue

stīpātor, -ōris *m.* bodyguard, attendant

stīpendiārius, -a, -um *adj.* performing military service; paying tribute; *n.sbst.* tax paid to an occupying military force

stīpendium, -(i)ī *n.* payment (*esp. for soldiers*); tribute, tax; military service, campaign

stīpes, -itis *m.* trunk, stump; tree; stick, club

stīpō 1. to pack tight; (+*abl.*) crowd (with); stuff (with)

stips, stipis *f.* small offering of money, financial gift

stipula, -ae *f.* stalk; stubble; reed-pipe

stipulātiō, -ōnis *f.* demand for a financial guarantee

stipulātiuncula, -ae *f.* small demand for a financial guarantee

stipulātor, -ōris *m.* money lender (on the strength of guarantees)

stipulor 1. *dep.* to demand a formal guarantee, stipulate; demand a formal guarantee from

stīria, -ae *f.* icicle

stirpitus *adv.* from the roots

stirps, -pis *f.* stem, stalk; shoot, sprout; stock, source; root, foundation

stīva, -ae *f.* plough-handle

stlatta, -ae *f.* large cargo-boat

stlattārius, -a, -um *adj.* brought by cargo-boat

stō, stetī, statum 1. to stand; stand up; remain, stay; be positioned, lie; stand firm, persist; be fixed; halt, stop; (+*abl./ gen.*) cost; (+*ab* +*abl.*) stand by; (+*per* +*acc.*) be due to (someone)

stola, -ae *f.* long upper garment (worn by matrons *or* religious figures)

stolātus, -a, -um *adj.* wearing a *stola*

stolidē *adv.* stupidly, obtusely

stolidus, -a, -um *adj.* stupid, obstuse, dull; inert

stomachicus, -ī *m.* one with a weak stomach

stomachor 1. *dep.* to be irritated, be angry; (+*acc.*) be angry at

stomachōsē *adv.* irritably, angrily

stomachōsus, -a, -um *adj.* irritable, angry

stomachus, -ī *m.* stomach; gullet; appetite; disposition, temper; annoyance, anger

storia (-ea), -ae *f.* mat of rushes, matting

strabō, -ōnis *m.* squinter

strāgēs, -is *f.* slaughter, bloodshed; destruction, overthrow; debris, carnage

strāgulum, -ī *n.* covering, blanket; saddle-cloth

strāgulus, -a, -um *adj.* used as bedding

strāmen, -inis *n.* straw covering; bedding

strāmentum, -ī *n.* (*usu. pl.*) straw covering; bedding; saddle; corn-stalk

strāmineus, -a, -um *adj.* made of straw

strangulō 1. to strangle; suffocate, choke; hold close

strangūria, -ae *f.* strangury

stratēgēma, -atis *n.* trick, stratagem

stratēgus, -ī *m.* general

stratiōticus, -a, -um *adj.* of *or* relating to a soldier; soldier-like

strātum, -ī *n.* coverlet, bedding; bed, couch; saddle-cloth; pavement

strātūra, -ae *f.* paving

strēn(u)a, -ae *f.* favourable omen; new year's gift

strēnuē *adv.* energetically, actively; briskly

strēnuitās, -ātis *f.* energetic activity

strēnuus, -a, -um *adj.* energetic, active; restless

strepitō 1. to make a lot of noise; clatter, rattle

strepitus, -ūs *m.* loud noise; creak; rumble; din; shouting, uproar

strepō, -uī, -itum 3. to make a loud noise; creak; rumble; shout (*esp. in protest*); (+*abl.*) resound (with)

striātus, -a, -um *adj.* grooved

strictim *adv.* closely, tightly; slightly, superficially

strictūra, -ae *f.* mass of iron

strīdō, -dī 3. or **-eō** 2. to make a shrill sound, whistle; shriek; creak; hiss

strīdor, -ōris *m.* shrill sound, whistling; shriek; creak; hiss

strīdulus, -a, -um *adj.* shrill-sounding, whistling, creaking

strigilis, -is *f.* tool for scraping the skin clean, strigil

strigō 1. to halt, stop

strigōsus, -a, -um *adj.* lean, thin; meagre

stringō, -nxī, -ctum 3. (+*dat.*) to bind (to), fasten (to); tighten, constrict; draw, bare (*esp. weapons*); pluck, clip; graze, brush; harm slightly

stringor, -ōris *m.* contraction (*from touching*)

strix, -igis (-īgis) *f.* screech-owl

stropha, -ae *f.* trick, device

strophiārius, -(i)ī *m.* maker *or* seller of breast-bands

strophium, -(i)ī *m.* breast-band

structilis, -is, -e *adj.* used for building

structor, -ōris *m.* mason, builder; waiter *or* carver

structūra, -ae *f.* act of building; masonry; building

struēs, -is *f.* pile, heap; pile of sacrificial cakes

struix, -īcis *f.* pile, heap

strūma, -ae *f.* goitre

strūmōsus, -a, -um *adj.* covered in goitres

struō, -xī, -ctum 3. to construct, put together; pile up; arrange; compose; contrive

strūteum, -ēī *n.* sparrow-apple, quince

strūthocamēlus, -ī *m.* ostrich

studeō 2. (+*dat.*) to devote oneself to, concentrate upon; favour, support; study

studiōsē *adv.* eagerly, zealously, assiduously

studiōsus, -a, -um *adj.* (+*gen./dat.* or +*ad* +*acc.*) eager (for), zealous; devoted (to); learned (in); studious; *m.sbst.* student; disciple

studium, -(i)ī *n.* eagerness, zeal; (+*gen.*) keenness (for), devotion (to); study, learning; pastime

stultē *adv.* stupidly; foolishly

stultiloquentia, -ae *f.* stupid talk, babbling

stultiloquium, -(i)ī *n.* stupid talk, babbling

stultiloquus, -a, -um *adj.* stupid talker, babbler

stultitia, -ae *f.* stupidity, folly; act of folly

stultividus, -a, -um *adj.* stupid in sight

stultus, -a, -um *adj.* stupid, dull; foolish, silly

stupefaciō, -fēcī, -factum 3. to make numb; stupefy

stupeō 2. to be numb; be stupefied; be astonished *or* dumbfounded at

stupescō 3. to become stupefied

stupiditās, -ātis *f.* stupidity

stupidus, -a, -um *adj.* numb; stupefied; stupid

stupor, -ōris *m.* numbness; stupefaction; stupidity; idiot

stuppa, -ae *f.* tow, hemp

stuppeus, -a, -um *adj.* made of tow

stuprātor, -ōris *m.* (+*gen.*) one who violates sexually

stuprō 1. to violate sexually; defile

stuprum, -ī *n.* dishonour; sexual defilement; incest

sturnus, -ī *m.* starling

suāda, -ae *f.* persuasion

suādēla, -ae *f.* persuasion

suādeō 2. (+*dat./acc.*) to advise, urge; advocate; (+*inf.*) urge (to); (+*acc.*+*inf.*) persuade (that)

suādus, -a, -um *adj.* persuasive

suāsiō, -ōnis *f.* advice; advisory speech; advocation

suāsor, -ōris *m.* adviser; advocate

suāsōria, -ae *f.* rhetorical exercise of giving advisory speeches in historical contexts

suāsum, -ī *n.* dark grey

suāsus, -ūs *m.* advice, persuasion

suāvidicus, -a, -um *adj.* speaking charmingly

suāviloquens, -ntis *adj.* speaking charmingly

suāviloquentia, -ae *f.* charm of speech

suāviolum, suāvior see **sāviolum, sāvior**

suāvis, -is, -e *adj.* sweet; sweet-sounding; sweet-smelling; attractive; charming, pleasant

suāvisāviātiō, -ōnis *f.* passionate kissing

suāvitās, -ātis *f.* sweetness; charm, pleasantness

suāviter *adv.* sweetly; charmingly, pleasantly

suāvitūdō, -inis *f.* sweetness, sweetheart

sub *prep.* (+*abl.*) under, beneath, below; at the foot of; near; in the reign of; (*of time*) during; (+*acc.*) under, along under; up to; (*of time*) just before, towards; straight after; **sub manum** to hand

subabsurdē *adv.* somewhat absurdly

subabsurdus, -a, -um *adj.* somewhat absurd

subaccūsō 1. to censure somewhat

subactiō, -ōnis *f.* breaking up

subaerātus, -a, -um *adj.* having copper below

subagrestis, -is, -e *adj.* somewhat rustic, rather unrefined

subālāris, -is, -e *adj.* carried under one's arm

subalbus, -a, -um *adj.* whitish

subamārus, -a, -um *adj.* somewhat bitter

subaquilus, -a, -um *adj.* darkish

subarroganter *adv.* somewhat arrogantly

subauscultō 1. to eavesdrop; listen secretly to

subbasilicānus, -ī *m.* one who lounges in a basilica

subbibō, -ī 3. to sip

subblandior 4. *dep.* (+*dat.*) to fawn upon flatteringly

subc- see **succ-** (other than below)

subcavus, -a, -um *adj.* cavernous

subcenturiō, -ōnis *m.* centurion's deputy

subcontumēliōsē *adv.* somewhat insultingly

subcrispus, -a, -um *adj.* somewhat curly *or* wavy

subcustōs, -ōdis *m.* deputy guard

subdēbilis, -is, -e *adj.* somewhat enfeebled

subdifficilis, -is, -e *adj.* somewhat difficult

subdiffīdō 3. to be somewhat mistrustful

subditīvus, -a, -um *adj.* (fraudulently) substituted, supposititious

subdō, -didī, -ditum 3. (+*dat.*) to place beneath, set under; substitute (*esp.* fraudulently); subject (to); expose (to)

subdoceō 2. to teach in addition

subdolē *adv.* deceitfully

subdolus, -a, -um *adj.* deceitful, crafty

subdomō 1. to subdue, tame

subdubitō 1. to be in some doubt

subdūcō, -duxī, -ductum 3. to draw up; haul (*ships*) onto land; (+*dat.*) withdraw (from); remove secretly, steal; calculate

subductiō, -ōnis *f.* hauling (*of ships*) onto land; calculation

subedō, -esse, -ēdī, -ēsum *v.irreg.* to eat away from beneath

subeō, -īre, -iī (-īvī), -itum 4. (+*dat./acc.*) to go under; undergo, suffer; approach; climb; follow, succeed; replace; come to aid; suggest itself (to); steal upon

sūber, -eris *n.* cork tree; cork

subērigō, -rexī, -rectum 3. to raise up somewhat

subf- see **suff-**

subg- see **sugg-**

subhorridus, -a, -um *adj.* somewhat rough

subiaceō 2. (+*dat.*) to lie below

sūbiciō (sub-), -iēcī, -iectum 3. to throw *or* set under; lay before; make subject (to); raise; subjoin (to); substitute (for); introduce fraudulently; interpose; suggest

subiectē *adv.* submissively

subiectiō, -ōnis *f.* placing under; fraudulent introduction

subiectō 1. to throw up from below; apply from below

subiector, -ōris *m.* (+*gen.*) one who introduces fraudulently

subiectus (subī-), -a, -um *adj.* situated below; exposed, open; subordinate; *m. sbst.* subordinate

subigitātiō, -ōnis *f.* titillation, fondling

subigitātrix, -īcis *f.* woman who arouses by fondling

subigitō 1. to arouse by fondling

subigō, -ēgī, -actum 3. (+*dat. or +sub* +*acc.*) to drive under; plough, cultivate; (+*ad/in +acc. or +inf.*) compel (to); train; subdue, suppress; knead, massage; sharpen

subimpudens, -ntis *adj.* somewhat impudent

subinānis, -is, -e *adj.* somewhat empty

subinde *adv.* immediately afterwards; repeatedly, now and again

subinsulsus, -a, -um *adj.* somewhat insipid

subinvideō 2. (+*dat. of person +acc. of thing*) to be somewhat envious (of someone) (for)

subinvīsus, -a, -um *adj.* somewhat unpopular

subinvītō 1. to request gently

subīrascor, -īrātus 3. *dep.* (+*dat.*) to be somewhat angry (at)

subīrātus, -a, -um *adj.* (+*dat.*) somewhat angry (at)

subitārius, -a, -um *adj.* suddenly formed *or* gathered; critical

subitō *adv.* suddenly; quickly, soon

subitus, -a, -um *adj.* sudden; suddenly done *or* formed; improvised; *n.sbst.* crisis, emergency

subiungō, -nxī, -nctum 3. (+*dat.*) to join *or* fix under; subjoin; make subject (to), subjugate (under)

sublābor, -lapsus 3. *dep.* to collapse; slip *or* ebb away; creep up

sublātē *adv.* loftily, grandly

sublātiō, -ōnis *f.* elevation, raising

sublectō 1. to wheedle, coax

sublegō, -lēgī, -lectum 3. to pick up; kidnap; eavesdrop; choose as a replacement

sublestus, -a, -um *adj.* weak, slight

sublevātiō, -ōnis *f.* alleviation

sublevō 1. to raise up, lift; support; assist, help; encourage; alleviate, mitigate

sublica, -ae *f.* wooden pile *or* stake

sublicius, -a, -um *adj.* supported by wooden piles; **pons sublicius** bridge over the Tiber, supposedly built by Ancus Martius

subligāculum, -ī *n.* actor's loin-cloth

subligar, -āris *n.* actor's loin-cloth

subligō 1. to bind; (+*dat.*) bind on; (+*abl.*) arm (with)

sublīme(n) *adv.* on high; up aloft

sublīmis, -is, -e *or* **-us, -a, -um** *adj.* elevated, high; lofty, sublime; grand; illustrious; *n.pl.sbst.* high place

sublīmitās, -ātis *f.* elevation, height; high place; grandeur

sublīmiter *adv.* on high, aloft; grandly

sublingulō, -ōnis *m.* 'dish-licker', scullion

sublinō, -lēvī, -litum 3. to smear over; **ōs sublinere** (+*dat.*) to trick, cheat

sublūceō 2. to gleam faintly; (+*dat.*) shine through

subluō, -uī, -ūtum 3. to wash the bottom of; flow at the base of

sublustris, -is, -e *adj.* somewhat light, dim

submānō 1. to be running with moisture below

submergō, -rsī, -rsum 3. to make sink, submerge

submerus, -a, -um *adj.* slightly diluted

subministrātor, -ōris *m.* supplier

subministrō 1. (+*dat.*) to supply (to), provide (for)

submissē *adv.* in a subdued manner; submissively

submissim *adv.* in a subdued manner

submissiō, -ōnis *f.* lowering; subordination

submissus, -a, -um *adj.* low, lowered; submissive; servile; gentle; (*of hair*) worn long

submittō, -mīsī, -missum 3. (+*dat.*) to send under; subject, subordinate (to); send secretly; send as help; allow to grow, rear; lower, diminish

submolestē *adv.* somewhat annoyingly

submolestus, -a, -um *adj.* somewhat annoying

submoneō 2. to advise privately

submōrōsus, -a, -um *adj.* somewhat morose

submoveō, -mōvī, -mōtum 2. to remove; drive off; expel, banish; exclude

submūtō 1. to substitute

subnectō, -xī, -xum 3. (+*dat.*) to bind under; subjoin; fasten up

subnegō 1. to refuse partly

subniger, -gra, -grum *adj.* blackish, swarthy

subnimium, -(i)ī *n.* 'under-greatcoat'

subnixus (-īsus), -a, -um *adj.* (+*abl.*) resting upon; relying upon; encouraged by

subnotō 1. to sign (*documents*); take particular notice of, mark

subnuba, -ae *f.* supplanted bride

subnūbilus, -a, -um *adj.* somewhat cloudy *or* dark

subō 1. (*of animals*) to be on heat

subobscēnus, -a, -um *adj.* somewhat indecent

subobscūrus, -a, -um *adj.* somewhat obscure

subodiōsus, -a, -um *adj.* somewhat tiresome

suboffendō 3. to cause some offence

suboleō 2. (+*acc.*) to whiff of

subolēs, -is f. sprout; offspring, progeny; generation; race

subolescō 3. to grow up

subolō see **suboleō**

suborior, subortus 4. dep. to arise (in succession)

subornō 1. (+abl.) to dress (in); equip (with); instruct secretly, suborn

subortus, -ūs m. springing up (in succession)

subp- see **supp-** (other than below)

subpaenitet 2. impers. (+acc. of person +gen. of thing) I feel some regret (for)

subpalpor 1. dep. (+dat.) to ingratiate oneself with

subpār, -aris adj. (+dat.) almost equal (to)

subparasītor 1. dep. (+dat.) to act as the parasite (of)

subparus, -ī m. women's shawl

subprōmus, -ī m. steward's assistant

subrancidus, -a, -um adj. somewhat putrid

subraucus, -a, -um adj. somewhat hoarse

subrectus, -a, -um adj. upright

subrēmigō 1. (+dat.) to paddle beneath

subrēpō, -repsī, -reptum 3. (+dat.) to creep up (to); creep in stealthily, insinuate oneself

subrīdeō, -sī, -sum 2. to smile

subrīdiculē adv. rather amusingly

subrigō, -exī, -ectum 3. to raise up, elect; rise up

subringor, -ictus 3. dep. to snarl a little

subripiō, -ipuī, -eptum 3. to steal, remove stealthily

subrogō 1. to elect as a substitute

subrubeō 2. to be tinged with red

subrūfus, -a, -um adj. reddish-haired

subruō, -uī, -utum 3. to overthrow; undermine, subvert

subrupiō see **subripiō**

subruptīcius, -a, -um adj. kidnapped

subrusticus, -a, -um adj. somewhat clumsy or boorish

subrutilus, -a, -um adj. reddish

subscrībō, -scripsī, -scriptum 3. (+dat.) to write below, append (to); enter, record; sign in support (of); aid in prosecution

subscriptiō, -ōnis f. subscript; signature; entry, recording (esp. of an offence)

subscriptor, -ōris m. co-prosecutor

subsecō, -uī, -tum 1. to cut away or back

subsellium, -(i)ī n. bench, low seat (esp. in a court); pl. the court(s)

subsentiō, -nsī, -nsum 4. to have a sneaking suspicion of

subsequor, -cūtus 3. dep. to follow after, follow up; succeed; conform with, imitate

subserviō 4. (+dat.) to be subject to, serve; support

subsessor, -ōris m. one who lies in wait

subsicīvus, -a, -um adj. spare, left over; performed at leisure; n.pl.sbst. remaining plot of land

subsidiārius, -a, -um adj. (of soldiers) supporting, reserve; m.pl.sbst. reserve soldiers

subsidium, -(i)ī n. additional troops, reserves; help, assistance; (+gen.) aid (for)

subsīdō, -sēdī 3. to sit down, sink; subside; remain, stay; wait in ambush

subsignānus, -a, -um adj. (of soldiers) reserve veteran

subsignō 1. to register (as security for a pledge); pledge

subsiliō, -uī 4. to leap up, spring up

subsistō, -stitī 3. (+acc./dat.) to stand firm (against); come to a stand, halt; stay behind, remain in place

subsortior 4. dep. to select (as a substitute) by lot

subsortītiō, -ōnis f. selection (of a substitute) by lot

substantia, -ae f. actual existence; constitution, essence

substernō, -trāvī, -trātum 3. (+dat.) to spread out under; spread out (as bedding) (for); cover the bottom of

substituō, -uī, -ūtum 3. (+dat.) to put before; substitute (for); name as a second heir

substō 1. to stand firm

substrictus, -a, -um adj. drawn in, contracted

substringō, -nxī, -ctum 3. to gather up, draw in; restrain, check

substructiō, -ōnis f. foundation, substructure

substruō, -uxī, -uctum 3. to build from below, lay a foundation

subsultim adv. with continual leaps

subsultō 1. to leap up continually

subsum, subesse v.irreg. (+dat.) to be

under; be beneath, at the base of; be near, at hand (to); underlie

subsūtus, -a, -um *adj.* stitched at the bottom, fringed

subtēmen (-tegmen), -inis *n.* weft (*of weaving*)

subter¹ *adv.* beneath, below

subter² *prep.* (+*acc./abl.*) below, beneath; along the underside of; at the base of

subterdūcō, -uxī, -uctum 3. to remove secretly

subterfugiō, -fūgī 3. to dodge, evade; slip away

subterlābor 3. *dep.* to flow beneath; slip away

subterō, -trīvī, -trītum 3. to wear away below

subterrāneus, -a, -um *adj.* subterranean

subtervolō 1. to fly up to

subtexō, -uī, -tum 3. (+*dat.*) to weave beneath; attach as an addition (to); (+*abl.*) cover below (with)

subtīlis, -is, -e *adj.* fine, slender; precise, exact; acute; refined; plain

subtīlitās, -ātis *f.* fineness; precision; acuteness

subtīliter *adv.* finely; precisely; acutely; plainly

subtimeō 2. to be somewhat afraid

subtrahō, -xī, -ctum 3. (+*dat.*) to drag from under; withdraw (from), remove (from); steal (from); rescue (from)

subtristis, -is, -e *adj.* somewhat sad

subturpiculus, -a, -um *adj.* slightly disgraceful

subturpis, -is, -e *adj.* somewhat disgraceful

subtus *adv.* beneath, below

subtūsus, -a, -um *adj.* beaten from beneath

subūcula, -ae *f.* under-tunic

sūbula, -ae *f.* cobbler's awl

subulcus, -ī *m.* swineherd

suburbānitās, -ātis *f.* state of being near the city (Rome)

suburbānus, -a, -um *adj.* situated near the city (Rome); suburban; *n.sbst.* suburban country dwelling

suburbium, -(i)ī *n.* suburban country (Rome)

suburgeō 2. to drive close (to)

subūrō 3. to burn slightly, singe

subvectiō, -ōnis *f.* carrying up, transportation

subvectō 1. to carry up (often)

subvectus, -ūs *m.* carrying up, transportation

subvehō, -xī, -ctum 3. to carry up, transport; *pass.* to travel upwards; sail upstream

subveniō, -vēnī, -ventum 4. (+*dat.*) to come to the aid of; assist, help; come to mind (for)

subventō 1. (+*dat.*) to come to the aid of

subvereor 2. *dep.* to be somewhat afraid

subversor, -ōris *m.* overthrower

subvertō, -tī, -sum 3. to overturn; overthrow, ruin

subvexus, -a, -um *adj.* sloping upwards

subvolō 1. to fly up

subvolturius, -a, -um *adj.* somewhat vulture-like

subvolvō 3. to roll up

subvortō see **subvertō**

succ- see **subc-** or **susc-** (other than below)

succēdō, -cessī, -cessum 3. (+*dat.*) to go under; approach; mount; succeed, follow; turn out well; (+*acc.*) to go up; approach

succendō, -dī, -sum 3. to set alight (from below); light; (*of passions etc.*) inflame

succenturiō 1. to supply as a reinforcement

succernō, -crēvī, -crētum 3. to sift

successiō, -ōnis *f.* succession

successor, -ōris *m.* successor

successus, -ūs *m.* successful outcome; success; approach

succīdāneus, -a, -um *adj.* substitute (for another) in sacrifice

succīdia, -ae *f.* joint of pork

succīdō¹, -ī 3. (+*dat.*) to give way (to), sink; fall under

succīdō², -dī, -sum 3. to cut down from beneath

succiduus, -a, -um *adj.* giving way beneath, sinking

succinctus, -a, -um *adj.* (+*abl.*) girdled (with); clothed (in); armed (with); succinct

succingō, -nxī, -nctum 3. to put in a girdle, gird up; arm; surround

succingulum, -ī *n.* girdle

succinō 3. (+*dat.*) to accompany in song; chime in; (+*acc.*) recite

succlāmātiō, -ōnis *f.* shout in response

succlāmō 1. (+*dat.*) to shout in response (to)

succollō 1. to carry on one's shoulders

succrescō, -ēvī 3. to grow from beneath; (+*dat.*) grow to replace

succumbō, -cubuī, -cubitum 3. (+*dat.*) to sink to the ground (under); lie down (under); give in (to), submit (to)

succurrō, -rrī, -rsum 3. (+*dat.*) to run to help; assist; come to mind (for); run beneath

succutiō, -ssī, -ssum 3. to shake from beneath

sūcidus, -a, -um *adj.* juicy

sūcinum, -ī *n.* amber

sūcinus, -a, -um *adj.* made of amber

sūcula, -ae *f.* windlass

sūcus, -ī *m.* juice; sap; taste; vigour

sūdārium, -(i)ī *n.* sweat-towel, handkerchief

sūdātiō, -ōnis *f.* sweating

sūdātōrius, -a, -um *adj.* causing sweat; *n. sbst.* sweating-room

sūdātrix, -īcis *f.* female who sweats

sudis, -is *f.* stake; spike

sūdō 1. to sweat; sweat over; (+*abl.*) be damp (with)

sūdor, -ōris *m.* sweat; toil, labour

sūduculum, -ī *n.* whipping-post

sūdus, -a, -um *adj.* (*of weather etc.*) bright; *n.pl.sbst.* bright sky

suescō (sŭe-), suēvī 3. (+*inf. or* +*dat.*) to become accustomed (to); habituate

suētus (sŭē-), -a, -um *adj.* (+*dat.*) accustomed (to); (+*inf.*) accustomed (to); usual, familiar

sūfēs, -ētis *m.* chief magistrate in Punic cities

suffarcinō 1. to stuff

suffectus, -a, -um *adj.* appointed as a replacement

sufferō, sufferre, sustulī, sublātum *v. irreg.* to suffer, endure; support; offer

sufferus, -a, -um *adj.* somewhat wild

sufficiō, -fēcī, -fectum 3. to put under; appoint; (+*dat.*) substitute (with); (+*abl.*) steep (with); (+*dat.*) be adequate (for), suffice (for); (+*inf. or* +*ut* +*subj.*) be capable (of)

suffīgō, -fixī, -fixum 3. (+*dat.*) to fix beneath; fix up (to)

suffīmen, -inis *n.* incense (used for fumigation)

suffīmentum, -ī *n.* incense (used for fumigation)

suffiō 4. to fumigate

sufflāmen, -inis *n.* drag (for braking a vehicle)

sufflāminō 1. to brake (*a vehicle*) with a drag

sufflāvus, -a, -um *adj.* somewhat yellow, slightly blonde

sufflō 1. to puff up; blow on; say boastfully

suffōcātiō, -ōnis *f.* suffocation

suffōcō 1. to stifle, suffocate; repress

suffodiō, -fōdī, -fossum 3. to dig beneath, tunnel under; jab from below

suffossiō, -ōnis *f.* tunnelling

suffrāgātiō, -ōnis *f.* support (*of a candidate*)

suffrāgātor, -ōris *m.* supporter (*of a candidate*)

suffrāgium, -(i)ī *n.* vote; voting; approval, support

suffrāgor 1. *dep.* (+*dat.*) to canvass for; vote for; support, approve

suffringō 3. to break the bottom of

suffugiō, -fūgī 3. to slip away from; take shelter

suffugium, -(i)ī *n.* shelter, refuge

suffulciō, -lsī, -ltum 4. to prop up from beneath

suffundō, -fūdī, -fūsum 3. to pour on *or* in; make well up; (+*abl.*) suffuse (with), stain (with)

suffūror 1. *dep.* to steal secretly

suffuscus, -a, -um *adj.* somewhat dusky

suffūsiō, -ōnis *f.* welling up; cataract

suggerō, -ssī, -stum 3. to pile up; (+*dat.*) attach (to); suggest

suggestum, -ī *n.* platform

suggestus, -ūs *m.* platform, dais; pile

suggillātiō, -ōnis *f.* (verbal) wounding

suggillō 1. to bruise; insult, affront

suggrandis, -is, -e *adj.* somewhat big, largish

suggredior, -ssus 3. *dep.* to approach; attack

sūgō, suxī 3. to suck (on *or* up)

suillus, -a, -um *adj.* of *or* relating to pigs

sulcātor, -ōris *m.* one who makes a furrow

sulcō 1. to make a furrow in, plough

sulcus, -ī *m.* furrow; rut; ditch

sullāturiō 4. to desire to act like Sulla

sulp(h)ur, -uris *n.* sulphur

sulp(h)urātus, -a, -um *adj.* treated with sulphur; *n.pl.sbst.* wood treated with sulphur

sulp(h)ureus, -a, -um *adj.* containing sulphur; like sulphur; sulphur-yellow

sultis = **sī voltis**

sum, esse, fuī *v.irreg.* to be; be living; exist; (+*dat.*) belong (to); *impers.* (+*inf.*) it is possible (to)

sūmen, -inis *n.* sow's udder

summ- see **subm-** (other than below)

summa, -ae *f.* total, sum; whole; sum of money; most important point; **ad summam** in short

summārium, -iī *n.* summary

summās, -ātis *adj.* of the most noble rank

summātim *adv.* summarily, briefly

summātus, -ūs *m.* state of supremacy

summē *adv.* in the highest degree, extremely

summula, -ae *f.* small amount of money

summum *adv.* at most; for the last time

summus, -a, -um *adj.* highest, uppermost; farthest; greatest; most excellent

sūmō, sumpsī, sumptum 3. to take up; choose; put on; procure; adopt; spend

sumptiō, -ōnis *f.* logical premiss

sumptuārius, -a, -um *adj.* of *or* relating to financial expenditure

sumptuōsē *adv.* costly; extravagantly

sumptuōsus, -a, -um *adj.* costly, expensive; extravagant

sumptus, -ūs (-ī) *m.* cost, expense; expenditure; resources

suō, suī, sūtum 3. to sew

suovetaurīlia, -ium *n.pl.* sacrifice of a pig, a ram and a bull

super¹ *adv.* over, above; on top; beyond; besides

super² *prep.* (+*acc.*) over, above; on top of; beyond; besides; (+*abl.*) over, above; about, concerning

superā see **suprā**

superābilis, -is, -e *adj.* surmountable; conquerable

superaddō, -idī, -itum 3. (+*dat.*) to affix (upon)

superans, -ntis *adj.* dominant; exceeding

superātor, -ōris *m.* conqueror

superbē *adv.* proudly; arrogantly

superbia, -ae *f.* pride, haughtiness; arrogance, disdain

superbificus, -a, -um *adj.* acting disdainfully

superbiō 4. (+*abl.*) to be proud (because of); (+*inf.*) disdain (to); be splendid

superbus, -a, -um *adj.* proud, haughty; arrogant, disdainful; magnificent, splendid

superciliōsus, -a, -um *adj.* covered with a stern expression

supercilium, -(i)ī *n.* eyebrow; arrogance; severity; ridge, brow

supercurrō 3. to outdo in yield

superēmineō 2. to overtop

superficiāria, -ae *f.* one who resides on another's land

superficiēs, -ēī *f.* top part; building

superfīgō, -fixī, -fixum 3. (+*dat.*) to fix on top (of)

superfīō, -fierī, -factus 3. to become superfluous; be left over

superfluō, -uxī 3. to overflow; be superfluous; abound (*in riches*)

superfulgeō 2. to shine down upon

superfundō, -fūdī, -fūsum 3. (+*dat.*) to pour over; *pass.* spill over *or* out

supergredior, -ssus 3. *dep.* to go beyond; exceed, surpass

superiaciō, -iēcī, -iectum (-iactum) 3. to throw on top of; transcend, surpass

superimmineō 2. to stand above menacingly

superimpōnō, -posuī, -positum 3. to place on top

superincidō 3. to fall on top

superincubō 1. to lie on top

superinduō, -uī, -ūtum 3. to put on over one's clothes

superingerō, -ssī, -stum 3. to heap on top

superiniciō, -iēcī, -iectum 3. to throw on top of

superinsternō, -strāvī, -strātum 3. to spread on top of

superior, -or, -us *compar.adj.* higher, upper; earlier, previous; older; stronger; better

superiūmentārius, -iī *m.* overseer of beasts of burden

superius *compar.adv.* above

superlābor 3. *dep.* to glide over

supernatō 1. to float on top of

superne *adv.* above; on top

supernus, -a, -um *adj.* upper, higher; terrestrial; celestial

superō 1. to climb over, pass; rise above, exceed; (+*abl.*) outdo (in); conquer, defeat; (+*dat.*) remain, survive; abound

superpendeō 2. to overhang

superpōnō, -posuī, -positum 3. to place on top; put in a higher position

superquam *conj.* (+*quod*) in addition to the fact (that)

superscandō 3. to climb over

superscrībō, -scrīpsī, -scrīptum 3. to write on top of (*as a correction*)

supersedeō (-sideō), -sēdī, -sessum 2. (+*dat.*) to sit upon; (+*dat./abl.*) abstain (from); (+*inf.*) forbear (to)

superstagnō 1. to overflow

supersternō, -strāvī, -strātum 3. to spread on top

superstes, -itis *adj.* (+*dat.*) remaining, surviving; standing over (*esp. as a victor*); standing by as a witness; *m.sbst.* witness

superstitiō, -ōnis *f.* religious awe, superstition

superstitiōsē *adv.* superstitiously

superstitiōsus, -a, -um *adj.* superstitious; ecstatic, inspired

superstitō 1. to remain, survive

superstō, -etī 1. (+*dat./abl./acc.*) to stand above *or* on top (of)

superstruō, -uxī, -uctum 3. to build upon

supersum, -esse, -fuī *v.irreg.* (+*dat.*) to remain, be left over; survive; be available (to); be superfluous (to); be superior (to); have the strength (for)

superurgeō 2. to apply pressure from above

superus, -a, -um *adj.* upper, higher; terrestrial; celestial; *m.pl.sbst.* the gods *or* the living; **dē** or **ex superō** from above

supervac(u)āneus, -a, -um *adj.* superfluous, unnecessary

supervacuus, -a, -um *adj.* superfluous, unnecessary; **ex supervacuō** or **in supervacuum** unnecessarily

supervādō 3. to go over, surmount

supervehōr, -ctus 3. *dep.* (+*acc.*) to sail over *or* past

superveniō, -vēnī, -ventum 4. (+*dat./ acc.*) to come on top (of); catch up (with); arrive (unexpectedly); supervene (upon); (+*acc.*) exceed

superventus, -ūs *m.* (unexpected) arrival

supervīvō, -ixī 3. (+*dat.*) to live longer (than)

supervolitō 1. to fly to and fro over; fly to and fro overhead

supervolō 1. to fly over; fly overhead

supīnō 1. to lie on one's back; tilt back; turn up (*soil*)

supīnus, -a, -um *adj.* lying on one's back, supine; upside-down; flat *or* gently sloping; uninterested, passive

suppa- see **subpa-**

suppeditātiō, -ōnis *f.* state of being available *or* at hand

suppeditō 1. to supply, make available; (+*dat.*) be at hand (for), come to aid

suppēdō 3. to fart quietly

sup(p)ellex, -ectilis *f.* furniture; equipment, outfit

suppernātus, -a, -um *adj.* hamstrung

suppetiae, -ārum *f.pl.* help, aid; **suppetiās venīre** (+*dat.*) to come to aid

suppetō, -īvī (-iī) 3. (+*dat.*) to be at hand (for), be available (to); suffice (for)

suppīlō 1. to steal; rob stealthily

suppingō, suppēgī, suppactum 3. (+*dat.*) to affix below

supplantō 1. to make stumble, trip up

supplēmentum, -ī *n.* supplement, filling up; military reinforcement

suppleō, -ēvī, -ētum 2. to make up, complete; replace, make up for

supplex, -icis *adj.* (+*gen. of person*) supplicating, entreating; *m.sbst.* suppliant

supplicātiō, -ōnis *f.* propitiation of a god; thanksgiving for military victory

suppliciter *adv.* in the manner of a suppliant

supplicium, -(i)ī *n.* propitiatory act *or* gift; supplication, entreaty; punishment; **supplicium dare** to pay the penalty; **supplicium sūmere** to exact punishment

supplicō 1. (+*dat.*) to make offerings (to), worship; beseech, entreat, supplicate

supplōdō, -sī, -sum 3. to stamp (*one's feet*)

supplōsiō, -ōnis *f.* stamping (*of feet*)

suppōnō, -posuī, -positum 3. (+*dat.*) to place under, put beneath; expose (to), make subject (to); add (to); substitute (for), counterfeit (as)

supportō 1. to convey

suppositīcius, -a, -um *adj.* substitute; pretend, sham

suppositiō, -ōnis *f.* fraudulent substitution (*esp. of children*)

suppostrix, -īcis *f.* (+*gen.*) female who fraudulently substitutes

suppressiō, -ōnis *f.* illegal retention (*of money*)

suppressus, -a, -um *adj.* low, subdued

supprimō, -pressī, -pressum 3. to press down, cause to sink; restrain, detain; suppress, conceal

suppudet 2. *impers.* (+*acc. of person* +*gen. of thing*) it causes some shame

suppūrātiō, -ōnis *f.* festering sore

suppūrō 1. to fester inside

suppus, -a, -um *adj.* upside-down

supputō 1. to reckon up

suprā¹ *adv.* above, on the top; beyond; more; before

suprā² *prep.* (+*acc.*) over, above; beyond; more than; before

suprālātiō, -ōnis *f.* exaggeration

suprālātus, -a, -um *adj.* over-the-top, exaggerated

suprāscandō 3. to climb over, surmount

suprāscriptus, -a, -um *adj.* written above as a correction

suprēmum *adv.* for the last time

suprēmus, -a, -um *adj.* highest; ultimate, last; critical, final; greatest; most important

sups- see **subs-**

supt- see **subt-**

sūra, -ae *f.* calf (of the leg)

surculus, -ī *m.* young shoot, twig; scion, cutting

surdaster, -tra, -trum *adj.* rather deaf

surditās, -ātis *f.* deafness

surdus, -a, -um *adj.* deaf, unhearing; muted, muffled; unheard

surgō, surrexī, surrectum 3. to rise, arise; get up, spring up; stand tall; swell; develop

surr- see **subr-**

sursum (-us) *adv.* upwards; above

sūs¹, suis *m./f.* pig, sow

sus², sa, sum *adj.* see **suus**

susc- see **succ-** (other than below)

suscenseō 2. (+*dat./acc.*) to be angry (at)

susceptiō, -ōnis *f.* undertaking

susceptum, -ī *n.* enterprise

suscipiō, -cēpī, -ceptum 3. to catch up; raise, lift up; support; adopt; take up, undertake; maintain

suscitō 1. to rouse, stir; raise, lift up; excite

suspectō 1. to gaze up at; be suspicious; (+*acc.*+*inf.*) suspect (that)

suspectus¹, -a, -um *adj.* arousing mistrust, suspected; supposed

suspectus², -ūs *m.* view from below; esteem, regard

suspendium, -(i)ī *n.* hanging oneself

suspendō, -dī, -sum 3. to hang, suspend; execute by hanging; support, prop up; break off; keep in suspense

suspensūra, -ae *f.* vaulted floor

suspensus, -a, -um *adj.* in suspense, uncertain; inconclusive; light, gentle; **in suspensō** undecided

suspicax, -ācis *adj.* suspicious, wary

suspiciō¹, suspexī, suspectum 3. to look up at; admire, respect; suspect; (+*acc.* +*inf.*) look up and see (that)

suspīciō², -ōnis *f.* suspicion, mistrust; slight suggestion; faint idea, inkling

suspīciōsē *adv.* in a manner arousing suspicion

suspīciōsus, -a, -um *adj.* full of suspicion, wary; arousing suspicion, suspicious

suspicor 1. *dep.* or **suspicō** 1. to suspect; surmise, imagine; (+*acc.*+*inf.*) suspect (that); imagine (that)

suspīrātus, -ūs *m.* deep breath, sigh

suspīritus, -ūs *m.* deep breath, sigh

suspīrium, -(i)ī *n.* deep breath, sigh

suspīrō 1. to breathe deeply, sigh; sigh for; breathe out

susque *adv.* **susque dēque** both up and down; indifferent

suss- see **subs-**

sustentātiō, -ōnis *f.* delay, deferment

sustentō 1. to hold up, support; maintain; hold back, restrain; withstand; delay

sustineō, -tinuī, -tentum 2. to hold up, support; maintain; hold back, restrain; withstand; delay; (+*inf.*) be able (to)

sustollō 3. to raise up, lift high; remove, snatch away

susurrō 1. to whisper, rustle; insinuate

susurrus¹, -ī *m.* whisper, rustle; insinuation

susurrus², **-a**, **-um** *adj*. whispering

sūta, **-ōrum** *n.pl*. sewn garment

sūtēlae, **-ārum** *f.pl*. tricks, stratagems

sūtilis, **-is**, **-e** *adj*. sewn together, stitched

sūtor, **-ōris** *m*. cobbler, shoemaker

sūtōrius, **-a**, **-um** *adj*. of *or* relating to a cobbler

sūtrīnus, **-a**, **-um** *adj*. of *or* relating to a cobbler

sūtūra, **-ae** *f*. stitch, seam

suus, **sua**, **suum** *adj*. his, her, its, their; independent; suitable, proper; favourable

sȳcophanta, **-ae** *m*. trickster, swindler

sȳcophantia, **-ae** *f*. deception, trickery

sȳcophantiōsē *adv*. deceptively, fraudulently

sȳcophantor 1. *dep*. (*+dat*.) to practise deception (upon)

syllaba, **-ae** *f*. syllable

syllabātim *adv*. syllable by syllable

syllogismus, **-ī** *m*. syllogism

symbola, **-ae** *f*. financial contribution to a communal meal

symbolus, **-ī** *m*. token *or* symbol (that forms a matching pair with another)

sympathīa, **-ae** *f*. affinity between elements of nature, sympathy

symphōnia, **-ae** *f*. group of singers *or* musicians, band

symphōniacus, **-a**, **-um** *adj*. that sings *or* plays in concert; *m./f.sbst*. singer, musician

symplegma, **-atis** *n*. erotic intertwining

symposium, **-(i)ī** *n*. drinking party

syngrapha, **-ae** *f*. written agreement to pay, promissory note

syngraphus, **-ī** *m*. written agreement, contract; passport

synhedrus, **-ī** *m*. councillor (of a Greek state)

synthesina, **-ae** *f*. loose-fitting garment, dressing-gown

synthesis, **-is** *f*. matching set; loose-fitting suit of clothes, dressing-gown

syrma, **-atis** *n*. long robe (*esp. worn by tragic actors*); tragedy

tabella, -ae f. board; tablet (for writing or inscribing); painting; placard

tabellārius, -a, -um adj. bearing a message; of or relating to voting; m.sbst. messenger

tābeō 2. to waste away, decay

taberna, -ae f. inn; hut; stall, shop

tabernāculum, -ī n. tent; **tabernāculum capere** to set up an augur's tent for taking auspices

tabernārius, -(i)ī m. innkeeper; shopkeeper

tābēs, -is f. wasting away, decay; discharge; disease

tābescō, tābuī 3. to waste away; putrefy; melt away

tābidus, -a, -um adj. wasting away, decaying; causing decay

tābificus, -a, -um adj. causing decay

tabula, -ae f. board; writing-tablet; painting; account; auction; pl. public records; **manum dē tabulā** enough!, stop!

tabulārium, -(i)ī n. archive; record-office

tabulārius, -(i)ī m. book-keeper, accountant

tabulātiō, -ōnis f. planking, flooring

tabulātum, -ī n. planking, decking; storey; layer (of vines)

tābum, -ī n. putrid discharge; plague

taceō 2. to be silent; stop speaking; be silent about

tacitē adv. silently, quietly; privately

taciturnitās, -ātis f. keeping silent

taciturnus, -a, -um adj. silent; taciturn

tacitus, -a, -um adj. silent; tacit; secret

tactilis, -is, -e adj. able to be touched, tangible

tactiō, -ōnis f. touching

tactus, -ūs m. touch, touching; influence

taeda, -ae f. pine-wood; (pine) torch

taedet, taesum est 3. impers. semi-dep. (+acc. of person +gen. of thing) to weary, tire

taedifer, -era, -erum adj. torch-bearing

taedium, -(i)ī n. (+gen.) weariness (of), disgust (with); boredom

taenia, -ae f. ribbon, headband

taeter, -tra, -trum adj. foul, horrible; monstrous

taetrē adv. foully

tagax, -ācis m. light-fingered, thievish

tālāria, -ium n.pl. winged sandals or ankles; base of ankle-length garment; instrument of torture

tālāris, -is, -e adj. stretching down to the ankles

tālārius, -a, -um adj. (perhaps) of or relating to games with dice

talassiō, -ōnis f. ritual cry given at weddings

tālea, -ae f. stake, bar

talentum, -ī n. Greek unit of weight; sum of money

tāliō, -ōnis f. retaliation in kind

tālis, -is, -e adj. such; of such a kind; (+qualis) such … (as)

tāliter adv. in such a way

tālitrum, -ī n. flick of the knuckles

talpa, -ae f. mole

tālus, -ī m. ankle; die (for games)

tam adv. to such a degree; (+adj./adv.) so; (+quam) so … (as)

tamarix, -īcis f. tamarisk

tamen adv. nevertheless; yet

tamendem adv. nevertheless

tamenetsī conj. even though

tametsī conj. even though; nevertheless

tammodo adv. just now

tamquam adv. just as; (+si or subj.) just as if

tandem adv. at last; after all

tangō, tetigī, tactum 3. to touch; border upon; arrive at; steal; taste; affect

tantillus, -a, -um adj. so little, so small; n. sg.sbst. so small an amount

tantisper adv. so long (as); for the meantime

tantopere or **tantō opere** adv. to such a degree, so much

tantulus, -a, -um adj. so little, so small; n. sg.sbst. so small an amount

tantum, -ī n. so much; acc. as adv. to such a degree; only; (+quod) only just

tantus, -a, -um adj. so great; (+quantus) so great … (as)

tantusdem, -tadem, -tundem adj. just so much; n.sg.sbst. just that amount; acc. as adv. just as much

tapēs, -ētos m. tapestry, woven hanging

tappētia n.pl. see **tapēs**

tardē adv. slowly; with delay

tardescō 3. to become slow

tardiloquus, -a, -um adj. slow-speaking

tardipēs, -edis adj. slow-footed, lame

tarditās, -ātis f. slowness; delay; mental slowness

tarditūdō, -inis f. slowness

tardiusculus, -a, -um adj. rather slow

tardō 1. to slow down, delay; check; loiter

tardus, -a, -um adj. slow; late; slow-witted

tarmes, -itis m. woodworm

tarpezīta, -ae m. banker

tat onomatopoeic sound of a door-knock

tata, -ae m. daddy, papa (child's speak)

tatae interj. hurrah!

tau indecl.n. the Greek letter tau

taurea, -ae f. leather whip

taureus, -a, -um adj. derived from a bull

taurifer, -era, -erum adj. producing bulls

tauriformis, -is, -e adj. having the form of a bull

taurīnus, -a, -um adj. derived from or like a bull; made of ox-hide

taurus, -ī m. bull

taxātiō, -ōnis f. assessment, valuation

taxeus, -a, -um adj. made or consisting of yew

taxillus, -ī m. small die

taxō 1. to rate, value; criticize

taxus, -ī f. yew tree

techina, -ae f. trick, artifice

technyphion, -iī m. small workroom

tectē adv. secretly, covertly

tector, -ōris m. plasterer

tectōriola, -ōrum n.pl. pieces of plasterwork

tectōrium, -(i)ī n. plaster; pl. pieces of plasterwork

tectōrius, -a, -um adj. of or relating to plastering; **opus tectōrium** plasterwork

tectum, -ī n. roof; dwelling

tectus, -a, -um adj. covered, roofed; hidden; secretive

teges, -etis f. mat made of rushes

tegetīcula, -ae f. small mat

teg(i)men, -inis n. covering

teg(i)mentum, -ī n. covering

tegō, texī, tectum 3. to cover; roof over; clothe; protect; conceal

tēgula, -ae f. roof-tile, tile

tegum- see **teg(i)m-**

tegus see **tergus**

tēla, -ae f. warp; spider's web; loom; plan

tēlinum, -ī n. ointment prepared from fenugreek

tellūs, -ūris f. land; country; earth

tēlum, -ī n. missile, spear; weapon

temerārius, -a, -um adj. rash, reckless; haphazard, random

temerātor, -ōris m. one who defiles

temere adv. recklessly; haphazardly; without reason; easily

temeritās, -ātis f. recklessness; boldness; haphazardness

temerō 1. to desecrate, dishonour; violate

tēmētum, -ī n. intoxicating drink

temnō 3. to despise, disdain

tēmō, -ōnis m. beam (of a wagon or plough); wagon

temperāmentum, -ī n. blend; compromise; restraint

temperans, -ntis adj. restrained, temperate

temperanter adv. with restraint

temperantia, -ae f. restraint, temperance

temperātē adv. with restraint

temperātiō, -ōnis f. blending; (+gen.) moderation (of); balanced arrangement

temperātor, -ōris m. one who tempers

temperātūra, -ae f. constitution; temperateness

temperātus, -a, -um adj. temperate; restrained

temperī see **temporī**

temperiēs, -ēī f. blend; (mild) climate

temperō 1. to temper; regulate; be restrained, temperate; (+*dat*.) be moderate towards *or* in; (+*ab* +*abl*. *or* +*quin* +*subj*.) refrain from

tempestās, -ātis *f*. season, period of time; weather; storm

tempestīvē (-ō) *adv*. at the right time, opportunely

tempestīvitās, -ātis *f*. seasonable quality

tempestīvus, -a, -um *adj*. in season; timely, opportune

templum, -ī *n*. consecrated land; temple; region; roof-plank

temporārius, -a, -um *adj*. temporary, occasional

temporī *adv*. at the right time, opportunely

temptābundus, -a, -um *adj*. testing in one's movements

temptāmen, -inis *n*. attempt; test

temptāmentum, -ī *n*. attempt; test

temptātiō, -ōnis *f*. attempt; (+*gen*.) attack (on/of)

temptātor, -ōris *m*. (+*gen*.) one who makes an attempt (on)

temptō 1. to feel; test, probe; try; make an attempt on; attack

tempus, -oris *n*. time; moment; season; right time; grammatical tense; forehead; temple

tēmulentus, -a, -um *adj*. drunk, inebriated

tenācitās, -ātis *f*. clinging, holding on

tenāciter *adv*. with a firm grip; stubbornly

tenax, -ācis *adj*. clinging; (+*gen*.) holding fast (to); restraining; niggardly; stubborn

tendicula, -ae *f*. snare cord

tendō, tetendī, tensum (-tum) 3. to stretch (out), extend; pull tight, draw; encamp; proceed (to); exert oneself; (+*inf*.) strive (to)

tenebrae, -ārum *f.pl*. darkness, gloom; obscurity; obscure business; ignorance

tenebric(ōs)us, -a, -um *adj*. dark, gloomy

tenebrōsus, -a, -um *adj*. dark, gloomy

tenellulus, -a, -um *adj*. rather tender, very delicate

tenellus, -a, -um *adj*. rather tender, somewhat delicate

teneō, -uī, -tum 2. to hold, keep fixed; contain; occupy, own; maintain

tener, -era, -erum *adj*. tender; soft; immature; gentle, effeminate

tenerascō 3. to become soft

tenerē *adv*. gently; sensitively

teneritās, -ātis *f*. immaturity, tenderness

teneritūdō, -inis *f*. immaturity, tenderness

tēnesmos, -ī *m*. bowel-pains

tenor, -ōris *m*. straight course; continuity; tenor; tone

tensa, -ae *f*. wagon used for procession of images of gods

tensus, -a, -um *adj*. taut, tense

tentīgō, -inis *f*. state of being (sexually) erect

tentō see **temptō**

tentōrium, -(i)ī *n*. tent

tentus see **tensus**

tenuiculus, -a, -um *adj*. rather thin

tenuis, -is, -e *adj*. thin, narrow; fine; slight; weak; subtle; plain; poor; trivial

tenuitās, -ātis *f*. thinness; fineness; subtlety; simplicity; poverty

tenuiter *adv*. thinly; scantily; weakly; plainly

tenuō 1. to thin, attenuate; wear down; rarefy; reduce, diminish

tenus¹ *prep*. (+*abl*./*gen*.) as far as, up to

tenus², -oris *n*. snare

tepefaciō, -fēcī, -factum 3. to make tepid, warm

tepefactō 1. to warm habitually

tepeō 2. to be tepid, warm; be lukewarm (*in passion*)

tepescō, tepuī 3. to grow tepid; become lukewarm, cool off (*in passion*)

tepidē *adv*. in a warm condition

tepidus, -a, -um *adj*. tepid, lukewarm

tepor, -ōris *m*. warmth, middling heat; lukewarmness (*of style*)

ter *adv*. three times, thrice

terdeciens (-ēs) *adv*. thirteen times

terebinthus, -ī *f*. terebinth tree; terebinth wood

terebrō 1. to drill a hole into, bore

terēdō, -inis *f*. woodworm (*or sim.*)

teres, -etis *adj*. rounded, smooth

tergeminus, -a, -um *adj*. threefold, triple

tergeō, tersī, tersum 2. to wipe, rub; wipe off; press

tergīnum, -ī *n*. ox-hide whip

tergiversātiō, -ōnis *f.* hesitation, reluctance

tergiversor 1. *dep.* to be reluctant, hesitate

tergō see **tergeō**

tergum, -ī *n.* back; hide; rear; **tergum dare** or **vertere** to take to flight

tergus, -oris *n.* back; hide

termentum, -ī *n.* sore from abrasion, blister

termes, -itis *m.* bough

terminātiō, -ōnis *f.* marking off (*territories*); limit; conclusion

terminō 1. to mark off (*territories*); restrict, delimit; conclude

terminus, -ī *m.* boundary marker; limit, end; conclusion

ternī, -ae, -a *pl.adj.* three each; three at once

terō, trīvī, trītum 3. to rub; wear down; thresh; use up; wear out

terra, -ae *f.* land, ground; earth; region; *pl.* planet earth

terrēnus, -a, -um *adj.* of or relating to dry land, terrestrial; consisting of soil or earth

terreō 2. to overpower with fear, terrify; (+*ab* +*abl.*) deter from

terrestris, -is, -e *adj.* of or relating to dry land, terrestrial; from the ground

terreus, -a, -um *adj.* born from the earth

terribilis, -is, -e *adj.* frightening, terrible

terricula, -ōrum *n.pl.* cause of fear, bogey

terrificō 1. to make frightened, terrify

terrificus, -a, -um *adj.* frightening, terrifying

terrigena, -ae *m./f.* one born from the earth

terriloquus, -a, -um *adj.* uttering terrifying words

territō 1. to scare (repeatedly), frighten

territōrium, -(i)ī *n.* land of a town, territory

terror, -ōris *m.* terror, dread; object of terror

ter(r)uncius, -(i)ī *m.* copper coin worth three *unciae*

tersus, -a, -um *adj.* neat; refined

tertiadecimānī, -ōrum *m.pl.* soldiers of the thirteenth legion

tertiānus, -a, -um *adj.* occurring every other day; *m.pl.sbst.* soldiers of the third legion

tertiō or **-um** *adv.* for a third time; thirdly

tertius, -a, -um *adj.* third; **nudius tertius** day before yesterday

tervenēficus, -ī *m.* triple-poisoner, archscoundrel

tesqua, -ōrum *n.pl.* wasteland(s)

tessella, -ae *f.* six-sided die

tessellō 1. to adorn with mosaics

tessera, -ae *f.* six-sided die; military tablet containing watchword; ticket for receipt of benefit (*esp. of corn*); hospitality token used for identification

tesserārius, -iī *m.* soldier entrusted with circulating *tesserae* from the general

tesserula, -ae *f.* small token for receipt of corn

testa, -ae *f.* earthenware vessel, brick or tile; shard; shell, covering

testāceus, -a, -um *adj.* made of earthenware bricks

testāmentārius, -a, -um *adj.* of or relating to wills; *m.sbst.* forger of wills

testāmentum, -ī *n.* will, testament

testātiō, -ōnis *f.* testifying

testātor, -ōris *m.* one who makes a will

testātus, -a, -um *adj.* well-attested, proved

testiculus, -ī *m.* testicle

testificātiō, -ōnis *f.* bearing witness; proof

testificor 1. *dep.* to testify to; give proof of; call to witness

testimōnium, -(i)ī *n.* testimony; proof

testis, -is *m./f.* witness, testifier; (+*gen.*) proof (of); spectator

testor 1. *dep.* to call to witness; bear witness; prove; make a will under witness

testū *n.abl.sg.* earthenware pot or lid

testūdineus, -a, -um *adj.* like a tortoise; made of tortoiseshell

testūdō, -inis *f.* tortoise, turtle; tortoiseshell; lyre; vault; military defensive cover (formed by shields held aloft or a wooden screen)

testula, -ae *f.* potsherd

tetrachmum, -ī *n.* Greek silver coin worth four *drachmae*

tetraō, -ōnis *m.* large game bird, black grouse

tetrarchēs, -ae *m.* minor king protected by Rome, tetrarch

tetrarchia, -ae *f.* kingdom of a tetrarch

tetrastichon, -ī *n.* poem of four lines, quatrain

tetricus, -a, -um *adj.* severe, forbidding

texō, -uī, -tum 3. to weave; intertwine; build; compose

textilis, -is, -e *adj.* made by weaving *or* plaiting; *n.sbst.* woven fabric

textor, -ōris *m.* weaver

textōrius, -a, -um *adj.* entangled

textrīnum, -ī *n.* weaving; weaving workshop

textrix, -īcis *f.* female weaver

textum, -ī *n.* woven fabric; framework; texture

textūra, -ae *f.* weaving; construction; texture

textus, -ūs *m.* (atomic) structure; piece of plaited work

thalamēgos, -os, -on *adj.* possessing cabins

thalamus, -ī *m.* chamber; marriage-bed; marriage

thalassicus (-inus), -a, -um *adj.* sea-green, aquamarine

thapsos, -ī *f.* poisonous shrub

theātrālis, -is, -e *adj.* of *or* relating to the theatre

theātrum, -ī *n.* theatre, place for performance; audience

thēca, -ae *f.* box, case

thema, -atis *n.* horoscope

theologūmena, -ōrum *n.pl.* theological discourses

theologus, -ī *m.* theologian

theoractus, -a, -um *adj.* struck by the gods, raving

thermae, -ārum *f.pl.* thermal baths

thermopōlium, -(i)ī *n.* place selling hot drinks

thermopōtō 1. to refresh with hot drinks

thermulae, -ārum *f.pl.* (small) thermal baths

thēsaurārius, -a, -um *adj.* concerned with treasure

thēsaurus, -ī *m.* vault, treasury; treasure, hoard

thēta *indecl.n.* the Greek letter *theta*; symbol of condemnation

thiasus, -ī *m.* Bacchic dance; group of Bacchic dancers

tholus, -ī *m.* circular building with a domed roof

thōrax, -ācis *m.* body armour, cuirass; waistcoat

thronos, -ī *m.* throne

thyius, -a, -um *adj.* made of citron wood

thymbra, -ae *f.* aromatic herb

thymum, -ī *n.* thyme

thynnus, -ī *m.* tunny fish

thyrsiger, -era, -erum *adj.* bearing the thyrsus

thyrsus, -ī *m.* ivy-covered wand associated with Bacchus

tiāra, -ae *f.* or **tiārās, -ae** *m.* Asian headdress

tībia, -ae *f.* reed-pipe, flute

tībiāle, -is *n.* shin-guard

tībīcen, -inis *m.* player of the *tibia*; pillar, prop

tībīcina, -ae *f.* female player of the *tibia*

tībīcinium, -(i)ī *n.* playing of the *tibia*

tigillum, -ī *n.* small plank

tignārius, -a, -um *adj.* concerned with timber; **faber tignārius** carpenter

tignum, -ī *n.* plank; timber

tigris, -is or **-idis** *f./m.* tiger; tiger-skin

tilia, -ae *f.* lime-tree

timefactus, -a, -um *adj.* made frightened, afraid

timens, -ntis *adj.* (+*gen.*) afraid (of)

---

timeō 2. (see also **metuō** and **vereor**)
a) with noun
   mortem timeo I fear death
b) with infinitive
   mori timeo I am afraid to die
c) with **nē** + subjunctive
   timeo ne moriar I fear that (lest) I may die

---

timidē *adv.* fearfully; cautiously

timiditās, -ātis *f.* timidity; instance of cowardliness

timidus, -a, -um *adj.* fearful; timid

timor, -ōris *m.* fear; object of fear

tinctilis, -is, -e *adj.* applied by dipping

tinctus, -ūs *m.* dipping

tinea, -ae *f.* grub, larva

tingō, -xī, -ctum 3. to dip, soak; (+*abl.*) imbue (with), dye (with)

tinia see **tinea**

tinnīmentum, -ī *n.* ringing sound

tinniō 4. to ring, jangle; sound shrilly

tinnītus, -ūs *m.* ringing sound, jangling

tinnulus, -a, -um *adj.* ringing, jangling

tintinnābulum, -ī *n.* bell

tintinnāculus, -a, -um *adj.* jangling

tintinō 1. to have a ringing sensation, ring

tīnus, -ī *f.* the shrub laurustinus

tippula, -ae *f.* kind of water-spider

tīrō, -ōnis *m.* newly enrolled soldier; novice

tīrōcinium, -(i)ī *n.* state of being a *tiro;* initial service; apprenticeship

tīrunculus, -ī *m.* mere beginner, recruit

tisana, -ae *f.* barley

tisanārium, -(i)ī *n.* barley-water (*or sim.*)

tītillātiō, -ōnis *f.* tickling; titillation

tītillō 1. to tickle; titillate

tittibilīcium, -(i)ī *n.* worthless item, bagatelle

titubanter *adv.* hesitatingly, falteringly

titubantia, -ae *f.* hesitation, unsteadiness

titubātiō, -ōnis *f.* tottering; hesitancy

titubō 1. to totter, be unsteady; stumble; waver

titulus, -ī *m.* placard, tablet; inscription; title; distinction; pretext

toculliō, -ōnis *m.* usurer

todillus, -a, -um *adj.* of *or* relating to small birds

tōfīnus, -a, -um *adj.* made of tufa

tōfus, -ī *m.* porous volcanic rock, tufa

toga, -ae *f.* formal Roman garment, toga; **toga candida** toga worn by political candidates; **toga praetexta** purple-edged toga worn by magistrates and children; **toga virīlis** toga worn by adults

togātārius, -iī *m.* actor in Roman comedy

togātulus, -ī *m.* mere toga-wearing client

togātus, -a, -um *adj.* wearing a toga; Roman; civilian; *f.sbst.* Roman comedy performed in togas

togula, -ae *f.* little *or* petty toga

tolerābilis, -is, -e *adj.* tolerable; passable; tolerant

tolerābiliter *adv.* tolerably; passably

tolerans, -ntis *adj.* (+*gen.*) tolerant (of)

toleranter *adv.* tolerantly, patiently

tolerantia, -ae *f.* tolerance, patience

tolerō 1. to support; sustain, maintain; endure, tolerate

tollenō, -ōnis *m.* mechanical crane

tollō, sustulī, sublātum 3. to lift, raise; take up (as one's own); rouse; remove; destroy

tolūtārius, -a, -um *adj.* jogging

tolūtim *adv.* at a jog

tomāculum, -ī *n.* sausage

tōmentum, -ī *n.* material for stuffing (*cushions etc.*)

tomus, -ī *m.* piece of papyrus

tondeō, totondī, tonsum 2. to clip, shear; prune

tonitrālis, -is, -e *adj.* (*perhaps*) of *or* relating to thunder

tonitrus, -ūs *m.* thunder

tonō, -uī 1. to thunder; speak thunderously

tonsa, -ae *f.* oar

tonsilis, -is, -e *adj.* able to be clipped; clipped, shorn

tonsillae, -ārum *f.pl.* tonsils

tonsitō 1. to shear

tonsor, -ōris *m.* barber

tonsōrius, -a, -um *adj.* of *or* relating to a barber

tonstrīcula, -ae *f.* little female barber

tonstrīna (tōs-), -ae *f.* barber's shop

tonstrix, -īcis *f.* female barber

tonsūra, -ae *f.* cutting

tonsus, -ūs *m.* style of hair, haircut

tōphus see **tōfus**

topiārium, -(i)ī *n.* landscape gardening

topiārius, -(i)ī *m.* landscape gardener

topica, -ōrum *n.pl.* discourses on commonplaces

toral, -ālis *n.* coverlet

torculum, -ī *n.* wine-press

toreuma, -atis *n.* carved *or* embossed work

tormentum, -ī *n.* rope; instrument of torture; catapult

tormina, -um *n.pl.* bowel-pains

torminōsus, -a, -um *adj.* suffering from colic

tornō 1. to turn on a lathe, round

tornus, -ī *m.* turner's lathe

torōsus, -a, -um *adj.* brawny, muscular

torpēdō, -inis *f.* sluggishness; cramp-fish

torpeō 2. to be numb, motionless; be sluggish, slothful

torpescō, -puī 3. to grow numb, become motionless; become slothful

torpidus, -a, -um *adj.* benumbed, stupefied

torpor, -ōris *m.* numbness; drowsiness; sloth

torquātus, -a, -um *adj.* wearing a collar, collared

torqueō, torsī, tortum 2. to twist, wind; turn, distort; hurl; torment

torquēs (-is), -is *m./f.* necklace (*of twisted metal*); wreath

torrens, -ntis *adj.* scorching hot; flowing headlong; *m.sbst.* torrent

torreō, torruī, tostum 2. to parch, dry up; roast, burn

torrescō 3. to be roasted

torridus, -a, -um *adj.* parched, roasted; desiccated

torris, -is *m.* firebrand

tortē *adv.* crookedly, twistingly

tortilis, -is, -e *adj.* twisted, twined

tortō 1. to keep bending, writhe

tortor, -ōris *m.* torturer; hurler (*of a sling*)

tortuōsus, -a, -um *adj.* sinuous; tortuous

tortus¹, -a, -um *adj.* bent, curved; curly

tortus², -ūs *m.* whirling, hurling; coil

torulus, -ī *m.* cord, band

torus, -ī *m.* couch, marriage-bed; marriage; palliasse; ridge; muscle

torvitās, -ātis *f.* fierceness, savageness

torvus, -a, -um *adj.* grim, fierce, savage

tōs- see **tons-**

tot *indecl.adj.* so many

totidem *indecl.adj.* just as many; (+*quot*) as many (as)

totiens (-ēs) *adv.* so often

tōtum, -īus *n.* the whole, entirety; **ex tōtō** utterly

tōtus¹, -a, -um *adj.* whole (of), all, entire

totus², -a, -um *adj.* so great (a)

toxicum, -ī *n.* poison

trabālis, -is, -e *adj.* of *or* relating to beams; as big as a tree-trunk

trabea, -ae *f.* purple and white robe worn by kings and *equites*

trabeātus, -a, -um *adj.* wearing a *trabea*

trabs, -bis *f.* tree-trunk; timber; boat

tractābilis, -is, -e *adj.* tangible; manageable; amenable

tractātiō, -ōnis *f.* handling; management; treatment, discussion

tractātor, -ōris *m.* masseur

tractātrix, -īcis *f.* masseuse

tractātus, -ūs *m.* management; treatment, discussion

tractim *adv.* gradually, at length

tractō 1. to drag about; handle; manipulate; manage; perform; treat, discuss; deliberate

tractum, -ī *n.* flock of wool

tractus, -ūs *m.* dragging along; drawing out; trail; expanse; region

trāditiō, -ōnis *f.* handing over; passing down (*of knowledge*)

trāditor, -ōris *m.* traitor

trādō, -didī, -ditum 3. to hand over, give up; hand down; entrust; report; propound

trādūcō, -duxī, -ductum 3. to bring across, lead over *or* past; transfer; pass (*time*); expose to ridicule

trāductiō, -ōnis *f.* transferral; passing (*of time*); exposure to ridicule

trāductor, -ōris *m.* one who changes (*status*)

trādux, -ucis *m.* vine-layer, vine-branch

trāf- see **transf-**

tragicē *adv.* tragically

tragicōmoedia, -ae *f.* drama combining tragic and comic elements

tragicus, -a, -um *adj.* of *or* relating to tragic drama; tragic; *m.sbst.* tragic actor

tragoedia, -ae *f.* tragedy; *pl.* bombastic style, histrionics

tragoedus, -ī *m.* tragic actor

trāgula, -ae *f.* hunting spear

tragus, -ī *m.* body odour from the armpits

trahax, -ācis *adj.* rapacious

trahea, -ae *f.* threshing sledge

trahō, -xī, -ctum 3. to drag, pull along; draw out; extend; draw in; attract; (+*in/ad* +*acc.*) assign (to)

trāiciō, -iēcī, -iectum 3. to throw across; convey over; cross over; transfer; transfix

trāiectiō, -ōnis *f.* transference; crossing over

trāiectus, -ūs *m.* crossing over; route across

trāl- see **transl-**

trāma, -ae *f.* warp, woof

trāmes, -itis *m.* path, course

trān- see **transn-**

tranquillē *adv.* calmly, tranquilly

tranquillitās, -ātis *f.* calmness, tranquillity

tranquillō 1. to calm down, make tranquil

tranquillus, -a, -um *adj.* calm, tranquil; *n. sbst.* calm weather *or* conditions

trans *prep.* (+*acc.*) across, over; beyond

transabeō, -īre, -īvī (-iī), -itum 4. to go beyond; transfix

transactor, -ōris *m.* negotiator

transadigō, -ēgī, -actum 3. to transfix; thrust (*sthg*) through (*sthg*)

transcendō, -dī, -sum 3. to climb across, cross over; pass over; transgress

transcīdō, -dī, -sum 3. to cut *or* flog all over

transcrībō, -scripsī, -scriptum 3. to copy, transcribe; transfer, assign

transcurrō, -rrī, -rsum 3. to run across *or* through; run the course of; hasten past

transcursus, -ūs *m.* rushing across

transd- see **trād-**

transenna, -ae *f.* lattice-work; bird net, trap

transeō, -īre, -īvī (-iī), -itum 4. to go across, pass (over); pass by; transgress; run over; surpass; (+*in* +*acc.*) be changed into

transerō, -uī, -tum 3. to transfer by grafting

transferō, -ferre, -tulī, -lātum *v.irreg.* to carry over, transport; transfer; change; translate

transfīgō, -fixī, -fixum 3. to transfix; thrust

transfigūrō 1. to change the form of, transform

transfodiō, -fōdī, -fossum 3. to dig through; transfix

transformis, -is, -e *adj.* changed in form, transformed

transformō 1. to change the form of, transform

transfretō 1. to cross the sea

transfuga, -ae *m.* deserter (*esp. to the enemy side*)

transfugiō, -fūgī 3. to go over to the enemy, desert; escape

transfugium, -(i)ī *n.* desertion (*to the enemy side*)

transfūmō 1. to pass through like smoke

transfundō, -ūdī, -ūsum 3. to transfer by pouring; transfer

transfūsiō, -ōnis *f.* transferral by pouring

transgredior (-grad-), -ssus 3. *dep.* to go across; move over (*esp. to the enemy*); surpass

transgressiō, -ōnis *f.* going across; hyperbaton, verbal inversion

transgressus, -ūs *m.* going across

transigō, -ēgī, -actum 3. to drive through; transfix; complete; settle

transiliō, -luī 4. to leap to the other side; leap over (*sthg*); pass over; transgress

transitiō, -ōnis *f.* going across; desertion (*to the enemy*); doorway

transitōrius, -a, -um *adj.* providing a passageway (*through*)

transitus, -ūs *m.* going across, passage; path across; transition; **in transitū** in passing

translātīcius, -a, -um *adj.* traditional, inherited; commonplace

translātiō, -ōnis *f.* transferral; transferred sense (*of words*)

translātīvus, -a, -um *adj.* transferable

translātor, -ōris *m.* one who transfers

translegō 3. to read through (aloud)

transloquor 3. *dep.* to recount in full

translūceō 2. to shine through *or* across

transmarīnus, -a, -um *adj.* of *or* relating to a country overseas, transmarine

transmeō 1. to travel over

transmigrō 1. to move residence

transmineō 2. to jut through the other side

transmissiō, -ōnis *f.* journey across

transmittō, -mīsī, -missum 3. to send across, transmit; cross over; give passage to; disregard

transmontānus, -a, -um *adj.* of *or* relating to the region over a mountain range

transmoveō, -mōvī, -mōtum 2. to move elsewhere, transfer

transmūtō 1. to change, transmute

transnatō 1. to swim across

transnō 1. to swim across; swim to the other side; glide across

transnōminō 1. (+*double acc.*) to rename (*sthg*) as (*sthg*)

transpadānus, -a, -um *adj.* situated across the river Po

transpectus, -ūs *m.* view through

transpiciō 3. to see through

transpōnō, -posuī, -positum 3. to move across

transportō 1. to convey across

transrhenānus, -a, -um *adj.* situated across the river Rhine

transs- see **trans-**

transtiberīnus, -a, -um *adj.* situated across the river Tiber

transtineō 2. to pass through

transtrum, -ī *n.* cross-beam; rower's bench

transultō 1. to leap across

transūmō 3. to take up from elsewhere, adopt

transuō, -uī, -ūtum 3. to transfix

transvēctiō, -ōnis f. conveying across; riding past

transvehō, -xī, -ctum 3. to convey across; carry past; *pass.* ride, sail across

transverberō 1. to strike through, transfix

transversārius, -a, -um *adj.* lying across, transverse

transversus, -a, -um *adj.* lying across, transverse; moving across; **ex/dē transversō** from the side; unexpectedly

transvolitō 1. to fly across

transvolō 1. to fly across *or* over

trapētus, -ī m. mill for pressing olives

trapezophorum, -ī n. ornamental table

trāsenna see **transenna**

trāv- see **transv-**

trecēnī, -ae, -a *pl.adj.* three hundred each; three hundred at a time

trecentēsimus, -a, -um *adj.* three-hundredth

trecentī, -ae, -a *pl.adj.* three hundred

trecentiens (-ēs) *adv.* three hundred times

trechedipnum, -ī n. Greek dining wear (*perhaps* slippers)

tredecim *indecl.adj.* thirteen

tremebundus, -a, -um *adj.* trembling; shivering

tremefaciō, -fēcī, -factum 3. to make tremble

tremendus, -a, -um *adj.* terrible, dreadful

tremescō 3. to tremble; (+*acc.*) quake at

tremō, -uī 3. to tremble; vibrate; (+*acc.*) quake at

tremor, -ōris m. trembling; vibrating; object of terror

tremulus, -a, -um *adj.* trembling; vibrating, shaking, quivering

trepidanter *adv.* anxiously

trepidātiō, -ōnis f. trepidation, anxiety

trepidē *adv.* agitatedly, anxiously

trepidō 1. to be in a state of panic; be anxious; tremble; hurry

trepidus, -a, -um *adj.* anxious, panic-stricken; agitated; trembling

trēs, trēs, tria *pl.adj.* three

tressis, -is m. three *asses*

triangulus, -a, -um *adj.* with three sides, triangular; *n.sbst.* triangle

triāriī, -ōrum m.pl. most experienced Roman soldiers, positioned in the third rank

tribas, -adis f. lesbian

tribolus, -ī m. thorny plant, caltrop

tribuārius, -a, -um *adj.* of *or* relating to a tribe

tribūlis, -is m. fellow-tribesman; poor person

tribulum, -ī n. threshing sledge

tribulus see **tribolus**

tribūnal, -ālis n. platform, dais; funeral monument; **prō/in tribūnālī** officially

tribūnātus, -ūs m. office of tribune

tribūnicius, -a, -um *adj.* of *or* relating to a tribune; *m.sbst.* former tribune

tribūnus, -ī m. tribune; military tribune

tribuō, -uī, -ūtum 3. to assign, allot; ascribe (to); grant; (+*dat.*) respect

tribus, -ūs f. tribe

tribūtārius, -a, -um *adj.* liable to pay tribute; of *or* relating to tribute

tribūtim *adv.* by tribes

tribūtiō, -ōnis f. distribution, allotting

tribūtum, -ī n. tax, tribute; offering

tribūtus¹, -ī m. tax, levy

tribūtus², -a, -um *adj.* arranged by tribes

trīcae, -ārum f.pl. trifles; troubles, problems

trīcēnī, -ae, -a *pl.adj.* thirty each; thirty at a time

trīcensimus (-ēsi-), -a, -um *adj.* thirtieth

triceps, -cipitis *adj.* having three heads

trichila, -ae f. summer-house

trichōrum, -ī n. one of three parts of a room *or* building

trīciens (-ēs) *adv.* thirty times

triclīnium, -(i)ī n. triangular arrangement of dining couches; dining room

trīcor 1. *dep.* to cause problems, play tricks

tricorpor, -oris *adj.* having three bodies

tricuspis, -idis *adj.* having three prongs

tridens, -ntis *adj.* having three prongs; *m. sbst.* trident

tridentifer, -erī m. trident-bearer

tridentiger, -era, -erum *adj.* bearing a trident

trīduum, -uī n. period of three days

triennia, -ium n.pl. triennial rites

triennium, -(i)ī n. period of three years

triens, -ntis *m*. third part; third of a *sex-tarius*; third of an *as*

trientābulum, -ī *n*. land given to lender of money (worth a third of his debt)

triērarchus, -ī *m*. commander of a trireme

triēris, -is *f*. trireme

trietēricus, -a, -um *adj*. triennial; *n.pl*. triennial rites

trietēris, -idis *f*. period of three years; triennial rite(s)

trifāriam *adv*. in three parts *or* ways

trifaucis, -is, -e *adj*. having three throats

trifidus, -a, -um *adj*. having three prongs

trifīlis, -is, -e *adj*. having three strands of hair

trifolium, -iī *n*. clover (*or sim*.)

triformis, -is, -e *adj*. having three forms

trifur, -ūris *m*. triple-thief

trifurcifer, -erī *m*. triple-rogue

trigeminus, -a, -um *adj*. born as a triplet; threefold

trīgintā *indecl.adj*. thirty

trigō(n), -ōnis *m*. three-player ball game; ball used in this game

trigōnālis, -is, -e *adj*. of *or* relating to the game *trigon*

trigōnum, -ī *n*. triangle

trilībris, -is, -e *adj*. weighing three pounds

trilinguis, -is, -e *adj*. having three tongues

trilix, -īcis *adj*. having a triple thread

trime(n)stris, -is, -e *adj*. lasting three months

trimetrus, -ī *m*. verse consisting of three *metra*

trimodius, -(i)ī *m*. measure of three *modii*

trīmulus, -a, -um *adj*. (only) three years old

trīmus, -a, -um *adj*. three years old

trīnī, -ae, -a *pl.adj*. three each; three at a time; *sg*. threefold

trinoctiālis, -is, -e *adj*. occurring three nights successively

trinōdis, -is, -e *adj*. having three knots

triōbulum, -ī *n*. three-obol piece

triōnēs, -um *m.pl*. constellations of Great and Little Bear

triparcus, -a, -um *adj*. triply stingy

tripart- see **tripert-**

tripectorus, -a, -um *adj*. having three chests

tripedālis, -is, -e *adj*. three feet broad

tripertītō *adv*. in three parts

tripertītus, -a, -um *adj*. tripartite

tripēs, -edis *adj*. having three feet *or* legs; *m.sbst*. three-legged piece of furniture

triplex, -icis *adj*. threefold, triple; tripartite; *n.sg.sbst*. triple amount

triplus, -a, -um *adj*. (+*gen*.) three times the amount (of)

tripudiō 1. to perform the *tripudium*

tripudium, -(i)ī *n*. ritual Roman dance; favourable omen, i.e. the frantic eating of corn by the sacred chickens

tripūs, -podis *m*. three-legged stand; the tripod seat of the Delphic priestess; Delphic oracle

triquetrus, -a, -um *adj*. triangular

trirēmis, -is, -e *adj*. having three banks of oars; *f.sbst*. trireme

triscurria, -ōrum *n.pl*. triple-buffoonery

triste *adv*. sorrowfully; sternly; painfully

tristiculus, -a, -um *adj*. rather sad

tristificus, -a, -um *adj*. inspiring sadness

tristis, -is, -e *adj*. sad, gloomy; grim, dismal; solemn, stern; bitter

tristitia, -ae or **-ēs, -ēī** *f*. unhappiness, sadness; sternness; sourness

trisulcus, -a, -um *adj*. having three forks

tritavos, -ī *m*. great-great-great-great-grandfather

trīticeia, -ae *f*. 'wheat-fish' (*pun on hordeia*)

trīticeus, -a, -um *adj*. consisting of wheat

trīticum, -ī *n*. wheat

trītor, -ōris *m*. rubber, polisher

trītūra, -ae *f*. threshing

trītus¹, -a, -um *adj*. well-worn, eroded; common; experienced

trītus², -ūs *m*. rubbing

triumphālis, -is, -e *adj*. of *or* relating to a triumph, triumphal; triumphant

triumphe *interj*. ritual cry greeting triumphant generals

triumphō 1. to celebrate a triumph; process in a triumph; triumph; (+*de* +*abl*.) exult (over)

triumphus, -ī *m*. triumphal procession of a victorious general granted by the senate; triumph; the cry *triumphe*

triumvir, -rī *m*. member of a board of three *or* triumvirate; *pl*. board of three

triumvirālis, -is, -e *adj*. of *or* relating to *triumviri*

triumvirātus, -ūs *m*. office of a *triumvir*

trivenēfica, -ae *f*. triple-poisoner, arch-witch

triviālis, -is, -e *adj.* of the cross-roads, commonplace

trivium, -(i)ī *n.* meeting point of three roads, cross-roads

trivius, -a, -um *adj.* of *or* relating to cross-roads

trochaeus, -ī *m.* trochee, metrical foot of a long syllable followed by a short

trochus, -ī *m.* hoop

troclea, -ae *f.* block and pulley(s) for lifting weights

tropa, -ae *f.* game of casting knucklebones into a hole

tropaeum, -ī *n.* trophy, victory monument; victory

trossulus, -ī *m.* coxcomb, fop

trucīdātiō, -ōnis *f.* butchering, massacre

trucīdō 1. to slaughter (*animals*); butcher, massacre (*humans*)

truculentē *adv.* fiercely, savagely

truculentia, -ae *f.* ferocity, savagery

truculentus, -a, -um *adj.* ferocious, savage

trudis, -is *f.* barge-pole, pointed staff

trūdō, -sī, -sum 3. to thrust, push; drive (into)

trulla, -ae *f.* ladle; fire-pan

truncō 1. to lop off, dismember; strip of foliage

truncus¹, -a, -um *adj.* mutilated, dismembered; deprived (*of foliage*)

truncus², -ī *m.* torso, trunk; tree-trunk

trūsō 1. to keep thrusting

trutina, -ae *f.* balance, weighing scales

trutinō 1. to weigh in a balance

trux, trucis *adj.* savage, harsh; cruel

trȳgonus, -ī *m.* sting-ray

tū (*acc.* **tē**, *gen.* **tuī**, *dat.* **tibī (tibi)**, *abl.* **tē**) *pron.* you; *pl.* see **vōs**

tuātim *adv.* in your own fashion

tuba, -ae *f.* trumpet (*used esp. in war*)

tūber, -eris *adj.* swelling, protuberance; fungus

tubicen, -inis *m.* trumpeter

tubula, -ae *f.* small trumpet

tubulātus, -a, -um *adj.* fitted with pipes

tubur, -uris *m.* exotic fruit (*perhaps* the medlar)

tuburcinor 1. *dep.* to eat greedily

tubus, -ī *m.* tube, vessel

tuccētum, -ī *n.* seasoned meat dish

tuditō 1. to strike repeatedly

tueor, tuitus 2. *dep.* or **tuor** 3. *dep.* to look at, regard; guard, protect; maintain

tugurium, -(i)ī *n.* hut, shack

tum *adv.* then, at that time; afterwards; besides; **cum ... tum** not only ... but also

tumefaciō, -fēcī, -factum 3. to make swell (*often with pride*)

tumeō 2. to become inflated, swell; be puffed up (*with pride*); be inflamed (*with pride*)

tumescō 3. to begin to inflate, swell

tumidus, -a, -um *adj.* swollen, protuberant; puffed up (*with pride*); inflamed (*with passion*)

tumor, -ōris *m.* swollen condition, swelling (*esp. of water*); arrogance; passion; turmoil

tumulō 1. to cover with a mound

tumulōsus, -a, -um *adj.* full of small hills

tumultuārius, -a, -um *adj.* suddenly drafted (*esp. of soldiers*); makeshift; haphazard

tumultuātiō, -ōnis *f.* tumult, uproar

tumultuor 1. *dep.* or **tumultuō** 1. to make an uproar, cause a disturbance

tumultuōsē *adv.* turbulently, confusedly

tumultuōsus, -a, -um *adj.* full of uproar, turbulent; met with panic

tumultus, -ūs *m.* uproar, commotion; insurrection, rebellion; confusion; passion

tumulus, -ī *m.* small hill; burial mound

tunc *adv.* then, at that very time; next

tundō, tutudī, tunsum (tūsum) 3. to strike, beat; crush

tunica, -ae *f.* sleeved garment for men and women, tunic; covering

tunicātus, -a, -um *adj.* wearing a tunic; covered

tunicula, -ae *f.* small *or* thin tunic

tuor see **tueor**

turba, -ae *f.* commotion, turmoil; throng; the mob, masses

turbāmentum, -ī *n.* means of causing turmoil

turbātē *adv.* in a confused manner

turbātiō, -ōnis *f.* commotion, disturbance

turbātor, -ōris *m.* one who stirs up commotion, disturber

turbātrix, -īcis *f.* female disturber

turbātus, -a, -um *adj.* in a state of turmoil

turbella, -ae *f.* minor disturbance

turbidē *adv.* in a confused manner; mutinously

turbidus, -a, -um *adj.* turbulent, wild; disordered; turbid, muggy; unruly

turbineus, -a, -um *adj.* rotating like a spinning-top

turbō[1] 1. to stir up, disturb; throw into disarray, upset; rouse, harry; be in a state of uproar

turbō[2], **-inis** *m.* spinning-top, whirling object; tornado; whirlpool; whirling

turbulentē *adv.* turbulently

turbulentus, -a, -um *adj.* turbulent, full of turmoil; riotous

turda, -ae *f.* female thrush

turdus, -ī *m.* thrush

tūreus, -a, -um *adj.* of *or* relating to incense

turgeō, tursī 2. to swell

turgescō 3. to begin to swell

turgidulus, -a, -um *adj.* rather swollen

turgidus, -a, -um *adj.* swollen, inflated

tūribulum, -ī *n.* censer for burning incense

tūricremus, -a, -um *adj.* burning incense

tūrifer, -era, -erum *adj.* bearing incense

tūrilegus, -a, -um *adj.* collecting incense

turma, -ae *f.* squadron (*of cavalry*); throng

turmālis, -is, -e *adj.* of *or* relating to a squadron (*of cavalry*); *m.sbst.* member of the same squadron

turmātim *adv.* in squadrons (*of cavalry*)

turpiculus, -a, -um *adj.* somewhat ugly *or* unpleasant

turpificātus, -a, -um *adj.* corrupted, befouled

turpilucricupidus, -a, -um *adj.* greedy for base profit

turpis, -is, -e *adj.* ugly; foul; shameful, base; obscene

turpiter *adv.* unpleasantly; dishonourably

turpitūdō, -inis *f.* ugliness; turpitude; disgrace

turpō 1. to disfigure; defile, pollute; bring dishonour on

turricula, -ae *f.* small tower; dice-box

turrifer, -era, -erum *adj.* bearing a tower

turriger, -era, -erum *adj.* bearing a tower

turris, -is *f.* tower, turret; elephant's howdah

turrītus, -a, -um *adj.* furnished with a tower *or* towers; formed like a tower

turtur, -uris *m.* turtle-dove

turturella, -ae *f.* little turtle-dove

tūs, tūris *n.* frankincense

tusculum, -ī *n.* little frankincense

tussiō 4. to cough repeatedly

tussis, -is *f.* cough

tūtāmen, -inis *n.* means of protection

tūtāmentum, -ī *n.* means of protection

tūtēla, -ae *f.* protection, custody; guardianship; guardian

tūtō *adv.* safely, free from harm

tūtor, -ōris *m.* guardian, protector

tūtor 1. *dep.* or **tūtō** 1. to keep safe, protect; maintain

tūtus, -a, -um *adj.* safe, free from risk *or* danger; vigilant

tuus, tua, tuum; *adj.* your; *m.pl.* your friends, relatives; *n.pl.* your possessions

tuxtax *onomatopoeic* sound of slapping

tympanizō 1. to play the *tympanum*

tympanotriba, -ae *m.* one who beats the *tympanum*

ty(m)panum, -ī *n.* small drum; revolving cylinder

tȳphōn, -ōnis *m.* whirlwind

typus, -ī *m.* embossed figure, bas-relief

tyrannicīda, -ae *m.* slayer of a tyrant

tyrannicus, -a, -um *adj.* instituted by a tyrant; despotic

tyrannis, -idis *f.* tyranny

tyrannoctonus, -ī *m.* slayer of a tyrant

tyrannus, -ī *m.* obtainer of monarchy by non-constitutional means, tyrant; despot, sovereign

tȳrotarīchos, -ī *m.* dish of cheese and salt-fish

über¹, überis *n*. udder; breast; rich, fertile soil

über², überis *adj*. rich, fertile, copious; luxuriant; valuable

überius *compar.adv*. more copiously, more abundantly

überō 1. to make fertile

übertās, -ātis *f*. fruitfulness; copiousness, abundance, richness

übertim *adv*. abundantly, copiously

ubi (ubī) *adv*. in what place?, where?; (*rel.*) in which, where

ubicumque (ubī-) *adv*. in whatever place?, wherever?; (*rel.*) in whatever place

ubilibet *adv*. wherever?, whenever?; (*rel.*) wherever, whenever

ubinam *adv*. where in the world?, wherever?

ubiquāque *adv*. in whatever place at all, everywhere

ubīque *adv*. in whatever place, wherever; everywhere

ubiubi *adv*. in whatever place, wherever

ubivīs *adv*. wherever you will, no matter where; whenever you will

ūdō, ūdōnis *m*. felt slipper

ūdus, ūda, ūdum *adj*. wet, damp, soaked

ulcerō 1. to make sore, make ulcerous

ulcerōsus, -a, -um *adj*. full of sores, ulcerous

ulciscor, ultus 3. *dep*. to take vengeance upon, punish; avenge

ulcus, -eris *n*. sore, ulcer; source of vexation

ulcusculum, -ī *n*. small sore, ulcer

ūlīgō, -inis *f*. marshland

ullus, -a, -um *adj*. any

ulmeus, -a, -um *adj*. made of elm

ulmitriba, -ae *m*. one who wears out elm whips (*by being flogged*)

ulmus, -ī *f*. elm, elm wood

ulna, -ae *f*. forearm, elbow

ulpicum, -ī *n*. garlic

ulterior, -or, -us *compar.adj*. farther away, more distant; further

ulterius *compar.adv*. farther away; to a greater extent, further

ultimō *superl.adv*. finally

ultimus, -a, -um *superl.adj*. farthest away, most distant; final, last; earliest; lowest in status

ultiō, -ōnis *f*. vengeance, retribution

ultor, -ōris *m*. avenger

ultrā¹ *prep*. (+*acc.*) beyond; after

ultrā² *adv*. beyond; further; thereafter; besides

ultrix, -īcis *f./n.adj*. avenging, vengeful; *f./n.sbst.* avenger

ultrō *adv*. to a point further away; conversely; in addition; of one's own accord; **ultrō citrō** to and fro

ulula, -ae *f*. owl, screech-owl

ululātus, -ūs *m*. howling, wailing, shrieking

ululō 1. to howl, wail, shriek; attend with howling

ulva, -ae *f*. swamp-grass, sedge

umbella, -ae *f*. parasol, sunshade

umbilīcus, -ī *m*. navel; centre, core; decorated end of cylinder around which papyrus was rolled

umbō, -ōnis *m*. protuberance, promontory; boss of a shield

umbra, -ae *f*. shade, shadow; ghost, phantom

umbrāc(u)lum, -ī *n*. shady place, shelter; parasol

umbrāticulus, -a, -um *adj*. living in the shade

umbrāticus, -a, -um *adj.* living in the shade

umbrātilis, -is, -e *adj.* carried out in the shade, done in retirement

umbrifer, -era, -erum *adj.* shade-bearing, shady

umbrō 1. to throw a shadow upon, shade

umbrōsus, -a, -um *adj.* full of shade, shadowy

ūmectō 1. to make wet, dampen

ūmeō 2. to be wet, be damp

umerus, -ī *m.* shoulder, upper-arm

ūmescō 3. to become wet

ūmidulus, -a, -um *adj.* rather wet, somewhat damp

ūmidus, -a, -um *adj.* wet, damp, moist

ūmifer, -era, -erum *adj.* full of moisture

ūmor, ūmōris *m.* moisture; liquid, fluid

umquam *adv.* at any time, ever

ūnā *adv.* together, at the same time

ūnaet- see **ūnet-**

ūnanimans, -ntis *adj.* of one mind, in accord

ūn(i)animus, -a, -um *adj.* of one mind, acting in unison

uncia, -ae *f.* twelfth; twelfth of an *as*; twelfth of a *sextarius*

unciārius, -a, -um *adj.* of *or* relating to a twelfth

unciātim *adv.* by twelfths, by *unciae*

uncīnātus, -a, -um *adj.* hooked, barbed

unciola, -ae *f.* mere twelfth

unctiō, -ōnis *f.* anointing

unctitō 1. to anoint habitually

unctor, -ōris *m.* anointer, masseur

unctōrium, -iī *n.* anointing room in a bath-house

unctum, -ī *n.* rich banquet, sumptuous food

unctūra, -ae *f.* anointing

unctus, -a, -um *adj.* anointed, oiled; oily, greasy

uncus¹, -ī *m.* hook

uncus², -a, -um *adj.* hooked

unda, -ae *f.* wave, billow; river, stream; water

unde *adv.* from where?, from what source?; (*rel.*) from which

undeciens (-ēs) *adv.* eleven times

undecim *indecl.adj.* eleven

undecimus, -a, -um *adj.* eleventh

undecimvir, -rī *m.* member of a committee of eleven

undecumque *adv.* from whatever direction

undēnī, -ae, -a *pl.adj.* eleven each; eleven at a time

undēnōnāgintā *indecl.adj.* eighty-nine

undeoctōgintā *indecl.adj.* seventy-nine

undēquadrāgintā *indecl.adj.* thirty-nine

undēquinquāgēsimus, -a, -um *adj.* forty-ninth

undēquinquāgintā *indecl.adj.* forty-nine

undēsexāgintā *indecl.adj.* fifty-nine

undētrīcēsimus, -a, -um *adj.* twenty-ninth

undētrīgintā *indecl.adj.* twenty-nine

undeunde *adv.* from wherever?; from somewhere or other

undēvīcēsimus, -a, -um *adj.* nineteenth

undēvīgintī, -ae, -a *indecl.adj.* nineteen

undique *adv.* from all sides, from every part; in all respects

undiqueversum (-vor-) *adv.* from every direction

undisonus, -a, -um *adj.* full of the sound of waves

undō 1. to surge, billow; gush; undulate

undōsus, -a, -um *adj.* full of waves, surging

ūnetvīcēsimānī, -ōrum *m.pl.* soldiers of the twenty-first legion

ūnetvīcēsimus, -a, -um *adj.* twenty-first

ungō, unxī, unctum 3. to smear with oil (*or sim.*), anoint

unguen, -inis *n.* fat, grease

unguentārius, -a, -um *adj.* of *or* relating to ointments; *m.sbst.* dealer in ointments, perfumer

unguentātus, -a, -um *adj.* anointed, perfumed

unguentum, -ī *n.* ointment, perfume

unguiculus, -ī *m.* fingernail, toenail

unguis, -is *m.* fingernail; claw, talon

ungula, -ae *f.* hoof, claw, talon

unguō see **ungō**

ūnicē *adv.* singularly, particularly

ūnicus, -a, -um *adj.* sole, single; unique, singular; *m./f.sbst.* only child

ūniformis, -is, -e *adj.* of only one kind

ūnigena, -ae *adj.* only (*one*) produced; *m./f.sbst.* sibling

ūnimanus, -a, -um *adj.* having one hand

ūniō, -ōnis *m.* large, single pearl

ūnisubsellium, -(i)ī *n.* bench for one person

ūnitās, -ātis *f.* uniformity

ūniter *adv.* so as to form one

ūniversālis, -is, -e *adj.* universal, general

ūniversē *adv.* generally

ūniversitās, -ātis *f.* entirety, whole; universe

ūniversus (-vor-), -a, -um *adj.* whole of, entire; collective; simultaneous; general, universal; *n.sg.sbst.* the whole, universe

ūnoculus, -ī *m.* one-eyed man

ūnomammius, -a, -um *adj.* having one breast

ūnorsum *adv.* all at once

unquam see **umquam**

ūnumquicquid *n.* every single thing

ūnus, ūna, ūnum (*gen.* **ūnius** or **ūnīus**, *dat.* **ūnī**) *adj.* one, a single; *m./f.sg.sbst.* someone

upupa, -ae *f.* hoopoe; pickaxe, mattock

urbānē *adv.* politely, with refinement; wittily

urbānitās, -ātis *f.* urban qualities, sophistication, refinement, good taste; wit

urbānus, -a, -um *adj.* of *or* relating to the city (*esp.* Rome); sophisticated, refined, witty; *m.sbst.* city-dweller

urbicapus, -ī *m.* captor of cities

urbicus, -a, -um *adj.* of *or* relating to the city (*esp.* Rome)

urbs, urbis *f.* city, large town; Rome

urceolus, -ī *m.* small pitcher, ewer

urceus, -ī *m.* pitcher, ewer

ūrēdō, -inis *f.* blight from frost

urg(u)eō, ursī 2. to press, squeeze; push, shove; weigh down; press hard; press on with; urge; threaten

ūrīna, -ae *f.* urine

ūrīnātor, -ōris *m.* diver

ūrīnor 1. *dep.* to dive, plunge under water

urna, -ae *f.* pitcher, urn, water jar; measure of half an *amphora*

urnula, -ae *f.* small pitcher

ūrō, ussī, ustum 3. to burn; roast, scorch; corrode; make sore; inflame (*with passions*)

ursa, -ae *f.* female bear

ursus, -ī *m.* bear

urtīca, -ae *f.* stinging nettle; jellyfish

ūrūca, -ae *f.* caterpillar

ūrus, ūrī *m.* wild ox

ūsitātē *adv.* in an everyday manner

ūsitātus, -a, -um *adj.* everyday, familiar, customary

uspiam *adv.* somewhere; anywhere

usquam *adv.* anywhere; in any direction; in any situation

usque *adv.* all the way; as far as; without interruption, continuously; thoroughly; (+*ad* +*acc.*) right up (to)

usquequāque *adv.* everywhere; in every respect

ussus see **ūsus**

ustor, -ōris *m.* burner of dead bodies

ustulō (-ilō) 1. to scorch, char

ūsūcapiō[1], -cēpī, -captum 3. to gain ownership by prolonged possession

ūsūcapiō[2], -ōnis *f.* gain of ownership by prolonged possession

ūsūra, -ae *f.* use, enjoyment; interest

ūsūrārius, -a, -um *adj.* offered on loan

ūsūrpātiō, -ōnis *f.* usurping, assumption; continued usage

ūsūrpō 1. to usurp, assume; put into practice; use continually; perceive

ūsus, ūsūs *m.* use, employment; practice; experience; customary interaction; utility; need; **ūsūs fructus** usufruct

---

ut *conj.*

1. **ut** + *indicative*

a) how, in what way? (question)
ut videtur avunculus meus? how does my uncle seem?

b) how (exclamation)
ut elegans est! how refined he is!

c) as, according as
ut optasti, ita est as you wished, so it is

d) when, as soon as
ut haec audivit, risit when he heard these things, he smiled

---

2. **ut** + *subjunctive*

a) to, in order to (result clause)
festinavit ad forum ut plus vini emeret he hurried to the market to buy more wine

b) so that (consecutive clause, marked by preceding sign-post word such as *tam, tantus, talis, tot, adeo, ita*)
tam callidus erat ut he was so cunning that

c) to (indirect command)

imperavit servis ut leonem necarent he ordered the slaves to kill the lion

d) that not (negative after verb of fearing) *vereor ut servus veniat* I fear that the slave is not coming

---

utcumque *conj.* in whatever manner, however; whenever; *adv.* as best one can; at any rate

ūtens, -ntis *adj.* having expendable money

ūtensilia, -ium *n.pl.* necessary provisions, essentials

uter¹, utra, utrum *adj.* which of two?; whichever of the two; either

ūter², ūtris *m.* leather bag; inflated bag (*to aid swimming*)

utercumque, utracumque, utrumcumque *adj.* whichever of the two

uterlibet, utralibet, utrumlibet *adj.* whichever of the two you wish

uterque, utraque, utrumque *pron.* each person of the two; *adj.* each ... of the two

uterus, -ī *m.* or **uterum, -ī** *n.* womb, uterus; abdomen, stomach

utervīs, utravīs, utrumvīs *adj.* whichever of the two you wish, either person

utī see **ut**

ūtibilis, -is, -e *adj.* that can be used

ūtilis, -is, -e *adj.* useful; profitable, advantageous; effective

ūtilitās, -ātis *f.* usefulness, utility; benefit, convenience, expediency

ūtiliter *adv.* usefully, profitably

utinam *part.* (*+subj.*) I wish that!; if only!, would that!

utīque *adv.* without doubt; necessarily; particularly; in any case

ūtor, ūsus 3. *dep.* (*+abl.*) to use make use of, employ; practise; experience; enjoy

utpote *part.* as is natural, as one would expect

utrāque *adv.* on both sides

utrārius, -(i)ī *m.* water-carrier

utriculārius, -(i)ī *m.* player of bagpipes (*or sim.*)

utrimque *adv.* on both sides

utrimquesecus *adv.* on both sides

utrō *adv.* in which direction (of two)?

utrobīque see **utrubīque**

utrōque *adv.* in both directions

utrōquevorsum *adv.* in both directions

utrubi *adv.* in which place (of two)?; in both places; on both sides; in both instances

utrubīque *adv.*

utrum *conj.* whether

utut *adv.* however

ūva, ūvae *f.* cluster of grapes; uvula; **ūva passa** raisin

ūvescō 3. to become wet

ūvidulus, -a, -um *adj.* rather wet

ūvidus, -a, -um *adj.* wet, damp, moist; drunk

ūvifer, -era, -erum *adj.* bearing grape-clusters

uxor, uxōris *f.* wife

uxorcula, -ae *f.* dear little wife

uxōrius, -a, -um *adj.* of *or* relating to a wife; devoted to one's wife

vacātiō, -ōnis f. (+*gen.*) freedom (from), exemption (from), immunity (from); holiday; soldier's payment to avoid certain duties

vacca, -ae f. cow

vaccīnium, -(i)ī n. blueberry, whortleberry

vacēfīō, -fierī, -factus v.irreg. to become empty

vacerrōsus, -a, -um adj. stupid (*literally* full of stakes)

vacillātiō, -ōnis f. swaying, rocking

vacillō 1. to sway, rock back and forth; stagger, stumble; be weak, unsound; waver, be in doubt

vacīvitās, -ātis f. (+*gen.*) emptiness (of), lack (of)

vacīvus, -a, -um adj. empty, vacant; (+*gen.*) free (from)

vacō 1. to be empty, vacant; (+*abl.*) be destitute (of), free (from); be at leisure; (+*dat.*) have time (for); *impers.* (+*dat.* +*inf.*) there is time (for one to)

vacuēfaciō, -fēcī, -factum 3. to make empty, vacate; (+*abl.*) empty (of)

vacuitās, -ātis f. (+*gen./abl.*) freedom (from)

vacuō 1. to make empty, vacate

vacuus, -a, -um adj. empty, void; unoccupied, vacant; (+*gen./abl.* or +*ab* +*abl.*) free (from), devoid (of); at leisure, free; (+*dat.*) free (for); unmarried; vain, useless

vadimōnium, -(i)ī n. promise of appearance of a defendant before a court of law, security

vādō, vāsī, vāsum 3. to go, proceed, rush

vador 1. *dep.* to accept sureties for a defendant's appearance in a court of law

vadōsus, -a, -um adj. full of shoals, shallow

vadum, -ī n. shallow place, shoal, ford; bottom (*of a body of water*); (*usu. pl.*) waters

vae interj. (*expressing pain*) alas!, woe!

vae- see **vē-**

vafer, vafra, vafrum adj. clever, cunning, crafty

vafrē adv. cleverly, cunningly

vafritia, -ae f. cleverness, cunning

vagē adv. in a widely wandering fashion

vāgīna, -ae f. scabbard, sheath; husk of grain

vāgiō 4. to wail, cry

vāgītus, -ūs m. wailing, crying

vagor¹ 1. *dep.* or **vagō** 1. to wander, roam, drift; disperse, spread far and wide; digress; waver, fluctuate

vāgor², -ōris m. wailing, crying

vagus, -a, -um adj. wandering, roaming, drifting; dispersed, scattered; discursive, diffuse; wavering, fluctuating; fickle

vāh interj. (*expressing pain*) ah!; (*expressing surprise*) wow!; (*expressing disdain*) oh!

vaha interj. (*expressing surprise*) wow!

valdē adv. greatly, very much, extremely; very much so

valedīcō, -dixī, -dictum 3. to say goodbye

valens, -ntis adj. strong, powerful, mighty; healthy, well; effective, potent

valenter adv. strongly, powerfully

valentulus, -a, -um adj. somewhat sturdy, strong

valeō 2. to be strong, powerful; be healthy, well; be potent; be valid; (+*inf.*) have the power (to); (+*acc.*) signify, mean; **valē(te)** goodbye, farewell

valescō 3. to become powerful; become healthy

valētūdinārium, -iī *n.* sickroom, infirmary

valētūdō, -inis *f.* bodily condition, state; good health; bad health, illness

valgus, -a, -um *adj.* knock-kneed

validē *adv.* powerfully; vigorously, vehemently

validus, -a, -um *adj.* powerful, strong, vigorous; healthy, well; potent, efficient; influential

vallāris, -is, -e *adj.* of or relating to a rampart; **corōna vallāris** garland awarded to the first soldier to cross the enemy rampart

vallēs (-is), -is *f.* valley, vale

vallō 1. to fortify with a rampart or palisade; hem in, surround; defend

vallum, -ī *n.* palisade of stakes set on a rampart; defence, barrier

vallus, -ī *m.* stake; palisade

valvae, -ārum *f.pl.* folding-door(s)

vānescō 3. to disappear, vanish; become useless

vānidicus, -a, -um *adj.* talking idly, chattering

vāniloquentia, -ae *f.* idle talk; boasting, bombast

vāniloquus, -a, -um *adj.* talking idly; boastful

vānitās, -ātis *f.* emptiness; pointlessness, futility; falsity, insincerity; boasting; foolishness

vānitūdō, -inis *f.* emptiness of speech, falsehood

vannus, -ī *f.* winnowing-fan

vānus, -a, -um *adj.* empty, insubstantial; illusory, hollow; pointless, futile; false, insincere; boastful; foolish

vapidē *adv.* flatly; **sē vapidē habēre** to be poorly, unwell

vapidus, -a, -um *adj.* flat, vapid

vapor, -ōris *m.* vapour, steam; heat, warmth

vapōrārium, -(i)ī *n.* steam-chamber (for heating a bath-house)

vapōrifer, -era, -erum *adj.* producing steam or vapour

vapōrō 1. to fill with vapour, steam; heat, warm; be hot

vappa, -ae *f.* flat or vapid wine; worthless man, good-for-nothing

vāpulāris, -is, -e *adj.* of or relating to beating

vāpulō 1. to be beaten, knocked about; be ruined, destroyed

vāra, -ae *f.* forked support

varians, -ntis *adj.* varied, of diverse parts

variantia, -ae *f.* variety, diversity

variātiō, -ōnis *f.* difference (of character)

vāricōsus, -a, -um *adj.* suffering from varicose veins

vāricus, -a, -um *adj.* with legs apart, straddling

variē *adv.* variously, differently; in a diverse manner; fluctuatingly, inconstantly

varietās, -ātis *f.* variety, diversity (of colour, quality etc.); pl. varieties; divergence; fluctuation, inconstancy

variō 1. to vary, diversify; variegate (in colour); change, alter; cause to fluctuate, alternate; differ; waver

varius, -a, -um *adj.* varied, diverse; variegated; different, conflicting; fluctuating, inconstant

varix, -icis *f.* varicose vein

vārus, -a, -um *adj.* bent apart; bow-legged; conflicting, differing

vas¹, vadis *m.* one who guarantees the appearance of a defendant in a court of law, surety

vās², vassis (vāsis) *n.* vessel, receptacle; pl. equipment, kit

vāsārium, -(i)ī *n.* allowance provided for soldiers

vasculārius, -(i)ī *m.* crafter of small vessels

vasculum, -ī *n.* small vessel

vastātiō, -ōnis *f.* ravaging, devastation

vastātor, -ōris *m.* ravager, devastator

vastātrix, -īcis *f.* female ravager

vastē *adv.* vastly, extensively; (of speech) roughly, without refinement

vastificus, -a, -um *adj.* ravaging, causing devastation

vastitās, -ātis *f.* devastation, desolation; wilderness; vastness, immensity

vastitiēs, -ēī *f.* state of devastation

vastō 1. to make desolate; ravage, devastate, destroy

vastus, -a, -um *adj.* deserted, empty; ravaged; vast, immense; awesome, extreme; rough, unrefined

vāsum see **vās²**

vātēs, -is *m./f.* prophet, seer; poet, bard

vāticinātiō, -ōnis *f.* prophecy, foretelling

vāticinātor, -ōris *m.* prophet, seer

vāticinor 1. *dep.* to engage in prophecy; rave, rant; predict

vāticinus, -a, -um *adj.* prophetic

vatillum, -ī *n.* coal-shovel

vātis see **vātēs**

vatius, -a, -um *adj.* knock-kneed

-ve *conj.* (*enclitic*) or

vēcordia, -ae *f.* derangement, madness, folly

vēcors, -rdis *adj.* deranged, mad, foolish

vectātiō, -ōnis *f.* (+*gen.*) travel (by)

vectīgal, -ālis *n.* payment to the state, tax; revenue, income

vectīgālis, -is, -e *adj.* of *or* relating to taxes; liable to taxation

vectiō, -ōnis *f.* (+*gen.*) transport (by)

vectis, -is *m.* bar, crowbar; bolt (of a door)

vectō 1. to transport, carry; *pass.* ride, travel

vector, -ōris *m.* carrier, transporter; passenger, rider

vectōrius, -a, -um *adj.* used for carrying *or* transporting

vectūra, -ae *f.* carriage, transport; passage-money

vegeō 2. to make vigorous, excite

vegetus, -a, -um *adj.* vigorous, excited, energetic; (*of the mind or thoughts*) fresh, lively

vēgrandis, -is, -e *adj.* puny, diminutive

vehemens, -ntis *adj.* violent, forceful; vigorous, impetuous; potent

vehementer *adv.* violently, forcefully; vigorously, impetuously; immensely, exceedingly

vehic(u)lum, -ī *n.* means of transport; cart, wagon

vehō, vexī, vectum 3. to carry, convey, bear; *pass.* (+*abl. of vehicle*) travel, ride, sail

vel *part.* or; *adv.* even, actually; at any rate; **vel ... vel** either ... or

vēlāmen, -inis *n.* covering, veil

vēlāmentum, -ī *n.* covering, veil; cover; olive branch wrapped in wool as offering of supplication

vēlārium, -lī *n.* curtain, awning

vēlātī, -ōrum *m.pl.* **accensī vēlātī** supernumerary troops, reserves

vēles, -itis *m.* (*usu. pl.*) light-armed soldier

vēlifer, -era, -erum *adj.* sail-bearing; sail-driving

vēlificātiō, -ōnis *f.* sailing

vēlificō 1. or **vēlificor** 1. *dep.* to sail; sail through; (+*dat.*) aim (for)

vēlitāris, -is, -e *adj.* of *or* relating to a light-armed soldier

vēlitātiō, -ōnis *f.* fighting tactics of a light-armed soldier

vēlitor 1. *dep.* to engage in abuse, wrangle

vēlivolus, -a, -um *adj.* flying with sails; full of flying sails

vellicō 1. to pluck, pinch, peck; carp at, taunt

vellō, vellī or **vulsī (vo-), vulsum (vo-)** 3. to pluck, tear out, pull up; extract, remove

vellus, -eris *n.* shorn wool, fleece; fur, hide

vēlō 1. to cover, clothe; veil, conceal

vēlōcitās, -ātis *f.* swiftness, rapidity

vēlōciter *adv.* swiftly, rapidly, quickly

vēlox, -ōcis *adj.* swift, rapid, quick

vēlum, -ī *n.* sail; curtain, awning; **vēla facere** to spread one's sails; **vēla dare** to give one's sails to the wind

velut(ī) *adv.* just as, even as; for instance; (+*subj.*) as though

vēm- see **vehem-**

vēna, -ae *f.* vein, blood-vessel; fissure, pore; channel, stream; vein (*of metal*), ore; store of talent

vēnābulum, -ī *n.* hunting-spear

vēnālicius, -a, -um *adj.* for sale, purchasable; *m.sbst.* slave-dealer

vēnālis, -is, -e *adj.* for sale, purchasable; available for rent, on hire; open to bribes, corrupt; *m.sbst.* slave

vēnāticus, -a, -um *adj.* of *or* used in hunting

vēnātiō, -ōnis *f.* hunting, hunt (*in the wild or an arena*); game, quarry

vēnātor, -ōris *m.* hunter

vēnātōrius, -a, -um *adj.* of *or* used in hunting

vēnātrix, -īcis *f.* huntress

vēnātūra, -ae *f.* hunting

vēnātus, -ūs *m.* hunting, hunt

vendibilis, -is, -e *adj.* that may be sold, vendible

venditātiō, -ōnis *f.* boasting, vaunting

venditātor, -ōris *m.* (+*gen.*) boaster (about), vaunter (of)

venditiō, -ōnis f. sale, vending

venditō 1. to offer for sale; advertise, cry up

venditor, -ōris m. seller, vendor; one who sells for bribes

vendō, -didī, -ditum 3. to sell, vend; sell for bribes; advertise, cry up

venēfica, -ae f. sorcery, magic; poisoning

venēficium, -(i)ī n. poisoning

venēficus, -a, -um adj. of or relating to sorcery; m./f.sbst. sorcerer or sorceress; m./f.sbst. poisoner

venēnārius, -iī m. poisoner

venēnātus, -a, -um adj poisonous; poisoned

venēnifer, -era, -erum adj. poison-carrying, venomous; magical

venēnō 1. to poison; bewitch

venēnum, -ī n. drug, potent substance; poison, poisoning; love-potion; dye

vēneō, vēnīre, vēniī, vēnitum 4. to be sold

venerābilis, -is, -e adj. worthy of respect, venerable; reverential

venerābundus, -a, -um adj. full of awe, reverent

venerātiō, -ōnis f. reverence, veneration, awe

venerātor, -ōris m. one who venerates

veneror 1. dep. or **venerō** 1. to revere, venerate, honour; (+ut +subj.) beseech reverently (that)

venia, -ae f. indulgence, allowance; kindness, favour; pardon; (+gen.) **(cum) bonā veniā** with (your etc.) good leave

veniō, vēnī, ventum 4. to come, approach; arise; come along; arrive

venn- see **vēn-**

vēnor 1. dep. to hunt; go hunting

vēnōsus, -a, -um adj. full of veins; shrivelled with age

venter, -tris m. belly, stomach, abdomen; bowels; womb; foetus

ventilō 1. to ventilate, fan; brandish, wave

ventiō, -ōnis f. coming, arrival

ventitō 1. to come frequently, resort

ventōsus, -a, -um adj. full of wind, windy; fast as the wind; vain, puffed up; fickle, volatile

ventriculus, -ī m. belly, stomach; ventricle

ventriōsus, -a, -um adj. pot-bellied

ventulus, -ī m. small wind, breeze

ventus, -ī m. wind, breeze

vēnūcula, -ae f. kind of grapevine

vēnum, vēnō m. (only acc. and dat.) for sale; **vēnum dare** (+acc.) to sell

vēnumdō (-ndō), -dedī, -datum 1. to put up for sale

venus, -eris f. loveliness, attractiveness, beauty; grace, charm

venustās, -ātis f. loveliness, attractiveness, beauty; grace, charm

venustē adv. attractively, charmingly

venustulus, -a, -um adj. somewhat charming

venustus, -a, -um adj. charming, attractive, graceful

veprēcula, -ae f. small thorn-bush

veprēs, -is m./f. thorn-bush

vēr, vēris n. spring, springtime; **vēr sacrum** festival involving sacrifice of firstlings

vērātrum, -ī n. hellebore

vērax, -ācis adj. speaking the truth, truthful

verbēna, -ae f. (usu. pl.) branch, twig (used esp. for religious purposes)

verbēnātus, -a, -um adj. carrying a branch or twig (for religious purposes)

verber, -eris n. (usu. pl.) whip, lash; thong of a sling; blow (of a whip); flogging

verberābilis, -is, -e adj. deserving a flogging

verberābundus, -a, -um adj. busy with flogging

verberātiō, -ōnis f. flogging

verbereus, -a, -um adj. of or relating to flogging

verberō[1] 1. to flog, lash; hammer, beat; attack, assail

verberō[2] **, -ōnis** m. one who deserves a flogging, scoundrel

verbivēlitātiō, -ōnis f. verbal skirmish

verbōsē adv. in many words, verbosely

verbōsus, -a, -um adj. full of words, talkative; prolix, verbose

verbum, -ī n. word; verb; saying; pl. utterance, talk; **verba dare** (+dat.) to trick, dupe

verculum, -ī n. 'dear little spring'

vērē adv. truly, really; correctly

verēcundē adv. modestly, bashfully; discreetly, with restraint

verēcundia, -ae f. modesty, bashfulness, shame; restraint; diffidence, uncertainty

verēcundor 1. *dep.* to be modest; (+*inf.*) be shy (to)

verēcundus, -a, -um *adj.* modest, bashful; restrained; diffident

verēdus, -ī *m.* swift breed of horse

vereor 2. *dep.* to be afraid of, fear; (+*inf.*) fear (to); (+*ne*/*ut* +*subj.*) fear (that/that not); show respect for, revere

verētrum, -ī *n.* penis

vergō 3. to bend; be inclined, slope; tend; draw to an end; make to bend down, tilt

vēridicus, -a, -um *adj.* speaking the truth

vēriloquium, -(i)ī *n.* use of genuine etymology

vērīsimilis, -is, -e *adj.* likely, probable

vēritās, -ātis *f.* truthful state, reality; truth; truthfulness, honesty; correctness

vēriverbium, -(i)ī *n.* speaking of the truth

vermiculātus, -a, -um *adj.* arranged in a worming fashion

vermiculus, -ī *m.* grub, maggot

vermina, -um *n.pl.* griping pains

verminātiō, -ōnis *f.* racking pain

verminō 1. to be racked

vermis, -is *m.* worm, grub

verna, -ae *m.* home-born slave, family slave; home-bred animal; common fellow

vernāculus, -a, -um *adj.* domestic; native, indigenous; proletarian, common; *m. sbst.* fool, dullard

vernīlis, -is, -e *adj.* obsequious like a slave

vernīlitās, -ātis *f.* servility; insolence

vernīliter *adv.* in a servile manner

vernō 1. to be spring; enjoy new life, grow green

vernula, -ae *m./f.* young home-born slave

vernus, -a, -um of *or* relating to spring, vernal

vērō *adv.* truly, really; certainly; to be sure, indeed; truthfully

verpa, -ae *f.* penis

verpus, -us *adj.* circumcised *or* with the foreskin retracted

verrēs, -is *m.* boar

verrīnus, -a, -um *adj.* of *or* relating to a boar

verrō, verrī, versum 3. to sweep, brush, drag; sweep clean; sweep together, collect

verrūca, -ae *f.* wart

verrūcōsus, -a, -um *adj.* covered with warts

verruncō 1. (+*adv.*) to turn out

versābundus, -a, -um *adj.* revolving, whirling around

versātilis, -is, -e *adj.* able to be rotated, revolving; versatile, varied

versicolor, -ōris *adj.* having changeable colour(s)

versiculus, -ī *m.* short line, small verse; *pl.* minor poem

versipellis, -is *m.adj.* able to change one's form *or* shape

versō 1. to make turn continually, spin, stir; turn, twist; brandish, shake; ponder, consider; *pass.* be about often, resort; be active; (+*in* +*abl.*) be involved (in), busy (with)

versum *adv.* turned towards, towards

versūra, -ae *f.* changing one's creditor to pay off a debt

versus¹, -ūs *m.* row, line; line of poetry *or* prose; turning step (*in a dance*)

versus² *adv.* see **versum**

versūtē *adv.* cunningly, cleverly

versūtia, -ae *f.* act of cunning, stratagem

versūtiloquus, -a, -um *adj.* craftily speaking, wily-tongued

versūtus, -a, -um *adj.* cunning, clever, wily

vertebra, -ae *f.* joint of the body

vertex, -icis *m.* whirlpool, eddy; crown of the head; peak of a hill, summit; celestial pole

verticōsus, -a, -um *adj.* full of whirlpools

vertīgō, -inis *f.* turning round, whirling; dizziness

vertō, -tī, -sum 3. to turn, turn round; turn back, reverse; put to flight, rout; overturn; (+*dat.*) transfer (to); translate; exchange; (+*in* +*acc.*) turn (into), change (into)

vertragus, -ī *m.* swift Gallic hound

verū, -ūs *n.* spit; javelin

veruīna, -ae *f.* spit, stake

vērum¹ *conj.* true, but; however, but

verum² *n.* see **verū**

vērumtamen (-unt-) *conj.* but even so, nonetheless

vērus, -a, -um *adj.* true, real, genuine; truthful, honest; just, proper; *n.sbst.* truth, fact

verūtum, -ī *n.* short spear, dart

verūtus, -a, -um *adj.* armed with a short spear

vervex, -ēcis *m.* male sheep, wether; idiot, dullard

vēsānia, -ae *f.* madness, insanity

vēsāniō 4. to be mad, be insane

vēsānus, -a, -um *adj.* mad, insane, frenzied

vescor 3. *dep.* (+*abl.*/*acc.*) to feed upon, consume; (+*abl.*) use, enjoy; eat food

vescus, -a, -um *adj.* thin, slender, small

vēsīca, -ae *f.* bladder; inflated bladder; lantern (made from a bladder); vagina

vēsīcula, -ae *f.* small bladder; bubble

vespa, -ae *f.* wasp

vesper, -eris (-erī) *m.* evening; the Evening Star; the west

vespera see **vesper**

vesperascō 3. to become evening

vespertīnus, -a, -um *adj.* of *or* relating to the evening; in the evening; western

vesperūgō, -inis *f.* the Evening Star

vester, -tra, -trum *adj.* belonging to you (*pl.*), your; concerning *or* relating to you

vestibulum, -ī *n.* enclosed space before a building, court-yard; entrance

vestīgium, -(i)ī *n.* sole of the foot; footprint, track; trace, vestige; route, trail; moment of time

vestīgō 1. to follow the trail of, track; investigate

vestīmentum, -ī *n.* item of clothing, garment; rug, blanket

vestiō 4. to cover, clothe; dress, adorn

vestipica, -ae *f.* female servant concerned with clothing

vestis, -is *f.* clothes, clothing; dress, attire; awning, drapery

vestītus, -ūs *m.* clothing, clothes; dress, attire; covering

veterāmentārius, -a, -um *adj.* of *or* relating to old things

veterānus, -a, -um *adj.* (*esp. of soldiers*) experienced, mature, veteran; *m.sbst.* veteran

veterārium, -iī *n.* wine-cellar

veterascō 3. to become old, longestablished

veterātor, -ōris *m.* experienced individual, old hand

veterātōriē *adv.* with experience, adroitly

veterātōrius, -a, -um *adj.* experienced; adroit, crafty

veterīnus, -a, -um *adj.* (*of animals*) used for draught

veternōsus, -a, -um *adj.* lethargic, drowsy; *m.sbst.* drowsy person

veternus, -ī *m.* lethargy, drowsiness; sloth; old age

vetō, vetuī (-āvī), vetitum 1. to prohibit, forbid; (+*acc.*+*inf.* or +*quin*/*ne* +*subj.*) forbid (someone to); reject, veto

vetulus, -a, -um *adj.* somewhat old, rather aged; *m.sbst.* old fellow; *f.sbst.* old woman

vetus, -eris *adj.* old, aged; veteran, experienced; long-established, ancient; *m.pl.sbst.* the ancients; *f.pl.sbst.* old shops in the Roman Forum; *n.sbst.* old saying *or* tale; *n.pl.sbst.* antiquity

vetustās, -ātis *f.* old age, maturity; antiquity; length of time

vetustus, -a, -um *adj.* long-established, ancient; archaic, old-fashioned

vexāmen, -inis *n.* upheaval, upset

vexātiō, -ōnis *f.* shaking, jolting; harassment, rough treatment

vexātor, -ōris *m.* one who causes trouble, harasser

vexillārius, -(i)ī *m.* standard-bearer; *pl.* reserve corps of veteran soldiers

vexillātiō, -ōnis *f.* detachment, corps

vexillum, -ī *n.* military standard, flag; detachment, corps

vexō 1. to shake, jolt; ravage, destroy; treat roughly, upset; harass, trouble

via, viae *f.* road, pathway; passage; course; way, method, means

viālis, -is, -e *adj.* of *or* relating to roads

viāticātus, -a, -um *adj.* furnished with necessary provisions for a journey

viāticum, -ī *n.* necessary provisions for a journey, travel expense; soldier's daily savings

viāticus, -a, -um *adj.* of *or* relating to a journey; **cēna viātica** farewell dinner

viātor, -ōris *m.* traveller; magistrate's messenger

vībix, -īcis *f.* weal, mark from a blow

vibrō 1. to brandish, wave; crimp, frizzle; hurl, thrust; rock, tremble; dart, flash; glitter, shimmer

vīburnum, -ī *n.* the wayfaring tree

vīcānus, -a, -um *adj.* living in a village; *m. pl.sbst.* villagers

vicārius, -a, -um *adj.* substitute, vicarious; *m.sbst.* substitute, successor; deputy servant

vīcātim *adv.* from village to village; from district to district

vice, vicem see **[vicis]**

vīcēnī, -ae, -a *pl.adj.* twenty each; twenty at a time

vīcens- see **vīcēs-**

vīcēsimānus, -a, -um *adj.* of *or* relating to the twentieth legion; *m.sbst.* soldier of the twentieth legion

vīcēsimārius, -a, -um *adj.* of *or* relating to a five-percent tax

vīcēsimus, -a, -um *adj.* twentieth; **vīcēsima pars** five-percent tax (*on manumissions etc.*)

vicia, -ae *f.* vetch

vīciēs (-ens) *adv.* twenty times

vīcīnālis, -is, -e *adj.* of *or* relating to the local inhabitants

vīcīnia, -ae *f.* neighbourhood, vicinity; neighbours; proximity; similarity

vīcīnitās, -ātis *f.* neighbourhood, vicinity; neighbours; (*+gen.*) proximity (to); similarity

vīcīnus, -a, -um *adj.* neighbouring; of *or* relating to a neighbour; similar, like; *m./f. sbst.* neighbour; *n.pl.sbst.* neighbourhood

[vicis], -is *f.* change, alternation; requital; turn; lot, fate; **per vicēs (-em)** by turns; **vicem** (*+gen.*) in the place (of), in the manner (of)

vicissātim *adv.* in turn

vicissim *adv.* in turn; reciprocally; conversely

vicissitūdō, -inis *f.* change, alternation; reciprocation

victima, -ae *f.* animal offered in sacrifice

victimārius, -(i)ī *m.* assistant at sacrifices

victitō 1. to stay alive, subsist

victor, -ōris *m.* conqueror, victor; *adj.* victorious

victōria, -ae *f.* victory; Victory as a personified goddess

victōriātus, -ī *m.* silver coin stamped with an image of Victory

victōriola, -ae *f.* small statue of Victory

victrīcia, -um *n.pl.adj.* victorious

victrix, -trīcis *f.* female conqueror, victress; *adj.* victorious

victum- see **victim-**

victus, -ūs *m.* food, nourishment; way of life

vīculus, -ī *m.* small village, hamlet

vīcus, -ī *m.* street *or* district of a town; village, hamlet

vidēlicet *adv.* evidently, clearly; of course (*often ironic*); namely; (*+acc.+inf.*) it is clear (that)

videō, vīdī, vīsum 2. to see; look at; perceive, notice; (*+acc.+inf.*) see (that); realize (that); consider; see to; (*+ne/ut +subj.*) take care (that); *pass.* seem, appear; *impers. pass.* (*+dat.*) seem good (to)

viduitās, -ātis *f.* widowhood; (*+gen.*) want (of), deprivation (of)

vīdulus, -ī *m.* trunk, sack

viduō 1. to widow; (*+abl./gen.*) deprive (of); empty

viduus, -a, -um *adj.* widowed; deprived of one's owner; (*+abl.*) deprived (of); *f.sbst.* widow

viētus, -a, -um *adj.* wrinkled, shrivelled

vigeō 2. to be lively, vigorous; flourish, thrive

vigescō 3. to become lively, grow vigorous

vīgēsis *indecl.m.* coin worth 20 *asses*

vigil, -ilis *adj.* awake; watchful, vigilant; *m./f.sbst.* sentry, watchman

vigilans, -ntis *adj.* watchful, vigilant

vigilanter *adv.* watchfully, vigilantly

vigilantia, -ae *f.* wakefulness; vigilance

vigilārium, -īī *n.* watchtower

vigilax, -ācis *adj.* wakeful, restless

vigilia, -ae *f.* (*usu. pl.*) wakefulness; watch, patrol; vigilance; one of the four divisions of the night

vigilō 1. to be *or* stay awake; be watchful, vigilant; work at whilst staying awake

vīgintī *indecl.adj.* twenty

vīgintīvirātus, -ūs *m.* office of the *vigintiviri*

vīgintīvirī, -ōrum *m.pl.* commission of twenty men set up by Caesar to distribute lands in Campania

vigor, -ōris *m.* liveliness, vigour

vīlica, -ae *f.* wife of the overseer of an estate

vīlicō 1. to oversee an estate

vīlicus, -ī *m.* overseer of an estate; steward, bailiff

vīlis, -is, -e *adj.* of low price, cheap; worthless; unimportant; low, mean; ordinary, common

vīlitās, -ātis *f.* lowness of price, cheapness; worthlessness

vīliter *adv.* at a low price, cheaply

villa, -ae f. country house or estate

villōsus, -a, -um adj. covered in hair, shaggy

villula, -ae f. small country house

villum, -ī n. small amount of wine

villus, -ī m. shaggy hair

vīmen, -inis n. pliant twig, osier; piece of wickerwork

vīmentum, -ī n. piece of wickerwork

vīmineus, -a, -um adj. made of wicker-work

vīn see **volō¹**

vīnāceum, -ī n. grape-stone

vīnārius, -a, -um adj. of or relating to wine; m.sbst. wine-dealer; n.sbst. wine-jar

vincibilis, -is, -e adj. that can be won

vinciō, vinxī, vinctum 4. to bind, fetter; tie together, bond; encircle, surround

vinclum see **vinculum**

vincō, vīcī, victum 3. to conquer, defeat; subdue, overcome; surpass, excel; sur-mount; outlast

vinculum, -ī n. bond, fetter, chain; restraint; fastening; connection, link

vindēmia, -ae f. grape-harvest; the year's grapes or wine

vindēmiātor, -ōris m. grape-harvester

vindēmiola, -ae f. little harvest

vindex, -icis m./f. protector, defender; protector of creditors; avenger

vindicātiō, -ōnis f. assertion of ownership; defending, avenging

vindiciae, -ārum f.pl. temporary owner-ship granted by a praetor

vindicō 1. to lay claim to, arrogate; claim as free, liberate; avenge, punish

vindicta, -ae f. ceremony in which a praetor manumits a slave by touching him with a rod; vengeance, punishment

vīnea, -ae f. vineyard; structure used to shelter besieging soldiers

vīnētum, -ī n. vineyard

vīnipollens, -ntis adj. mighty through wine

vīnitor, -ōris m. vineyard worker

vinnulus, -a, -um adj. charming, ingrati-ating

vīnolentia, -ae f. inebriation from wine

vīnolentus, -a, -um adj. inebriated from wine; wine-flavoured

vīnōsus, -a, -um adj. full of wine, inebri-ated; wine-flavoured; wine-loving

vīnum, -ī n. wine; wine-drinking; grape

viola, -ae f. the flower violet; the colour violet

violābilis, -is, -e adj. that can be wounded, vulnerable; that can be outraged

violārium, -(i)ī n. plantation or bed of violets

violārius, -(i)ī m. one who dyes cloth(es) violet

violātiō, -ōnis f. profanation, violation

violātor, -ōris m. profaner, violator

violens, -ntis adj. violent, impetuous

violenter adv. violently, impetuously; furiously

violentia, -ae f. violence, vehemence, impetuosity; fury, aggression

violentus, -a, -um adj. violent, vehement, impetuous; furious, aggressive

violō 1. to treat violently, injure; profane, defile; infringe, violate

vīpera, -ae f. poisonous snake, viper

vīpereus, -a, -um adj. of or relating to a viper; made of vipers, snaky

vīperīnus, -a, -um adj. of or relating to a viper

vir, virī m. man, adult male; husband; individual; soldier

virāgō, -inis f. man-like woman; heroic woman, war-maiden

virectum, -ī n. area of greenery

vireō 2. to be green, verdant; be fresh, vigorous

virescō 3. to grow green, become verdant

virga, -ae f. green twig, shoot; rod, stick; pl. rods used in lictors' fasces; genealogical branch; stripe

virgātor, -ōris m. one who beats with a rod

virgātus, -a, -um adj. made of twigs; striped, streaked

virgētum, -ī n. thicket of brushwood

virgeus, -a, -um adj. made of twigs

virgidēmia, -ae f. rod-harvest (i.e. a good beating)

virginālis, -is, -e adj. of or like a maiden

virginārius, -a, -um adj. of or relating to maidens

virgineus, -a, -um adj. of or like a maiden; frequented by maidens; virginal; of or relating to virgins

virginitās, -ātis f. maidenhood; virginity

virgō, -inis f. girl of a marriageable age, maiden; virgin

virgula, -ae *f.* small twig, shoot; small rod

virgulta, -ōrum *n.pl.* brushwood, thicket

virgultus, -a, -um *adj.* covered with brushwood

virguncula, -ae *f.* young maiden

viridans, -ntis *adj.* green; healthy

virid(i)ārium, -(i)ī *n.* garden of flowers, pleasure-garden

viridis, -is, -e *adj.* green; verdant, healthy; vigorous, youthful; *n.pl.sbst.* shrubs, greenery

viridītās, -ātis *f.* greenness; vigour, youthfulness

virīlis, -is, -e *adj.* of *or* relating to a man, virile; masculine; manly, courageous; appropriate for an individual man

virīlitās, -ātis *f.* manhood, masculinity

virīliter *adv.* in a virile manner, courageously

virīpotens, -ntis *adj.* mighty in force, powerful

virītim *adv.* man by man, individually

virōsus, -a, -um *adj.* stinking, rank

virtūs, -ūtis *f.* manliness, valour; bravery, courage; excellence; moral virtue, goodness; **virtūte** (*+gen.*) thanks (to)

vīrus, -ī (*sg. only*) *n.* venom, poison; bitter taste, acridity; slime

vīs, vīs (*pl.* **vīrēs, -ium**) *f.* force, violence, vigour; large number; ability, power; influence; meaning, essence; *pl.* troops, forces

viscātus, -a, -um *adj.* covered with bird-lime

viscerātiō, -ōnis *f.* distribution of sacrificial meat

viscō 1. to catch in bird-lime

viscum, -ī *n.* mistletoe; bird-lime

viscus, -eris *n.* (*usu. pl.*) flesh of the body; internal bodily organs; womb; child; innermost part

vīsiō, -ōnis *f.* image (*visual or mental*)

vīsitō 1. to see often; visit

vīsō, vīsī 3. to go to see, visit; go and look; examine, consider

vispillō, -ōnis *m.* gravedigger for the poor

vīsum, -ī *n.* sight, appearance

vīsus, -ūs *m.* sight, vision; sight, appearance

vīta, -ae *f.* life; way of life; career; soul

vītābilis, -is, -e *adj.* that should be avoided

vītābundus, -a, -um *adj.* evasive in one's actions; (*+acc.*) attempting to avoid

vītālis, -is, -e *adj.* of *or* relating to life; living; life-giving, vital; *n.pl.sbst.* vital parts

vītāliter *adv.* vitally

vītātiō, -ōnis *f.* (*+gen.*) avoidance (of)

vitellus, -ī *m.* little calf; egg yolk

vīteus, -a, -um *adj.* of *or* relating to vines

vīticula, -ae *f.* vine-shoot

vītifer, -era, -erum *adj.* vine-bearing

vītigenus, -a, -um *adj.* produced from the vine

vitiō 1. to spoil, impair; invalidate, falsify; deflower, debauch

vitiōsē *adv.* faultily, defectively

vitiōsitās, -ātis *f.* viciousness, corruption

vitiōsus, -a, -um *adj.* full of faults, flawed, defective; debauched, corrupt

vītis, -is *f.* grape-vine; vine-shoot; centurion's staff of vine wood

vītisator, -ōris *m.* planter of vines

vitium, -(i)ī *n.* fault, flaw; moral defect, vice; deflowering

vītō 1. to shun, avoid

vītor, -ōris *m.* wickerworker

vitreārius, -(i)ī *m.* glass-worker

vitreus, -a, -um *adj.* made of glass; glasslike; *n.sbst.* piece of glassware

vītricus, -ī *m.* stepfather

vitrum, -ī *n.* glass; woad

vitta, -ae *f.* ritual headband; marriage headband

vittātus, -a, -um *adj.* wearing a headband

vitula, -ae *f.* young cow, calf

vitulīnus, -a, -um *adj.* of a calf *or* its flesh; *f.sbst.* veal

vītulor 1. *dep.* to shout in joy, rejoice

vitulus, -ī *m.* male calf

vituperābilis, -is, -e *adj.* blameworthy, censurable

vituperātiō, -ōnis *f.* criticism, censure

vituperātor, -ōris *m.* one who criticizes, censurer

vituperō 1. to find fault with, criticize; regard as invalid

vīvācitās, -ātis *f.* tenacity of life, longevity

vīvārium, -(i)ī *n.* enclosure for living creatures, preserve, aquarium

vīvax, -ācis *adj.* tenacious of life, long-lived; life-giving

vīvescō 3. to come to life; become lively

vīvidus, -a, -um *adj.* living, animated; lively, vigorous; lifelike

vīvirādix, -īcis *f.* rooted cutting, quickset

vīvō, vixī, victum 3. to live; spend one's life; survive, live on; be active, lively; live to the full

vīvus, -a, -um *adj.* alive, living; lifelike; alight; lively; native, natural

vix *adv.* with difficulty; barely, scarcely

vixdum *adv.* scarcely yet, only just

vocābulum, -ī *n.* word; noun; name, appellation

vōcālis, -is, -e *adj.* able to speak, articulate; tuneful, sonorous; *f.sbst.* vowel

vocāmen, -inis *n.* name, appellation

vocātiō, -ōnis *f.* dinner invitation

vocātor, -ōris *m.* dispatcher of dinner invitations

vocātus, -ūs *m.* calling, summons; invitation

vōciferātiō, -ōnis *f.* clamour, shout

vōciferor 1. *dep.* to cry out, shout; voice loudly, scream

vocitō 1. to name habitually, call usually; summon often

vocīvus see **vacīvus**

vocō 1. to call, summon; call upon, invoke; invite; demand; name, call; challenge

vōcula, -ae *f.* small voice

volaemum, -ī *n.* type of pear

volāticus, -a, -um *adj.* flying, swift; fickle

volātilis, -is, -e *adj.* flying; fleeting

volātus, -ūs *m.* flight

volens, -ntis *adj.* willing, voluntary; favourable, welcome

volg- see **vulg-**

volitō 1. to fly about, flit; rush around

volō¹, velle, voluī *v.irreg.* to want, desire; (+*inf.*) wish (to); mean, imply; **vīs(ne)?** or **vīn?** (+*inf.*) don't you want (to)?

volō² 1. to fly, glide; rush, speed

volō³, -ōnis *m.* volunteer soldier

volsellae, -ārum *f.pl.* tweezers

volt- see **vult-**

volūbilis, -is, -e *adj.* rotating, revolving; rolling, flowing; unstable, inconstant

volūbilitās, -ātis *f.* rotation, revolution; rolling; fluency; roundness; instability

volūbiliter *adv.* fluently

volucer, -cris, -cre *adj.* flying, winged; swift; fleeting, transitory; *f./m.sbst.* bird

volūmen, -inis *n.* coil, twist; roll of papyrus, book

voluntārius, -a, -um *adj.* willing, voluntary; done of one's own accord; *m.pl.sbst.* volunteer soldiers

voluntās, -ātis *f.* wish, will; desire, intent, purpose; choice; disposition

volup *adv.* pleasurably, delightfully

voluptābilis, -is, -e *adj.* causing pleasure, delightful

voluptārius, -a, -um *adj.* of *or* relating to pleasure; pleasurable; devoted to pleasure, sensual

voluptās, -ātis *f.* pleasure, delight, joy; sex; *pl.* public shows, entertainments

voluptuōsus, -a, -um *adj.* causing pleasure, delightful

volūtābrum, -ī *n.* wallowing place

volūtābundus, -a, -um *adj.* wallowing

volūtātiō, -ōnis *f.* wallowing, rolling; turmoil, commotion

volūtō 1. to cause to roll; toss about; consider, ponder; *pass.* wallow, roll about

volvō, -vī, -ūtum 3. to cause to roll, turn round; roll forward; unroll (*a book*), read; experience; consider, ponder

vōmer, -eris *m.* ploughshare

vomica, -ae *f.* boil, ulcer

vōmis see **vōmer**

vomitiō, -ōnis *f.* vomiting, spewing

vomitō 1. to vomit continually

vomitor, -ōris *m.* one who vomits

vomitus, -ūs *m.* vomiting; vomit

vomō, -uī, -itum 3. to spew, vomit; belch out; be sick

vorāgō, -inis *f.* abyss, chasm

vorax, -ācis *adj.* consuming, devouring; greedy, ravenous

vorō 1. to consume greedily, devour

vors- see **vers-**

vorsōria, -ae *f.* rope used to change direction of a ship's course

vort- see **vert-**

vōs (*acc.* **vōs**, *gen.* **vestrī (-um)**, *dat./abl.* **vōbīs**) *pron.* you (*pl.*); you (*sg.*) and your associates

voster see **vester**

vōtifer, -era, -erum *adj.* vow-bearing, votive

vōtīvus, -a, -um *adj.* of *or* relating to a vow, votive

votō see **vetō**

vōtum, -ī *n.* vow; votive offering; prayer, wish

voveō, vōvī, vōtum 2. to vow, promise; (+*acc.*+*inf.*) pray (that); wish for, pray for

vox, vōcis *f.* voice; spoken utterance; saying; word; language; sound

vulgāris, -is, -e *adj.* common, ordinary; common, frequent; well-known; low, unrefined

vulgātor, -ōris *m.* one who makes common, divulger

vulgātus, -a, -um *adj.* common, ordinary; well-known

vulgivagus, -a, -um *adj.* widely wandering

vulgō[1] 1. to make common, divulge; spread about

vulgō[2] *adv.* commonly; frequently; publicly; altogether

vulgus, -ī (*acc. sometimes* **-um**) *n.* common people, public; crowd, mob

vulnerābilis, -is, -e *adj.* vulnerable

vulnerātiō, -ōnis *f.* wounding

vulnerō 1. to wound, injure

vulnificus, -a, -um *adj.* causing wounds

vulnus, -eris *n.* wound, injury, blow

vulpēcula, -ae *f.* little fox

vulpēs, -is *f.* fox

vulticulus, -ī *m.* look, facial expression

vultuōsus, -a, -um *adj.* with exaggerated facial expression, grimacing

vultur, -uris *m.* vulture

vulturīnus, -a, -um *adj.* of *or* like a vulture

vulturius, -(i)ī *m.* vulture; unlucky throw (*in game of dice*)

vultus, -ūs *m.* look, expression; face; appearance

vulva, -ae *f.* womb; vagina; sow's womb (*a culinary delicacy*)

X

xenium, -iī *n.* gift from host to guest

xērampelinus, -a, -um *adj.* dark red

xiphiās, -ae *m.* swordfish

xysticus, -ī *m.* athlete

xystus, -ī *m.* outdoor walk

zāmia, -ae *f.* damage, injury

zēlotypus, -a, -um *adj.* jealous, prone to jealousy

zōdiacus, -a, -um *adj.* of *or* relating to the zodiac; **orbis zōdiacus** the zodiac

zōna, -ae *f.* girdle, belt; celestial zone

zōnārius[1]**, -a, -um** *adj.* of *or* relating to belts

zōnārius[2]**, -(i)ī** *m.* girdle-maker

zōnula, -ae *f.* small girdle

zōthēca, -ae *f.* recess, alcove

zōthēcula, -ae *f.* small alcove

ENGLISH–LATIN
DICTIONARY

a, an aliquis, -qua, -quid, quīdam, quaedam, quiddam

abandon (*people*) dēserō, -uī, -tum 3.,
(dē)relinquō, (dē)relīquī, (dē)relictum 3.,
dēstituō, -uī, -ūtum 3.; (*things*) dēsistō,
dēstitī 3.; (+*dat.*) dēsum, deesse, dēfuī *v.
irreg.*; omittō, omīsī, omissum 3.

abdicate abdicō 1., ēiūrō 1.

abdication abdicātiō, -ōnis *f.*

abdomen abdōmen, -inis *n.*

abide dūrō 1., permaneō, -nsī, -nsum 2.;
abide by (+*abl.*) stō, stetī 1.

ability ops, opis *f.*, facultās, -ātis *f.*, potestās, -ātis *f.*; (*mental*) ingenium, -(i)ī *n.*

abject humilis, -is, -e, abiectus, -a, -um

abjure abiūrō 1., recūsō 1.

able potens, -ntis; (*mentally*) ingeniōsus, -a,
-um

able (to), am (+*inf.*) possum, posse, potuī
v.irreg., valeō 2.; (know how to) (+*inf.*)
sciō 4.

abnormal mīrus, -a, -um, singulāris, -is, -e,
novus, -a, -um

abode domicilium, -(i)ī *n.*

abolish aboleō, -lēvī, -litum 2., tollō, sustulī, sublātum 3., dēleō, dēlēvī, dēlētum
2.

abominable abōminandus, -a, -um, ātrox,
-ōcis, dētestābilis, -is, -e

abound (in) (+*abl.*) abundō 1.; (+*abl.*) circumfluō, -xī 3.

about¹ (*adv.*) circā, fer(m)ē, circiter

about² (*prep.*) (+*acc.*) circum, circā; (concerning) (+*abl.*) dē, super

above¹ (*adv.*) super, suprā; **from above**
dēsuper

above² (*prep.*) (+*acc.*) super, suprā; (*poetic*)
(+*abl.*) super

abroad (to the outside) forās; (outside)
forīs

abrupt (steep) arduus, -a, -um, praeruptus,
-a, -um, abruptus, -a, -um; *see also* **sudden**

absence absentia, -ae *f.*

absent absens, -ntis

absent (from), am (+*abl. or* +*ab* +*abl.*)
absum, abesse, āfuī *v.irreg.*

absolutely plānē, omnīnō

absolve absolvō, -vī, -ūtum 3.

absorb absorbeō, -buī (*or* -psī), -ptum 2.,
(ex)hauriō, -sī, -sum 4.

abstain (from) (+*abl. or* +*ab* +*abl.*) abstineō, abstinuī, abstentum 2.

abstinence continentia, -ae *f.*, temperantia, -ae *f.*, abstinentia, -ae *f.*

abstinent temperātus, -a, -um, abstinens,
-ntis

abundance (of) (+*gen.*) plūrimum, -ī *n.*,
cōpia, -ae *f.*, ūbertās, -ātis *f.*

abundant largus, -a, -um, amplus, -a, -um

abuse¹ (*noun*) (insult) maledictum, -ī *n.*,
convīcium, -(i)ī *n.*

abuse² (*v.*) (insult) maledīcō, -dixī, -dic-
tum 3.; (misuse) (+*abl.*) abūtor, abūsus 3.
dep.

abusive maledīcens, -ntis, contumēliōsus,
-a, -um

accept accipiō, accēpī, acceptum 3., recipiō, recēpī, receptum 3.

access aditus, -ūs *m.*, accessus, -ūs *m.*

accident cāsus, -ūs *m.*; **by accident** cāsū,
forte, fortuitō

acclaim acclāmō 1.

accommodate accommodō 1., adiuvō,
-ūvī, -ūtum 1.

accompany comitor 1. *dep.*, prōsequor,
-secūtus 3. *dep.*

accomplice socius, -(i)ī *m.*, satelles, -itis *m.*

accord, of my own ultrō, meā (*etc.*) sponte

accordingly itaque, igitur, ergō

account ratiō, -ōnis *f.*; (narrative) narrātiō,

-ōnis *f.*; **take into account** (+*gen.*) ratiōnem habeō 2.; **on account of** (+*acc.*)
propter, ob
accurate dīligens, -ntis, accūrātus, -a, -um
accurately dīligenter, cūrā
accuse accūsō 1., insimulō 1., postulō 1.
accuser accūsātor, -ōris *m.*, petītor, -ōris *m.*
accustom assuēfaciō, -fēcī, -factum 3.
accustomed, am (+*inf.*) soleō, solitus 2.
semi-dep.
accustomed, become consuescō, -suēvī,
-suētum 3.
ache dolor, -ōris *m.*, angor, -ōris *m.*
achieve conficiō, -fēcī, -fectum 3., perficiō,
-fēcī, -fectum; (reach) perveniō, -vēnī,
-ventum 4.
achievement actum, -ī *n.*, factum, -ī *n.*,
successus, -ūs *m.*, rēs gesta, rēī gestae *f.*
acknowledge agnoscō, agnōvī, agnōtum
3.; (admit) confiteor, confessus 2. *dep.*
acorn glans, -ndis *f.*
acquire adipiscor, adeptus 3. *dep.*, assequor, assecūtus 3. *dep.*, consequor, consecūtus 3. *dep.*
acquit absolvō, -vī, -ūtum 3., purgō 1.
acquittal absolūtiō, -ōnis *f.*, līberātiō, -ōnis
f.
across[1] (*adv.*) trans
across[2] (*prep.*) (+*acc.*) trans, per
act[1] (*v.*) agō, ēgī, actum 3., faciō, fēcī, factum 3.; (behave) (+*adv.*) mē (*etc.*) gerō
(gessī, gestum 3.)
act[2] (*noun*), **action** actum, -ī *n.*, factum, -ī
n.; (*legal*) causa, -ae *f.*, actiō, -ōnis *f.*; (*of a
play*) actus, -ūs *m.*
actor actor, -ōris *m.*, mīmus, -ī *m.*
actress mīma, -ae *f.*
actual vērus, -a, -um
actually rē vērā, vērē
acute acūtus, -a, -um, ācer, ācris, ācre,
sagax, -ācis
adapt accommodō 1., aptō 1.
add addō, addidī, additum 3., accommodō
1., adiungō, -xī, -ctum 3.
address appellō 1., alloquor, allocūtus 3.
dep.; (deliver a speech) verba faciō (fēcī,
factum 3.)
adduce addūcō, adduxī, adductum 3.,
prōferō, -ferre, -tulī, -lātum *v.irreg.*
adequate idōneus, -a, -um, aptus, -a, -um,
iustus, -a, -um
adequately aptē, satis

adhere (+*dat.* or +*in* +*acc.*) (in)haereō, -sī,
-sum 2.
adjacent contiguus, -a, -um, vīcīnus, -a,
-um
administer administrō 1., prōcūrō 1.
administration prōcūrātiō, -ōnis *f.*,
administrātiō, -ōnis *f.*, regimen, -inis *n.*
admirable (ad)mīrābilis, -is, -e, laudābilis,
-is, -e
admiration admīrātiō, -ōnis *f.*, laus, -dis *f.*
admire admīror 1. *dep.*
admirer admīrātor, -ōris *m.*
admission aditus, -ūs *m.*, accessus, -ūs *m.*
admit permittō, -mīsī, -missum 3., intrōdūcō, -duxī, -ductum 3.; (confess) confiteor, confessus 2. *dep.*
admonish (ad)moneō 2.
adolescence adolescentia, -ae *f.*
adolescent adolescens, -ntis *m.*
adopt adoptō 1., adsūmō, adsumpsī,
adsumptum 3.
adore veneror 1. *dep.*, colō, coluī, cultum
3.; (love) amō 1.
adorn (ex)ornō 1.
adult adultus, -ī *m.*
adulterer adulter, -rī *m.*, moechus, -ī *m.*
adulteress adultera, -ae *f.*, moecha, -ae *f.*
adultery adulterium, -(i)ī *n.*, stuprum, -ī *n.*
advance[1] (*noun*) prōgressus, -ūs *m.*
advance[2] (*v.*) prōgredior, -gressus 3. *dep.*,
prōcēdō, -cessī, -cessum 3.
advantage ēmolumentum, -ī *n.*, opportūnitās, -ātis *f.*, ūtilitās, -ātis *f.*; (profit)
commodum, -ī *n.*, fructus, -ūs *m.*, lucrum,
-ī *n.*
advantageous opportūnus, -a, -um, fructuōsus, -a, -um, quaestuōsus, -a, -um,
ūtilis, -is, -e
adverse adversus, -a, -um, infensus, -a,
-um, contrārius, -a, -um
adversity rēs adversae, rērum adversārum
f.pl.
advise (ad)moneō 2.; (+*dat.*) consilium dō
(dedī, datum 1.)
adviser suāsor, -ōris *m.*, consiliārius, -(i)ī *m.*
advocate auctor, -ōris *m.*, patrōnus, -ī *m.*;
(legal) causidicus, -ī *m.*
affair rēs, rēī *f.*, cāsus, -ūs *m.*, negōtium,
-(i)ī *m.*
affect (*people*) commoveō, -mōvī, -mōtum
2., afficiō, affēcī, affectum 3., tangō,

tetigī, tactum 3.; (*things*) efficiō, effēcī, effectum 3.; *see also* **pretend**

affection affectus, -ūs *m.*; (love) cāritās, -ātis *f.*, amor, amōris *m.*

affix affīgō, affixī, affixum 3., alligō 1.

affliction dolor, -ōris *m.*, aegritūdō, -inis *f.*

afraid timidus, -a, -um, pavidus, -a, -um, territus, -a, -um

afraid (of), am timeō 2., metuō, -uī 3., (per)timescō, -muī 3., vereor, veritus 2. *dep.*

after[1] (*prep.*) (+*acc.*) post; (according to) ad

after[2] (*conj.*) postquam (post ... quam)

afternoon post merīdiānum tempus; **in the afternoon** post merīdiem

afterwards post, posthāc, posteā, deinde

again rursus, rursum; (a second time) iterum

against (+*acc.*) contrā, adversus (-um)

age (period) aetās, -ātis *f.*, aevum, -ī *n.*; (*of things*) vetustās, -ātis *f.*; **old age** senectūs, -ūtis *f.*

aggravate (ag)gravō 1., exulcerō 1.

agile velox, -ōcis, agilis, -is, -e

agitate concitō 1., quatiō, quassum 3., vibrō 1.; (disturb) perturbō, sollicitō 1.

ago (+*acc.*) abhinc

agree (with) (+*cum* +*abl.*) consentiō, consensī, consensum 4.; (+*cum* +*abl.*) congruō, -uī 3.

agreeable acceptābilis, -is, -e, acceptus, -a, -um

agreement pactum, -ī *n.*, concordia, -ae *f.*, consensus, -ūs *m.*

agriculture agricultūra, -ae *f.*, agricultiō, -ōnis *f.*

aid[1] (*noun*) auxilium, -(i)ī *n.*, ops, opis *f.*, subsidium, -(i)ī *n.*

aid[2] (*v.*) (ad)iuvō, -ūvī, -ūtum 1.; (+*dat.*) opem ferō (ferre, tulī, lātum *v.irreg.*); **come to aid** (+*dat.*) subveniō, -vēnī, -ventum 4.

aim intendō, -dī, -tum 3.

aim at petō, petīvī (-iī), petītum 3.

air āēr, āeris *m.*, aethēr, -eris *m.*

alert vigil, -ilis, alacer, -cris, -cre

alien externus, -a, -um, peregrīnus, -a, -um, adventīcius, -a, -um, aliēnus, -a, -um, aliēnigenus, -a, -um, hospitus, -a, -um

alike[1] (*adj.*) pār, paris, similis, -is, -e

alike[2] (*adv.*) pariter, similiter

alive vīvus, -a, -um

all cunctus, -a, -um, omnis, -is, -e

allegiance fidēs, -ēī *f.*

alleviate allevō 1.

alliance societās, -ātis *f.*, foedus, -eris *n.*

allow patior, passus 3. *dep.*, sinō, sīvī, situm 3.; (+*dat.*) permittō, -mīsī, -missum 3.; (grant) concēdō, -cessī, -cessum 3.

allowed, it is (+*dat.*+*inf.*) licet 2. *impers.*

allure alliciō, allexī, allectum 3.

allurement invītāmentum, -ī *n.*, blandīmentum, -ī *n.*

alluring blandus, -a, -um

ally socius, -(i)ī *m.*

almighty omnipotens, -ntis

almost fer(m)ē, paene, prope

alone[1] (*adj.*) sōlus, -a, -um, ūnus, ūna, ūnum

alone[2] (*adv.*) modo, sōlum, tantum

along (+*acc.*) praeter, secundum

aloud clārē, magnā vōce

already iam

also quoque, etiam; (besides) praetereā

altar āra, ārae *f.*, altāria, -um *n.pl.*

alter (com)mūtō 1., novō 1., corrigō, -rexī, -rectum 3.

alternately invicem, per vicēs, alternīs

although quamquam; (+*subj.*) cum, ut

altogether omnīnō

always semper

am (are, is, be) sum, esse, fuī *v.irreg.*; *see also* **exist**

amass accumulō 1., aggerō 1.

amaze (ob)stupefaciō, -fēcī, -factum 3.

amazed (ob)stupefactus, -a, -um, attonitus, -a, -um, stupidus, -a, -um

ambassador lēgātus, -ī *m.*

ambiguous anceps, ancipitis, ambiguus, -a, -um, dubius, -a, -um

ambition ambitiō, -ōnis *f.*, glōria, -ae *f.*

ambush insidiae, -ārum *f.pl.*

amiable amābilis, -is, -e, cōmis, -is, -e

among(st) (+*acc.*) inter, apud; (+*abl.*) in

amphitheatre amphitheātrum, -ī *n.*

ample amplus, -a, -um

amuse oblectō 1., dēlectō 1.

ancestors maiōres, -um *m.pl.*; (*poetic*) patrēs, -um *m.pl.*

anchor ancora, -ae *f.*

ancient vetus, veteris, vetustus, -a, -um, antīquus, -a, -um, priscus, -a, -um, pristinus, -a, -um

and et, -que, ac (*before consonants*), atque
(*before vowels*)

anger[1] (*noun*) īra, īrae **f.**, īrācundia, -ae **f.**,
indignātiō, -ōnis **f.**

anger[2] (*v.*) irrītō 1., lacessō, -īvī (-iī), -ītum
3.

angle angulus, -ī **m.**

angry (with), am (+*dat.*) īrascor, īrātus 3.
dep., suscenseō 2., stomachor 1. *dep.*

animal animal, -ālis **n.**, bestia, -ae **f.**, fera,
-ae **f.**

annihilate dēleō, -ēvī, -ētum 2., exstinguō,
-nxī, -nctum 3.

announce (an)nuntiō 1.

annoy vexō 1., lacessō, -īvī (-iī), -ītum 3.,
irrītō 1.

annoyance vexātiō, -ōnis **f.**, molestia, -ae **f.**

annoyed, am aegrē *or* graviter ferō (ferre,
tulī, lātum *v.irreg.*)

annual anniversārius, -a, -um, annuus, -a,
-um

annually quotannīs

another alius, -a, -um; (*of two*) alter, -era,
-erum; **belonging to another** aliēnus,
-a, -um; **at another time** aliās; **in
another place** alibī; **to another place**
aliō

answer[1] (*noun*) responsum, -ī **n.**

answer[2] (*v.*) respondeō, -dī, -sum 2.

ant formīca, -ae **f.**

antiquated obsolētus, -a, -um, priscus, -a,
-um, antīquus, -a, -um

antiquity (age) vetustās, -ātis **f.**; (ancient
period) antīquitās, -ātis **f.**

anxiety sollicitūdō, -inis **f.**, cūra, -ae **f.**,
pavor, -ōris **m.**, anxietās, -ātis **f.**

anxious sollicitus, -a, -um, anxius, -a, -um;
anxious for (+*dat.*) studiōsus, -a, -um

any, anyone, anything quisquam, quae-
quam, quidquam (quicquam), ullus, -a,
-um; (any at all) ecquis, -is, -id; (any you
like) quīvīs, quaevīs, quidvīs, quīlibet,
quaelibet, quidlibet

anywhere usquam; (anywhere at all) ubivīs; **to anywhere** quōquam

apart seōrsum

apologize (for) excūsō 1.; (+*gen.*) veniam
petō (-īvī (-iī), -ītum 3.)

apparent *see* **obvious**

appeal to obtestor 1. *dep.*, obsecrō 1.

appear appāreō 2., conspiciō, -spexī,
-spectum 3.; (seem) videor, vīsus 2. *dep.*

appearance faciēs, -ēī **f.**, speciēs, -ēī **f.**,
aspectus, -ūs **m.**, habitus, -ūs **m.**

appease plācō 1.

appetite appetentia, -ae **f.**, appetītiō, -ōnis
f.

applaud (ap)plaudō, -sī, -sum 3., conclāmō
1., collaudō 1.

applause plausus, -ūs **m.**, laus, laudis **f.**

apple mālum, -ī **n.**

appoint creō 1.; (*times etc.*) dicō 1., destinō
1.

apprehend compre(he)ndō, -dī, -sum 3.;
(*mentally*) intellegō, -xī, -ctum 3.

approach[1] (*noun*) adventus, -ūs **m.**, aditus,
-ūs **m.**, accessus, -ūs **m.**

approach[2] (*v.*) (+*dat. or* +*ad* +*acc.*) adeō,
adīre, adīvī (adiī), aditum 4., accēdō,
accessī, accessum 3., appropinquō 1.

appropriate aptus, -a, -um, accommodātus, -a, -um, idōneus, -a, -um

approve (ap)probō 1.

approximately (+*acc.*) circā

arbiter arbiter, -trī **m.**, disceptātor, -ōris **m.**

arch arcus, -ūs **m.**

archer sagittārius, -(i)ī **m.**

ardent ardens, -ntis, vehemens, -ntis, fervens, -ntis

ardently vehementer, ardenter

ardour ardor, -ōris **m.**, fervor, -ōris **m.**

arena arēna, -ae **f.**

argue (dis)serō, -uī, -tum 3.

argument disputātiō, -ōnis **f.**

arise (ad)orior, (ad)ortus 4. *dep.*, surgō,
surrexī 3., nascor, nātus 3. *dep.*

arm bracchium, -(i)ī **n.**, lacertus, -ī **m.**;
upper arm armus, -ī **m.**

armed armātus, -a, -um

armour arma, -ōrum **n.pl.**, armātūra, -ae **f.**

armpit āla, ālae **f.**

army exercitus, -ūs **m.**, cōpiae, -ārum **f.pl.**

around (+*acc.*) circā

arrest compre(he)ndō, -dī, -sum 3.

arrival adventus, -ūs **m.**

arrive adveniō, advēnī, adventum 4., perveniō, -vēnī, -ventum 4.

arrogance arrogantia, -ae **f.**, superbia, -ae **f.**

arrow sagitta, -ae **f.**

art ars, artis **f.**, artificium, -(i)ī **n.**

artist artifex, -ficis **m.**

as (when) ut, quandō, sīcut; (as much *etc.*
as) quam, ac (*before consonants*), atque

(*before vowels*); (*while*) dum; **as though** tamquam; **as if** quasi

ascertain cognoscō, -nōvī, -nitum 3., discō, didicī 3.

ash[1] (*of a fire*) cinis, -eris *m.*

ash[2] (*tree*) fraxinus, -ī *f.*

ashamed, am *see* **shame, feel**

ask quaerō, -sīvī, -sītum 3., petō, -īvī (-iī), -ītum 3.; (inter)rogō 1.

ask for *see* **demand**[2]

aspect facies, -ēī *f.*

ass asinus, -ī *m.*, asellus, -ī *m.*

assail oppugnō 1., aggredior, aggressus 3. *dep.*

assassin sīcārius, -(i)ī *m.*

assault *see* **attack**

assemble (come together) coeō, coīre, coīvī (coiī), coitum 4., conveniō, -vēnī, -ventum 4.; (bring together) *see* **gather**

assembly conventus, -ūs *m.*

assert affirmō 1.

assign assignō 1.

assist (ad)iuvō, -ūvī, -ūtum 1., auxilior 1. *dep.*

assistant adiūtor, -ōris *m.*, auxiliātor, -ōris *m.*, minister, -trī *m.*

astonished attonitus, -a, -um

astronomer astrologus, -ī *m.*

astronomy astrologia, -ae *f.*, astronomia, -ae *f.*

at (+*acc.*) ad, apud; (+*abl.*) in

attach affīgō, affixī, affixum 3., alligō 1.

attack[1] (*noun*) impetus, -ūs *m.*, oppugnātiō, -ōnis *f.*

attack[2] (*v.*) (+*acc.*) aggredior, aggressus 3. *dep.*, oppugnō 1.; (+*dat.*) adorior, adortus 4. *dep.*; (in speech) (+*in* +*acc.*) invehor, invectus 3. *dep.*

attacker oppugnātor, -ōris *m.*

attain perveniō, -vēnī, -ventum 4., adipiscor, adeptus 3. *dep.*, assequor, assecūtus 3. *dep.*

attempt[1] (*noun*) cōnātus, -ūs *m.*, inceptum, -ī *n.*

attempt[2] (*v.*) cōnor 1. *dep.*, tentō (temptō) 1.

attend comitor 1. *dep.*, prōsequor, -secūtus 3. *dep.*

attendant minister, -trī *m.*; (companion) comes, -itis *m.*, satelles, -itis *m.*, stīpātor, -ōris *m.*

attentive intentus, -a, -um, attentus, -a, -um

attract attrahō, -xī, -ctum 3., alliciō, allexī, allectum 3.

attractive formōsus, -a, -um, blandus, -a, -um

auction auctiō, -ōnis *f.*

audacity ferōcia, -ae *f.*, audācia, -ae *f.*

augur augur, -uris *m./f.*

aunt (*paternal*) amīta, -ae *f.*; (*maternal*) mātertera, -ae *f.*

auspicious *see* **fortunate**

authentic certus, -a, -um, vērus, -a, -um

authority auctōritās, -ātis *f.*, imperium, -(i)ī *n.*

autumn autumnus, -ī *m.*

autumnal autumnālis, -is, -e

auxiliary auxiliāris, -is, -e

avarice *see* **greed**

avenge ulciscor, ultus 3. *dep.*, vindicō 1.; (+*dat.*) parentō 1.

avenger ultor, -ōris *m.*, vindex, -icis *m.*

average medius, -a, -um, mediocris, -is, -e

avert āvertō, -tī, -sum 3., arceō 2.

avoid vītō 1., dēfugiō, dēfūgī 3.R

awake (*someone*) excitō 1.

aware of, am sentiō, sensī, sensum 4., animadvertō, -tī, -sum 3.

away from (+*abl.*) ē *or* ex

awe reverentia, -ae *f.*

awful ātrox, -ōcis, dīrus, -a, -um, terribilis, -is, -e

axe secūris, -is *f.*

axis, axle axis, axis *m.*

B

baby infans, -ntis *m./f.*
bachelor caelebs, -libis *m.*
back tergum, -ī *n.*, dorsum, -ī *n.;* **on one's back** supīnus, -a, -um
backward(s) retrō, retrorsum
bacon lardum, -ī *n.*
bad malus, -a, -um; (wicked) prāvus, -a, -um, improbus, -a, -um, turpis, -is, -e
badly male; (wickedly) prāvē, turpiter, improbē
badness *see* **wickedness**
bag saccus, -ī *m.*, sarcina, -ae *f.*
baggage impedīmenta, -ōrum *n.pl.*, sarcinae, -ārum *f.pl.*
baker pistor, -ōris *m.;* (*female*) pistrix, -īcis *f.*
bakery pistrīnum, -ī *n.*
balance lībra, -ae *f.*, lanx, lancis *f.*
bald calvus, -a, -um, glaber, -bra, -brum
ball pila, -ae *f.*
band (*of men*) manus, -ūs *f.*
bandit latrō, -ōnis *m.*
banish ēiciō, ēiēcī, ēiectum 3., relegō 1., expellō, expulī, expulsum 3.
bank (*of a river*) rīpa, -ae *f.*, ōra, ōrae *f.;* (*of earth*) agger, -eris *m.;* (*of money*) (mensa) argentāria, -ae *f.*
banker argentārius, -(i)ī *m.*
bar asser, -eris *m.*
barb hāmus, -ī *m.*
barbarian barbarus, -ī *m.*
barbaric barbarus, -a, -um; (wild, savage) crūdēlis, -is, -e, immānis, -is, -e, ferus, -a, -um, saevus, -a, -um
barber tonsor, -ōris *m.;* **barber's shop** tonstrīna, -ae *f.*
bard vātēs, -is *m.*
bare nūdus, -a, -um; (mere) merus, -a, -um
barely vix, aegrē
bargain paciscor, pactus 3. *dep.*

bark¹ (*noun*) cortex, -icis *m.*, liber, librī *m.*
bark² (*v.*) lātrō 1.
barley hordeum, -ī *n.*
barn horreum, -ī *n.*
barracks castra, -ōrum *n.pl.*
barrel cūpa, -ae *f.; see also* **vessel**
barren sterilis, -is, -e, infēcundus, -a, -um
barricade intersēpiō, -īvī (-iī), -tum 4., inaedificō 1.
barrier saeptum, -ī *n.*
base¹ (*noun*) fundāmentum, -ī *n.*, basis, -is *f.*, rādix, -īcis *f.*
base² (*adj.*) turpis, -is, -e, humilis, -is, -e
basely turpiter
bashful *see* **shy**
basket quālus, -ī *m.*, sporta, -ae *f.*, corbis, -is *f.;* (*poetic*) calathus, -ī *m.*
bath bal(i)neum, -ī *n.*, alveus, -ī *m.;* **baths** balneae, -ārum *f.pl.*
bathe lavō 1., abluō, -uī, -ūtum 3.
batter *see* **beat**
battle proelium, -(i)ī *n.*, pugna, -ae *f.;* **line of battle** aciēs, -ēī *f.;* **join battle** proelium committō (-mīsī, -missum 3.)
battlement pinna, -ae *f.*
bay¹ (inlet) sinus, -ūs *m.*
bay² (tree) laurea, -ae *f.*, laurus, -ī (-ūs) *f.*
be *see* **am**
beach lītus, -oris *n.*, acta, -ae *f.*, arēna, -ae *f.*
beak rostrum, -ī *n.*
beam¹ (*noun*) trabs, -bis *f.*, tignum, -ī *n.;* (*of light*) radius, -(i)ī *m.*
beam² (*v.*) *see* **shine**
bean fāba, -ae *f.*
bear¹ (*noun*) (*male*) ursus, -ī *m.;* (*female*) ursa, -ae *f.*
bear² (*v.*) ferō, ferre, tulī, lātum *v.irreg.*, portō 1., gestō 1.; (suffer) patior, passus 3. *dep.*, perferō, -ferre, -tulī, -lātum *v.irreg.*, tolerō 1.; (*a child*) parō, peperī, partum 3.

beard barba, -ae *f.*
beast bestia, -ae *f.*, fera, -ae *f.*, bēlua, -ae *f.*;
  beast of burden iūmentum, -ī *n.*
beat pellō, pepulī, pulsum 3., pulsō 1.,
  verberō 1., percutiō, -ssī, -ssum 3.; (am
  victorious over) vincō, vīcī, victum 3.,
  superō 1.
beaten, am vāpulō 1.
beautiful formōsus, -a, -um, pulc(h)er,
  -c(h)ra, -c(h)rum, bellus, -a, -um, venustus, -a, -um; (*of places*) amoenus, -a, -um
beautify (ex)ornō 1.
beauty formitūdō, -inis *f.*, faciēs, -ēī *f.*,
  pulc(h)ritūdō, -inis *f.*, venustās, -ātis; (*of
  places*) amoenitās, -ātis *f.*
beaver castor, -oris *m.*
because quod, quia, quoniam; (+*subj.*)
  cum; **because of** (+*acc.*) propter, ob
become fīō, fierī, factus *v.irreg.*, nascor,
  nātus 3. *dep.*, orior, ortus 4. *dep.*
becomes (me), it mē (*etc.*) decet 2. *impers.*
bed lectus, -ī *m.*, cubīle, -is *n.*; (*of a river*)
  alveus, -ī *m.*
bedroom cubiculum, -ī *n.*
bee apis, apis *m.*
beech fāgus, -ī *f.*
before[1] (*prep.*) (+*acc.*) ante; (+*abl.*) prae,
  prō
before[2] (*conj.*) antequam (ante … quam),
  priusquam (prius … quam)
before(hand) anteā, antehāc, ante, prius
beg ōrō 1., rogō 1., obsecrō 1., petō, -īvī
  (-iī), -ītum 3., flāgitō 1.; (*as a pauper*)
  mendīcō 1.
beget generō 1., prōcreō 1., gignō, genuī,
  genitum 3.
beggar pauper, -eris *m.*, mendīcus, -ī *m.*
begin incipiō, incēpī, inceptum 3., coepī,
  coeptum 3. (*only in pf.*), incohō 1., instituō, -uī, -ūtum 3.
beginner tīrō, -ōnis *m.*
beginning initium, -(i)ī *n.*, incipium, -(i)ī
  n.
beguile dēcipiō, dēcēpī, dēceptum 3.,
  fallō, fefellī, falsum 3.
behave (+*adv.*) mē (*etc.*) gerō (gessī, gestum
  3.)
behaviour gestus, -ūs *m.*, mōrēs, -um *m.pl.*
behead dētruncō 1.
behind[1] (*adv.*) post, pōne, retrō
behind[2] (*prep.*) (+*acc.*) post, pōne

behold aspiciō, aspexī, aspectum 3., spectō
  1., intueor, intuitus 2. *dep.*
belch[1] (*noun*) ructus, -ūs *m.*
belch[2] (*v.*) (ē)ructō 1.
belief fidēs, -ēī *f.*; (opinion) opīniō, -ōnis *f.*
believe crēdō, -didī, -ditum 3.; (+*dat.*)
  fidem habeō 2.
bell tintinnābulum, -ī *n.*
belly abdōmen, -inis *n.*, alvus, -ī *f.*, venter,
  -tris *m.*
belong (to) (+*ad* +*acc.*) pertineō, -tinuī,
  -tentum 2.
beloved dīlectus, -a, -um
below[1] (*adv.*) subter, infrā
below[2] (*prep.*) (+*acc.*) subter, infrā
belt zōna, -ae *f.*; (*poetic*) cingulum, -ī *n.*
benches (*of a ship*) transtra, -ōrum *n.pl.*
bend (in)flectō, (in)flexī, (in)flexum 3.,
  inclīnō 1.
beneath *see* **below**[2]
beneficial ūtilis, -is, -e
benefit (+*dat.*) prōsum, prōdesse, prōfuī *v.*
  irreg.
bent curvus, -a, -um, flexus, -a, -um
bequest lēgātum, -ī *n.*
bereaved orbus, -a, -um
berry acinus, -ī *m.*, bāca, -ae *f.*
beseech *see* **beg**
beside (+*acc.*) prope, iuxtā; (except) (+*acc.*)
  praeter
besides praetereā
besiege obsideō, obsēdī, obsessum 2.;
  (assail) oppugnō 1.
besieger obsessor, -ōris *m.*
best optimus, -a, -um
bestir incitō 1., excitō 1.
betray prōdō, -didī, -ditum 3., trādō, -didī,
  -ditum 3.
better melior, -or, -us, potior, -or, -us
between (+*acc.*) inter
bewail dēfleō, -ēvī, -ētum 2., dēplōrō 1.
beware caveō, cāvī, cautum 2.
beyond[1] (*adv.*) ultrā, suprā
beyond[2] (*prep.*) (+*acc.*) praeter, ultrā,
  extrā, trans
bid iubeō, iussī, iussum 2.; petō, -īvī (-iī),
  -ītum 3., rogō 1.; (+*dat.*) imperō 1.
bide *see* **wait**
big grandis, -is, -e, magnus, -a, -um, vastus,
  -a, -um
bill (*legal*) rogātiō, -ōnis *f.*; (beak) rostrum,
  -ī *n.*

billow

billow fluctus, -ūs *m.*
bind (al)ligō 1., vinciō, vinxī, vinctum 4., obstringō, -nxī, -ctum 3.; (make liable) obligō 1.
bird āles, ālitis *m./f.*, avis, avis *f.*, volucris, -is *f.*
birth ortus, -ūs *m.*, nātiō, -ōnis *f.*
bit morcellum, -ī *n.*
bite¹ (*noun*) morsus, -ūs *m.*
bite² (*v.*) mordō, momordī, morsum 3.
biting mordax, -ācis, mordens, -ntis, ācer, ācris, ācre
bitter acerbus, -a, -um, amārus, -a, -um, asper, -era, -erum, acidus, -a, -um
bitterly amārē, acerbē
bitterness acerbitās, -ātis, amāritūdō, -inis *f.*
black āter, ātra, ātrum, niger, nigra, nigrum
blacksmith faber, fabrī *m.*
bladder vēsīca, -ae *f.*
blame¹ (*noun*) culpa, -ae *f.*, vituperātiō, -ōnis *f.*, reprehensiō, -ōnis *f.*
blame² (*v.*) vituperō 1., reprehendō, -dī, -sum 3., accūsō 1.; (*poetic*) culpō 1.
blank vacuus, -a, -um
blemish *see* **blot**
blind caecus, -a, -um, oculīs captus, -a, -um
blindness caecitās, -ātis *f.*
blister pustula, -ae *f.*, vēsīca, -ae *f.*
block obstruō, -xī, -ctum 3., occlūdō, -sī, -sum 3., oppleō, -ēvī, -ētum 2.
blockade obsidiō, -ōnis *f.*
blood sanguis, -inis *m.*, cruor, -ōris *m.*
bloodshed caedēs, -is *f.*
bloody cruentus, -a, -um
bloom¹ (*noun*) flōs, flōris *m.*
bloom² (*v.*) flōreō 2., vigeō 2.; **come into bloom** flōrescō 3.
blooming flōridus, -a, -um, flōrens, -ntis
blot litūra, -ae *f.*; (*of character*) vitium, -(i)ī *n.*, mendum, -ī *n.*
blow¹ (*noun*) plāga, -ae *f.*, ictus, -ūs *m.*; (*of fortune*) calamitās, -ātis *f.*
blow² (*v.*) flō 1., aspīrō 1., (ex)hālō 1.
blue caeruleus, -a, -um
blunt hebes, -etis
boar verrēs, -is *m.*; (*wild*) aper, aprī *m.*
board tabula, -ae *f.*
boast glōrior 1. *dep.*; **boast of** iactō 1.
boastful glōriōsus, -a, -um
boasting glōriātiō, -ōnis *f.*, iactātiō, -ōnis *f.*

boat nāvis, -is *f.*, linter, -tris *f.*, scapha, -ae *f.*; (*poetic*) cumba, -ae *f.*
bodily corporeus, -a, -um, corporālis, -is, -e
body corpus, -oris *n.*; (*of soldiers*) manus, -ūs *f.*; **small body** corpusculum, -ī *n.*
bodyguard satelles, -itis *m.*, custōs, -ōdis *m./f.*
boil (reach boiling-point) ferveō, ferbuī 2., (ex)aestuō 1.; (heat to boiling-point) coquō, coxī, coctum 3.
bold audax, -ācis, fortis, -is, -e, ferox, -ōcis, animōsus, -a, -um
bold, am audeō, ausus 2. *semi-dep.*
boldly audacter, ferōciter, animōsē
boldness audācia, -ae *f.*, ferōcia, -ae *f.*, confīdentia, -ae *f.*
bond ligāmentum, -ī *n.*, vinculum, -ī *n.*
bone os, ossis *n.*
book liber, librī *m.*, caudex (cō-), -icis *m.*, volūmen, -inis *n.*
bookcase scrīnium, -(i)ī *n.*, pegma, -atis *n.*
bookseller bibliopōla, -ae *m.*
boot calceus, -ī *m.*
booty praeda, -ae *f.*, spolium, -(i)ī *n.*
border¹ (*noun*) margō, -inis *m.*, labrum, -ī *n.*, fīnis, -is *m.* (*esp.pl.*)
border² (*v.*) (+*dat.* or +*ad* +*acc.*) attingō, attigī, attactum 3., adiaceō 2.
born, am nascor, nātus 3. *dep.*
borrow mūtuor 1. *dep.*
boss bulla, -ae *f.*, umbō, -ōnis *m.*
both ambō, ambae, ambō, uterque, utraque, utrumque; **both ... and** et ... et
bottle ampulla, -ae *f.*, lagōna (lagoena), -ae *f.*
bound modus, -ī *m.*, terminus, -ī *m.*
boundary *see* **border¹**
bovine būbulus, -a, -um
bow arcus, -ūs *m.*; (*of a ship*) prōra, -ae *f.*
bowl pelvis, -is *f.*, patera, -ae *f.*
box arca, -ae *f.*, capsa, -ae *f.*
boxer pugil, -ilis *m.*
boy puer, -rī *m.*
boyhood pueritia, -ae *f.*
boyish puerīlis, -is, -e
bracelet armilla, -ae *f.*
braid plectō, -xī, -xum 3.
brain cerebrum, -brī *n.*
bramble rubus, -ī *m.*, vepris, -is *m.* (*esp.pl.*)
branch rāmus, -ī *m.*, virga, -ae *f.*
brand notō 1.
brandish iactō 1., vibrō 1.

brave fortis, -is, -e, audax, -ācis, animōsus, -a, -um

brave, am audeō, ausus 2. *semi-dep.*

bravely fortiter, audacter

bravery fortitūdō, -inis *f.*, virtūs, -ūtis *f.*, constantia, -ae *f.*

brazen a(h)ēneus, -a, -um

breach perfringō, -frēgī, -fractum 3.

bread pānis, -is *m.*

breadth lātitūdō, -inis *f.*

break[1] (*noun*) intervallum, -ī *n.*

break[2] (*v.*) frangō, frēgī, fractum 3., rumpō, rūpī, ruptum 3.; (*laws*) violō 1.

break off abrumpō, abrūpī, abruptum 3.

break out ērumpō, ērūpī, ēruptum 3.

break up dissipō 1.

breakfast i(āi)entāculum, -ī *n.*, prandium, -(i)ī *n.*

breast pectus, -oris *n.*, animus, -ī *m.*

breastplate lōrīca, -ae *f.*, thōrax, -ācis *m.*

breath anima, -ae *f.*, hālitus, -ūs *m.*, spīritus, -ūs *m.*

breathe spīrō 1., hālō 1.

breed gens, gentis *f.*, genus, -eris *n.*, nātiō, -ōnis *f.*

breeze aura, -ae *f.*

brevity brevitās, -ātis *f.*

bribe corrumpō, -rūpī, -ruptum 3., pervertō, -tī, -sum 3.

bribery ambitus, -ūs *m.*, largitiō, -ōnis *f.*

brick later, -eris *m.*

bridal nuptiālis, -is, -e

bride sponsa, -ae *f.*

bridegroom sponsus, -ī *m.*

bridge pons, pontis *m.*; **little bridge** ponticulus, -ī *m.*

brief brevis, -is, -e

briefly breviter, strictim

bright lūcidus, -a, -um, clārus, -a, -um, candidus, -a, -um, splendidus, -a, -um

brightness candor, -ōris *m.*, fulgor, -ōris *m.*, splendor, -ōris *m.*, nitor, -ōris *m.*

brim labrum, -ī *n.*, margō, -inis *m.*, limbus, -ī *m.*

bring (af)ferō, (af)ferre, (at)tulī, (al)lātum *v.irreg.*, (ad)dūcō, (ad)duxī, (ad)ductum 3., (ap)portō 1.

bring away auferō, auferre, abstulī, ablātum *v.irreg.*

bring out prōdūcō, -duxī, -ductum 3.

brittle fragilis, -is, -e

broad lātus, -a, -um, amplus, -a, -um

bronze[1] (*noun*) aes, aeris *n.*

bronze[2] (*adj.*) a(h)ēneus, -a, -um

brooch fībula, -ae *f.*

broth iūs, iūris *n.*

brothel lupānar, -āris *n.*

brother frāter, -tris *m.*

brother-in-law lēvir, -ri *m.*

brown fuscus, -a, -um

bruised līvidus, -a, -um

brutal saevus, -a, -um, ferus, -a, -um, immānis, -is, -e

brutality immānitās, -ātis *f.*

bucket situla, -ae *f.*, (h)ama, -ae *f.*

build aedificō 1., construō, -xī, -ctum 3.

building aedificātiō, -ōnis *f.*, aedificium, -(i)ī *n.*

bulk magnitūdō, -inis *f.*, amplitūdō, -inis *f.*

bull taurus, -ī *m.*

bullock iuvencus, -ī *m.*

burden onus, oneris *n.*

burdensome onustus, -a, -um, gravis, -is, -e

burial sepultūra, -ae *f.*, humātiō, -ōnis *f.*

burn flagrō 1., ūrō, ussī, ustum 3.; (am on fire) ardeō, arsī, arsum 2.

burn down cremō 1.

burning incendium, -(i)ī *n.*

bury sepeliō, -īvī (-iī), sepultum 4., interimō, -ēmī, -emptum 3., obruō, -uī, -utum 3., operiō, -uī, -tum 4.

bush frutex, -icis *f.*

business negōtium, -(i)ī *n.*, rēs, reī *f.*, causa, -ae *f.*

busy negōtiōsus, -a, -um, occupātus, -a, -um

but sed, at, tamen

butcher[1] (*noun*) lanius, -(i)ī *m.*

butcher[2] (*v.*) caedō, cecīdī, caesum 3., trucīdō 1., mactō 1., iugulō 1.

butterfly pāpiliō, -ōnis *m.*

buy emō, ēmī, emptum 3.

by (+*acc.*) ad, apud, prope, iuxtā

bye avē(te)

byre būbīle, -is *n.*

C

cabbage brassica, -ae *f.*, caulis, -is *f.*
cabinet armārium, -(i)ī *n.*
cable ancorāle, -is *n.*
cage cavea, -ae *f.*
cake placenta, -ae *f.*
calamity *see* **disaster**
calculate computō 1.
calf (*male*) vitulus, -ī *m.*; (*female*) vitula, -ae *f.*
call vocō 1.; (name) appellō 1., nōminō 1., dīcō, dixī, dictum 3.
calm[1] (*noun*) quiēs, -ētis *f.*, tranquillitās, -ātis *f.*, pax, pācis *f.*
calm[2] (*v.*) tranquillus, -a, -um, quiētus, -a, -um, placidus, -a, -um, sēdātus, -a, -um
calmly aequō animō, placidē
camp castra, -ōrum *n.pl.*; **pitch camp** castra pōnō (posuī, positum 3.)
can (+*inf.*) possum, posse, potuī *v.irreg.*, valeō 2.; (know how to) (+*inf.*) sciō 4.
candid simplex, -icis, apertus, -a, -um, candidus, -a, -um
candidate candidātus, -ī *m.*
cane (h)arundō, -inis *f.*, calamus, -ī *m.*
cannot (+*inf.*) nequeō, nequīvī (-iī), nequītum 4.
cap pilleus, -ī *m.*
capability facultās, -ātis *f.*, capācitās, -ātis *f.*
capacious amplus, -a, -um, capax, -ācis
captain gubernātor, -ōris *m.*
capture capiō, cēpī, captum 3., compre(he)ndō, -dī, -sum 3.
care (anxiety) cūra, -ae *f.*, sollicitūdō, -inis *f.*; (diligence) cūra, -ae *f.*, dīligentia, -ae *f.*
carefree sēcūrus, -a, -um
careful accūrātus, -a, -um, dīligens, -ntis
carefully accūrātē, dīligenter
caress (ad)mulceō, -lsī, -lsum 2., blandior 4. *dep.*

carriage currus, -ūs *m.*, raeda, -ae *f.*; (*general*) vehiculum, -ī *n.*
carry portō 1., ferō, ferre, tulī, lātum *v. irreg.*, vehō, vexī, vectum 3.
carry across transportō 1.
carry away asportō 1., auferō, auferre, abstulī, ablātum *v.irreg.*
carry out exportō 1.; (enact) exsequor, exsecūtus 3. *dep.*, conficiō, -fēcī, -fectum 3.
cart plaustrum, -ī *n.*
case causa, -ae *f.*, rēs, reī *f.*
cast *see* **throw**
castle arx, arcis *f.*, castellum, -ī *n.*
cat fēlēs, -is *f.*, aelūrus, -ī *m.*
catalogue index, -icis *m.*
catch capiō, cēpī, captum 3., compre(he)ndō, -dī, -sum 3.; (*an illness*) in morbum cadō (cecidī, cāsum 3.)
cattle pecus, -oris *n.*; (single head of cattle) pecus, -udis *f.*
cause[1] (*noun*) causa, -ae *f.*, rēs, reī *f.*
cause[2] (*v.*) (+*ut*+*subj.*) faciō, fēcī, factum 3., efficiō, effēcī, effectum 3.
caution cautiō, -ōnis *f.*, cūra, -ae *f.*; **lack of caution** temeritās, -ātis *f.*, imprūdentia, -ae *f.*
cavalry equitēs, -um *m.pl.*, equitātus, -ūs *m.*
cave antrum, -ī *n.*, caverna, -ae *f.*, cavea, -ae *f.*, spēlunca, -ae *f.*
cease (to/from) (+*inf.*) dēsinō, dēsīvī (-iī), dēsitum 3.; (+*abl. or* +*inf.*) dēsistō, dēstitī 3.
ceaseless perpetuus, -a, -um, continuus, -a, -um, adsiduus, -a, -um
cedar cedrus, -ī *f.*
celebrate celebrō 1.
celestial aetherius, -a, -um, caelestis, -is, -e, dīvīnus, -a, -um

cell carcer, -eris *n.*, cella, -ae *f.*, cubiculum, -ī *n.*

centre medium, -(i)ī *n.*, media pars, mediae partis *f.*

centurion centuriō, -ōnis *m.*

century saeculum, -ī *n.*, centum annī (-ōrum *m.pl.*)

ceremony caerimōnia, -ae *f.*, rītus, -ūs *m.*

certain certus, -a, -um, fīdus, -a, -um, stabilis, -is, -e, status, -a, -um

certainly certō, certē, haud dubiē

chain catēna, -ae *f.*, vinculum, -ī *n.*

chair sella, -ae *f.*, cathedra, -ae *f.*, sedīle, -is *n.*

chalk crēta, -ae *f.*

chamber cubiculum, -ī *n.*, cella, -ae *f.*

chance cāsus, -ūs *m.*, fors, fortis *f.*, occāsiō, -ōnis *f.*, opportūnitās, -ātis *f.*, fortūna, -ae *f.*; **by chance** cāsū, forte

change (com)mūtō 1., convertō, -tī, -sum 3.

changeable inconstans, -ntis, mūtābilis, -is, -e, varius, -a, -um

channel fretum, -ī *n.*, fossa, -ae *f.*, canālis, -is *m.*

character ingenium, -(i)ī *n.*, nātūra, -ae *f.*, indolēs, -is *f.*; **noble character** virtūs, -ūtis *f.*; (*of an alphabet*) littera, -ae *f.*

charge[1] (*noun*) (attack) impetus, -ūs *m.*; (price) pretium, -(i)ī *n.*; (accusation) crīmen, -inis *n.*; (command) mandātum, -ī *n.*

charge[2] (*v.*) (+*in* +*acc.*) invādō, -sī, -sum 3.; (+*in* +*acc.*) impetum faciō (fēcī, factum 3.); (accuse) accūsō 1., insimulō 1.

chariot currus, -ūs *m.*

charm dulcēdō, -inis *f.*, venustās, -ātis *f.*, lepōs, -ōris *m.*, ēlegantia, -ae *f.*; (spell) carmen, -inis *n.*

chase *see* **hunt**

chase away abigō, abēgī, abactum 3.

chaste castus, -a, -um, pudīcus, -a, -um

chastity castitās, -ātis *f.*, pudīcitia, -ae *f.*

cheap vīlis, -is, -e

cheat (dē)fraudō 1., dēcipiō, dēcēpī, dēceptum 3., fallō, fefellī, falsum 3.

cheer clāmor, -ōris *m.*

cheerful hilaris, -is, -e, laetus, -a, -um

cheese cāseus, -ī *m.*

chef coquus, -ī *m.*

cherry-tree cerasus, -ī *f.*

chest arca, -ae *f.*, cista, -ae *f.*; (*of the body*) pectus, -oris *n.*

chestnut tree castanea, -ae *f.*

chew mandūcō 1.

chicken pullus, -ī *m.*

chief dux, dūcis *m.*, princeps, -cipis *m.*

chieftain rēgulus, -ī *m.*

child puer, -rī *m.*; **children** līberī, -ōrum *m. pl.*, puerī, -ōrum *m.pl.*; *see also* **son** *and* **daughter**

childhood pueritia, -ae *f.*

chin mentum, -ī *n.*

chip assula, -ae *f.*

choice (*act*) ēlectiō, -ōnis *f.*, dēlectus, -ūs *m.*; (*faculty*) optiō, -ōnis *f.*

choose optō 1., ēligō, ēlēgī, ēlectum 3., dēligō, dēlēgī, dēlectum 3.

chord nervus, -ī *m.*

circle circ(ul)us, -ī *m.*, orbis, -is *m.*, corōna, -ae *f.*

circumstance rēs, reī *f.*, tempus, -oris *n.*

citadel arx, arcis *f.*

citizen cīvis, -is *m./f.*

citizenship cīvitās, -ātis *f.*

city urbs, urbis *f.*; (town) oppidum, -ī *n.*

civic cīvicus, -a, -um, cīvīlis, -is, -e

claim vindicō 1., postulō 1.

claimant petītor, -ōris *m.*

clap *see* **applaud**

clarity clāritās, -ātis *f.*

class classis, -is *f.*, genus, -eris *n.*, ordō, -inis *m.*

claw unguis, -inis *m.*

clay argilla, -ae *f.*

clean pūrus, -a, -um, mundus, -a, -um; (*morally*) castus, -a, -um

cleanse purgō 1.

clear[1] (*adj.*) clārus, -a, -um, lūcidus, -a, -um; (obvious) manifestus, -a, -um, plānus, -a, -um, perspicuus, -a, -um

clear[2] (*v.*) expediō 4., purgō 1.

clear away āmoveō, āmōvī, āmōtum 2., dētergeō, -sī, -sum 2.

clearly clārē, lūcidē, plānē

cleave scindō, scidī, scissum 3., (dif)findō, (dif)fidī, (dif)fissum 3.

clemency clēmentia, -ae *f.*

clever callidus, -a, -um, intelligens, -ntis, astūtus, -a, -um, sollers, -rtis

cliff scopulus, -ī *m.*, rūpēs, -is *f.*, cautēs (cōtēs), -is *f.* (*esp.pl.*)

climb[1] (*noun*) ascensus, -ūs *m.*

climb² (*v.*) scandō, -dī, -sum 3., ascendō, -dī, -sum 3.

cling (to) (*+dat.*) (ad)haereō, -sī, -sum 2.

cloak pallium, -(i)ī *n.*, amiculum, -ī *n.*

clod glaeba, -ae *f.*

close claudō, -sī, -sum 3.; (shut up) interclūdō, -sī, -sum 3.

close to (*+acc.*) prope, iuxtā

cloth textum, -ī *n.*

clothe (in) (*+abl.*) vestiō 4., amiciō, amictum 4.

clothing vestītus, -ūs *m.*, vestīmentum, -ī *n.*, vestis, -is *f.*, amictus, -ūs *m.*

cloud nūbēs, -is *f.*; **raincloud** nimbus, -ī *m.*

clumsy ineptus, -a, -um, inhabilis, -is, -e

coachman aurīga, -ae *m.*, raedārius, -(i)ī *m.*

coal carbō, -ōnis *m.*

coast lītus, -oris *n.*, ōra, ōrae *f.*, acta, -ae *f.*

cock gallus, -ī *m.*

coffin arca, -ae *f.*, capsulus, -ī *m.*

coin nummus, -ī *m.*

cold¹ (*noun*) frīgus, -oris *n.*, algor, -ōris *m.*

cold² (*adj.*) frīgidus, -a, -um, glacidus, -a, -um

collar-bone iugulum, -ī *n.*

colleague collēga, -ae *m.*

collect colligō, collēgī, collectum 3.

collection caterva, -ae *f.*, grex, gregis *m.*

collide (with) (*+cum +abl.*) conflīgō, -flixī, -flictum 3.

colonnade porticus, -ūs *f.*

colony colōnia, -ae *f.*

colour¹ (*noun*) color, -ōris *m.*

colour² (*v.*) colōrō 1., tingō, -xī, -ctum 3.

column columna, -ae *f.*; **marching column** agmen, -inis *n.*

comb pecten, -inis *m.*

combat pugna, -ae *f.*, certāmen, -inis *n.*

combination coniunctiō, -ōnis *f.*

combine coniungō, -xī, -ctum 3., misceō, miscuī, mixtum 2.

come veniō, vēnī, ventum 4., accēdō, accessī, accessum 3.

come about *see* **happen**

come close proximō 1., adeō, adīre, adīvī (adiī), aditum 4.

come often ventitō 1.

come on! age (*pl.* agite)

come upon *see* **find**

comedy cōmoedia, -ae *f.*

comfort adlevō 1., (con)sōlor 1. *dep.*

command¹ (*noun*) imperium, -(i)ī *n.*, mandātum, -ī *n.*, iussum, -ī *n.*

command² (*v.*) (*+dat.*) imperō 1., iubeō, iussī, iussum 2.; (*armies*) (*+dat.*) praesum, praeesse, praefuī *v.irreg.*

commander praefectus, -ūs *m.*, dux, dūcis *m.*, imperātor, -ōris *m.*

commemorate celebrō 1.

commend laudō 1., commendō 1., probō 1.

commerce merx, mercis *f.* (*usu.pl.*), commercium, -(i)ī *n.*

commit (entrust) committō, -mīsī, -missum 3., mandō 1.; (do) faciō, fēcī, factum 3.; (*wrongdoings etc.*) peccō 1., errō 1.

common (shared) commūnis, -is, -e, pūblicus, -a, -um; (commonplace) frequens, -ntis, vulgāris, -is, -e

community cīvitās, -ātis *f.*, rēspūblica, rēīpūblicae *f.*

compact crassus, -a, -um, densus, -a, -um

companion comes, -itis *m.*, sodālis, -is *m.*, socius, -(i)ī *m.*

compare (with) (*+cum +abl.*) conferō, -ferre, -tulī, -lātum *v.irreg.*, comparō 1.

compel cōgō, coēgī, coactum 3., compellō, -pulī, pulsum 3.

compete certō 1., contendō, -dī, -tum 3.

competition certāmen, -inis *n.*, contentiō, -ōnis *f.*

complaint querimōnia, -ae *f.*, querēla, -ae *f.*, questus, -ūs *m.*

complete plēnus, -a, -um, absolūtus, -a, -um, integer, -gra, -grum

completely omnīnō, prorsus

comply (with) (*+dat.*) obsequor, obsecūtus 3. *dep.*

compose compōnō, -posuī, -positum 3.

composed of, am (*+abl. or +ex +abl.*) constō, constitī 1., consistō, constitī 3.

comprehend contineō, -tinuī, -tentum 2., complector, -plexus 3. *dep.*; (realize) intellegō, -xī, -ctum 3.

conceal abdō, abdidī, abditum 1., cēlō 1., occultō 1.

conceive concipiō, -cēpī, -ceptum 3.

concern (*+ad +acc.*) attineō, attinuī, attentum 2.; **it concerns me** meā (*etc.*) rēfert (rēferre, rētulī *v.irreg.*)

concerning (*+abl.*) dē

condemn condemnō 1., damnō 1.

condemnation condemnātiō, -ōnis *f.*,
damnātiō, -ōnis *f.*

condition status, -ūs *m.*, condiciō, -ōnis *f.*,
sors, sortis *f.*; (term) condiciō, -ōnis *f.*

conduct (dē)dūcō, (dē)duxī, (dē)ductum
3.; administrō 1.

confederacy foedus, -eris *n.*

confess confiteor, confessus 2. *dep.*, fateor,
fessus 2. *dep.*

confidence fīdūcia, -ae *f.*, fidēs, -ēī *f.*

confidence (in), have confīdō, -fīsus 2.
semi-dep.; (+*dat.*) fidem habeō 2.

confiscate pūblicō 1.

conflict certāmen, -inis *n.*, pugna, -ae *f.*

confound confundō, -fūdī, -fūsum 3.

confuse confundō, -fūdī, -fūsum 3.,
(per)turbō 1.

confusion confūsiō, -ōnis *f.*, (per)turbātiō,
-ōnis *f.*

congratulate (+*dat.*) grātulor 1. *dep.*

congregate congregor 1. *dep.*, conveniō 4.

connect alligō 1., connectō, -xī, -xum 3.

connected continuus, -a, -um, connexus,
-a, -um

conquer vincō, vīcī, victum 3., superō 1.

conqueror victor, -ōris *m.*

conscience conscientia, -ae *f.*

consent consensus, -ūs *m.*

conserve (con)servō 1.

consider arbitror 1. *dep.*, ponderō 1., consīderō 1., contemplor 1. *dep.*

consideration arbitrātiō, -ōnis *f.*, consīderātiō, -ōnis *f.*

consist of (+*ex* +*abl.*) constō, constitī 1.

conspire (against) (+*contrā* +*acc.*) coniūrō 1., conspīrō 1.

constant constans, -ntis, stabilis, -is, -e,
firmus, -a, -um; *see also* **faithful**

construct faciō, fēcī, factum 3., fabricor 1.
dep.

consul consul, -lis *m.*

consulship consulātus, -ūs *m.*

consult consulō, -uī, -tum 3., consultō 1.

consume consūmō, -sumpsī, -sumptum 3.

contain contineō, -tinuī, -tentum 2.,
capiō, cēpī, captum 3., compre(he)ndō,
-dī, -sum 3.

contemplate contemplor 1. *dep.*

contemporary aequālis, -is *m.*

contempt contemptus, -ūs *m.*, fastīdium,
-(i)ī *n.*

contend certō 1., contendō, -dī, -sum 3.,
pugnō 1.

contest certāmen, -inis *n.*, pugna, -ae *f.*,
contentiō, -ōnis *f.*

continent continens, -ntis *m.*

continual perpetuus, -a, -um, adsiduus, -a,
-um, continuus, -a, -um

continually perpetuō, adsiduē

continue continuō 1., prōdūcō, -duxī,
-ductum 3.

contract pactum, -ī *n.*, conventiō, -ōnis *f.*

contrary contrārius, -a, -um, adversus, -a,
-um

contrive inveniō, invēnī, inventum 4.,
excōgitō 1., māchinor 1. *dep.*

control[1] (*noun*) imperium, -(i)ī *n.*, potestās, -ātis *f.*

control[2] (*v.*) gubernō 1., regō, rēgī, rectum
3., regnō 1., moderor 1. *dep.*

convenient commodus, -a, -um, idōneus,
-a, -um, habilis, -is, -e

converse (with) (+*cum* +*abl.*) colloquor,
collocūtus 3. *dep.*

convex convexus, -a, -um

cook[1] (*noun*) coquus, -ī *m.*, magīrus, -ī *m.*

cook[2] (*v.*) coquō, coxī, coctum 3.

copious abundans, -ntis, largus, -a, -um

copper aes, aeris *n.*

copy exemplum, -ī *n.*

cord restis, -is *f.*, fūnis, -is *m./f.*, chorda, -ae
f.

cork cortex, -icis *m./f.*

corn frūmentum, -ī *n.*

corner angulus, -ī *m.*

corpse cadāver, -eris *n.*

correct corrigō, -rexī, -rectum 3.

cost (+*abl.*) constō, constitī 1.

costly pretiōsus, -a, -um, cārus, -a, -um

cough tussis, -is *f.*

council concilium, -(i)ī *n.*, consilium, -(i)ī
n.

count calculō 1., numerō 1.

country patria, -ae *f.*; (territory) fīnēs, -ium
m.pl., agrī, -ōrum *m.pl.*

countryside rūs, rūris *m.*; **in the countryside** rūrī

courage audācia, -ae *f.*, virtūs, -ūtis *f.*, fortitūdō, -inis *f.*, constantia, -ae *f.*

courageous audax, -ācis, fortis, -is, -e,
animōsus, -a, -um

courageously audacter, fortiter

course cursus, -ūs *m.*; (*of food*) ferculum, -ī *n.*

court area, -ae *f.*; (*royal*) aula, -ae *f.*

cousin (*paternal*) patruēlis, -is *m./f.*; (*maternal*) (con)sobrīnus, -ī *m.*, (con)sobrīna, -ae *f.*

cover operiō, -uī, -tum 4., tegō, texī, tectum 3.

cow bōs, bovis *m./f.*, vacca, -ae *f.*

cowardice ignāvia, -ae *f.*, timiditās, -ātis *f.*

cowardly ignāvus, -a, -um, timidus, -a, -um

cowherd armentārius, -(i)ī *m.*, bubulcus, -ī *m.*

crab cancer, -crī *m.*

crack rīma, -ae *f.*

cradle cūnābula, -ōrum *n.pl.*, cūnae, -ārum *f.pl.*

craftsman artifex, -ficis *m.*, opifex, -ficis *m.*

crag *see* **cliff**

cramped angustus, -a, -um, artus, -a, -um

crash fragor, -ōris *m.*, strepitus, -ūs *m.*

crawl rēpō, repsī, reptum 3., serpō, serpsī, serptum 3.

craziness āmentia, -ae *f.*, dēmentia, -ae *f.*

crazy āmens, -ntis, dēmens, -ntis

create creō 1., gignō, genuī, genitum 3., faciō, fēcī, factum 3.

creature animal, -ālis *n.*

credit fidēs, -ēī *f.*

creep *see* **crawl**

crest iuba, -ae *f.*, cresta, -ae *f.*

crime crīmen, -inis *n.*, facinus, -oris *n.*, scelus, -eris *n.*, dēlictum, -ī *n.*, flāgitium, -(i)ī *n.*, maleficium, -(i)ī *n.*

criminal scelestus, -a, -um, scelerātus, -a, -um

crisis discrīmen, -inis *n.*, tempus, -oris *n.*

criticize vituperō 1.

crooked prāvus, -a, -um

crop¹ (*noun*) messis, -is *f.*, frūgēs, -um *f.pl.*

crop² (*v.*) tondō, totondī, tonsum 3.

cross¹ (*noun*) crux, crucis *f.*

cross² (*v.*) trāiciō, trāiēcī, trāiectum 3., transgredior, -gressus 3. *dep.*

crow cornix, -īcis *f.*

crowd multitūdō, -inis *f.*, turba, -ae *f.*

crown corōna, -ae *f.*, diadēma, -atis *n.*

crude crūdus, -a, -um, rudis, -is, -e, incultus, -a, -um

cruel crūdēlis, -is, -e, ātrox, -ōcis, barbarus, -a, -um, saevus, -a, -um

cruelly crūdēliter, ātrōciter

cruelty crūdēlitās, -ātis *f.*, saevitia, -ae *f.*

crumb mīca, -ae *f.*

crush opprimō, oppressī, oppressum 3.

cry (weep) lacrimō 1., plōrō 1.; (shout) (con)clāmō 1., vōciferor 1. *dep.*

cub catulus, -ī *m.*

cudgel mulcō 1.

cultivate colō, coluī, cultum 3.

culture cultus, -ūs *m.*, cultūra, -ae *f.*

cunning¹ (*noun*) versūtia, -ae *f.*, calliditās, -ātis *f.*

cunning² (*adj.*) versūtus, -a, -um, vafer, vafra, vafrum, callidus, -a, -um

cup pōculum, -ī *n.*

cupboard armārium, -(i)ī *n.*

curb frēnō 1., cohibeō 2.

cure¹ (*noun*) remedium, -(i)ī *n.*, medicāmen, -inis *n.*

cure² (*v.*) sānō 1., medeor 2. *dep.*

curse imprecātiō, -ōnis *f.*

curved curvus, -a, -um, flexus, -a, -um

cushion pulvīnar, -āris *n.*

custom mōs, mōris *m.*, institūtum, -ī *n.*, ūsus, ūsūs *m.*

customary ūsitātus, -a, -um, solitus, -a, -um

customer emptor, -ōris *m.*

cut secō, secuī, sectum 1., caedō, cecīdī, caesum 3.

D

dagger pūgiō, -ōnis *m.*, sīca, -ae *f.*
daily¹ (*adj.*) cottidiānus (quōt-), -a, -um
daily² (*adv.*) cottidiē (quōt-), in diēs
dainty ēlegans, -ntis, dēlicātus, -a, -um
dam mōlēs, -is *f.*, agger, -eris *m.*
damage¹ (*noun*) damnum, -ī *n.*, dētrīmentum, -ī *n.*, noxa, -ae *f.*, incommodum, -ī *n.*; **damages** (legal) līs, lītis *f.*
damage² (*v.*) *see* **harm**²
damp ūmidus, -a, -um
dance¹ (*noun*) saltātiō, -ōnis *f.*
dance² (*v.*) saltō 1.
danger perīculum, -ī *n.*, discrīmen, -inis *n.*
dangerous perīculōsus, -a, -um, infestus,
-a, -um
dare audeō, ausus 2. *semi-dep.*
daring¹ (*noun*) audācia, ferōcia
daring² (*adj.*) audax, -ācis, ferox, -ōcis,
fortis, -is, -e
daringly audacter
dark (shady) cālīginōsus, -a, -um, obscūrus,
-a, -um, tenebrōsus, -a, -um; (*in colour*)
āter, ātra, ātrum, fuscus, -a, -um, niger,
nigra, nigrum
darken obscūrō 1., occaecō 1.
darkness tenebrae, -ārum *f.pl.*, cālīgō, -inis
f., obscūritās, -ātis *f.*
dart iaculum, -ī *n.*, tēlum, -ī *n.*
date diēs, diēī *m./f.*, tempus, -oris *n.*
daughter fīlia, -ae *f.*; (*poetic*) nāta, -ae *f.*
daughter-in-law nūrus, -ūs *f.*
dawn (prīma) lux, (prīmae) lūcis *f.*, dīlūculum, -ī *n.*, aurōra, -ae *f.*
day diēs, diēī *m./f.*; **for the day** in diem;
late in the day multō diē; **by day** interdiū; **period of two/three days** bīduum/
trīduum, -ī *n.*; **on the day before** prīdiē;
on the day after postrīdiē
dead mortuus, -a, -um, exanimis, -is, -e

(-us, -a, -um); **the dead** inferī, -ōrum *m.*
pl.
deadly lētālis, -is, -e, fātālis, -is, -e, mortifer,
-era, -erum, exitiālis, -is, -e
deaf surdus, -a, -um, auribus (*or* aure)
captus, -a, -um
deafness surditās, -ātis *f.*
deal out distribuō, -uī, -ūtum 3.
dealer negōtiātor, -ōris *m.*
dear cārus, -a, -um, pretiōsus, -a, -um
death mors, mortis *f.*, fūnus, -eris *n.*, lētum,
-ī *n.*, obitus, -ūs *m.*, nex, necis *f.*
debate¹ (*noun*) disputātiō, -ōnis *f.*, disceptātiō, -ōnis *f.*
debate² (*v.*) dēlīberō 1., disceptō 1., disputō 1.
debauchery stuprum, -ī *n.*
debt aes aliēnum, aeris aliēnī *n.*; **cancellation of debts** tabulae novae, tabu-
lārum novārum *f.pl.*
debtor dēbitor, -ōris *m.*
decay¹ (*noun*) tābēs, -is *f.*
decay² (*v.*) tābescō, tābuī 3., marcescō 3.
deceit fraus, -dis *f.*, fallācia, -ae *f.*, dolus, -ī
m.
deceitful fraudulentus, -a, -um, fallax,
-ācis, dolōsus, -a, -um
deceive dēcipiō, dēcēpī, dēceptum 3.,
fallō, fefellī, falsum 3., ēlūdō, -sī, -sum 3.,
fraudō 1.
decency honestās, -ātis *f.*
decent honestus, -a, -um, decens, -ntis
decide constituō, -uī, -ūtum 3., dēcernō,
dēcrēvī, dēcrētum 3., (dī)iūdicō 1.
decision dēcrētum, -ī *n.*, sententia, -ae *f.*,
dīiūdicātiō, -ōnis *f.*
declaim dēclāmō 1.
declare dēclārō 1., affirmō 1., praedicō 1.;
declare war bellum indīcō (indixī,
indictum 3.)

decline nōlō, nōlle, nōluī *v.irreg.*, recūsō 1.
decorate exornō 1., decorō 1.
decrease (make smaller) dēminuō, -uī, -ūtum 3.; (become smaller) dēcrescō, dēcrēvī, dēcrētum 3.
decree[1] (*noun*) dēcrētum, -ī *n.*, ēdictum, -ī *n.*; (*of the senate*) senātūsconsultum, -ī *n.*
decree[2] (*v.*) dēcernō, dēcrēvī, dēcrētum 3., ēdīcō, ēdixī, ēdictum 3.
dedicate consecrō 1.
deed factum, -ī *n.*, actum, -ī *n.*, rēs gesta, rēī gestae *f.*
deep altus, -a, -um, profundus, -a, -um
deeply altē, penitus
deer cervus, -ī *m.*
defeat[1] (*noun*) clādēs, -is *f.*
defeat[2] (*v.*) *see* **conquer**
defence praesidium, -(i)ī *n.*, dēfensiō, -ōnis *f.*
defend dēfendō, -dī, -sum 3., tueor, tuitus 2. *dep.*, tūtor 1. *dep.*
defendant reus, reī *m.*
deficiency *see* **lack**[2]
defile maculō 1., foedō 1., violō 1., spurcō 1.
definite certus, -a, -um, status, -a, -um, constitūtus, -a, -um
degree gradus, -ūs *m.*, ordō, -inis *m.*; **to some degree** aliquantum
degrees, by gradātim
deity deus, deī *m.*, nūmen, -inis *n.*
delay[1] (*noun*) mora, -ae *f.*, cunctātiō, -ōnis *f.*
delay[2] (*v.*) (make delayed) dētineō, dētinuī, dētentum 2., (re)moror 1. *dep.*, tardō 1.; (dally) cunctor 1. *dep.*, cessō 1.; (hesitate) dubitō 1.
deliberate dēlīberō 1., consīderō 1., consultō 1.
deliberately consultō, consīderātē
deliberation dēlīberātiō, -ōnis *f.*, consultātiō, -ōnis *f.*
delicacy ēlegantia, -ae *f.*
delicate ēlegans, -ntis, mollis, -is, -e, dēlicātus, -a, -um, tener, -era, -erum
delicious dulcis, -is, -e, suāvis, -is, -e
delight voluptās, -ātis *f.*, dēlectātiō, -ōnis *f.*
delightful iūcundus, -a, -um, suāvis, -is, -e, grātus, -a, -um
delights, it mē (*etc.*) iuvat 1. *impers.*, mē (*etc.*) dēlectat 1. *impers.*

demand[1] (*noun*) postulātiō, -ōnis *f.*, flāgitātiō, -ōnis *f.*
demand[2] (*v.*) postulō 1., poscō, poposcī 3., flāgitō 1.
demonstrate dēmonstrō 1., doceō, -uī, -tum 2., probō 1.
den specus, -ūs *m.*, latibulum, -ī *n.*
denounce increpō, -uī 1., vituperō 1.; (*legal*) accūsō 1.
dense densus, -a, -um, creber, -bra, -brum, crassus, -a, -um; *see also* **stupid**
deny abnuō, -uī, -ūtum 3., negō 1.
depart abeō, abīre, abīvī (abiī), abitum 4., abscēdō, abscessī, abscessum 3., ēgredior, ēgressus 3. *dep.*, excēdō, excessī, excessum 3., dēmigrō 1.
departure abitus, -ūs *m.*, discessus, -ūs *m.*, prōfectiō, -ōnis *f.*
depend (on) (+*ex* +*abl.*) pendeō, pependī, pensum 2.
deplore dēplōrō 1., dēfleō, dēflēvī, dēflētum 2.
deport dēportō 1.
deprecate dēprecor 1. *dep.*
deprive (of) (+*abl.*) prīvō 1., adimō, adēmī, ademptum 3., spoliō 1.
depth altitūdō, -inis *f.*
deputy lēgātus, -ūs *m.*
derive (+*ab* +*abl.*) trahō, -xī, -ctum, dēdūcō, dēduxī, dēductum 3.
descend dēscendō, -dī, -sum 3.
descendant prōgnātus, -ī *m.*
descent dēscensus, -ūs *m.*; (*family*) orīgō, -inis *f.*, genus, -eris *n.*
describe dēscrībō, dēscripsī, dēscriptum 3., dēpingō, -nxī, -ctum 3., dēmonstrō 1., ēnarrō 1.
desert dēserō, -uī, -tum 3., dēstituō, -uī 3., relinquō, relīquī, relictum 3.
deserter transfuga, -ae *m.*, perfuga, -ae *m.*
deserve mereor, meritus 2. *dep.* or mereō 2.
deservedly meritō, iūre
deserving (of) (+*abl.* or *gen.*) dignus, -a, -um
design *see* **plan**
desire[1] (*noun*) appetentia, -ae *f.*, appetītus, -ūs *m.*, cupīditās, -ātis *f.*
desire[2] (*v.*) optō 1., cupiō 4., appetō, -īvī (-iī), -ītum 3., dēsīderō 1.
desirous (of) (+*gen.*) cupidus, -a, -um, studiōsus, -a, -um, avidus, -a, -um
despair[1] (*noun*) dēspērātiō, -ōnis *f.*

despair² (*v.*) dēspērō 1.
despise contemnō, -mpsī, -mptum 3.,
dēspiciō, dēspexī, dēspectum 3., aspernor
1. *dep.*
despoil (of) (+*abl.*) spoliō 1.
destiny fātum, -ī *n.*, sors, sortis *f.*
destitution egestās, -ātis *f.*, inopia, -ae *f.*
destroy exscindō, -cidī, -cissum 3., dēleō,
-ēvī, -ētum 2., perdō, -didī, -ditum 3.,
ēvertō, -tī, -sum 3.
destruction exitium, -(i)ī *n.*, perniciēs, -ēī
f., ēversiō, -ōnis *f.*
destructive exitiōsus, -a, -um, perniciōsus,
-a, -um
detain retineō, retinuī, retentum 2.
determine dēcernō, dēcrēvī, dēcrētum 3.,
cōnstituō, -uī, -ūtum 3.
detest *see* **hate**
devastate (dē)vastō 1., (dē)populor 1. *dep.*
develop crescō, crēvī, crētum 3., adolescō,
adolēvī, adultum 3.
devoted (to) (+*dat.*) studiōsus, -a, -um,
dēditus, -a, -um
devotion studium, -(i)ī *n.*
devour (dē)vorō 1., consūmō, -sumpsī,
-sumptum 3.
dew rōs, rōris *m.*
dictate dictō 1.
dictator dictātor, -ōris *m.*
die morior, mortuus 3. *dep.*, (diem) obeō,
obīre, obīvī (obiī), obitum 4., (vītā)
excidō, -dī 3.
differ discrepō 1., dissentiō, -sī, -sum 4.,
differō, differre, distulī, dīlātum *v.irreg.*
difference discrīmen, -inis, *n.*, differentia,
-ae *f.*
different dissimilis, -is, -e, alius, -a, -um,
varius, -a, -um
differently dissimiliter, aliter, variē
difficult difficilis, -is, -e, arduus, -a, -um
difficulty difficultās, -ātis *f.*; **with difficulty** aegrē, vix, difficulter (-ciliter)
dig fodiō, fōdī, fossum 3.
dig up effodiō, -ōdī, -ossum 3.
dignity dignitās, -ātis *f.*, gravitās, -ātis *f.*,
honestās, -ātis *f.*
diligent *see* **careful**
dim obscūrus, -a, -um; (blunt) hebes, -etis
din strepitus, -ūs *m.*
dine cēnō 1.
dinner cēna, -ae *f.*; (*morning meal*) prandium, -(i)ī *n.*

dip mergō, -sī, -sum 3., tingō, -xī, -ctum 3.
dire ātrox, -ōcis, dīrus, -a, -um
direct¹ (*v.*) dīrigō, dīrexī, dīrectum 3.,
gubernō 1., regō, rexī, rectum 3., administrō 1.
direct² (*adj.*) rectus, -a, -um
directly rectā
dirt caenum, -ī *n.*, sordēs, -is *f.*
dirty sordidus, -a, -um, illōtus, -a, -um,
luteus, -a, -um
disadvantage incommodum, -ī *n.*
disadvantageous incommodus, -a, -um,
inīquus, -a, -um
disaffected (ab)aliēnātus, -a, -um
disagree (with) (+*cum* or *ab* +*abl.*) dissentiō, -sī, -sum 4., discrepō 1.
disagreeable molestus, -a, -um, iniūcundus, -a, -um, gravis, -is, -e
disagreement dissensiō, -ōnis *f.*, dissidium, -(i)ī *n.*
disallow vetō, vetuī, vetitum 1.
disappear abolescō, -lēvī, -lētum 3., ēvānescō, -nuī 3.
disapprove commendō 1., improbō 1.
disaster calamitās, -ātis *f.*, cāsus, -ūs *m.*,
clādēs, -is *f.*
disastrous perniciōsus, -a, -um, calamitōsus, -a, -um
disc orbis, -is *m.*
discharge (*duties*) (+*acc./abl.*) fungor,
functus 3. *dep.*
discipline disciplīna, -ae *f.*, studium, -(i)ī *n.*
discord discordia, -ae *f.*, dissidium, -(i)ī *n.*
discordant dissonus, -a, -um, discors, -rdis
discourage (+*ab* or *dē* +*abl.*) dēterreō 2.
discover reperiō, repperī, repertum 4.,
inveniō, invēnī, inventum 4., cognoscō,
-nōvī, -nitum 3.
discoverer inventor, -ōris *m.*
discovery inventiō, -ōnis *f.*; (thing discovered) inventum, -ī *n.*
discretion prūdentia, -ae *f.*, iūdicium, -(i)ī
n.
discuss disserō, -uī, -tum 3., dēlīberō 1.,
disceptō 1., agitō 1.
discussion disceptātiō, -ōnis *f.*
disease morbus, -ī *m.*, aegritūdō, -inis *f.*
disgrace¹ (*noun*) ignōminia, -ae *f.*, turpitūdō, -inis *f.*, infāmia, -ae *f.*, dēdecus, -oris
n.
disgrace² (*v.*) dēdecorō 1.

disgraceful turpis, -is, -e, inhonestus, -a, -um

dish patella, -ae *f.*, lanx, lancis *f.*

dishonest improbus, -a, -um, fraudulentus, -a, -um

dishonestly improbē, fraudulenter

dishonesty improbitās, -ātis *f.*, fraus, -dis *f.*

dishonour *see* **disgrace**

dislike[1] (*noun*) odium, -(i)ī *n.* fastīdium, -(i)ī *n.*

dislike[2] (*v.*) fastīdiō 4.

disloyal infīdus, -a, -um, improbus, -a, -um

dismiss ablegō 1., dīmittō, dīmīsī, dīmissum 3.

dismissal dīsmissiō, -ōnis *f.*

disorder tumultus, -ūs *m.*, confūsiō, -ōnis *f.*, (per)turbātiō, -ōnis *f.*

disperse (go apart) dīlābor, dīlapsus 3. *dep.*; (send apart) dissipō 1., dispellō, -pulī, -pulsum 3.

display ostendō, -dī, -sum (-tum) 3., ostentō 1., exhibeō 2.

displease (+*dat.*) displiceō 2.

disregard[1] (*noun*) neglegentia, -ae *f.*, incūria, -ae *f.*

disregard[2] (*v.*) neglegō, -xī, -ctum 3., omittō, omīsī, omissum 3.

disrespect insolentia, -ae *f.*

disrespectful insolens, -ntis

dissemble dissimulō 1.

dissension discordia, -ae *f.*, sēditiō, -ōnis *f.*

dissimilar *see* **different**

distance spatium, -(i)ī *n.*, longinquitās, -ātis *f.*, intervallum, -ī *n.*; **at a distance** longē, procul

distant longinquus, -a, -um, remōtus, -a, -um

distinct distinctus, -a, -um, disiunctus, -a, -um, sēparātus, -a, -um; *see also* **clear**[1]

distinction discrīmen, -inis *n.*; (honour) honōs (-or), -ōris *m.*, decus, -oris *n.*

distinguish distinguō, -nxī, -nctum 3., dīiūdicō 1.

distinguished praeclārus, -a, -um, insignis, -is, -e

distribute distribuō, -uī, -ūtum 3., dīvidō, dīvīsī, dīvīsum 3.

district regiō, -ōnis *f.*, terra, -ae *f.*

distrust (+*dat.*) diffīdō, diffīsus 3. *semi-dep.*

distrustful diffīdens, -ntis, suspīciōsus, -a, -um

disturb (per)turbō 1., commoveō, -mōvī, -mōtum 2.

disturbance tumultus, -ūs *m.*, turbātiō, -ōnis *f.*

ditch fossa, -ae *f.*

divide dīvidō, dīvīsī, dīvīsum 3., abiungō, -nxī, -nctum 3., sēiungō, -nxī, -nctum 3., partiō 4. *or* partior 4. *dep.*

divine dīvīnus, -a, -um, dī(v)us, -a, -um, caelestis, -is, -e, sacer, sacra, sacrum, sanctus, -a, -um

do faciō, fēcī, factum 3., efficiō, effēcī, effectum 3., agō, ēgī, actum 3., gerō, gessī, gestum 3.

doctor medicus, -ī *m.*

document litterae, -ārum *f.pl.*, tabula, -ae *f.*, instrūmentum, -ī *n.*

doe cerva, -ae *f.*

doer actor, -ōris *m.*, auctor, -ōris *m.*

dog canis, -is *m./f.*

dolphin delphīnus, -ī *m.*

donkey asellus, -ī *m.*, asinus, -ī *m.*

door iānua, -ae *f.*, forēs, -ium *m.pl.*, ostium, -(i)ī *n.*, valvae, -ārum *f.pl.*; **backdoor** postīcum, -ī *n.*

double duplex, -icis, geminus, -a, -um, anceps, ancipitis

doubt[1] (*noun*) dubium, -(i)ī *n.*, dubitātiō, -ōnis *f.*; **without doubt** sine dubiō, haud dubiē

doubt[2] (*v.*) (ad)dubitō 1.

dove columba, -ae *f.*, palumbēs, -is *m./f.*

down from (+*abl.*) dē

downwards deōrsus (-um), dēsuper

dowry dōs, dōtis *m.*

drag trahō, -xī, -ctum 3.

dragon dracō, -ōnis *m.*, serpens, -ntis *f.*

drain exhauriō, -sī, -sum 4.; (*fields*) siccō 1.

draw trahō, -xī, -ctum 3., dūcō, duxī, ductum 3.; (*weapons*) stringō, -nxī, -ctum 3.; (*liquids*) exhauriō, -sī, -sum 4.

draw near *see* **approach**[2]

draw up (*soldiers*) instruō, -uxī, -uctum 3.; (*laws*) scrībō, scripsī, scriptum 3.

dread *see* **fear**

dreadful *see* **awful**

dream[1] (*noun*) somnium, -(i)ī *n.*

dream[2] (*v.*) somniō 1., dormitō 1.

dress[1] (*noun*) vestis, -is *f.*, vestītus, -ūs *m.*

dress[2] (*v.*) vestiō 4.

drill perforō 1., terebrō 1.

drink[1] (*noun*) pōtiō, -ōnis *f.*, pōtus, -ūs *m.*

drink² (*v.*) bibō, bibī, bibitum 3., pōtō 1.

drip stillō 1.

drive agō, ēgī, actum 3., pellō, pepulī, pulsum 3., agitō 1.; (travel) (in)vehor, (in)vectus 3. **dep.**

drive away abigō, abēgī, abactum 3., exigō, exēgī, exactum 3., fugō 1.

drive back repellō, repulī, repulsum 3.

drive out expellō, expulī, expulsum 3., exturbō 1.

driver raedārius, -(i)ī *m.*, aurīga, -ae *m.*

drop (let go) dēmittō, dēmīsī, dēmissum 3.; (give up) omittō, omīsī, omissum 3.

drop gutta, -ae *f.*, stilla, -ae *f.*

drunk ēbrius, -a, -um, tēmulentus, -a, -um

dry¹ (*adj.*) siccus, -a, -um, āridus, -a, -um

dry² (*v.*) (make dry) siccō 1.; (dry up) ārescō, āruī 3.

duck anas, anatis *f.*

dull hebes, -etis, obtūsus, -a, -um; (stupid) tardus, -a, -um, brūtus, -a, -um

duly rīte

dumb mūtus, -a, -um

dung merda, -ae *f.*, stercus, -oris *n.*

during (+*acc.*) per, inter

dusk crepusculum, -ī *n.*

dusky fuscus, -a, -um

dust pulvis, -eris *m.*

duty officium, -(i)ī *n.*, mūnus, -eris *n.*; (piety) pietās, -ātis *f.*, religiō, -ōnis *f.*

dwarf nānus, -ī *m.*

E

each quisque, quaeque, quidque (quicque), omnis, -is, -e; **each of two** uterque,
utraque, utrumque; **from each side**
utrimque; **in each direction** utrōque

eager (for) (+*gen.*) cupidus, -a, -um, alacer,
-cris, -cre, avidus, -a, -um, studiōsus, -a,
-um; *see also* **keen**

eagerly cupidē, studiōsē

eagerness cupīditās, -ātis *f.*, studium, -(i)ī
n., aviditās, -ātis *f.*, ardor, -ōris *m.*

eagle aquila, -ae *f.*

ear auris, -is *f.*

ear of corn spīca, -ae *f.*, arista, -ae *f.*

early¹ (*adj.*) (in the day) mātūtīnus, -a,
-um; mātūrus, -a, -um

early² (*adv.*) (in the day) māne; mātūrē

earn mereor 2. *dep. or* mereō 2.

earnestly magnopere, vehementer

earth (ground) terra, -ae *f.*, humus, -ī *f.*,
solum, -ī *n.*; (planet) terrārum orbis, -is
m., tellūs, -ūris *f.*

earthquake terrae mōtus, -ūs, *m.*

easily facile

east oriens, -ntis *m.*

easy facilis, -is, -e; (relaxed) placidus, -a,
-um, tranquillus, -a, -um

eat edō, esse, ēdī, ēsum *v.irreg.*; (+*abl.*)
vescor 3. *dep.*

edge margō, -inis *m.*, labrum, -ī *n.*, ōra, ōrae
f.

educate doceō, docuī, doctum 2., ērudiō
4., instituō, -uī, -ūtum 3., ēducō 1.

education ēducātiō, -ōnis *f.*, ērudītiō, -ōnis
f., doctrīna, -ae *f.*, litterae, -ārum *f.pl.*

eel anguilla, -ae *f.*

effect¹ (*v.*) efficiō, effēcī, effectum 3., faciō,
fēcī, factum 3.

effect² (*noun.*) ēventus, -ūs *m.*, effectus, -ūs
m.

effective, efficient efficax, -ācis

effort opera, -ae *f.*, labor, -ōris *m.*, cōnātus,
-ūs *m.*

egg ōvum, ōvī *n.*

eight octō

eighteen duodēvīgintī

eighth octāvus, -a, -um; **eight times**
octiens (-iēs)

eighty octōgintā

either (of two) alteruter, -tra, -trum, uterque, utraque, utrumque; **either ... or** aut
... aut, vel ... vel

elated ēlātus, -a, -um

elbow cubitum, -ī *n.*

elect optō 1., ēligō, ēlēgī, ēlectum 3., creō
1., dēsignō 1.

election comitia, -ōrum *n.pl.*

elegant ēlegans, -ntis, bellus, -a, -um,
comptus, -a, -um

elegy elegeia (-gīa), -ae *f.*

elephant elephantus, -ī *or* elephans (-ās),
-ntis *m.*

eleven undecim; **eleven times** undeciens
(-iēs)

elm ulmus, -ī *f.*

eloquence ēloquentia, -ae *f.*

eloquent ēloquens, -ntis, fācundus, -a,
-um

else¹ (*adj.*) alius, -a, -um

else² (*adv.*) (otherwise) aliter; (besides)
praetereā

elsewhere alibī

embankment agger, -eris *m.*

embark nāvem conscendō (-dī, -sum 3.)

embrace amplector, amplexus 3. *dep.*,
complector, complexus 3. *dep.*

emend ēmendō 1., corrigō, -rexī, -rectum
3.

emendation ēmendātiō, -ōnis *f.*

emerge ēmergō, -sī, -sum 3., appāreō 2.

emergency discrīmen, -inis *n.*, cāsus, -ūs *m.*

emperor imperātor, -ōris *m.*, princeps, -cipis *m.*, dominus, -ī *m.*

empire imperium, -(i)ī *n.*, principātus, -ūs *m.*, regnum, -ī *n.*

employ (+*abl.*) ūtor, ūsus 3. *dep.*; (+*acc.*) ūsurpō 1.

empty inānis, -is, -e, vacuus, -a, -um, cassus, -a, -um; (vain) vānus, -a, -um

encamp castra pōnō (posuī, positum 3.)

encourage adhortor 1. *dep.*, cohortor 1. *dep.*, excitō 1.

end[1] (*noun*) fīnis, -is *m.*, exitus, -ūs *m.*

end[2] (*v.*) (bring to an end) fīniō 4.; (+*dat.*) fīnem impōnō (imposuī, impositum 3.)

endanger perīclitor 1. *dep.*

endless infinītus, -a, -um, aeternus, -a, -um, perpetuus, -a, -um

endurance patientia, -ae *f.*, tolerantia, -ae *f.*

endure patior, passus 3. *dep.*, tolerō 1., perferō, perferre, pertulī, perlātum *v.irreg.*

enemy (*public*) hostis, -is *m.*; (*private*) inimīcus, -a, -um

energetic strēnuus, -a, -um, impiger, -gra, -grum

energy vigor, -ōris *m.*, impetus, -ūs *m.*, contentiō, -ōnis *f.*, vīs, vīs *f.*

engage (with) (+*cum* +*abl.*) congredior, congressus 3. *dep.*

engine machīna, -ae *f.*

enjoy (+*abl.*) fruor, fructus 3. *dep.*, gaudeō, gāvīsus 2. *semi-dep.*; (have) (+*abl.*) ūtor, ūsus 3. *dep.*

enlist conscrībō, -scripsī, -scriptum 3.

enmity inimīcitia, -ae *f.*, odium, -(i)ī *n.*, invidia, -ae *f.*

enormous immānis, -is, -e, ingens, -ntis, vastus, -a, -um, immensus, -a, -um

enough satis, sat; **more than enough** nimis; **not enough** parum

enquire quaerō, quaesīvī, quaesītum 3., (inter)rogō 1., sciscitō 1.

enter ingredior, ingressus 3. *dep.*, intrō 1., ineō, inīre, inīvī (iniī), initum 4.

enthusiastic fervidus, -a, -um, vehemens, -ntis, ardens, -ntis

entirely omnīnō, plānē, prorsus

entrance aditus, -ūs *m.*

entreat ōrō 1., obsecrō 1., precor 1. *dep.*, rogō 1.

entreaty precēs, -um *f.pl.*, obsecrātiō, -ōnis *f.*

entrust mandō 1., permittō, -mīsī, -missum 3., commendō 1.

envy[1] (*noun*) invidia, -ae *f.*, malevolentia, -ae *f.*, līvor, -ōris *m.*

envy[2] (*v.*) (+*dat.*) invideō, invīsī, invīsum 2.

epigram epigramma, -atis *n.*

equal[1] (*noun*) aequus, -a, -um, pār, paris, aequālis, -is, -e

equal[2] (*v.*) (ad)aequō 1.

equality aequālitās, -ātis *f.*

equally aequē, pariter

equip instruō, -xī, -ctum 3., armō 1., ornō 1.

equipment arma, -ōrum *n.pl.*, instrūmenta, -ōrum *n.pl.*

err errō 1., peccō 1.

error error, -ōris *m.*, peccātum, -ī *n.*, errātum, -ī *n.*

escape[1] (*v.*) effugiō, effūgī 3., ēvādō, -sī, -sum 3.

escape[2] (*noun*) fuga, -ae *f.*, effugium, -(i)ī *n.*

escort[1] (*noun*) comitātus, -ūs *m.*

escort[2] (*v.*) comitor 1. *dep.*, prōsequor, -secūtus 3. *dep.*, dēdūcō, dēduxī, dēductum 3.

especially praesertim, praecipuē, potissimum

establish instituō, -uī, -ūtum 3.; (make firm) confirmō 1., stabiliō 4.; (prove) probō 1.

estate villa, -ae *f.*, fundus, -ī *m.*, praedium, -(i)ī *n.*

esteem aestimō 1., putō 1.

estimate aestimō 1., censeō 2.

eternal aeternus, -a, -um, perpetuus, -a, -um, sempiternus, -a, -um

eternally perpetuō, in aeternum

eternity aeternitās, -ātis *f.*

ether aether, -eris *m.*

evade vītō 1., (ef)fugiō, (ef)fūgī 3.

even[1] (*adj.*) plānus, -a, -um, pār, paris, aequus, -a, -um

even[2] (*adv.*) etiam, vel, quoque; **not even** nē ... quidem; **even if** et(iam) sī

evening[1] (*noun*) vesper, -erī (-eris) *m. or* vespera, -ae *f.*; **in the evening** vesperī

evening[2] (*adj.*) vespertīnus, -a, -um

ever umquam; (always) semper, perpetuō

every, everyone omnis, -is, -e, quisque,

quaeque, quidque (quicque); **from every side** undique

everywhere ubīque, passim

evidence indicium, -(i)ī *n.*, argūmentum, -ī *n.*

evil¹ (*noun*) malum, -ī *n.*, incommodum, -ī *n.*

evil² (*adj.*) malus, -a, -um, improbus, -a, -um, prāvus, -a, -um

exact¹ (*adj.*) exactus, -a, -um, dīligens, -ntis

exact² (*v.*) **(from)** (+*ab* +*abl.*) exigō, exēgī, exactum 3.

exaggerate augeō, auxī, auctum 2.

examine perspiciō, -spexī, -spectum 3., investīgō 1., (per)scrūtor 1. *dep.*

example exemplum, -ī *n.*, exemplar, -āris *n.*, specimen, -inis *n.*; **for example** verbī causā, exemplī grātiā

exasperate irrītō 1., exasperō 1.

exceed superō 1., antestō, -stetī 1., excēdō, excessī, excessum 3.

excellent excellens, -ntis, optimus, -a, -um, praestans, -ntis, praeclārus, -a, -um

excellently excellenter, optimē, praeclārē

except praeter

excessive nimius, -a, -um, immodicus, -a, -um

exchange (per)mūtō 1.

excite concitō 1., excitō 1., commoveō, -mōvī, -mōtum 2.

excited trepidus, -a, -um

excited, am trepidō 1., concursō 1.

exclaim exclāmō 1., (con)clāmō 1.

excrement merda, -ae *f.*, stercus, -oris *n.*

excuse excūsō 1., (ex)purgō 1.; *see also* **pardon²**

execution supplicium, -(i)ī *n.*

executioner carnifex, -ficis *m.*

exercise exerceō 2.

exertion labor, -ōris *m.*, sūdor, -ōris *m.*, contentiō, -ōnis *f.*, cōnātus, -ūs *m.*

exhale (ex)hālō 1.

exhausted dēfessus, -a, -um, confectus, -a, -um

exhort *see* **encourage**

exile (man) exul, -lis *m.*, profugus, -ī *m.*; (state) exilium, -(i)ī *n.*

exile, am an exulō 1.

exist sum, esse, fuī *v.irreg.*, exsistō, exstitī 3.

exit¹ (*noun*) exitus, -ūs *m.*, ēgressus, -ūs *m.*

exit² (*v.*) *see* **go out**

expect exspectō 1., prōvideō, -vīdī, -vīsum 2., spērō 1.

expediency ūtilitās, -ātis *f.*

expedient ūtilis, -is, -e, commodus, -a, -um

expel abigō, abēgī, abactum 3., expellō, expulī, expulsum 3.

expense impendium, -(i)ī *n.*, sumptus, -ūs *m.*

expensive cārus, -a, -um, sumptuōsus, -a, -um, pretiōsus, -a, -um

experience experior, expertus 4. *dep.*, patior, passus 3. *dep.*

experienced perītus, -a, -um, expertus, -a, -um, exercitātus, -a, -um

expert artifex, -icis *m.*

expiate luō, luī 3., expiō 1.

explain expōnō, exposuī, expositum 3., explicō 1., ēnōdō 1.

express exprimō, expressī, expressum 3., significō 1., dēmonstrō 1.

expression (*of the face*) vultus, -ūs *m.*; (*of speech*) vox, vōcis *f.*, locūtiō, -ōnis *f.*, verbum, -ī *n.*

expurgate (ex)purgō 1.

extend (make wider) extendō, -dī, -sum 3.; (am spread out) pateō 2.

extensive amplus, -a, -um, lātus, -a, -um, magnus, -a, -um

external externus, -a, -um, exterior, -or, -us

extreme summus, -a, -um, ultimus, -a, -um, maximus, -a, -um, extrēmus, -a, -um

exult in (+*abl.*) exsultō 1., gestiō 1., glōrior 1. *dep.*, laetor 1. *dep.*

eye oculus, -ī *m.*; (*poetic*) ocellus, -ī *m.*, lūmen, -inis *n.*

eyebrow supercilium, -(i)ī *n.*

F

face¹ (*noun*) faciēs, -ēī *f.*, vultus, -ūs *m.*, ōs, ōris *n.*

face² (*v.*) (a)spectō 1.; *see also* **meet**

fact rēs, reī *f.*, factum, -ī *n.*

faction factiō, -ōnis *f.*, pars, partis *f.*

factory officīna, -ae *f.*, fabrica, -ae *f.*

fade ēvānescō, -nuī 3.

fail (+*dat.*) dēsum, deesse, dēfuī *v.irreg.*, dēficiō, dēfēcī, dēfectum 3.; (not to succeed) concidō, -cidī, -cīsum 3.

failure dēfectiō, -ōnis *f.*

faint collābor, -lapsus 3. *dep.*

fair aequus, -a, -um, iustus, -a, -um; *see also* **beautiful**

fairly aequē, iustē; (slightly) mediocriter

fairness aequitās, -ātis *f.*

faith fidēs, -ēī *f.*, fidēlitās, -ātis *f.*

faithful fidēlis, -is, -e

fall¹ (*noun*) cāsus, -ūs *m.*, lapsus, -ūs *m.*

fall² (*v.*) cadō, cecidī, cāsum 3., dēlābor, dēlapsus 3. *dep.*, ruō, ruī, rutum 3.; (die) pereō, perīre, perīvī (-iī), peritum 4., occidō, -idī, -īsum 3.

fall ill aegrescō 3.

fall into (+*in* +*acc.*) incidō, incidī, incīsum 3.

false falsus, -a, -um, fictus, -a, -um, commentīcius, -a, -um; (lying) mendax, -ācis, fallax, -ācis, perfidus, -a, -um

falsehood mendācium, -(i)ī *n.*, falsum, -ī *n.*

falsely falsō, perperam

fame fāma, -ae *f.*, glōria, -ae *f.*, laus, -dis *f.*

familiar nōtus, -a, -um, familiāris, -is, -e

family familia, -ae *f.*, gens, gentis *f.*, domus, -ūs *f.*, cognātiō, -ōnis *f.*

famine famēs, -is *f.*, (cibī) inopia, -ae *f.*

famous fāmōsus, -a, -um, (prae)clārus, -a, -um, illustris, -is, -e

far procul, longē; **by far** multō, longē; **as far as** (+*abl.*) tenus

fare (*for travel*) vectūra, -ae *f.*; (food) cibus, -ī *m.*, victus, -ūs *m.*

farewell valē(te), avē(te)

farm fundus, -ī *m.*, praedium, -(i)ī *m.*, ager, agrī *m.*, villa, -ae *f.*

farmer agricola, -ae *m.*, cultor, -ōris *m.*, arātor, -ōris *m.*

farming agricultūra, -ae *f.*, rēs rusticae, rērum rusticārum *f.pl.*

fashion mōs, mōris *m.*, consuētūdō, -inis *f.*, rītus, -ūs *m.*; (*of dress*) ornātus, -ūs *m.*, habitus, -ūs *m.*

fast¹ (*adj.*) vēlox, -ōcis, rapidus, -a, -um, celer, -era, -erum, citus, -a, -um, pernix, -īcis; (firm) firmus, -a, -um, stabilis, -is, -e

fast² (*adv.*) celeriter, rapidē

fasten (al)ligō 1., (af)fīgō, affixī, affixum 3.

fasten together *see* **bind**

fat¹ (*noun*) arvīna, -ae *f.*, adeps, adipis *f.*

fat² (*adj.*) crassus, -a, -um, obēsus, -a, -um, pinguis, -is, -e, sagīnātus, -a, -um

fatal perniciōsus, -a, -um, fātālis, -is, -e, lētālis, -is, -e, fūnestus, -a, -um, exitiōsus, -a, -um

fate fātum, -ī *n.*, sors, sortis *f.*, fortūna, -ae *f.*

father pater, patris *m.*, genitor, -ōris *m.*, parens, -ntis *m.*

father-in-law socer, -erī *m.*

fatherland patria, -ae *f.*

fatigue lassitūdō, -inis *f.*, (dē)fatīgātiō, -ōnis *f.*

fatigued (dē)fessus, -a, -um, lassus, -a, -um

fault culpa, -ae *f.*, vitium, -(i)ī *n.*, noxa, -ae *f.*, menda, -ae *f.*, peccātum, -ī *n.*

faultless innocens, -ntis, integer, -gra, -grum

favour¹ (*noun*) grātia, -ae *f.*, favor, -ōris *m.*, benevolentia, -ae *f.*; (act) beneficium, -(i)ī *n.*

favour² (*v.*) (+*dat.*) faveō, fāvī, fautum 2.,
suffrāgor 1. *dep.*

favourable commodus, -a, -um, idōneus,
-a, -um, secundus, -a, -um, faustus, -a,
-um

favourably commodē, prosperē

fawn upon adulor 1. *dep.*

fear¹ (*noun*) metus, -ūs *m.*, timor, -ōris *m.*,
terror, -ōris *m.*, pavor, -ōris *m.*

fear² (*v.*) timeō 2., metuō, metuī 3., pertimescō, -muī 3., vereor, veritus 2. *dep.*

fearful timidus, -a, -um, pavidus, -a, -um,
trepidus, -a, -um; (frightful) dīrus, -a,
-um, terribilis, -is, -e

feast epulae, -ārum *f.pl.*, convivium, -(i)ī *n.*

feather penna, -ae *f.*, pinna, -ae *f.*, plūma,
-ae *f.*

fee mercēs, -ēdis *f.*

feed alō, aluī, altum 3., nūtriō 4., pascō,
pāvī, pastum 3.; (+*abl.*) vescor 3. *dep.*

feel tangō, tetigī, tactum 3., temptō 1.;
(experience) sentiō, sensī, sensum 4.,
percipiō, -cēpī, -ceptum 3.

female¹ (*noun*) fēmina, -ae *f.*, mulier, -ris *f.*

female², feminine (*adj.*) muliebris, -is, -e,
fēmineus, -a, -um

fence saepēs, -is *f.*

fertile fēcundus, -a, -um, ferax, -ācis, ūber,
-ris

festival diēs festus, diēī festī *m.*, feriae,
-ārum *f.pl.*

fetch addūcō, adduxī, adductum 3.,
(af)ferō, (af)ferrē, (at)tulī, (al)lātum *v.*
irreg., apportō 1.

fetters catēna, -ae *f.*, compes, -edis *f.*, vinculum, -ī *n.*

fever febris, -is *f.*

few paucī, -ae, -a, rārī, rārae, rāra; **very few**
perpaucī, -ae, -a

fewer minus

fickle levis, -is, -e, inconstans, -ntis, mūtābilis, -is, -e, varius, -a, -um

field ager, agrī *m.*, arvum, -ī *n.*, campus, -ī
m.

fierce ferox, -ōcis, ferus, -a, -um, ātrox,
-ōcis, saevus, -a, -um, trux, trucis, immānis, -is, -e

fiercely ferōciter, ātrōciter

fiery flammeus, -a, -um, igneus, -a, -um

fifteen quindecim; **fifteen times** quindeciens (-iēs)

fifth quintus, -a, -um

fiftieth quinquāgensimus (-gēs-), -a, -um

fifty quinquāgintā

fig fīcus, -ī *m.*

fight¹ (*noun*) pugna, -ae *f.*, certāmen, -inis
n.

fight² (*v.*) (dē)pugnō 1., dīgladior 1. *dep.*,
proelior 1. *dep.*, bellō 1.; (*to the death*)
dīmicō 1.; (*a battle*) proelium committō
(-mīsī, -missum 3.)

fighter pugnātor, -ōris *m.*

fig-tree fīcus, -ī (-ūs) *f.*

figure figūra, -ae *f.*, forma, -ae *f.*, faciēs, -ēī
f.; (image) imāgō, -inis *f.*

file¹ (*noun*) līma, -ae *f.*

file² (*v.*) līmō 1., (ex)poliō 4.

fill oppleō, opplēvī, opplētum 2., impleō,
implēvī, implētum 2., compleō, com-
plēvī, complētum 2.

final ultimus, -a, -um, extrēmus, -a, -um

finally postrēmō, dēnique

find reperiō, repperī, repertum 4., inveniō,
invēnī, inventum 4.

find out cognoscō, -nōvī, -nitum 3.

fine formōsus, -a, -um, pulc(h)er, -c(h)ra,
-c(h)rum, bellus, -a, -um; *see also* **thin**

finger digitus, -ī *m.*

finish perficiō, -fēcī, -fectum 3., conficiō,
-fēcī, -fectum 3., absolvō, -vī, -ūtum 3.;
(put an end to) terminō 1., fīniō 4.

fir abies, -etis *f.*

fire ignis, -is *m.*, incendium, -(i)ī *n.*,
flamma, -ae *f.*; (spirit) ardor, -ōris *m.*

firm firmus, -a, -um, solidus, -a, -um, constans, -ntis, stabilis, -is, -e

firmly firmē, solidē, constanter

firmness firmitūdō, -inis *f.*, stabilitās, -ātis
f.

first prīmus, -a, -um; (first of two) *see* **former**

first name praenōmen, -inis *n.*

firstly prīmum, prīmō

fish piscis, -is *m.*

fisherman piscātor, -ōris *m.*

fishing-rod (h)arundō, -inis *f.*

fist pugnus, -ī *m.*

fit aptō 1., accommodō 1.

fit out (ex)ornō 1., instruō, -uxī, -uctum 3.

fitted aptus, -a, -um, habilis, -is, -e, idōneus, -a, -um, commodus, -a, -um

five quinque; **five times** quinquiens (-iēs);
five-year period lustrum, -ī *n.*, quinquennium, -(i)ī *n.*

fix (set in place) (dē)fīgō, (dē)fīxī, (dē)fīxum 3.; (mend) reparō 1.

fixed fixus, -a, -um, certus, -a, -um, firmus, -a, -um

flag signum, -ī *n.*, vexillum, -ī *n.*

flame flamma, -ae *f.*

flank latus, -eris *n.*

flash micō 1., splendeō 2., fulgeō, fulsī, fulsum 2.

flask uter, utris *m.*, ampulla, -ae *f.*

flat aequus, -a, -um, plānus, -a, -um

flats, block of insula, -ae *f.*

flatter blandior 4. *dep.*, adulor 1. *dep.*; (+*dat.*) assentior, assensus 4. *dep.*

flattery adulātiō, -ōnis *f.*, blanditia, -ae *f.*

flavour sapor, -ōris *m.*, sūcus, -ī *m.*

flaw mendum, -ī *n.*, vitium, -(i)ī *n.*

flawless *see* **faultless**

flax līnum, -ī *n.*

flee (ef)fugiō, (ef)fūgī 3.

fleece vellus, -eris *n.*

fleet classis, -is *f.*

fleeting fugax, -ācis, fluxus, -a, -um

flesh cārō, carnis *f.*, corpus, -oris *n.*, viscera, -um *n.pl.*

flight (fleeing) fuga, -ae *f.*; (flying) volātus, -ūs *m.*, lapsus, -ūs *m.*

fling iaciō, iēcī, iactum 3., prōiciō, prōiēcī, prōiectum 3., iaculor 1. *dep.*

flint silex, -icis *m.*

float innō 1., (in)natō 1., lābor, lapsus 3. *dep.*, fluitō 1.

flock¹ (*noun*) grex, gregis *m.*, pecus, -oris *n.*

flock² (*v.*) confluō, -xī 3., convolō 1., congregor 1. *dep.*

flood¹ (*noun*) inundātiō, -ōnis *f.*, ēluviō, -ōnis *f.*

flood² (*v.*) inundō 1.

floor pavīmentum, -ī *n.*, solum, -ī *n.*

flour farīna, -ae *f.*

flow fluō, fluxī, fluxum 3., lābor, lapsus 3. *dep.*, mānō 1.

flower¹ (*noun*) flōs, flōris *m.*, flosculus, -ī *m.*

flower² (*v.*) flōreō 2., (ef)flōrescō 3.

flowing fluens, -ntis, mānans, -ntis

flute tībia, -ae *f.*

flute-player tībīcen, -inis *m.*

fly¹ (*noun*) musca, -ae *f.*

fly² (*v.*) volō 1., volitō 1.

fog cālīgō, -inis *f.*, nebula, -ae *f.*

fold (com)plicō 1.

follow (con)sequor, (con)secūtus 3. *dep.*, consector 1. *dep.*

food cibus, -ī *m.*, nūtrīmentum, -ī *n.*, esca, -ae *f.*, victus, -ūs *m.*, alimentum, -ī *n.*

fool scurra, -ae *m.*

foolish stultus, -a, -um, ineptus, -a, -um, insipiens, -ntis, fatuus, -a, -um

foot pēs, pedis *m.*

foot-soldier pedes, -itis *m.*

for¹ (*prep.*) (instead of) (+*abl.*) prō; (because of) (+*acc.*) praeter, ob

for² (*conj.*) enim, nam, namque, etenim; (because) quia, quod

forage pābulor 1. *dep.*

forbid vetō, vetuī, vetitum 1., prohibeō 2.

force¹ (*noun*) vīs, vīs *f.*, mōmentum, -ī *n.*, impetus, -ūs *m.*; (*of men*) manus, -ūs *f.*, cōpiae, -ārum *f.pl.*

force² (*v.*) coerceō 2., cōgō, coēgī, coactum 3.

ford vadum, -ī *n.*

forehead frons, -ntis *m.*

foreign externus, -a, -um, adventīcius, -a, -um, aliēnigenus, -a, -um, barbarus, -a, -um, hospitus, -a, -um, peregrīnus, -a, -um

foreigner advena, -ae *m./f.*, barbarus, -ī *m.*, hospes, -itis *m.*, peregrīnus, -ī *m.*

foresee praesentiō, -sī, -sum 4., prōvideō, -vīdī, -vīsum 2., prōspiciō, -spexī, -spectum 3.

forest silva, -ae *f.*, saltus, -ūs *m.*

foretell praedīcō, -dixī, -dictum 3.

forget (+*gen./acc.*) oblīviscor, oblītus 3. *dep.*, dēdiscō, dēdicī 3.

forgive (+*dat.*) ignoscō, ignōvī, ignōtum 3.; (+*dat.*) veniam dō (dedī, datum 1.)

fork forca, -ae *f.*

form¹ (*noun*) faciēs, -ēī *f.*, forma, -ae *f.*, figūra, -ae *f.*

form² (*v.*) (ef)fingō, -nxī, -ctum 3., (con)formō 1., faciō, fēcī, factum 3.

former pristinus, -a, -um, prior, -or, -us; **the former ... the latter** ille (illa, illud) ... hīc (haec, hoc)

formerly anteā, ante, quondam, ōlim

fort castellum, -ī *n.*, arx, arcis *f.*

fortieth quadrāgensimus (-gēs-), -a, -um

fortification castellum, -ī *n.*, mūnīmentum, -ī *n.*

fortify (com)mūniō 4.

fortunate fēlix, -īcis, beātus, -a, -um, fortūnātus, -a, -um
fortunately fēlīciter
fortune fortūna, -ae *f.*, fors, fortis *f.*; **good
fortune** fēlīcitās, -ātis *f.*; *see also* **wealth**
forty quadrāgintā
forum forum, -ī *n.*
forward porrō
foster-mother nūtrix, -īcis *f.*
foul *see* **horrible**
found fundō 1., constituō, -uī, -ūtum 3.
foundation fundāmenta, -ōrum *n.pl.*
fountain fons, fontis *m.*, caput, capitis *n.*
four quattuor; **four times** quater, quartum; **four year period** quadriennium,
-(i)ī *n.*
fourteen quattuordecim
fourth quartus, -a, -um
fox vulpēs, -is *f.*; **little fox** vulpēcula, -ae *f.*
fragile fragilis, -is, -e
fragment fragmentum, -ī *n.*
fraud fraus, -dis *f.*, fallācia, -ae *f.*, dolus, -ī
m.
free¹ (*adj*). līber, -era, -erum, solūtus, -a,
-um; (without cost) grātuitus, -a, -um
free² (*v.*) līberō 1., solvō, -vī, -ūtum 3.,
expediō 4.
freedman lībertus, -ī *m.*
freedom lībertās, -ātis *f.*; (*of choice*) arbitrium, -(i)ī *n.*
freely līberē, solūtē
freeze gelidō 1.
frenzied furens, -ntis, vēsānus, -a, -um,
āmens, -ntis
frenzy furor, -ōris *m.*, āmentia, -ae *f.*
frequent frequens, -ntis, creber, -bra,
-brum
frequently saepe, frequenter, crebrō
fresh recens, -ntis, novus, -a, -um
friend amīcus, -ī *m.*, sodālis, -is *m.*; (*female*)
amīca, -ae *f.*

friendly cōmis, -is, -e, amīcus, -a, -um,
benevolus, -a, -um, benignus, -a, -um
friendship amīcitia, -ae *f.*, hospitium, -(i)ī
n.
fright terror, -ōris *m.*, metus, -ūs *m.*, pavor,
-ōris *m.*
frighten (ex)terreō 2.
frightening terrificus, -a, -um, horridus,
-a, -um, terribilis, -is, -e
frog rāna, -ae *f.*
from (+*abl.*) ā *or* ab, ē *or* ex, dē
from where unde
front frons, -ntis *m.*; **in front (of)** (+*gen.*) ā
fronte; (+*acc.*) ante
frost gelū, -ūs *n.*, pruīna, -ae *f.*
frugal frūgī *indecl.adj.*, parcus, -a, -um
fruit fructus, -ūs *m.*, frux, frūgis *f.*, pōmum,
-ī *n.*
fruitful fēcundus, -a, -um
full (of) (+*abl./gen.*) plēnus, -a, -um,
refertus, -a, -um, replētus, -a, -um; (*of
food*) satur, -ris
fully plēnē, abundanter
fun lūdus, -ī *m.*, iocus, -ī *m.*
fund fiscus, -ī *m.*, pecūnia, -ae *f.*
funeral fūnus, -eris *n.* (*esp.pl.*)
funny ioculāris, -is, -e
fur pellis, -is *f.*
furious furens, -ntis, rabidus, -a, -um, furiōsus, -a, -um
furiously rabidē
furnace fornax, -ācis *f.*
furniture sup(p)ellex, -lectilis *f.*, apparātus, -ūs *m.*
further ulterius, longius, amplius;
(besides) praetereā
fury furor, -ōris *m.*, īra, īrae *f.*, rabiēs, -ēī *f.*
futile vānus, -a, -um, inānis, -is, -e, futtilis,
-is, -e
future futūrum, -ī *n.*; **in future** in futūrum,
in posterum

G

gain[1] (*noun*) lucrum, -ī *n.*, ēmolumentum, -ī *n.*, ūtilitās, -ātis *f.*, quaestus, -ūs *m.*, praemium, -(i)ī *n.*

gain[2] (*v.*) adipiscor, adeptus 3. *dep.*, assequor, assecūtus 3. *dep.*, consequor, -secūtus 3. *dep.*, nanciscor, na(n)ctus 3. *dep.*, lucror 1. *dep.*

gait incessus, -ūs *m.*, ingressus, -ūs *m.*

gall bīlis, -is *f.*, fel, fellis *n.*

gambler āleātor, -ōris *m.*

gambling ālea, -ae *f.*

game lūdus, -ī *m.*, lūsiō, -ōnis *f.*

gap hiātus, -ūs *m.*, lacūna, -ae *f.*

gape (in)hiō 1.

garden hortus, -ī *m.*; **small garden** hortulus, -ī *m.*

garland corōna, -ae *f.*

garlic ālium, āl(i)ī *n.*

garrison praesidium, -(i)ī *n.*

gas vapor, -ōris *m.*

gate (*of a city*) porta, -ae *f.*; (*of a house*) iānua, -ae *f.*

gatekeeper iānitor, -ōris *m.*

gather (come together) coeō, coīre, coīvī (coiī), coitum 4., conveniō, -vēnī, -ventum 4.; (bring together) conferō, conferre, contulī, collātum *v.irreg.*, colligō, -lēxī, -lectum 3., congregō 1.

gaze conspectus, -ūs *m.*, obtūtus, -ūs *m.*

gem lapillus, -ī *m.*, gemma, -ae *f.*

general[1] (*noun*) dux, dūcis *m.*, imperātor, -ōris *m.*

general[2] (*adj.*) commūnis, -is, -e, pūblicus, -a, -um, vulgāris, -is, -e, generālis, -is, -e; **in general** ad summam, commūniter, universē

generally plērumque, fer(m)ē, vulgō

generate gignō, genuī, genitum 3., prōcreō 1., generō 1.

generation (age) aetās, -ātis *f.*, saeculum, -ī *n.*

generous līberālis, -is, -e, mūnificus, -a, -um, benignus, -a, -um

gentle mītis, -is, -e, clēmens, -ntis, mollis, -is, -e, lēnis, -is, -e, mansuētus, -a, -um

gentleness lēnitās, -ātis *f.*, mansuētūdō, -inis *f.*, clēmentia, -ae *f.*

gently lēniter, molliter, suāviter, mansuētē, mīte

genuine sincērus, -a, -um, germānus, -a, -um

gesture gestus, -ūs *m.*, mōtus, -ūs *m.*

get capiō, cēpī, captum 3., perveniō, -vēnī, -ventum 4., nanciscor, na(n)ctus 3. *dep.*, adipiscor, adeptus 3. *dep.*, consequor, -secūtus 3. *dep.*

get away *see* **escape**

get back recipiō, recēpī, receptum 3.

ghost mānēs, -ium *m.pl.*, umbra, -ae *f.*, phasma, -atis *n.*

gift dōnum, -ī *n.*; (*poetic*) mūnus, -eris *n.*

girl puella, -ae *f.*, virgō, -inis *f.*

give dō, dedī, datum 1., dōnō 1., praebeō 2., largior 4. *dep.*

give back reddō, -didī, -ditum 3.

give up āmittō, āmīsī, āmissum 3., relinquō, relīquī, relictum 3.; (hand over) trādō, -didī, -ditum 3.

glad laetus, -a, -um, hilaris, -is, -e

glad (at), am (+*abl.*) gaudeō, gāvīsus 2. *semi-dep.*

glade saltus, -ūs *m.*, silva, -ae *f.*

gladiator gladiātor, -ōris *m.*

glass vitrum, -ī *n.*

glen (con)vallis, -is *f.*

gloomy *see* **shady**

glory glōria, -ae *f.*, laus, -dis *f.*, decus, -oris *n.*

glow ardeō, arsī, arsum 2., flagrō 1.

gluttonous *see* **greedy**

gnaw (ar)rōdō, -sī, -um 3.

go eō, īre, īvī (iī), itum 4., vādō, vāsī, vāsum 3., gradior, gressus 3. *dep.*; (*poetic*) meō 1.

go around ambeō, ambīre, ambīvī (-iī), ambitum 4.

go away *see* **depart**

go back *see* **return**[2]

go in *see* **enter**

go out exeō, exīre, exīvī (exiī), exitum 4., ēgredior, ēgressus 3. *dep.*, excēdō, excessī, excessum 3.

go under subeō, subīre, subīvī (-iī), subitum 4.

goat caper, caprī *m.*, hircus, -ī *m.*; **she-goat** capra, -ae *f.*, capella, -ae *f.*

goblet scyphus, -ī *m.*, pōculum, -ī *n.*

god deus, deī *m.*, dīvus, dīvī *m.*, nūmen, -inis *n.*

goddess dea, deae *f.*, dīva, -ae *f.*

godlike dīvīnus, -a, -um

gold aurum, -ī *n.*

golden aureus, -a, -um

good[1] (*noun*) bonum, -ī *n.*, salūs, -ūtis *f.*, ūtilitās, -ātis *f.*; **goods** (merchandise) merx, mercis *f.*; (property) bona, -ōrum *n. pl.*

good[2] (*adj.*) bonus, -a, -um, probus, -a, -um, benignus, -a, -um; (*morally*) honestus, -a, -um; (useful) commodus, -a, -um, ūtilis, -is, -e

goodbye valē(te), avē(te)

goodness virtūs, -ūtis *f.*, bonitās, -ātis *f.*, probitās, -ātis *f.*, benignitās, -ātis *f.*

goodwill benevolentia, -ae *f.*, voluntās, -ātis *f.*

goose anser, -eris *m.*

gossip rūmōrēs, -um *m.pl.*, sermō, -ōnis *m.*

govern gubernō 1., regō, rexī, rectum 3., regnō 1., administrō 1., gerō, gessī, gestum 3., (prō)cūrō 1., temperō 1.; (+*dat.*) praesum, praeesse, praefuī *v.irreg.*

government imperium, -(i)ī *n.*, regnum, -ī *n.*; (governing) administrātiō, -ōnis *f.*, prōcūrātiō, -ōnis *f.*, regimen, -inis *n.*

governor praefectus, -ūs *m.*, gubernātor, -ōris *m.*, rector, -ōris *m.*

grace grātia, -ae *f.*, favor, -ōris *m.*; *see also* **charm**

graceful ēlegans, -ntis, venustus, -a, -um, lepidus, -a, -um

gracefully ēleganter, venustē, lepidē

grade gradus, -ūs *m.*

gradually gradātim, paulātim, sensim

grain mīca, -ae *f.*; (*of corn*) frūmentum, -ī *n.*

granary horreum, -ī *n.*, granārium, -(i)ī (*esp.pl.*)

granddaughter neptis, -is *f.*

grandfather avus, avī *m.*

grandmother avia, -ae *f.*

grandson nepōs, -ōtis *m.*

grant permittō, -mīsī, -missum 3., concēdō, -cessī, -cessum 3.

grape acinus, -ī *m.*; **bunch of grapes** ūva, ūvae *f.*

grapevine vītis, -is *f.*

grass herba, -ae *f.*, grāmen, -inis *n.*

grateful grātus, -a, -um

grave sepulc(h)rum, -ī *n.*; (*place of cremation*) bustum, -ī *n.*

great magnus, -a, -um, grandis, -is, -e, ingens, -ntis, amplus, -a, -um, vastus, -a, -um; *see also* **famous**; **so great** tantus, -a, -um

great-granddaughter proneptis, -is *f.*

great-grandfather proavus, -ī *m.*; **great-great-grandfather** abavus, -ī *m.*

great-grandmother proavia, -ae *f.*; **great-great-grandmother** abavia, -ae *f.*

great-grandson pronepōs, -ōtis *m.*

greatly maximē, vehementer, valdē, magnopere

greatness magnitūdō, -inis *f.*, amplitūdō, -inis *f.*

greed (*for food*) gula, -ae *f.*, edācitās, -ātis *f.*; (*for anything*) avāritia, -ae *f.*, aviditās, -ātis *f.*, cupīditās, -ātis *f.*

greedy (*for food*) vorax, -ācis, edax, edācis, gulōsus, -a, -um; (*for anything*) avidus, -a, -um, avārus, -a, -um, cupidus, -a, -um

green viridis, -is, -e, virens, -ntis, prasinus, -a, -um

greet salūtō 1.; (+*dat.*) salūtem dīcō (dixī, dictum 3.)

greeting (con)salūtātiō, -ōnis *f.*

grey cānus, -a, -um; **grey-blue** glaucus, -a, -um, caesius, -a, -um

grief aegritūdō, -inis *f.*, maestitia, -ae *f.*, dolor, -ōris *m.*, luctus, -ūs *m.*, maeror, -ōris *m.*

grieve maereō 2., lūgeō, luxī, luctum 2., doleō 2.

grin *see* **smile**

grind molō, -uī, -itum 3.
groan[1] (*noun*) gemitus, -ūs *m.*
groan[2] (*v.*) gemō, gemuī, gemitum 3.
groin inguen, inguinis *n.*
ground humus, -ī *f.*, terra, -ae *f.*, solum, -ī *n.*; **on the ground** humī; *see also* **reason**
group caterva, -ae *f.*, grex, gregis *m.*, circulus, -ī *m.*
grow (ac)crescō, (ac)crēvī, (ac)crētum 3.; (mature) adolescō, adolēvī, adultum 3., pūbescō 3.; (raise) colō, coluī, cultum 3., alō, aluī, altum 3.
growth auctus, -ūs *m.*, incrēmentum, -ī *n.*
guard[1] (*noun*) custōs, -ōdis *m.*, excubiae, -ārum *f.pl.*; (protection) custōdia, -ae *f.*, praesidium, -(i)ī *n.*
guard[2] (*v.*) dēfendō, -dī, -sum 3., custōdiō

4., tueor, tuitus 2. *dep.*; (+*dat.*) praesideō, -sēdī 2.
guess coniectō 1., dīvīnō 1., auguror 1. *dep.*
guest (*male*) hospes, -itis *m.*; (*female*) hospita, -ae *f.*
guide[1] (*noun*) dux, dūcis *m.*
guide[2] (*v.*) dūcō, duxī, ductum 3., gubernō 1., regō, rexī, rectum 3.
guile dolus, -ī *m.*
guilt noxia, -ae *f.*, culpa, -ae *f.*, vitium, -(i)ī *n.*
guilty nocens, -ntis, noxius, -a, -um, sons, sontis
gulf sinus, -ūs *m.*
gulp hauriō, -sī, -sum 4.
gymnasium palaestra, -ae *f.*, gymnasium, -(i)ī *n.*

H

habit mōs, mōris *m.*, consuētūdō, -inis *f.*, ūsus, ūsūs *m.*

hail¹ (*noun*) grandō, -inis *m.*

hail² (*v.*) salūtō 1., appellō 1.

hair (*single*) capillus, -ī *m.*, pīlus, -ī *m.*; (*collective*) crīnis, -is *m.*, coma, -ae *f.*, caesariēs, -ēī *f.*

hairy pīlōsus, -a, -um, capillātus, -a, -um, comātus, -a, -um

half dīmidium, -(i)ī *n.*

hall ātrium, -(i)ī *n.*

halt consistō, constitī 3.

hammer malleus, -ī *m.*

hand manus, -ūs *f.*, palma, -ae *f.*; **right hand** dext(e)ra, -ae *f.*; **left hand** sinistra, -ae *f.*, laeva, -ae *f.*

hand over trādō, -didī, -ditum 3.

handle¹ (*noun*) ansa, -ae *f.*, manubrium, -(i)ī *n.*, capulus, -ī *m.*

handle² (*v.*) tractō 1.

handsome formōsus, -a, -um, pulc(h)er, -c(h)ra, -c(h)rum, venustus, -a, -um, bellus, -a, -um

hang pendeō, pependī, pensum 2.

hang back cessō 1.

hang on (*+dat. or +ad +acc.*) (ad)haereō, -sī, -sum 2.

hang over (*+dat.*) impendeō, -dī, -sum 2.; (*+dat.*) immineō 2.

hang up suspendeō, -dī, -sum 2.

happen fīō, fierī, factus *v.irreg.*, accidō, accidī, accīsum 3., ēveniō, ēvēnī, ēventum 4., contingō, -tigi, -tactum 3.

happiness laetitia, -ae *f.*, fēlīcitās, -ātis *f.*

happy laetus, -a, -um, beātus, -a, -um, hilaris, -is, -e, fēlix, -īcis, fortūnātus, -a, -um

harbour portus, -ūs *m.*

hard dūrus, -a, -um, rigidus, -a, -um; *see also* **difficult**

harden dūrō 1.

hardly aegrē, vix

hardship incommodum, -ī *n.*, inopia, -ae *f.*, molestiae, -ārum *f.pl.*, labor, -ōris *m.*, aerumna, -ae *f.*

hare lepus, -oris *m.*

harm¹ (*noun*) dētrīmentum, -ī *n.*, damnum, -ī *n.*

harm² (*v.*) laedō, -sī, -sum; (*+dat.*) noceō 2.

harmful noxius, -a, -um, nocens, -ntis

harmonious concors, -rdis, congruens, -ntis

harmony concordia, -ae *f.*, concentus, -ūs *m.*, consensus, -ūs *m.*

harp lyra, -ae *f.*

harsh asper, -era, -erum, acerbus, -a, -um, austērus, -a, -um, sevērus, -a, -um, immītis, -is, -e, dūrus, -a, -um; (*of sound*) absonus, -a, -um, raucus, -a, -um

harshness sevēritās, -ātis *f.*, asperitās, -ātis *f.*, acerbitās, -ātis *f.*

harvest messis, -is *f.*

harvester messor, -ōris *m.*

haste celeritās, -ātis *f.*, properātiō, -ōnis *f.*

hasten properō 1., festīnō 1., contendō, -dī, -tum 3., mātūrō 1.

hastily properē, properanter

hasty praeceps, -cipitis, (prae)properus, -a, -um

hat pilleus, -ī *m.*, petasus, -ī *m.*

hate ōdī, ōsum 3. (*only in pf.*), contemnō, -mpsī, -mptum 3.

hatred odium, od(i)ī *n.*, invidia, -ae *f.*, inimīcitia, -ae *f.*

have habeō 2., teneō, tenuī, tentum 2.

hay faenum, -ī *n.*

hazard cāsus, -ūs *m.*, perīculum, -ī *n.*, fors, fortis *f.*

head caput, capitis *n.*; (mind) *see* **heart** *or* **mind**; *see also* **leader**

headdress mitra, -ae *f.*
headlong praeceps, -cipitis
heal sānō 1., medeor 2. *dep.*
health sānitās, -ātis *f.*, salūs, -ūtis *f.*, valētudō, -inis *f.*; **am in good health** valeō 2.
healthy sānus, -a, -um, validus, -a, -um, salvus, -a, -um
heap¹ (*noun*) acervus, -ī *m.*, agger, -ris *m.*, mōlēs, -is *f.*, cumulus, -ī *m.*
heap² (*v.*) acervō 1., cumulō 1., congerō, -ssī, -stum 3.
hear (ex)audiō 4., auscultō 1.; **hear of** cognoscō, -nōvī, -nitum 3.
hearer audītor, -ōris *m.*
hearsay fāma, -ae *f.*, rūmor, -ōris *m.*
heart cor, cordis *n.*; (spirit) animus, -ī *m.*, mens, mentis *f.*, pectus, -oris *n.*; (inner part) interiōra, -um *n.pl.*
hearth focus, -ī *m.*, camīnus, -ī *m.*
heat¹ (*noun*) calor, -ōris *m.*, aestus, -ūs *m.*, ardor, -ōris *m.*, fervor, -ōris *m.*
heat² (*v.*) calefaciō, -fēcī, -factum 3., inflammō 1.
heat up calescō 3.
heaven caelum, -ī *n.*, polus, -ī *m.*, aether, -ris *m.*, axis, axis *m.*
heavenly caelestis, -is, -e, dīvīnus, -a, -um, aetherius, -a, -um
heaviness pondus, -eris *n.*, gravitās, -ātis *f.*
heavy gravis, -is, -e, onustus, -a, -um, ponderōsus, -a, -um
hedge saepēs, -is *f.*
heedless incautus, -a, -um, temerārius, -a, -um, neglegens, -ntis
heedlessly incautē, temere, neglegenter
heel calx, -cis *f.*
height altitūdō, -inis *f.*, prōcēritās, -ātis *f.*
heir hērēs, -ēdis *m.*
heiress hērēs, -ēdis *f.*
helmet cassis, -is *m.*, galea, -ae *f.*
helmsman gubernātor, -ōris *m.*
help¹ (*noun*) auxilium, -(i)ī *n.*, ops, opis *f.*, subsidium, -(i)ī *n.*
help² (*v.*) (ad)iuvō, (ad)iūvī, (ad)iūtum 1.; (+*dat.*) subveniō, -vēnī, -ventum 4.
helper auxiliātor, -ōris *m.*, adiūtor, -ōris *m.*
hen gallīna, -ae *f.*
hence hinc
herald praecō, -ōnis *m.*, praenuntius, -(i)ī *m.*
herd grex, gregis *m.*, armentum, -ī *n.*, caterva, -ae *f.*

herdsman pastor, -ōris *m.*, armentārius, -(i)ī *m.*; *see also* **cowherd** *and* **shepherd**
here hīc
hereafter posthāc
hero herōs, -ōos *m.*
heroine hērōis, -idos *f.*
hesitate haesitō 1., dubitō 1., cunctor 1. *dep.*
hesitation haesitātiō, -ōnis *f.*, dubitātiō, -ōnis *f.*, cunctātiō, -ōnis *f.*
hexameter hexameter, -tri *m.*
hidden occultus, -a, -um, absconditus, -a, -um
hide¹ (*noun*) pellis, -is *f.*, vellus, -eris *n.*, corium, -(i)ī *n.*
hide² (*v.*) abdō, abdidī, abditum 3., cēlō 1., abscondō, -dī, -ditum 3., occultō 1.; (*emotions*) dissimulō 1.
hiding place latebra, -ae *f.* (*esp.pl.*), latibulum, -ī *n.*
high altus, -a, -um, sublīmis, -is, -e, (ex)celsus, -a, -um
hill collis, -is *m.*, tumulus, -ī *m.*
hilly montuōsus, -a, -um
hilt capulus, -ī *m.*
himself *etc.* ipse, ipsa, ipsum
hinder impediō 4., retardō 1.; (+*dat.*) obstō, obstitī 1., obsistō, obstitī 3.
hindrance impedīmentum, -ī *n.*
hip coxa, -ae *f.*, coxendix, -īcis *f.*
hire condūcō, -duxī, -ductum 3.
hiss sībilō 1.
history histōria, -ae *f.*, rēs gestae, rērum gestārum *f.pl.*, annālēs, -ium *m.pl.*
hit pellō, pepulī, pulsum 3., pulsō 1., verberō 1., feriō 4., tundō, tutudī, tunsum (tūsum) 3., percutiō, -ssī, -ssum 3.
hither hūc
hoarse raucus, -a, -um
hoe sarculum, -ī *n.*
hog porcus, -ī *m.*, sūs, suis *m./f.*
hold teneō, tenuī, tentum 2., habeō 2., obtineō, obtinuī, obtentum 2., gestō 1.; *see also* **contain**
hold back retineō, retinuī, retentum 2.
hole cavum, -ī *n.*, lacūna, -ae *f.*, forāmen, -inis *n.*
holiday diēs festus, diēī festī *m.*, fēriae, -ārum *f.pl.*
hollow (con)cavus, -a, -um, cassus, -a, -um, vacuus, -a, -um

holy sacer, sacra, sacrum, sanctus, -a, -um, augustus, -a, -um

home domus, -ūs *f.*, domicilium, -(i)ī *n.*; **at home** domī; **homewards** domum

honest probus, -a, -um, vērus, -a, -um, sincērus, -a, -um, candidus, -a, -um

honesty probitās, -ātis *f.*, vēritās, -ātis *f.*, sincēritās, -ātis *f.*, fidēs, -ēī *f.*

honey mel, mellis *n.*

honour honestās, -ātis *f.*, fidēs, -ēī *f.*; (dignity) dignitās, -ātis *f.*

honour (with) honōrō 1., colō, coluī, cultum 3.; (+*abl.*) ornō 1.

honourable honestus, -a, -um, honōrificus, -a, -um; (honoured) honōrātus, -a, -um

hoof ungula, -ae *f.*

hook hāmus, -ī *m.*, uncus, -ī *m.*

hoop circulus, -ī *m.*, trochus, -ī *m.*

hope[1] (*noun*) spēs, speī *f.*

hope[2] (*v.*) spērō 1.

horn cornū, -ūs *n.*

horrible horrendus, -a, -um, nefārius, -a, -um, foedus, -a, -um, ātrox, -ōcis

horribly foedē

horror timor, -ōris *m.*, horror, -ōris *m.*, pavor, -ōris *m.*

horse equus, equī *m.*, caballus, -ī *m.*; (mare) equa, -ae *f.*

horseman eques, -itis *m.*

host hospes, -itis *m.*; *see also* **enemy**

hostage obses, obsidis *m.*

hostile hostīlis, -is, -e, inimīcus, -a, -um, infestus, -a, -um, hosticus, -a, -um

hot calidus, -a, -um, fervidus, -a, -um, aestuōsus, -a, -um

hot, am caleō, -uī 2., ferveō, ferbuī 2., aestuō 1.

hot, become calescō 3., fervescō 3.

hot, make calefaciō, -fēcī, -factum 3.

hotly ardenter

hound canis, -is *m./f.*

hour hōra, -ae *f.*

house domus, -ūs *f.*, aedēs, -ium *f.pl.*, aedificium, -(i)ī *n.*, domicilium, -(i)ī *n.*; (country house) villa, -ae *f.*

household familia, -ae *f.*, domus, -ūs *f.*

how (*exclam.*) ut, quam; (*interrog.*) quōmodo, quemadmodum, quī; (+*adj.*/*adv.*) quam; **how many** quot; **how great** quantus, -a, -um

how often quotiens (-iēs)

however[1] (*adv.*) quamvīs, quamlibet

however[2] (*conj.*) tamen, autem, sed, at

howl ululō 1.

huge immānis, -is, -e, ingens, -ntis, vastus, -a, -um, immensus, -a, -um

hum fremō, -uī, -itum 3., murmurō 1.

human hūmānus, -a, -um, mortālis, -is, -e; **human being** homō, hominis *m.*

humble humilis, -is, -e, obscūrus, -a, -um; (modest) modestus, -a, -um, moderātus, -a, -um

humour (+*dat.*) grātificor 1. *dep.*, obsequor, obsecūtus 3. *dep.*, indulgeō, -sī, -sum 2.

hundred centum; **hundred times** centiens (-iēs)

hunger famēs, -is *f.*, inedia, -ae *f.*

hungry ēsuriens, -ntis, iēiūnus, -a, -um

hunt vēnor 1. *dep.*, consector 1. *dep.*

hunter vēnātor, -ōris *m.*

hurl *see* **throw**

hurriedly festīnanter, properē, raptim

hurry festīnō 1., mātūrō 1., properō 1.; (make faster) accelerō 1., mātūrō 1., incitō 1.

hurt[1] (*adj.*) saucius, -a, -um

hurt[2] (*v.*) laedō, -sī, -sum 3.; (+*dat.*) noceō 2.; (*feelings*) offendō, -dī, -sum

husband marītus, -ī *m.*, vīr, virī *m.*, coniunx, -iugis *m.*

hut cāsa, -ae *f.*, mapālia, -ium *n.pl.*, tugurium, -(i)ī *n.*

I ego (*acc.* mē, *gen.* meī, *dat.* mihī (mihi), *abl.* mē); **I myself** equidem, ego ipse, egomet

ice gelū, -ūs *n.*, glaciēs, -ēī *f.*

icy gelidus, -a, -um, frīgidus, -a, -um

idle vacuus, -a, -um, ignāvus, -a, -um, segnis, -is, -e, ōtiōsus, -a, -um; (useless) inūtilis, -is, -e, vānus, -a, -um, inānis, -is, -e, irritus, -a, -um

idleness ōtium, ōt(i)ī *n.*, ignāvia, -ae *f.*, segnitia, -ae *f.*

if sī; **as if** quasi; **if only** sī modo; **but if** quod sī

ignorance inscītia, -ae *f.*, inscientia, -ae *f.*, ignōrātiō, -ōnis *f.*

ignorant (+*gen.*) inscius, -a, -um, ignārus, -a, -um, indoctus, -a, -um

ignorant of, am ignōrō 1.

ignorantly inscienter, indoctē

ignore neglegō, -xī, -ctum 3., praetereō, -īre, -īvī (-iī), -itum 4.

ill aeger, aegra, aegrum, aegrōtus, -a, -um

ill, am aegrōtō 1.

ill-disposed malevolus, -a, -um

illness aegritūdō, -inis *f.*, morbus, -ī *m.*

illuminate illustrō 1., illūminō 1.

illustrious praeclārus, -a, -um, praestans, -ntis, illustris, -is, -e, splendidus, -a, -um, eximius, -a, -um

ill-will malevolentia, -ae *f.*

image imāgō, -inis *f.*, figūra, -ae *f.*, simulācrum, -ī *n.*, speciēs, -ēī *f.*

imaginary *see* false

imagine mente *or* animō concipiō (-cēpī, -ceptum 3.), excōgitō 1., putō 1.

imitate imitor 1. *dep.*, effingō, -nxī, -ctum 3., aemulor 1. *dep.*

imitation imitātiō, -ōnis *f.*, aemulātiō, -ōnis *f.*; (copy) imāgō, -inis *f.*, simulācrum, -ī *n.*

immediately statim, prōtinus, confestim

immense *see* huge

immortal immortālis, -is, -e, sempiternus, -a, -um, aeternus, -a, -um

immutable immūtābilis, -is, -e

impassable invius, -a, -um, impedītus, -a, -um, insuperābilis, -is, -e

impiety impietās, -ātis *f.*, scelus, -eris *n.*

impious impius, -a, -um, scelestus, -a, -um

implore ōrō 1., implōrō 1., rogō 1., obsecrō 1., obtestor 1. *dep.*

imply significō 1.

import importō 1., invehō, -xī, -ctum

important gravis, -is, -e, necessārius, -a, -um, magnus, -a, -um

impression impressiō, -ōnis *f.*; *see also* copy *and* opinion

improve corrigō, -rexī, -rectum 3., meliōrem faciō (fēcī, factum 3.), excolō, excoluī, excultum 3.

improvident imprōvidus, -a, -um, imprūdens, -ntis, incautus, -a, -um

impulse impulsus, -ūs *m.*, impetus, -ūs *m.*, stimulus, -ī *m.*

impunity, with impūne

impure impūrus, -a, -um, contāminātus, -a, -um, incestus, -a, -um

impurity impūritās, -ātis *f.*, incestus, -ūs *m.*

in (+*abl.*) in

inanimate inanimus, -a, -um

incense tūs, tūris *n.*

incite (in)citō 1., stimulō 1., incendō, -dī, -sum 3.

inclination inclīnātiō, -ōnis *f.*; (propensity) voluntās, -ātis *f.*, studium, -(i)ī *n.*

incline inclīnō 1.

include inclūdō, -sī, -sum 3., contineō, -tinuī, -tentum 2., complector, complexus 3. *dep.*, compre(he)ndō, -dī, -sum 3.

inconvenient incommodus, -a, -um, inopportūnus, -a, -um

incorrect falsus, -a, -um, mendōsus, -a, -um; (morally wrong) *see* **wicked**

increase (become larger) (ac)crescō, (ac)crēvī, (ac)crētum 3., gliscō 3.; (make larger) augeō, auxī, auctum 2., amplificō 1.

indecisive anceps, ancipitis, dubius, -a, -um

indeed vērō, sānē

indicate (dē)monstrō 1., indicō 1.

indication indicium, -(i)ī *n.*, signum, -ī *n.*, argūmentum, -ī *n.*, significātiō, -ōnis *f.*

indictment crīmen, -inis *n.*, accūsātiō, -ōnis *f.*

indifference negligentia, -ae *f.*, incūria, -ae *f.*

indifferent dissolūtus, -a, -um, remissus, -a, -um

indignant indignans, -ntis

indignation īra, īrae *f.*, indignātiō, -ōnis *f.*

individual singulāris, -is, -e, proprius, -a, -um

induce addūcō, adduxī, adductum 3., impellō, impulī, impulsum 3., persuādeō, -sī, -sum 2.

indulge (+*dat.*) indulgeō, -lsī, -lsum 2.

indulgence venia, -ae *f.*, indulgentia, -ae *f.*

indulgent indulgens, -ntis, benignus, -a, -um

ineffectual invalidus, -a, -um, irritus, -a, -um

inept ineptus, -a, -um

inexperienced imperītus, -a, -um, rudis, -is, -e, ignārus, -a, -um

inexplicable inexplānābilis, -is, -e, inexplicābilis, -is, -e

infamous infāmis, -is, -e, flāgitiōsus, -a, -um

infamy ignōminia, -ae *f.*, infāmia, -ae *f.*, dēdecus, -oris *n.*

infant infans, -ntis

infantry peditēs, -um *m.pl.*

infertile sterilis, -is, -e, infēcundus, -a, -um

infinite infīnītus, -a, -um

infinity infīnītās, -ātis *f.*

inflate inflō 1.

influence auctōritās, -ātis *f.*, potentia, -ae *f.*, pondus, -eris *n.*, vīs, vīs *f.*

inform nuntiō 1., certiōrem faciō (fēcī, factum 3.), doceō, -uī, -tum 2.

informer index, -icis *m.*

inhabit incolō, incoluī, incultum 3., habitō 1.

inhabitant incola, -ae *m.*, habitātor, -ōris *m.*

inheritance hērēditās, -ātis *f.*

inhuman inhūmānus, -a, -um, crūdēlis, -is, -e

injure *see* **harm**[2]

injury *see* **harm**[1]

ink ātrāmentum, -ī *n*

inn taberna, -ae *f.*, dēversōrium, -(i)ī *n.*, hospitium, -(i)ī *n.*

inner *see* **internal**

innkeeper cāupō, -ōnis *m.*

innocent insons, -ntis, innocens, -ntis; (*morally*) castus, -a, -um, integer, -gra, -grum

inquire *see* **enquire**

insane āmens, -ntis, dēmens, -ntis, insānus, -a, -um, furiōsus, -a, -um

insanity āmentia, -ae *f.*, dēmentia, -ae *f.*, insānia, -ae *f.*, furor, -ōris *m.*

inside[1] (*adv.*) intus

inside[2] (*prep.*) (+*acc.*) intrā; (+*abl.*) in

insolent insolens, -ntis, arrogans, -ntis, superbus, -a, -um

inspiration afflātus, -ūs *m.*

instance exemplum, -ī *n.*, specimen, -inis *n.*

instantly statim, prōtinus, confestim, continuō

instead of (+*abl.*) prō; (+*gen.*) vicem

institution institūtum, -ī *n.*, mōs, mōris *m.*; (body) sodālitās, -ātis *f.*

instrument instrūmentum, -ī *n.*, māchina, -ae *f.*

insult contumēlia, -ae *f.*

integrity integritās, -ātis *f.*, sanctitās, -ātis *f.*, innocentia, -ae *f.*

intellect mens, mentis *f.*, intelligentia, -ae *f.*, ingenium, -(i)ī *n.*, sagācitās, -ātis *f.*

intend (to) (+*inf.*) in animō habeō 2., cōgitō 1.

intentionally consultō, consiliō

interfere (with) (+*dat.*) interveniō, -vēnī, -ventum 4.

internal interior, -or, -us, intestīnus, -a, -um

internally intus, penitus

interpret interpretor 1. *dep.*, explānō 1.

interpreter interpres, -etis *m./f.*

interrupt interpellō 1., interrumpō, -rūpī, -ruptum 3.

into (+*acc.*) in

introduce intrōdūcō, -duxī, -ductum 3., indūcō, induxī, inductum 3., invehō, -xī, -ctum 3.

invade (+*in* +*acc.*) invādō, -sī, -sum 3.

invasion irruptiō, -ōnis *f.*, incursiō, -ōnis *f.*

invent fingō, finxī, fictum 3., inveniō, invēnī, inventum 4., reperiō, repperī, repertum 4.

invisible caecus, -a, -um

invite invītō 1., vocō 1.

invoke advocō 1., implōrō 1.

involved (in) (+*in* +*abl.*) versor 1. *dep.*

inwardly introrsus (-um), intrinsecus

iron[1] (*noun*) ferrum, -ī *n.*

iron[2] (*adj.*) ferreus, -a, -um

island insula, -ae *f.*

ivory ebur, eboris *n.*

ivy hedera, -ae *f.*

J

jail carcer, -eris *n.*, vincula, -ōrum *n.pl.*
jar olla, -ae *f.*, urna, -ae *f.*, amphora, -ae *f.*, dolium, -(i)ī *n.*
javelin tēlum, -ī *n.*, pīlum, -ī *n.*, iaculum, -ī *n.*
jaw bucca, -ae *f.*, māla, -ae *f.*, maxilla, -ae *f.*
jealous invidus, -a, -um
jealous of, am (+*dat.*) invideō, invīsī, invīsum 2., aemulor 1. *dep.*
jealousy invidia, -ae *f.*, aemulātiō, -ōnis *f.*
jest *see* **joke**
jest, in per iocum, iocō
jester scurra, -ae *m.*, maccus, -ī *m.*
jewel gemma, -ae *f.*
job labor, -ōris *m.*, opus, operis *n.*; (post) officium, -(i)ī *n.*
join cōpulō 1., (col)ligō 1., adiungō, -xī, -ctum 3.
joke¹ (*noun*) iocus, -ī *m.*
joke² (*v.*) iocor 1. *dep.*, ioculor 1. *dep.*, cavillor 1. *dep.*

journey iter, itineris *n.*, via, viae *f.*, cursus, -ūs *m.*
joy laetitia, -ae *f.*, gaudium, -(i)ī *n.*
joyful hilaris, -is, -e, laetus, -a, -um
judge¹ (*noun*) iūdex, -icis *m.*, arbiter, -trī *m.*, aestimātor, -ōris *m.*
judge² (*v.*) censeō, -uī, -um 2., iūdicō 1., existimō 1.
judgement iūdicium, -(i)ī *n.*, arbitrium, -(i)ī *n.*, consilium, -(i)ī *n.*
jug olla, -ae *f.*, urceus, -ī *m.*
jump saliō 4.
just¹ (*adj.*) iustus, -a, -um, aequus, -a, -um
just² (*adv.*) modo, sōlum, tantum; **just now** nūperrimē, recens; **just as** sīcut(ī), ita
justice iustitia, -ae *f.*, iūs, iūris *n.*
justification causa, -ae *f.*, excūsātiō, -ōnis *f.*
justly meritō, iustē, iūre

K

keel carīna, -ae *f.*

keen alacer, -cris, -cre, ācer, ācris, ācre, acūtus, -a, -um, perspicax, -ācis

keenly ācriter, acerbē, acūtē

keenness alacritās, -ātis *f.*, aciēs, -ēī *f.*, perspicācitās, -ātis *f.*

keep (con)servō 1., teneō, tenuī, tentum 2., custōdiō 4.; (*promises*) (*+abl.*) stō, stetī 1.

keep back (from) (*+abl.*) prohibeō 2., arceō 2.

keeper custōs, -ōdis *m.*, cūrātor, -ōris *m.*

key clāvis, -is *f.*

kick calcitrō 1.

kidneys rēnēs, -um *m.pl.*

kill interficiō, -fēcī, -fectum 3., (ē)necō 1., occīdō, -sī, -sum 3., caedō, -sī, -sum 3., trucīdō 1.

kind¹ (*noun*) genus, -eris *n.*, gens, gentis *f.*, modus, -ī *m.*; **of such a kind** tālis, -is, -e; **by kinds** generātim

kind² (*adj.*) cōmis, -is, -e, amīcus, -a, -um, benignus, -a, -um, benevolus, -a, -um, clēmens, -ntis

kindle incendō, -dī, -sum 3., inflammō 1.

kindly benignē, cōmiter, amīcē, clementer

kindness bonitās, -ātis *f.*, benevolentia, -ae *f.*, benignitās, -ātis *f.*, cōmitās, -ātis *f.*; **act of kindness** beneficium, -(i)ī *n.*

king rex, rēgis *m.*; **minor king** rēgulus, -ī *m.*

kingdom regnum, -ī *n.*

kingly rēgālis, -is, -e, rēgius, -a, -um

kiss¹ (*noun*) osculum, -ī *n.*, bāsium, -(i)ī *n.*, s(u)āvium, -(i)ī *n.*

kiss² (*v.*) osculor 1. *dep.*, bāsiō 1., s(u)āvior 1. *dep.*

kitchen culīna, -ae *f.*

knee genū, -ūs *n.*

knife culter, -trī *m.*

knight eques, equitis *m.*

knot¹ (*v.*) nōdō 1., nectō, nexī, nexum 3.

knot² (*noun*) nōdus, -ī *m.*, vinculum, -ī *n.*

know sciō 4., nōvī, nōtum 3. (*pf. of* noscō); **get to know** cognoscō, cognōvī, cognitum 3.; **not to know** ignōrō 1.

knowledge scientia, -ae *f.*, cognitiō, -ōnis *f.*, doctrīna, -ae *f.*, disciplīna, -ae *f.*

known nōtus, -a, -um

knuckle articulus, -ī *m.*

L

labour¹ (*noun*) labor, -ōris *m.*, opera, -ae *f.*,
opus, operis *n.*
labour² (*v.*) labōrō 1., operam dō (dedī,
datum 1.), opus faciō (fēcī, factum 3.)
lack¹ (*v.*) (+*abl.*) careō 2., egeō 2.
lack² (*noun*) inopia, -ae *f.*, egestās, -ātis *f.*
ladder scāla, -ae *f.* (*esp.pl.*)
laden onustus, -a, -um, gravis, -is, -e
lady mulier, -ris *f.*, fēmina, -ae *f.*; **lady of
the house** domina, -ae *f.*, māterfamiliās,
mātrisfamiliās *f.*
lake lacus, -ūs *m.*, lacūna, -ae *f.*
lamb (*male*) agnus, -ī *m.*; (*female*) agna, -ae *f.*
lame claudus, -a, -um
lament lāmentor 1. *dep.*
lamentation lāmentātiō, -ōnis *f.*, plōrātus,
-ūs *m.*, querēla, -ae *f.*, complōrātiō, -ōnis *f.*
lamp lūcerna, -ae *f.*
land humus, -ī *f.*, tellūs, -ūris *f.*, terra, -ae *f.*;
(cultivated land) solum, -ī *n.*, ager, agrī *m.*
landlord caupō, -ōnis *m.*
language lingua, -ae *f.*, sermō, -ōnis *m.*;
(style) ōrātiō, -ōnis *f.*, dictiō, -ōnis *f.*
languid languidus, -a, -um, lassus, -a, -um
large grandis, -is, -e, magnus, -a, -um,
amplus, -a, -um
last¹ (*adj.*) ultimus, -a, -um, postrēmus, -a,
-um, extrēmus, -a, -um; (most recent)
proximus, -a, -um
last² (*v.*) dūrō 1., permaneō, -sī, -sum 2.
last, at tandem, dēmum, postrēmum
lasting diūturnus, -a, -um, perennis, -is, -e
stabilis, -is, -e
late¹ (*adj.*) sērus, -a, -um; (recent) recens,
-ntis
late² (*adv.*) sērō
lately nūper
laugh rīdeō, rīsī, rīsum 2., cachinnō 1.
laughter rīsus, -ūs *m.*, cachinnus, -ī *m.*
laurel laurus, -ī *f.*, laurea, -ae *f.*

lavish profūsus, -a, -um, prōdigus, -a, -um,
sumptuōsus, -a, -um
law lex, lēgis *f.*, iūs, iūris *n.*
lawful lēgitimus, -a, -um
lawsuit līs, lītis *m.*, contrōversia, -ae *f.*,
causa, -ae *f.*
lawyer advocātus, -ī *m.*, causidicus, -ī *m.*,
iūrisconsultus (iūre-), -ī *m.*
lay pōnō, posuī, positum 3., (col)locō 1.
lay down (dē)pōnō, dēposuī, dēpositum 3.
lay waste vastō 1.
laziness pigritia, -ae *f.*, segnitia, -ae *f.*,
ignāvia, -ae *f.*
lazy piger, pigra, pigrum, segnis, -is, -e,
ignāvus, -a, -um
lead¹ (*noun*) plumbum, -ī *n.*
lead² (*v.*) dūcō, duxī, ductum 3.
lead back redūcō, reduxī, reductum 3.
lead out ēdūcō, ēduxī, ēductum 3.
leader dux, dūcis *m.*, ductor, -ōris *m.*
leaf folium, -(i)ī *n.*, frons, -ndis *f.*; (*of a book*)
pāgina, -ae *f.*, schēda, -ae *f.*
lean inclīnō, inclīvī, inclītum 3.
leap saliō 4.
learn (ē)discō, (ē)didicī 3., cognoscō, -nōvī,
-nitum 3.
learned doctus, -a, -um, ērudītus, -a, -um,
litterātus, -a, -um
learning doctrīna, -ae *f.*, ērudītiō, -ōnis *f.*
leather corium, -(i)ī *n.*
leave abeō, abīre, abīvī (abiī), abitum 4.,
abscēdō, abscessī, abscessum 3., dīgredior, dīgressus 3. *dep.*; (abandon) relinquō, relīquī, relictum 3., omittō, omīsī,
omissum 3., dēstituō, -uī, -ūtum 3.
left (remaining) reliquus, -a, -um; **left**
(side) sinister, -tra, -trum, laevus, -a, -um
leg crūs, crūris *n.*
legate lēgātus, -ī *m.*
legion lēgiō, -ōnis *f.*

leisure ōtium, ōt(i)ī *n.*
leisurely ōtiōsē, lentē
lend commodō 1.
length longitūdō, -inis *f.*; (*of time*) longinquitās, -ātis *f.*
lengthen ēlongō 1., prōdūcō, -duxī, -duc-
tum 3.
lenient clēmens, -ntis, lēnis, -is, -e, mītis,
-is, -e
less minus
lessen (dē)minuō, -uī, -ūtum 3.
let ablocō 1.; (allow) sinō, sīvī 3., patior,
passus 3. *dep.*
letter epistula, -ae *f.*, litterae, -ārum *f.pl.*,
charta, -ae *f.*; (*of the alphabet*) littera, -ae *f.*
level aequus, -a, -um, plānus, -a, -um, pār,
paris
levy dēlectus, -ūs *m.*
liable prōnus, -a, -um, obnoxius, -a, -um
liberty lībertās, -ātis *f.*
library bibliothēca, -ae *f.*
lick lingō, linxī, linctum 3., lambō, lambī 3.
lie[1] (*noun*) mendācium, -(i)ī *n.*, falsum, -ī *n.*
lie[2] (*v.*) mentior 4. *dep.*; (recline) iaceō,
iacuī, iactum 2., cubō, -uī, -itum 1.
life vīta, -ae *f.*, anima, -ae *f.*
lift (sub)levō 1., tollō, sustulī, sublātum 3.
light[1] (*noun*) lūmen, -inis *n.*, lux, lūcis *f.*
light[2] (*adj.*) levis, -is, -e
lighten (make less heavy) exonerō 1.;
(make more illuminated) illustrō 1.
lightly leviter
lightning fulmen, -inis *n.*, fulgur, -uris *n.*
like[1] (*adj.*) (+*dat./gen.*) similis, -is, -e, pār,
paris
like[2] (*v.*) amō 1., dīligō, dīlexī, dīlectum 3.
like[3] (*adv.*) (+*gen.*) similiter, modō
limb artus, -ūs *m.*, membrum, -ī *n.*
limit fīnis, -is *m.*, līmes, -itis *m.*, terminus, -ī
m., modus, -ī *m.*
limp claudicō 1.
line līnea, -ae *f.*; (*of battle*) aciēs, -ēī *f.*;
(marching column) agmen, -inis *n.*; (*of
poetry*) versus, -ūs *m.*
linger cunctor 1. *dep.*, cessō 1., moror 1.
dep.
link vinculum, -ī *n.*
lion leō, leōnis *m.*
lip lābia, -ae *f.*, labrum, -ī *n.*
liquid[1] (*noun*) ūmor, ūmōris *m.*, liquidus, -ī
m.
liquid[2] (*adj.*) liquidus, -a, -um

list tabula, -ae *f.*, index, -icis *f.*
listen (to) audiō 4., auscultō 1.
literature litterae, -ārum *f.pl.*
little parvus, -a, -um, exiguus, -a, -um
little, a paulum, aliquant(ul)um; **too
little** parum
live vīvō, vixī, victum 3., spīrō 1., sum, esse,
fuī *v.irreg.*
live at colō, coluī, cultum 3., habitō 1.
lively vegetus, -a, -um, vehemens, -ntis,
alacer, -cris, -cre
liver iecur, iocineris *n.*
load onus, oneris *n.*
loaf pānis, -is *m.*
loan mūtuum, -ī *n.*
location locus, -ī *m.*
lofty altus, -a, -um, ēlātus, -a, -um,
(ex)celsus, -a, -um, sublīmis, -is, -e
log lignum, -ī *n.*, stīpes, -itis *m.*
lone, lonely sōlus, -a, -um, ūnus, ūna,
ūnum; (*of places*) āvius, -a, -um, dēsertus,
-a, -um
long longus, -a, -um; (*of time*) diūtinus, -a,
-um, longinquus, -a, -um, longus, -a, -um
look aspectus, -ūs *m.*; (appearance) faciēs,
-ēī *f.*, speciēs, -ēī *f.*
look (at) spectō 1., aspiciō, aspexī, aspectum 3., intueor, intuitus 2. *dep.*, contemplor 1. *dep.*
loom tēla, -ae *f.*
loose laxus, -a, -um, remissus, -a, -um
loosen (re)laxō 1., remittō, remīsī, remissum 3., resolvō, -vī, -ūtum 3.
lord dominus, -ī *m.*
lose āmittō, āmīsī, āmissum 3., perdō,
-didī, -ditum 3.
loss damnum, -ī *n.*, dētrīmentum, -ī *n.*,
iactūra, -ae *f.*
lot sors, sortis *f.*, fortūna, -ae *f.*
loud magnus, -a, -um, clārus, -a, -um
loudly clārē, magnā vōce
love[1] (*noun*) amor, amōris *m.*, cāritās, -ātis
f., studium, -(i)ī *n.*
love[2] (*v.*) amō 1., dīligō, dīlexī, dīlectum 3.;
(+*dat.*) studeō 2.
lovely venustus, -a, -um, amābilis, -is, -e,
pulc(h)er, -c(h)ra, -c(h)rum
lover amātor, -ōris *m.*, amans, -ntis *m.*;
(*female*) amātrix, -īcis *f.*
low abiectus, -a, -um, dēmissus, -a, -um; (*of
character*) humilis, -is, -e, obscūrus, -a,
-um, turpis, -is, -e

lower dēmittō, dēmīsī, dēmissum 3.
loyal fidēlis, -is, -e, fīdus, -a, -um
loyalty fidēlitās, -ātis *f.*, fidēs, -ēī *f.*
luck fortūna, -ae *f.*, cāsus, -ūs *m.*, fortūna, -ae *f.*
lucky fēlix, -īcis, fortūnātus, -a, -um, faustus, -a, -um

lung pulmō, -ōnis *m.* (*usu.pl.*)
lust libīdō, -inis *f.*, cupīditās, -ātis *f.*
luxurious luxuriōsus, -a, -um, lautus, -a, -um, dēlicātus, -a, -um
luxury luxuria, -ae *f.*, luxus, -ūs *m.*, lautitia, -ae *f.*
lyre lyra, -ae *f.*, fīdes, -is *f.*

machine māchina, -ae *f.*, māchinātiō, -ōnis *f.*

mad āmens, -ntis, dēmens, -ntis, insānus, -a, -um, vēsānus, -a, -um, furiōsus, -a, -um

mad, am furō 3., insāniō 4.

madly dēmenter, insānē, furiōsē

madness āmentia, -ae *f.*, dēmentia, -ae *f.*, insānia, -ae *f.*, vēcordia, -ae *f.*, furor, -ōris *m.*

magic[1] (*noun*) ars magica, artis magicae *f.*

magic[2] (*adj.*) magicus, -a, -um, mīrus, -a, -um

magician magus, -ī *m.*

magnificent (generous) magnificus, -a, -um, mūnificus, -a, -um; (outstanding) praeclārus, -a, -um, splendidus, -a, -um

magnitude magnitūdō, -inis *f.*

maidservant ancilla, -ae *f.*, famula, -ae *f.*

mainland continens, -ntis *m.*, terra, -ae *f.*

mainly plērumque, potissimum, praecipuē

maintain sustineō, sustinuī, sustentum 2., (con)servō 1.; (assert) vindicō 1., affirmō 1.

make faciō, fēcī, factum 3., creō 1., efficiō, effēcī, effectum 3., fabricor 1. *dep.*

maker fabricātor, -ōris *m.*

male masculus, -a, -um, mās, maris; (*of men alone*) virīlis, -is, -e

malice malevolentia, -ae *f.*, malignitās, -ātis *f.*, invidia, -ae *f.*

malignant malevolus, -a, -um, malignus, -a, -um, indignus, -a, -um

man homō, hominis *m.*, vir, virī *m.*; **man by man** virītim

manage prōcūrō 1., tractō 1., administrō 1.

management prōcūrātiō, -ōnis *f.*, tractātiō, -ōnis *f.*, administrātiō, -ōnis *f.*, cūra, -ae *f.*

manifest *see* **obvious**

manner via, viae *f.*, modus, -ī *m.*, ratiō, -ōnis *f.*; (character) mōrēs, -um *m.pl.*

many multī, -ae, -a, frequentēs, -ium; **very many** permultī, -ae, -a, plūrimī, -ae, -a; **so many** tot; **as many** quot; **so many times** totiens (-iēs); **as many times** quotiens (-iēs)

map tabula, -ae *f.*

maple acer, aceris *n.*

marble marmor, -oris *n.*

march[1] (*noun*) iter, itineris *n.*

march[2] (*v.*) prōgredior, -gressus 3. *dep.*, iter faciō (fēcī, factum 3.), proficiscor, -profectus 3. *dep.*

mark (distinctive) signum, -ī *n.*, indicium, -(i)ī *n.*; (blemish) nota, -ae *f.*, macula, -ae *f.*

market forum, -ī *n.*, macellum, -ī *n.*

marriage mātrimōnium, -(i)ī *n.*, coniugium, -(i)ī *n.*, cōnūbium, -(i)ī *n.*

marry (*of a man*) dūcō, duxī, ductum 3.; (*of a woman*) (+*dat.*) nūbō, nupsī, nuptum 3.

marsh palūs, -ūdis *f.*

martial bellicōsus, -a, -um, mīlitāris, -is, -e

mason faber, fabrī *m.*

mass mōlēs, -is *m.*, massa, -ae *f.*; (*of people*) multitūdō, -inis *f.*, turba, -ae *f.*

massacre[1] (*noun*) trucīdātiō, -ōnis *f.*, caedēs, -is *f.*, interneciō, -ōnis *f.*, strāgēs, -is *f.*

massacre[2] (*v.*) trucīdō 1., caedō, cecīdī, caesum 3.

mast mālus, -ī *m.*

master dominus, -ī *m.*; (*of the house*) paterfamiliās, patrisfamiliās *m.*; (teacher) magister, -trī *m.*

mat stōrea, -ae *f.*

material māteria, -ae *f.*

mathematics mathēmatica, -ae *f.*

matter rēs, rēī *f.*, māteria, -ae *f.*, causa, -ae *f.*; (substance) corpus, -oris *n.*

mature mātūrus, -a, -um, adultus, -a, -um

maybe fortasse, forsitan

meagre petilus, -a, -um, macer, macra, macrum, exīlis, -is, -e, iēiūnus, -a, -um

meal cēna, -ae *f.*; *see also* **breakfast, dinner**

mean (average) medius, -a, -um; (poor) abiectus, -a, -um, sordidus, -a, -um, humilis, -is, -e; (unkind) *see* **cruel**

meaning sententia, -ae *f.*, vīs, vīs *f.*, significātiō, -ōnis *f.*

meanwhile interim, intereā

measure (per)mētior 4. *dep.*

measure out mētor 1. *dep.*

meat cārō, carnis *f.*, pulpa, -ae *f.*

medicine medicāmentum, -ī *n.*, medicīna, -ae *f.*, remedium, -(i)ī *n.*

mediocre *see* **average**

meet (+*dat.*) obviam eō (īre, īvī (iī), itum 4.); (+*in* +*acc.*) incidō, -idī, -īsum 3.

meet together conveniō, -vēnī, -ventum 4., concurrō, -rrī, -rsum 3.

meeting contiō, -ōnis *f.*, concursiō, -ōnis *f.*, congressiō, -ōnis *f.*

melt (become liquid) liquescō, licuī 3., liquēfīō, -fierī, -factus *v.irreg.*, tābescō, tābuī 3.

memorable memorābilis, -is, -e

memory memoria, -ae *f.*, recordātiō, -ōnis *f.*

mention[1] (*noun*) mentiō, -ōnis *f.*, commemorātiō, -ōnis *f.*

mention[2] (*v.*) (com)memorō 1.; (+*gen.*) mentiōnem faciō (fēcī, factum 3.)

merchant mercātor, -ōris *m.*

merciful misericors, -rdis, clēmens, -ntis, lēnis, -is, -e

mercy misericordia, -ae *f.*, clēmentia, -ae *f.*, venia, -ae *f.*

mere merus, -a, -um, pūrus, -a, -um, sōlus, -a, -um, ūnus, ūna, ūnum

merely modo, sōlum, tantum

merit virtūs, -ūtis *f.*, meritum, -ī *n.*, dignitās, -ātis *f.*

message nuntius, -(i)ī *m.*

messenger nuntius, -(i)ī *m.*, tabellārius, -(i)ī *m.*

metal metallum, -ī *n.*

method ratiō, -ōnis *f.*, modus, -ī *m.*, via, viae *f.*

midday merīdiēs, -ēī *m.*

middle medius, -a, -um

midnight media nox, mediae noctis *f.*

might rōbur, -oris *n.*, vīs, vīs *f.*

migrate migrō 1., abeō, abīre, abīvī (abiī), abitum 4., discēdō, -cessī, -cessum 3.

mild clēmens, -ntis, lēnis, -is, -e, mītis, -is, -e

mile mille *or* mīlia (passuum)

military mīlitāris, -is, -e, bellicus, -a, -um

milk[1] (*noun*) lac, lactis *n.*

milk[2] (*v.*) mulgeō, mulsī 2.

mill mola, -ae *f.* (*esp.pl.*), pistrīnum, -ī *n.*

mind mens, mentis *f.*, animus, -ī *m.*, ingenium, -(i)ī *n.*

mine metallum, -ī *n.* (*usu.pl.*)

mine *see* **my**

mingle *see* **mix**

mint ment(h)a, -ae *f.*; (*for money*) monēta, -ae *f.*

minute pusillus, -a, -um, exiguus, -a, -um, minūtus, -a, -um

miracle mīrāculum, -ī *n.*

mirror speculum, -ī *n.*

miserable miser, -era, -erum, aerumnōsus, -a, -um, tristis, -is, -e, miserābilis, -is, -e

mislead dēcipiō, dēcēpī, dēceptum 3., fallō, fefellī, falsum 3.

miss (feel the absence of) dēsīderō 1., requīrō, requīsīvī (-iī), requīsītum 3.

miss out praetermittō, -mīsī, -missum 3., omittō, omīsī, omissum 3.

missile missile, -is *n.*, tēlum, -ī *n.*

mist cālīgō, -inis *f.*, nebula, -ae *f.*

mistake error, -ōris *m.*, errātum, -ī *n.*, peccātum, -ī *n.*

mistake, make a errō 1., peccō 1.

mistress domina, -ae *f.*; (*of the house*) māterfamiliās, mātrisfamiliās *f.*; (teacher) magistra, -ae *f.*

misty cālīginōsus, -a, -um, nebulōsus, -a, -um

mix (com)misceō, (com)miscuī, (com)mixtum 2.

mixture permixtiō, -ōnis *f.*; (act of mixing) mixtūra, -ae *f.*

moan gemō, gemuī, gemitum 3.

mock dērīdeō, -sī, -sum 2., cavillor 1. *dep.*; (+*dat.*) illūdeō, -sī, -sum 2.

moderate[1] (*adj.*) modicus, -a, -um, mediocris, -is, -e; moderātus, -a, -um, modestus, -a, -um, temperātus, -a, -um; *see also* **average**

moderate[2] (*v.*) moderor 1. *dep.*; (+*dat.*) temperō 1.

modern novus, -a, -um, recens, -ntis

modest pudens, -ntis, modestus, -a, -um, verēcundus, -a, -um

modesty pudor, -ōris *m.*, modestia, -ae *f.*, verēcundia, -ae *f.*

mole talpa, -ae *f.*; (*on the body*) naevus, -ī *m.*

money aes, aeris *n.*, pecūnia, -ae *f.*, nummī, -ōrum *m.pl.*, argentum, -ī *n.*

money-box fiscus, -ī *m.*

monster bēlua, -ae *f.*, portentum, -ī *n.*, monstrum, -ī *n.*

month mensis, -is *m.*

monument monumentum, -ī *n.*

moon lūna, -ae *f.*

moral mōrālis, -is, -e, bene mōrātus, -a, -um, honestus, -a, -um, probus, -a, -um

more[1] (*adj.*) *sg.* (+*gen.*) plūs; *pl.* plūrēs, -ēs, -a

more[2] (*adv.*) potius, magis, ultrā

moreover praetereā, ultrō

morning *see* **dawn**

morning, in the māne

mortal mortālis, -is, -e

most maximē, plūrimum

mother māter, mātris *f.*, parens, -ntis *f.*; (*poetic*) genetrix, -īcis *f.*

mother-in-law socrus, -ūs *f.*

motherly māternus, -a, -um

motion mōtiō, -ōnis *f.*, mōtus, -ūs *m.*

mount conscendō, -dī, -sum 3., ascendō, -dī, -sum 3.

mountain mons, montis *m.*

mournful (*full of sorrow*) maestus, -a, -um, tristis, -is, -e, flēbilis, -is, -e

mouse mūs, mūris *m.*

mouth ōs, ōris *n.*; (*of a river*) ostium, -(i)ī *n.*

move (com)moveō, (com)mōvī, (com)mōtum 2.

much[1] (*adj.*) multus, -a, -um; **too much** nimius, -a, -um

much[2] (*adv.*) multum, valdē; **too much** nimis

mucus mūcus, -ī *m.*

mud līmus, -ī *m.*, lutum, -ī *n.*, caenum, -ī *n.*

mule hinnus, -ī *m.*, mūlus, -ī *m.*

multitude multitūdō, -inis *f.*, turba, -ae *f.*, massa, -ae *f.*

murder caedēs, -is *f.*, nex, necis *f.*, occīsiō, -ōnis *f.*

murmur murmur, -uris *n.*, fremitus, -ūs *m.*

muscle musculus, -ī *m.*, nervus, -ī *m.*

mushroom fungus, -ī *m.*, bōlētus, -ī *m.*

music cantus, -ūs *m.*

must (+*acc.*+*inf.*) necesse est (esse, fuit *v. irreg.*); (+*inf.*) dēbeō 2., opus est (esse, fuit *v.irreg.*); *or use gerundive of verb*

mute mūtus, -a, -um

mutiny sēditiō, -ōnis *f.*, mōtus, -ūs *m.*

mutual mūtuus, -a, -um

my, mine meus, mea, meum

mysterious sēcrētus, -a, -um, occultus, -a, -um

mystery (*of religion*) mystērium, -(i)ī *n.*

myth fābula, -ae *f.*

N

nail¹ (*v.*) cōnfīgō, -fīxī, -fixum 3., affīgō, affīxī, affixum 3.

nail² (*noun*) unguis, -is *m.*; (*for hammering*) clāvus, -ī *m.*

naked nūdus, -a, -um

name¹ (*noun*) nōmen, -inis *n.*, vocābulum, -ī *n.*; (repute) fāma, -ae *f.*; **first name** praenōmen, -inis *n.*; **family name** cognōmen, -inis *n.*

name² (*v.*) nōminō 1., appellō 1., nuncupō 1.

nape cervix, -īcis *f.*, collum, -ī *n.*

narrate (ē)narrō 1., memorō 1.

narrow angustus, -a, -um, artus, -a, -um

nasty gravis, -is, -e, malus, -a, -um, turpis, -is, -e, foedus, -a, -um

nation gens, gentis *f.*, nātiō, -ōnis *f.*, cīvitās, -ātis *f.*, populus, -ī *m.*, rēspūblica, -ae *f.*

national patrius, -a, -um

native indigena, -ae *m.*

nature nātūra, -ae *f.*; (*of a person*) ingenium, -(i)ī *n.*, indolēs, -is *f.*

naval nāvālis, -is, -e, nauticus, -a, -um

navigate nāvigō 1.

near¹ (*adv.*) prope, propter, iuxtā

near² (*prep.*) (+*acc.*) prope, ad, propter, iuxtā

nearly fer(m)ē, paene, prope

necessarily necessāriō (-ē)

necessary necessārius, -a, -um; **it is necessary (to)** (+*inf.*) necessum est

neck cervix, -īcis *f.*, collum, -ī *n.*; *see also* **throat**

necklace monīle, -is *n.*

need¹ (*noun*) necessitās, -ātis *f.*

need² (*v.*) requīrō, -īsīvī (-iī), -īsītum 3.; (lack) (+*abl.*) careō, -uī 2., egeō, eguī 2.

need, there is (+*abl.*) opus est

needle acus, acūs *f.*

neglect neglegō, -xī, -ctum 3., omittō,

omīsī, omissum 3., pratermittō, -mīsī, -missum 3.

negligence neglegentia, -ae *f.*, incūria, -ae *f.*, indiligentia, -ae *f.*

neigh hinniō 4.

neighbour vīcīnus, -ī *m.*

neighbourhood vīcus, -ī *m.*, vīcīnia, -ae *f.*

neighbouring vīcīnus, -a, -um, fīnitimus, -a, -um, propinquus, -a, -um

neither¹ (*pron.*) neuter, -tra, -trum

neither² (*conj.*) neque, nec; **neither ... nor** neque ... neque (nec ... nec)

nest nīdus, -ī *m.*

net rēte, -is *n.*, plaga, -ae *f.* (*esp.pl.*)

nettle urtīca, -ae *f.*

never numquam

nevertheless nihilōminus, (at)tamen

new novus, -a, -um, recens, -ntis, insolitus, -a, -um

newcomer advena, -ae *m./f.*

next¹ (*adj.*) proximus, -a, -um, insequens, -ntis, posterus, -a, -um

next² (*adv.*) posteā, deinde

nice suāvis, -is, -e, dulcis, -is, -e

night nox, noctis *f.*, tenebrae, -ārum *f.pl.*; **by night** nocte, noctū

nightingale luscinia, -ae *f.*

nine novem; **nine time** noviens (-iēs)

nineteen undēvīgintī

ninety nōnāgintā

ninth nōnus, -a, -um

nipple papilla, -ae *f.*

no¹, none (*adj.*) nullus, -a, -um

no² (*adv.*) nōn, minimē; **no rather** immō (vērō)

noble praeclārus, -a, -um, līberālis, -is, -e, honestus, -a, -um, pulcherrimus, -a, -um; (*of birth*) nōbilis, -is, -e, generōsus, -a, -um; **nobles** optimātes, -um *m.pl.*

nobody nēmō, nēminis, nullus, -a, -um

nocturnal nocturnus, -a, -um
nod nūtō 1.
noise sonitus, -ūs *m.*, crepitus, -ūs *m.*
none *see* **no¹**
nonsense nūgae, -ārum *f.pl.*, ineptiae,
-ārum *f.pl.*
nor neque, nec
northern aquilōnius, -a, -um
nose nāsus, -ī *m.*, nārēs, -ium *m.pl.*
nostril nāris, -is *m.* (*usu.pl.*)
not nōn
note¹ (*noun*) annotātiō, -ōnis *f.*
note² (*v.*) annotō 1.
notebook commentārius, -(i)ī *m.*, adversāria, -ōrum *n.pl.*
nothing nihil (nīl), -lī *n.*
notice animadvertō, -tī, -sum 3.

nourish alō, aluī, altum 3., nūtriō 4.
now nunc, iam; **now ... now** modo ...
modo
nowhere nusquam
nude nūdus, -a, -um
numb torpens, -ntis
numb, am torpeō 2.
numb, grow torpescō 3.
number numerus, -ī *n.*
numbness torpor, -ōris *m.*
numerous frequens, -ntis, crēber, -bra,
-brum, plūrimī, -ae, -a (*only in pl.*)
nurse¹ (*v.*) alō, aluī, altum 3., nūtriō 4.,
foveō, fōvī, fōtum 2.
nurse² (*noun*) nūtrix, -īcis *f.*
nut nux, nucis *f.*
nymph nympha, -ae *f.*

O

oak quercus, -ūs *f.*, rōbur, -uris *n.*; **holm-oak** īlex, īlicis *f.*; **made of oak** quernus, -a, -um, īlignus, -a, -um

oar rēmus, -ī *m.*, tonsa, -ae *f.*

oath iūsiūrandum, iūrisiūrandī *n.*

obedience oboedientia, -ae *f.*, obsequium, -(i)ī *n.*

obedient (+*dat.*) oboediens, -ntis, obsequens, -ntis

obey (+*dat.*) pāreō 2., oboediō 4., obsequor, obsecūtus 3. *dep.*

object¹ (*noun*) rēs, reī *f.*; *see also* **purpose**

object² (*v.*) recūsō 1., repugnō 1.

objection recūsātiō, -ōnis *f.*

observe observō 1., spectō 1., contemplor 1. *dep.*; (*customs etc.*) (con)servō 1.

obstinate pertinax, -ācis, obstinātus, -a, -um

obstruct obstruō, -xī, -ctum 3.; (+*dat.*) obstō, obstitī 1.

obtain adipiscor, adeptus 3. *dep.*, consequor, consecūtus 3. *dep.*, nanciscor, na(n)ctus 3. *dep.*

obvious manifestus, -a, -um, perspicuus, -a, -um

occasion tempus, -oris *n.*, occāsiō, -ōnis *f.*

occupy teneō, tenuī, tentum 2., occupō 1., capiō, cēpī, captum 3., habeō 2.

occur accidō, accidī, accīsum 3., fīō, fierī, factus *v.irreg.*

occurrence cāsus, -ūs *m.*, ēventum, -ī *n.*

ocean ōceanus, -ī *m.*

octopus polypus, -ī *m.*

odour odor, odōris *m.*

off (+*acc.*) extrā; (out of) (+*abl.*) ē *or* ex

offence (fault) peccātum, -ī *n.*, dēlictum, -ī *n.*; (*feeling*) offensiō, -ōnis *f.*

offend offendō, -dī, -sum 3., laedō, -dī, -sum 3.; (commit a fault) peccō 1.

offer offerō, offerre, obtulī, oblātum *v.irreg.*, dēferō, dēferre, dētulī, dēlātum *v. irreg.*, praebeō 2.

office officium, -(i)ī *n.*, mūnus, -eris *n.*

officer tribūnus, -ī *m.*, praefectus, -ī *m.*

offspring prōlēs, -is *m.*, prōgeniēs, -ēī *f.*

often saepe, crēbrō; **so often** totiens (-iēs); **how often** quotiens (-iēs)

oh (*of anguish, pain*) ah, (e)heu; (*of surprise*) hem, prō(h)

oil oleum, -ī *n.*

old vetus, veteris, vetustus, -a, -um, antīquus, -a, -um, priscus, -a, -um, pristinus, -a, -um; (*of people*) senex, -is, grandis, -is, -e

old age senectūs, -ūtis *f.*

olive olea, -ae *f.*, olīva, -ae *f.*

omen ōmen, ōminis *n.*

omit omittō, omīsī, omissum 3., praetermittō, -mīsī, -missum 3.

on (+*abl.*) in; (concerning) (+*abl.*) dē; (*of time use abl. alone*)

once semel; (formerly) ōlim, quondam, aliquandō; **at once** simul, statim, prōtinus

one ūnus, ūna, ūnum, aliquis, -qua, -quid

one by one singulātim

one hundred centum

one thousand mille

onion caepa, -ae *f.*, bulbus, -ī *m.*

only¹ (*adj.*) singulāris, -is, -e, ūnicus, -a, -um

only² (*adv.*) modo, sōlum, tantum

onset impetus, -ūs *m.*, incursus, -ūs *m.*

open¹ (*adj.*) apertus, -a, -um, patens, -ntis; *see also* **candid**

open² (*v.*) aperiō, -uī, -tum 4., patefaciō, -fēcī, -factum 3., solvō, -vī, -ūtum 3.

open, am pateō 2.

openly palam, apertē

opinion opīniō, -ōnis *f.*, sententia, -ae *f.*, iūdicium, -(i)ī *n.*

opponent adversārius, -(i)ī *m.*

opportunity occāsiō, -ōnis *f.*, facultās, -ātis *f.*, cōpia, -ae *f.*

oppose repugnō 1., resistō, restitī 3.; (+*dat.*) obstō, obstitī 1.; (+*dat.*) adversor 1. *dep.*

opposite (+*acc.*) adversus (-um), contrā

oppress vexō 1., premō, pressī, pressum 3.

oppression vexātiō, -ōnis *f.*

or aut, vel, -ve; **either ... or** aut ... aut, vel ... vel

oracle ōrāculum, -ī *n.*

orator ōrātor, -ōris *m.*

order[1] (*noun*) ordō, -inis *m.*

order[2] (*v.*) iubeō, iussī, iussum 2.; (+*dat.*) imperō 1.; (set in order) ordinō 1., compōnō, -posuī, -positum 3.

ordinary ūsitātus, -a, -um, vulgāris, -is, -e, commūnis, -is, -e

organize ordinō 1., compōnō, -posuī, -positum 3.

origin orīgō, -inis *f.*, initium, -(i)ī *n.*, fons, fontis *m.*

other alius, -a, -um; (other of two) alter, -era, -erum

other's aliēnus, -a, -um

otherwise aliter

ours noster, -tra, -trum

out (*adv.*) forās, extrā

out of (+*abl.*) ē *or* ex, dē; (+*acc.*) extrā

outdo superō 1., vincō, vīcī, victum 3.

outrage iniūria, -ae *f.*, flāgitium, -(i)ī *n.* contumēlia, -ae *f.*

outside[1] (*adj.*) externus, -a, -um, exterus, -a, -um

outside[2] (*adv.*) extrā, forīs

outstanding *see* **illustrious**

oven camīnus, -ī *m.*, furnus, -ī *m.*

over (+*acc.*) trans, per, super

overcome superō 1., vincō, vīcī, victum 3.

overthrow ēvertō, -tī, -sum 3., perdō, -didī, -ditum 3., opprimō, oppressī, oppressum 3.

overwhelm obruō, -ī, -tum 3., opprimō, oppressī, oppressum 3.

owe dēbeō 2.

owing to (+*acc.*) propter, ob

owl noctua, -ae *f.*, ulula, -ae *f.*, būbō, -ōnis *m.*

own[1] (*adj.*) proprius, -a, -um

own[2] (*v.*) possideō, possēdī, possessum 2., teneō, tenuī, tentum 2., habeō 2.

ox bōs, bovis *m.*

oyster ostrea, -ae *f.*

P

pace passus, -ūs *m.*, gradus, -ūs *m.*; *see also* **speed**

pacify pācō 1., plācō 1., sēdō 1.

pack sarcina, -ae *f.*; *see also* **crowd**

packet fasciculus, -ī *m.*

pact *see* **treaty**

page pāgina, -ae *f.*

pail situla, -ae *f.*, hama, -ae *f.*

pain dolor, -ōris *m.*

painful molestus, -a, -um, acerbus, -a, -um

paint[1] (*noun*) pigmentum, -ī *n.*

paint[2] (*v.*) (dē)pingō, -nxī, -ctum 3.; (*dye*) colōrō 1., fūcō 1.

painting pictūra, -ae *f.*, tabula (picta), -ae (pictae) *f.*

palace (domus) rēgia, (domūs) rēgiae *f.*; (*poetic*) palatium, -(i)ī *n.*

pale, pallid pallidus, -a, -um

paleness, pallor pallor, -ōris *m.*

palm palma, -ae *f.*

palm tree palma, -ae *f.*

pamphlet libellus, -ī *m.*

pan patina, -ae *f.*, patella, -ae *f.*

panic pavor, -ōris *m.*, terror, -ōris *m.*

paper charta, -ae *f.*, papyrus, -ī *m.*

parcel fascis, -is *m.*, fasciculus, -ī *m.*

pardon[1] (*noun*) venia, -ae *f.*

pardon[2] (*v.*) (+*dat. of person* +*acc. of thing*) ignōscō, ignōvī, ignōtum 3., condōnō 1.

parent parens, -ntis *m./f.*

park hortus, -ī *m.* (*usu.pl.*)

parrot psittacus, -ī *m.*

part pars, partis *f.*, membrum, -ī *n.*; (*of a play*) persōna, -ae *f.*, partēs, -um *f.pl.*; **for my part** equidem

particle mīca, -ae *f.*, particula, -ae *f.*

particularly praesertim, praecipuē, magnopere

partly partim, parte

partner socius, -(i)ī *m.*, consors, -rtis *m.*

party festum, -ī *n.*; (*of men*) factiō, -ōnis *f.*, secta, -ae *f.*, manus, -ūs *f.*

pass[1] (*noun*) saltus, -ūs *m.*, angustiae, -ārum *f.pl.*

pass[2] (*v.*) (*spatially*) praetergredior, -gressus 3. *dep.*, praetereō, -īre, -īvī (-iī), -itum 4., transgredior, -gressus 3. *dep.*; (*time*) dēgō, dēgī 3., agō, ēgī, actum 3.; (*laws*) perferō, -ferre, -tulī, -lātum *v.irreg.*

pass over *see* **omit**

passage transitus, -ūs *m.*, transgressiō, -ōnis *f.*; (*of a book*) locus, -ī *m.*

passion īra, īrae *f.*; *see also* **lust**

passionate īrātus, -a, -um, concitātus, -a, -um, vehemens, -ntis

past[1] (*adj.*) praeteritus, -a, -um

past[2] (*prep.*) (+*acc.*) praeter, trans

pastry crustum, -ī *n.*

path sēmita, -ae *f.*, via, viae *f.*, trāmes, -itis *m.*

pathless invius, -a, -um

patience patientia, -ae *f.*, tolerantia, -ae *f.*

patient patiens, -ntis, tolerans, -ntis

patiently patienter, toleranter

pause mora, -ae *f.*, intervallum, -ī *n.*

paw pēs, pedis *m.*

pay[1] (*noun*) stīpendium, -(i)ī *n.*, mercēs, -ēdis *f.*

pay[2] (*v.*) (ex)solvō, -vī, -ūtum 3., numerō 1., pendeō, pependī, pensum 2.

pea pīsum, -ī *n.*

peace pax, pācis *f.*, ōtium, ōt(i)ī *n.*, concordia, -ae *f.*

peaceful placidus, -a, -um, quiētus, -a, -um, tranquillus, -a, -um

peacock pāvō, -ōnis *m.*

pear pirum, -ī *n.*

pear tree pirus, -ī *f.*

pearl margarīta, -ae *f.*, bāca, -ae *f.*

pedestal fundāmentum, -ī *n.*, basis, -is *f.*

pedestrian pedes, -itis *m.*
pelvis pelvis, -is *f.*
pen stilus, -ī *m.*, calamus, -ī *m.*
penalty poena, -ae *f.*, multa, -ae *f.*, damnum, -ī *n.*
penetrate penetrō 1.
peninsula paeninsula, -ae *f.*
penis membrum, -ī *n.*, cauda, -ae *f.*; (*poetic*) fascinum, -ī *n.* (*or* -us, -ī *m.*), mentula, -ae *f.*, pēnis, -is *m.*, verpa, -ae *f.*
people populus, -ī *m.*, gens, gentis *f.*, plebs, plēbis *f.*, hominēs, -um *m.pl.*
pepper piper, -eris *n.*
perceive sentiō, -sī, -sum 4., intellegō, -xī, -ctum 3., percipiō, -cēpī, -ceptum 3.
perennial perennis, -is, -e
perfect perfectus, -a, -um, integer, -ğra, -grum
perfection perfectiō, -ōnis *f.*
perfectly perfectē
perform fungor, functus 3. *dep.*, faciō, fēcī, factum 3., agō, ēgī, actum 3., perficiō, -fēcī, -fectum 3., exsequor, exsecūtus 3. *dep.*
performance (per)functiō, -ōnis *f.*, exsecūtiō, -ōnis *f.*; (*on a stage*) fābula, -ae *f.*
perfume unguentum, -ī *n.*, odor, odōris *m.*
perhaps fortasse, fors(it)an
peril perīculum, -ī *n.*
perilous perīculōsus, -a, -um
period spatium, -(i)ī *n.*, tempus, -oris *n.*, aetās, -ātis *f.*
perish pereō, -īre, -īvī (-iī), -itum 4., intereō, -īre, -īvī (-iī), -itum 4.
perjury periūrium, -(i)ī *n.*
permanence stabilitās, -ātis *f.*, constantia, -ae *f.*
permanent stabilis, -is, -e, perpetuus, -a, -um, diūturnus, -a, -um
permissible concessus, -a, -um, licitus, -a, -um
permission licentia, -ae *f.*, potestās, -ātis *f.*
permit sinō, sīvī, situm 3.; (+*dat.*) permittō, -mīsī, -missum 3.
perpetrate committō, -mīsī, -missum 3., faciō, fēcī, factum 3.
perpetual perpetuus, -a, -um, perennis, -is, -e
perpetually perpetuō
persecute insector 1. *dep.*, persequor, -secūtus 3. *dep.*

perseverance constantia, -ae *f.*, persevērantia, -ae *f.*
persist persevērō 1.
persistence persevērantia, -ae *f.*, pertinācia, -ae *f.*
persistent persevērans, -ntis, pertinax, -ācis
persistently persevēranter, pertināciter
person persōna, -ae *f.*, homō, -inis *m.*, caput, capitis *n.*
personality nātūra, -ae *f.*
perspire sūdō 1.
persuade (+*dat.*) persuadeō, -sī, -sum 2.
persuasion persuāsiō, -ōnis *f.*
pest pestis, -is *f.*
pestilence pestilentia, -ae *f.*
petty levis, -is, -e
philologist grammaticus, -ī *m.*
philosopher sapiens, -ntis *m.*, philosophus, -ī *m.*
philosophy sapientia, -ae *f.*, philosophia, -ae *f.*
phrase locūtiō, -ōnis *f.*
physical corporālis, -is, -e, corporeus, -a, -um
physician medicus, -ī *m.*, physicus, -ī *m.*, clīnicus, -ī *m.*
pick carpeō, carpsī, carptum 2., dēligō, dēlēgī, dēlectum 3.
pick out ēligō, ēlēgī, ēlectum 3., excerpō, -psī, -ptum 3.
picture pictūra, -ae *f.*, figūra, -ae *f.*, imāgō, -inis *f.*
piece fragmentum, -ī *n.*, pars, partis *f.*
pier mōlēs, -is *f.*
pierce perfodiō, -fōdī, -fossum 3., transfīgō, -fixī, -fixum 3., perforō 1., pungō, pepugī, punctum 3.
piety religiō, -ōnis *f.*, pietās, -ātis *f.*
pig porcus, -ī *m.*, sūs, suis *m.*; (sow) porca, -ae *f.*, sūs, suis *f.*
pigeon columba, -ae *f.*, palumbēs, -is *f.*
piglet porcellus, -ī *m.*
pigsty hara, -ae *f.*
pile massa, -ae *f.*, mōlēs, -is *m.*, acervus, -ī *m.*, cumulus, -ī *m.*
pile up accumulō 1., coacervō 1., exstruō, -uxī, -uctum 3.
pillage (dē)populātiō, -ōnis *f.*, rapīna, -ae *f.*
pillar columen, -inis *n.*, columna, -ae *f.*
pillow cervīcal, -ālis *n.*, pulvīnus, -ī *m.*
pin acus, acūs *f.*

pinch vellicō 1.
pine pīcea, -ae *f.*, pīnus, -ūs *f.*
pious pius, pia, pium, religiōsus, -a, -um, sanctus, -a, -um
pipe fistula, -ae *f.*; (musical) tībia, -ae *f.*, fistula, -ae *f.*
pirate praedō, -ōnis *m.*, pīrāta, -ae *m.*
pit fossa, -ae *f.*, fovea, -ae *f.*
pitch (tar) pix, picis *f.*
pitch camp castra pōnō (posuī, positum 3.)
pitchfork furca, -ae *f.*
pity[1] (*noun*) misericordia, -ae *f.*
pity[2] (*v.*) (+*gen.*) mē (*etc.*) miseret 2. *impers.*
place[1] (*noun*) locus, -ī *m.*; **in another place** alibī
place[2] (*v.*) pōnō, posuī, positum 3., (col)locō 1.
plague pestis, -is *f.*, pestilentia, -ae *f.*
plain[1] (*noun*) campus, -ī *m.*
plain[2] (*adj.*) perspicuus, -a, -um, clārus, -a, -um; (obvious) manifestus, -a, -um, plānus, -a, -um
plainly perspicuē, clārē
plait nectō, nex(u)ī, nexum 3., implicō, -āvī *or* -uī, -ātum 1., plectō, plexī, plexum 3.
plan[1] (*noun*) consilium, -(i)ī *n.*, prōpositum, -ī *n.*, dēsignātiō, -ōnis *f.*
plan[2] (*v.*) cōgitō 1., consilium capiō (cēpī, captum 3.); (intend) (+*inf.*) in animō habeō 2.
planet stella, -ae *f.*, errans, -ntis *m.*
plank tabula, -ae *f.*
plant herba, -ae *f.*, planta, -ae *f.*
plate catillus, -ī *m.*
play[1] (*noun*) lūsus, -ūs *m.*; (*on a stage*) fābula, -ae *f.*
play[2] (*v.*) lūdō, lūsī, lūsum 3.
player lūsor, -ōris *m.*
plead excūsō 1.
pleasant iūcundus, -a, -um, suāvis, -is, -e grātus, -a, -um, dulcis, -is, -e; (*of places*) amoenus, -a, -um
pleasantly iūcundē, suāviter
please dēlectō 1.; (+*dat.*) placeō 2.; **it pleases (me)** mihī (*etc.*) libet 2. *impers.*
pleasure voluptās, -ātis *f.*
plot[1] (*noun*) insidiae, -ārum *f.pl.*, coniūrātiō, -ōnis *f.*; (*of land*) agellus, -ī *m.*
plot[2] (*v.*) coniūrō 1.
plough[1] (*noun*) arātrum, -ī *n.*

plough[2] (*v.*) arō 1.
ploughman arātor, -ōris *m.*
pluck carpō, -psī, -ptum 3.
plum prūnum, -ī *n.*
plum tree prūnus, -ī *f.*
plunder praedor 1. *dep.*, dīripiō, dīripuī, dīreptum 3., harpagō 1.
plunge (dē)mergeō, -rsī, -rsum 2.
poem carmen, -inis *n.*, poēma, -atis *n.*
poet poēta, -ae *m.*
poetic poēticus, -a, -um
point punctum, -ī *n.*; (sharp point) aciēs, -ēī *f.*; (main point) caput, capitis *n.*, cardō, -inis *m.*
point out (dē)mōnstrō 1., indicō 1., ostendō, -dī, -sum (-tum) 3.
poison venēnum, -ī *n.*, vīrus *n.* (*only nom. and acc.sg.*)
poisonous noxius, -a, -um
pole contus, -ī *m.*, asser, -ris *m.*; (planetary) polus, -ī *m.*
polish (ex)poliō 4.
polite hūmānus, -a, -um, cōmis, -is, -e, urbānus, -a, -um
politician magistrātus, -ūs *m.*
pond, pool lacūna, -ae *f.*, stagnum, -ī *n.*
poop puppis, -is *f.*
poor pauper, -eris, miser, -ra, -rum, exīlis, -is, -e, inops, -pis
poppy papāver, -eris *n.*
popular grātus, -a, -um; (of or for the people) populāris, -is, -e
pork porcīna, -ae *f.*
port portus, -ūs *m.*
portent portentum, -ī *n.*, monstrum, -ī *n.*, ōmen, ōminis *n.*
position locus, -ī *m.*, situs, -ūs *m.*, status, -ūs *m.*; *see also* **rank**
possess possideō, possēdī, possessum 2., occupō 1., habeō 2.
possibility facultās, -ātis *f.*
possible, it is fierī potest (potuit *v.irreg.*)
possibly fortasse
postpone differō, differre, distulī, dīlātum *v.irreg.*
pot olla, -ae *f.*, matella, -ae *f.*, vās, vassis *n.*
pour fundō, fūdī, fūsum 3.
pour in infundō, infūdī, infūsum 3.
poverty paupertās, -ātis *f.*, inopia, -ae *f.*, egestās, -ātis *f.*
power potentia, -ae *f.*, potestās, -ātis *f.*, vīrēs, -ium *f.pl.*

powerful potens, -ntis, validus, -a, -um
practice ūsus, ūsūs *m.*, consuētūdō, -inis *f.*,
exercitātiō, -ōnis *f.*
practise exerceō 2., factitō 1.
praetor praetor, -ōris *m.*
praetorship praetūra, -ae *f.*
praise¹ (*noun*) laus, -dis *f.*
praise² (*v.*) laudō 1.
praiseworthy laudābilis, -is, -e
pray ōrō 1., precor 1. *dep.*, veneror 1. *dep.*
prayers precēs, -um *f.pl.*
precede antecēdō, -cessī, -cessum 3.;
(*+dat.*) anteeō, -īre, -īvī (-iī), -itum 4.,
praeeō, -īre, -īvī (-iī), -itum 4.
precious pretiōsus, -a, -um, cārus, -a, -um
predict praedīcō, -dixī, -dictum 3., auguror
1. *dep.*
prefer posthabeō 2., antepōnō, -posuī,
-positum 3.; (prefer to) (*+inf.*) mālō,
mālle, māluī *v.irreg.*
pregnant praegnans, -ntis, gravidus, -a,
-um
prepare (com)parō 1.
prepared (for) (*+ad+acc.*) parātus, -a, -um
presence of, in the (*+abl.*) cōram
present¹ (*noun*) dōnum, -ī *n.*, mūnus, -eris
n.
present² (*adj.*) praesens, -ntis, instans,
-ntis; **at present** nunc, in praesentī
present, am adsum, adesse, adfuī *v.irreg.*
presently mox, brevī (tempore)
preserve (con)servō 1.
press premō, pressī, pressum 3.; *see also*
urge
press on (*+dat.*) instō, institī 1.
presume coniciō, coniēcī, coniectum 3.,
sūmō, sumpsī, sumptum 3.
pretend simulō 1., fingō, finxī, fictum 3.
pretty bellus, -a, -um, formōsus, -a, -um,
pulc(h)er, -c(h)ra, -c(h)rum
prevent prohibeō 2.; (*+quōminus/quīn*
+subj.) impediō 4.; (*+dat. +quōminus etc.*)
obstō, obstitī 1.
previously anteā, antehāc
price pretium, -(i)ī *n.*
pride superbia, -ae *f.*, glōria, -ae *f.*
priest sacerdōs, -ōtis *m.*
prince rēgulus, -ī *m.*, princeps, -cipis *m.*
prison carcer, -eris *n.*, vincula, -ōrum *n.pl.*
prisoner captīvus, -ī *m.*
private prīvātus, -a, -um, sēcrētus, -a, -um
privately sēcrētō, clam

prize pretium, -(i)ī *n.*
problem quaestiō, -ōnis *f.*
proceed pergō, perrexī, perrectum 3.,
prōcēdō, -cessī, -cessum 3.
procession pompa, -ae *f.*, agmen, -inis *n.*
produce ēdō, ēdidī, ēditum 3., pariō,
peperī, partum 3., ferō, ferre, tulī, lātum
v.irreg.
product fructus, -ūs *m.*
profit lucrum, -ī *n.*, fructus, -ūs *m.*, ēmolumentum, -ī *n.*
progress prōgredior, prōgressus 3. *dep.*
prologue prologus, -ī *m.*
prolong prōdūcō, -duxī, -ductum 3.
promise¹ (*noun*) prōmissum, -ī *n.*
promise² (*v.*) polliceor, pollicitus 2. *dep.*,
prōmittō, -mīsī, -missum 3.
prompt alacer, -cris, -cre, promptus, -a, -um
proof argūmentum, -ī *n.*, documentum,
-(i)ī *n.*
proper rectus, -a, -um, iustus, -a, -um,
decōrus, -a, -um
property bona, -ōrum *n.pl.*, rēs, reī *f.*
prose orātiō (solūta), -ōnis (solūtae) *f.*
prosper flōreō 2.
prosperity fortūna, -ae *f.*, fēlīcitās, -ātis *f.*
prosperous fortūnātus, -a, -um, fēlix, -īcis,
secundus, -a, -um
prostitute meretrix, -īcis *f.*, scortum, -ī *n.*,
lēna, -ae *f.*
protect dēfendō, -dī, -sum 3., tueor, tuitus
2. *dep.*, custōdiō 4.
protector dēfensor, -ōris *m.*, custōs, -ōdis
m.
proud superbus, -a, -um, insolens, -ntis,
arrogans, -ntis
proudly superbē
prove probō 1., dēmonstrō 1.; (test)
experior, expertus 4. *dep.*
provide praebeō 2., parō 1.
provide for (*+dat.*) prōvideō, -vīdī, -vīsum
2.
providence prōvidentia, -ae *f.*
province prōvincia, -ae *f.*
provisions cibus, -ī *m.*, frūmentum, -ī *n.*,
commeātūs, -uum *m.pl.*
provoke lacessō, -īvī (-iī), -ītum 3., irrītō 1.,
vexō 1., excitō 1.
prow prōra, -ae *f.*
prudence prūdentia, -ae *f.*
prudent prūdens, -ntis, cautus, -a, -um
public pūblicus, -a, -um, commūnis, -is, -e

public, in forīs, in prōpatulō
publish (dī)vulgō 1.; (*books*) ēdō, ēdidī, ēditum 3.
pull trahō, traxī, tractum 3., tractō 1.
pulsate palpitō 1., vibrō 1., micō, -uī 1.
punish (+*dē* +*abl.*) poenās sūmō (sumpsī, sumptum 3.), pūniō 4.
punished, am poenās dō (dedī, datum 1.)
punishment poena, -ae *f.*, supplicium, -(i)ī *n.*
pup catulus, -ī *m.*
pupil discipulus, -ī *m.*; (*of the eye*) pūpilla, -ae *f.*, aciēs, -ēī *f.*
pure castus, -a, -um, pūrus, -a, -um, merus, -a, -um, integer, -gra, -grum

purification purgātiō, -ōnis *f.*, lustrātiō, -ōnis *f.*
purify (ex)pūrgō 1.
purple purpureus, -a, -um
purpose consilium, -(i)ī *n.*, prōpositum, -ī *n.*
pursue persequor, -secūtus 3. *dep.*, insequor, insecūtus 3. *dep.*, insectō 1.
pus pūs, pūris *n.*
push trūdō, -sī, -sum 3., impellō, impulī, impulsum 3.
put down dēpōnō, dēposuī, dēpositum 3.
put pōnō, posuī, positum 3.
put up with *see* **tolerate**
puzzle aenigma, -atis *n.*, nōdus, -ī *m.*
pyre rogus, -ī *m.*

Q

quantity quantitās, -ātis *f.*, numerus, -ī *m.*; (large quantity) vīs, vīs *f.*, pondus, -eris *n.*
quarrel¹ (*noun*) rixa, -ae *f.*, iurgium, -(i)ī *n.*
quarrel² (*v.*) rixor 1. *dep.*, iurgō 1., altercor 1. *dep.*
queen rēgīna, -ae *f.*
quench exstinguō, -nxī, -nctum 3.
question¹ (*noun*) quaesītum, -ī *n.*, quaestiō, -ōnis *f.*, interrogātum, -ī *n.*
question² (*v.*) (inter)rogō 1., dubitō 1.
quick celer, -ris, -re, citus, -a, -um, vēlox, -ōcis, rapidus, -a, -um, pernix, -īcis, alacer, -cris, -cre
quickly celeriter, cito, vēlōciter

quiet¹ (*noun*) quiēs, -ētis *f.*, tranquillitās, -ātis *f.*, pax, pācis *f.*
quiet² (*adj.*) quiētus, -a, -um, tranquillus, -a, -um, pācātus, -a, -um, placidus, -a, -um
quiet, keep quiescō, quiēvī, quiētum 3., sileō 2.
quietly quiētē, tranquillē, tacitē
quite satis; (completely) omnīnō, admodum; **not quite** parum, vix
quiver¹ (*noun*) pharetra, -ae *f.*
quiver² (*v.*) tremō, -uī 3., trepidō 1.
quivering tremebundus, -a, -um, tremulus, -a, -um

R

rabbit cūniculus, -ī *m.*
race (nation) gens, gentis *f.*, genus, -eris *n.*, propāgō, -inis *f.*, nātiō, -ōnis *f.*; (competition) cursus, -ūs *m.*, certāmen, -inis *n.*
radish rādix, -īcis *f.*, raphanus, -ī *m.*
rage[1] (*noun*) īra, īrae *f.*, furor, -ōris *m.*, rabiēs, -ēī *f.*, saevitia, -ae *f.*
rage[2] (*v.*) furō 3., saeviō 4.
rain pluvia, -ae *f.*; (heavy rain) imber, imbris *m.*
rainbow arcus, -ūs *m.*
rains, it pluit 3. *impers.*
raise (ē)levō 1., tollō, sustulī, sublātum 3., ērigō, ērexī, ērectum 3., sublevō 1.; *see also* **increase**
rake rastellus, -ī *m.*
ram ariēs, -etis *m.*
rampart vallum, -ī *n.*, agger, -ris *m.*
random, at temere
range seriēs, -ēī *f.*, ordō, -inis *m.*
rank status, -ūs *m.*, gradus, -ūs *m.*; (*of an army*) ordō, ordinis *m.*
ransom redimō, redēmī, redemptum 3.
rapid rapidus, -a, -um, celer, -ris, -re, citus, -a, -um, velox, -ōcis
rare rārus, -a, -um, singulāris, -is, -e, eximius, -a, -um; *see also* **thin**
rarely rārō
rash temerārius, -a, -um, incautus, -a, -um, inconsultus, -a, -um, praeceps, -cipitis
rashly temere, inconsultē
rashness temeritās, -ātis *f.*
rate aestimō 1., censeō, -uī, -um 2.
rather potius, prius
rather, would (+*inf.*) mālō, mālle, māluī *v. irreg.*
ravage (dē)populor 1. *dep.*, (per)vastō 1.
raw crūdus, -a, -um, incoctus, -a, -um
ray radius, -(i)ī *m.*, iubar, -aris *n.*
reach (+*ad* +*acc.*) adveniō, advēnī, adven-

tum 4., attingō, attigī, attactum; *see also* **touch**
read legō, lēgī, lectum 3., ēvolvō, -vī, -ūtum 3.
read through perlegō, -lēgī, -lectum 3.
readily libenter, promptē, facile
ready (for) (+*ad* +*acc.*) parātus, -a, -um, promptus, -a, -um
reality vēritās, -ātis *f.*
realize intellegō, -xī, -ctum 3., mente (*or* animō) concipiō (-cēpī, -ceptum 3.), cognōscō, cognōvī, cognitum 3., sentiō, -sī, -sum 4., compre(he)ndō, -dī, -sum 3.
really rē ipsā (*or* vērā)
reap (dē)metō, (dē)messuī, (dē)messum 3.
reaper messor, -ōris *m.*
rear tergum, -ī *n.*
reason causa, -ae *f.*, ratiō, -ōnis *f.*; (faculty of reason) mens, mentis *f.*, ratiō, -ōnis *f.*
reasoning ratiō, -ōnis *f.*, ratiōcinātiō, -ōnis *f.*
rebellion rebelliō, -ōnis *f.*, dēfectiō, -ōnis *f.*, sēditiō, -ōnis *f.*
rebuild restituō, -uī, -ūtum 3., reficiō, refēcī, refectum 3.
rebuke increpō, -uī 1., repre(he)ndō, -dī, -sum 3., vituperō 1.
recall revocō 1.; (recall to mind) recordor 1. *dep.*, in animum (*or* memoriam) revocō 1.
receive accipiō, accēpī, acceptum 3., recipiō, recēpī, receptum 3.
recent recens, -ntis, novus, -a, -um
recently nūper, recens
recite recitō 1., prōnuntiō 1.
recline recumbō, recubuī, recubitum 3.
recognize cognōscō, cognōvī, cognitum 3., agnōscō, agnōvī, agnitum 3.
record historia, -ae *f.*, monumentum, -ī *n.*, tabulae, -ārùm *f.pl.*; *pl.* annālēs, -ium *m. pl.*, fastī, -ōrum *m.pl.*

recover recipiō, recēpī, receptum 3.,
recuperō 1., reparō 1.
recruit (*military*) tīrō, -ōnis *m.*
red ruber, rubra, rubrum, russus, -a, -um,
rubens, -ntis, rubidus, -a, -um
reduce (dē)minuō, -uī, -ūtum 3.
reed (h)arundō, -inis *f.*, calamus, -ī *m.*
refer referō, referre, rettulī, re(l)lātum *v.
irreg.*, tribuō, -uī, -ūtum 3.
reflect repercutiō, -ssī, -ssum 3.
refuge perfugium, -(i)ī *n.*, portus, -ūs *m.*
refuse recūsō 1., repudiō 1.; (deny)
(dē)negō 1.; (refuse to) (+*inf.*) nōlō, nōlle,
nōluī *v.irreg.*
refute redarguō, -uī 3., refūtō 1.
regal rēgālis, -is, -e, rēgius, -a, -um
regard spectō 1., observō 1.; *see also* **concern**
region regiō, -ōnis *f.*, locus, -ī *m.*
regret doleō 2.; mē (*etc.*) paenitet 2.
impers.; (miss) dēsīderō 1.
regularly constanter
reign regnō 1., imperō 1.
rein habēna, -ae *f.*
reinforcements novae cōpiae, novārum
cōpiārum *f.pl.*, subsidium, -(i)ī *n.*
reject repudiō 1., aspernor 1. *dep.*, respuō,
-ī 3.
rejoice (in) (+*abl.*) gaudeō, gāvīsus 2. *semi-
dep.*, laetor 1. *dep.*
relate (ē)narrō 1., commemorō 1., trādō,
-didī, -ditum 3.
relative propinquus, -ī *m.*, cognātus, -ī *m.*;
(*female*) propinqua, -ae *f.*, cognāta, -ae *f.*
release līberō 1., laxō 1., exsolvō, -vī,
-ūtum 3.; (*of a slave*) manūmittō, -mīsī,
-missum 3.
relieve sublevō 1., exonerō 1., laxō 1.
religion religiō, -ōnis *f.*
religious religiōsus, -a, -um, sanctus, -a,
-um
reluctant invītus, -a, -um
relying (on) (+*abl.*) frētus, -a, -um
remain (re)maneō, (re)mansī, (re)mansum
2., moror 1. *dep.*; (am left) superō 1.,
supersum, -esse, -fuī *v.irreg.*
remaining reliquus, -a, -um, superstes,
-etis
remedy remedium, -(i)ī *n.*, medicīna, -ae *f.*,
medicāmentum, -ī *n.*
remember (com)meminī (*only in pf.*),
recordor 1. *dep.*, memorō 1.

remind (ad)moneō 2.
remorse paenitentia, -ae *f.*
remorse, feel mē (*etc.*) paenitet 2. *impers.*
remote longinquus, -a, -um, remōtus, -a,
-um, disiunctus, -a, -um
remove removeō, remōvī, remōtum 2.,
auferō, auferre, abstulī, ablātum *v.irreg.*,
ablēgō 1.; (*one's home*) commigrō 1.
renew renovō 1., reparō 1., reficiō, refēcī,
refectum 3., integrō 1.
renown fāma., -ae *f.* glōria, -ae *f.*, nōmen,
-inis *n.*
rent (hire) condūcō, -duxī, -ductum 3.
rent out (ab)locō 1.
repair reparō 1., reficiō, refēcī, refectum 3.,
restituō, -uī, -ūtum 3.
repay solvō, -vī, -ūtum 3., reddō, -didī,
-ditum 3.
repeat iterō 1., redintegrō 1.
repeatedly identidem, iterum atque
iterum
repel repellō, reppulī, repulsum 3., fugō 1.
replace repōnō, reposuī, repositum 3.,
restituō, -uī, -ūtum 3.
reply respondeō, -dī, -sum 2.
report renuntiātiō, -ōnis; *see also* **rumour**
repress opprimō, oppressī, oppressum 3.
reproach increpō, -uī 1., repre(he)ndō, -dī,
-sum 3., increpitō 1., incūsō 1.
republic rēspūblica, rēīpūblicae *f.*, cīvitās,
-ātis *f.*
reputation existimātiō, -ōnis *f.*, fāma, -ae
f., laus, -dis *f.*, nōmen, -inis *n.*, glōria, -ae *f.*
request petō, petīvī (-iī), petītum 3., rogō
1., poscō, poposcī 3., precor 1. *dep.*,
implōrō 1., postulō 1.
require requīrō, -īsīvī (-iī), -īsītum 3.;
(+*abl.*) egeō, eguī 2.; (demand) postulō 1.,
poscō, poposcī 3.
rescue servō 1., līberō 1., exsolvō, -vī,
-ūtum 3.
resentment īra, īrae *f.*
reserves (military) subsidia, -ōrum *n.pl.*
resign (+*abl.*) mē (*etc.*) abdicō 1., abeō,
abīre, abīvī (abiī), abitum 4.; (give up)
concēdō, -cessī, -cessum 3.
resist (+*dat.*) resistō, restitī 3., repugnō 1.,
obstō, obstitī 1., adversor 1. *dep.*
resolution obstinātiō, -ōnis *f.*, constantia,
-ae *f.*; *see also* **plan**[1]
resolve dēcernō, dēcrēvī, dēcrētum 3.,
statuō, -uī, -ūtum 3., destinō 1.

resources opēs, opum *f.pl.*, pecūnia, -ae *f.*; *see also* **help**[1]

respect[1] (*noun*) observantia, -ae *f.*, reverentia, -ae *f.*

respect[2] (*v.*) observō 1., revereor 2. *dep.*, colō, coluī, cultum 3.

respectable honestus, -a, -um, venerābilis, -is, -e

respond respondeō, -dī, -sum 2.

rest[1] (*noun*) (relaxation) quiēs, -ētis *f.*, ōtium, ōt(i)ī *n.*, tranquillitās, -ātis *f.*, pax, pācis *f.*

rest[2] (*noun*) (remainder) reliquum, -ī *n.*, residuum, -ī *n.*

rest[3] (*v.*) (re)quiescō, (re)quiēvī, (re)quiētum 3., ōtior 1. *dep.*, cessō 1.; *see also* **place**[2]

rest on (+*abl.*) nītor, nīsus 3. *dep.*

restore redintegrō 1., restituō, -uī, -ūtum 3., reficiō, refēcī, refectum 3.

result ēventus, -ūs *m.*, ēventum, -ī *n.*, fructus, -ūs *m.*, consequentia, -ae *f.*, exitus, -ūs *m.*

retain retineō, retinuī, retentum 2., conservō 1.

retake recipiō, recēpī, receptum 3.

return[1] (*noun*) reditus, -ūs *m.*, regressus, -ūs *m.*

return[2] (*v.*) (go back) redeō, redīre, redīvī (-iī), reditum 4., remigrō 1., revertor, revertus 3. *dep.*; (give back) reddō, reddidī, redditum 3., restituō, -uī, -ūtum 3., referō, referre, rettulī, relātum *v.irreg.*

reveal patefaciō, -fēcī, -factum 3., ēvulgō 1.

reversal commūtātiō, -ōnis *f.*, conversiō, -ōnis *f.*, vicissitūdō, -inis *f.*

revolt dēfectiō, -ōnis *f.*, mōtus, -ūs *m.*, sēditiō, -ōnis *f.*, rebelliō, -ōnis *f.*

reward praemium, -(i)ī *n.*, fructus, -ūs *m.*, mercēs, -ēdis *f.*

rib costa, -ae *f.*

ribbon fascia, -ae *f.*, redimīculum, -ī *n.*

rich dīvēs (dīs), dīvitis (dītis), opulentus, -a, -um, locuplēs, -ētis, fortūnātus, -a, -um, pecūniōsus, -a, -um

riches dīvitiae, -ārum *f.pl.*, opēs, opum *f.pl.*, fortūnae, -ārum *f.pl.*, pecūnia, -ae *f.*

riddle aenigma, -atis *n.*

ride (equō) vehor, vectus 3. *dep.*, equitō 1.

rider vector, -ōris *m.*

ridge iugum, -ī *n.*

right dexter, -t(e)ra, -t(e)rum; (correct)

rectus, -a, -um, probus, -a, -um, aequus, -a, -um, iustus, -a, -um; **right hand** dext(e)ra; **on the right** dext(e)rā, ad dext(e)ram

rightly rectē, iūre, iustē

rigorous sevērus, -a, -um, dūrūs, -a, -um

rigour sevēritās, -ātis *f.*, dūritia, -ae *f.*

rim ōra, ōrae *f.*

ring orbis, -is *m.*, circulus, -ī *m.*; (*of a finger*) ānulus, -ī *m.*

riot tumultus, -ūs *m.*, mōtus, -ūs *m.*, turba, -ae *f.*

rip scindō, scidī, scissum 3., dīvellō, dīvellī, dīvulsum 3.

ripe mātūrus, -a, -um, tempestīvus, -a, -um

ripen (become ripe) mātūrescō, -ruī 3., adolescō, adoluī, adultum 3.; (make ripe) mātūrō 1.

rise (ex)surgō, (ex)surrexī, (ex)surrectum 3., orior, ortus 4. *dep.*; *see also* **increase**

risk perīclitor 1. *dep.*

rite rītus, -ūs *m.*

rival rīvālis, -is *m.*, aemulus, -ī *m.*

rivalry rīvālitās, -ātis *f.*, aemulātiō, -ōnis *f.*, certāmen, -inis *n.*

river flūmen, -inis *n.*, fluvius, -(i)ī *m.*, amnis, -is *m.*

road via, viae *f.*, iter, itineris *n.*

roam vagor 1. *dep.*, errō 1., pālor 1. *dep.*

roar fremō, -uī, -itum 3., vōciferor 1. *dep.*, mūgiō 4.

roaring fremitus, -ūs *m.*, mūgitus, -ūs *m.*

rob dēspoliō 1.; (engage in robbery) latrōcinor 1. *dep.*

robber latrō, -ōnis *m.*, praedō, -ōnis *m.*, fūr, fūris *m.*

robbery latrōcinium, -(i)ī *n.*

robe vestis, -is *f.*

rock saxum, -ī *n.*, rūpēs, -is *f.*, scopulus, -ī *m.*

rod virga, -ae *f.*

roll[1] (*noun*) volūmen, -inis *n.*

roll[2] (*v.*) (ē)volvō, -vī, -ūtum 3., volūtō 1.; volvor, volūtus 3. *dep.*

roof tectum, -ī *n.*, culmen, -inis *n.*

room cella, -ae *f.*, cubiculum, -ī *n.*, conclāve, -is *n.*; (space) spatium, -(i)ī *n.*, locus, -ī *n.*

root rādix, -īcis *f.*; (base) fons, fontis *m.*

  from the roots (i.e. completely) rādīcitus

rope fūnis, -is *m.*, restis, -is *f.*

rose rosa, -ae *f.*
rostrum tribūnal, -ālis *n.*
rot putrescō 3., tābescō, tābuī 3.
rotten putridus, -a, -um, putrēfactus, -a, -um
rough asper, -era, -erum, horridus, -a, -um, hirsūtus, -a, -um
round¹ (*adj.*) rotundus, -a, -um, orbiculā-tus, -a, -um
round² (*prep.*) (+*acc.*) circā, circum
rouse excitō 1., stimulō 1.
rout fundō, fūdī, fūsum 3., fugō 1., dissipō 1.
route via, viae *f.*, iter, itineris *n.*
row rēmigō 1.
rower rēmex, -igis *m.*
royal rēgālis, -is, -e, rēgius, -a, -um
royalty regnum, -ī *n.*
rub fricō, -uī, -tum 1., terō, trīvī, trītum 3.
rub out dēleō, dēlēvī, dēlētum 2.
rubbish quisquiliae, -ārum *f.pl.*
rude (*in manners*) insolens, -ntis, petulans, -ntis
ruin¹ (*noun*) exitium, -(i)ī *n.*, perniciēs, -ēī *f.*, interitus, -ūs *m.*, clādēs, -is *f.*, calamitās,

-ātis *f.*, ruīna, -ae *f.*; (*of buildings*) ruīnae, -ārum *f.pl.*, parietinae, -ārum *f.pl.*
ruin² (*v.*) perdō, -didī, -ditum 3., pervertō, -tī, -sum 3.; (+*dat.*) pessum dō (dedī, datum 1.)
rule gubernō 1., regō, rexī, rectum 3., regnō 1.; (+*dat.*) dominor 1. *dep.*; (+*dat.*) imperō 1.
ruler dominus, -ī *m.*, rex, rēgis *m.*, rector, -ōris *m.*
rumour fāma, -ae *f.*, rūmor, -ōris *m.*, sermō, -ōnis *m.*
run currō, cucurrī, cursum 3., volō 1.; (*of liquids*) fluō, fluxī, fluxum 3.
run about cursō 1., cursitō 1.
run away aufugiō 4.; (*in battle*) terga dō (dedī, datum 1.)
run out excurrō, ex(cu)currī, excursum 3.
runner cursor, -ōris *m.*
rural rusticus, -a, -um, agrestis, -is, -e
rush ruō, ruī, rutum 3., currō, cucurrī, cursum 3.
rust robīgō, -inis *f.*; (*of iron*) ferrūgō, -inis *f.*
rustic *see* **rural**

S

sack¹ (*noun*) coleus, -ī *m.*, saccus, -ī *m.*
sack² (*v.*) dīripiō, dīripuī, dīreptum 3.,
  spoliō 1.
sacred sacer, sacra, sacrum, sanctus, -a,
  -um
sacrifice¹ (*noun*) sacrificium, -(i)ī *n.*,
  sacrum, -ī *n.*; (loss) iactūra, -ae *f.*
sacrifice² (*v.*) mactō 1., sacrificō 1.,
  immolō 1.; (give up for) (+*acc.*+*dat.*)
  posthabeō 2.; (carry out a sacrifice) sacra
  faciō (fēcī, factum 3.)
sad tristis, -is, -e, maestus, -a, -um
saddle strātum, -ī *n.*
sadness tristitia, -ae *f.*, maestitia, -ae *f.*
safe tūtus, -a, -um, salvus, -a, -um, incolumis, -is, -e
safety salūs, -ūtis *f.*, incolumitās, -ātis *f.*
sail¹ (*noun*) vēlum, -ī *n.*
sail² (*v.*) nāvigō 1.; (set sail) vēla dō (dedī,
  datum 1.)
sailing nāvigātiō, -ōnis *f.*
sailor nauta, -ae *f.*
sake of, for the (+*gen.*) causā, grātiā;
  (+*acc.*) propter
salary mercēs, -ēdis *f.*
saliva salīva, -ae *f.*
salmon salmō, -ōnis *m.*
salt sāl, salis *m.*
salted salsus, -a, -um
salute salūtō 1.
same īdem, eadem, idem; **at the same
  time** simul; **in the same place** ibidem
sanctify consecrō 1.
sanctuary dēlūbrum, -ī *n.*, fānum, -ī *n.*
sand (h)arēna, -ae *f.*
sandal solea, -ae *f.*, crepida, -ae *f.*
sandy (h)arēnōsus, -a, -um
satchel loculus, -ī *m.*
satisfactory grātus, -a, -um, idōneus, -a,
  -um

satisfied (with) (+*abl.*) contentus, -a, -um
sausage tomāculum, -ī *n.*
savage saevus, -a, -um, ferus, -a, -um,
  inhūmānus, -a, -um, ātrox, -ōcis
savagery ferōcitās, -ātis *f.*, inhūmānitās,
  -ātis *f.*
save (con)servō 1.
saw serra, -ae *f.*
say dīcō, dixī, dictum 3., āiō *v.irreg.*,
  inquam *v.irreg.*; **say that ... not** negō 1.
saying dictum, -ī *n.*
scale¹ (*noun*) lanx, -cis *f.*; (pair of scales)
  lībra, -ae *f.*; (step) gradus, -ūs *m.*; (*of a fish*)
  squāma, -ae *f.*
scale² (*v.*) ascendō, -dī, -sum 3.
scandal calumnia, -ae *f.*, infāmia, -ae *f.*,
  opprobrium, -(i)ī *n.*
scanty exiguus, -a, -um, exīlis, -is, -e,
  tenuis, -is, -e
scar cicātrix, -īcis *f.*
scarce rārus, -a, -um
scarcely vix, aegrē
scatter spargō, -sī, -sum 3., dissipō 1.; (go
  apart) dissipor 1. *dep.*
scene spectāculum, -ī *n.*
scent odor, odōris *m.*
sceptre scēptrum, -ī *n.*
scheme ratiō, -ōnis *f.*, ars, artis *f.*, dolus, -ī
  m.
school (*for boys*) lūdus, -ī *m.*, gymnasium,
  -(i)ī *n.*; (*for men*) schola, -ae *f.*
schoolmaster magister, -trī *m.*
science doctrīna, -ae *f.*, disciplīna, -ae *f.*
scold admoneō 2., obiūrgō 1., increpō, -uī,
  -itum 1.
scorn spernō, sprēvī, sprētum 3., contemnō, -mpsī, -mptum 3.
scorpion scorpiō, -ōnis *m.*
scout explōrātor, -ōris *m.*, speculātor, -ōris
  m.

scrape, scratch rādō, rāsī, rāsum 3.
scream[1] (*noun*) clāmor, -ōris *m.*, ululātus, -ūs *m.*
scream[2] (*v.*) clāmō 1., ululō 1.
screen vēlāmentum, -ī *n.*, ōbex, ōbicis *m./f.*
scribe scrība, -ae *m.*
scroll volūmen, -inis *n.*
scythe falx, falcis *f.*
sea mare, maris *n.*, aequor, -oris *n.*, pontus, -ī *m.*, pelagus, -ī *n.*, altum, -ī *n.*
seal (stamp) signum, -ī *n.*; (animal) phōca, -ae *f.*
search (carry out a search) investīgō 1., scrūtor 1. *dep.*; (carry out a search of) excutiō, -ssī, -ssum 3.
search for quaerō, -sīvī (-iī), -sītum 3.
seashore lītus, -oris *n.*, acta, -ae *f.*
season tempestās, -ātis *f.*, hōra, -ae *f.*
seat sēdēs, -is *f.*, sedīle, -is *n.*
seaweed alga, -ae *f.*
second alter, -era, -erum, secundus, -a, -um; **for a second time** iterum
secret arcānus, -a, -um, sēcrētus, -a, -um, occultus, -a, -um
secretly sēcrētō, occultē, clam
section pars, -tis *f.*
secure tūtus, -a, -um, firmus, -a, -um
securely tūtō
sediment faex, -cis *f.*
see videō, vīdī, vīsum 2., cernō, crēvī, crētum 3., spectō 1.; (realize) intellegō, -xī, -ctum
seed sēmen, -inis *n.*, grāmen, -inis *n.*
seek petō, -īvī (-iī), petītum 3., quaerō, -sīvī (-iī), -sītum 3.
seem videor, vīsus 2. *dep.*
seer vātēs, -is *m./f.*
seize rapiō, -uī, -tum 3., compre(he)ndō, -dī, -sum 3., arripiō, arripuī, arreptum 3.
seldom rārō
select *see* **choose**
self-confidence fīdūcia, -ae *f.*, confīdentia, -ae *f.*
self-control temperantia, -ae *f.*
selfish avārus, -a, -um
sell vendō, -idī, -itum 3.
senate senātus, -ūs *m.*
senate house cūria, -ae *f.*
send mittō, mīsī, missum 3.
send away dīmittō, dīmīsī, dīmissum 3.
send back remittō, remīsī, remissum 3.
send for arcessō, -īvī (-iī), -ītum 3.

send into intrōmittō, -mīsī, -missum 3., immittō, immīsī, immissum 3.
senile senīlis, -is, -e
sense[1] (*noun*) sensus, -ūs *m.*; (meaning) sententia, -ae *f.*, vīs, vīs *f.*; **good sense** prūdentia, -ae *f.*
sense[2] (*v.*) sentiō, -sī, -sum 4.
sensible prūdens, -ntis; (tangible) sensibilis, -is, -e
sentence sententia, -ae *f.*, iūdicium, -(i)ī *n.*
sentry vigil, -lis *m.*, custōs, -ōdis *m.*
separate disiungō, -xī, -ctum 3., sēparō 1., dīvidō, dīvīsī, dīvīsum 3., sēgregō 1.
separately seorsum, sēparātim
sepulchre sepulc(h)rum, -ī *n.*
serene tranquillus, -a, -um, placidus, -a, -um
serenity tranquillitās, -ātis *f.*
series ordō, -inis *m.*, seriēs, -ēī *f.*
serious gravis, -is, -e, sevērus, -a, -um, sērius, -a, -um
serpent serpens, -ntis *f.*, dracō, -ōnis *m.*
servant (*male*) famulus, -ī *m.*, servus, -ī *m.*; (*female*) famula, -ae *f.*, serva, -ae *f.*, ancilla, -ae *f.*; (*male assistant*) minister, -trī *m.*; (*female assistant*) ministra, -ae *f.*
serve serviō 4.; (*food/drink*) ministrō 1.
service servitium, -(i)ī *n.*; (military) mīlitia, -ae *f.*, stīpendia, -ōrum *n.pl.*; **good service** beneficium, -(i)ī *n.*
servile servīlis, -is, -e
servitude servitūs, -ūtis *f.*
set[1] (*noun*) numerus, -ī *m.*, grex, gregis *m.*, congeriēs, -ēī *f.*
set[2] (*v.*) locō 1., pōnō, posuī, positum 3., sistō, stitī, statum 3.
set free līberō 1.
set out proficiscor, profectus 3. *dep.*
settle constituō, -uī, -ūtum 3., compōnō, -posuī, -positum 3.
settlement (*of people*) colōnia, -ae *f.*; (*of disputes*) compositiō, -ōnis *f.*
settler colōnus, -ī *m.*
seven septem; **seven times** septiens (-iēs)
seventeen septendecim
seventh septimus, -a, -um
seventy septuāgintā
several aliquot, complūrēs, -ēs, -a
severe dūrus, -a, -um, sevērus, -a, -um, gravis, -is, -e, austērus, -a, -um, ācer, ācris, ācre, asper, -ra, -rum

severity sevēritās, -ātis *f.*, gravitās, -ātis *f.*, asperitās, -ātis *f.*

sew serō, -uī, -tum 3.

sewer cloāca, -ae *f.*

sex (gender) sexus, -ūs *m.*; (intercourse) coitus, -ūs *m.*

shade, shadow umbra, -ae *f.*; (*of the dead*) mānēs, -ium *m.pl.*

shady umbrōsus, -a, -um, obscūrus, -a, -um, opācus, -a, -um

shaggy hirsūtus, -a, -um

shake vibrō 1., labefactō 1., quatiō, -ssī, -ssum 3., agitō 1.; *see also* **shiver**

shake off excutiō, -ssī, -ssum 3.

shallow brevis, -is, -e, vadōsus, -a, -um

shallows vada, -ōrum *n.pl.*

shame pudor, -ōris *m.*, ignōminia, -ae *f.*

shame, feel mē (*etc.*) pudet 2. *impers.*

shameful turpis, -is, -e, ignōminiōsus, -a, -um

shamefully turpiter

shamelessness impudentia, -ae *f.*

shape faciēs, -ēī *f.*, figūra, -ae *f.*, forma, -ae *f.*

share¹ (*noun*) pars, -tis *f.*, portiō, -ōnis *f.*

share² (*v.*) commūnicō 1.; (give a share of) partior 4. *dep.*

sharp ācer, ācris, ācre, acūtus, -a, -um

sharpen acuō, acuī, acūtum 3.

sharpness aciēs, -ēī *f.*, acūmen, -inis *n.*

shatter quassō 1., perfringō, -frēgī, -fractum 3.

shave rādō, rāsī, rāsum 3.

sheep ovis, ovis *f.*

sheet (*of cloth*) linteum, -ī *n.*; (*of metal*) lāmina, -ae *f.*; (*of paper*) schida, -ae *f.*, charta, -ae *f.*, pāgina, -ae *f.*

shell concha, -ae *f.*

shelter¹ (*noun*) perfugium, -(i)ī *n.*, suffugium, -(i)ī *n.*, tegmen, -inis *n.*

shelter² (*v.*) tegō, texī, tectum 3., dēfendō, -dī, -sum 3.

shepherd pastor, -ōris *m.*, ovīliō, -ōnis *m.*

shield scūtum, -ī *n.*, clipeus, -ī *m.*

shin tībia, -ae *f.*

shine fulgeō, -sī, -sum 2., lūceō, luxī 3.

shining fulgens, -ntis, splendidus, -a, -um, lūcidus, -a, -um

ship nāvis, -is *f.*

shipwreck naufragium, -(i)ī *n.*

shipwrecked naufragus, -a, -um

shiver tremō, -uī 3., horreō 2.

shoe calceus, -ī *m.*

shoemaker sūtor, -ōris *m.*

shop taberna, -ae *f.*

shore ōra, ōrae *f.*, lītus, -oris *n.*, acta, -ae *f.*

short brevis, -is, -e; **for a short time** paulisper

shortage inopia, -ae *f.*

shorten curtō 1., contrahō, -xī, -ctum 3.

shortly *see* **soon**

shortness brevitās, -ātis *f.*

should (+*inf.*) dēbeō 2.

shoulder (h)umerus, -ī *m.*

shout¹ (*noun*) clāmor, -ōris *m.*

shout² (*v.*) clāmō 1., vōciferor 1. *dep.*

show¹ (*noun*) spectāculum, -ī *n.*, lūdī, -ōrum *m.pl.*

show² (*v.*) (dē)monstrō 1., indicō 1.

show off mē (*etc.*) iactō 1.

shower imber, imbris *m.*

shrewd acūtus, -a, -um, sagax, -ācis, ācer, ācris, ācre

shrine dēlūbrum, -ī *n.*, fānum, -ī *n.*

shrink from dētrectō 1.

shun (ē)vītō 1.

shut claudō, -sī, -sum 3., operiō, -uī, -tum 4.

shy verēcundus, -a, -um, timidus, -a, -um, pudibundus, -a, -um

shyly verēcundē, timidē

shyness verēcundia, -ae *f.*, pudor, -ōris *m.*

sick aeger, aegra, aegrum, aegrōtus, -a, -um

sick, am aegrōtō 1.; (feel sick) nauseō 1.

sickle falx, -cis *f.*

sickness aegritūdō, -inis *f.*, morbus, -ī *m.*; (feeling) nausea, -ae *f.*

side latus, -eris *n.*, pars, -tis *f.*; **on both sides** utrimque; **on all sides** undique

siege obsidiō, -ōnis *f.*, oppugnātiō, -ōnis *f.*

sieve crībrum, -ī *n.*

sigh suspīrium, -(i)ī *n.*

sight (seeing) aspectus, -ūs *m.*; (faculty) vīsus, -ūs *m.*; (thing seen) spectāculum, -ī *n.*, aspectāmen, -inis *n.*, speciēs, -ēī *f.*

sign signum, -ī *n.*, ōmen, ōminis *n.*, indicium, -(i)ī *n.*, nota, -ae *f.*; (trace) vestīgium, -(i)ī *n.*; *see also* **portent**

signal signum, -ī *n.*

signify significō 1.

silence silentium, -(i)ī *n.*

silent silens, -ntis, tacitus, -a, -um; (*in character*) taciturnus, -a, -um

silent, am sileō 2., taceō 2.

silently tacitē

silly fatuus, -a, -um, stultus, -a, -um, ineptus, -a, -um

silver argentum, -ī *n.*

similar similis, -is, -e

simulate simulō 1.

sin peccātum, -ī *n.*, dēlictum, -ī *n.*

sin, commit peccō 1.

since[1] (*adv.*) abhinc, posteā

since[2] (*prep.*) (+*abl.*) ē *or* ex, ā *or* ab

since[3] (*conj.*) postquam; (because) quod, quia; (+*subj.*) cum

sincere sincērus, -a, -um, apertus, -a, -um

sinew nervus, -ī *m.*

sing canō, cecinī, cantum 3., cantō 1.

singer cantor, -ōris *m.*, cantrix, -īcis *f.*

single ūnus, ūna, ūnum, sōlus, -a, -um, ūnicus, -a, -um; (unmarried) caelebs, -libis

sink (push down) (dē)mergō, -sī, -sum 3., dēprimō, dēpressī, dēpressum 3.; (go down) dēsīdō, dēsēdī, dēsessum 3., dēscendō, -dī, -sum 3.

sip gustō 1.

sister soror, -ōris *f.*

sister-in-law glōs, glōris *f.*

sisterly sorōrius, -a, -um

sit sedeō, sēdī, sessum 2.

sit down consīdō, -sēdī, -sessum 3.

site situs, -ūs *m.*, locus, -ī *m.*

situated situs, -a, -um

six sex; **six times** sexiens (-iēs)

sixteen sēdecim

sixth sextus, -a, -um

sixty sexāgintā

size magnitūdō, -inis *f.*, amplitūdō, -inis *f.*, mensūra, -ae *f.*

skill perītia, -ae *f.*, sollertia, -ae *f.*, ars, artis *f.*

skilled perītus, -a, -um, doctus, -a, -um, sollers, -tis

skin cutis, -is *m.*; (hide) pellis, -is *f.*

skull caput, capitis *n.*

sky caelum, -ī *n.*, aether, -ris *m.*

slack laxus, -a, -um, remissus, -a, -um

slacken (make loose) remittō, remīsī, remissum 3.; (become loose) laxor 1. *dep.*

slander calumnia, -ae *f.*, obtrectātiō, -ōnis *f.*

slaughter[1] (*noun*) caedēs, -is *f.*, strāgēs, -is *f.*

slaughter[2] (*v.*) caedō, cecīdī, caesum 3., trucīdō 1., mactō 1.

slave servus, -ī *m.*, famulus, -ī *m.*; (domestically born slave) verna, -ae *m.*

slave-woman serva, -ae *f.*, ancilla, -ae *f.*, famula, -ae *f.*

slavery servitūs, -ūtis *f.*

slay necō 1., occīdō, -dī, -sum 3., interficiō, -fēcī, -fectum 3.

sleep[1] (*noun*) somnus, -ī *m.*

sleep[2] (*v.*) dormiō 4.

sleepiness sopor, -ōris *m.*

sleepless insomnis, -is, -e, vigil, -lis

slice secō, -uī, -tum 1.

slide lābor, lapsus 3. *dep.*

slime līmus, -ī *m.*, lutum, -ī *n.*

slip lābor, lapsus 3. *dep.*

slippery lūbricus, -a, -um

slope clīvus, -ī *m.*, dēclīvitās, -ātis *f.*

slow tardus, -a, -um, lentus, -a, -um, longus, -a, -um

slowly tardē, lentē

sly callidus, -a, -um, vafer, vafra, vafrum, versūtus, -a, -um, astūtus, -a, -um

slyness astūtia, -ae *f.*

small parvus, -a, -um, minūtus, -a, -um, exiguus, -a, -um

smaller minor, -or, -us

smallest minimus, -a, -um

smart (neat) concinnus, -a, -um, nitidus, -a, -um

smartness nitor, -ōris *m.*

smell odor, odōris *m.*; (sense) odōrātus, -ūs *m.*

smelly olidus, -a, -um

smile[1] (*noun*) rīsus, -ūs *m.*

smile[2] (*v.*) surrīdeō, -rīsī, -rīsum 2.

smoke fūmus, -ī *m.*

smooth lēvis, -is, -e, plānus, -a, -um, placidus, -a, -um

smoothly lēniter, placidē

snack cēnula, -ae *f.*

snail cochlea, -ae *f.*

snake anguis, -is *m.*, serpens, -ntis *f.*, dracō, -ōnis *m.*; **sea snake** nātrix, -īcis *f.*

snare laqueus, -ī *m.*, plaga, -ae *f.*

snatch rapiō, -uī, -tum 3.

sneeze[1] (*noun*) sternūtāmentum, -ī *n.*

sneeze[2] (*v.*) sternuō, -ī 3.

snort fremitus, -ūs *m.*

snow nix, nivis *f.*

snows, it ningit, -xit 3. *impers.*

so sīc, ita; (+*adj.*/*adv.*) tam; (+*v.*) adeō; **so big, much** tantus, -a, -um; **so many** tot; **so many times** totiens; **so that** (+*subj.*) ut

soap sāpō, -ōnis *m.*
society societās, -ātis *f.*
sod (*of grass*) caespes, -itis *m.*
soft mollis, -is, -e, lēnis, -is, -e, mītis, -is, -e, dēlicātus, -a, -um
soften molliō 4., lēniō 4.
softly molliter, lēniter
softness mollitia, -ae *f.*
soil humus, -ī *f.*, solum, -ī *n.*, terra, -ae *f.*
solace sōlātium, -(i)ī *n.*
sold, am vēneō, vēnīre, vēnīvī (-iī), vēnitum 4.
soldier mīles, -itis *m.*; (footsoldier) pedes, -itis *m.*
solemn sollemnis, -is, -e, gravis, -is, -e, sanctus, -a, -um
solemnity gravitās, -ātis *f.*, sanctitās, -ātis *f.*
solid solidus, -a, -um, firmus, -a, -um
solitude sōlitūdō, -inis *f.*
solve solvō, -vī, -ūtum 3., explicō 1., ēnōdō 1.
some aliquī, -qua, -quod (*esp.pl.*); *pl.* nōnnullī, -ae, -a
somehow aliquā
someone, something aliquis, -qua, -quid
sometimes interdum, nōnnumquam
somewhere alicubi; **somewhere else** alibī; **to somewhere** aliquō
son fīlius, -(i)ī *m.*, nātus, -ī *m.*
son-in-law gener, -rī *m.*
song cantus, -ūs *m.*, carmen, -inis *n.*
soon mox, brevī (tempore), cito; **as soon as possible** quam prīmum
soot fūlīgō, -inis *f.*
soothe (dē)lēniō 4.
sore ulcus, -eris *n.*
sorrow dolor, -ōris *m.*, maestitia, -ae *f.*, luctus, -ūs *m.*
sorry for, feel (+*gen. of thing*) mē (*etc.*) paenitet 2. *impers.*, mē (*etc.*) piget 2. *impers.*
sort genus, -eris *n.*
soul anima, -ae *f.*, animus, -ī *m.*; (heart) cor, cordis *n.*
sound sonus, -ūs *m.*, sonitus, -ūs *m.*; (loud sound) fremitus, -ūs *m.*, fragor, -ōris *m.*
soup iūs, iūris *n.*
sour acerbus, -a, -um, amārus, -a, -um
source fons, fontis *m.*, orīgō, -inis *f.*
south merīdiēs, -ēī *f.*
southern austrālis, -is, -e
sow sūs, suis *f.*, scrōfa, -ae *f.*

space spatium, -(i)ī *n.*, locus, -ī *m.*; *see also* **void**
spacious amplus, -a, -um, lātus, -a, -um, capax, -ācis
spare (+*dat.*) parcō, pepercī, parsum 3., temperō 1.
sparing parcus, -a, -um
sparkle scintilla, -ae *f.*
sparrow passer, -eris *m.*
speak loquor, locūtus 3. *dep.*, dīcō, dixī, dictum 3., ōrātionem habeō 2.
speaker ōrātor, -ōris *m.*
spear hasta, -ae *f.*, framea, -ae *f.*
special proprius, -a, -um, praecipuus, -a, -um
species genus, -eris *n.*
spectacle spectāculum, -ī *n.*
spectator spectātor, -ōris *m.*
speech ōrātiō, -ōnis *f.*, contiō, -ōnis *f.*; (faculty of speech) lingua, -ae *f.*
speed vēlōcitās, -ātis *f.*, celeritās, -ātis *f.*
speedily celeriter, vēlōciter, cito
spell cantus, -ūs *m.*, carmen, -inis *n.*
spend (ex)pendeō, -sī, -sum 2., ērogō 1.; (*time*) terō, trīvī, trītum 3., agō, ēgī, actum 3., consūmō, -sumpsī, -sumptum 3.
spice condīmentum, -ī *n.*
spider arānea, -ae *f.*
spiderweb arāneum, -ī *n.*
spine spīna, -ae *f.*
spirit spīritus, -ūs *m.*, animus, -ī *m.*, anima, -ae *f.*; (vigour) vigor, -ōris *m.*, vīs, vīs *f.*
spit[1] (*noun*) verū, -ūs *n.*
spit[2] (*v.*) spuō, spuī, spūtum 3., spūtō 1.
splendid splendidus, -a, -um, insignis, -is, -e
splinter assula, -ae *f.*, fragmentum, -ī *n.*
split findō, fīdī, fissum 3.
spoil praeda, -ae *f.*, spolium, -(i)ī *n.*
sponge spongia, -ae *f.*
spontaneously ultrō, meā (*etc.*) sponte
sport lūdus, -ī *m.*
spot macula, -ae *f.*; *see also* **place**[1]
spotted maculōsus, -a, -um
spread (expand) pateō 2.; (move apart) pandō, pandī, pansum (passum) 3., extendō, -dī, -sum (-tum) 3.
sprig virga, -ae *f.*
spring[1] (*noun*) vēr, vēris *n.*
spring[2] (*v.*) saliō 4., orior, ortus 4. *dep.*
spring from (+*abl.*) exorior, exortus 4. *dep.*
sprinkle aspergō, -sī, -sum 3.

spur calcar, -āris *n.*
spy speculātor, -ōris *m.*, explōrātor, -ōris *m.*
squadron (*of cavalry*) turma, -ae *f.*, āla, ālae *f.*
squander dissipō 1., consūmō, -sumpsī, -sumptum 3., effundō, effūdī, effūsum 3.
square quadrātum, -ī *n.*
squeeze premō, pressī, pressum 3.
stable¹ (*noun*) stabulum, -ī *n.*
stable² (*adj.*) firmus, -a, -um, stabilis, -is, -e
staff baculum, -ī *n.*, virga, -ae *f.*, scīpiō, -ōnis *m.*
stag cervus, -ī *m.*
stage scaena, -ae *f.*, pulpitum, -ī *n.*
stain macula, -ae *f.*, lābēs, -is *f.*
stair scālae, -ārum *f.pl.*, gradūs, -uum *m.pl.*; (single stair) scāla, -ae *f.*
stake pālus, -ī *m.*
stalk culmus, -ī *m.*
stammer balbūtiō 4.
stamp signum, -ī *n.*, nota, -ae *f.*
stand stō, steti 1.; *see also* **stay**
stand by (+*dat.*) assistō, astitī 3.
standard signum, -ī *n.*; (benchmark) norma, -ae *f.*
star stella, -ae *f.*, sīdus, -eris *n.*, astrum, -ī *n.*
stare obtūtus, -ūs *m.*
start¹ (*noun*) incipium, -(i)ī *n.*
start² (*v.*) incipiō, incēpī, inceptum 3.
starvation famēs, -is *f.*
state status, -ūs *m.*, condiciō, -ōnis *f.*; (country) rēspūblica, rēīpūblicae *f.*, cīvitās, -ātis *f.*
station statiō, -ōnis *f.*, locus, -ī *m.*
statue statua, -ae *f.*, effigiēs, -ēī *f.*
statute lex, lēgis *f.*
stay (per)maneō, (per)mansī, (per)mansum 2.
steadiness constantia, -ae *f.*
steady stabilis, -is, -e, firmus, -a, -um, constans, -ntis
steal fūror 1. *dep.*, clepō, -psī, -ptum 3., surripiō, -ripuī, -reptum 3.
stealth furtum, -ī *n.*
stealthily furtim, clam
steam vapor, -ōris *m.*, fūmus, -ī *m.*
steel ferrum, -ī *n.*, chalybs, -bis *m.*, adamās, -antis *m.*
steep arduus, -a, -um, praeruptus, -a, -um
steepness arduum, -ī *n.*
steer gubernō 1., regō, rexī, rectum 3.

step¹ (*noun*) gradus, -ūs *m.*, passus, -ūs *m.*;
  step by step gradātim
step² (*v.*) gradior, gressus 3. *dep.*
stepdaughter prīvigna, -ae *f.*
stepfather vītricus, -ī *m.*
stepmother noverca, -ae *f.*
stepson prīvignus, -ī *m.*
sterile sterilis, -is, -e, infēcundus, -a, -um
sterility sterilitās, -ātis *f.*
stern¹ (*noun*) puppis, -is *f.*
stern² (*adj.*) sevērus, -a, -um, dūrus, -a, -um
sternly sevērē, dūriter
stick baculum, -ī *n.*, fustis, -is *m.*
stick to (+*dat.*) adhaereō, -sī, -sum 2.
stiff rigidus, -a, -um
still¹ (*adj.*) immōtus, -a, -um, quiētus, -a, -um, tranquillus, -a, -um
still² (*adv.*) etiam, adhūc
stimulate stimulō 1., excitō 1.
sting aculeus, -ī *m.*
stinking foetidus (fēt-), -a, -um
stir up concitō 1., stimulō 1., excitō 1., cieō, cīvī, citus 2., commoveō, -mōvī, -mōtum 2.
stomach stomachus, -ī *m.*, alvus, -ī *f.*, venter, -trī *m.*
stone¹ (*noun*) lapis, -dis *m.*, saxum, -ī *n.*; (gem) lapillus, -ī *m.*, gemma, -ae *f.*
stone² (*adj.*) lapideus, -a, -um, saxeus, -a, -um
stonemason lapicīda, -ae *m.*
stop consistō, constitī 3., fīniō 4.
store¹ (*noun*) cōpia, -ae *f.*
store² (*v.*) repōnō, reposuī, repositum 3.
store-room horreum, -ī *n.*, apothēca, -ae *f.*
storm tempestās, -ātis *f.*, procella, -ae *f.*
story fābula, -ae *f.*, narrātiō, -ōnis *f.*
stove camīnus, -ī *m.*
straight (dī)rectus, -a, -um
straighten corrigō, correxī, correctum 3.
strain¹ (*noun*) contentiō, -ōnis *f.*, labor, -ōris *m.*
strain² (*v.*) (ē)nītor, (ē)nīsus 3. *dep.*
strait fretum, -ī *n.*; *pl.* angustiae, -ārum *f.pl.*
strange mīrus, -a, -um, novus, -a, -um, insolitus, -a, -um
stranger advena, -ae *m./f.*, hospēs, -itis *m.*, peregrīnus, -ī *m.*
strangle strangulō 1.
straw strāmentum, -ī *n.*
stray vagor 1. *dep.*, aberrō 1.

stream fluvium, -(i)ī *n.*, flūmen, -inis *n.*, amnis, -is *m.*

street via, viae *f.*, platea, -ae *f.*

strength vīrēs, -ium *f.pl.*, valentia, -ae *f.*, rōbur, -oris *n.*

strengthen corrōborō 1., (con)firmō 1.

stress ictus, -ūs *m.*

stretch tractus, -ūs *m.*, spatium, -(i)ī *n.*

stretch out porrigō, porrexī, porrectum 3., extendō, -dī, -tum (-sum) 3.

strict sevērus, -a, -um, austērus, -a, -um, rigidus, -a, -um

stride passus, -ūs *m.*, gradus, -ūs *m.*

strife discordia, -ae *f.*

strike pellō, pepulī, pulsum 3., pulsō 1., verberō 1., feriō 4.

string chorda, -ae *f.*, nervus, -ī *m.*, resticula, -ae *f.*

strip (dē)nūdō 1.

strong fortis, -is, -e, rōbustus, -a, -um, firmus, -a, -um, validus, -a, -um

struggle luctor 1. *dep.*, certō 1., (ē)nītor, (ē)nīsus 3. *dep.*

study¹ (*noun*) studium, -(i)ī *n.*

study² (*v.*) (+*dat.*) operam dō (dedī, datum 1.), studeō 2.

stuff māteria, -ae *f.*

stunned attonitus, -a, -um

stupid stultus, -a, -um, hebes, -etis

stupidity stultitia, -ae *f.*

stupidly stultē

stutter balbūtiō 4.

submit (+*dat.*) obtemperō 1., pāreō 2.

subsist sustentor 1. *dep.*

substance māteria, -ae *f.*, corpus, -oris *n.*, rēs, reī *f.*

substantial solidus, -a, -um; *see also* **important**

subtle subtīlis, -is, -e

subtlety subtīlitās, -ātis *f.*

successful (*of people*) fēlix, -īcis; (*of things*) secundus, -a, -um

successfully fēlīciter, prosperē

successive continuus, -a, -um, perpetuus, -a, -um

such tālis, -is, -e

suck sūgō, suxī, suctum 3.

sudden subitus, -a, -um, repentīnus, -a, -um

suddenly subitō, repente

suffer patior, passus 3. *dep.*, tolerō 1., ferō, ferre, tulī, lātum *v.irreg.*

suffering dolor, -ōris *m.*

sufficiently satis

suggest admoneō 2., subiciō, subiēcī, subiectum 3.

suitable idōneus, -a, -um, aptus, -a, -um

sulphur sulfur, -uris *n.*

sum summa, -ae *f.*

summer¹ (*noun*) aestās, -ātis *f.*

summer² (*adj.*) aestīvus, -a, -um

summit culmen, -inis *n.*, vertex, -icis *m.*

summon (con)vocō 1., arcessō, -īvī (-iī), -ītum 3.

sun sōl, sōlis *m.*

sunny aprīcus, -a, -um

superstition religiō, -ōnis *f.*, superstitiō, -ōnis *f.*

supper cēna, -ae *f.*

supplies commeatus, -ūs *m.*

supply (with) (+*abl.*) suppeditō 1., praebeō 2.

support¹ (*noun*) subsidium, -(i)ī *n.*, firmāmentum, -ī *n.*

support² (*v.*) fulciō, fultus 4., sustentō 1., firmō 1.

supporter fautor, -ōris *m.*

suppose existimō 1., pōnō, posuī, positum 3., opīnor 1. *dep.*

sure certus, -a, -um, fīdus, -a, -um

surely certō; (+*question*) nōnne; **surely not** num

surname cognōmen, -inis *n.*

surpass antecēdō, -cessī, -cessum 3., anteveniō, -vēnī, -ventum 4., (ex)superō 1.

surprise opprimō, oppressī, oppressum 3., dēpre(he)ndō, -dī, -sum 3.

surprised attonitus, -a, -um, mīrātus, -a, -um

surrender trādō, -didī, -ditum 3., concēdō, -cessī, -cessum 3.

surround circumveniō, -vēnī, -ventum 4., cingō, -xī, -ctum 3., circumdō, -dedī, -datum 1.

survive supersum, -esse, -fuī *v.irreg.*

suspect suspicor 1. *dep.*

suspend suspendeō, -dī, -sum 2.

suspicion suspīciō, -ōnis *f.*

suspicious suspicax, -ācis, suspīciōsus, -a, -um

sustain sustineō, -tinuī, -tentum 2.; (nourish) alō, aluī, altum 3., sustentō 1.

swallow¹ (*noun*) hirundō, -inis *f.*

swallow² (*v.*) dēvorō 1.

swamp palūs, -ūdis *f.*
swan cycnus, -ī *m.*, olor, olōris *m.*
swear iūrō 1.
sweat[1] (*noun*) sūdor, -ōris *m.*
sweat[2] (*v.*) sūdō 1.
sweep (con)verrō, -rrī, -rsum 3.
sweet suāvis, -is, -e, dulcis, -is, -e
swell tumeō 2., inflō 1.

swift celer, -ris, -re, rapidus, -a, -um, vēlox, -ōcis
swim nō, nāvī, nātum 1., natō 1.
swindle fraus, -dis *f.*
sword gladius, -(i)ī *m.*; (*poetic*) ensis, -is *m.*
sympathy concordia, -ae *f.*, misericordia, -ae *f.*
system ratiō, -ōnis *f.*, formula, -ae *f.*

T

table mensa, -ae *f.*, quadra, -ae *f.*
tablet tabula, -ae *f.*, tabella, -ae *f.*
tactics bellī ratiō, -ōnis *f.*, rēs mīlitāris, reī mīlitāris *f.*
tail cauda, -ae *f.*, pēnis, -is *m.*
take capiō, cēpī, captum 3., tollō, sustulī, sublātum 3., sūmō, sumpsī, sumptum 3., rapiō, -uī, -tum 3., compre(he)ndō, -dī, -sum 3.; (by assault) expugnō 1.; *see also* **lead**
take away abdō, abdidī, abditum 3., adimō, adēmī, ademptum 3., auferō, auferre, abstulī, ablātum *v.irreg.*, ēripiō, ēripuī, ēreptum 3.
take down dēmō, dempsī, demptum 3.
take in accipiō, accēpī, acceptum 3., recipiō, recēpī, receptum 3.; (*mentally*) *see* **understand**
take up sūmō, sumpsī, sumptum 3., suscipiō, -cēpī, -ceptum 3.
tale fābula, -ae *f.*, narrātiō, -ōnis *f.*
talent (ability) ingenium, -(i)ī *n.*, facultās, -ātis *f.*; (*of money*) talentum, -ī *n.*
talk loquor, locūtus 3. *dep.*, sermōcinor 1. *dep.*
talkative loquax, -ācis, garrulus, -a, -um
tall altus, -a, -um, (ex)celsus, -a, -um, prōcērus, -a, -um
tame¹ (*adj.*) mītis, -is, -e, mansuētus, -a, -um, domitus, -a, -um, placidus, -a, -um
tame² (*v.*) domō, -uī, -itum 1., mansuēfaciō, -fēcī, -factum 3., frēnō 1.
tar pix, picis *f.*
task opus, operis *n.*, labor, -ōris *m.*, negōtium, -(i)ī *n.*, pensum, -ī *n.*
taste¹ (*noun*) gustus, -ūs *m.*; sapor, -ōris *m.*; (sense of taste) gustātus, -ūs *m.*
taste² (*v.*) (dē)gustō 1.
tavern caupōna, -ae *f.*, taberna, -ae *f.*
tax vectigal, -ālis *n.*, tribūtum, -ī *n.*

teach doceō, -uī, -tum 2., instruō, -uxī, -uctum 3., instituō, -uī, -ūtum 3.
teacher magister, -trī *m.*, doctor, -ōris *m.*, praeceptor, -ōris *m.*
tear¹ (*noun*) lacrima, -ae *f.*, flētus, -ūs *m.*
tear² (*v.*) (dī)scindō, (dī)scidī, (dī)scissum 3., (dī)lacerō 1., (dī)laniō 1., (dī)vellō, (dī)vellī, (dī)vulsum 3.
tedious longus, -a, -um, lentus, -a, -um, molestus, -a, -um
tell dīcō, dixī, dictum 3., narrō 1., referō, referre, rettulī, re(l)lātum *v.irreg.*; (bid) iubeō, iussī, iussum 2.; (+*dat.*) imperō 1.
temperance moderātiō, -ōnis *f.*, continentia, -ae *f.*, modestia, -ae *f.*, temperantia, -ae *f.*
temperate moderātus, -a, -um, continens, -ntis, modestus, -a, -um, temperans, -ntis, sōbrius, -a, -um
temple aedēs, -is *f.*, dēlūbrum, -ī *n.*, templum, -ī *n.*, fānum, -ī *n.*
ten decem; **ten times** deciens (-iēs)
tenacious tenax, -ācis, pertinax, -ācis
tenacity tenācitās, -ātis *f.*, pertinācia, -ae *f.*
tend colō, coluī, cultum 3., cūrō 1.
tender dēlicātus, -a, -um, mollis, -is, -e, tener, -era, -erum
tendon nervus, -ī *m.*
tent tabernāculum, -ī *n.*, contubernium, -(i)ī *n.*
tenth decimus, -a, -um
term (condition) condiciō, -ōnis *f.*, lex, lēgis *f.*; *see also* **word**
terminate (come to an end) terminor 1. *dep.*, fīnior 4. *dep.*
terrestrial terrēnus, -a, -um, terrestris, -is, -e
terrible terribilis, -is, -e, ātrox, -ōcis, horribilis, -is, -e, dīrus, -a, -um

territory fīnēs, -ium *m.pl.*, regiō, -ōnis *f.*, ager, agrī *m.*, terra, -ae *f.*

terror terror, -ōris *m.*, pavor, -ōris *m.*, timor, -ōris *m.*, metus, -ūs *m.*

test temptō 1., explōrō 1., experior, expertus 4. *dep.*, perspiciō, -spexī, -spectum 3.

testify dēclārō 1., testor 1. *dep.*

than quam *or use abl. of compared object*

thank (+*dat.*) grātiam (*or* grātēs) agō (ēgī, actum 3.)

that[1] (*pron.*) (*demonstrative*) ille, -a, -ud, is, ea, id; **that of yours** iste, ista, istud; (*relative*) quī, quae, quod

that[2] (*conj.*) *use acc.+inf.*; (*after verbs of fearing*) nē; **in order that** (+*subj.*) ut

theatre theātrum, -ī *n.*

theft furtum, -ī *n.*

then tum, tunc; (next) deinde, posteā, tum

thence inde, illinc

theory ratiō, -ōnis *f.*, ars, artis *f.*, doctrīna, -ae *f.*

there ibi, illīc; **to there** eō, illūc; **from there** inde, illinc

therefore igitur, itaque, ergō

thick densus, -a, -um, crassus, -a, -um, spissus, -a, -um, pinguis, -is, -e

thicket dūmētum, -ī *n.*

thickly dēnsē, spissē, crēbrō

thief fūr, fūris *m.*

thieve fūror 1. *dep.*

thigh femur, -oris (-inis) *n.*

thin tenuis, -is, -e, exīlis, -is, -e, gracilis, -is, -e

thing rēs, reī *f.*

think putō 1., opīnor 1. *dep.*, cōgitō 1., reor, ratus 2. *dep.*, existimō 1.

third tertius, -a, -um; **for the third time** tertium

thirst sitis, -is *f.*

thirsty sitiens, -ntis

thirteen tredecim

thirty trīgintā

this hīc, haec, hoc; **in this way** sīc

thistle carduus, -ī *m.*

thither eō, illūc

thorn spīna, -ae *f.*

thoroughly omnīnō, prorsus, penitus, funditus

thought cōgitātiō, -ōnis *f.*, animus, -ī *m.*; (idea) nōtiō, -ōnis *f.*, consilium, -(i)ī *n.*, cōgitātum, -ī *n.*

thousand mille (*pl.* mīlia)

thrash verberō 1.

thread fīlum, -ī *n.*, līnum, -ī *n.*

threat minae, -ārum *f.pl.*, comminātiō, -ōnis *f.*

threaten (+*dat.*) immineō 2.; (+*dat.*) impendeō, -dī, -sum 2.; (+*dat.*) instō, institī 1.; **threaten with** (+*acc. of thing* +*dat. of person*) (com)minor 1. *dep.*, dēnuntiō 1.

three trēs, trēs, tria

threshold līmen, līminis *n.*

thrice ter

throat faucēs, -um *f.pl.*, guttur, -uris *n.*, iugulum, -ī *n.*

throb palpitō 1., saliō 4.

throng multitūdō, -inis *f.*, turba, -ae *f.*

through (+*acc.*) per

throw iaciō, iēcī, iactum 3., mittō, mīsī, missum 3.

throw down dēiciō, dēiēcī, dēiēctum 3., praecipitō 1.

thrush turda, -ae *f.*

thumb pollex, -icis *m.*

thunder[1] (*noun*) tonitrus, -ūs *m.*, fragor, -ōris *m.*

thunder[2] (*v.*) tonō, -uī 1.

thunderbolt fulmen, -inis *n.*

thus sīc, ita

tickle titillō 1.

tide aestus, -ūs *m.*

tidy mundus, -a, -um, concinnus, -a, -um

tie ligō 1., nectō, nex(u)ī, nexum 3.

tile tēgula, -ae *f.*, testa, -ae *f.*

till[1] (*v.*) colō, coluī, cultum 3., arō 1.

till[2] (*prep.*) (+*acc.*) (usque) ad

till[3] (*conj.*) *see* **until**

timber lignum, -ī *n.*

time tempus, -oris *n.*, hōra, -ae *f.*, tempestās, -ātis *f.*, aevum, -ī *n.*; **at that time** tum, tunc; **in good time** ad tempus; **at the same time** simul; **once upon a time** ōlim

timid timidus, -a, -um, trepidus, -a, -um, pavidus, -a, -um

timidly timidē, trepidē

tire (make tired) (dē)fatīgō 1.

tired (dē)fessus, -a, -um, lassus, -a, -um, (dē)fatīgātus, -a, -um

title titulus, -ī *m.*, inscriptiō, -ōnis *f.*, nōmen, -inis *n.*

to (+*acc.*) ad, in

today hodiē
toe digitus, -ī *m.*
toga toga, -ae *f.*
together ūnā, simul
toil[1] (*noun*) labor, -ōris *m.*, opera, -ae *f.*
toil[2] (*v.*) (ē)labōrō 1.
toilet latrīna, -ae *f.*
token signum, -ī *n.*
tolerable tolerābilis, -is, -e, patibilis, -is, -e
tolerance tolerantia, -ae *f.*, patientia, -ae *f.*
tolerate tolerō 1., patior, passus 3. *dep.*, ferō, ferre, tulī, lātum *v.irreg.*
tomb sepulc(h)rum, -ī *n.*, tumulus, -ī *m.*
tomorrow crās
tone tonus, -ī *m.*
tongue lingua, -ae *f.*
tonight hāc nocte
too quoque, etiam; **too much** nimis, nimium; **too little** parum
tool instrūmentum, -ī *n.*, ferrāmentum, -ī *n.*
tooth dens, dentis *m.*
top culmen, -inis *n.*, apex, apicis *m.*, cacū-men, -inis *n.*, vertex, -icis *m.*
torch fax, facis *f.*, taeda, -ae *f.*
tortoise testūdō, -inis *f.*
torture[1] (*noun*) cruciātus, -ūs *m.*, tormen-tum, -ī *n.*
torture[2] (*v.*) (ex)cruciō 1., (ex)torqueō, -rsī, -rtum 2.
torturer carnifex, -icis *m.*, tortor, -ōris *m.*
total tōtus, -a, -um, summus, -a, -um, cunctus, -a, -um, ūniversus, -a, -um
touch tangō, tetigī, tactum 3., attingō, attigī, attactum 3.; (*of emotions*) flectō, flexī, flexum 3., commoveō, commōvī, commōtum 2., attingō, attigī, attactum 3.
tough dūrus, -a, -um, lentus, -a, -um
tow trahō, traxī, tractum 3.
toward(s) (+*acc.*) ad, in, adversus; (+*dat.*) obviam; (concerning) (+*acc.*) ergā, contrā
tower turris, -is *f.*, arx, arcis *f.*
town oppidum, -ī *n.*, urbs, urbis *f.*, mūni-cipium, -(i)ī *n.*
townsman oppidānus, -ī *m.*, cīvis, -is *m.*
trace, track vestīgium, -(i)ī *n.*, indicium, -(i)ī *n.*
trade mercātūra, -ae *f.*, commercium, -(i)ī *n.*
train exerceō 2., exercitō 1., instituō, -uī, -ūtum 3.

training disciplīna, -ae *f.*, exercitātiō, -ōnis *f.*
traitor prōditor, -ōris *m.*
transact agō, ēgī, actum 3., gerō, gessī, gestum 3.
translate convertō, -tī, -sum 3., interpretor 1. *dep.*, reddō, -didī, -ditum 3.
trap laqueus, -ī *m.*
travel vehor, vectus 3. *dep.*, iter faciō (fēcī, factum 3.)
traverse lustrō 1., peragrō 1.
tray ferculum, -ī *n.*
treachery perfidia, -ae *f.*, prōditiō, -ōnis *f.*, fraus, -dis *f.*
treasure gāza, -ae *f.*, thēsaurus, -ī *m.*, opēs, opum *f.pl.*
treat tractō 1.
treaty foedus, -eris *n.*, pactum, -ī *n.*, con-ventum, -ī *n.*
tree arbor, -oris *f.*
tremble *see* **shiver**
trench fossa, -ae *f.*
trial iūdicium, -(i)ī *n.*, quaestiō, -ōnis *f.*
tribe gens, gentis *f.*, nātiō, -ōnis *f.*, trībus, -ūs *f.*, cīvitās, -ātis *f.*
tribune tribūnus, -ī *m.*
tribute tribūtum, -ī *n.*
trick dolus, -ī *m.*, fraus, -dis *f.*, ars, artis *f.*, fallācia, -ae *f.*, vafrāmentum, -ī *n.*
trifling levis, -is, -e, tenuis, -is, -e
triumph triumphus, -ī *m.*, victōria, -ae *f.*
trivial *see* **trifling**
troops cōpiae, -ārum *f.pl.*, mīlitēs, -um *m. pl.*
trouble molestiae, -ārum *f.pl.*, labor, -ōris *m.*
troublesome molestus, -a, -um
trousers brācae, -ārum *f.pl.*
truce indūtiae, -ārum *f.pl.*
true vērus, -a, -um, germānus, -a, -um
truly vērē
trumpet tuba, -ae *f.*, būcina, -ae *f.*
trunk truncus, -ī *m.*; *see also* **box**
trust fidēs, -ēī *f.*, fīdūcia, -ae *f.*
trustworthy fīdus, -a, -um, fidēlis, -is, -e
truth vēritās, -ātis *f.*, vērum, -ī *n.*
try (at)temptō ((at)tentō) 1., cōnor 1. *dep.*, experior, expertus 4. *dep.*
tube fistula, -ae *f.*
tune carmen, -inis *n.*, modī, -ōrum *m.pl.*
tunic tunica, -ae *f.*
turf caespes, -itis *m.*
turn (con)vertō, -tī, -sum 3., flectō, flexī,

flexum 3.; (become) (+*adj./noun*) vertor, versus 3. *dep.*

turn back revertor, -rsus 3. *dep.*

turn out ēveniō, ēvēnī, ēventum 4., ēvādō, -sī, -sum 3.

turnip rāpum, -ī *n.*

turret turris, -is *f.*

turtle testūdō, -inis *f.*

turtle dove turtur, -uris *m.*

tutor *see* **teacher**

tweak vellicō 1.

twelve duodecim

twentieth vīcensimus, -a, -um

twenty vīgintī

twice bis

twig virga, -ae *f.*, rāmulus, -ī *n.*

twilight crepusculum, -ī *n.*

twin geminus, -a, -um

twine implicō 1., nectō, nex(u)ī, nexum 3.

two duo, duae, duo; **two-year period** biennium, -(i)ī *n.*

two-footed bipēs, bipedis

two-headed biceps, bicipitis

type genus, -eris *n.*

tyranny dominātiō, -ōnis *f.*

tyrant tyrannus, -ī *m.*, rex, rēgis *m.*

U

ugly turpis, -is, -e, dēformis, -is, -e, foedus, -a, -um

ulcer ulcus, -eris *n.*

unable, am (+*inf.*) nequeō, nequīre, nequīvī, nequītum 4., nōn possum (posse, potuī *v.irreg.*)

unarmed inermis, -is, -e, nūdus, -a, -um

unavoidable inēvītābilis, -is, -e

unaware nescius, -a, -um, ignārus, -a, -um

uncertain incertus, -a, -um, dubius, -a, -um, ambiguus, -a, -um, anceps, ancipitis

unchangeable *see* **immutable**

uncivilized barbarus, -a, -um, ferus, -a, -um, incultus, -a, -um, immānis, -is, -e

uncle (mother's brother) avunculus, -ī *m.*; (father's brother) patruus, -ī *m.*

uncommon *see* **rare**

unconquerable invictus, -a, -um

uncover reperiō, repperī, repertum 4.

under (+*abl.*) sub, subter; (to under) (+*acc.*) sub

undergo subeō, subīre, subīvī (-iī), subitum 4., patior, passus 3. *dep.*, tolerō 1., perferō, -ferre, -tulī, -lātum *v.irreg.*

understand intellegō, -xī, -ctum 3., animō *or* mente percipiō (-cēpī, -ceptum 3.)

undertake suscipiō, -cēpī, -ceptum 3., incipiō, incēpī, inceptum 3.

undertaking inceptum, -ī *n.*

undeserved immeritus, -a, -um, iniustus, -a, -um

undoubtedly certē, haud dubiē, sine dubiō

unequal impār, -aris, dissimilis, -is, -e

unfair iniustus, -a, -um, inīquus, -a, -um

unfaithful infidēlis, -is, -e, perfidus, -a, -um

unfasten (re)solvō, -vī, -ūtum 3.

unfavourable adversus, -a, -um, inīquus, -a, -um, infaustus, -a, -um

unfriendly inimīcus, -a, -um, aliēnus, -a, -um

unhappy miser, -era, -erum, infēlix, -īcis, infortūnātus, -a, -um

unharmed incolumis, -is, -e, tūtus, -a, -um, salvus, -a, -um, integer, -gra, -grum

unheard inaudītus, -a, -um

unimportant levis, -is, -e

unite (bring together) cōpulō 1., misceō, miscuī, mixtum 2., congregō 1., consociō 1.

universal commūnis, -is, -e, ūniversus, -a, -um

unjust iniustus, -a, -um, inīquus, -a, -um, iniūriōsus, -a, -um

unjustly iniustē, inīquē, iniūriā

unkind sevērus, -a, -um, crūdēlis, -is, -e

unknown incognitus, -a, -um, inexplōrātus, -a, -um, ignōtus, -a, -um

unless nisi

unlucky infēlix, -īcis, infortūnātus, -a, -um

unmarried caelebs, -libis

unoccupied apertus, -a, -um, vacuus, -a, -um

unpleasant iniūcundus, -a, -um, incommodus, -a, -um, molestus, -a, -um

unpopularity infāmia, -ae *f.*, invidia, -ae *f.*, offensiō, -ōnis *f.*

unprotected apertus, -a, -um, indēfēnsus, -a, -um

unripe immātūrus, -a, -um, crūdus, -a, -um, acerbus, -a, -um

unsafe infestus, -a, -um, perīculōsus, -a, -um

unstable levis, -is, -e, inconstans, -ntis

unsuccessful infēlix, -īcis

unsuccessfully infēlīciter

unsuspecting inopinans, -ntis, incautus, -a, -um

untie (dis)solvō, -vī, -ūtum 3.

until[1] (*prep.*) (+*acc.*) (usque) ad
until[2] (*conj.*) dōnec, dum, quoad
untouched integer, -gra, -grum, intactus, -a, -um
unusual inūsitātus, -a, -um, insolitus, -a, -um
unwell aeger, aegra, aegrum, infirmus, -a, -um
unwilling invītus, -a, -um
unwise insipiens, -ntis
unworthy (of) (+*abl.*/*gen.*) indignus, -a, -um
up (*adv.*) sursum (-us)
upright (ē)rectus, -a, -um
uproar tumultus, -ūs *m.*
upwards sursum (-us)
urge (ad)hortor 1. *dep.*, incitō 1., stimulō

1.; (+*dat.*) instō, institī 1.
urgently vehementer, magnopere
use[1] (*noun*) ūsus, ūsūs *m.*, ūsūra, -ae *f.*
use[2] (*v.*) (+*abl.*) ūtor, ūsus 3. *dep.*; (+*acc.*) adhibeō 2., ūsūrpō 1.
useful ūtilis, -is, -e, idōneus, -a, -um, commodus, -a, -um, aptus, -a, -um
usefulness ūtilitās, -ātis *f.*
useless vānus, -a, -um, inūtilis, -is, -e, inānis, -is, -e
usual ūsitātus, -a, -um, solitus, -a, -um, consuētus, -a, -um
usually fer(m)ē, plērumque
utmost extrēmus, -a, -um, summus, -a, -um, ultimus, -a, -um
utterance dictum, -ī *n.*
utterly penitus, funditus, omnīnō

V

vacant vacuus, -a, -um
vague incertus, -a, -um, ambiguus, -a, -um,
  dubius, -a, -um
vain (empty) inānis, -is, -e, vānus, -a, -um;
  (pointless) irritus, -a, -um, vānus, -a, -um;
  (vainglorious) glōriōsus, -a, -um; **in vain**
  frustrā, nequīquam
vale, valley vallis, -is *f.*
valuable pretiōsus, -a, -um
value¹ (*noun*) pretium, -(i)ī *n.*, aestimātiō,
  -ōnis *f.*
value² (*v.*) (+*gen. of price*) faciō, fēcī, factum
  3., aestimō 1., dūcō, duxī, ductum 3.
vanish (ē)vānescō, -nuī 3.
vapour vapor (-ōs), -ōris *m.*, nebula, -ae *f.*
variety varietās, -ātis *f.*, dīversitās, -ātis *f.*
various varius, -a, -um, dīversus, -a, -um
variously variē, dīversē
vary variō 1., mūtō 1.
vase vās, vassis *n.*, urceus, -ī *m.*
vast ingens, -ntis, amplus, -a, -um, vastus,
  -a, -um, lātus, -a, -um, immensus, -a, -um
vastness amplitūdō, -inis *f.*, immensitās,
  -ātis *f.*
vegetable (h)olus, -eris *n.*
vehicle vehiculum, -ī *n.*; *see also* **carriage**
veil¹ (*noun*) vēlāmen, -inis *n.*, flammeolum,
  -ī *n.*
veil² (*v.*) tegō, texī, tectum 3., vēlō 1.
vengeance ultiō, -ōnis *f.*, vindicātiō, -ōnis
  f.
vengeance, take *see* **avenge**
verdict iūdicium, -(i)ī *n.*, sententia, -ae *f.*
verse versus, -ūs *m.*
very valdē, admodum, maximē, summē;
  very much magnopere
vessel alveus, -ī *m.*, olla, -ae *f.*, vās, vassis *n.*,
  amphora, -ae *f.*, orca, -ae *f.*, dolium, -(i)ī
  n.; *see also* **ship**
veteran veterānus, -a, -um

vibration tremor, -ōris *m.*, vibrātiō, -ōnis *f.*,
  mōtus, -ūs *m.*
victim victima, -ae *m.*, hostia, -ae *f.*
victor victor, -ōris *m.*, triumphus, -ī *m.*
victory victōria, -ae *f.*
view¹ (*noun*) aspectus, -ūs *m.*, aciēs, -ēī *f.*;
  (opinion) sententia, -ae *f.*, opīniō, -ōnis *f.*,
  iūdicium, -(i)ī *n.*
view² (*v.*) aspiciō, aspexī, aspectum 3.,
  contemplor 1. *dep.*
vigorous ācer, ācris, ācre, strēnuus, -a, -um,
  vīvidus, -a, -um, fortis, -is, -e
vigorously ācriter, strēnuē, fortiter
vigour vīs, vīs *f.*, vigor, -ōris *m.*, nervī,
  -ōrum *m.pl.*
vile turpis, -is, -e, vīlis, -is, -e, foedus, -a,
  -um, nēquam (*indecl.adj.*)
vileness turpitūdō, -inis *f.*, foeditās, -ātis *f.*
village vīcus, -ī *m.*, pāgus, -ī *m.*
villager vīcānus, -ī *m.*, pāgānus, -ī *m.*,
  agrestis, -is *m.*
vine vītis, -is *f.*
vinegar acētum, -ī *n.*
violate violō 1.
violence vīs, vīs *f.*, violentia, -ae *f.*, saevitia,
  -ae *f.*
violent violentus, -a, -um, vehemens, -ntis,
  saevus, -a, -um
violently per vim, violenter, vehementer,
  saevē
violet viola, -ae *f.*
virgin virgō, -inis *f.*
virtue virtūs, -ūtis *f.*, honestās, -ātis *f.* probitās, -ātis *f.*, bonitās, -ātis *f.*
vision (sense of sight) vīsus, -ūs *m.*, aspectus, -ūs *m.*
visit vīsō, vīsī, vīsum 3., frequentō 1.
voice vox, vōcis *f.*
void¹ (*noun*) ināne, -is *n.*
void² (*adj.*) inānis, -is, -e, vacuus, -a, -um

voluntarily ultrō, sponte
vote[1] (*noun*) suffrāgium, -(i)ī *n.*, sententia, -ae *f.*
vote[2] (*v.*) suffrāgium *or* sententiam ferō (ferre, tulī, lātum *v.irreg.*)
vow[1] (*noun*) vōtum, -ī *n.*, dēvōtiō, -ōnis *f.*, prōmissum, -ī *n.*

vow[2] (*v.*) voveō, vōvī, vōtum 2., (dē)spondeō, -sī, -sum 2., prōmittō, -mīsī, -missum 3.

voyage nāvigātiō, -ōnis *f.*

vulgar vulgāris, -is, -e, plēbeius, -a, -um

vulture vultur, -uris *m.*

W

wage(s) aes, aeris *n.*, mercēs, -ēdis *f.*
stīpendium, -(i)ī *n.*

wage war bellō 1., belligerō 1., bellum
gerō (gessī, gestum 3.)

waggon plaustrum, -ī *n.*, carrus, -ī *m.*

wail lāmentor 1. *dep.*, (com)plōrō 1.

wailing plōrātus, -ūs *m.*, lāmentātiō, -ōnis
f.

wait maneō, mansī, mansum 2., moror 1.
dep.; (wait for) exspectō 1., praestōlor 1.
dep.

wake (cause to wake) excitō 1., suscitō 1.

walk ambulō 1., gradior, gressus 3. *dep.*

wall mūrus, -ī *m.*; (*of a city*) moenia, -um *n.*
pl.; (*of a house*) pariēs, -etis *m.*

wander vagor 1. *dep.*, errō 1., pālor 1. *dep.*

want (need) (+*abl./gen.*) egeō, eguī 2.,
careō, -uī 2., indigeō 2.; (+*acc.*) dēsīderō
1., requīrō, requīsīvī (-iī), requīsītum 3.

want (to) (+*inf.*) volō, velle, voluī *v.irreg.*

war bellum, -ī *n.*; **declare war** bellum
indīcō (indixī, indictum 3.)

warfare mīlitia, -ae *f.*

warlike bellicōsus, -a, -um, mīlitāris, -is, -e,
ferox, -ōcis

warm calidus, -a, -um; (lukewarm) tepidus,
-a, -um

warm, am caleō 2.

warm, become calescō 3.

warmth calor, -ōris *m.*, aestus, -ūs *m.*;
(slight warmth) tepor, -ōris *m.*

warn (ad)moneō 2.

warrior mīles, -itis *m.*, bellātor, -ōris *m.*

wart verrūca, -ae *f.*

wary prūdens, -ntis, cautus, -a, -um

wash lavō, lāvī, lautum (lōtum, lūtum) 1.

wasp vespa, -ae *f.*

waste consūmō, -sumpsī, -sumptum 3.,
dissipō 1., profundō, -dī, -sum 3.; (*land*)

(dē)vastō 1., populor 1. *dep.*; (*time*) terō,
trīvī, trītum 3.

watch spectō 1., aspiciō, aspexī, aspectum
3., observō 1.; (stay awake) vigilō 1.

watchman vigil, -lis *m.*, custōs, -ōdis *m.*

water aqua, -ae *f.*, liquor, -ōris *m.*, unda, -ae
f., lympha, -ae *f.*

wave[1] (*noun*) fluctus, -ūs *m.*, unda, -ae *f.*

wave[2] (*v.*) (brandish) vibrō 1., agitō 1.,
iactō 1.; (undulate) fluctuō 1.

waver vacillō 1., fluctuō 1., dubitō 1.

wax cēra, -ae *f.*

waxen cēreus, -a, -um

way iter, itineris *n.*, via, viae *f.*, cursus, -ūs
m.; (manner) ratiō, -ōnis *f.*, modus, -ī *m.*;
(custom) mōs, mōris *m.*, institūtum, -ī *n.*;
in this way sīc, ita

weak dēbilis, -is, -e, infirmus, -a, -um,
invalidus, -a, -um, confectus, -a, -um,
imbēcillus, -a, -um

weakly infirmē

weakness dēbilitās, -ātis *f.*, infirmitās, -ātis
f., imbēcillitās, -ātis *f.*

wealth dīvitiae, -ārum *f.pl.*, opēs, opum *f.*
pl., opulentia, -ae *f.*

wealthy opulentus, -a, -um, dīvēs, dīvitis
(dītis), locuplēs, -ētis

weapon tēlum, -ī *n.*; **weapons** arma,
-ōrum *n.pl.*

wear gestō 1., gerō, gessī, gestum 3., portō
1.

wear down (con)terō, (con)trīvī, (con)trī-
tum 3.

weariness (dē)fatīgātiō, -ōnis *f.*, lassitūdō,
-inis *f.*

weary (dē)fessus, -a, -um, lassus, -a, -um,
languidus, -a, -um

weary of, am mē (*etc.*) taedet 2. *impers.*

weasel mustēla, -ae *f.*

weather tempestās, -ātis *f.*, caelum, -ī *n.*

weave (con)texō, (con)texuī, (con)textum 3.

weaver textor, -ōris *m.*

web tēla, -ae *f.*

weep fleō, flēvī, flētum 2., lacrimō 1., lāmentor 1. *dep.* (dē)plōrō 1.

weep over (+*dat.*) illacrimō 1., (dē)fleō, (dē)flēvī, (dē)flētum 2.

weigh ponderō 1., pendō, pependī, pensum 3., pensō 1.; *see also* **consider**

weight pondus, -eris *n.*, gravitās, -ātis *f.*, onus, oneris *n.*

welcome grātus, -a, -um, acceptus, -a, -um, exoptātus, -a, -um

welfare salūs, -ūtis *f.*, ūtilitās, -ātis *f.*

well[1] (*noun*) puteus, -ī *m.*

well[2] (*adj.*) sānus, -a, -um, integer, -gra, -grum, salvus, -a, -um, valens, -ntis

well[3] (*adv.*) bene, rectē

well, am bene valeō 2.

well-disposed benevolus, -a, -um

well-known nōtus, -a, -um, pervulgātus, -a, -um, fāmōsus, -a, -um

west occidens, -ntis *m.*

western occidentālis, -is, -e, occiduus, -a, -um

wet madidus, -a, -um, ūmidus, -a, -um

whale balaena, -ae *f.*, cētus, -ī *m.*

what, whatever *see* **who, whoever**

wheat trīticum, -ī *n.*

wheel rota, -ae *f.*

when (*interrog.*) quandō; (*conj.*) cum, ubi, ut

whence unde

where ubi, quā

where to quō

wherever ubicumque, quācumque

whether utrum, an; **whether ... or** utrum ... an

which quis, quis, quid; **which of two** uter, utra, utrum; (*rel. pron.*) quī, quae, quod

while, whilst dum, quoad, dōnec; **for a while** paulisper

whip[1] (*noun*) lōrum, -ī (*esp.pl.*), flagellum, -ī *n.*

whip[2] (*v.*) verberō 1.

whirlwind turbō, -ōnis *m.*, vortex, -icis *m.*

whisper[1] (*noun*) susurrus, -ūs *m.*

whisper[2] (*v.*) (in)susurrō 1.

whistle[1] (*noun*) sībilus, -ī *m.*

whistle[2] (*v.*) sībilō 1.

white albus, -a, -um, candidus, -a, -um, niveus, -a, -um

whiten (de)albō 1.

whither quō

who, what quis, quis, quid; **which of two** uter, utra, utrum; (*rel.pron.*) quī, quae, quod

whoever, whatever quīcumque, quae-cumque, quidcumque, quisquis, quis-quis, quidquid (quicquid)

whole tōtus, -a, -um, ūniversus, -a, -um, omnis, -is, -e, cunctus, -a, -um

wholly omnīnō, prorsus

why cūr, quamobrem, quārē, quid

wicked improbus, -a, -um, nefārius, -a, -um, prāvus, -a, -um, malus, -a, -um, scelestus, -a, -um, nēquam (*indecl.adj.*)

wickedness improbitās, -ātis *f.*, nēquitia, -ae *f.*, prāvitās, -ātis *f.*, malitia, -ae *f.*; (act) scelus, -eris *n.*

wide amplus, -a, -um, lātus, -a, -um, laxus, -a, -um

widow vidua, -ae *f.*

widower viduus, -ī *m.*

width amplitūdō, -inis *f.*, lātitūdō, -inis *f.*, laxitās, -ātis *f.*

wife uxor, uxōris *f.*, marīta, -ae *f.*, coniunx, -iugis *f.*

wild saevus, -a, -um, ferus, -a, -um, incultus, -a, -um, ferox, -ōcis

will voluntās, -ātis *f.*, consilium, -(i)ī *n.*, studium, -(i)ī *n.*; (testament) testāmentum, -ī *n.*

willing volens, -ntis, libens, -ntis, promptus, -a, -um

willingly libenter

willow sālix, -icis *f.*

win vincō, vīcī, victum 3., superō 1.; *see also* **gain**

wind ventus, -ī *m.*, anima, -ae *f.*, flātus, -ūs *m.*

window fenestra, -ae *f.*

wine vīnum, -ī *n.*

wing āla, ālae *f.*, penna, -ae *f.*; (*of an army*) cornū, -ūs *n.*

winter[1] (*noun*) hiem(p)s, -mis *f.*, brūma, -ae *f.*

winter[2] (*adj.*) hibernus, -a, -um, hiemālis, -is, -e, brūmālis, -is, -e

wipe tergeō, -sī, -sum 2., dētergeō, -sī, -sum 2.

wisdom sapientia, -ae *f.*, prūdentia, -ae *f.*

wise sapiens, -ntis, prūdens, -ntis
wish volō, velle, voluī *v.irreg.*, cupiō 4.,
(ex)optō 1.
wish, do not nōlō, nōlle, nōluī *v.irreg.*
with (+*abl.*) cum
within[1] (*adv.*) intrō, intus
within[2] (*prep.*) (+*acc.*) intrā, inter; (+*abl.*)
in
without (+*abl.*) sine; (+*acc.*) extrā
withstand resistō, restitī 3.; (+*dat.*) obstō,
obstiti 1.
witness testis, -is *m.*
witty lepidus, -a, -um, salsus, -a, -um
wolf lupus, -ī *m.*; **shewolf** lupa, -ae *f.*
woman mulier, -ris *f.*, fēmina, -ae *f.*; **old
woman** anus, anūs *f.*; (young woman) *see*
girl
womb uterus, -ī *m.*, alvus, -ī *f.*
wonder (ad)mīror 1. *dep.*
wonderful mīrificus, -a, -um, mīrus, -a,
-um, (ad)mīrābilis, -is, -e
wood (material) lignum, -ī *n.*; (forest) silva,
-ae *f.*, nemus, -oris *n.*, saltus, -ūs *m.*
wooden ligneus, -a, -um
wool lāna, -ae *f.*
word verbum, -ī *n.*, vocābulum, -ī *n.*, vox,
vōcis *f.*, nōmen, -inis *f.*
work[1] (*noun*) labor, -ōris *m.*, opus, -eris *n.*,
factum, -ī *n.*, pensum, -ī *n.*, opera, -ae *f.*;
work of art ars, artis *f.*, artificium, -(i)ī *n.*
work[2] (*v.*) (ē)labōrō 1., operor 1. *dep.*
workplace fabrica, -ae *f.*, officīna, -ae *f.*
world terrārum orbis, -is *m.*, mundus, -ī *m.*,
terrae, -ārum *f.pl.*
worm vermis, -is *m.*, lumbrīcus, -ī *m.*

worse[1] (*adj.*) peior, -or, -us, dēterior, -or,
-us, inferior, -or, -us
worse[2] (*adv.*) peius, dēterius
worship adōrō 1., colō, coluī, cultum 3.,
veneror 1. *dep.*
worst pessimus, -a, -um
worth pretium, -(i)ī *n.*, aestimātiō, -ōnis *f.*,
cāritās, -ātis *f.*
worthless vīlis, -is, -e, inūtilis, -is, -e
worthy (of) (+*abl.*/*gen.*) dignus, -a, -um
would that (ō) utinam
wound[1] (*noun*) vulnus, -eris *n.*, plāga, -ae *f.*
wound[2] (*v.*) vulnerō 1., sauciō 1.
wounded vulnerātus, -a, -um, saucius, -a,
-um
wrap involvō, -vī, -ūtum 3., amiciō 4., vēlō
1.
wrench (from) (+*dat.*) extorqueō, -sī,
-tum 2.
wrestle (col)luctor 1. *dep.*
wretched miser, -era, -erum, maestus, -a,
-um, miserābilis, -is, -e
wrinkle rūga, -ae *f.*
write scrībō, scrīpsī, scrīptum 3.
write down annotō 1.
writer scriptor, -ōris *m.*, auctor, -ōris *m.*;
(scribe) scrība, -ae *m.*
wrong[1] (*noun*) iniūria, -ae *f.*; (act of wickedness) nefās (*indecl.n.*)
wrong[2] (*adj.*) prāvus, -a, -um, perversus,
-a, -um, iniustus, -a, -um, falsus, -a,
-um
wrong, do peccō 1., dēlinquō, dēlīquī,
dēlictum 3.
wrongdoing peccātum, -ī *n.*, errātum, -ī *n.*
wrongly male, prāvē, perperam, falsō

yawn oscitō 1., hiō 1.
year annus, -ī *m.*
yearly[1] (*adj.*) annuus, -a, -um
yearly[2] (*adv.*) quotannīs
yearn *see* **desire**[1]
yellow lūridus, -a, -um, fulvus, -a, -um, flāvus, -a, -um, lūteus, -a, -um
yes ita (vērō), sānē, certē
yesterday herī
yesterday's hesternus, -a, -um
yet (*however*) tamen, sed, at; (*temporal*) adhūc, etiamnunc; **not yet** nōndum
yew taxus, -ī *f.*
yield cēdō, cessī, cessum 3., dō, dedī, datum 1.

yoke iugum, -ī *n.*
yolk vitellus, -ī *m.*
you *sg.* tū (*acc.* tē, *gen.* tuī, *dat.* tibī, *abl.* tē); *pl.* vōs (*acc.* vōs, *gen.* vestrī *or* vestrum, *dat./abl.* vōbīs)
young iuvenis, -is, -e, iūnior, -or, -us, parvus, -a, -um, novus, -a, -um; (*young man*) *see* **youth**[1]
your (*of one*) tuus, tua, tuum, (*of more than one*) vester, -tra, -trum; **that of yours** iste, ista, istud
youth[1] (*man*) iuvenis, -is *m.*, adolescens, -ntis *m.*, puer, -rī *m.*
youth[2] (*young age*) iuventūs, -ūtis *f.*, adolescentia, -ae *f.*, pueritia, -ae *f.*

Z

zeal studium, -(i)ī *n.*, fervor, -ōris *m.*,
industria, -ae *f.*, ardor, -ōris *m.*

zealous studiōsus, -a, -um, fervidus, -a,
-um, ardens, -ntis

Latin Words and Phrases in Common Use

ā fortiōrī	by a stronger reason
ā posteriōrī	from what comes later, reasoning from effects to causes; inductive
ā priōrī	from what comes before, reasoning from causes to effects; deductive
ā verbīs ad verbera	from words to blows
ab incūnābulīs	from the cradle
ab initiō	from the beginning
ab ōvō	from the egg
ab urbe conditā (AUC)	from the founding of the city (of Rome)
ad absurdum	to the point of absurdity
ad astra	to the stars
ad fēminam	to the individual (woman); personal
ad hoc	to this end, for this purpose
ad hominem	to the individual (man); personal
ad infīnītum	to infinity, for ever
ad initium	at the beginning
ad libitum (ad lib.)	at one's pleasure, at will
ad maiōrem Deī glōriam (AMDG)	to the greater glory of God
ad nauseam	to the point of disgust
ad rem	to the point
ad vītam aeternam	for all time
addenda et corrigenda	things to be added and corrected
adsum	I am here
aegrōtat	he/she is ill
Agnus Deī	Lamb of God
ālea iacta est	the die is cast
alma māter	nurturing mother
alternīs diēbus (alt. dieb.)	every other day, on alternate days
amō, amās, amat	I love, you love, he/she/it loves
amor vincit omnia	love conquers all
anguis in herbā	snake in the grass
Annō Dominī (AD)	in the year of our Lord
annuit coeptīs	he (God) has favoured our undertakings
annus horribilis	a dreadful year
annus mīrābilis	a wonderful year
ante bellum	before the war
ante cibum (a.c.)	before food
ante merīdiem (a.m.)	before noon

apparātus criticus	critical apparatus (textual notes)
arma virumque canō	arms and the man I sing
ars est cēlāre artem	the art/skill is to conceal the art
ars grātiā artis	art for art's sake
ars longa, vīta brevis	art is long, life is short
audēre est facere	to dare is to do
aurea mediocritās	the golden mean
aut vincere aut morī	either to conquer or to die
avē atque valē	hail and farewell
avē Caesar, moritūrī tē salūtant	hail Caesar, those who are about to die salute you
avē Maria	hail Mary
Baccalaureus Artium (BA)	Bachelor of Arts
Baccalaureus Scientiae (BSc)	Bachelor of Science
bis dat quī cito dat	he gives twice who gives quickly
bis vīvit quī bene vīvit	he lives twice who lives well
bonā fidē	in good faith, sincerely
brevis esse labōrō, obscūrus fīō	I strive to be brief, but become obscure
carpe diem	pluck the day, seize the opportunity
cavē canem	beware of the dog
caveat emptor	let the buyer beware
cavendō tūtus	safe by taking care
cēdant arma togae	let arms give way to the toga
cēterīs paribus	other things being equal
circā/circum (c. or circ.)	about
cīvis Rōmānus sum	I am a Roman citizen
cōgitō ergō sum	I think, therefore I am
commūne bonum	the common good
compos mentis	in control of one's mind, sound of mind
confer (cf.)	compare
contrā mundum	against the world
Corpus Christī	the body of Christ
corpus dēlictī	the body of the crime, i.e. evidence
corrigenda	things to be corrected
cui bonō?	in whose interest?
cum grānō salis	with a grain of salt
cum laude	with praise
curriculum vītae (CV)	the course of one's life
damnātiō memoriae	damnation of memory
dē factō	in reality
dē gustibus nōn est disputandum	there can be no arguing regarding tastes
dē iūre	by law, official
dē mortuīs nīl nisi bonum	of the dead (speak) nothing but good
dē profundīs	from the depths
Deī grātiā (DG)	by the grace of God
dēlenda est Carthāgō	Carthage must be destroyed
Deō volente (DV)	God willing
deus ex māchinā	god from a machine
Deus vōbiscum	God be with you!
Diēs Īrae	day of wrath; Judgement Day
diēs nātālis	birthday
dīra necessitās	grim necessity

Dīvīnitātis Doctor (DD)	Doctor of Divinity
docendō discitur	one learns through teaching
Doctor Litterārum (D.Lit./Litt.)	Doctor of Literature/Letters
Domine, dīrige nōs	Lord, direct us
Dominus illūminātiō mea	the Lord is my light
dracō dormiens numquam titillandus	never tickle a sleeping dragon
drāmatis persōnae	the characters in a play
dulce est dēsipere in locō	it is a sweet thing to be frivolous on occasion
dulce et decōrum est prō patriā morī	it is a sweet and noble thing to die for one's country
dum spīrō, spērō	while I draw breath, I have hope
dum vīvimus, vīvāmus	while we live, let us live
ē plūribus ūnum	from many, one
Ecce Homō!	Behold the Man!
ergō bibāmus	therefore let us drink
errāre hūmānum est	to err is human
esse quam vidērī	to be rather than to seem
estō perpetua	let her be everlasting
et alia (et al.)	and other things
et aliae/aliī (et al.)	and others
et cētera (etc. or &c.)	and the rest
et in Arcadiā ego	I too (i.e. death) am in Arcadia
et tū, Brūte!	you too, Brutus!
ex cathedrā	from the chair, i.e. with authority
ex grātiā	as a favour
ex librīs	from the library (of)
ex mōre	according to custom
ex officiō	according to one's office
ex post factō	after the fact
ex silentiō	from silence
ex tempore	off the cuff, without preparation
excelsior	higher
exeat	let him/her go out
exemplī grātiā (e.g.)	for the sake of example
exeunt omnēs	all go out (*stage direction*)
facta, nōn verba	deeds, not words
fāta viam invenient	the Fates will find a way
festīnā lentē	make haste slowly
fīat lux	let there be light
Fideī Dēfensor (FD or Fid. Def.)	Defender of the Faith
fīnis corōnat opus	the end crowns the work
flagrante dēlictō	with the crime blazing, in the very act of a crime
flōreat	let it flourish
flōruit (fl. or flor.)	he/she flourished
fons et orīgō	source and origin
fons vītae sapientia	wisdom is the source of life
fortēs fortūna adiuvat	fortune favours the brave
forsan et haec ōlim meminisse iuvābit	perhaps at some point it will be pleasant to recall even these things
fortūna caeca est	fortune is blind
Gallia est omnis dīvīsa in partēs trēs	the whole of Gaul is divided into three parts

gaudeāmus igitur, iuvenēs dum sumus	let us rejoice therefore, while we are young
genius locī	the spirit of the place
glōria in excelsīs Deō	Glory to God in the highest
Graecia capta ferum victōrem cēpit	Greece, having been captured, made a conquest of her wild conqueror
habeās corpus	you may have the body
habēmus Pāpam	we have a Pope
hīc iacet	here lies
honōris causā	for the sake of honour, i.e. honorary
horror vacuī	fear of emptiness
ibidem (ibid.)	in the same place
id est (i.e.)	that is to say
Iēsus hominum salvātor (IHS)	Jesus saviour of mankind
Iēsus Nazarēnus Rex Iudaeōrum (INRI)	Jesus of Nazareth, King of the Jews
imprimātur	let it be printed
in absentiā	in one's absence
in āctū	in practice
in aeternum	for ever
in camerā	in the chamber, in secret *or* private
in capite	in chief
in extensō	in full, at full length
in extrēmīs	in dire straits, at the point of death
in fīne	in short, to conclude
in hōc signō vincēs	by this sign you shall conquer
in infīnītum	to infinity
in locō parentis	in the place of a parent
in mediās rēs	into the midst of things
in memoriam	to the memory of
in nuce	in a nutshell
in ōvō	in the egg
in perpetuum	for all time
in plēnō	in full
in principiō	in the beginning
in propriā persōnā	in one's own person
in saxō condita	founded on rock
in sitū	in its original place
in statū pūpillārī	in the state of being a pupil
in terrōrem	as a warning
in tōtō	in all, completely
in transitū	in passing
in uterō	in the uterus
in vīnō vēritās	truth in wine
in vitrō	in glass, i.e. in a test-tube
infrā dignitātem (infra dig.)	beneath one's dignity
inter alia	among other things
inter aliōs	among other persons
inter nōs	between ourselves
inter parēs	between equals
inter sē	between themselves
inter vīvōs	between the living
ipsō factō	by the fact itself, by that very fact
iūniōrēs ad labōrēs	juniors to the chores

labōrāre est ōrāre	to work is to pray
lapsus linguae	a slip of the tongue
laus Deō	praise be to God
Lēgum Doctor (LLD)	Doctor of Laws
lingua franca	a common language
litterātī	men of letters
locō citātō (loc. cit.)	in the place cited
locum tenens	occupying another's position
locus classicus	classic passage (of writing)
lupus est homō hominī	man is a wolf to man
lux mea Christus	Christ is my light
Magister Artium (MA)	Master of Arts
Magister Philosophiae (MPhil)	Master of Philosophy
magnā cum laude	with great praise
magnum opus	great work, masterpiece
malā fidē	in bad faith
manus manum lavat	one hand washes another
margarītās ante porcōs	pearls before swine
mea (maxima) culpa	my own (very great) fault
Medicīnae Doctor (MD)	Doctor of Medicine
membrum virīle	the penis
mementō morī	remember that you are to die
mens agitat mōlem	mind stirs up matter
mens rea	guilty mind
mens sāna in corpore sānō	a sound mind in a sound body
mīlitat omnis amans	every lover is a soldier
mīrābile dictū/vīsū	marvellous to relate/to behold
miserēre meī	have mercy on me
modus operandī	a way of operating
modus vīvendī	a way of living
mors omnibus commūnis	death is common to all
mortuī nōn mordent	the dead do not bite
mūtātīs mūtandīs	with the necessary changes
nē plūs ultrā	no further
nēmō mē impūne lacessit	no one provokes me with impunity
nihil ad rem	nothing to do with the matter
nīl dēspērandum	nothing to be despaired of, i.e. don't despair
nīl hominī certum est	nothing is certain for man
nōlī mē tangere	don't touch me
nōn compos mentis	not of sound mind
nōn nōbīs sōlum	not only for ourselves
nōn omnia possumus omnēs	we cannot all do everything
nōn omnis moriar	I shall not entirely die
nōn palma sine pulvere	no palm (glory) without dust (work)
nōn placet	it is not pleasing
nōn sequitur	it does not follow
nosce tē ipsum	know yourself
notā bene (NB)	note well
nunc dīmittis	now you send forth
nunc est bibendum	now is the time to drink
O tempora, O mōrēs!	what times, what customs!
obiit	he/she died

obiter dictum	something said along the way
ōderint dum metuant	let them hate as long as they fear
ōdī et amō	I hate and I love
omnia praeclāra rāra	all the best things are rare
omnia vincit amor	love conquers all
omnibus vīribus cōnābor	I will try my utmost
opere citātō (op. cit.)	in the work cited
opus Deī	the work of God
ōrā et labōrā	pray and work
pāce	with peace, without wishing to offend
pānem et circensēs	bread and circuses
Pater Noster	Our Father
paucīs verbīs	in a few words
pax vōbiscum	peace be with you
pecūnia nōn olet	money does not have a scent
per annum	yearly
per ardua ad astra	through difficulty to the stars
per capita	by heads, per person
per contrā	on the other side
per diem	daily
per fās et nefās	by right and wrong
per mensem	monthly
per ōs (p.o.)	by mouth
per parēs	by one's equals
per prōcūrātiōnem (per pro. or p.p.)	through the agency (of)
per sē	by *or* of itself
perīculum in morā	peril in delay
persōna nōn grāta	unacceptable *or* unwelcome person
Philosophiae Doctor (PhD)	Doctor of Philosophy
pinxit (pinx. or pnxt)	he/she painted it
placet	it is pleasing
possunt quia posse videntur	they can because it seems that they can
post cibum (p.c.)	after food
post coitum	after sexual intercourse
post factum	after the event
post hoc, ergō propter hoc	after this, therefore because of this
post merīdiem (p.m.)	after noon
post mortem	after death
post partum	after childbirth
post scriptum (PS)	written afterwards
post tenebrās, lux	after darkness, light
praemonitus, praemūnītus	forewarned is forearmed
prīmā faciē	at first sight
prīmus inter parēs	first among equals
prō bonō pūblicō	for the public good
prō formā	for form's sake
prō hāc vice	for this occasion
prō ratā	proportionally
prō rē nātā (p.r.n.)	as the occasion arises, as needed
prō tantō	so far
prō tempore (pro tem.)	temporarily
proximē accessit	he/she came next, i.e. was runner-up

quater in diē (q.i.d.)	four times a day
quī docet discit	he who teaches learns
quid prō quō	one thing for another
quis custōdiet ipsōs custōdēs?	who shall guard the guards themselves?
quō vādis, Domine?	where are you going, Lord?
quod erat dēmonstrandum (QED)	which was to be demonstrated
quod scripsī, scripsī	that which I have written, I have written
quod vidē (q.v.)	which see
quondam	former
quot hominēs, tot sententiae	there are as many opinions as there are men
rāra avis	a rare bird
reductiō ad absurdum	reduction to the absurd
requiescat in pāce (RIP)	may he/she rest in peace
rēs ipsa loquitur	the thing speaks for itself
respice fīnem	look to the end
Rōmānī īte domum!	Romans go home!
rūs in urbe	the countryside in the city
sanctum sanctōrum	the holy of holies
sapere audē	dare to be wise
scīlicet (sc.)	namely
scripsit (script)	he/she wrote it
sculpsit (sc.)	he/she carved it
semper fidēlis	always faithful
senātus populusque Rōmānus (SPQR)	the senate and people of Rome
sensū lātō	in a broad sense
sensū strictō	in a narrow sense
sī vīs pācem, parā bellum	if you want peace, prepare for war
sīc semper tyrannīs	thus always to tyrants
sīc transit glōria mundī	thus passes away the glory of the world
sine diē	without a day, indefinitely
sine dubiō	without doubt
sine quā nōn	without which not, i.e. something indispensable
spērō meliōra	I hope for better things
status (in) quō	the state in which, existing conditions
stet	let it stand
sub iūdice	under a judge
sub poenā	under penalty of
sub rosā	under the rose, i.e. secretly, in confidence
sub speciē aeternitātis	under the sight of eternity
suī generis	of one's own kind
summā cum laude	with the highest praise
summum bonum	the greatest/supreme good
suprā	above
tabula rāsa	a blank tablet
tempus fugit	time flies
ter in diē (t.i.d.)	three times a day
terminus ante quem	limit before which
terminus post quem	limit after which
terra firma	solid ground
terra incognita	unknown land
timeō Danaōs et dōna ferentēs	I fear Greeks even when they bear gifts

tū nē cēde malīs	do not give in to misfortunes
ubi mel ibi apēs	where there is honey there are bees
ubi Petrus ibi ecclēsia	where there is Peter (a rock) there is a church
ultima ratiō	final sanction
ultimus Rōmānōrum	the last of the Romans
ultrā vīrēs	beyond the powers, without authority
urbī et orbī	to the city and the world
ut infrā (ut inf.)	as below
ut pictūra poēsis	a poem like a picture
ut suprā (ut sup.)	as above
vae victīs	woe to the conquered
vēnī, vīdī, vīcī	I came, I saw, I conquered
ventīs secundīs	with a favourable wind
verbātim ac litterātim	word for word and letter for letter
versus (v. or vs.)	against
vice versā	with the positions being reversed
victor lūdōrum	winner of the games
vidē (v.)	see
vidēlicet (viz)	that is to say; to wit; namely
videō meliōra probōque, dēteriōra sequor	I see better things and approve of them, but I follow worse things
vincet amor patriae	love of one's homeland will prevail
vincit quī patitur	he that endures conquers
virginibus puerīsque	for girls and boys
virtūs praemium optimum	virtue is the best reward
vīta mūtātur, non tollitur	life is changed, not taken away
vīvā vōce (viva)	with living voice; an oral examination
vīvat rex/rēgīna	long live the king/queen
vox populī (vox pop)	the voice of the people

List of Latin Proper Names

Gods and Goddesses

Aeolus, -ī *m.* god of the winds
Aesculāpius, -(i)ī *m.* god of medicine; son of Apollo
Amor, Amōris *m.* see Cupīdō
Apollō, -inis *m.* god of prophecy, poetry and music, sun-god; son of Jupiter and Leto
Bacchus, -ī *m.* god of wine
Bellōna, -ae *f.* goddess of war; sister of Mars
Bona Dea *f.* goddess of chastity and fertility, worshipped by women
Bromius, -(i)ī *m.* alternative title of Bacchus, god of wine
Camēnae, -ārum *f.pl.* Roman goddesses associated with inspiration
Cerēs, -eris *f.* goddess of agriculture, corn and the growth of fruits; mother of Proserpine
Cupīdō, -inis *m.* god of love; son of Mars and Venus
Cybelē, -ēs *f.* Phrygian mother goddess, Magna Mater
Cytherēa, -ae *f.* Venus
Diāna, -ae *f.* virgin goddess of hunting and childbirth, moon-goddess; twin sister of Apollo
Dīs, Dītis *m.* Pluto, god of the underworld
Discordia, -ae *f.* goddess of discord
Fāma, -ae *f.* goddess of fame and rumour
Faunus, -ī *m.* god of flocks and shepherds
Flōra, -ae *f.* goddess of flowers and springtime
Fortūna, -ae *f.* goddess of fortune
Iacchus, -ī *m.* Bacchus
Iānus, -ī *m.* two-headed god of beginnings and gateways
Iūnō, -ōnis *f.* goddess of marriage and patroness of women; wife and sister of Jupiter
Iuppiter, Iovis *m.* king of the Gods
Larēs, -ium *m.pl.* household gods
Līber, -ī *m.* Bacchus
Lībera, -ae *f.* Proserpine
Libitīna, -ae *f.* goddess associated with funerals
Lūcīna, -ae *f.* goddess of childbirth
Magna Māter *f.* Cybele, Phrygian Mother Goddess
Māia, -ae *f.* mother of Mercury
Mānēs, -ium *m.pl.* the shades of the dead, gods of the underworld
Mars, Martis *m.* god of war; father of Romulus
Māvors, -ortis *m.* Mars
Mercurius, -(i)ī *m.* messenger of the gods; god of merchants, thieves, verbal communication and lyre-playing; son of Jupiter and Maia

Minerva, -ae *f.* goddess of wisdom and creative arts; daughter of Zeus
Monēta, -ae *f.* goddess of the mint (title of Juno)
Neptūnus, -ī *m.* god of the sea
Ops, Opis *f.* goddess of plenty; wife of Saturn
Orcus, -ī *m.* god of the underworld, Pluto
Palēs, -is *f.* goddess of shepherds and flocks
Pān, Pānos *m.* god of shepherds and woods; son of Mercury
Parcae, -ārum *f.pl.* the (three) Fates
Penātēs, -ium *m.pl.* household gods
Plūtō(n), -ōnis *m.* king of the Dead, god of the underworld; husband of Proserpine
Pōmōna, -ae *f.* goddess of fruit and fruit trees
Portūnus, -ī *m.* god of harbours
Priāpus, -ī *m.* god of fertility, gardens and vineyards
Prōserpina, -ae *f.* queen of the Dead; daughter of Ceres, wife of Pluto
Quirīnus, -ī *m.* name given to Romulus, founder of Rome, after his deification
Sāturnia, -ae *f.* Juno, daughter of Saturn
Sāturnus, -ī *m.* god of agriculture; father of Jupiter
Sīlēnus, -ī *m.* drunken companion and tutor of Bacchus
Silvānus, -ī *m.* god of woods and trees
Terminus, -ī *m.* god of boundaries
Trivia, -ae *f.* Diana *or* Hecate
Venus, -eris *f.* goddess of love; mother of Aeneas by Anchises
Vertumnus, -ī *m.* god of the seasons and their produce
Vesta, -ae *f.* goddess of the hearth and household
Vulcānus (Volc-), -ī *m.* blacksmith god; son of Jupiter and Juno

Countries, Islands and Regions

Aegyptus, -ī *f.* Egypt
Āfrica, -ae *f.* Africa
Arabia, -ae *f.* Arabia
Asia, -ae *f.* Asia
Attica, -ae *f.* Attica
Ausonia, -ae *f.* Italy
Bīthȳnia, -ae *f.* Bithynia (province of Asia Minor; below Black Sea)
Boeōtia, -ae *f.* Boeotia
Britannia, -ae *f.* Britain
Calabria, -ae *f.* Calabria (southeast Italy)
Calēdonia, -ae *f.* Scotland
Campānia, -ae *f.* Campania
Cantium, -ī *n.* Kent
Cappadocia, -ae *f.* Cappadocia (Asia Minor)
Capreae, -ārum *f.pl.* Capri
Cilicia, -ae *f.* Cilicia
Colchis, -idis *f.* Colchis (east of Black Sea)
Corcȳra, -ae *f.* Corfu
Crēta, -ae *f.* Crete
Cyprus, -ī *f.* Cyprus
Dācia, -ae *f.* Dacia (Romania)
Dēlos, -ī *f.* Delos
Dīa, Dīae *f.* Naxos

Etrūria, -ae f. Etruria
Eurōpa, -ae f. Europe
Galatia, -ae f. Galatia
Gallia, -ae f. Gaul
Germānia, -ae f. Germany
Graecia, -ae f. Greece
Hibēria, -ae f. Spain
Hibernia, -ae f. Ireland
Hispānia, -ae f. Spain
Italia, -ae f. Italy
Ithaca, -ae f. Ithaca
Iūdaea, -ae f. Judaea
Latium, -īī n. Latium
Libya, -ae (Libyē, -ēs) f. Libya
Lycia, -ae f. Lycia
Lydia, -ae f. Lydia
Macedonia, -ae f. Macedonia
Magna Graecia f. Greek colonies of southern Italy
Mesopotamia, -ae f. Asian country between the Tigris and Euphrates
Mona, -ae f. Anglesey; Isle of Man
Nōricum, -ī n. Noricum (country between the Danube and Alps)
Paros, -ī f. Paros (one of the islands of the Cyclades)
Parthia, -ae f. Parthia
Pharus (-os), -ī f. Pharos (island next to Alexandria; famous for lighthouse; home to
   Proteus, the old man of the sea)
Pīeria, -ae f. Pieria (Macedonia)
Prōvincia, -ae f. Provence
Rhodos (-us), -ī f. Rhodes
Samnium, -īī n. Samnium (central Italy)
Scythia, -ae f. Scythia (Black Sea)
Sēres, -um m.pl. China
Syria, -ae f. Syria
Thessalia, -ae f. Thessaly (northern Greece)
Thrāc(i)a, -ae (Thrācē, -ēs) f. Thrace
Thūlē, -ēs f. Thule (most northerly of all islands)
Trīnacria, -ae f. Sicily
Trōas, -adis f. Troad
Tyrr(h)ēnia, -ae f. Etruria
Umbria, -ae f. Umbria

Inhabitants

Belgae, -ārum m.pl. Belgians
Celtae, -ārum m.pl. Celts
Graecī, -ōrum m.pl. Greeks
Helvetiī, -ōrum m.pl. Helvetii (Swiss)
Parthī, -ōrum m.pl. Parthians
Pelasgī, -ōrum m.pl. Greeks
Persae, -ārum m.pl. Persians
Phryges, -um m.pl. Phrygians, Trojans
Poenī, -ōrum m.pl. Carthaginians

Rōmānī, -ōrum *m.pl.* Romans
Rutulī, -ōrum *m.pl.* Rutulians (Latium)
Sabīnī, -ōrum *m.pl.* Sabines (central Italy)
Scythae, -ārum *m.pl.* Scythians (Black Sea)
Siculī, -ōrum *m.pl.* Sicilians
Umbrī, -ōrum *m.pl.* Umbrians
Volscī, -ōrum *m.pl.* Volscians (south Latium)

Cities and Towns

Alba Longa *f.* Alba Longa (Latium)
Alexandrīa, -ae *f.* Alexandria (Egypt)
Aquae Sulis *f.* Bath
Arīminum, -ī *n.* Rimini
Augusta Treverōrum *f.* Trier
Bērȳtus, -ī *f.* Beirut
Brundisium, -īī *n.* Brindisi (southeast Italy)
Bȳzantium, -īī *n.* Istanbul
Callēva Atrebātum *f.* Silchester
Carthāgō, -inis *f.* Carthage
Corinium, -īī *n.* Cirencester
Corinthus, -ī *f.* Corinth
Corstopitum, -ī *n.* Corbridge
Cȳrēnae, -ārum *f.pl.* Cyrene (North Africa)
Delphī, -ōrum *m.pl.* Delphi
Dēva, -ae *f.* Chester
Dōdōna, -ae *f.* Dodona
Eborācum, -ī *n.* York
Ēpīrus (-os), -ī *f.* Epirus
Gādēs, -ium *f.pl.* Cadiz
Glēvum, -ī *n.* Gloucester
Hierosolyma, -ōrum *n.pl.* Jerusalem
Īlios, -ī *f.* Ilium, Troy
Īlium (-on), -īī *n.* Ilium, Troy
Isca, -ae *f.* Caerleon
Lāvīnium, -(i)ī *n.* Lavinium (Latium)
Londinium, -(i)ī *n.* London
Lutētia, -ae *f.* Paris
Massilia, -ae *f.* Marseilles
Mediolānum, -ī *n.* Milan
Melita, -ae (Melitē, -ēs) *f.* Malta
Mycēnae, -ārum *f.pl.* (**Mycēnē, -ēs** *f.*) Mycenae
Neāpolis, -is *f.* Naples
Ōstia, -ae *f.* (**Ōstia, -ōrum** *n.pl.*) Ostia
Panormus, -ī *m.* Palermo (Sicily)
Patavium, -īī *n.* Padua
Patrae, -ārum *f.pl.* Patras (Greece)
Pergamum¹, -ī *n.* (**Pergama, -ōrum** *n.pl.*) citadel of Troy, Troy
Pergamum², -ī *n.* Pergamum (Mysia)
Pharsālus (-os), -ī *f.* Pharsalus (Thessaly)
Philippī, -ōrum *m.pl.* Philippi (Macedonia)

Phrygia, -ae *f.* Phrygia, Troy
Pompeiī, -ōrum *m.pl.* Pompeii (Campania)
Puteolī, -ōrum *m.pl.* Pozzuoli (Campania)
Rōma, -ae *f.* Rome
Sīdōn, -ōnis (-ōnos) *f.* Sidon (Phoenicia)
Sparta, -ae *f.* Sparta (southern Greece; celebrated for frugality)
Sybaris, -is *f.* Sybaris (southern Italy; notorious for extravagance)
Syrācūsae, -ārum *f.pl.* Syracuse (Sicily)
Tarentum, -ī *n.* Taranto (southern Italy)
Thēbae, -ārum *f.pl.* Thebes (1. Greece: seven-gated, 2. Egypt: hundred-gated)
Tomis, -is *f.* (**Tomī, -ōrum** *m.pl.*) Tomis (on the Black Sea)
Trōia, -ae *f.* Troy
Verulamium, -iī *n.* St Albans

Seas, Rivers and Springs

Albis, -is *m.* river Elbe
Arar, Araris *m.* river Saône
Arnus, -ī *m.* river Arno
Castalia, -ae *f.* Castalia (spring associated with inspiration; on Mt Parnassus)
Dānuvius, -iī *m.* Upper Danube
Hadria, -ae *m.* Adriatic Sea
Hellēspontus, -ī *m.* Hellespont, Dardanelles
Hippocrēnē, -ēs *f.* Hippocrene (spring associated with inspiration; on Mt Parnassus)
Ister, Istrī *m.* Lower Danube
Lēthē, -ēs *f.* river Lethe (underworld)
Liger, Ligeris *m.* river Loire
Mare Aegaeum *n.* Aegean Sea
Mare Atlanticum *n.* Atlantic
Mare inferum *n.* Tyrrhenian Sea
Mare Iōnium *n.* Ionian Sea
Mare nostrum *n.* Mediterranean
Mare superum *n.* Adriatic Sea
Nīlus, -ī *m.* Nile
Padus, -ī *m.* river Po
Pēnēus, -ī *m.* river Peneus (Thessaly)
Phlegethōn, -ontis *m.* river Phlegethon (underworld)
Pontus, -ī (Euxīnus) *m.* Black Sea
Propontis, -idos (-idis) *f.* sea of Marmora
Rhēnus, -ī *m.* river Rhine
Rhodanus, -ī *m.* river Rhône
Rubicō(n), -ōnis *m.* Rubicon (stream marking boundary between Italy and Cisalpine Gaul)
Sabrīna, -ae *f.* river Severn
Scamander, -drī *m.* river Scamander (Troy)
Sequāna, -ae *f.* river Seine
Simoīs, -entis *m.* river Simois (Troy)
Styx, Stygis (Stygos) *f.* river Styx (underworld)
Tāmesis, -is *m.* river Thames
Tib(e)ris, -is (Tiberīnus, -ī) *m.* river Tiber

Mountains

Aetna, -ae (Aetnē, -ēs) *f.* Mt Aetna (volcano; Sicily)
Alpēs, -ium *f.pl.* the Alps
Caucasus, -ī *m.* Caucasus mountains
Cynthus, -ī *m.* Mt Cynthus (Delos; sacred to Apollo)
Dictē, -ēs *f.* Mt Dicte (Crete)
Eryx, Erycis *m.* Mt Eryx (Sicily)
Helicōn, -ōnis *m.* Mt Helicon (Boeotia; sacred to Apollo and the Muses)
Hymettus (-os), -ī *m.* Mt Hymettus (near Athens)
Īda, Īdae (Īdē, Īdēs) *f.* Mt Ida (1. near Troy, 2. Crete)
Mons Āpennīnus *m.* Apennine mountain range (Italy)
Olympus, -ī *m.* Mt Olympus (northern Greece; home of the Gods)
Parnā(s)sus (-os), -ī *m.* Mt Parnassus (central Greece; sacred to Apollo and the Muses)
Pēlion, -iī *n.* Mt Pelion (Thessaly)
Taurus, -ī *m.* Taurus mountain range (southeast Turkey)
Tāygetus, -ī *m.* (**Tāygeta, -ōrum** *n.pl.*) Taygetus mountain range (southern Greece)
Vesuvius, -iī *m.* Mt Vesuvius (volcano; near Pompeii)

Winds

Āfricus, -ī *m.* Southwest wind
Aquilō, -ōnis *m.* North wind
Auster, Austrī *m.* South wind
Boreās, -ae *m.* North wind
Caurus (Cōrus), -ī *m.* Northwest wind
Favōnius, -ī *m.* West wind
Notus (-os), -ī *m.* South wind
Septentriō, -ōnis *m.* North wind
Zephyrus, -ī *m.* West wind

Days of the Week

diēs Sōlis day of the sun: Sunday
diēs Lūnae day of the moon: Monday
diēs Martis day of Mars: Tuesday
diēs Mercuriī day of Mercury: Wednesday
diēs Veneris day of Venus: Thursday
diēs Iovis day of Jupiter: Friday
diēs Sāturnī day of Saturn: Saturday

Months of the Year

(mensis) Iānuārius, -iī *m.* January
(mensis) Februārius, -iī *m.* February
(mensis) Martius, -iī *m.* March
(mensis) Aprīlis, -is *m.* April
(mensis) Māius, -iī *m.* May
(mensis) Iūnius, -iī *m.* June

(mensis) Iūlius, -iī *m.* July; formerly *Quintilis*
(mensis) Augustus, -ī *m.* August; formerly *Sextilis*
(mensis) September, -bris *m.* September
(mensis) Octōber, -bris *m.* October
(mensis) November, -bris *m.* November
(mensis) December, -bris *m.* December

Common First Names

A. = Aulus
C. = Gāius
Cn. = Gnaeus
D. = Decimus
L. = Lūcius
M. = Marcus
M'. = Mānius
P. = Publius
Q. = Quintus
S. (Sex.) = Sextus
T. = Titus
Ti. (Tib.) = Tiberius

Chronology of Roman Emperors

JULIO-CLAUDIANS

Augustus (Octavian) 27 BC–AD 14
Tiberius 14–37
Gaius (Caligula) 37–41
Claudius 41–54
Nero 54–68

YEAR OF THE FOUR EMPERORS

Galba 68–9
Otho 69
Vitellius 69
Vespasian 69–79

FLAVIANS

Vespasian 69–79
Titus 79–81
Domitian 81–96

Nerva 96–8
Trajan 98–117
Hadrian 117–38

ANTONINES

Antoninus Pius 138–61
Marcus Aurelius 161–80
    with Lucius Verus 161–9 and Commodus from 177
Commodus 180–92

Pertinax 193
Didius Julianus 193
Pescennius Niger 193
Clodius Albinus 193

SEVERANS

Septimius Severus 193–211
    with Caracalla from 198 and Geta from 209
Caracalla 211–17
    with Geta 211–12
Opellius Macrinus 217–18
    with Diadumenianus 218
Elagabalus 218–22
Alexander Severus 222–35
Maximinus Thrax 235–8

Gordian I 238
Gordian II 238
Balbinus 238
Pupienus 238
Gordian III 238–44
Philip the Arab 244–9
    with his son Philip 247–9
Trajan Decius 249–51
Trebonianus Gallus and Volusianus 251–3
Valerian and Gallienus 253–60
Gallienus 260–68
Claudius II Gothicus 268–70
Aurelian 270–75
Tacitus 275–6 and Florianus 276
Probus 276–82
Carus 282–3
Carinus and Numerianus 283–4

THE TETRARCHY

Diocletian [East] 284–305
Maximian [West] 286–305
Galerius [East] 305–11
Constantius I Chlorus [West] 305–6
Severus [West] 306–8
Maxentius [Rome] 306–12
Licinius [West] 308–11
Maximinus Daia [East] 309/10–11

Constantine the Great [West] and Licinius [East] 311–24

Constantine the Great 324–37
Constantine II, Constantius II and Constans 337–40
Constantius II and Constans 340–50
Constantius II 350–61
Julian the Apostate 361–3
Jovian 363–4
Valentinian I and Valens 364–75
    with Gratian 367–75
Valens, Gratian and Valentinian II 375–8
Theodosius I (the Great) 379–95
    with Gratian and Valentinian II 379–83

with Valentinian II and Arcadius 383–92
with Arcadius and Honorius 392–5

In 395 the Roman Empire is formally split into two separate entities

WESTERN EMPIRE 395–476

Honorius 395–423
Johannes 423–5
Valentinian III 425–55
Petronius Maximus 455
Avitus 455–6
Majorian 457–61
Libius Severus 461–5
Anthemius 467–72
Olybrius 472
Glycerius 473–4
Julius Nepos 474–5
Romulus Augustulus 475–6

The Western Roman Empire is brought to an end by the deposition of Romulus in 476

EASTERN EMPIRE 395–1453

Arcadius 395–408
Theodosius II 408–50
Marcian 450–57
Leo I 457–74
Leo II 474
Zeno 474–91

The Eastern Roman Empire continues from Zeno until the fall of Constantinople in 1453

Chronology of Latin Writers
(from Plautus to Suetonius)

Plautus	(Titus Maccius Plautus), comic playwright from Umbria (254–184 BC)
Ennius	(Quintus Ennius), epic poet and tragedian from southern Italy (c. 239–169 BC)
Cato the Elder	(Marcus Porcius Cato), Italian statesman, orator, moral reformer, prose writer (234–149 BC)
Pacuvius	(Marcus Pacuvius), tragedian and painter from southern Italy (c. 220–130 BC)
Terence	(Publius Terentius Afer), comic playwright, perhaps born in Carthage (c. 185–159 BC)
Lucilius	(Gaius Lucilius), Roman satirical poet (180–102/1 BC)
Accius	(Lucius Accius), tragedian and poet from Umbria (170–c. 86 BC)
Varro	(Marcus Terentius Varro), celebrated polymath: poet, satirist, antiquarian, grammarian (116–27 BC)
Nepos	(Cornelius Nepos), biographer and historian from Cisalpine Gaul (c. 110–24 BC)
Cicero	(Marcus Tullius Cicero), statesman, orator and philosopher (106–43 BC)
Caesar	(Gaius Julius Caesar), general, statesman, orator and historian (100–44 BC)
Lucretius	(Titus Lucretius Carus), philosophical poet (c. 94–55 BC)
Sallust	(Gaius Sallustius Crispus), historian (86–35 BC)
Catullus	(Gaius Valerius Catullus), neoteric poet (c. 84–54 BC)
Virgil	(Publius Vergilius Maro), Rome's most important poet, writing in the genres of pastoral, didactic and epic poetry; from Cisalpine Gaul (70–19 BC)
Gallus	(Gaius Cornelius Gallus), soldier and enigmatic pioneer of elegiac love poetry (70/69–27/6 BC)
Horace	(Quintus Horatius Flaccus), poet from south Italy, famed for his lyric poetry, the *Odes* (65–8 BC)

Livy	(Titus Livius), Roman historian, author of a history of Rome in 142 books, from north-east Italy (59 BC–AD 17)
Tibullus	(Albius Tibullus), Roman elegiac poet (c. 55–19 BC)
Propertius	(Sextus Propertius), elegiac poet from Umbria (c. 50 BC to between 16 and 2 BC)
Seneca the Elder	(Marcus Annaeus Seneca), Latin rhetorician, from Cordoba, Spain; father of Lucius Annaeus Seneca (c. 50 BC–AD 40)
Vitruvius	(Vitruvius Pollio), Roman architect and engineer, author of the 10-book treatise, *De architectura* (fl. c. 50 BC)
Ovid	(Publius Ovidius Naso), influential Roman poet, famed for the *carmen et error* ('a poem and an error of judgement') that resulted in his banishment from Rome to the Black Sea (43 BC–AD 17)
Seneca the Younger	(Lucius Annaeus Seneca), Roman philosopher and moralist, tutor to the emperor Nero; from Cordoba, Spain (c. 4 BC–AD 65)
Pliny the Elder	(Gaius Plinius Secundus), polymathic author of the *Naturalis Historia* in 37 books; uncle and adoptive father of the Younger Pliny (AD 23/4–79)
Silius Italicus	(Tiberius Catius Asconius Silius Italicus), epic poet and politician (c. AD 26–103)
Persius	(Aulus Persius Flaccus), satirical poet from Etruria (AD 34–62)
Quintilian	(Marcus Fabius Quintilianus), Spanish-born professional teacher of rhetoric (c. AD 35–c. 95)
Lucan	(Marcus Annaeus Lucanus), epic poet from Cordoba, Spain; forced to take his own life by the emperor Nero (AD 39–65)
Columella	(Lucinus Iunius Moderatus Columella), Spanish-born writer of a 12-book treatise on agriculture (fl. c. AD 50)
Petronius	(Gaius Petronius Arbiter), pioneer of the genre of the Roman novel; forced to take his own life by the emperor Nero (died AD 66)
Martial	(Marcus Valerius Martialis), Spanish-born epigrammatic poet (c. AD 40–103/4)
Statius	(Publius Papinius Statius), Roman poet from Naples (c. AD 45–c. 96)
Tacitus	(Publius? Cornelius Tacitus), politician and major Roman historian, born in Narbonese or Cisalpine Gaul (c. AD 56–c. 118)
Juvenal	(Decimus Iunius Iuvenalis), Roman satirical poet (c. AD 60–140)
Pliny the Younger	(Caius Caecilius Secundus), successful politician and orator, celebrated as the author of 10 books of letters (c. AD 61/2–c. 113)
Valerius Maximus	author of handbook of 'memorable deeds and sayings' for the use of orators (c. 1st century AD)
Suetonius	(Gaius Tranquillus Suetonius), imperial biographer and antiquarian (c. AD 69 to after 122)

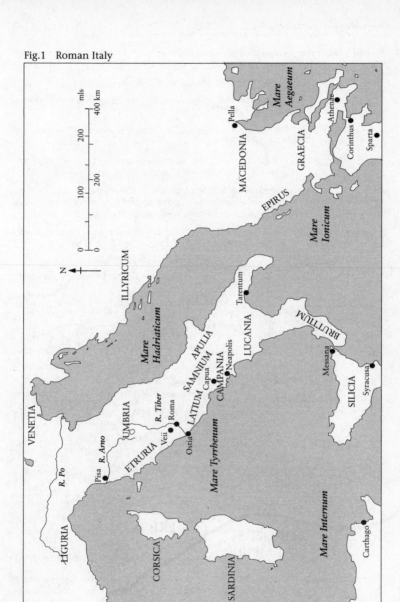

Fig.1 Roman Italy

Fig.2 The Roman Empire (under Trajan)

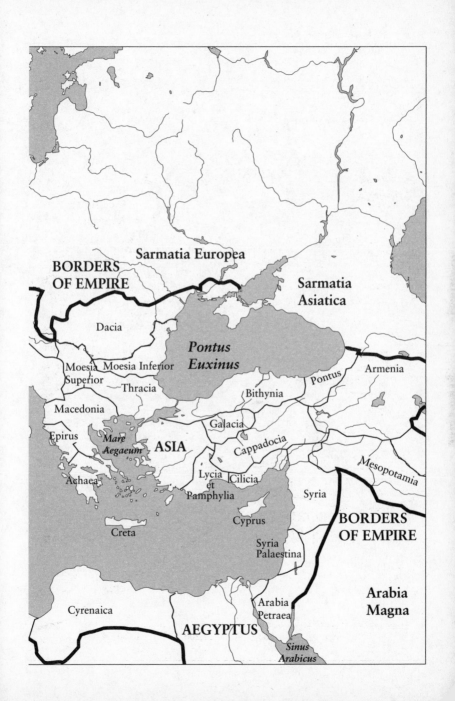

Fig.3 Roman Britain

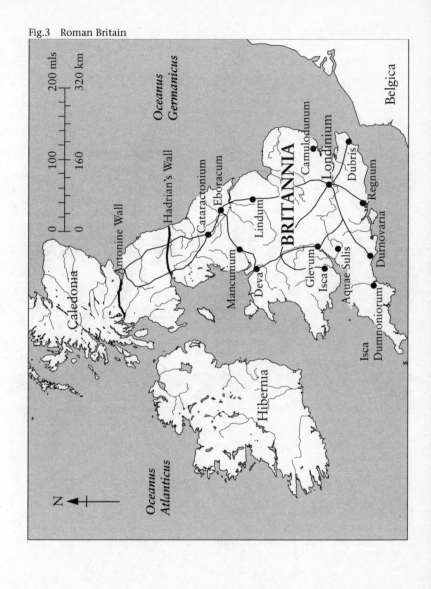

Fig.4　The City of Rome

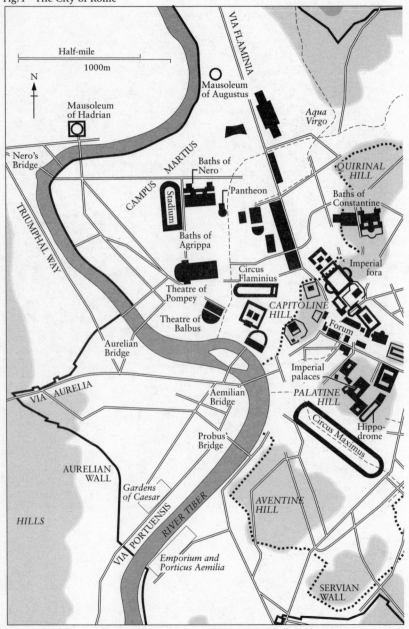

Half-mile
1000m

N

Mausoleum of Hadrian

Nero's Bridge

TRIUMPHAL WAY

VIA FLAMINIA

Mausoleum of Augustus

Aqua Virgo

CAMPUS MARTIUS

Baths of Nero

Stadium

Pantheon

QUIRINAL HILL

Baths of Constantine

Baths of Agrippa

Imperial fora

Circus Flaminius

Theatre of Pompey

CAPITOLINE HILL

Theatre of Balbus

Forum

Aurelian Bridge

VIA AURELIA

Aemilian Bridge

Imperial palaces

PALATINE HILL

Hippo-drome

Circus Maximus

Probus' Bridge

AURELIAN WALL

Gardens of Caesar

VIA PORTUENSIS

RIVER TIBER

AVENTINE HILL

HILLS

Emporium and Porticus Aemilia

SERVIAN WALL

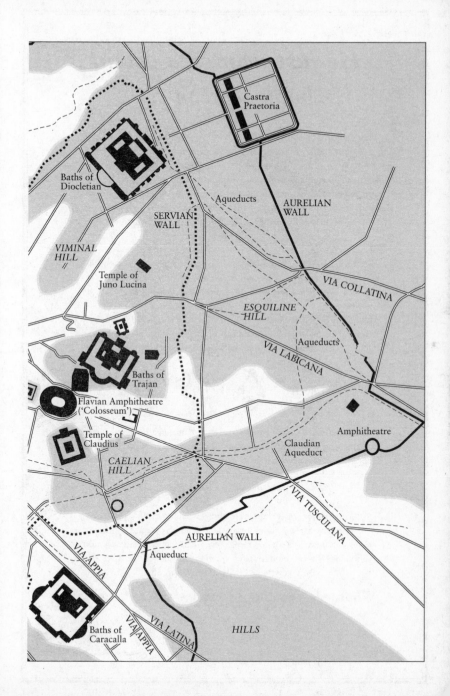

He just wanted a decent book to read ...

Not too much to ask, is it? It was in 1935 when Allen Lane, Managing Director of Bodley Head Publishers, stood on a platform at Exeter railway station looking for something good to read on his journey back to London. His choice was limited to popular magazines and poor-quality paperbacks – the same choice faced every day by the vast majority of readers, few of whom could afford hardbacks. Lane's disappointment and subsequent anger at the range of books generally available led him to found a company – and change the world.

'We believed in the existence in this country of a vast reading public for intelligent books at a low price, and staked everything on it'
Sir Allen Lane, 1902–1970, founder of Penguin Books

The quality paperback had arrived – and not just in bookshops. Lane was adamant that his Penguins should appear in chain stores and tobacconists, and should cost no more than a packet of cigarettes.

Reading habits (and cigarette prices) have changed since 1935, but Penguin still believes in publishing the best books for everybody to enjoy. We still believe that good design costs no more than bad design, and we still believe that quality books published passionately and responsibly make the world a better place.

So wherever you see the little bird – whether it's on a piece of prize-winning literary fiction or a celebrity autobiography, political tour de force or historical masterpiece, a serial-killer thriller, reference book, world classic or a piece of pure escapism – you can bet that it represents the very best that the genre has to offer.

Whatever you like to read – trust Penguin.

PENGUIN REFERENCE LIBRARY

THE PENGUIN DICTIONARY OF CLASSICAL MYTHOLOGY

EDITED BY PIERRE GRIMAL

'An essential source' *Library Journal*

Who bore children by a bear and was transformed into a bird as punishment? Why exactly did Zeus turn his lover into a cow? Classical myth is a vibrant and entertaining world, and Pierre Grimal's seminal text *The Penguin Dictionary of Classical Mythology* is indisputably the finest guide available. Meticulously researched and thoroughly cross-referenced, the text is accessible and informative, sweeping in its breadth and comprehensive in its detail. You will find the no less than *four* versions of the beautiful *Helen*'s birth, as well as lengthy explanations of all the major figures and events – from *Odysseus* to *Heracles* to *Troy* to the *Jason* and the *Argonauts*.

- Discusses all the heroes and heroines of Homer, Sophocles, Aeschylus and Euripides (amongst many others), from *Venus* to *Pandora* via *Apollo* and *Aphrodite*

- Demonstrates how and where classical mythology has resurfaced and influenced the works of later painters and writers, from Freud to James Joyce

- Includes comprehensive cross-referencing and genealogical tables to show the complex links between different characters and myths

ONLY PENGUIN GIVES YOU MORE

PENGUIN HISTORY

PAGANS AND CHRISTIANS
IN THE MEDITERRANEAN WORLD FROM THE SECOND CENTURY AD
TO THE CONVERSION OF CONSTANTINE
ROBIN LANE FOX

'This brilliant book is a wholly unexpected and central contribution to its subject.
What is more it is readable and rereadable, even gripping' Peter Levi, *Spectator*

How did Christianity compare and compete with the cults of the pagan gods in the
Roman Empire? This scholarly work from award-winning historian, Robin Lane
Fox, places Christians and pagans side by side in the context of civil life and
contrasts their religious experiences, visions, cults and oracles. Leading up to the
time of the first Christian emperor, Constantine, the book aims to enlarge and
confirm the value of contemporary evidence, some of which has only recently
been discovered.

'A massive and humane study. On my shelf it will rest with pride between Edward
Gibbon and Peter Brown' Charles Thomas, *Daily Telegraph*

'Here is richness indeed …on the one hand a magisterial analysis and
reconstruction of an apparently remote and alien society, on the other a detailed
study of the single most significant process in our history and still the most
important determinant of our present attitudes and beliefs'
Donald Earl, *The Times*

'This book is important indeed' Henry Chadwick, *Financial Times*

PENGUIN HISTORY

THE CLASSICAL WORLD
ROBIN LANE FOX

The classical civilizations of Greece and Rome dominated the world some forty lifetimes before our own, and they continue to intrigue, inspire and enlighten us. From Greece in the eighth century BC to Rome at the time of Julius Caesar and Augustus in the first century BC, their art and architecture, drama and epics, philosophy and politics have been the foundation of much of what we value today. Their heroes, from Achilles to Alexander, are still powerfully evoked in our modern culture, films and writing.

The Classical World brilliantly describes the vast sweep of history in which these two great civilizations ruled – from the epic poems of Homer and the beginning of literacy through the foundation of Athenian democracy and the turbulent empire-building of Alexander the Great to the establishment of the Roman Republic, the rise of Christianity, and the challenges this new faith faced in the Roman imperial age.

For those who are new to this enthralling subject and for the many who continue to share his fascination with classical Greece and Rome, Robin Lane Fox's account is a wonderfully exciting historical tour of two of the greatest empires the world has ever seen.

Praise for Robin Lane Fox

Pagans and Christians

'Brilliant…it is readable and rereadable, even gripping' *Spectator*

'This open-hearted and learned book is one that any scholar of the ancient world and of early Christianity would be proud to have written… Lane Fox has opened his pages to let in an entirely new world' *The New York Review of Books*

'Here is richness indeed… a magisterial analysis' *The Times*

PENGUIN HISTORY

ALEXANDER THE GREAT
ROBIN LANE FOX

'So enjoyable and well-written ... Fox's book became my main guide through Alexander's amazing story' Oliver Stone

Tough, resolute, fearless, Alexander was a born warrior and ruler of passionate ambition who understood the intense adventure of conquest and of the unknown. When he died in 323 BC aged thirty-two, his vast empire comprised more than two million square miles, spanning from Greece to India. His achievements were unparalleled – he had excelled as leader to his men, founded eighteen new cities and stamped the face of Greek culture on the ancient East. The myth he created is as potent today as it was in the ancient world.

Robin Lane Fox's superb account searches through the mass of conflicting evidence and legend to focus on Alexander as a man of his own time. Combining historical scholarship and acute psychological insight, it brings this colossal figure vividly to life.

'I do not know which to admire most, his vast erudition or his imaginative grasp of so remote and complicated a period and such a complex personality' *Sunday Times*

'A magnificent, compelling epic ... He has honoured him splendidly' *Sunday Telegraph*

'An achievement of Alexandrian proportions' *New Statesman*

PENGUIN CLASSICS

THE CONQUEST OF GAUL
CAESAR

> 'The enemy were overpowered and took to flight.
> The Romans pursued as far as their strength enabled them to run'

Between 58 and 50 BC Julius Caesar conquered most of the area now covered by France, Belgium and Switzerland, and invaded Britain twice, and *The Conquest of Gaul* is his record of these campaigns. Caesar's narrative offers insights into his military strategy and paints a fascinating picture of his encounters with the inhabitants of Gaul and Britain, as well as lively portraits of the rebel leader Vercingetorix and other Gallic chieftains. *The Conquest of Gaul* can also be read as a piece of political propaganda, as Caesar sets down his version of events for the Roman public, knowing he faces civil war on his return to Rome.

Revised and updated by Jane Gardner, S. A. Handford's translation brings Caesar's lucid and exciting account to life for modern readers. This volume includes a glossary of persons and places, maps, appendices and suggestions for further reading.

Translated by S. A. Handford
Revised with a new introduction by Jane F. Gardner

Penguin Classics

THE ANNALS OF IMPERIAL ROME
TACITUS

'Nero was already corrupted by every lust, natural and unnatural'

The Annals of Imperial Rome recount the major historical events from the years shortly before the death of Augustus to the death of Nero in AD 68. With clarity and vivid intensity Tacitus describes the reign of terror under the corrupt Tiberius, the great fire of Rome during the time of Nero and the wars, poisonings, scandals, conspiracies and murders that were part of imperial life. Despite his claim that the *Annals* were written objectively, Tacitus' account is sharply critical of the emperors' excesses and fearful for the future of imperial Rome, while also filled with a longing for its past glories.

Michael Grant's fine translation captures the moral tone, astringent wit and stylish vigour of the original. His introduction discusses the life and works of Tacitus and the historical context of the *Annals*. This edition also contains a key to place names and technical terms, maps, tables and suggestions for further reading.

Translated with an introduction by Michael Grant

PENGUIN CLASSICS

THE AGRICOLA *AND* THE GERMANIA
TACITUS

> 'Happy indeed were you, Agricola,
> not only in your glorious life but in your timely death'

The Agricola is both a portrait of Julius Agricola – the most famous governor of Roman Britain and Tacitus' well-loved and respected father-in-law – and the first detailed account of Britain that has come down to us. It offers fascinating descriptions of the geography, climate and peoples of the country, and a succinct account of the early stages of the Roman occupation, nearly fatally undermined by Boudicca's revolt in AD 61 but consolidated by campaigns that took Agricola as far as Anglesey and northern Scotland. The warlike German tribes are the focus of Tacitus' attention in *The Germania*, which, like *The Agricola*, often compares the behaviour of 'barbarian' peoples favourably with the decadence and corruption of Imperial Rome.

Harold Mattingly's translation brings Tacitus' extravagant imagination and incisive wit vividly to life. In his introduction, he examines Tacitus' life and literary career, the governorship of Agricola, and the political background of Rome's rapidly expanding Empire. This edition also includes a select bibliography, and maps of Roman Britain and Germany.

Translated with an introduction by H. Mattingly
Translation revised by S. A. Handford

PENGUIN CLASSICS

THE LETTERS OF THE YOUNGER PLINY

> 'Of course these details are not important enough for history …
> you have only yourself to blame for asking for them'

A prominent lawyer and administrator, Pliny (*c*. AD 61–113) was also a prolific letter-writer, who numbered among his correspondents such eminent figures as Tacitus, Suetonius and the Emperor Trajan, as well as a wide circle of friends and family. His lively and very personal letters address an astonishing range of topics, from a deeply moving account of his uncle's death in the eruption that engulfed Pompeii and observations on the early Christians – 'a desperate sort of cult carried to extravagant lengths' – to descriptions of everyday life in Rome, with its scandals and court cases, and of his own life in the country. Providing a series of fascinating views of imperial Rome, his letters also offer one of the fullest self-portraits to survive from classical times.

Betty Radice's definitive edition was the first complete modern translation of Pliny's letters. In her introduction, she examines the shrewd, tolerant and occasionally pompous man who emerges from these.

Translated with an introduction by Betty Radice

PENGUIN CLASSICS

—

THE RISE OF THE ROMAN EMPIRE
POLYBIUS

> 'If history is deprived of the truth,
> we are left with nothing but an idle, unprofitable tale'

In writing his account of the relentless growth of the Roman Empire, the Greek statesman Polybius (*c.* 200–118 BC) set out to help his fellow-countrymen understand how their world came to be dominated by Rome. Opening with the Punic War in 264 BC, he vividly records the critical stages of Roman expansion: its campaigns throughout the Mediterranean, the temporary setbacks inflicted by Hannibal and the final destruction of Carthage in 146 BC. An active participant in contemporary politics, as well as a friend of many prominent Roman citizens, Polybius was able to draw on a range of eyewitness accounts and on his own experiences of many of the central events, giving his work immediacy and authority.

Ian Scott-Kilvert's translation fully preserves the clarity of Polybius' narrative. This substantial selection of the surviving volumes is accompanied by an introduction by F. W. Walbank, which examines Polybius' life and times, and the sources and technique he employed in writing his history.

Translated by Ian Scott-Kilvert

Selected with an introduction by F. W. Walbank

PENGUIN SUBJECT DICTIONARIES

Penguin's Subject Dictionaries aim to provide two things: authoritative complimentary reference texts for the academic market (primarily A level and undergraduate studies) *and* clear, exciting and approachable reference books for general readers on subjects outside the core curriculum.

Academic & Professional

ACCOUNTING
ARCHEOLOGY
ARCHITECTURE
BUILDING
BUSINESS
CLASSICAL MYTHOLOGY
CRITICAL THEORY
ECONOMICS
INTERNATIONAL RELATIONS
LATIN
LITERARY TERMS & THEORY
MARKETING (forthcoming)
MEDIA STUDIES
MODERN HISTORY
PENGUIN HUMAN BIOLOGY (forthcoming)
PHILOSOPHY
PSYCHOLOGY
SOCIOLOGY

Scientific, Technical and Medical

BIOLOGY
CHEMISTRY
CIVIL ENGINEERING
COMPUTING
ELECTRONICS
GEOGRAPHY
GEOLOGY
MATHEMATICS
PHYSICAL GEOGRAPHY
PHYSICS
PSYCHOANALYSIS
SCIENCE
STATISTICS

English Words & Language

CLICHÉS
ENGLISH IDIOMS
PENGUIN ENGLISH GRAMMAR
PENGUIN RHYMING DICTIONARY
PROVERBS
SYNONYMS & ANTONYMS
SYNONYMS & RELATED WORDS
ROGET'S THESAURUS
THE COMPLETE PLAIN WORDS
THE PENGUIN A–Z THESAURUS
THE PENGUIN GUIDE TO PLAIN ENGLISH
THE PENGUIN GUIDE TO PUNCTUATION
THE PENGUIN WRITER'S MANUAL
USAGE AND ABUSAGE

Religion

BIBLE
ISLAM (forthcoming)
JUDAISM (forthcoming)
LIVING RELIGIONS
RELIGIONS
SAINTS
WHO'S WHO IN THE AGE OF JESUS

General Interest

BOOK OF FACTS
FIRST NAMES
MUSIC
OPERA
SURNAMES (forthcoming)
SYMBOLS
THEATRE

Penguin Reference – making knowledge everybody's property